RUNNING ON EMPTY

McGill-Queen's Studies in Ethnic History
Series One: Donald Harman Akenson, Editor

McGill-Queen's Studies
in Ethnic History
Series Two: John Zucchi, Editor

Running on Empty

Canada and the Indochinese Refugees,
1975–1980

Michael J. Molloy, Peter Duschinsky,
Kurt F. Jensen, and Robert J. Shalka

McGill-Queen's University Press
Montreal & Kingston • London • Chicago

ISBN 978-0-7735-4880-0 (cloth)
ISBN 978-0-7735-4881-7 (paper)
ISBN 978-0-7735-5063-6 (ePDF)
ISBN 978-0-7735-5064-3 (ePUB)

Legal deposit first quarter 2017
Bibliothèque nationale du Québec

Reprinted 2017

Printed in Canada on acid-free paper that is 100% ancient forest free
(100% post-consumer recycled), processed chlorine free

This book has been published with the help of a grant from the Canadian
Federation for the Humanities and Social Sciences, through the Awards to
Scholarly Publications Program, using funds provided by the Social Sciences
and Humanities Research Council of Canada. Funding has also been received
from the Canadian Immigration Historical Society.

McGill-Queen's University Press acknowledges the support of the Canada
Council for the Arts for our publishing program. We also acknowledge the
financial support of the Government of Canada through the Canada Book
Fund for our publishing activities.

Lyrics from "Running on Empty" by Jackson Browne published with
permission of Drive Music Publishing, 12650 Riverside Drive, Ste 200,
Studio City, CA 91607.

Cover image: Courtesy of Margaret Tebbutt

Library and Archives Canada Cataloguing in Publication

Molloy, Michael J., author
Running on empty : Canada and the Indochinese refugees, 1975–1980 /
Michael J. Molloy, Peter Duschinsky, Kurt F. Jensenm and Robert J. Shalka.

(McGill-Queen's studies in ethnic history. Series two ; 41)
Includes bibliographical references and index.
Issued in print and electronic formats.
ISBN 978-0-7735-4880-0 (hardback).
–ISBN 978-0-7735-4881-7 (paperback).
–ISBN 978-0-7735-5063-6 (PDF).
–ISBN 978-0-7735-5064-3 (ePUB)

1. Refugees–Indochina–History. 2. Refugees–Canada–History.
3. Refugees–Services for–Canada. 4. Indochinese–Relocation–Canada–
History. I. Duschinsky, Peter, 1943–, author II. Jensen, Kurt F. (Kurt
Frank), 1946–, author III. Shalka, Robert J., 1945–, author IV. Title.
V. Series: McGill-Queen's studies in ethnic history. Series two ; 41

HV640.5.I5M65 2017   325'.2109590971   C2016-906721-1
                                                 C2016-906722-X

This book is dedicated to Canada's immigration officials who endured great hardships while rescuing refugees in Southeast Asia, and whose diligence, dedication, and ingenuity ensured that the refugees were welcomed on arrival in Canada and settled across the country by generous sponsors and communities. Few of these men and women view their actions as exceptional, yet they made an enormous difference to the lives of the 70,000 Indochinese refugees who arrived in Canada between 1975 and 1980.

We also dedicate this book to three outstanding leaders: to the late Flora MacDonald and to former immigration ministers Ron Atkey and Lloyd Axworthy. The authors acknowledge with sadness the passing of the Honourable Ron Atkey on 9 May 2017.

CONTENTS

Ronald Atkey

This book is the quintessential and comprehensive history of an important time in recent Canadian history: 1975 to 1980. It is highly focused on the "boat people" – refugees to Canada from Vietnam, along with refugees from Laos and Cambodia. Within its covers there are important lessons for governments, organizations, and individuals trying to come to grips with an even larger refugee movement from Syria in the twenty-first century.

I had the good fortune to be minister of employment and immigration from 1979 to 1980 when Canada made its grand gesture to successfully resettle 50,000 boat people to Canada in an eighteen-month period. While I came into this politically as a new minister on 4 June 1979, a lot of the groundwork had been already been done by a group within the department, much of it led by Michael Molloy. It is fitting that he is now the driving force to mobilize veterans from the department to publish this book under the auspices of the Canadian Immigration Historical Society and McGill-Queen's University Press. In that context, I am honoured to have been asked by Michael to provide a perspective to this book in a brief foreword.

First, this initiative to provide humanitarian assistance to large numbers of people in distress was an opportunity for Canadian society to come together to provide effective relief in a way that was unprecedented. Yes, government officials led the way in establishing structures, personnel, and resources. But it was communities across Canada – provinces, municipalities, faith-based groups, and neighbourhoods in large and small towns – that made it all happen. This was a clear example of Canada performing at its best.

Second, never have I seen in my career as an academic, lawyer, or politician a situation where public servants in Canada have gone so far beyond the call of duty to make sure that a humanitarian political objective, established by a newly elected government, has been implemented to the fullest within the time frame and budgets established. This book carefully documents this heroic achievement and chronicles the cooperation with predecessor and successor governments.

Third, but for this book, a lot of fascinating stories from the refugee camps in Southeast Asia, the staging centres in Edmonton and Montreal, and the Canadian communities where resettlement took place would have been lost. Now they will be part of Canada's historical record.

Canada's humanitarian tradition in resettling refugees goes back to the nineteenth century with the Irish and has continued into the twentieth century with the Armenians, Mennonites, Ukrainians, Poles, Hungarians, Czechs, Ugandans, Chileans, Vietnamese, and Kosovars. Only occasionally have we badly dropped the ball, as happened with the Jewish boat people in the 1930s. This book provides context for perhaps the largest and most ambitious refugee resettlement effort in Canada's history. It is arguably the most successful effort in terms of receiving in Canada a large group of highly motivated immigrants who are now making significant contributions to our society. This is a story that will be told by others in the years ahead.

The profound value of *Running on Empty* is that it demonstrates the can-do spirit of Canada in all its parts. It is a very important part of our immigration history. To ignore it in grappling with today's refugee crises should be unthinkable.

The Honourable Ronald Atkey, PC, QC

PREFACE AND ACKNOWLEDGMENTS

The Canadian Immigration Historical Society (CIHS) exists to support, encourage, and promote research into the history of Canadian immigration and to stimulate interest in and further the appreciation and understanding of immigration and refugee issues, especially as these influence Canada's development and our position in the world. This book is the result of a partnership between CIHS and veteran officers of those government departments responsible for all aspects of immigration. Between 1975 and 1980, many of these officers were based at Canadian diplomatic missions in Southeast Asia and travelled to makeshift camps in distant parts of the region to select refugees from Vietnam, Laos, and Cambodia for resettlement in Canada and to arrange their transportation to Canada. Others performed the refugees' medical and security clearances, matched refugees with sponsors, welcomed the refugees on arrival in Canada, and facilitated their reception by Canadian sponsors and government representatives across the country. Coordinating this complex and difficult operation was a team of officers based at Immigration Headquarters in Ottawa.

Excellent books exist on the Indochinese refugee movement. W. Courtland Robinson's *Terms of Refugee: The Indochinese Exodus and the International Response* (London & New York: Zed Books 1998) provides a comprehensive study of the whole movement, focusing heavily on the American program. Howard Adelman's *Canada and the Indochinese Refugees* (Regina: L.A. Weigl Educational Associates 1982) supplies a Canadian perspective. However, to date, the role of Canada's Department of Immigration and its partner agencies has not been recorded in any depth. Four decades ago, nearly 70,000 Indochinese refugees were resettled in Canada in a few short years, in large part through the hard work of Canadian officials whose experiences were largely unrecorded and in danger of being lost. This omission was particularly regrettable as the Indochinese refugee resettlement movement to Canada was based on a unique co-operation: officials at all levels of government worked with thousands of ordinary Canadians who volunteered their time, effort, and money to sponsor Indochinese refugees.

This book was written using archival research combined with accounts of the personal experiences of former government officials. Three members of CIHS with experience in selecting refugees, managing refugee programs abroad, and foreign intelligence work, as well as writing and academic research, agreed to join Michael Molloy, the president of CIHS, as authors. Molloy, Canada's former ambassador to Jordan, was Immigration's senior coordinator of the Indochinese refugee movement in 1979–80. Robert Shalka has a doctorate in history and served as a visa officer at the Canadian Embassy in Bangkok during the peak years of the Indochinese refugee movement in 1978–80. Peter Duschinsky (himself once a youthful refugee to Canada) has writing and research experience and managed refugee programs in Africa and Europe in the 1980s and '90s. Kurt Jensen, an adjunct professor at Carleton University, was an intelligence expert with the Department of Foreign Affairs. Somewhat later, Gail Kirkpatrick Devlin, a professional editor, joined the writing team.

The research team of Duschinsky and Jensen worked extensively to identify and photograph relevant files at Library and Archives Canada (LAC) and at the Research and Evaluation Bureau at Citizenship and Immigration Canada. Robert Shalka arranged for the Privy Council Office to release a number of critical Cabinet memoranda from the 1975–80 period. Laura May Roth, a research assistant funded in part by the University of Ottawa's Graduate School of Public and International Affairs, undertook with great skill the task of cataloguing the documentation. Together with material from the CIHS Indochinese Document Collection (cited as CIHS Collection), this documentation became the core of the book's historical section, written by Molloy, Duschinsky, and Jensen. To augment these official documents, Molloy invited more than forty former Canadian officials who had worked on the Indochinese movement to write about their experiences. The narratives prepared by these officials were edited by Jensen, Molloy, and Duschinsky. Drawing on firsthand experience, Shalka wrote two chapters on the Bangkok operation and created much of the book's chronology.

In the course of preparing this book, CIHS, in cooperation with York University's Centre for Refugee Studies, hosted a conference on the Indochinese refugee movement of 1975–80 and the launch of Canada's Private Refugee Sponsorship Program. Held at York University, 20–23 November 2013, the conference brought together for three days of intense discussion former federal, provincial, and municipal officials, academics, journalists, sponsors, community leaders and organizers, religious leaders, and former Vietnamese, Sino-Vietnamese, Laotian, and Cambodian refugees. The conference's proceedings, recorded on video, along with interviews of the participants and a number of short documentaries, may be accessed at http//indochinese.apps01.yorku.ca/conference/. The authors gained important information, insights, and inspiration through their participation in the conference. As well, the conference's discussions provided considerable additional material used in writing this book.

We cannot name all those who contributed to the successful settlement of nearly 70,000 Indochinese in Canada between 1975 and 1980. Many have passed away, while others have retired and could not be contacted. Those who contributed to the movement's success and to this book include many of the hardy souls who served in Southeast Asia, mainly members of Canada's Immigration Foreign Service and volunteers from the domestic immigration service, officers of the Quebec Immigration Service, RCMP liaison officers, and immigration doctors from the Department of National Health and Welfare.

We received contributions from colleagues who worked at Immigration Headquarters in Ottawa and at Employment and Immigration's regional offices and Canada Employment and Immigration Centres in various parts of the country. We also received accounts from public servants who matched refugees with sponsors and made the refugees welcome at the reception centres at the Canadian Forces bases in Montreal and Edmonton (in close partnership with members of the Canadian Forces), and from refugee liaison officers who coordinated settlement services at the communities level.

The book was discussed with the former minister of immigration, Ron Atkey, who provided a number of useful insights and was kind enough to provide the foreword. We were saddened when the former secretary of state for external affairs, Flora MacDonald, passed away as the book neared completion.

The personal accounts provided by the following colleagues who participated in the Indochinese Refugee movement from 1975 to 1980 brought the experience to life: Ernest Allen, Naomi Alboim, Deborah Ashford, John Baker, Gordon Barnett, Serge Bergevin, Tove Bording, Captain Bryan Brown, Kenneth Brown, Rev. Linda Butler, Ronald Button, Donald Cameron, Gerry Campbell, Joyce Cavanagh-Wood, Guy Cuerrier, Jean Paul Deslisle, Doug Dunnington, David Elder, Michael Fitzpatrick, Florent Fortin, John M. "Gibby" Gibson, Marius Grinius, Dr Brian Gushulak, Richard Hawkshaw, Elizabeth Heatherington, R. Scott Heatherington, Dr Earl Hershfield, Lucile Horner, William Janzen, Susan Lopez, Elizabeth Marshall, Richard Martin, Marlene Massey, John McEachern, Susan McKale, Hulene Montgomery, Scott Mullin, Cheryl Munroe, Donald Myatt, Martha Nixon, Murray Oppertshauser, Jim Pasman, Ian Rankin, David Ritchie, Charles Rogers, Robert Shalka, William Sheppit, Thomas Steel, Ralph Talbot, Margaret Tebbutt, Ian Thompson, Leopold Verboven, and John Wilkins. We are most grateful that they took the time to record their experiences.

Advice, information, and recommendations were received from Howard Adelman, Michael Casasola (UNHCR Ottawa office), Ian Hamilton, Ernest Hébert, Al Lukie, William Lundy, Norm Olson, Bill Marks, Rene Pappone, Gavin Stewart, and Ian Thompson. Stephen Fielding conducted interviews with William Sheppit and the late Tove Bording, and Max Brem provided access to an interview he conducted with Murray Oppertshauser and Robert Shalka in 1980.

Graduate students from the University of Ottawa made significant contributions. Marie Alice Belmont provided a term paper on the origins of the private sponsorship program, while Dara Marcus supplied the account of the *Hai Hong* episode, and Laura May Roth prepared the first draft of the chapter on rescue at sea.

Many individuals worked behind the scenes on this book. These included our editor Gail Kirkpatrick Devlin, and our general organizer, editor, and fact-checker Jo Molloy. Editorial expertise for several chapters was provided by Christiana Epp Duschinsky. The Graduate School of Public and International Affairs of the University of Ottawa generously provided a series of competent research assistants, including Janet Tsu Ji, Laura May Roth, Sarah Tayyem, Sarah Voegeli, Erika Bennett, and Sabrina Arrizza. We are indebted to Sarah Simpkin, the GIS and geography librarian at University of Ottawa, for the fine maps.

Michael McCormick of CIC's Research and Evaluation Branch, visa officers Kathleen Sigurdson and Zal Karkaria, and historian Laura Madokoro read parts of the manuscript, suggesting corrections and advising on presentation.

Umit Kiziltan, Michael McCormick, and Eleanor Berry of the Citizenship and Immigration Research and Evaluation Branch supported our efforts from the start and were instrumental in helping us gain access to departmental files not open to the public at Library and Archives Canada. The extensive archival research that underpins this book was conducted with the assistance of LAC's ever-efficient and helpful staff. We are grateful to the Privy Council Office for providing access to critical Cabinet documents.

The book has been sponsored and financially supported by the CIHS and its board of directors: Anne Arnott, James Bissett, Brian Casey, Roy Christensen, Hector Cowan, Valerie de Montigny, Brian Davis, Gail Devlin, Charlene Elgee, Raphael Girard, Gerry Maffre, Ian Rankin, Kathleen Sigurdson, Dianne Burrows, and Gerry Van Kessel. The authors are present or past members of the board.

We are grateful to the Toronto-Dominion Bank for a generous contribution to assist with publication costs and to a grant from the Canadian Federation for the Humanities and Social Sciences, through the Awards to Scholarly Publications Program, using funds provided by the Social Sciences and Humanities Research Council of Canada.

We should note that three of the contributions to the book were submitted in French, and it was the authors' intention to include them in that language. However, our publishers were not able to accommodate chapters in more than one language. The contributors kindly agreed to having their submissions translated into English; the original French versions may be found at cihs-shic.ca/indochina.

We were exceedingly fortunate in our single attempt to find a publisher. Within forty-eight hours of submitting our "immodest proposal" for this book, we received a positive and highly encouraging response from Jacqueline Mason of McGill-Queen's University Press.

The skill, patience, knowledge, and kindness of Jacqueline, Ryan Van Huijstee, Maureen Garvie, Natalie Blanchere, and their colleagues at MQUP, and our indexer, Celia Braves, in guiding us through the process is deeply appreciated. We are also grateful to a number of anonymous contributors who came to our rescue at the last moment.

The authors wish to express their gratitude to their wives, Jo Molloy, Christiana Epp Duschinsky, Jill Jensen, and Elena Gudyrenko, for their constant support and encouragement during this lengthy endeavour.

We are very grateful to all who have contributed in so many ways to this long-running enterprise. We take responsibility for any errors and imperfections.

Michael J. Molloy, Peter Duschinsky, Kurt F. Jensen, and Robert J. Shalka
Ottawa, September 2016

ABBREVIATIONS AND TERMINOLOGY

Abbreviations

ADM	Assistant Deputy Minister (Executive Director)
ARVN	Army of the Republic of Vietnam
ASEAN	Association of Southeast Asian Nations
CD	Diplomatic Corps
CEC	Canada Employment Centre
CEIC	Canadian Employment and Immigration Commission
CIA	Central Intelligence Agency (US)
CIC	Canada Immigration Centre
CIDA	Canadian International Development Agency
CIHS	Canadian Immigration Historical Society
CM	Circular Memorandum
CP Air	Canadian Pacific Airlines
COFI	Centres d'orientation et de formation des immigrants
CR	Convention Refugee Seeking Resettlement Class
CRS	Catholic Relief Services
CSIS	Canadian Security Intelligence Service
CSQ	Certificat de sélection du Québec
DC	Designated Class
DC1	Designated Class member settled by the government.
DC2	Designated Class member sponsored or nominated by a relative
DC3	Designated Class member sponsored by a private sponsor
DC4	Designated Class member sponsored under the Joint Assistance Program

DC5	Designated Class members with sufficient resources to cover own settlement costs
DCS	Demande de certificat de sélection
DEA	Department of External Affairs
DG	Director General
DISERO	Disembarkation Resettlement Offers
DK	Democratic Kampuchea
DM	Deputy Minister/Chairman
DMP	Designated Medical Practitioner (Roster Doctor)
DMR	Destination Matching Request
DND	Department of National Defence
E&I	Employment and Immigration Canada (also CEIC)
FC	Family Class
FRP	Family Reunification Program
FSO	Foreign Service Officer
GAR	Government Assisted Refugee
ICDC	Indochinese Designated Class
ICEM/ICM	Intergovernmental Committee on European Migration, which became Intergovernmental Committee on Migration (ICM) in 1980 and International Organization for Migration (IOM) in 1989.
ICRC/IRC	International Committee of the Red Cross/ International Red Cross
IDHQ	Immigration Department Headquarters (NHQ)
IDP	Immigration and Demographic Policy Group
IFAP	The Asia Pacific division of CEIC's Foreign Branch responsible Asia operations
IMM8	Application for Permanent Residence in Canada
IMM1000	Immigrant Record of Landing /Visa
IMM1009	Family Class sponsorships
IMM1010	Assisted Relative undertakings
IMM1314	Indochinese Designated Class Processing Record and Visa
IMM1354/1355	Immigrant Assessment Record
IOM	International Organization for Migration
IPO	Immigration Program Officer (locally engaged)
IRP	Indochinese Refugee Program

ISAP	Immigrant Settlement and Adaptation Program
JAP	Joint Assistance Program – difficult cases where CEIC paid settlement costs and a private sponsor provided hands-on support
JVA	Joint Voluntary Agency
KR	Khmer Rouge
KRP	Cambodian relatives sponsored or nominated
KRS	Cambodian Refuges
LES	Locally Engaged Staff
LIT	Laotian in Thailand
LO	Liaison Officer (RCMP)
LPSA	Longue-Pointe Staging Area
M&I	Department of Manpower and Immigration
MA	Master Agreement
MC	Memorandum to Cabinet
MCC	Mennonite Central Committee (of Canada)
MIQ	Ministry of Immigration Quebec/Ministère de l'Immigration du Québec
MP	Member of Parliament
MP	Minister's Permit
MRCS	Malaysian Red Crescent Society
MSF	Medécins Sans Frontières
NAT	Notification of Arrival Telex
NCC	National Citizens' Coalition
NGO	Non-Governmental Organization
NHQ	National Headquarters (of CEIC)
NHW	National Health and Welfare
O-I-C	Officer-in-Charge (Immigration Program Manager)
ODP	Orderly Departure Program (US)
OGDS	Other governmental departments
OM	Oppressed Minority
PCO	Privy Council Office
PDRL	People's Democratic Republic of Laos
PI	Prospective Immigrant
PSR	Privately Sponsored Refugee
PVL	Promise of Visa Letter
QIS/SIQ	Quebec Immigraton Service/Service de l'Immigration du Québec

RCMP	Royal Canadian Mounted Police
RCMP LO	RCMP Liaison Officer
RDG	Regional Director General
RLO	Refugee Liaison Officer
RMC	Refugee Matching Centre
RO	Regional Office
RSAC	Refugee Status Advisory Committee
RTG	Royal Thai Government
RTPYC	Royal Tanjung Pinang Yacht Club
RVN	Republic of Vietnam
SBE	Small Boat Escapee (Boat Person)
SSEA	Secretary of State for External Affairs (Foreign Minister)
STM	Jetfoil company in Macau
TB	Tuberculosis
TBS	Treasury Board Secretariat
TD	Temporary Duty
TFDPT	Task Force for Displaced Persons in Thailand
TJP	Tanjung Pinang
TL	Travel Loan
TOR	Thailand Overland Refugees
2-I-C	Second-in-Charge (Deputy Immigration Program Manager)
UNBRO	United Nations Border Relief Organization
UNHCR	United Nations High Commissioner for Refugees
USAF	United States Air Force
USINS	United States Immigration and Naturalization Services
USSR	Union of Soviet Socialist Republics
VC	Viet Cong
VNP	Vietnamese relatives, sponsored or nominated
VNP/KRP	Vietnam Khmer Republic Program
VNQ	Vietnamese Refugees, others
VO	Visa Officer (Canadian immigration officer serving abroad)
WCRP	World Conference on Religion and Peace

Immigration Terminology

For the purposes of this book, the visa offices located at various Canadian missions in Southeast Asia are identified with the prefix E&I (for Employment and Immigration) and the name of the city where they were located (e.g., E&I Singapore, E&I Hong Kong).

Affirmation for Visa	one-page document issued in emergencies to refugees, stateless people, and others lacking passports or travel documents.
furthered	medical decision delayed for treatment or additions tests.
paper screening	initial assessment of an immigration application using the point system.
post	Canadian government offices abroad: embassies, high commissions, commission (Hong Kong), consulates; now called missions.
posting/posted	assignment to a post for set period of at least one year.
Stage B	security and criminality screening
staging areas	Canadian reception centres for a special movement of refugees.

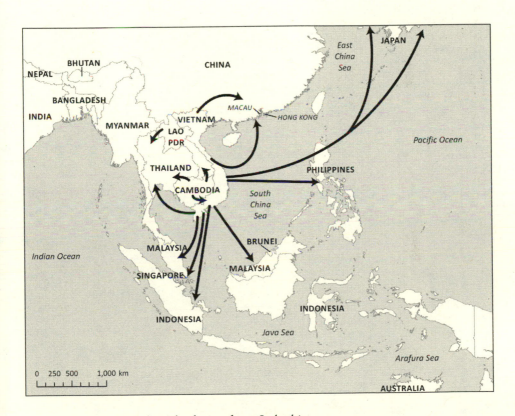

Exodus of refugees from Indochina, 1975–1995

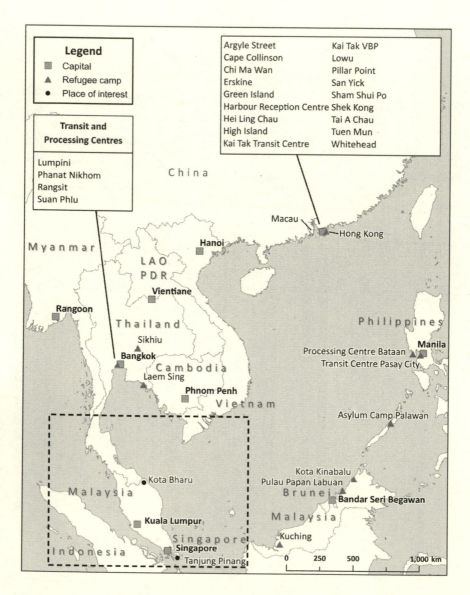

Legend
■ Capital
▲ Refugee camp
● Place of interest

Transit and
Processing Centres

Lumpini
Phanat Nikhom
Rangsit
Suan Phlu

Argyle Street   Kai Tak VBP
Cape Collinson   Lowu
Chi Ma Wan   Pillar Point
Erskine   San Yick
Green Island   Sham Shui Po
Harbour Reception Centre Shek Kong
Hei Ling Chau   Tai A Chau
High Island   Tuen Mun
Kai Tak Transit Centre Whitehead

China

Macau

Hong Kong

Hanoi

LAO
PDR

Vientiane

Rangoon

Myanmar

Thailand

Sikhiu

Bangkok

Cambodia

Laem Sing

Phnom Penh

Vietnam

Philippines

Manila

Processing Centre Bataan
Transit Centre Pasay City

Asylum Camp Palawan

Kota Kinabalu
Pulau Papan Labuan

Brunei

Bandar Seri Begawan

Kota Bharu

Malaysia

Malaysia

Kuala Lumpur

Kuching

Singapore

Singapore

Indonesia

Tanjung Pinang

0   250   500   1,000 km

Vietnamese boat people camps, Southeast Asia, 1975–1980s

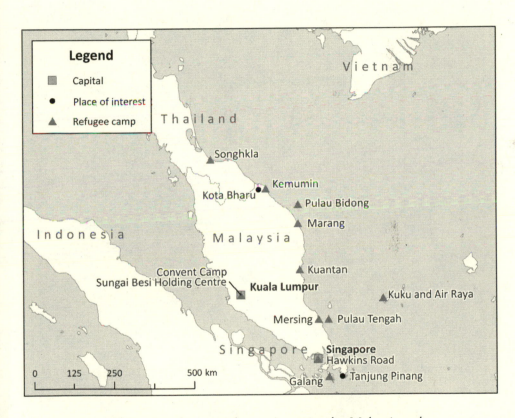

Vietnamese boat people camps, peninsular Malaysia and Indonesia, 1975–1980

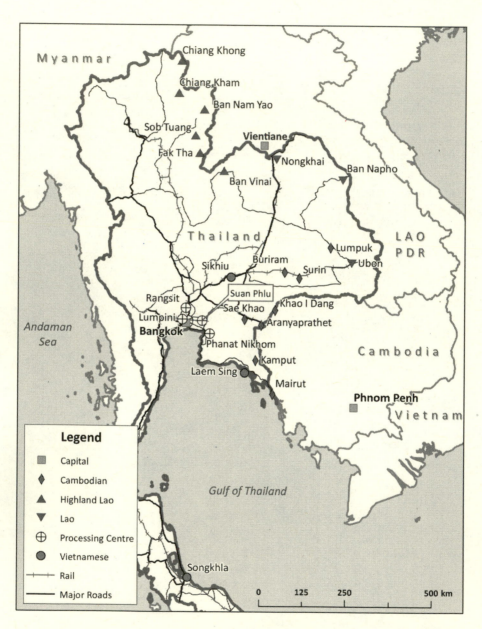

Indonesian refugee camps, Thailand, 1975–1980s

RUNNING ON EMPTY

Running on, running on empty
Running on, running blind
Running on, running into the sun,
But I'm running behind.

Jackson Browne

INTRODUCTION

Jackson Browne's 1977 hit song "Running on Empty" became the anthem of Canadian immigration officials during the Indochinese refugee operation of 1979–80. It was in the mind of refugee coordinator Mike Molloy as fatigue set in late at night, knowing that however much he and his colleagues had accomplished in the course of the day, there would be twice as many challenges to be met and problems to be solved the following day. It reflects the state of Canada's immigration officers and their Quebec colleagues in distant jungle camps, far from their bases in Singapore and Bangkok, as they accepted that tomorrow the tropical heat would still be there, the makeshift conditions would not have changed and, most importantly, the desperate refugees needing Canada's help would still be waiting. As total exhaustion embraced them, as they were "running on empty," they performed their duties with compassion, determination, and speed. The challenges seemed insurmountable, but every officer involved remained unwavering in his or her commitment to meet the enormous quotas and ensure that the never-ending succession of charter flights left for Canada with no seat unoccupied. What more could be asked of them?

Between 1975 and 1980 approximately 70,000 Indochinese refugees were resettled in Canada, including over 60,000 in 1979–80 alone. The latter remains the largest refugee movement compressed into so short a time frame in Canadian history. Forty years later, the great majority of these former refugees and their descendants are valued and productive Canadian citizens. This rapid resettlement of large numbers of desperate people, most of whom initially spoke little or no English or French, was only possible because of the openness and generosity of the Canadian people who themselves were only beginning to evolve into a truly multicultural society. That generosity became the trigger that led the United Nations High Commissioner for Refugees to award the Nansen Medal, the refugee equivalent of the Nobel Prize, to the "People of Canada" in 1986.[1]

The resettlement in Canada of Indochinese refugees grew out of a partnership between the Canadian public and its governments. The many ordinary Canadians who sponsored refugees through faith communities, municipalities, and ad hoc agencies and as groups of private individuals joined forces with the various levels of governments. These included officials of the Canadian Immigration Department, its federal partner departments and agencies, and provincial officials. Through a massive cooperative effort, they brought the refugees to Canada from half a world away and helped them settle in this country. What was a collaboration of committed public and government agencies proved a success and evolved into a template for future refugee movements. This partnership approach to solving refugee crises was, and remains, uniquely Canadian.

Of course, the people most profoundly affected by the resettlement process were the refugees themselves. The largest group was of Vietnamese and Sino-Vietnamese origin, with other sizeable groups from Cambodia and Laos. At the core of the Indochinese refugee resettlement story is the suffering and courage of the refugees who risked their lives on the open seas and in the jungles of Southeast Asia to escape from oppressive regimes in their home countries. It is also the story of struggle and sacrifice to build new lives for themselves and their children in a strange, distant wintery land far from their tropical homes.

The Canadian public reacted with unprecedented compassion to the government's July 1979 decision to admit 50,000 Indochinese refugees. Citizens' groups, faith communities, municipalities, and ordinary Canadians generated over 7,600 sponsorships on behalf of almost 40,000 refugees, of whom 32,281 arrived in Canada in 1979–80. Many of those involved in volunteer and sponsorship programs for the refugees have recorded their experiences in religious publications and local and national newspapers and periodicals reflecting the broad grassroots nature of the sponsorship movement. A valuable portrait of the sponsorship effort is found in Howard Adelman's *Canada and the Indochinese Refugees* (Regina: L.A. Weigl Educational Associates 1982).

The struggles of refugees in adapting to life in Canada, especially during the first ten years after arrival, are documented in various academic papers and monographs.[2] These studies, focusing on the experience of refugees and the institutions and sponsors that assisted them, have reached a number of important conclusions about their integration into Canadian society. Refugees from Vietnam, Cambodia, and Laos often found their early years in Canada difficult. They came from cultures significantly different from Canada's English and French founding cultures. Their views of family cohesion, their religious beliefs, and their approaches to gender relations often differed from Canadian norms. Most importantly, their mother tongues were so dissimilar to Canada's Indo-European languages that most Indochinese adults had severe difficulties in learning English or French. As a result, many refugees had to accept low-level jobs that resulted in their initial economic and social integration below the status they enjoyed at home. However, the great social cohesion within their families and their ethnic groups and the emphasis that most placed on education meant that their children have risen rapidly into the Canadian middle class and, some four decades later, are proud Canadians.

Despite the academic attention focused on the refugees' initial settlement and integration experience, the manner in which they were selected, processed, transported to Canada, and received upon arrival has not yet been recorded. The contributions and experiences of the many government officials, including elected officials and public servants, involved in this great project are the focus of this study. The evolution of Canadian immigration law and policy, including key decisions made at the Cabinet, ministerial, and senior bureaucratic levels, is recorded throughout the book. The work of government officials is largely framed through and by parliamentary legislation and administrative rules and regulations. As elected officials are influenced by the actions and opinions of civil society and the media, we have also described developing public attitudes towards the Indochinese refugees and the lingering opposition to their acceptance.

The goal of this book is to make available, in a format accessible to the general reader and helpful to scholars in Canadian and migration studies, the context and the process through which 70,000 refugees were brought to Canada and settled here between the fall of Saigon in April 1975 and December 1980. The book records how, on short notice, Canada's Immigration Department was able to implement the political decision to accept 50,000 (increased to 60,000) refugees at the height of the Indochinese refugee crisis of 1979–80.

The challenge was formidable: locate, identify, document, screen, transport, receive, match with sponsors, destine and resettle 60,000 Vietnamese, Cambodian, and Laotian refugees located in seventy camps spread over seven countries and territories surrounding the South China Sea, all by December 1980.

This narrative speaks to Canadian values and reinforces the idea that the resettlement of refugees is something that Canadians – in political life, in the public service, and in their communities and institutions – do well. We hope this book will inspire others, including refugee communities, sponsors and sponsoring organizations, settlement agencies, and provincial and municipal institutions, to tell their part of this great Canadian story.

Canada's Vietnamese, Laotian, and Cambodian communities, in partnership with various universities and museums, are currently organizing to record their own stories. Notable among these efforts are the Indochinese Refugee Movement Project at York University's Centre for Refugee Studies and the Hearts of Freedom project based at Carleton University. These projects are designed to collect and preserve the stories of the refugees and their sponsors. The Hearts of Freedom project intends to publish a volume of firsthand accounts of the refugee experience. The Canadian Immigration Historical Society is participating in these efforts.

Many crucial government documents dealing with the Indochinese movement, inaccessible for more than thirty years, were released in time to support the preparation of this book. We believe there is benefit in seeing firsthand the information the decision-makers had before them when making policy, and so, where appropriate, these sources have been extensively quoted. The Indochina section of CIHS's website, www.cihs-shic.ca, makes available many key documents and an archive of photographs, taken for the most part by officers who served in Southeast Asia. The website also includes the full text and statistical tables contained in the report the Immigration Department issued when the 1979–80 movement concluded.[3]

Jargon is the bane of bureaucratic administrations. We have made efforts to eliminate immigration jargon from the book wherever possible, and to aid in overcoming the inevitable intrusion of such language, we have provided a list of common abbreviations and technical terms following the acknowledgments.

Similarly, there are terms employed in this book that require clarification. The media and others often referred to the refugees at this time as "boat people" or Vietnamese refugees. The reality was more complicated. While ethnic Vietnamese were the largest group admitted to Canada, many of the boat people were members of the Chinese minority in Vietnam. And while the Cambodian and Laotian refugees escaped to Thailand across the Mekong River and were referred to as "overland refugees," the rest of the world had difficulty understanding these distinctions. Some scholars have objected to the use of the terms "Indochina" and "Indochinese," noting that these were colonial terms invented by the French to describe their now non-existent Southeast Asian empire of Vietnam, Cambodia, and Laos. The objection is valid, but these terms were widely employed before and during the period with which the book is concerned. The refugees today increasingly refer to themselves as a group as "Southeast Asian refugees," but that term ignores the fact that there are at least eleven countries that are collectively referred to as Southeast Asia. Most importantly, no matter how archaic the use of "Indochina" or "Indochinese" may be, there is no other word that collectively identifies the three countries, Vietnam, Cambodia, and Laos, from which the refugees we are concerned with fled. As inappropriate as the two terms may now be, they provide a necessary element of clarity and are used throughout the book for the ease of the reader who will, we hope, more easily comprehend the region and populations to which they refer.

Ron Atkey, the Cabinet minister who played a decisive role in determining the nature of the movement in 1979–80, has written the foreword to this book. Atkey, and a succession of capable immigration ministers during the crucial years of 1975 to 1980, led the Canadian response to the Indochinese refugee challenge. Robert Andras (Liberal), the first of these ministers, oversaw the design of the Immigration Act, 1976, and directed the Canadian response to the refugees created by the victory of communist forces in 1975 in Indochina. His successor, Bud Cullen (Liberal), managed the implementation of the act (including the creation of the Indochinese Designated Class and the introduction of the private refugee sponsorship program), and ordered the Immigration Department to intervene on behalf of refugees on the stricken freighter *Hai Hong* in late 1978. Cullen also stimulated Canada's resettlement efforts for Indochinese refugees by including them in the first Annual Refugee Plan for 1979. Under the leadership of ministers Andras and Cullen, over 9,000 Indochinese refugees were resettled in Canada between 1975 and 1978. In July 1979, under the newly elected Progressive Conservative government of Joe Clark, Atkey, in partnership with the secretary of state for external affairs, Flora MacDonald, persuaded their Cabinet colleagues to authorize the admission of 50,000 more refugees and challenged Canadians to sponsor them. The response of Canadians to this challenge exceeded all expectations. Finally, Lloyd Axworthy (Liberal) increased the overall target by 10,000 in the spring of 1980 and saw the arrival of the last of 60,049 refugees in December 1980, thereby meeting Canada's commitment.

When the Indochinese refugee crisis erupted in 1978, the facilities and human resources needed to administer refugee resettlement were for the most part contained within the Employment and Immigration Commission[4] and were therefore responsible to one minister. Other federal bodies, including National Health and Welfare, the Royal Canadian Mounted Police, External Affairs, and National Defence, provided medical examinations, security/criminality screening, overseas diplomatic and administrative support, and reception facilities and services for the arriving refugees. The Province of Quebec was unique in that it had its own overseas selection, settlement, and language training services. Regardless of political sensitivities, federal and Quebec officials worked together closely, especially in the field abroad.

Cabinet and bureaucratic records do not reveal the real time, real world decision-making or personal experiences that are critical to understanding the success of initiatives described in the following pages. To supplement government documents, a number of former frontline officials who found themselves involved in Canada's response to the refugee crisis abroad and in Canada have recorded their experiences for this book. Their personal accounts are the core of parts 2 and 3. Descriptions of their experiences are at times heart-wrenching and always dramatic. The stories of frontline Canadian officials, together with the historical account in chapters 1 to 10, provide a unique and comprehensive portrait of a large, complex, and ultimately successful refugee resettlement operation in an era before cellphones, computers, and the Internet. Officials had to operate with limited guidance from policy-makers and senior officials in responding to widely differing environments and rapidly evolving circumstances.

Running on Empty tells a long story with many twists and turns and distinct phases or facets. The story has its roots in French imperialism, complicated by World War II and the Japanese occupation of Indochina. The early postwar period saw conflict between national aspirations and an attempted resumption of colonialism. The Cold War became a factor in a complex tale where the rights and wrongs of the protagonists were often forgotten. Throughout, the people of the region were the victims. It is impossible to assign altruistic motives to any of the warring participants; the hardships and dangers facing the local populations were evident. It was the events of early 1975, however, that provided the catalyst for a massive outflow of refugees from Vietnam, Cambodia, and Laos, and it was the large outflow of Vietnamese boat people starting in 1978, and continuing through 1979 and 1980, that triggered the international response to the crisis in which Canada and its citizens played a major role.

Running on Empty is divided into three parts: first, a historical overview from 1975 to 1980, second, recollections of officials who served in Southeast Asia, and third, recollections of officials involved in the reception and resettlement of refugees after arrival. Part 1 begins with a concise history (chapter 1) of how Canadian immigration and refugee policy evolved from the end of World War II to 1975. It describes the race-based, Eurocentric policy that focused on the admission of Europeans displaced by the war to meet Canadian labour market needs. In 1956, the decision to admit 37,000 Hungarian refugees set a critical precedent. Changing values and growing awareness of human rights eventually led to the removal of most racial barriers (1962), and the introduction of the point system (1967), which injected a degree of consistency and fairness into the immigration system. The government's decision to sign the UN Refugee Convention and Protocol (1969) led to the adoption of a coherent refugee policy, extending Canadian refugee resettlement beyond Europe and leading to the admission of refugees from Uganda, Chile, and, in 1975, Vietnam and Cambodia. Chapter 2 deals with the immediate consequences for Canada of the communist victory in Laos, Cambodia, and Vietnam in early 1975. It describes unsuccessful efforts to evacuate relatives of Vietnamese already in Canada, and cooperative efforts that resulted in the transportation of 120 orphans from Cambodia and Vietnam to Canada on two flights in the final days before the communist takeover. Chapter 3 describes little-known Canadian operations that moved refugees to Canada from Guam and various refugee centres in the United States, and the negative impact on Canadian public opinion and political will of the arrival in Canada of a notorious Vietnamese general. It traces small-scale operations in Southeast Asia in late 1976 and 1977, during a period when the refugee problem had dropped off the public radar and appeared to be fading away. At the same time, the phenomenon of the boat people was emerging as a serious challenge to the neighbouring countries of Southeast Asia. Chapter 4 deals with the coming into effect of the 1976 Immigration Act, the first Canadian legislation to include refugee provisions. The chapter describes the establishment of a resettlement system for Convention Refugees, the humanitarian "designated classes," designed to target and simplify the selection of specific refugee groups, and the introduction of the private refugee sponsorship system.

The pivotal year of 1978 is the subject of chapter 5, documenting a dawning recognition that the refugee situation would get much worse before it got better. It describes governmental efforts to establish small resettlement programs for boat people and overland refugees in Thailand, to promote the new sponsorship system, and to sensitize the public to an impending crisis. The chapter concludes with a description of the impact of the *Hai Hong* affair and the decision to resettle refugees from the derelict freighter. Chapter 6 examines the signing of the first master agreement between the Mennonite Central Committee and the government to facilitate refugee sponsorship, followed by a series of incremental decisions by the Trudeau and Clark governments culminating in the July 1979 decision to admit 50,000 refugees, and the government's challenge to Canadian civil society to sponsor large numbers of the refugees. The existing refugee processing systems were inadequate to handle the dramatic deluge of refugees, and chapter 7 describes the modifications and innovations introduced to match tens of thousands of refugees with thousands of sponsors, streamline documentation, transport and receive the refugees, and coordinate community-level resettlement efforts. Chapter 8 describes the rapid expansion of refugee selection in Southeast Asia to meet burgeoning sponsorship demands. As the number of refugee sponsorships exceeded governmental expectation (and budget), and a national organization launched a media campaign against the admission of so many Asian refugees, the government concluded that it could not exceed the 50,000 target without provoking a backlash. It announced that it would cut back on its commitment to government assisted refugees. This decision, and the reaction of civil society, are described in chapter 9. This section ends with chapter 10, describing how, following the Clark government's defeat, the incoming immigration minister, Lloyd Axworthy, decided to add another 10,000 government-assisted refugees. The story continues until the final flight brings in the last of the 60,000 refugees to Canada in December 1980.

The focus changes in part 2 with a series of firsthand accounts written by men and women directly involved in the selection and processing of refugees in Southeast Asia. Chapter 11 looks at the earliest days of the Singapore operation (1975–77), which at that time also included Thailand, through the eyes of two enterprising officers tasked with searching an enormous territory to find relatives of Indochinese refugees already in Canada. Chapter 12 is an overview of the Singapore-based refugee operation, covering Malaysia and Indonesia, written in the summer of 1980 by a visa officer (and former journalist) at the end of a three-year assignment. The report, never submitted to Immigration Headquarters, contains a remarkably candid account of the most complex operation in Southeast Asia. Chapter 13 recounts the experiences of visa officers in tracking down and selecting refugees in Malaysia, Indonesia, Brunei, and the Anambas Islands during the height of the 1979–80 resettlement operation. This chapter also includes contributions on the security and medical screening processes. Chapter 14 contains an insightful memoir of the officer responsible for coordination of Canadian resettlement operations in Malaysia. The firsthand accounts in these chapters provide poignant and graphic descriptions of the challenges, hardships, joys, and sorrows of the young men and women who delivered the program in Malaysia, Indonesia, and Brunei out of the Singapore visa office.

Chapters 15 and 16, written by an officer who helped establish the refugee operation in Thailand in late 1979, capture the challenges of creating a resettlement program staffed to deal with twenty families a month but almost immediately tasked with processing 18,000 refugees. These chapters include detailed information on how the refugee selection process actually functioned and adapted to changing demands. Chapter 17 supplies firsthand accounts of what it was like to work in the camps of Thailand processing a diverse caseload of Vietnamese boat people, along with Cambodians, Laotians, and people from the Hill Tribes.

Memoirs of officers involved in the refugee operations in Hong Kong, Macau, and Manila make up chapter 18. The Indochinese refugee movement was the first in which officers of the Quebec Immigration Service worked alongside their federal colleagues; the memoirs of two QIS officers in chapter 19 reveal a pattern of camaraderie and cooperation enlivened by occasional disagreements.

With thousands of refugees fleeing in small boats, the issue of what to do with those rescued on the high seas by passing merchant ships was a continuing problem. Chapter 20 records the challenges faced by Canadian visa officers based far from Southeast Asia in responding to refugees carried to the Persian Gulf and to Turkey by their rescuers. This chapter also includes a rare account by the British captain of a Canadian-owned ship, recording his frustration with trying to find a country willing to permit the refugees he had rescued to go ashore.

Part 3 shifts the focus from Southeast Asia to Canada. The government made an early decision to establish staging areas at military bases in Edmonton and Montreal where the refugee aircraft charters would land. Refugees would spend anywhere from three to five days at the staging areas. Their documentation would be completed, and they had a chance to rest, be outfitted with seasonal clothing, and receive orientation before proceeding to their sponsors and destinations. Chapter 21 includes accounts written by managers of these unique operations overseen by both the Canadian military and the Immigration Department.

Chapter 22 covers a variety of perspectives on coordinating sponsorship, community reception, and the provision of settlement services at the provincial and community levels. The chapter illustrates how officials from all levels of government and a wide variety of religious and community institutions came together, without a master plan, to ensure services were put in place for the benefit of both refugees and sponsors. A unique federal contribution was the recruitment of fifty-five experienced community workers as refugee liaison officers (RLOs). Two RLOs working in different environments recount their experiences in chapter 23. While an account of how the refugees adapted to Canada is beyond the scope of this volume, chapter 24 succinctly surveys the findings of various studies, done for the most part a decade after the majority of the refugees arrived in Canada. The studies, which restricted their scope to the experiences of refugees in specific parts of the country, reveal how hard it was for many to learn English and French and the detrimental impact of this difficulty on their employment prospects. The studies also revealed some surprising findings about the relative merits of the private sponsorship and government settlement programs from the refugees' perspectives. This chapter also notes that there has been almost no work done by academics on the settlement and integration experiences of the Indochinese refugees in the past thirty years and that, given the size of the community and the challenges its members faced, a new round of academic studies would not be amiss.

To conclude, the authors offer a number of insights based on Canada's largest ever resettlement effort.

For two decades, from 1957 onwards, the Hungarian refugee movement served as the precedent used in public discourse to legitimize subsequent resettlement operations. Given both its magnitude and the hands-on involvement of so many Canadians, the Indochinese movement subsequently replaced the Hungarian operation as the standard by which future Canadian resettlement programs for refugees would be judged. The bold decision of the Clark government to accept 50,000 refugees in July 1979 paid off when Canadians took up the challenge and opportunity afforded by the as-yet-untried private sponsorship program, which remains to this day a pillar of Canada's approach to refugee resettlement. We hope this volume will demonstrate how the bold political leadership and enthusiastic public response to the plight of those who fled Vietnam, Cambodia, and Laos in 1979 and 1980 rested on the creativity of the public servants who developed the policy framework and the robust and flexible bureaucratic tools capable of bringing 60,000 refugees to Canada. We also hope that the narratives in parts 2 and 3 provide some insights into the character, quality, and capabilities of our colleagues who implemented the policy in Canada and abroad.

As this book was being completed, Canadians were motivated by the Syrian civil war to once again respond to a massive population displacement. Efforts to sensitize the public and the government to this new crisis were, in part, a result of decisions made at the 2013 conference on the Indochinese movement at York University mentioned in the preface. As the media and civil society leaders appealed to Canadians to once more take advantage of the private sponsorship program in reaching out to the Syrian refugees, the precedent established in 1979 and 1980 for the Indochinese movement was invariably invoked. This linking of past to present was deliberate. It was particularly visible in Toronto where Lifeline Syria, the organization created to encourage private sponsorships, was not only named after its 1979 predecessor, Operation Lifeline, but also drew on many of the organizational structures and operational techniques developed forty years earlier. The committee formed by the mayors of Canada's cities to coordinate their efforts on behalf of the Syrians harkens back to the pioneering efforts of the mayors of Windsor, Ottawa, and Vancouver in providing community-based leadership in the 1970s. Other examples abound.

Throughout Canada's history, immigration has been an important driver of fundamental change. This book examines the roles of Canadian political leaders and officials in facilitating the arrival of 70,000 refugees from Vietnam, Cambodia, and Laos between 1975 and 1980. Of course the story did not end there, and refugees from the countries that once comprised Indochina continued to arrive in Canada until 1992, bringing the total movement to something like 130,000 souls. After a very hard struggle, they settled in well, and they and their children are found in all sectors of Canadian life. Like most refugees, they arrived with nothing, so the only way they could go was up. Their story, like the stories of other immigrants and refugees who have found their way to Canada, deserves a place in the greater Canadian story.

Running on Empty records an extraordinary moment in Canada's history. It illustrates the confluence of insightful political direction, creative public-service policy execution, and a popular groundswell among Canadians. Coming together in common purpose, they set a standard that continues to inspire humanitarian actions on behalf of the displaced and persecuted.

PART ONE

A History of Canada's
Involvement with the Indochinese
Refugees, 1975–1980

I

The Historical Evolution of Canada's Refugee Policy between World War II and the Immigration Act, 1976

Canada's capacity to resettle 70,000 Indochinese refugees between 1975 and 1980 – the largest single refugee movement to Canada – can best be understood by viewing it in the context of the evolution of Canadian refugee policy since World War II.[1] Between 1947 and 1976, Canada resettled approximately 300,000 refugees and displaced persons without any reference to refugees in Canadian immigration legislation. This feat was possible because of a well-functioning professional network of immigration offices abroad and in Canada and a series of often inventive ad hoc measures adopted by successive governments and supported by the Canadian body politic.

When Prime Minister Mackenzie King relaunched Canada's immigration program following the Great Depression and World War II, his vision was geographically and racially exclusive, limited to Europe and Europeans. In a speech on 1 May 1947, he maintained, "The people of Canada do not wish as a result of mass immigration to make a fundamental alteration in the character of our population. Large scale immigration from the Orient would change the fundamental composition of the Canadian population."[2] At the same time, Mackenzie King recognized Canada's moral obligation to assist the masses of displaced persons in the refugee camps of postwar Europe. On his instructions, from 1947 to 1951, the Canadian Government Immigration Mission, working with the International Refugee Organization and the Canadian Christian Committee for Refugees, processed the admission to Canada of 163,000 Europeans displaced by the war. Authority for the movement was based on a series of Orders-in-Council that specified the numbers and occupations of the persons to be admitted. As the postwar refugee crisis slowly abated, another 23,000 stateless Europeans were admitted to Canada between 1952 and 1956.[3]

Canada had been involved in the drafting of the UN Refugee Convention, opened for signature in 1951. However, Cabinet declined to ratify the Convention for fear that it would inhibit Canada's ability to deport people on national security grounds. The Convention defined a refugee as someone who was outside his country of nationality and, as a result of events in Europe before 1951, had a well-founded fear of persecution because of race, religion, nationality, membership of a particular social group, or political opinion. Canada established its own refugee definition after 1951, drawing on the UN Convention definition but focusing on people fleeing countries under the domination of the Soviet Union.[4]

That same year saw the launch of the Office of the UN High Commissioner for Refugees and its logistical counterpart, the Intergovernmental Committee for European Migration, the latter situated outside the UN structure, away from Soviet interference. Canada was involved in the creation of both. The following year, Parliament passed the Immigration Act, 1952, which said a great deal about who could not be admitted to Canada but had little to say about who could. Authority to decide immigrant admission policy was vested in the minister of immigration, who continued to maintain Canada's preference for European immigration.

With respect to refugee policy, the government expected and hoped that once the postwar refugee crisis was resolved, the refugee problem would fade away. In 1959, during World Refugee Year, Canada admitted 1,300 individuals from the dwindling refugee camps of Europe, including 211 in need of treatment for tuberculosis. However, even as the refugee camps of Europe were virtually emptied, new refugee challenges emerged. In late 1956, Hungary revolted against Soviet domination. When the USSR crushed the Hungarian Revolution, Cabinet, emboldened by strong support from the Canadian public and media, mandated Canada's immigration minister at the time, Jack Pickersgill, to fly to Vienna and personally organize departmental officials, cut formalities to the bone, and move 37,000 refugees to Canada. The Hungarian refugee movement set a precedent for Canada's can-do approach to future refugee crises.

At the same time, Canada's Europe-based approach to immigration and refugee policy was being reconsidered. By the 1960s, Canadian values were changing. A racially based, Europe-centred immigration policy was not consistent with Canada's self-image in the world as a progressive middle power, and it contradicted Prime Minister John Diefenbaker's Canadian Bill of Rights. Ellen Fairclough, the country's first female immigration minister, oversaw the drafting of new immigration regulations that removed the most racist provisions from Canada's immigration program.[5] The authority to admit immigrants to Canada devolved to immigration officials abroad on the basis of general instructions. When the government released a test balloon for immigration reform in its White Paper on Immigration[6] in 1966, Canada had not been involved in a serious refugee movement for a decade. Yet, based on the perception of changed Canadian values, the white paper recommended distinct refugee legislation and the ratification of the 1951 UN Refugee Convention.

Radical change in the immigration program occurred in 1967 with the introduction of the point system for the selection of economic immigrants – a genuine Canadian innovation.[7] It was followed by the rapid expansion of the immigration network in Asia, the Middle East, Latin America, the Caribbean, and Africa, none of them traditional sources of immigration to Canada. Within a year, Canadian officials were implementing a policy of "universality," interviewing applicants for immigration in over one hundred countries, using criteria defined by the point system and consistent family reunification policies. Coincidentally, as Canada's immigration policy became universal in scope, 1967 also saw the United Nations launch a protocol to the UN Refugee Convention that made the convention universal rather than Europe-centred in application.

In August 1968, the Soviet Union ended Czechoslovakia's effort to reform its communist system. Russian tanks rolled into Prague, and Canada, on the basis of a Cabinet decision, accepted 11,000 Czechoslovak refugees escaping Soviet tyranny.

Canada ratified the UN Refugee Convention and Protocol in 1969, and in 1970 Cabinet reviewed the implications of this ratification, noting that while the immigration system had been universal since the introduction of the point system, the refugee system had remained focused exclusively on European refugees. Based on the Cabinet review,[8] a comprehensive set of instructions on how to select refugees for resettlement under the universality policy was issued to immigration officials on 2 January 1971. The 1970 policy had three main elements:

1 Canada abandoned its own refugee definition and adopted the UN Refugee Convention's definition: resettlement activities were no longer confined to Europe.

2 The point system would be used to assess refugees' prospects for successful establishment on the understanding that officers had and were encouraged and expected to use their discretionary authority to override the system in favour of refugees, given the extra assistance available to them on arrival.[9]

3 The Oppressed Minority policy provided for the selection of oppressed people who were not refugees according to the UN definition because they were still in their home countries.[10]

These instructions for dealing with refugees would be quickly tested. When Britain appealed to Canada for assistance in coping with the expulsion of Uganda's Asian community in August 1972, Prime Minister Pierre Trudeau announced the decision to assist in terms profoundly different from those used by Mackenzie King twenty-five years previously: "We are prepared to offer an honourable place in Canadian life to those Ugandan Asians who come to Canada ... I am sure that [they] will ... by their abilities and industry, make an ... important contribution to Canadian society."[11] The team sent to Kampala moved 5,000 Ugandan Asians to Canada in sixty days.[12] Another 2,000, from refugee camps in Europe, would follow.

The next major refugee movement followed the Pinochet coup that replaced Salvador Allende's leftist government in Chile with a right-wing military dictatorship. Dogged by controversy from the start, the Chilean movement was politically controversial and technically complex to deliver. A leaked controversial assessment of left-wing elements in Chile by the Canadian ambassador outraged churches and human-rights advocates who coalesced into a new, assertive community of refugee advocates. Over the succeeding years and under constant criticism, Canada's Immigration Department extracted 7,000 distressed Chileans in three streams: Chileans in neighbouring countries (Convention Refugees), Chileans directly from Chile under the Oppressed Minority policy, and two hundred political prisoners direct from Chilean prisons, along with their families. A fourth stream of Chileans appeared at Canadian airports as asylum seekers, a new phenomenon for Canada.

Then, starting in April 1975 after communist victories in Cambodia, Laos, and Vietnam, Canada participated in a refugee resettlement movement from distant Southeast Asia, which in 1979–80 would become the largest refugee movement in our history.

It is important to note that the 1952 Immigration Act, conceived as an enforcement tool during a time when most Canadians assumed, like Mackenzie King, that the nature of our population would never change, had remained in place – despite Ellen Fairclough's reforms, the introduction of the point system, the universalization of the immigration system, the signing of the UN Refugee Convention and Protocol, the 1970 refugee policy, and the arrival of refugees and immigrants from all parts of the world. The main virtue of the 1952 act was that it did not hinder Canada's use of discretionary means to manage refugee crises. However, Canada's place in the world changed in the 1960s and '70s, a change expressed through the adoption of universal, non-discriminatory approaches to human rights and immigration. The country needed immigration legislation that better reflected its values and its citizens' demands for more progressive, open, and transparent approaches to refugees and immigrants.

The drafting of the Immigration Act, 1976 under the supervision of Liberal minister Robert Andras was preceded by extensive public consultations on immigration. Hundreds of submissions were received, and a joint parliamentary committee held public hearings across the country. The newly formed community of refugee advocates had strong views about Canadian resettlement and asylum policies and took full advantage of the consultative process to make them known. As passed by Parliament in 1976 (the year after Saigon fell and the first wave of Indochinese refugees arrived in Canada), the new act broke so completely with its 1952 predecessor that it took two years to design the regulations, administrative instructions, and tools needed to implement it. The new legislation provided for a range of refugee provisions (described in chapter 4) that would profoundly impact how Canada dealt with the second wave of Indochinese refugees in 1979 and 1980.[13]

2

The Fall of Saigon and Canada's Response

The International Context

After a series of interconnected wars lasting almost three decades, the dominant role of the West in Indochina came to an end in the spring of 1975. The Indochinese wars were part of the protracted post–World War II national liberation struggles of Third World nations ruled as colonies by European powers. More importantly, the Indochinese liberation struggles became a part of the Cold War, the ideologically based, worldwide showdown between the United States and the USSR, the two superpowers to emerge from the destruction of World War II. Once the Chinese communists had defeated the nationalist Guomindang in 1949, Communist China emerged as a powerful state and joined the USSR in supporting the emergence of a communist and nationalist anti-colonial movement in northern Vietnam that opposed France, the colonial power weakened by World War II. Initially, the United States had been reluctant to support France's attempt to continue to control Indochina. However, once China and the USSR declared their support of North Vietnam, Americans saw South Vietnam as the second potential "domino"[1] to fall to communism in Asia. Following the defeat of France, the United States became involved in the war to contain the newly established North Vietnamese state and stop the spread of communism.[2]

The Indochinese wars have been the subject of a large number of scholarly analyses, eyewitness accounts, and media reporting – enough material to fill a small library. This is not the place to attempt to repeat the many controversies regarding the war's aims and its conduct, the 1973 Paris Peace Accords, and the communist victory in Indochina. It should, however, be noted that close to four decades after the war's end, passionate scholarly debate about it continues.[3] The victory of North Vietnam and its guerilla ally in South Vietnam, the Viet Cong, followed the US strategy of military disengagement in Vietnam in the early 1970s. As agreed through the Paris Peace Accords in 1973, the United States withdrew all of its troops from Vietnam. But instead of a ceasefire and negotiations between the government of South Vietnam and the communist Viet Cong aiming at a peaceful resolution of the conflict – the other principal paper elements of the Peace Accords – North Vietnam redoubled its attacks against the weakened government of South Vietnam. At the same time, the Khmer Rouge in Cambodia and the Pathet Lao in Laos successfully brought to a close their wars against the governments in Phnom Penh and Vientiane. South Vietnam, Cambodia, and Laos fell to the communists in quick succession. By early May 1975, all of former French Indochina was ruled by communist governments.[4]

An unplanned consequence of these long-term Cold War conflicts was large population movements.[5] Arguably, the large-scale US involvement in Indochina started with a population movement. The Geneva Accords of 1954 that put the seal on the French defeat, establishing the communist regime in North Vietnam and the French-supported Republic of Vietnam in the south, also allowed major population exchanges between the two parts of the now divided country. The accords allowed the people of Vietnam a long period of grace – three hundred days – in which to choose where they wished to reside. During this period, close to one million northerners – the great majority of them civilians – moved to the south, while between 14,000 and 45,000 civilians and about 100,000 communist fighters moved from the south to the north. A large part of the north-south movement was accomplished through transports of people by the French military and the US Navy in an operation christened by the Americans "Passage to Freedom," a name that reflected the US Cold War ideological commitment. Those taking advantage of Operation Passage to Freedom were predominantly Catholic and middle class. These factors would remain important elements of population movements for the next thirty-five years. Under the pressure of civil wars and advancing communist armies and ideologies as well as US bombing, many of the population

movements both within Indochina and from Indochina to third countries would consist of ethnic and class minorities, including Catholics
from North Vietnam, Vietnamese from Cambodia, Hill Tribes, including Hmong, from Laos, middle-class commercial people from all of
Indochina, and Chinese from Vietnam.[6]

In the decades of conflict following Operation Passage to Freedom,
but still before the fall of Saigon, very large numbers were displaced
within Indochina. Gil Loescher in his book *The* UNHCR *and World
Politics* estimates that some twenty million people were uprooted at
one time or another within Vietnam, and there was an enormous
rural-to-urban exodus.[7] The population of Saigon grew by about two
million through the influx of rural populations. In Cambodia, by the
time the Khmer Rouge marched into Phnom Penh, there were some
two to three million internally displaced persons in a total population
of 7.5 million.[8] The total human cost of the civil war in Cambodia between the Lon Nol government and the Khmer Rouge, as well as the
Viet Cong incursions and the US bombing campaign between 1970
and 1975, is estimated to be 500,000 dead and two million internally
displaced.[9] In Vietnam, by the time the North Vietnamese forces
closed in on Saigon in April 1975, more than half of South Vietnam's
population had been uprooted at least once.[10] And though the war
ended at the end of April, hundreds of thousands of Vietnamese were
soon on the move again.

It is important to note how the international community and the
UNHCR, its main multilateral refugee protection institution, regarded
the population displacements in Indochina on the eve of the fall of
Saigon. While the 1951 Statute of the Office of the UNHCR seeks to
provide "the necessary legal protection for refugees" and to "seek permanent solutions for the problems of refugees," for decades the international refugee protection system found it difficult to move
beyond the refugee definition referring to individuals rather than to
groups of people forced to flee conflicts.[11] At first, during the late
1960s, the UNHCR considered the political impediments of becoming
embroiled in Indochina to be too great and played only a very minor
role in assisting refugees. However, by the early 1970s and especially
after 1975, facing ever-increasing demands by displaced people, the
UNHCR, under US pressure, had to assume a greater role in Indochina.[12] Yet, when called upon to help with the large-scale flight of
Indochinese, the UNHCR was reluctant to refer to these people as

"refugees," preferring to use terms like "displaced persons from Indo-China outside their country of origin" or "persons leaving the Indo-China peninsula in small boats."[13]

Most of the world, including the UNHCR, considered Indochina to be an American problem and initially resisted the internationalization of the emerging refugee crisis. None of the countries of the Southeast Asia region were signatories to the UN Refugee Convention. In the period immediately following the fall of Saigon, the UNHCR believed that the repatriation of refugees or, failing that, local integration, was the preferred solution to the emerging crisis.[14] Thus, immediately after the fall of Saigon, most of the international community showed little interest or willingness to take large-scale measures to deal with the refugee outflow. Initially, although it always considered the escaping Vietnamese and Cambodians to be refugees, it too was reluctant to accept them for resettlement. However, as the scope of the emergency became evident, the United States reacted with a massive resettlement program in America and requested the international community to share the burden of permanently resettling refugees. Most western allies did not react positively; Canada, on the basis of humanitarian considerations, did.[15]

Canada's Evolving Policies in Response to the Imminent Fall of Saigon and the Emerging Indochinese Refugee Crisis, 1975

By the beginning of April 1975, Canada's foreign policy establishment realized that South Vietnam would fall to the communists within weeks. The initial diplomatic assessment of Canada's relations with the new regime, based on a report from the embassy in Washington, was that Canada's "future relations with a communist-dominated South Vietnam or a unified Vietnamese state would not be important," and the new Vietnam would have "no bilateral interests for Canada."[16] The same assessment also noted that requests had been received from the US State Department regarding a multilateral international response to resettle refugees fleeing the communist takeover: "Would Canada agree to participate in a broadly based refugee program in which ... Australia, Britain ... and perhaps a few other countries would be interested?" It was recognized that such a program would be US-led rather than sponsored by the UN, given sensitivities within the UN due to strongly opposing views on the new Vietnamese government.[17]

Therefore it should be emphasized that during the final days of South Vietnam and following the fall of Saigon, Canada's main role in Vietnam was not political or economic. It rapidly evolved into a humanitarian and refugee-related role, falling within the policy and operational purview of the Department of Manpower and Immigration. In response to strong representations by Vietnamese residing in Canada, the government agreed in April 1975 to admit their family members. Then, on 1 May 1975, immediately after the fall of Saigon, the government agreed, in response to a request from the United States, to admit refugees from Cambodia and South Vietnam. Thus, Canada's initial reaction to the refugee crisis, occasioned by the conquest of South Vietnam by the North Vietnamese, included not only "relatives sponsored or nominated by Canadian Citizens or residents" but also 2,000 individuals considered to be Convention refugees from camps in the United States and 1,000 others in Southeast Asia.[18]

Canada had to react rapidly to assist the United States in clearing the camps around Asia and the Pacific, where the great masses of refugees were initially accommodated in makeshift camps. Immigration Minister Robert Andras recognized that "public association with the United States in such a program may, having regard to the United States' role in Vietnam, have undesirable features."[19] However, he emphasized to Cabinet that, following well-established Canadian traditions, "humanitarian considerations ought to be regarded as paramount."[20] In order to demonstrate the even-handed nature of Canada's program, Andras highlighted the similarity of Canada's humanitarian efforts in South Vietnam and Chile. What was important in both of these movements was that Canada acted "solely to alleviate human distress, without regard to political or any other considerations." That in one instance refugees were fleeing from a right-wing military coup and in another a communist conquest did not matter.[21]

Canada's policy position was developed to meet the refugee emergency in Indochina, independent of its political causes. The challenge facing the Department of Manpower and Immigration was to project resettlement operations to locations in Asia and the United States where refugees had arrived through their own initiative or as a result of American rescue efforts. Decisions made by working-level officials in the field made it possible to move thousands of refugees quickly in chaotic and swiftly changing postwar conditions.[22]

Events Leading up to the Evacuation of Saigon

On the immigration side, two closely related operational efforts had unfolded during the last weeks before the final evacuation of the Canadian Embassy in Saigon. First, Immigration Department Head-quarters in Ottawa, beginning in early April 1975, had to react to the rapidly developing and still largely unexpected refugee emergency in Vietnam. At the time, Canada had "a very small Vietnamese commu-nity, mainly located in Quebec: there were only 1,204 Vietnamese im-migrants landed in Canada during the five preceding years."[23] As well, there was a core of approximately 1,300 French-speaking Vietnamese students studying in Quebec and another two hundred in the rest of Canada. Despite these apparently small numbers, as the situation in South Vietnam deteriorated at the beginning of April, a delegation of Vietnamese students travelled from Montreal to Ottawa and demon-strated in front of Parliament, asking the federal government to help their besieged compatriots in Vietnam. The government reacted pos-itively, deciding that those on student visas could apply for perma-nent residence,[24] and ordering immigration offices across the country to remain open over the weekend to accept family sponsorships. The small Vietnamese community quickly generated thousands of spon-sorships that were telexed directly to the embassy in Saigon.[25] Tove Bording described the situation in Ottawa:

> The small team on the Asia Pacific desk could not cope and the whole Headquarters' Foreign Service contingent swung into ac-tion. The Minister, Bob Andras, moved from his office on the 11th floor of the Bourque Building in Ottawa to the office of the Director General of the Foreign Service on the second floor, in order to be readily available to deal with issues as they arose. Everyone was working 14–16 hour days and Allan Gotlieb, the Deputy Minister, had food sent in from Nates, Ottawa's iconic delicatessen across the street ... Two officers slept at the Exter-

nal Affairs communications centre to ensure incoming and out-going messages were dealt with promptly. It was decided to allow any Vietnamese and Cambodians already in Canada, re-gardless of their status here, to remain.[26]

Secondly, members of the Immigration Department's contingent in Southeast Asia – first from Singapore and then from Hong Kong – were instructed to proceed to Saigon to process visa applications. The Canadian High Commission in Singapore had primary responsibility for visa processing work in South Vietnam, and on or just after 1 April 1975, Gavin Stewart at Immigration HQ phoned John Baker, a young visa officer in Singapore, in the middle of the night, asking him to get on a plane to Saigon as quickly as possible. He told Baker that the Canadian Embassy in Washington had been advised by the Ameri-cans that they could foresee the collapse of the Republic of Vietnam government within weeks. Even before Baker's plane landed, it was evident to him that Saigon was under siege. On the approach to Saigon's Tan Son Nhut Airport, he "could see billowing black smoke close by." On landing, he learned that a USAF C-5A Galaxy, then the largest plane in the world, had just crashed with nearly 250 Viet-namese orphans and dozens of caregivers on board.[27] Some 115 of them survived the crash.

Baker's first challenge was to attempt to contact all persons with ac-tive immigration cases even as the city was surrounded by North Viet-namese forces. He asked one of the local embassy employees to try to contact all the applicants. This was feasible for those in or close to Saigon; but it was impossible to contact those outside the immediate surroundings of the city. The country was crumbling, along with cru-cial infrastructure and services, including phones and mail delivery. All the same, the South Vietnamese government and the military con-tinued to function almost to the end of April. This is important to note, because as Ernest Hébert, Canada's chargé d'affaires in Saigon, observed, "customs, immigration and security were performing their duty normally and no one could leave the country without a passport and a Vietnamese exit permit."[28]

More challenges lay ahead. The next big obstacle would be the exit permits required by the South Vietnamese authorities. People may have been ready to receive their visas, but exit permits to leave Viet-nam were almost impossible to obtain, except for those with connections and sufficient resources.[29] In the weeks before the fall of Saigon "the South Vietnamese Government was determined, as a matter of policy and survival, to prevent by all possible means and at all cost the departure of their own citizens [in order] not to demoralize and de-motivate its soldiers in the combat zones."[30] The exit permit require-ment was enforced at Vietnam's airports at gunpoint until the last days of the regime. Even on 24 April, as the remaining Canadian con-tingent left on the last Canadian flight leaving Saigon, they had to pass through four South Vietnamese Army checkpoints enforcing strict document controls.[31]

Meanwhile, the high-pressure work being performed in Canada was bearing fruit: each morning, the Canadian Embassy in Saigon re-ceived from headquarters a long roll (twenty to thirty feet) of telex paper with the names of people sponsored by Canadian relatives and friends. These lists often contained incomplete names and incomplete addresses and rarely included dates of birth. With each passing day, the rolls grew longer, the names on them serving as an index of those the embassy was supposed to contact. Of the desperate crowds show-ing up at the embassy each day, only a miniscule number of people could be matched with the names on the lists. The streets of Saigon were becoming increasingly tense, with artillery and rocket fire in the distance. Electrical power at the embassy was intermittent. Even as staff worked twelve-hour days in chaotic circumstances, little progress was being made in handling the crowds and finding people named on the ever-growing lists.[32]

Canadian officials attempted to find solutions to the worsening sit-uation. Canadian Forces flights, diverted to the South Vietnam emer-gency, ferried visa officers back and forth between Saigon and Hong Kong, but little evident progress was made on the ground.[33] On 8 April, John Baker flew to Hong Kong and back to Saigon the next day with Ernest Allen, the deputy immigration manager in Hong Kong. Allen assisted with the evacuation of a group of Canadians from Saigon and flew back to Hong Kong with them. But there was no way to meet the demand for visas by panicked people sponsored by relatives and friends in Canada. As Allen observed, at the airport on 9 April, virtually no Vietnamese showed up to attempt to leave with the Canadian evacuees. The Vietnamese simply could not obtain either passports or exit permits in the deteriorating situation and were not allowed to leave by their own authorities.[34]

Charles Rogers, the manager of the Hong Kong Visa Office, under-stood that the Canadian government had committed to resettle any South Vietnamese fleeing the fall of South Vietnam who had connec-tions to Canada and whose relatives in Canada had submitted their names to the immigration authorities. On the other hand, like all other Canadian officials observing the chaos in South Vietnam, he realized that connecting the lists of names received from Canada with the people in South Vietnam was terribly difficult and becoming less feasible each day as the communist forces closed in and conditions deteriorated. Moreover, many of the people had already fled the coun-try, so trying to locate them was a fruitless task. Amidst this turmoil, a practical solution was needed.

Knowing that many of the people on the telex roles from head-quarters were desperate enough to try to get out of Vietnam by any means, Rogers decided to provide them with a blanket visa approval if in some way they could get to a Canadian diplomatic representative in Vietnam or somewhere else. He devised a so-called Promise of Visa Letter (PVL) which guaranteed holders a Canadian visa if they could present themselves with the document to any Canadian diplomatic representative.[35] The PVL provided the hope of passage to Canada to desperate Vietnamese relatives of Canadian residents in the turmoil of the last days of South Vietnam.

By the second week of April, the tiny Canadian Embassy in Saigon could no longer manage the daily influx of lists of names from Canada. As a result, the lists were sent to Hong Kong, where PVLs were writ-ten for all the persons on the lists – a gargantuan task – and the letters were hand-carried by Canadian officers Margaret Tebbutt, Bill Bow-den, and Donald Cameron on Canadian military flights to Saigon, where they were mailed to the persons concerned. Over a two-week period, Canada's mission in Hong Kong produced some 3,500 PVLs, covering between 14,000 and 15,000 individuals, all of them mailed even as the fighting engulfed the South Vietnamese capital. Vietnamese refugees in possession of a PVL continued to show up in camps and other locations throughout Southeast Asia decades after the fall of Saigon.[36] It is impossible to estimate how many of the PVL were even-tually honoured. Undoubtedly, given the chaotic conditions under which they were mailed, the actual number used by refugees was rel-atively low.[37] However, the PVL did serve a real, practical purpose, holding out hope that eventually the refugee family would be united with Canadian relatives.

The Final Evacuation of South Vietnam

The US Evacuation of Saigon

While it is not the main subject of this book, the US evacuation of Saigon was the central event in the final days of South Vietnam and, as such, affected activities of the smaller diplomatic missions, including Canada's. Within a large segment of the population of South Vietnam that had served in the Government of Vietnam's military and bureaucracy or were part of the heavily Chinese or Catholic commercial and professional middle classes, as well as the large numbers of remaining US business and aid people, there was great fear of the conquering North Vietnamese forces. This fear was well founded. Reports were circulating in the capital of cruel punishments in areas captured by the invading forces against any Americans and all people deemed to be US collaborators or class enemies; the cruelties meted out by the Viet Cong when it briefly captured Hue during the Tet offensive were remembered.[38]

During March 1975, South Vietnam had rapidly unravelled: "The South suddenly began to lose the war faster than the North could win it." Panic set in. "In some areas, desperate South Vietnamese soldiers … turned their rage on South Vietnamese citizens in an ugly orgy of violence and murder."[39] On 29 March, the airport in Danang, South Vietnam's second-largest city, was the scene of terrifying violence as South Vietnamese soldiers fired on masses of civilians, including women and children, attempting to get on a departing commercial aircraft. On the morning of 29 April, Operation Frequent Wind began evacuating remaining American personnel and Vietnamese civilians from Tan Son Nhut Airport: "When the last Marines were airlifted from the roof of the American Embassy on the morning of April 30, they left behind more than four hundred Vietnamese waiting to be airlifted out of the compound."[40]

The Danang airport incident of 29 March, the crash of the USAF "baby flight" on 4 April, and the desperate Vietnamese civilians left behind on the roof of the US embassy were the sad ending to the Americans' long war in Indochina. In the final accounting, the large remaining US military presence and well-established infrastructure in Vietnam – a battalion of Marines, the Seventh Fleet waiting just off the coast, military helicopters ferrying out Americans still left in Vietnam – could not prevent the American evacuation from becoming badly disorganized. CIA analyst Frank Snepp, in his notorious memoir – notorious because Snepp was attacked by the US government and eventually convicted by the US Supreme Court for violating his CIA non-disclosure agreement – "excoriates the tardy, improvised nature of the evacuation and laments the many Vietnamese working for the Americans that were left behind."[41]

On the early morning of 30 April, with several US commercial contract aircraft still at Tan Son Nhut Airport, and with many Vietnamese still clamouring to leave, the United States pulled the plug and moved all American personnel out of Vietnam. In his report on the last days of Saigon before the fall, *New York Times* reporter Fox Butterfield, a seasoned foreign correspondent, described with extraordinary vividness an aspect of the evacuation that would soon become all too familiar: Vietnamese people fleeing the country by boat.

> About 71,000 Vietnamese abandoned their homes, their possessions, and often their families, and put out to sea in tiny fishing boats or ungainly barges in hopes of finding the Seventh Fleet. How they knew where we were is a mystery. The first day, Tuesday, we were only 17 miles off the coast near Vung Tau, at the mouth of the Saigon River. By Wednesday we had moved out to 40 miles and later, because of the rumored sighting of a North Vietnamese gunboat, to 70 miles. But they came anyway. When we awoke on Wednesday morning there were 20 fishing boats off our starboard, all crammed with people, many of whom looked like poor fishermen. The [USS] Mobile had orders to take on people only by helicopter and we had to refuse them. Some United States sailors openly protested, asking their officers why we were leaving them. A Vietnamese Roman Catholic priest in the bow of one wooden fishing craft bent to his knees and prayed to us to take him aboard. But we could not and the boats were pointed in the direction of the rest of the fleet where half a dozen merchant ships under char-

ter to the Military Sealift Command were embarking evacuees from boats.[42]

Thus, with the experience of almost two decades in Vietnam, with a large military force of seasoned Marines, with the world's largest and most technically advanced navy waiting off-shore, the United States found the evacuation of South Vietnam extremely difficult. Could the tiny Canadian diplomatic representation do better?

The Final Canadian Evacuation of Saigon

After John Baker returned to his home office in Singapore, his place was taken by Donald Cameron, a young visa officer based in Hong Kong. The much larger Hong Kong visa office could afford the absence of an officer better than could Singapore. Cameron describes the last days of South Vietnam, before the fall of Saigon:

> I was directed by Charles Rogers on 14 April to go to Saigon to relieve John Baker so that he could return to his one-person office in Singapore. The Canadian Forces were not flying to Saigon that day, and I took an Air Vietnam flight with very few passengers, many of whom were Americans based in Hong Kong sent to close down their companies' operations in Vietnam.
>
> On arrival at the Embassy, I was immediately placed in the lobby along with Baker and the locally engaged Consular Assistant to answer questions from the crowd of Vietnamese who swarmed the place. I spent much of my time during the morning hours when the Embassy was open to the public standing in the lobby and repeating, "Sans passport et sans visa de sortie il n'y a rien à faire." [Without a passport or an exit visa, nothing can be done.][43]

Of course, passports or exit visas were almost impossible to obtain during the last days of South Vietnam.

In April 1975, with the defeat of South Vietnam rapidly approaching, External Affairs in Ottawa ordered the Canadian Embassy in Saigon, headed by chargé d'affaires Ernest Hébert, to evacuate. The chargé saw his responsibility as staying in Saigon as long as it was possible to ensure that all Canadians would be safely evacuated. All remaining Canadians who wished to leave flew out of the virtually deserted Tan Son Nhut Airport on a Canadian Forces c-130 aircraft on 24 April.[44] According to Hébert, 25 April would have been the last day for a safe final evacuation, so the handful of remaining Canadians left at almost the last possible moment.[45]

Hébert was harshly criticized by Peter Kent of the CBC, among others, for not allowing more Vietnamese nationals to leave on the last Canadian flights out of Saigon, and for being strict in the application of the rule that Vietnamese nationals needed a passport and an exit permit to leave with the evacuating Canadians.[46] Was the media criticism well-founded? The facts are that, unlike the Americans, Canada had only a tiny mission with extremely limited capacities on the ground. Second, Canada had no effective security arrangements of any kind in Saigon. Even with the large resources of the US Marine Corps and the US Navy, the Americans could not effectively control the evacuation of an enormous number of panicked people. Therefore, Canada had to act cautiously, in line with established international norms. Finally, as has been noted above and most importantly, the overwhelming majority of South Vietnamese were not permitted to obtain passports or exit permits by the South Vietnamese authorities. Kent either did not know about, or chose to ignore, the US experience at the Danang airport on 29 March and the fact that South Vietnamese civilians could not obtain passports or exit permits. The Canadian Embassy managed to do what it could under very difficult circumstances: there were two Canadian "baby flights" in April and eleven Vietnamese nationals were on the last Canadian flight from Saigon.[47] As Ernest Allen reported on one of the flights a week before the final evacuation flight on 24 April, "Our arrival at Tan Son Nhut occurred uneventfully, and I recall being surprised at the relative calm of the airport, despite South Vietnam's government being in absolute turmoil and its army in defeat. The atmosphere at Tan Son Nhut would change from composure to one of total chaos within the month as the city fell to the AVN. Adhering to Canada's unwritten policy regarding embassy closures and evacuations, "never the first, never the last, and always in good company," our actions in Saigon that day were in step with those of Australia and the United States, which were also evacuating civilian nationals."[48] In fact, Canada was among the last to evacuate. By 26 April, the airport had been bombed and made inoperative, and an orderly evacuation through the airport would have been impossible.[49]

The Baby Flights

The events of April in Saigon demonstrated that Canadian officials had the capacity to react, at times in a highly innovative manner – witness the Promise of Visa Letters – to extreme challenges. This demonstrated capacity would serve well when Canadian officers were asked to respond to the enormous challenges of an overwhelming movement of Vietnamese boat people as well as thousands of Cambodian and Laotian refugees in the camps of Thailand in 1979–80. The rapid transport to Canada of two groups of war orphans, the so-called baby flights, saw private Canadian individuals, Canadian officials abroad and in Canada, and even the relatives of those officials, act in tandem to swiftly move endangered orphan children to Canada and deliver them to adoptive parents. This strategy foreshadowed the cooperation between the Canadian government and the Canadian people that was to become the hallmark of the Indochinese refugee movement in 1979–80.

The baby flights did not occur in a vacuum: "From 1970 to 1974, over 1,400 adoptions of Vietnamese children in the United States had been arranged ... The US Operation Babylift was initiated on 2 April in response to the emergency situation ... in South Vietnam. Prospective adopting U.S. parents were concerned that Vietnamese orphans already selected for adoption, who might be physically endangered by active hostilities, would not be able to leave Vietnam expeditiously if normal, lengthy Vietnamese exit procedures and U.S. immigration procedures were followed."[50] Apparently under US pressure, in early April the adoption laws in Vietnam had all been waived, and the only document required was an embassy's note certifying that all the children on the flights listed had an adoption family abroad and were taken care of financially and otherwise.[51] The US government sent a number of military aircraft during April 1975 to ferry children out of besieged Saigon:

A total of 2,547 orphans were processed under "Operation Babylift," the great majority flown from Saigon to Clark Air Force Base in the Philippines between April 2 and April 19. Of this total, 1,945 went on to the USA and 602 to other countries, including over 120 to Canada. Many of the orphans were of mixed race, including African American-Vietnamese children, a legacy of the US military's long years in Vietnam. A number of highly motivated aid workers, including Americans, Australians, Germans and other nationalities participated in the American Operation Babylift. Tragically, the operation started with a terrifying disaster when a US Air Force C-5A crashed soon after taking off, killing 135 of the orphans and escorts on board.[52]

Several Canadian organizations were involved with saving Indochinese children, including a private group called Families for Children (FFC) based in Montreal, Quan Yung Foundation based in Ontario, and the provincial Ministry of Community and Social Services responsible for international adoptions in Ontario. The activities of Naomi Bronstein and Eloise and Anna Charet for Families for Children and Victoria Leach and Helen Allen of the Ontario government should be highlighted.[53]

The First Canadian Baby Flight

The first Canadian baby flight was atypical in a number of ways. Most of the children on it were not Vietnamese or of mixed race but Cambodian – although some were Vietnamese survivors of the crash of the US Galaxy baby flight. By the time the group of Cambodian babies arrived in Saigon in late March or early April (exact date unknown), they had already been through one evacuation. Eloise and Anna Charet had brought the children to Saigon from Phnom Penh on one of the last US flights out of Cambodia, operated by the "Flying Tigers," a fearless bunch of American flyers leaving the Cambodian capital just before the Khmer Rouge marched in. The children came from the Canada House orphanage established in Phnom Penh by Naomi Bronstein's Families for Children group. Bronstein, a young Canadian woman with a husband and children in Montreal, had established the Phnom Penh orphanage using her own family's money as well as resources she had obtained from various international and Canadian sources. The Charet sisters, two very young (twenty-two and twenty), idealistic Quebecers, went to Phnom Penh at Christmas 1974 and ran Canada House until the advance of the Khmer Rouge forced them to flee Cambodia with "their" babies.[54]

On learning that the Cambodian babies had been brought to Saigon, Bronstein quickly joined the Charet sisters, who were taking care of over fifty Cambodian babies in the South Vietnamese capital now under siege. Bronstein managed to get places for the orphans on the US baby flight that was to leave Saigon on 4 April 1975. Meanwhile, a Canadian CF-130 military flight had arrived in Saigon on that same day from Hong Kong to help with an early Canadian evacuation effort. After conferring with the Canadian chargé d'affaires, Ernest Hébert, Bronstein realized that there would be places for the Cambodian orphans on the Canadian flight back to Hong Kong, so she gave up her orphans' places on the US flight to make spaces available on the US plane for babies being flown from Vietnam to California.[55]

The US plane that crashed was the one that the three women were supposed to take with the babies. A documentary film about her shows a distraught Naomi Bronstein looking for live infants in the wreckage of the enormous crashed Galaxy aircraft and later shows her sobbing at the airport as babies are being loaded into the Canadian plane leaving for Hong Kong. Some of the babies she managed to get on the Canadian flight were tiny Vietnamese survivors of the crash.[56] The flight to Hong Kong with the babies, their caretakers – including Bronstein and the Charet sisters – and other Canadian evacuees occurred safely. Reports from the plane, however, talk of crowded conditions, with a Canadian woman attempting to pacify three babies on her lap all the way from Saigon to Hong Kong.[57] RCAF Major Bob Nicholson, the pilot of the flight, recalls "the scene in the air above verdant Vietnam, the Hercules transformed into a nursery with babies in large cardboard cartons tied down with cargo straps. Everyone pitched in to help – flight engineers, navigators and pilots."[58]

The staff of the Canadian Commission in Hong Kong immediately recognized the urgency of the situation. On the Saigon flight's arrival on 5 April, they put the group up in a hotel and worked overnight to get all the documentation (Minister's Permits under Section 7(2)c of the 1952 Immigration Act) in order so that the babies could leave for Canada on a scheduled flight leaving shortly.[59] When Elizabeth Heatherington left her flat that afternoon in Hong Kong to see if her visa officer husband, Scott Heatherington, had time for a supper break, she had no idea that in a few hours she, along with other Canadian diplomatic wives, would be on a flight to Vancouver accompanying dozens of orphaned children.

"Um ... I need some volunteers." Meryl 'Bud' Clark, the Commissioner for Canada in Hong Kong, approached me quietly. I had gone to the Causeway Bay Hotel to see if my husband Scott might have a quick moment for some supper. He and his colleagues had been working non-stop since the news that babies and orphans would arrive in HK before a new flight to Canada.

I replied "Of course" to Mr. Clark – not quite sure what sort of help he required, but thinking it would concern the children. He continued, "I need some escorts to travel to Canada with the babies – are you able to do this?" "Yes," I replied. Mr. Clark rounded up several other spouses of officers at the Commission – Sandra Cameron (wife of Donald Cameron, who had been in Vietnam to organize the lift), Marilyn Quigley (wife of Garnet Quigley), Jackie Missler, wife of RCMP officer Art Missler, and me.

Bud Clark had approached me about 3 p.m. That same evening we left Hong Kong with the "Baby Lift."

The old Kai Tak Airport in Hong Kong was never fancy. It was a survivor of the Second World War, cement, wood and tin painted yellow. We hurried into the building to meet with the staff from the airline and then boarded the plane.

It was a regularly scheduled flight. Inside the aircraft, the first class passengers were at the front, with economy next, followed by a section for us. Behind our seats there was a group of tourist passengers at the back and they were aghast as they saw us come into the cabin. Not only were we carrying armloads of children, who were obviously unwell, it was noisy, people were shouting at each other, and it was not an easy scene. I recall one couple cringing from my advances as I took my seat with my crying babies, which included one child with a ghastly rash (not contagious, but of course they did not know that at the time). However, I did reassure them of this, but they seemed quite horrified. Perhaps the airline had not told them what was happening, and that this was also a "mercy flight." At one point I thought that some people would deplane, and that might actually have happened – I cannot be sure. All of a sudden we were all trying to settle the babies, while the crew members were running around trying to get a semblance of calm to ensure takeoff would be on time.

We were on our way. The children were upset during takeoff due to the noise and change of air pressure, but they eventually calmed down. We kept on feeding them, first with a milk mixture, and then with water. This meant that there were frequent diaper changes and no time to sit and reflect.

During the flight there was some movement with the children as we tried to maximize their space and comfort. At one point there was an issue with our luggage, and things were moved around the cabin. I was anxious to keep an eye on the official documents I was carrying, but I remembered my instructions and kept them safe in a diaper bag. I did not take my eye off that diaper bag until Vancouver (even foregoing the washroom!).

The flight itself now seems like a dream. There was no time for sleep or relaxation as there was so much to do. I recall being concerned over my charges, just hoping they would make it to Canada. One baby in particular had very laboured breathing. But there were also warm, endearing recollections: after one meal one of the older children walked around collecting "Smarties" from the dessert on our dinner trays! She was absolutely beautiful – a young slim girl, perhaps around seven or eight, with olive skin, freckles and blondish curly hair! A combination of the American Midwest and the elegance of Southeast Asia.

Soon it was time to land. The children had been active during the flight, but "mine" did sleep from time to time. I could not believe that we had actually touched down. The whole aircraft must have sighed with relief. The regular passengers disembarked first. Some even said "Goodbye and good luck" ... but many did not speak to us.

Coming off the plane was awkward, and I was anxious to find the Immigration officer to hand over the documents and then make sure my children could have some space. It was chaotic. Hundreds of people had lined up behind a barrier – they were trying to touch and almost grab the babies. I felt very protective and hung on to the four I had, now well-balanced in my arms with the diaper bag on my back (along with my own small bag). Then the Immigration officer came up and asked me where the documents were. I was enormously happy to give him the package. And all of a sudden the NGO ladies found the liaison officers for the children and two babies were taken from me very quickly. The other two would stay with me until Montreal. All of a sudden I felt quite light – and missing those two small creatures.

There did not seem to be much time in transit. We boarded another aircraft which seemed so calm compared to the chaos and stress of the first one. Now there were just three escorts (instead of four) and of course fewer babies too. Sandra Cameron was continuing with "her" baby to Toronto, while Marilyn Quigley and I went on to Montreal. The flight seemed so uneventful and we landed during a snowstorm in Montreal. It was late. The welcoming committee was much smaller, and finally I said goodbye to "my" last two babies. They had seemed calmer and had even slept intermittently.

I was now on my own. As the airport was about to close, I ran to see if I could catch the last flight to Ottawa. I had not had time to alert my parents or any friends of my arrival. I quickly searched for a pay phone (no mobile phones then) but without success, as the boarding was being announced for Ottawa. I ran to the gate but it had just closed!

Returning to the ticket counter, thankfully still open although it was close to midnight, I asked the agent what I could do. She suggested I take a hotel in Montreal or "overnight it" at the airport. Another agent said that the last Greyhound bus usually stopped on the highway, and I could probably catch it if I ran!

Outside the airport it was cold and snowing. I was only wearing a light sweater-vest, brown cords and a white blouse. (I remember what I was wearing!) There was no shelter, but I just knew I had to get this bus, if it came. Amazingly, out of the snow I could see the misty lights and the shape of the bus approaching out of the storm; it was like a dream.[60]

The Second Canadian Baby Flight

In the early 1970s, stories about abandoned Vietnamese children, many of them the socially outcast biracial offspring of US soldiers, began to spread in Canada. Potential adoptive parents started to inquire about the possibility of adopting these orphans.[61] Victoria Leach, Ontario's adoption coordinator, accompanied by Helen Allen, the province's adoption information officer, travelled to South Vietnam in 1973 to research the needs of these Vietnamese orphans and the modalities for international adoptions from Vietnam. Slowly, in the course of the next two years, a few Vietnamese children were adopted by Ontario families.[62]

In February 1975, as the military situation in South Vietnam rapidly deteriorated, Leach was again back in Vietnam and confirmed the need for rescuing orphaned children, some "abandoned at orphanage gates, others ... left in churches and hotel lobbies or on Embassy steps." On her return trip to Canada, she was able to bring nine children back with her.

Two months later, Leach received a telegram from Friends for All Children (FFAC), a central child support agency in besieged Saigon, asking if Ontario could place five hundred babies. She immediately formed a team, consisting of herself, Helen Allen, two doctors, and a nurse, and proceeded to Saigon. Arriving during the immediate aftermath of the American baby flight crash, she went where there was need, including an orphanage almost in enemy territory. She was ferried around Saigon and its surroundings by Father Aarts, a Dutch priest. In a few days, she had managed to gather almost sixty orphans, some of them ill, needing the immediate attention of Dr Ward, a Canadian doctor. Her travel with the children from Saigon to Hong Kong was facilitated by Ernest Hébert, whose professionalism and goodwill she appreciated and to whom she expressed her gratitude. Like the Canadian baby flight one week before, she, the babies, and her team flew to Hong Kong on a CF-130. Charles Rogers, the officer-in-charge of the Canadian visa office in Hong Kong, was on the flight with her. The details of the flight are similar to the previous Canadian baby flight: "babies in cardboard boxes strapped to the floor, two babies to a box." Evidently Canadian military cargo planes were not designed to transport infants.

The children and their escorts left Saigon on Friday, 11 April, and departed Hong Kong for Canada on Sunday, 13 April, with Minister's Permits under Section 7(2)c of the 1952 Immigration Act.[63] This documentation is made clear on the flight manifest, implying that the Hong Kong visa office must again have worked through the weekend. Two of the Canadian doctors on Leach's team had stayed in Hong Kong and prepared for the medical reception and clearance of the children in the short time available there. Leach does not mention any special problems on the flight to Vancouver, except that two of the children, too ill to travel, stayed in a Hong Kong hospital and followed on a later flight. Leach states that in addition to her team, she had some other volunteers on the flight to Canada.

The Significance of the Canadian Baby Flights

At this late date, it is impossible to state exactly how many Indochinese orphan children came to Canada on the baby flights. According to Hébert's figures, there were sixty-two children on the first flight and sixty-nine on the second.[64] We do not have the flight manifest for the first flight, but according to the Hong Kong flight manifest for the second, only fifty-six orphans were on the onward leg to Canada. There are indications that some of the orphans who left Saigon on the CF-130 flights were adopted in countries other than Canada. On the other hand, there are indications that some orphans made it to Canada not on group flights but as individuals accompanied by adoptive parents or other escorts. All in all, we believe that approximately 120 orphans ended up with adoptive families in Canada.

The orphan flights demonstrated the incredible humanity of people like Victoria Leach and her Ontario team, Naomi Bronstein, Eloise Charet, and Anna Charet. These people represent the best of Canada's humanitarian spirit. As well, when Canada's chargé in Saigon and Canadian visa officers and their spouses in Saigon and Hong Kong were called on to help abandoned children in a war-torn country, they performed admirably.

We should end with an important point. What matters most is that the babies of 1975 are now living meaningful lives as adult Canadians. The documentary film about Naomi Bronstein includes a reunion of the children from the first baby flight, filmed twenty-five years after their arrival in Canada. It shows well-adjusted young Canadian women and men, many of them professionals, all of them apparently happy.[65] That they survived and are thriving is due to the cooperative efforts of private Canadian individuals, Canadian officials in Canada, Canadian visa officers and their spouses, and last but by no means least, Canada's chargé d'affaires in Saigon during the last days of the Republic of South Vietnam.

No small achievement.

3

The First Wave, 1975–1977

The Beginnings of the Post-1975 Refugee Movement
to Canada

Following the Canadian government's commitment to resettle Vietnamese refugees in Canada after the conquest of South Vietnam by North Vietnamese forces, Canadian officialdom reacted rapidly to implement the government's decision.[1] In 1975–76, the years immediately following the fall of Saigon, Canada "admitted nearly 7000 refugees from Vietnam and Cambodia. This included more than 4200 relatives of Canadian Citizens and landed immigrants, and more than 2300 persons as Convention Refugees with no relatives in Canada."[2]

Later, in 1979–80, Canada admitted 60,000 Indochinese refugees. In comparison, the number of Vietnamese refugees it accepted during the earlier period may appear to be small, but Canada was one of very few countries to react immediately to the refugee outflow following the communist victory and was second only to the United States in terms of the number of Vietnamese refugees accepted in 1975–76. As well, the initial Canadian effort in Indochina was on par with the 7,069 refugees resettled from Uganda in 1972–73 and the 7,016 from South America in 1973–79. In terms of numbers of refugees accepted, the total was exceeded only by the Hungarian (37,000 in 1956–57) and Czechoslovakian (11,000 in 1968–69) refugee movements.

In 1975, there was relatively little popular or political support in Canada for the movement of Indochinese refugees. The general feeling of Canadian commentators and media was that the war in Indochina was the United States' war and that it was up to the Americans to deal with the results of the war's loss, including the major outflow of refugees. Neither the UNHCR nor most western observers expected the refugee outflow to last, and the UNHCR initially believed the problem would be resolved by repatriation. However, in the case of the Vietnamese refugees evacuated by the US Navy, or leaving Vietnam on their own, usually in small boats as Vietnam fell, the Americans had little choice. Very rapidly, they were faced with 125,000 refugees in temporary accommodations at Clark Air Force base in the Philippines as well as in Guam, who needed to be moved as quickly as possible to camps on the US mainland.

That repatriation was not a possible solution was conclusively demonstrated after some 1,500 Vietnamese refugees on the Pacific island of Guam rioted because of camp conditions and demanded to be sent back to Vietnam. The Americans complied and shipped them back. Vietnamese authorities immediately sent the entire contingent of returnees to re-education camps. It is not known how many survived. After this incident, while the UNHCR still continued to voice hope for eventual repatriation, the option became a dead letter until well into the 1980s.[3]

Canada's main effort was in resettling refugees from Guam and from camps in the United States, including Camp Pendleton, California; Fort Chaffee, Arkansas; Ellis Air Force Base, Florida; and Indiantown Gap, Pennsylvania; as well as camps in Hong Kong. This assistance was welcomed by the beleaguered Americans. That Canada's motivation was entirely humanitarian and not political is demonstrated in several ways. First, Cabinet stated that no precedence would be given to Indochinese refugees over Chilean refugees and that refugees fleeing a right-wing coup would continue to be treated with the same consideration as refugees fleeing a communist takeover of power. Secondly, while the initial refugee outflow overland to Thailand from Laos and Cambodia was somewhat larger than that from Vietnam, no major consideration was given in 1975 to accepting large numbers of Laotian or Cambodian refugees for resettlement in developed countries, including Canada. Following the UNHCR views, it was felt that, since local integration and eventual repatriation of these refugees in Thailand was a real possibility and the preferred humanitarian solution, no resettlement in third countries outside the region was required or desirable. As well, while priority was at first given to refugees with family in Canada, the resettlement program rapidly accepted many as Convention refugees on a humanitarian basis.

A number of factors should be emphasized concerning the 1975–76 Vietnamese refugee movement to Canada. The people who selected and sent the refugees to Canada were dedicated Canadian officials, few in number and with limited resources. They had a strong sense of adventure and were ready to be on the road at a moment's notice. They were able to innovate because the system in place at the time provided them with latitude in how they performed their tasks, as long as they selected the refugees and sent them to Canada as quickly as possible. Their accounts of their activities reflect a belief of being involved in something worthwhile. These factors characterized the movement from its beginnings and would carry over to the much larger Indochinese refugee movement of 1979–80.

Of the 7,000 Indochinese refugees sent to Canada in 1975–76, relatively few were processed though Canadian missions in Asia aside from that in Hong Kong. The Canadian High Commission in Singapore selected only 107, the Canadian Embassy in Manila selected forty, and at that stage there was no immigration presence at the Canadian Embassy in Bangkok.[4] This meant that during the initial two years of the Indochinese Refugee Program, the bulk of the burden of refugee selection fell on Canada's commission in Hong Kong, which mounted the operation in Guam, and on consulates or roving teams in the United States.

Refugee Operations Abroad, 1975–77

Guam

Within two days of the fall of Saigon, on 2 May 1975 a Canadian team arrived from Hong Kong on the island of Guam. Guam is a small – about 544 square kilometres – Micronesian island in the Pacific Ocean belonging to the United States. The Americans had had military bases on the island since World War II. Thousands of Vietnamese refugees were flown to Guam daily from Clark Air Force Base in the Philippines as well as directly from US aircraft carriers. American facilities on the island were never meant to accommodate such an influx, and they were bursting at the seams.[5] In the words of Charles Rogers, Canada's immigration manager in Hong Kong, who led the Canadian team to Guam: "We were advised to bring 'everything we would need,' as nothing was available on the island in the way of equipment or staff."[6] At the abandoned airfield that served as the Guam refugee processing site, several thousand refugees were housed in large tents, and the Canadians quickly commandeered a "SEA" hut.[7] The Canadian team consisted of two Canada-based immigration foreign service officers, Charles Rogers and Scott Heatherington; one locally engaged immigration assistant, Rebecca Wong; a Canadian Health and Welfare doctor, Nick Kyriakides; and a communicator, Mel Swenson. Joyce Cavanagh, an immigration foreign service officer, joined the team a few days later from headquarters in Canada. It is a sad reflection of conditions on Guam that Dr Kyriakides contracted dengue fever in Guam and died of complications from the disease within a year.[8]

Accounts by Canadian officers provide a sense of the challenge of operating in Guam: "The Americans had many thousands of Vietnamese refugees housed in tents ... Securing space in which to conduct interviews was challenging ... we solved our space problem by appropriating a very primitive plywood gatehouse at the entrance to the base. This became the Canadian processing centre. During the first few days we got ourselves up and running with a very low-tech operation."[9]

Joyce Cavanagh describes the difficulties of the work, but even more, the sense of adventure, comradeship, and teamwork that the Canadian officers on the island brought to a challenging task:

All staff were lodged in the same condo in Guam. It was where we slept, did laundry and, at night, prepared files and visas.

When I arrived at the tent city, which housed thousands of refugees and where foreign Missions set up shop to do their immigration selection, I marveled at its vastness. Run by the US military, it was acres and acres of tents, with a few trailers here and there which served as offices. It was very hot and dusty. The military checked on us regularly and were eager to supply any item which they could reasonably provide: an extra chair, tables, water. After all, we were helping them solve a problem: remove refugees from Guam as expeditiously as possible, prior to monsoon season.

Some of my colleagues from Hong Kong had already been there for several days when I arrived, and they had a hut set up to serve as our interviewing space. Translators were hired from among the refugees, and there was a brisk turnover as some got visas, left and were replaced. I particularly remember three sisters, two of whom worked for us, and later settled in Ottawa. I seem to recall that the eldest had worked at our Embassy in Saigon.

The work was relentless; people lined up, were questioned about relatives or employers in Canada, and if they looked like they might have potential, they filled out application forms. If they passed a rudimentary immigration interview, they were shuffled along through the Stage B (security) and medical processes. (Our doctor thought all the Canadians should be taking Valium!)

On my first day at the tent camp, I asked my colleagues in the late morning for directions to the toilets. They gaped at me. No one knew. Apparently in the days previous to my arrival, not one of these men, and they were all men, had ever thought to use the facilities! Hard workers they were!

Each evening, after a long day at the tent city, the team went to dinner at one of the local restaurants, and then we headed back to the condo to work on the visas, the flight manifests, transportation loans and other paperwork.

The refugees were flown to Canada on chartered planes that arrived frequently and had to be full when they left Guam. Our targets were clear: fill that plane arriving in two days' time. An officer or two had to travel to the airport for each flight, check the documents, make sure everyone was on board who was supposed to be, and do a final head count. It is amazing how difficult it is to do an accurate head count of people on a plane. Overlooked babies were the most difficult to account for; now you see them, now you don't. And the planes, in my memory, always left at night, so that you were doing airport duty after an already long work day.[10]

An essential element of the operation on Guam was arranging transportation to Canada. Rapid, well-organized, and controlled air transportation to Canada would remain a central element in ensuring that the refugee movement was well coordinated and functioned smoothly. The Guam experience followed immediately upon the end of the war and the large, uncontrolled outflow of refugees; there was no time to make transportation arrangements with agencies or airlines prior to the Canadian processing team's arrival on the island. The team made arrangements in coordination with Immigration Headquarters in Ottawa. This aspect of the movement's administration was in fact more difficult in 1975 than it would become during the much larger refugee movement of 1979–80. By then, Canada could count on the highly professional assistance of the Intergovernmental Committee for European Migration (ICEM). In 1975, the Canadian officers had to count on their own initiative and expertise and help from their colleagues in Ottawa. Scott Heatherington describes transportation from Guam at this time: "We quickly realized that we were going to have to charter planes from Canada and that we had to ensure they flew with a full load of passengers. The challenges of processing 1,401 persons over two and a half weeks seems incomprehensible in retrospect but did not faze us at the time. We worked like demons to accomplish the task and we met and transported our clients to charters: Pan Am on May 7, CAF on May 9, Transair on May 12, Air Canada on May 14, Nord Air on May 16, CP on May 19, PWA on May 21 and Transair on May 23. Then we flew back to Hong Kong, not realizing at the time the magnitude of our accomplishment."[11]

Then there was Joyce Cavanagh's flight from Guam to Wake Island and back in the same day. Picture a petite young woman from the Ottawa Valley being transported on a US military aircraft to get a group of Vietnamese stranded on a coral atoll in the middle of the Pacific Ocean. Return air distance between Guam and Wake Island was 4,900 km – just under the flight distance between Vancouver, BC, and St John's, Newfoundland. But here is the adventure in her words:

While some of us were working on Guam, we heard that a few Vietnamese had found their way to Wake Island and were to be admitted to Canada. I was the officer designated to fly to Wake, gather up these people, and bring them back to Guam. During the return flight I was to assist them in completing their IMM8s [application forms] and any other necessary documentation.

The United States provided a C-130 [Hercules] for this voyage. Needless to say, this was a new experience for me. The empty plane was vast, noisy and cold and I had nothing to do but sit in my sling seat for the duration. I was given a box lunch that included an orange, so I ate all save the orange which I decided might be needed on the return flight. Sad to report, when I arrived on Wake, the orange was confiscated; this made no sense to me as both Guam and Wake were US territories.

Once again I have to confess that I had no idea where Wake was, but when I got there, after what seemed like hours in that bleak hold, I realized that it was nowhere: a spit of land in a vast ocean, with nothing much except a runway.

We were on Wake for about an hour, just long enough to get folks on board and begin the return trip. At that point I moved into high gear, handing out forms, fielding questions, moving about the plane to help where able. The more I got done in the air, the quicker these people could have their cases processed once back on Guam. I believe there might have been 25 extended families on that flight. As the air crew was busy flying the plane, I was on my own to scurry around that dim and chilly hold. No food was served, but of course such a large craft does have a toilet facility, so at least that was not a concern.[12]

A final note on the Guam operations, provided by team manager Charles Rogers, sums up these hectic three weeks: "We were slightly sad to close down our little operation, as by the third week we had it down to a science. Still, we were all exhausted, and the delights of Guam (whatever they may be) had long since palled. We processed some 1,800 persons and shipped 1,403 to Canada in exactly three weeks. Most of them will make fine immigrants. We all thought it was worthwhile; we were proud to be associated with the operation, and touched at the gratitude expressed by the Americans."[13]

Hong Kong and the Clara Maersk/Truong Xuan Incident

In May 1975, the Danish ship *Clara Maersk* arrived in Hong Kong full of Vietnamese refugees – the earliest such incident following the fall of Saigon and a prelude of things to come. It is the first major example of what would become typical elements of the "boat people" phenomenon. While a large number of small vessels filled with refugees left Vietnam during late April and early May 1975, the *Truong Xuan*, a Vietnamese freighter whose captain managed to slip out of Saigon harbour on the last day before the fall, was the only large freighter to leave Vietnam during the final battle. It did so with over 3,700 refugees on board. The *Truong Xuan* was not helped by passing US Navy ships, and it fell to the captain of a private commercial ship, the *Clara*

Maersk, to rescue the refugees as the *Truong Xuan* was sinking. Unfortunately, this became a typical feature of the boat people's experience. It was something of a lottery: while some refugees were picked up by passing ships, many were not and perished at sea.

Although the refugee camp experience was not a pleasant one anywhere, the *Clara Maersk*'s passengers were relatively lucky. They ended up in Hong Kong, where, in the early days following April 1975, Hong Kong authorities gave them temporary status. Canadian officials showed up at the Hong Kong refugee camps early and maintained their activities over the coming months. Interestingly, while Pham Ngoc Luy, captain of the stricken Vietnamese freighter, was resettled in the United States, the bulk of his extended family was resettled in Canada.[14]

A few excerpts from Captain Luy's account of the *Truong Xuan*'s odyssey provide a taste of the boat peoples' experience, which was to be repeated thousands of times during the years after 1975:

> Our first SOS telegram was sent out on May 2: "From the captain of Truong Xuan. Water leaking into engine room. Stop. Danger of sinking. Stop. More than three thousand Vietnamese fleeing the Communists are suffering from hunger and thirst. Stop. Many children are sick. Request for emergency rescue."
>
> In just ten minutes, Thanh [the ship's communicator] announced that *Clara Maersk* (OWIK) of Denmark had received our SOS message. I was constantly in the telecommunications room waiting for response. "Has Truong Xuan communicated with the American Seventh Fleet?"
>
> "No. We don't know their frequency."
>
> The day before, when the USS *Washington* and a ship of the American Seventh Fleet approached Truong Xuan in the afternoon, everybody was so happy; some took out their bottle of drinking water and poured it from head to foot, and some washed their hands with it. But these two ships had gone away.[15]

And then, the refugees were in a Hong Kong camp. Captain Luy continues his story:

> "We, more than three thousand refugees, wish to express our gratitude to her Majesty, to the people, the Government and the Governor of Hong Kong, for having the humanitarian kindness

to help us. We wish, however, to ask you to assure us that you will not return us to Viet Nam or send us to any Communist country."

The Hong Kong representative stood up at once and said he would return in an hour with an answer. We guessed that he left to discuss with the Governor of Hong Kong. Forty-five minutes later, he came back and announced: "No, no, no. Never will we return you to Viet Nam or send you to any Communist countries."

At the beginning of June 1975, Phuong Lan sponsored our whole family to come to Canada. Lan, who was my daughter Giang's high school classmate, had been a student in Canada and was living in Toronto. Our entire family was allowed to immigrate to Canada. We bid farewell to our son Pham Truc Lam, our daughters Pham Thu Giang and Pham Ngoc Dung, and Dung's husband, who also decided to go to Canada. My wife was crying as she gave each of them some money.[16]

Don Cameron provides a description of his first impression of the *Clara Maersk* and the Canadian response to the boat's arrival in Hong Kong:

Queen Elizabeth was making the first visit of a British monarch to Hong Kong on May 5 when I went up to The Peak in Hong Kong to see her crossing the harbour in the Governor's launch from Kai Tak airport. In the distance to the south I could see the *Clara Maersk* off Repulse Bay. Never had I seen a ship with so many people on board. With no room to lie down, all were standing on every surface from decks to containers to the top of the superstructure. I continue to wonder how they had all survived on the much smaller *Truong Xuan* ...

The Commission for Canada immediately sought permission to visit the Vietnamese refugees to determine if any had relatives in Canada or were holders of the Promise of Visa Letters which had been mailed to persons in Vietnam sponsored by relatives in Canada.

I recall going to the refugees' camp at Shek Kong in the New Territories. This was the headquarters of the British Army's 48th Gurkha Infantry Brigade and was well organized with excellent security, sanitation and facilities for housing and feeding large numbers. The Brigadier's wife (a Mrs. Whitehead) was present to ensure that the Vietnamese were well looked after and that we had access to the facilities we needed ... Interviews and processing of the refugees continued with a number of the Visa Officers in Hong Kong, including Margaret Tebbutt, Bill Bowden, and Scott Heatherington. Brian Beaupré and Joyce Cavanagh arrived on temporary duty from Canada to assist with the interviews.

Our quick response to the [*Clara Maersk*] crisis allowed us to transport to Canada several groups of refugees before the Hong Kong government authorized Vietnamese with the right of abode in Hong Kong to leave the camps. The Hong Kong media did not shy away from headlining this fact.[17]

The Canadian visa officer team in Hong Kong continued over the next several years with the ongoing task of visiting the refugee camps in Hong Kong, searching for sponsored refugees and holders of Promise of Visa Letters, but also selecting many unsponsored refugees for resettlement in Canada. Compared with the exuberant experience of the three-week Guam mission, this was routine visa officer work. As the fall of South Vietnam slowly receded from media and public consciousness, the work became the backbone of Canada's Indochinese refugee resettlement efforts. It provided valuable professional experience that paid off during the hectic, high-pressure years of 1979–80.

Camps in the United States and the General Dang Van Quang Affair

Camp Pendleton

In the spring of 1975, with the Pacific rainy season and its typhoons approaching, the US authorities, facing the prospect of muddy and flooded camps in Guam and the Philippines, were rapidly evacuating Vietnamese refugees to camps on the US mainland. Canada, through its consulates in the continental United States, continued the work of selecting Vietnamese refugees in these camps. The first and most important Indochinese refugee camp was Camp Pendleton in southern California near San Diego. While refugee selection and processing work in Camp Pendleton had little of the challenges and risks of the work in Southeast Asia, it was still stressful and demanding.

Marlene Massey, then a brand-new visa officer assigned to the consulate in Los Angeles, describes the beginnings of the operation. She characterizes Pendleton as "as a model of teamwork, organization and improvisation."[18] At the same time she notes that accommodations near the camp were somewhat difficult, especially for a young female officer:

> On Friday evening, I got a call from John Sheardown,[19] advising me to pack a bag because I would be going down to Pendleton for a few days to help set up operations there ... John picked me up at my hotel, and off we drove. Roughly 50 miles down the road, he informed me that motel accommodation was a bit tight just at the moment around Pendleton, and we would therefore be sharing a room for the night. The thought did cross my mind that this wasn't quite what I thought the Department meant when it talked about having to be adaptable. John assured me, however, that the room had twin beds, and that he'd brought his pajamas. The mind boggles at the alternative. At any rate, we arrived at our flamingo pink accommodation, and settled in for the night. And, to be fair, in discussing things with HQ the next day, John did confirm that I had been "a perfect gentleman."[20]

Massey adds that "it was a tremendous achievement to get that first group of Vietnamese up the escalator and onto that airplane, fully documented."[21] She spent only three weeks at the camp, travelling back and forth between Pendleton and the Canadian Consulate General in Los Angeles. She performed all the tasks involved in getting refugees selected and processed – ensuring that they were medically examined and the security clearances were done – and in getting them on the plane to Canada. It is amazing to think that in May 1975, all these tasks could be done in a matter of days, especially if we compare the 1975 processing times with those at the time of the writing of this book. For Massey, the three weeks spent in Pendleton and LA were "a real lesson in how to improvise, how to set up an office on the run, and how to pull staff such as those in the LA office into emergency mode."[22]

Joyce Cavanagh, at the end of the operation in Guam, island-hopped her way across the Pacific from Guam to Camp Pendleton to join two officers, Gibby Gibson and Bill Kolbeins, as the refugee selection and processing team at Camp Pendleton just as Massey was leaving. Some of Cavanagh's experiences in California are worth recalling.

> Working conditions in California were far superior to what I had seen [in Guam]. We had a decent trailer, toilet facilities, and we had evenings free! As it happened, we were a very jolly bunch at Camp Pendleton, in no small measure because of the time Gibby Gibson, who could make anything fun, was with us. We sampled the local restaurants and even ventured to San Diego on at least one occasion. Doctors, Fuzzies [RCMP], and Immigration officers all wined and dined together and generally had a good time in addition to working hard during daytime.
>
> The US Marines, who own and run the base, were very efficient and accommodating, they made our lives as pleasant as possible and ensured that our working conditions were conducive to getting people out of the United States as quickly as possible. The refugees were divided by nationality within Pendleton: Vietnamese, Cambodians, and Laotians. We had to find interpreters of course, and again it was a continuing challenge as they were soon visaed and departed for the delights of Edmonton and Moose Jaw.[23]

For Cavanagh, Pendleton was not only a place of work. It was also the place where she met her life partner, "a tall, handsome [American] border patrolman,"[24] and was transformed from Joyce Cavanagh to Joyce Cavanagh-Wood, affirming that even in the midst of high pressure work, the private lives of Canadian officers abroad continued.

Operations in Other US Refugee Camps

Indochinese refugee processing in the Central and Eastern United States was initially conducted by the small Canadian visa office at the consulate in New Orleans. Very soon after the fall of Saigon, refugees were transported to Fort Chaffee, a military camp in Arkansas, and processed for settlement within the United States as well as Canada. Conditions at Fort Chaffee were chaotic. The lone Canadian officer was constantly surrounded and overwhelmed by dozens of recent arrivals from Indochina. One of the earliest refugees accepted in Fort

Chaffee was Lieutenant General Dang Van Quang, a high-ranking South Vietnamese officer sponsored by family in Montreal. General Dang left for Montreal on 15 May 1975. His arrival in Canada caused a political storm with long-term repercussions. (See next section.) The officer who accepted Quang was quietly transferred out. Murray Oppertshauser was then assigned to take over the processing of Indochinese refugees in the camps of the American South and the Gulf of Mexico region. During an intense period of about ten weeks, Oppertshauser was constantly on the move between Arkansas, Florida, Pennsylvania, and the Eglin Air Force Base on the coast of the Gulf of Mexico. He selected refugees and arranged for their medical examinations and transportation to Canada.

After finishing his activities in the American South, Oppertshauser learned from US authorities of a large group of refugees at a military base in Indiantown Gap, Pennsylvania, some with possible contacts in Canada. During another intense period of five weeks, he and his team processed Indochinese refugees at this Appalachian army camp. They were assisted by Health and Welfare doctors Monty Palmer and Roger LeClair.[25]

The General Dang Van Quang Affair

Lieutenant General Dang Van Quang was a highly placed officer in the Army of the Republic of Vietnam (South Vietnam). As a special assistant for military and security affairs to the last president of South Vietnam, Nguyen Van Thieu, he worked in close cooperation with the US military in Vietnam. It is alleged that in a military operation in 1966 he got into a conflict with the CIA and earned its enmity.[26] He was one of the high-ranking South Vietnamese officers evacuated by helicopter from the US Embassy as Saigon was being occupied by North Vietnamese forces.[27] Soon after leaving Vietnam, General Dang arrived in the refugee camp in Fort Chaffee, Arkansas. On 15 May 1975, about two weeks after his departure from Southeast Asia, he was on his way to Montreal to join his wife and three sons who were already in Canada. One of his sons had been studying in Montreal, and the rest of his family got their visas in Saigon during the last chaotic weeks before Saigon fell.[28]

Immediately after his arrival in Montreal, serious allegations were made "by Asian scholars and by members of the growing Vietnamese refugee colony" against General Dang as a corrupt drug dealer and torturer.[29] The story became a media event in Canada, and Immigration Minister Robert Andras, under pressure "from Members of Parliament, academic circles, the press," had a deportation order issued against the general on or about 7 July 1975.[30] The United States would not accept Dang back, so he remained in Canada with part of his family until 1989, working as a janitor and dishwasher, when he was finally allowed, a sick man, back into the United States to live out the rest of his days in California.[31]

This seemingly minor incident involving a single high-profile, possibly undesirable refugee had a seriously negative impact on Canada's policy vis-à-vis Indochinese refugees. The incident embarrassed Canada's government. The fact that the United States would not accept General Dang back led Canadian politicians and policy-makers to conclude that they needed to be more cautious before undertaking further major efforts to help Indochinese refugees. After Canada's initial 1975 commitment was fulfilled, refugees, especially those with family connections, continued to be admitted, but there was little appetite, public or political, for serious engagement. The General Dang affair played a large part in producing this lull in the Indochinese movement to Canada. Only in the second half of 1978, with the re-emergence of the boat people problem on a large scale, and the deterioration of the situation on the Thai-Cambodian border, did Canada again seriously start to recommit to accepting significant numbers of Indochinese refugees.

Transition, 1976–77: Facing the "Boat People" Phenomenon and the Problems of the Thai Camps

By mid-1976 it appeared to many observers – including most of the international community as well as the international media – that the Indochinese refugee outflow was drawing to a close. Cambodia was hermetically sealed under the vicious regime of the Khmer Rouge. The new communist government of united Vietnam had full political control of the country and was not allowing refugees to escape in large numbers. While thousands of Lao and Cambodian refugees were languishing in Thai camps, it was generally assumed that this was Thailand's problem and that these refugees would either be repatriated or would integrate into Thai society. Yet even as the larger world, including Canada, was lulled into a sense of complacency, indications were emerging that the Indochinese refugee crisis was far from over.

While the two-person team at the Canadian visa office in Singapore, manager Tove Bording and visa officer Bill Sheppit, processed very few Indochinese refugees from 1975 to 1977, the office "was responsible for the area from Burma through Thailand, Laos, Cambodia, Malaysia, Brunei, Singapore and Indonesia"[32] and kept an eye on developments in this enormous region. As Bill Sheppit recalls, "Starting in early 1976, we saw the arrival of small boats up and down the Malay Peninsula (including Thailand) as well as along the southeastern Thai coast. Boat occupants who were not raped by pirates and reached the coast were detained at the local police stations of the towns. Some arrivals were detained on offshore islands in Malaysia and Indonesia."[33] Sheppit and Bording also went into distant primitive camps far removed from indigenous Thai communities. Seeing firsthand that no local integration was taking place, they reported on this to Immigration Headquarters in Ottawa.

Meanwhile, reports were arriving at western capitals and the UNHCR, documenting the increase in the outflow of small and medium-sized refugee boats from Vietnam escaping conditions in the newly united communist country. Commercial ships were picking up refugees on the high seas and, once they had them on board, had to feed and house them. By late 1976, under pressure of growing refugee numbers, Southeast Asian countries were reluctant to allow these refugee boats to land or to take refugees off the vessels.

In January 1977, the *Roland*, a converted minesweeper, attempted to take refugees from Malaysian camps to Australia but was turned around and steamed back to Malaysia. In the same month, the *Leap Dal*, an old coastal oil tanker, picked up refugees, mostly Laotians, in Thailand, again intending to sail to Australia. Neither boat was initially allowed to land anywhere; it took an international meeting to determine the fate of the refugees on the two boats. The boats' organizer, the World Conference on Religion and Peace (WCRP), an ecumenical NGO, was strongly criticized by the UNHCR and national governments.[34] As more stories like this received widespread media attention, western nations gradually became aware that the Indochinese refugee problem was not going away. However, the attitude of Southeast Asian countries was hardening toward the refugees as the number of boats ferrying them increased. In a note of 31 January 1977, the Malaysian government informed the UNHCR that it would no longer harbour Vietnamese displaced persons in Malaysia and that all such Vietnamese displaced persons would have to leave the country within six months.[35]

While Canada remained willing to accept boat people with a Canadian family connection, in 1976–77 the Canadian policy establishment remained reluctant to undertake significant additional Indochinese refugee-related initiatives. The lesson learned through the General Dang Van Quang affair played no small role in maintaining this reluctance. In October 1976, Kirk Bell, director general of recruitment and selection, wrote to a colleague that Canada had "done its part in the Indochina problem except perhaps for help with the 'small boats' people if they had relatives in Canada."[36] Nevertheless, that same month, Immigration Minister Bud Cullen was informed that there were 180 places left over in the quota for 1,000 refugees from outside the United States established in May 1975; it was agreed that these could be used by Canadian visa offices in Southeast Asia for boat people who met the UN Refugee Convention definition and had the potential to establish themselves successfully in Canada.[37] It was a small gesture but one that kept Canada involved, albeit modestly.

Throughout 1976 and 1977, boat departures continued to increase to such an extent that all of the Southeast Asian countries, including Thailand, Malaysia, and Indonesia, were suffering from serious refugee reception fatigue. At the same time, providing for something like 100,000 overland refugees in Thailand was placing a heavy burden on Thai resources. The general feeling among first countries of asylum was that after the initial willingness to help on the part of a few resettlement countries like the United States and Canada, resettlement possibilities and the willingness to share the burdens of resolving the Indochinese refugee problem were diminishing.

In the course of 1977, American authorities realized that something needed to be done and hoped that action could be taken in an internationally coordinated manner. As the problem continued to grow and fester, the United States announced in the summer of 1977 that it would accept another 15,000 refugees, including 8,000 from camps in Thailand and 7,000 boat people.

The deteriorating situation did not go unnoticed in Ottawa. On 6 May 1977, Deputy Minister Allan Gottlieb sent a long memorandum to Minister Cullen, informing him that two distinct refugee problems had emerged in Southeast Asia. There were now 76,000 refugees in Thailand, including Vietnamese, Cambodians, Laotians, and Laotian Hill Tribes.[38] Because of the large number and their low educational level, the UNHCR believed resettlement was not a practical solution; "The most effective and economical contribution Canada can make to the solution of this problem is to support the UNHCR both financially and diplomatically in persuading the Thai government to initiate a large-scale integration program."[39]

At the same time Gottlieb reported that Vietnamese were arriving in small boats and were being held in makeshift camps in the surrounding countries, and their plight was "particularly severe."[40] UNHCR saw little prospect for resettling these people in Southeast Asia, and the Malaysian government had informed UNHCR that boat refugees arriving after 30 June 1977 would be pushed out to sea.

Gottlieb indicated that since April 1976 Canada had resettled 6,600 Vietnamese and Cambodian refugees, but fewer than three hundred had come in 1977. He noted that France was accepting 1,000 Indochinese refugees a month, the United States was taking 100 families a month, and the Australians had just admitted 550. The 180 places transferred to the visa offices in Southeast Asia in 1976 had now been filled. A large-scale resettlement program was not warranted, but pressure to do more, from MPs Jake Epp and Douglas Roche and the Canadian Laotian and Cambodian associations, was building. Laotians had not been included in the program that began in 1975. An appeal from UNHCR was anticipated. Gottlieb recommended, and the minister agreed, that the last 450 places remaining from the 1975 quota for Indochinese refugees in the United States be transferred to the visa offices in Southeast Asia and, in addition, provision be made for 100 Laotians. Treasury Board would provide $262,000 to cover the 450 boat people, and CEIC[41] would fund the Laotians under the Ongoing Refugee Program. No additional funding would be available for language training; refugees who needed it would have to wait their turn.

With this decision, the government had wrung the last numbers out of Minister Andras's May 1975 commitment to admit 3,000 refugees without relatives. Once more, it was a modest commitment, but it kept Canada in the game. In addition, the number of boat people at the time was not all that large. Informed of the decision before it was announced publicly, UNHCR advised Canadian officials that there were, as of 15 July 1977, 500 boat people in Japan, 2,700 in Malaysia, 500 in the Philippines, 1,500 in Thailand, and 300 in Indonesia[42] – small numbers, compared to what would come.

On 2 August 1977, Cullen announced a decision to admit an additional 450 Indochinese refugees.[43] The press release stated that Canada had accepted 6,700 Indochinese refugees since May 1975, including 428 "small boat escapees" since January 1976.

A few days later, on 18 August, Robert Demling, the minister at the US Embassy in Ottawa, called on Richard Tait, Canada's executive director of immigration and demographic policy. Demling made "a formal démarche to urge that Canada accept more Vietnamese refugees" and explained that the United States "was launching a concerted drive to persuade the international community to undertake new commitments."[44] This initiative on the part of the United States signalled the beginning of a change in the attitude of resettlement countries, including Canada, towards the resolution of the Indochinese refugee dilemma. With the 1975 allocation for 3,000 refugees beyond those with relatives in Canada now exhausted, the next steps would require a new policy initiative.

4

The Immigration Act, 1976:
New Provisions for Refugees

I am not betraying or conveying a bias whatsoever, I want to start
developing a new policy, new legislation, by trying to define the
objective of immigration in the national self-interest of Canada. And
I don't accept that self-interest is necessarily selfish, nor necessarily
so cold as to exclude compassion, but it is basic ... More recently,
though, particularly in the 1970s, we have had a discernible effort
to develop Canadian refugee activity in a framework of policy
and principle[d] guidelines.

Robert Andras, describing his approach to developing
the 1976 Immigration Act.[1]

At the same time as the communist victories in Southeast Asia were
taking place, Canada was in the process of developing and then implementing the first new Canadian immigration legislation since 1952.[2]
The refugee provisions of the 1976 Immigration Act would have profound implications for the magnitude and scope of Canada's future involvement with the Indochinese refugees, providing a new set of tools
and a law-based framework for future resettlement programs.

When he initiated the process of developing new immigration legislation for Canada, Robert Andras, then minister of manpower and
immigration, described the 1952 Immigration Act, which he was determined to replace, as "devoid of policy." The old act was written "in
the language of the turn of the century, designed for the slow, casual
immigration movement by boat, or dog team, or whatever travel was
available in the early 1900s. I found it was discriminatory and it had
some extraordinarily disgusting clauses in it, about which, thank
goodness, current practice did not conform."[3]

Andras's deputy minister, Allan Gottlieb, brought in a brilliant officer from the Department of External Affairs, Richard Tait, to lead the most open and broadly consultative national dialogue on immigration in Canada's history. Hundreds of written submissions were received from other levels of government, academics, faith communities, institutions, and private individuals. A four-volume green paper, "The Canadian Immigration and Population Study,"[4] was widely circulated and touched off a second series of submissions. While officials, nervous about potential controversy, advised him to get on with quietly launching the legislation, Andras decided more consultations were required. He established a joint parliamentary committee of the Senate and House of Commons, which held thirty-five public hearings across the country. The hearings provided opportunities for seriously interested groups to air their views. They also attracted extremist groups from both ends of the political spectrum who had the effect of driving parliamentarians to the centre.

Thanks to the extensive preparations, opportunities for the airing of views, and the involvement of parliamentarians in the consultative process, the new immigration act, which for the first time spelled out the objectives and underlying principles of Canada's immigration and refugee policy, was presented to the House of Commons as Bill-c24. The act passed through the legislative process fairly smoothly and became law in 1976. Once the act was passed by Parliament, it took two years to get the supporting regulations, operational instructions, procedures, and systems in place. Canada had resettled 300,000 refugees and displaced persons between the end of World War II and 1976 with no reference whatsoever to refugees in Canadian law. The new act created, for the first time, a legislative and regulatory framework for Canada's refugee resettlement programs.

Building on Experience and Putting Refugees in the Law

The previous decade had seen considerable change and innovation in Canada's approach to refugee issues, and these developments helped shape the thinking that went into the new immigration act. In 1969, Canada ratified the 1951 UN Refugee Convention and its 1967 Protocol. The following year, 1970, Cabinet decided that Canada would extend its refugee resettlement activities beyond Europe. It adopted the UN Refugee Convention's definition for identifying refugees for both asylum and resettlement purposes. It laid out new rules for selecting refugees using the "point system,"[5] which officials were instructed to apply in a generous manner, making liberal use of their discretionary powers, given the extra assistance available to refugees after arrival in Canada.[6] Cabinet had also approved an "Oppressed Minority" policy to facilitate the admission of people who were not technically Convention refugees but were being oppressed within their own countries.[7]

The rapid succession of refugee crises requiring Canadian intervention (Czechoslovakia, Uganda, Latin America, and now Southeast Asia) had convinced policy-makers and officials alike that refugee crises in which resettlement formed part of the solution could no longer be regarded as infrequent episodic disturbances but were an ongoing reality. Although ad hoc responses to past refugee crises had served reasonably well, there was pressure from within government and interested sectors of Canadian society, in particular the major churches and their designated refugee advocates, to enshrine in law more of the fundamentals of Canadian immigration policy and practice, including those that applied to refugees.

The 1976 Immigration Act formally incorporated into Canadian law many of the policy developments of the previous years, including the Convention definition of a refugee as someone who, "by reason of a well-founded fear of persecution for reasons of race, religion, nationality, membership of a particular social group or political opinion, is outside the country of his nationality and is unable or, by reason of such fear, is unwilling to avail himself of the protection of that country."[8] In addition, the act set out a series of immigration objectives for Canada including, in Section 3(g), a commitment "to fulfil Canada's international legal obligations with respect to refugees and to uphold its humanitarian tradition with respect to the displaced and persecuted."[9]

The "legal obligations" related to Canada's responsibilities as a signatory to the 1951 Refugee Convention and 1967 Protocol and applied to the treatment and protection to be accorded to asylum seekers spontaneously arriving at Canada's borders. They underpinned the establishment of the Refugee Status Advisory Committee (RSAC), the predecessor of the Immigration and Refugee Board, to adjudicate claims to refugee status within Canada.[10] The procedures to be followed in asylum applications were also spelled out in the act. "Humanitarian tradition" referred to the long-standing Canadian practice of organizing resettlement programs for refugees and other displaced people and bringing them to Canada under official resettlement initiatives. Section 6 of the act defined the framework for the selection of various categories of immigrants. Section 6(2) provided for the admission of "any Convention refugee and any person who is a member of a class designated by the Governor in Council as a class, the admission of members of which would be in accordance with Canada's humanitarian tradition with respect to the displaced and persecuted."[11] This section acknowledged the reality that while many of those seeking resettlement would be victims of persecution who had fled their countries of origin (i.e., Convention refugees), there could be other circumstances where Canada might want to intervene but where the Convention definition might not apply. Examples from recent experience had included people who were internally displaced or oppressed or who might have been displaced across borders by something other than persecution, for example, by war. At the regulatory level, Section 6(2) led to the creation of a Convention Refugee Seeking Resettlement Class (CR) and to three additional "designated classes" to deal with existing problems where the Convention definition was not appropriate for the task at hand.

The final element of the 1976 act's shaping of Canada's resettlement activities made provision for a formal arrangement whereby interested persons or organizations could sponsor the admission of Convention refugees or members of designated classes.

The Convention Refugee Cornerstone

The Convention Refugee Seeking Resettlement Class was regarded as the cornerstone of Canada's resettlement regime. In the course of deliberations about how to frame this class in regulations, it was decided that Canada's CR class would be reserved for people who met the Convention definition but who did not have a settlement option or durable solution.[12] It would not apply to CRs who had been recognized and given permanent residency in another country. As a result, the regulations created this class for those Convention refugees who "[have] not become permanently resettled and [are] unlikely to be voluntarily repatriated or locally resettled."[13]

In considering the selection criteria that should apply to Convention refugees selected abroad, the designers of the CR regulation were constrained by Section 6(1), which stated that Convention refugees and members of the Family and Independent Classes could be accepted if they complied with the various regulations that determined whether or not they could become successfully established in Canada. Parliament was seeking a refugee resettlement system more structured and generous than what had gone before but remained reluctant to accept those not able to become self-sufficient within a reasonable time frame. After consultations with various refugee advocacy organizations, it was decided that Convention refugees selected under Canada's resettlement programs and members of designated classes would be exempt from the formal application of the point system. When considering whether a refugee could become successfully established in Canada, visa officers were to include factors such as age, education, occupation, skill level, and presence of family, but would not assign points as part of the decision-making process. Officers were also to take into account the extra assistance available to refugees upon arrival in Canada from government and other sources. This decision went a step beyond the system created by Cabinet in 1970, in that visa officers could now accept on their own authority, without the concurrence of their supervisors, refugees who did not qualify under the point system.

The selection system for the CR class involved a two-step process. First, visa officers were required to determine "eligibility," which required them to determine whether the applicants met the Convention definition, i.e., had a well-founded fear of persecution for reasons of race, religion, nationality, membership of a particular social group, or political opinion. This was a serious matter involving a careful and often lengthy interview to bring out the person's story and assess its merits and credibility. Having determined that the person met the Convention definition, officers then moved on to "admissibility" by assessing whether, with the assistance available from government or private sources, the refugee had a reasonable prospect for successfully establishing in Canada. Refugees, like all other immigrants, were subject to statutory requirements related to health, criminality, and security.

The Designated Classes

Canada had been using the UN Refugee Convention definition to identify refugees for its resettlement programs since 1970, and while the UN definition worked well in many situations, it had limitations. It did not apply to people facing oppression who were still within their own countries. This, for example, was the case of the Ugandan Asians who were threatened with expulsion but who had not yet been expelled when the Canadian team arrived in Uganda to assist them. Nor did it apply in the case of many Chileans who were being persecuted but were unable to flee across an international border. The Convention definition focused on persecution but not on the plight of people fleeing war or its aftermath or generalized violence. Canadian officials had even encountered people the government wished to resettle who objected to being categorized as refugees.[14]

Given this experience, the Refugee Policy Division eagerly seized the opportunity offered by Section 6(2) of the act to create alternative humanitarian classes, "the admission of which would be in accordance with Canada's humanitarian tradition with respect to the displaced and persecuted." Three designated classes were created:

• The Political Prisoner and Oppressed Persons Designated Class. This designation was intended for oppressed people Canada wished to assist who were still in their own countries.
• The Self-Exiled Person Designated Class. This class targeted citizens of Soviet bloc countries who had managed to escape from their countries and would be punished if they returned home or who had been stripped of their citizenship when permitted to depart.[15]
• The Indochinese Designated Class. In this designation, the issue of persecution was sidestepped on the grounds that whatever the motivation for fleeing, large numbers of Indochinese refugees had to be resettled rapidly if the Southeast Asian asylum countries were to keep their shores and borders open and, pragmatically, examining each person for a well-founded fear of persecution would simply take too much time.

The advent of the designated classes provided a regulation-based tool that permitted the government to define a group (as opposed to an individual) it wished to resettle with great specificity and thereby signal to its officers precisely whom they were to target and the conditions under which to accept them. In practice it had the effect of greatly simplifying the selection process: the government had determined who was eligible for consideration, and visa officers could concentrate on who was admissible.[16]

The Indochinese Designated Class

During the initial phase of the Indochinese movement from 1975 to 1978, the refugee selection system approved by Cabinet in 1970, along with a generous interpretation of the family sponsorship rules, was applied by officers processing refugees in Southeast Asia, Hong Kong, and Guam and at various military bases in the United States. By the end of 1976, Southeast Asian refugees accepted for resettlement in Canada included more than 4,200 relatives of Canadian citizens and permanent residents as well as 2,300 people with no Canadian relatives, who were selected as Convention refugees.[17]

The two-year period allotted by the government to the Immigration Department to implement the 1976 act coincided with an initial lull in Indochinese refugee selection in late 1976 and early 1977 when the crisis appeared to subside and come to an end. By September 1976 the Indochinese operation of 1975 was fading from memory. Issues relating to the Chilean refugee movement that had begun in 1973 had given rise to a new generation of assertive refugee advocates, who consumed vastly more time and political energy, thanks to a series of well-orchestrated lobbying efforts, public meetings, and letter-writing campaigns. In early 1977 the boat people phenomenon was just emerging, but it was unclear whether this was the last gasp of the Indochinese refugee phenomenon or the start of something new. However, by the fall of 1977, the steady stream of refugees had not abated. CEIC's Refugee Policy Division had begun to operate on the assumption that a new and large resettlement effort was inevitable, although it had no notion of how large that effort would become.

Consideration was given to whether a designated class could be designed to simplify the process of selecting and processing refugees in Southeast Asia. As mentioned above, determining whether someone is a Convention refugee is a complex matter requiring a detailed and time-consuming interview. The idea of Canadian visa officers trying to sort out from a crowd on a beach who was fleeing persecution and who had left for other reasons was as absurd as it was inefficient. The visa offices and the media were reporting that the Southeast Asian countries of asylum were pushing refugee boats back to sea, often with catastrophic results. Whether the boat people were Convention refugees or not was irrelevant at this stage. What did matter was that the Southeast Asian governments would only allow people to land safely if they were confident that the refugees would be quickly removed to resettlement countries. To speed up the process, officials concluded that Canada needed a designated class for the boat people that set aside the Convention definition. At that stage the department's attention was focused exclusively on Vietnamese boat people, in the mistaken assumption that Laotian and Cambodian refugees in Thailand would eventually be repatriated or locally integrated in Thailand.

Accordingly, a memorandum of 14 March 1978 from the Refugee Policy Division to CEIC's Legal Services provided "the essentials of a proposed 6(2) regulation for the admission of Vietnamese Small Boat Escapees under a special movement."[18] This regulation would apply to the planned Small Boat Escapee program under which fifty families a month would be admitted to Canada. The idea of limiting the designated class to boat escapees was quickly overtaken by events later that month when, during a visit to Canada, the new UN High Commissioner for Refugees Poul Hartling made the "surprising" request that Canada begin to resettle overland refugees from Thailand in addition to Vietnamese boat people.[19] In response, the Legal Affairs Branch was directed to draft a designated class regulation that would apply to Indochinese refugees generally. The regulation defined members of the Indochinese Designated Class as people who were "citizens or habitual residents of a country listed in the schedule [Democratic Kampuchea (Cambodia), People's Democratic Republic of Laos, and Socialist Republic of Vietnam], have left their country of citizenship or habitual residence subsequent to April 30, 1975, have not become permanently resettled, are unwilling or unable to return to their country of citizenship or former habitual residence, are outside Canada and seeking resettlement in Canada."[20]

Members of the Indochinese Designated Class would, like members of the Convention Refugee in Need of Resettlement Class, be exempt from the point system, be eligible for the same range of settlement assistance available to CRs, and, most importantly, be eligible for sponsorship under the new private refugee sponsorship program (see below). This regulation, with its focused definition and flexible selection criteria, provided the legal basis for the admission of 60,000 refugees into Canada between 1979 and 1980, plus tens of thousands more in subsequent years.

The Indochinese Designated Class came into effect in December 1978 just as the Indochinese refugee crisis began to dominate the attention of the world. It would be amended twice, first in 1979 to facilitate the admission of unaccompanied minors, and again in the late 1980s, when the international community decided it was time, because of changed circumstances, to restrict resettlement to those who complied with the more stringent requirements of the Convention definition under the Comprehensive Plan of Action.[21]

The Private Refugee Sponsorship Program

The involvement of churches, ethnic communities, and even employers in sponsoring refugees had been a feature of Canada's refugee resettlement programs before and after World War II until the early 1960s. The Canadian government encouraged interested organizations to offer assistance to refugees, including postwar displaced persons (1947–52) and Hungarians (1956–57), and during International Refugee Year (1959–60). As the system was not rooted in law, the government was able to turn sponsorships on and off at will. In 1957, after the arrival of a large number of immigrants, mostly British nationals and Hungarian refugees, it severely reduced immigrant intake because of an economic recession and suspended refugee sponsorships. By the late 1960s, private refugee sponsorship had fallen into disuse. It had not been used in the Czechoslovak or Ugandan refugee movements, although in the latter case the Canadian team in Kampala received a large number of telegrammed offers of assistance to individual Ugandan Asians from friends and relatives in Canada; these were accepted at face value by the visa officers when making selection decisions.[22]

The Chilean refugee crisis following the coup against the socialist Allende government brought into existence a new community of Canadian refugee advocates who were intensely concerned about human rights violations in Chile (and elsewhere) and deeply suspicious of governmental action and motivation. In the absence of a sponsorship program, the only option available was for those interested in a particular group of refugees to demonstrate, organize letter-writing campaigns, and lobby the government to alter selection criteria, speed up processing, and expand the numbers to be admitted. The prolonged and intensive controversy accompanying Canada's response to the Chilean refugees led policy-makers in Ottawa to consider reintroducing a refugee sponsorship option to channel public concern into direct action.

The 1976 Immigration Act[23] empowered the government to introduce regulations with respect to people "seeking to facilitate the admission or arrival in Canada of a Convention Refugee or a person who is a member of a designated class" and to establish the requirements for "the provision of an undertaking to assist any such Convention refugee or person ... in becoming successfully established in Canada."[24] The design of the sponsorship system was directed by Kirk Bell, director general of the Immigration Department's Recruitment and Selection Branch (R&S), assisted by the Refugee Policy Division. Mike Molloy and Linda Butler developed the basic principles, while Carla Thorlakson led a team that designed the processes and procedures.[25]

Bell had two objectives. First, he wished to create a vehicle to allow citizens and organizations to participate directly in resettling refugees and members of designated classes. Secondly, the 1976 act required an Annual Immigration Levels Plan, and it was eventually decided that the plan would include an Annual Refugee Plan setting out the numbers the government intended to resettle in a given year. Bell worried that the plan would generate controversy among refugee advocates over the size of the intake and the numbers allocated to different refugee populations. Under the sponsorship program that he envisaged, privately sponsored refugees would be considered over and above the target announced by the government, thus increasing Canada's overall intake of refugees. Sponsors would be free to focus on any refugee population as long as those sponsored met the Convention definition or were members of a designated class.[26]

Discussions on a sponsorship program began within the Recruitment and Selection Branch in early 1977. On 19 August 1977, Bell circulated a paper containing the main features of the proposed private sponsorship system.[27] The proposal suggested the types of organizations entitled to sponsor refugees, the guarantees required, and the procedures to verify, approve, and act upon sponsorship applications. The program's operational principles had their genesis in ad hoc sponsorship projects for Soviet Jews by the Jewish Immigrant Aid Society (JIAS) for their resettlement in Canada between 1974 and 1976, and a pilot project with B'nai B'rith for a group of Soviet Jews stranded in Italy in 1977–78.[28] Dr Joseph Kage of the Jewish Immigrant Aid Society, a consistent advocate of the establishment of a refugee sponsorship program since 1967,[29] had repeatedly demonstrated that Soviet Jews brought to Canada at JIAS's request were efficiently resettled at no cost to the Canadian taxpayer.

During a thaw in the Cold War confrontation between the East and West Blocs in the 1970s, Soviet authorities had permitted Soviet Jews to leave the Soviet Union, ostensibly to settle in Israel. Stripped of their Soviet citizenship upon leaving the country and not having resettled anywhere, the Soviet Jews could be considered as refugees. Most sought resettlement in Canada, the United States, or Australia immediately upon arrival in Western Europe, mainly Vienna and Rome. A few Soviet Jews initially immigrated to Israel, found integrating difficult, and returned to Rome. By 1977 they were still there, unable to claim refugee status because they had settled, however briefly, in Israel. The Canadian chapter of B'nai B'rith requested that Canada admit the residual group of seventy-five families who remained stranded in Rome.[30]

Jack Manion, the deputy minister of employment and immigration, proposed that the department field test the new refugee sponsorship system on the B'nai B'rith request before introducing the program.[31] He recommended that the sponsorship scheme should rely on national organizations responsible for the identification of needy groups of refugees and displaced persons but that the actual sponsorship should come from local groups providing services directly to the immigrant or refugee. The system would be "tailored to the Ongoing Program," the term applied primarily to people escaping the East Bloc countries, but would be "considerably streamlined" for future special refugee movements that might arise.[32] An agreement on the package of services to be provided had also to be defined. In the case of the pilot project, local B'nai B'rith chapters would be required to arrange accommodation, acquire initial food and clothing, and provide general reception and resettlement assistance. They would meet the families at the airport as well as assist in registering them for medical insurance, social security numbers, schooling for children, and in-depth counselling and personal support aimed at helping them adapt to an independent, self-supporting life in Canada.[33]

Five months later, Manion advised Minister Cullen that the pilot project involving the resettlement of Soviet Jews demonstrated that the assistance and services asked of the sponsors were reasonable and acceptable and that the operational procedures were sound.[34] The project had been enthusiastically welcomed by the UNHCR. Manion's memorandum was accompanied by a paper called "Sponsorship Provisions for Refugee and Humanitarian Cases," outlining the elements of the new sponsorship program. If the minister approved the paper, said Manion, the necessary forms and instructions for field offices in Canada and abroad could be ready by April 1978. The department would prepare a pamphlet for prospective sponsors and hold briefings for interested voluntary organizations and groups.

The Sponsorship Provisions paper ultimately defined the sponsorship program. It defined persons eligible for the private refugee sponsorship program as "those having a well-founded fear of persecution on the grounds of race, religion, nationality, or membership in a particular social group or political opinion, i.e. Convention refugees,"[35] and members of designated classes. The criteria for the program included the following elements:

- Sponsoring organizations and groups could name individuals whom they wanted to assist or simply specify a religious, ethnic, or other affinity category they wished to help.
- Sponsoring groups could be legally incorporated organizations or informal groups of at least five people, all of whom were Canadian citizens or permanent residents and eighteen years of age or older.
- Groups had to make adequate arrangements in the community of reception for the settlement of the refugees.
- Sponsors must demonstrate they had sufficient financial resources and had made preparations for lodging, care, and maintenance and resettlement assistance.
- Groups could not be in default of other refugee or humanitarian sponsorship applications.
- Sponsors were to meet refugee families upon arrival and pro-

vide counselling and initial orientation to life in Canada where necessary and assistance in seeking employment. Some newcomers might also require additional assistance, such as day-care arrangements.
• Sponsors would be cautioned that sponsoring a newcomer was a grave responsibility likely to be a key determinant in the success or failure of the newcomers in adapting to life in Canada.

An information campaign began in April to promote public participation in and support for the sponsorship plan. Director General Bell and Michael Molloy made visits to Ottawa, Halifax, Hamilton, Windsor, and Toronto in April 1978 to meet with leaders of voluntary organizations. Assistant Deputy Minister (ADM) Richard Tait reported on the results of the consultations to Deputy Minister Manion on 28 April 1978.[36] Most potential sponsors reacted positively and were delighted to have direct influence on the selection of refugees. Concerns were raised by some about the substantial financial commitment required; groups often expected their financial responsibility to cease after a few weeks or months and were worried about year-long commitments in the midst of a difficult employment climate. Some groups, particularly churches and human rights organizations, expressed concern with the lack of flexibility to account for unforeseen circumstances, while others wanted a form of sponsorship limited to non-material services such as orientation, counselling, and moral support. Tait's view was that, although much was asked of sponsoring groups, and some potential participants had reservations about what was required, the format should be allowed to prove itself.[37] Manion agreed.

In the intervening months, details of the sponsorship program were provided to the department's regional offices and Canada Immigration Centres. A useful exchange ensued, clarifying, for example, that the sponsorship program was designed to assist refugees and designated classes abroad;[38] it did not apply to refugee claimants already in Canada wishing to benefit from protection under the Refugee Convention. The resources that sponsors needed to have on hand when applying to sponsor had to equal the amount of money given by CEIC's Adjustment Assistance Program for a minimum three-month period; a group also had to be capable of generating resources to meet the refugees' needs for at least one year.

Language training and classes taught by the Canada Manpower Training Plan (and the living allowances that went along with these courses) were available to both sponsored refugees and government assisted refugees. After completing the courses, refugees remained the responsibility of the sponsoring organizations if they had not found employment and if they had been in Canada less than a year.

In the case of national sponsoring organizations, the department's regional offices were responsible for assessing the plans of organizations' branches within the region. Depending on the economic, housing, and labour market conditions, minor variations in the requirements were permitted from one region to another. It was acknowledged that in some cases departmental assistance would be required and would take the form of Adjustment Assistance. Such assistance was to be provided when there was a breakdown in sponsorship.

The campaign to promote the new refugee sponsorship program continued over the summer and into the fall of 1978. On 26 September, all senators and members of Parliament received a letter about the Thailand Overland Refugee Program, under which Canada had agreed to accept twenty families a month from Thailand, describing the new refugee sponsorships program. The letter emphasized the importance of organizations and groups willing to sponsor, thereby augmenting the government's stated commitment to this group.[39] Also during the summer of 1978, Molloy made visits to the western provinces with a threefold message: the Indochinese refugee situation was getting worse; Indochinese refugees already arriving at Canada Employment Centres across the country would benefit from the support of volunteers; and the new sponsorship program provided a way for Canadians to assist directly. These messages were reinforced by a paper entitled "Canada's Special Refugee Program for Indochinese Small-Boat Escapees."[40] Molloy's visits inspired organizations such as the Edmonton Interfaith Immigration Committee to host a series of workshops[41] over the fall and winter of 1978–79 to familiarize congregations and parishes with both the growing refugee problem and the new refugee sponsorship program.

On 28 September 1978, Executive Director Calvin Best, accompanied by Molloy and his successor as director of refugee policy, Doug Hill, met with bishops of the Catholic Church's Migration Commission to discuss their involvement in the sponsorship program.[42] At first somewhat reluctant to commit themselves, the bishops were impressed with Best's passionate presentation of the merits of the program, and within weeks Catholics across Canada received the church's endorsement of the program.[43]

Two weeks later, Manion wrote to the leaders of major religious denominations to outline refugee sponsorships and their impact on the refugee programs.[44] Responses, particularly from the local Catholic institutions, were positive. The Mennonite Central Committee of Ontario expressed strong interest and requested 250 sponsorship brochures[45] and other related material for their annual meeting in November 1978. Articles explaining sponsorship began to appear in church and ethnic newspapers. Letters were also prepared for the heads of major service clubs across Canada.

The designers of the program envisioned two major sponsorship streams. The first would include large, well-established organizations with formal master agreements on behalf of their constituent groups to facilitate a high number of sponsorships with minimal formalities. This partnership concept was particularly well received by church groups. The second sponsorship stream was to be used by local organizations and local groups of at least five individuals. In these cases, the capacity of the potential sponsors in terms of funding and ability to resettle refugees would be subject to review by the local Canada Immigration Centre.

Negotiations for the first of the master agreements were initiated by the Mennonite Central Committee of Canada (MCC) in early 1979.[46] The recollections of the two negotiators provide a fascinating record of how trust was quickly established between the two sides and how that trust altered the stance of the Immigration Department and the shape of the sponsorship program.

Gordon Barnett, negotiating on behalf of the Immigration Department, recalls that his early instructions were to be very tough:

Initially, the Department intended to negotiate an agreement which would assign all responsibility for the sponsored refugees to the sponsor [ed. note: despite Manion's decision to the contrary]. In particular the Federal Language Training Program would not be available to sponsored refugees and if the training was made available then there would be no allowances. My negotiating instructions from Cal [Best, assistant deputy minister] were along the following lines … [If] they want to get involved let's give them lots of opportunity to be involved. If they sponsor they get to settle the refugee; we keep government programs for government refugees. Maybe we have to provide language training but we should refuse initially and certainly no federal payments [for] either training allowances or adjustment assistance should be given.

As negotiations progressed and the goodwill of MCC became evident this approach changed and both sides readily accepted to do what each would do best. Bill [Janzen] negotiated in such good faith it was embarrassing to play the cards I had been given. When I got back to Kirk [Bell, director general] I told him that I thought we had this wrong. Negotiating with MCC demonstrated only their complete commitment to help against our reluctance to give anything up and our meanness. I thought we should adopt a different, more cooperative approach. Kirk was on side with this and agreed to talk to Cal.

Later in the day I got called up to Cal's office. Kirk was there. Cal was unhappy as he thought I had been persuaded to go against his instructions to offload everything onto the sponsors. I produced the first draft that Bill and I had prepared and pointed out that we were not even providing seats for language training. Cal wondered, having negotiated the deal, why did I want to give it all away? Kirk took it from there and when we left Cal's office I was instructed to have the Department provide training and allowances.

In the end we put together an agreement that had the individual sponsoring groups provide the day-to-day hands-on care, the national organizations would mitigate any unusual costs or difficulties and the Department would provide an overall structure that included language training and allowances and a willingness to take over from the sponsors any cases that were exceptionally costly or requiring unusual professional services. This willingness to assist each other worked both ways and for many of the more difficult families a mix of Departmental money and hands-on care provided by sponsors became the norm. It may well be that had the first agreement not been negotiated with a group as openly altruistic and sincerely helpful as MCC the National Sponsorship Agreements would have been less cooperative.[47]

The view from across the table is provided by William Janzen, the negotiator on behalf of MCC:

I was privileged to have a role in those negotiations which took place early 1979. I had been instructed by colleagues in MCC's Winnipeg head office to arrange a meeting with senior Immigration officials to look for better mechanisms for bringing in refugees from Southeast Asia, whose tragic situation was filling the news at this time. The officials were most open. The meeting took place on February 2, 1979. The assistant Deputy Minister, Cal Best, chaired it. With him were Kirk Bell and Gordon Barnett. On our side were John Wieler, Arthur Driedger, Robert Koop, Don Friesen and I. In that meeting we sketched the outline of an agreement. Gordon Barnett and I were then asked to write it up. We met three or four times within the next few weeks, always checking with our respective colleagues. But things came together quickly. The agreement was formally approved by the MCC Executive Committee in a telephone conference on February 14 and signed in the Winnipeg MCC offices on March 5 by our Executive Director, J.M. Klassen, and the Minister of Immigration, the Hon. Bud Cullen.

The agreement runs to eleven pages but its essence is simple. It arose from the fact that the new Immigration law, which came into force in April 1978, contained a provision – in section 6(2) in the act and section 7 in the Regulations – whereby any five individuals could sponsor a refugee if they accepted full liability for the refugee and his or her accompanying dependents for one year. Many people, though interested, were afraid of this liability. What would they do in a worst case scenario? With the Master Agreement (M.A.), MCC accepted this liability. As a result, local groups, or congregations, if they obtained a letter of authorization from MCC, did not have to worry about being liable. Also, if congregations obtained such letters, then Immigration officials did not have to screen them to see if they were reliable. The M.A. also spelled out what MCC would do, what the government would do, how communications would flow between the congregations and local Immigration offices and with the Embassies abroad, etc. Once the M.A. was signed, Mennonite congregations across Canada got to work with exceptional energy and commitment. Also, within weeks most of the other national church bodies had signed virtually identical M.A.s.[48]

Janzen attributed MCC's eagerness to negotiate a sponsorship agreement to a number of factors. Many Mennonites, including some of the MCC board members, had themselves been refugees. MCC had sponsored refugee members of its own community, mainly from the Soviet Union and Eastern Europe in the 1920s (21,000) and others after World War II (7,000). The Mennonites were confident in their relationship with the federal government based on previous successful partnerships in other fields, viewed their church as "a body that could act in society," and had extensive experience working in Vietnam stretching back to 1954. Finally, Janzen noted that, unlike some other church leaderships, the Mennonites did not view the sponsorship concept as a ploy to let the government off the hook, nor did they share the view, common to many of the more left-wing refugee advocates of the time, that the government was hard on refugees from right-wing regimes and soft on refugees from left-wing regimes.[49]

The day following the signing of the MCC master agreement, instructions for the processing of applications to sponsor from groups covered by the master agreements were approved by Calvin Best and subsequently sent to CEIC's regional offices, Canada Immigration Centres, and visa offices abroad.[50] The process was initially complex:[51]

• When a local constituent group of an organization with a master agreement approached a Canada Immigration Centre (CIC) with a request to sponsor a refugee, only the existence of a Letter of Agreement with the national organization had to be confirmed.

• A representative of the constituent group signed an affirmation form, which was sent by the CIC to the appropriate visa office, providing the name of the group and its address, whether named or unnamed refugees were to be selected, the number of people the group was willing to accept, and other relevant information.

• Refugees identified for sponsorship had to signify that they would accept the assistance of the sponsoring group.
• Once refugee applicants had accepted a sponsorship offer, the visa office sent a telex to the appropriate CIC specifying the names, dates of birth, nationality, occupational profiles, and language ability of working-aged members and the estimated processing time.
• The CIC passed the information to the sponsoring group, which then confirmed, approved, or rejected the proposed refugee.
• If it agreed, the group's representative signed a confirmation document, which the CIC sent to the visa office.
• The visa offices proceeded with travel arrangements and informed the CIC (and thence the sponsors).

Sponsors had to be flexible about the type of person they requested, since visa officers only had one chance to interview a refugee before arrival. Processing time, during this period when there were relatively few sponsorships, would often take no more than two months – exceptionally rapid by today's standards.

The Mennonite Master Agreement of 5 March 1979 was quickly followed by agreements with the Presbyterian Church of Canada (9 March 1979) and the Council of Christian Reformed Churches of Canada (5 April 1979). Leadership at this early stage was provided by Rev. Arie van Eek and Peter Swart of the Christian Reformed Church, along with Bishops Plourde (Ottawa), Wendle (Renfrew), and Remi de Roo (Victoria). By the end of August, twenty-eight national church organizations and Catholic or Anglican dioceses had signed master agreements, and by March 1981 the total had reached forty-seven.[52]

While the speed with which churches and other organizations concluded sponsorship agreements was impressive, the pace with which sponsorship committees were formed across Canada during the remainder of 1979 to take advantage of the new avenue for directly assisting boat people and other refugees was simply astonishing. The initial signers of sponsorship master agreements lost no time. By the end of June, CEIC had received 388 sponsorships for 1,609 refugees. By the end of 1979, 5,456 sponsorships had been received for 29,269 refugees, far surpassing the target of 21,000 that had been set by the government in July 1979.

TABLE 4.1
Initial sponsorships, spring 1979

Sponsor	Sponsorship applications	Refugees sponsored
Mennonites	203	1,009
Presbyterians	14	79
Lutherans	3	15
Christian Reformed	45	208

Source: Briefing Book, Indochinese Refugee Task Force, July 1979,
CIHS Collection.

TABLE 4.2
Sponsorship by month, 1 June 1979 to 31 December 1979

Month	Number of sponsoring groups	Number of refugees sponsored
June	388	1,609
July	359	2,201
August	1,420	8,263
September	1,076	5,745
October	932	4,968
December	493	2,443
Total, 1979	5,456	29,269

Source: Employment and Immigration Canada, *Indochinese Refugees:
The Canadian Response, 1979 and 1980* (Ottawa: Department of Supply
and Services 1982), 28.

Impact of the 1976 Immigration Act

Making the fulfillment of Canada's legal obligations to refugees and its humanitarian tradition toward the displaced and persecuted an objective of the 1976 Immigration Act underpinned the development of a legal framework that replaced the ad hoc measures and administrative processes that had served up to that point. Through the Indochinese Designated Class, the government sent a powerful policy signal and provided the Immigration Department with a selection tool that was precisely targeted, robust, and flexible.

While the designated class is no longer part of its regulatory framework, Canada has applied the basic concept in recent times to efficiently process large numbers of Bhutanese refugees in Nepal and Iraqi refugees scattered about the Middle East. These groups were accorded prima facie recognition as refugees, allowing visa officers to concentrate on assessing *admissibility* (health, criminality, and security) and settlement potential, not *eligibility* for the Convention Refugee Class.[53]

The decision to launch the sponsorship program coincided with a national trend towards social activism focusing on the active engagement of individuals in support of causes they embraced. The program's success reflected the timely confluence of government policy and public mobilization around an idea. And coming as it did just as Canadians became aware of the unfolding tragedy in Southeast Asia, the sponsorship program gave Canadians the means to convert their concern for the refugees into direct action.

It is worth noting that the private sponsorship program is one of the few elements of the 1976 Immigration Act to survive largely unchanged to this day. It has been frequently examined by other governments seeking to strengthen their resettlement programs, but it has not been easy to transplant it elsewhere, less because of its design than the value system in Canada that underpins it.[54] It is widely admired by refugee advocates in other countries, and well it should be. A study published in 2003 concluded that the largest agents of resettlement in the world were, first, the US government, second, the Australian government, and third, Canadian private sponsors; the Government of Canada was in fourth place, with all others trailing far behind.[55]

5

Ramping Up for Crisis, 1978

In 1978, conditions in Vietnam, Cambodia, and Laos deteriorated. Natural disasters and serious food shortages followed each other. Hostility was growing between Vietnam and both Cambodia and China; ethnic cleansing of Vietnam's Chinese minority, continued repression of those associated with the defunct South Vietnamese and Laotian regimes, and the genocide perpetrated by the Khmer Rouge in Democratic Kampuchea (Cambodia) prompted increasing numbers of people to flee overland to Thailand or by boat. Refugee boat arrivals in Malaysia, Indonesia, Brunei, Philippines, Hong Kong, and Macau escalated rapidly. In Canada, the redesign of the refugee resettlement system took place against dawning recognition that the increasing flow of people in Southeast Asia was moving in the direction of a major refugee crisis.

In November 1977, Immigration Minister Bud Cullen had agreed to a "metered" approach, whereby fifty "small boat escapees" (assigned the code SBE for statistical identification purposes) would be admitted each month, funded from within CEIC's existing resources.[1] Up to that point, Canadian resettlement activity in Southeast Asia focused on family reunification or using up the last of the commitment to resettle 3,000 unsponsored refugees made in May 1975. While the commitment to fifty per month was modest, it represented a new initiative and recognition that the Indochinese refugee problem had entered a new phase. The public announcement was delayed pending a response from Quebec Immigration Minister Jacques Couture regarding Quebec's participation. On 13 January 1978, Deputy Minister Jack Manion informed Cullen that Quebec would accept 30 per cent of this new movement and wished to participate in their selection.[2] Manion advised that the time had come to inform the other provinces and the public, and that a second announcement should be made when the first group arrived in Quebec under this new program.

The memorandum also informed the minister that the mayor of Windsor[3] had set up a committee to assist Indochinese refugees destined to that city and that the Canadian Catholic Organization for Development and Peace, operating out of the office of Archbishop Carney in Vancouver, "had expressed an interest in setting up a nationwide program of assistance for Boat escapees."[4] These events, as it turned out, were the leading edge of renewed public interest in the boat people.

On 17 January 1978, Richard Tait, the executive director (ADM) of immigration and demographic policy, wrote to CEIC regional directors general across Canada regarding refugee resettlement activities in the coming year and signalled a subtle but important shift in the Canadian approach to refugees. Tait's message summed up CEIC management's understanding of the growing problem in Southeast Asia. It began by informing the directors general that, while economic and labour market conditions would likely result in reduction of the total numbers of immigrants who would be admitted in 1978, international events would result in the admission of a substantial number of refugees and displaced persons:[5]

> Our most significant special program will involve the acceptance of up to 50 families each month of Vietnamese small boat escapees. You are no doubt aware that since the Communist takeover in South Vietnam in April, 1975, some 10,000 persons have fled that country by sea. Heedless of the risks involved, the numbers of escapees have increased recently by some 1,500 persons per month. The acceptance of these people by countries in Southeast Asia has generally been poor and there are confirmed reports of small boat escapees being refused permission to land and forced back to sea. The Minister recently agreed to our continuing participation in a concerted international effort to assist in relieving the plight of these people. Although not large, our commitment, when viewed against the 6,800 Vietnamese refugees already accepted by Canada, is expected to have a definite impact in resolving the problem by encouraging international resettlement efforts.[6]

Tait went on to note that Cabinet approval had not been sought for the Vietnamese Small Boat Escapee program, and as a result there would be no special allocation of resources for language or occupational training. He stated that despite careful selection abroad, "the very nature of these special movements will no doubt tax your resources." He stressed the need for Canada Employment Centre counsellors "to assist in the resettlement of refugees and other displaced persons with patience and in the spirit in which they were accepted for residence in this country."[7] Tait's memo also advised the directors general that out of a commitment to resettle 7,000 Chilean refugees (including two hundred political prisoners), over 5,800 had arrived, and Canada would continue to "extend liberal consideration" to large numbers of Eastern Europeans seeking refuge in Western Europe under the Ongoing Refugee Program.[8]

Tait's message constituted a fundamental shift in the way the refugee component of the overall immigration program was perceived by the department. Under the new immigration act, resettlement of refugees was now a legislated objective of the Immigration Department. For the first time in Canada's history, the refugee program was accorded sufficient priority to be exempted from a decision to reduce labour market immigration due to economic conditions. In fact, it was expected to increase despite those conditions.

The Indochinese commitment grew serendipitously from fifty people a month to fifty families a month. When Michael Molloy, the director of refugee policy, briefed Donald Cameron of the Foreign Branch's Asia Pacific Division (IFAP) on the fifty-person commitment, Cameron replied, "Surely you mean fifty families, not fifty people." After that, "fifty families" was quietly inserted into all official communications, including the official press release issued by the minister on 26 January 1978.[9] No one objected.

The program (as well as the increase) was officially communicated to the Department of External Affairs in a letter of 2 February 1978, from CEIC's Kirk Bell to Geoffrey Pearson, director general of the UN Bureau, asking that the Canadian Mission in Geneva advise the UNHCR of the new program. According to Bell, it had been "decided to increase our intake from 50 persons to 50 families each month in order to make a more substantial contribution to the alleviation of this problem."[10] Bell's letter asked that UNHCR be advised that the refugees would be selected by Canadian missions in Singapore,

Manila, and Hong Kong at a ratio of 35: 10: 5 and that refugees would have to meet normal immigration medical requirements. Priority would be given to those with relatives in Canada, those sponsored by Canadian organizations, and those whose occupational skills or ability to speak English or French "would ensure their successful establishment."[11]

Tait's blithe assertion that Canada's small commitment would "have a definite impact in resolving the problem by encouraging international resettlement efforts" was rapidly vindicated.[12] Lionel Rosenblatt of the US State Department wrote to Tait on 10 February 1978, expressing appreciation for the new Canadian program, which American officials had pointed to in hearings before a House of Representative subcommittee. According to Rosenblatt, "When we finally hammer out a long-range program you can be assured that the continuing Canadian role will have been a key precursor. In a sense the Canadian program can be said to have a multiplier potential beyond its own magnitude."[13]

Instructions for the new SBE program had been sent to Singapore, Manila, and Hong Kong by the Asia Pacific Bureau on 18 January 1978, but results were slow in coming. By April, only two refugees had been approved. Kirk Bell wrote to Joe Bissett, director general of the Foreign Branch, seeking an explanation.[14] In part, the problem arose from a misunderstanding on the part of the E&I team in Singapore, who assumed that fifty families were to be put into process each month, when Ottawa was expecting fifty families to arrive. At the same time, officials in Ottawa at the most senior levels had little understanding of the challenges faced by E&I Singapore with only two officers responsible for servicing scattered and difficult-to-reach refugee camps in Thailand, Malaysia, and Indonesia.

A report to the minister on 7 June 1978 suggested that because of family and historical ties, the majority of the "escapees" preferred to go the United States, France, or Australia and that the visa offices were now accepting more than the established monthly target to offset attrition.[15] Tougher American criteria for people with links to other countries were expected to help. Supporting infrastructure was thin on the ground, and in many cases the United States, Australia, Canada, and France were interviewing and processing the same cases. It was not until March 1978 that the UNHCR's "blue card" registration system, recording which countries had interviewed each case, was implemented in Malaysia; it was applied in Thailand in the summer of 1978, but only to Vietnamese boat people. Until these measures were in place, all of the resettlement countries put work into cases that ultimately went somewhere else. It would be several months before the SBE program was performing as envisaged, and it would then be quickly overtaken by events. As it was, the first large group to arrive under the fifty SBE families a month program was a group of forty-nine boat people rescued by a Greek freighter and taken to Mombasa, Kenya, where they were processed by the Canadian High Commission in Nairobi.[16]

The situation in Southeast Asia deteriorated further. In March, citing its communist ideology, the Vietnamese government nationalized all private businesses and began to move urban dwellers to rural "New Economic Zones." As the commercial class consisted largely of ethnic Chinese, the pressure on this community increased and would in the months that followed manifest itself in large numbers of ethnic Chinese returning, under compulsion, to China, while others fell prey to the organizers of a series of "large boats," arranged with the collusion of Vietnamese officials and Chinese business interests in Hong Kong. By July, China claimed to have accepted the return of 160,000 ethnic Chinese refugees and in retaliation cancelled all aid to Vietnam and closed its borders.

Up until April 1978, the Canadian strategy for Southeast Asia was based on a two-pronged approach, focusing on resettlement of Vietnamese boat people while providing funds to UNHCR for what it was hoped (naively, as it turned out) would be a local resettlement effort for the overland (Lao and Cambodian) refugees in Thailand. With the visit of the UN High Commissioner for Refugees Poul Hartling in March 1978, that position began to shift. In a memorandum to Minister Cullen, dated 26 April 1978, Deputy Minister Manion noted that the latest estimates indicated there were 99,000 overland refugees in Thailand, including 82,000 Lao, 14,000 Cambodians, and 3,000 Vietnamese: "Because of the large numbers involved and the fact that most of these people would have considerable difficulties adapting to life in industrialized countries, the appropriate solution appears to be resettlement in Thailand."[17]

Manion went on: "You will recall that during his visit to Canada, the new United Nations High Commissioner for Refugees, Poul Hartling, requested that we undertake to resettle a number of overland refugees in addition to our current small-boat escapee program. Given that the strategy indicated above was worked out in conjunction with the UNHCR, this request is rather surprising. However, because of this request, plus a growing interest in the fate of the overland refugees on the part of Members of Parliament and various Canadian organizations, we have asked our officials in Singapore and Thailand for an assessment of the situation with a view to identifying groups who will have to be resettled outside of that country."[18] Manion concluded that he thought the Laotians could probably stay in Thailand but that the Vietnamese would have to leave, as might most of the Cambodians, "because of the capricious actions of the Cambodian authorities."[19]

Following consultations with the embassies in Southeast Asia on 8 June, Immigration Minister Bud Cullen and Secretary of State for External Affairs Don Jamieson went to Cabinet seeking authority and funding for a new program for overland refugee families in Thailand. Justification for the program centred on the Cambodian government's violations of human rights and the plight of Cambodian refugees in Thailand.[20] The Memorandum to Cabinet of 8 June asked for approval to initiate a new special movement of twenty refugee families a month. To fund the new program, the memorandum sought Treasury Board approval for $2.4 million to cover the costs, including $1,462,000 for Adjustment Assistance allowances to the refugees, $803,000 for language training, and $76,000 for implementation costs. Reading the memorandum some forty years later, one is struck by its cautious and tentative wording. Senior officials at both External Affairs and Employment and Immigration, in their advice to ministers, were not prepared to recommend large scale third-country resettlement, at least from Thailand. The object of Cabinet's consideration was to "examine what, if any, additional Canadian action can be taken concerning (a) the Cambodian Government's violations of human rights and (b) the plight of Cambodian refugees in Thailand, against the background of Canadian interest in the area and our global response to refugee problems including our current assistance to Indochinese refugees."[21]

The first item was given short shrift with a frank admission that "prospects ... were limited" for any possible and effective action to improve the human rights situation in Cambodia. That said, Canada would continue to pursue the issue at the United Nations in the absence of any other avenues. The second item for consideration offered more possibilities. Cabinet was asked to meet the short-term needs of Cambodian and Laotian refugees in Thailand by approving a new program for Indochinese refugees in that country.[22] It was recommended that Canada admit refugee families at a metered rate of twenty families per month from Thai camps to an "unannounced total of 1000 persons." Selection would focus on "those among the Indochinese population in Thailand who are capable of successful establishment in Canada."[23] Employment and Immigration would seek the help of voluntary agencies and churches to assist the new immigrants in becoming established in Canada with the backing of federal government funds (over $3 million). It was expected that this modest resettlement program would demonstrate to both the Thai authorities and the international community that Canada had a continued concern and commitment to refugees in Thailand.

In looking to long-term solutions, the memorandum's authors noted that there were approximately 100,000 Indochinese refugees in Thailand. Fourteen thousand were Cambodians, most of whom had been in Thailand since 1975. The remaining 86,000 comprised Hill Tribe people from Laos, Lowland Lao, and a small number of Vietnamese – the Vietnamese being "the least liked by the Thais and the most readily adaptable to settlement in third countries."[24] Of the rest, the majority were described as "illiterate subsistence farmers who are unsuitable for resettlement in industrialized third countries." Accordingly, the memorandum argued that the "most sensible long-term solution [for this population of Lao and Cambodians] would appear ... to be permanent resettlement in Thailand." Cabinet was asked to approve immediate discussions with other governments that would, ultimately, encourage the Thai government to devise a plan for permanent resettlement, on the understanding that the international community would contribute substantially to its implementation. Why it was believed that the Thai government would accept such a proposal was not explained. It was also proposed that the Canadian ambassador in Bangkok raise the possibility of local resettlement with the Thai authorities "at the appropriate time."[25]

Following discussions with the provinces, on 20 July 1978, Cabinet approved the proposals put forward in the memorandum. Beyond specifying a metered intake of up to twenty families per month from Thailand, Cabinet left the details to the departments responsible. The program in Thailand was clearly envisaged as low key and minimal, signalling a modest commitment.[26]

The memorandum had also recommended making a cash donation of up to $1 million to UNHCR towards its $18 million Indochinese appeal (noting that CIDA was recommending $500,000). It sought authority to engage other governments in a discussion about resettling most of the refugees within Thailand, along with authorization for the Canadian ambassador in Thailand to advise the Thai authorities that Canada would provide financial support to a resettlement program in Thailand.[27] The process of obtaining final approval for this small increase in the Canadian resettlement commitment in Southeast Asia dragged on for two months. While the general approach was approved in a report to Cabinet on 15 June, the decision regarding the resettlement program and its costs would require further Cabinet discussion.[28]

On 10 July, Treasury Board reported to Cabinet that it had considered the report and recommended that the program to resettle twenty families go ahead but that CEIC absorb all the costs within its existing resources. It did, however, recommend approval of a $500,000 contribution by CIDA to UNHCR, with the possibility of a further $500,000 if the need still existed and if an evaluation of the first donation showed positive results.[29] CEIC Minister Bud Cullen pushed back at another Cabinet meeting on 13 July. Noting the minister's statement that CEIC had insufficient funds to absorb the costs of the proposed new resettlement program, Cabinet referred the matter back to Treasury Board, which considered the matter again on 19 July.[30] Treasury Board recommended that CEIC try to absorb the costs, with the possibility that a shortfall could be addressed in subsequent Supplementary and Main Estimates. Cabinet agreed.[31]

On 26 July, following the Cabinet decision, Cullen wrote to High Commissioner Hartling advising that implementation of the SBE program was approaching the full complement of fifty families arriving in Canada each month, and that the new program for twenty overland refugee families from Thailand had been approved and would commence, perhaps in October "as soon as sufficient resources have been deployed for the program."[32] Implicit in this undertaking was a decision to split responsibility for delivery of immigration and refugee programs between the existing E&I visa office at the Canadian High Commission in Singapore and a new visa office to be established at the embassy in Bangkok. E&I Singapore would retain responsibility for

Malaysia, Singapore, and Indonesia, while the new unit in Bangkok would cover Thailand and Burma. Two officers, Murray Oppertshauser and Robert Shalka, would arrive in Bangkok on 11 November 1978 to establish the visa office.[33]

Instructions were despatched in early August to CEIC regional offices across Canada informing them about the new program and announcing that for planning purposes it was expected that each month thirteen families would be directed to Quebec, two each to British Columbia and Ontario, and the remaining family in accordance with opportunities in other regions. The new movement was assigned the program identifier code TOR (Thailand Overland Refugees) to distinguish it from the Small Boat Escapee (SBE) movement.[34] With the opening of the CEIC facility in Bangkok, SBE monthly targets were reallocated between the posts in Southeast Asia: Singapore, thirty-five families; Manila, five; Hong Kong, five; and Bangkok, five, plus twenty TOR families.[35]

In compliance with the Cabinet directive that CEIC seek the cooperation of voluntary agencies and churches in assisting local CECs to help the arriving Indochinese refugees, a paper titled "The Small Boat Escapee Program"[36] had been prepared and distributed across the country.[37] An accompanying message from W.K. Bell, dated 13 September 1978, stated, "It should be noted that we are not insisting on formal refugee sponsorship in these cases because we are committed to a set intake each month regardless of whether sponsorships are forthcoming."[38] Bell went on to stress that CEIC was looking for voluntary assistance in helping the refugees with the adjustments they would have to make on arrival.

Despite the assurances given to High Commissioner Hartling, the flow of refugees to Canada under the SBE program had fallen far short of the target of fifty families a month, and there was concern in Ottawa about how this was affecting the perception of Canada's efforts in Southeast Asia and among other resettlement countries. With an international meeting on resettlement scheduled for 20 September in Kuala Lumpur, Malaysia, J.B. Bissett, director general, Foreign Branch, wrote to J.C. Cross, director general, Settlement, on 28 August, informing him that despite the initiation of the program in January, administrative problems arising from the referral of refugees to multiple resettlement countries had resulted in significant attrition.[39] Consequently, only 167 cases totalling 283 persons had arrived, creating a shortfall of 233 cases. Bissett asked Cross whether the settlement system could cope if the monthly rate of arrivals of SBE families was increased by twenty cases a month for the next five months (i.e., seventy families a month). Bissett wanted to announce the increased level of activity at the meeting in Kuala Lumpur to reassure UNHCR and participating members of the international community that Canada was committed to meeting its objectives. Cross agreed and notified the regional offices accordingly.⁴⁰

A number of developments that summer had prompted much thought and discussion within the Refugee Affairs Division of CEIC. The sponsorship program had been launched, and efforts to promote it among religious organizations and the voluntary sector were going better than expected, despite opposition from refugee advocates in a couple of mainline churches. The regulations for both the new Convention Refugee Class and the three designated classes had been drafted and were working their way through the regulatory approval process. The recommendation to accept fifty boat families had proceeded smoothly because CEIC was able to fund it from existing resources. By contrast, the work that had gone into the struggle to launch and fund the modest program for twenty TOR families a month, and the meagre disproportionate result achieved, led to the conclusion that there had to be a better way to obtain authorization, and above all, funding, for the growing portfolio of resettlement programs. If Canada was now going to be in the business of resettling refugees from various parts of the world, it needed a better planning and funding mechanism both for needs that could be foreseen and for the emergencies that would inevitably occur.

Section 7 of the 1976 act required that, after consultations with the provinces regarding demographic and labour-market needs, and with other individuals, organizations, and institutions as appropriate, the government must table in Parliament its immigration levels plan for the coming year sixty days before the end of the preceding year. Conversations between Ivan Timonin of the Demographic Policy Division, responsible for putting together the first (1979) Levels Plan, and Michael Molloy of Refugee Affairs led to the idea of inserting an annual refugee plan into the larger immigration levels plan. Jack Manion first floated this idea in a letter of 13 July 1978 to Allan Gottlieb, the under-secretary of External Affairs, expressing an interest in closer interdepartmental coordination on refugee matters and the possibility of an annual refugee plan. In his reply, Gottlieb informed Manion that discussions on international humanitarian relief and assistance were already taking place between External Affairs and CIDA, with a view to developing guidelines to facilitate coordinated Canadian responses to appeals from UNHCR and the International Red Cross. Gottlieb welcomed Manion's proposal for ongoing and regular consultations between External Affairs, CIDA, and CEIC. Gottlieb also expressed cautious support for the idea of an annual refugee plan, noting that "any plan and budget would require a considerable degree of flexibility in order to deal [with] unforeseen refugee situations that would undoubtedly occur."[41]

The support of both deputy ministers for better interdepartmental coordination on refugee matters and for an annual refugee plan led to a paper titled "Towards an Integrated Canadian Refugee Policy," written by Molloy and circulated by W.K. Bell on 14 September 1978.[42] The paper argued that a more formal mechanism was needed to integrate the foreign policy, refugee policy, and funding of humanitarian relief elements of Canada's refugee efforts. Resettlement and financial assistance to refugee relief needed to be integrated into a foreign policy framework and would lead to better use of resources and more leverage in managing international organizations. At the same time the paper argued that the creation of an annual refugee plan would make it easier for the government and its domestic and external partners to plan and manage their own responsibilities toward refugees.

The paper was widely circulated, and the first draft of an annual refugee plan for 1979 was sent to Manion by Executive Director Cal Best on 30 October 1978.[43] Best reported to Manion that the idea of using the plan to advance interdepartmental coordination on the refugee file was still an objective, although CIDA was not keen to have other departments involved in making decisions on the allocation of its funds. CIDA had, however, created a Humanitarian Emergency Relief Unit – a step in the right direction. As will be seen in the following chapter, the adoption by Cabinet of the 1979 Annual Refugee Plan in December 1978 marked the beginning of serious re-engagement with the Indochinese refugee problem and initiated the practice of having Cabinet review and authorize funding for the totality of Canada's predictable resettlement activities each year.

Conditions in Vietnam worsened, and pressure on the Chinese minority in particular intensified with a dispute over whether the 1.7

million ethnic Chinese still living in Vietnam should be considered citizens of China or Vietnam. In September, the first of a series of "big boats," the freighter *Southern Cross*[44] with 1,200 refugees on board, departed southern Vietnam. The ship sailed to Terengganu in Malaysia, arriving during the UNHCR resettlement conference. After being supplied with food, it was escorted away by the Malaysian navy. The Singaporean navy blocked entry to that country, and the *Southern Cross* was eventually beached on the uninhabited Indonesian island of Pengibu. In response to an appeal from UNHCR, E&I Singapore's O-I-C Ian Hamilton sought and quickly received approval from Ottawa to select cases of Canadian interest at the earliest opportunity, and then scrounged unused SBE quotas from Hong Kong and Manila.[45] The *Southern Cross* eventually sank, and the refugees were transferred to Tanjung Pinang, a thirteen-hour voyage, by the Indonesian navy. Hamilton led the first resettlement team to reach the refugees, and his report provides a graphic picture of a rapidly evolving situation:

> Further to our tel log 129, 4 Oct., have completed selection interviews of *Southern Cross* refugees, Oct. 11 and 12. Canada was first selection team to arrive Tanjung Pinang 24 hours after refugees arrived by Indonesian naval vessel. Interest in CDA extremely high. UNHCR and Indonesian officials expressed thanks for prompt CDN [action]. In all, 35 families were selected for further processing for a total of 81 people. In general, calibre of refugees accepted very high. Virtually all had language capability in English, French or both languages. Of 81 selected 41 claimed relatives in CDA in the Assisted Relative Class. QIS [Quebec Immigration Service] Fortin concurs in the selection of 22 *Southern Cross* for Québec. A point of interest is that of 1200 plus escapees on *Southern Cross* only 94 were ethnic Vietnamese. Remainder Chinese.
>
> Indonesian and UNHCR officials currently cooperating on construction of new refugee camp in Tanjung Pinang which will replace old rubber warehouse currently housing refugees. Completion date will be in one or two months. With increased landings noted in Malaysia and hardening of S[inga]porean attitude we are receiving reports of landings on small Indonesian islands. Latest report indicated 300 refugees from a remote island

which are to be transported to Tanjung Pinang near future. [It is] apparent 1979/80 travel schedule must consider increased att[en-tio]n to Indonesian camps as well as camps on island of Borneo (East Malaysia and Indonesia). Increase frequency of landings are also reported.[46]

Dramatic as it was, the *Southern Cross* episode would come to be seen as a dress rehearsal for much more significant events involving a second "big boat" in November. Pressure continued to mount; October saw the worst flooding in Vietnamese history, and the rice crop came in 7.5 million tons short of requirements.

As the SBE program gained traction and with the Bangkok office about to open, new instructions were sent to E&I Hong Kong, Manila, and Singapore along with others in the region in a circular memorandum (CM) dated 25 October 1978. The CM, which consolidated previous instructions, emphasized the need for careful selection, noting that no special allocations had been made for language training for SBEs and that unemployment levels in Canada were at their highest since the 1940s. Prepared in full knowledge that the Indochinese Designated Class was about to come into effect, the CM noted that Vietnamese selected under the program did not have to comply with the UN Convention definition. It indicated that preference should be given to those who met normal immigrant section criteria (i.e., capable of successful establishment). Other "desirable" applicants who failed to meet normal criteria, including francophones, could be accepted if they had above-average personal qualities or skills in demand, family configurations that would permit rapid self-sufficiency, willingness to take any employment on arrival, or offers of assistance from voluntary organizations or the Province of Quebec. It also required that cases of senior military or governmental employees of the former government of South Vietnam, along with those whose earlier activities might be subject to adverse comment, must be referred to Ottawa for decision.

While parts of the CM would become obsolete in a few months as the metered approach was abandoned with Cabinet's decision to launch a much larger Canadian effort under the 1979 annual refugee plan, the policy it laid out with regard to families would endure well into the next decade and would distinguish the Canadian program from its US and Australian counterparts: "For the purpose of this pro-

gram, a 'family' is defined as the husband and the wife and their un-
married sons or daughters under the age of 21 years. Other relatives
beyond the nuclear family are to be statistically recorded as separate
families and *every effort is to be made not to separate extended families in the selection process"*[47] (emphasis added). As will be seen in the
chapters dealing with operations in Southeast Asia, the instruction to
avoid separating extended families became a bedrock principle energetically applied by Canadian visa officers.

Skipping ahead, in December 1978 a second CM, penned by Carla
Thorlakson of the Refugee Affairs Division, would acquaint visa offices with three new designated classes approved by the Governor-
in-Council. The CM reaffirmed that those selected under the designated classes, while exempt from the need to comply with the UN
Convention definition, would have benefits equivalent to those accorded Convention Refugee status. These included exemption from
the points system, access to assisted travel loans, eligibility for sponsorship by private groups, and access to enhanced settlement services.
The Indochinese Designated Class, the CM advised the visa offices in
Southeast Asia, "provides an eligibility definition broad enough to en-
compass both the small boat escapees and the overland refugees in
Thailand. Our experience in dealing with Indo-Chinese refugees indicates that it is not realistic to require each boat escapee or overland
refugee to establish that he or she has personally been subject to some
for[m] of persecution as envisaged by the UN Refugee Convention.
The fact that they have managed to escape, survived the voyage, and
are now existing in one of the camps in Southeast Asia is sufficient
reason for them to merit our consideration on a humanitarian basis."[48]
This understanding of the circumstances of the Indochinese refugees
and the approach to be taken by Canadian visa officers was to shape
Canada's resettlement activities in Southeast Asia for the next decade.

Turning Point: The *Hai Hong*

In November 1978 the arrival off the Malaysian coast of the Hai
Hong, *a crippled freighter carrying 2,500 refugees, was to touch off a
series of events that would have a profound impact on how Indochinese refugees were perceived by Canada's public, media, and government and lead to a fundamental policy shift. The history of this episode*

and its effect on Canadian perceptions and policy thus merits detailed examination; the CIHS *is grateful to Dara Marcus for this account, which forms the basis for the rest of this chapter.*[49]

The Hong Kong–based syndicate that had fitted out the *Southern Cross* decided to purchase a second ship and sell passage to more Vietnamese wishing to flee their government's oppression.[50] The *Hai Hong*, built in Panama in 1948, was officially purchased for scrap metal in 1978 and sent to Hong Kong for demolition. Instead, it docked in Vietnam. Arrangements were made to pick up 1,200 passengers willing to pay for their freedom and, as with the *Southern Cross* venture, take them to Hong Kong. Vietnamese government officials, aware of the racket and more than willing to cooperate for a healthy share of the profits, forced the captain to take on an additional 1,300 passengers. The majority of those fleeing were ethnic Chinese, the persecuted business class. Each refugee paid sixteen bars of gold (roughly US$3,200 at that time): ten to Vietnamese officials and six to the boat syndicate. With close to 2,500 passengers on board and inadequate supplies for even half that number, the *Hai Hong* departed Vietnam on 24 October 1978.

The boat headed out of the Mekong Delta towards Hong Kong. However, Typhoon Rita blew the *Hai Hong* off course and damaged its engine. Unable to continue, and with insufficient food or water for the 2,500 passengers, the vessel spent several days trying to land on various Indonesian islands but was repeatedly turned away by authorities. Finally, unable to go farther, the ship dropped anchor near Port Klang off Malaysia. As the passengers had paid Vietnamese authorities in order to leave their country, Malaysia, like Indonesia, would not consider the passengers to be legitimate refugees and refused to allow the ship to dock. Malaysia feared that if it accepted the *Hai Hong* passengers as refugees, it would encourage similar refugee trafficking ventures. The *Hai Hong* remained anchored off Malaysia's coast, where the UNHCR and the Red Crescent monitored the situation and provided vital medical supplies and food.

Malaysia, already struggling with a large refugee population, insisted that for every new refugee, one refugee currently housed in a Malaysian camp would have to be accepted for resettlement by another country or be voluntarily repatriated. As days passed, conditions on board the *Hai Hong* deteriorated; two people had died during the voyage and a third died while it was anchored off Port

Klang. With no bathing facilities and very crowded conditions, most passengers had rashes and other skin problems. Reporters allowed on board by the Malaysian authorities described the brutal conditions on the vessel, stating that "We literally walked on top of people – men, women, children, and the elderly, stretched or crouched, noticeably exhausted and shaken, but exhibiting, without exception, a great dignity."[51]

The international community, including Canada, expressed sympathy for the passengers' plight, but at this stage no government was willing to propose a real solution. Malaysia, frustrated with the lack of assistance from the international community, announced that it intended to tow the disabled boat out into open waters and abandon its passengers to their fate. At this time, refugee camps were overflowing and thousands of boat people were dying at sea. If no country was willing to solve the problem of the 2,500 people on the damaged *Hai Hong*, the outlook for those on board was bleak.

There was little initial indication that Canada would play a significant role in resolving the *Hai Hong* situation. The economy was doing poorly, which, as the crisis developed, would lead some to express concern that new immigrants would take jobs from Canadians and that refugee resettlement costs would lead to tax increases. The unemployment rate was the highest it had been in decades, and there were complaints that people who had lived in Canada for generations were "going hungry and [had] no work and yet our government [was bringing] these people here."[52] And at the time, although the newspapers were covering the *Hai Hong* plight, there was no support in the press for Canada resettling the refugees. A *Toronto Star* editorial argued that Canada was not a suitable environment: "A Vietnamese peasant would find it all but impossible to adjust himself to this different world, culture, and climate," so the Canadian government should "induce our Malaysian friends to take in some of the sick and hapless human cargo."[53] There were also debates about whether the passengers could be considered legitimate refugees in the first place, "because of reports that the ship [was] owned by a syndicate" that charged for passage.[54]

However, as the days passed there were some suggestions that Canada might consider accepting some *Hai Hong* passengers if they held Promise of Visa Letters that Canadian officials had handed out before the fall of Saigon, along with others who had relatives residing in Canada.[55] Canadian authorities stated that Canada might even be willing to take others, pending "results of an investigation into the plight of the refugees by the UN commission."[56] At the same time it was known that there were tens of thousands of people already waiting in camps for resettlement arrangements, including more than 35,000 in Malaysia alone. Minister Cullen questioned whether priority should be given to the *Hai Hong* passengers as the acceptance of refugees straight from the vessel could be seen as bypassing those who had been waiting in the camps for years.

Quebec Steps In

Earlier that year, on 20 February, Minister Cullen and Quebec Immigration Minister Jacques Couture had signed the Cullen-Couture Agreement, based on the provision in the 1976 Immigration Act allowing provinces to make individual immigration agreements with the federal government.[57] The agreement allowed Quebec to choose and recruit its own immigrants in the interest of reinforcing its traditional French language and culture. The province had not yet taken advantage of this agreement, but Couture perceived the lack of movement by the international community regarding the *Hai Hong* passengers as an opportunity for Quebec to make use of the agreement. On 15 November, after the Quebec National Assembly "voted unanimously ... to ask federal government permission to accept" some of these refugees,[58] Couture announced that Quebec "would be willing to accept at least 200 *Hai Hong* refugees, or 30% of the number Canada accepted, if that number exceeded 200."[59] Quebec already had a sizeable Vietnamese population, and many Vietnamese spoke French. As a member of the separatist Parti Québécois, Couture was able to use this announcement to showcase Quebec's willingness and ability to act separately in the international arena.

Meanwhile, the UNHCR and various governments, including Canada, continued discussions with the Malaysians about what to do. The UNHCR had declared that it considered the passengers aboard the troubled vessel to be legitimate refugees, and High Commissioner Poul Hartling "began to pressure the Malaysians to allow [the *Hai Hong* passengers] to go ashore."[60] However, Malaysia continued to refuse to recognize the passengers as refugees, and, not having signed the UN Convention relating to the Status of Refugees, was under no obligation to comply with the UNHCR request. The other countries

continued attempting to convince Malaysia to allow the *Hai Hong* to
remain anchored safely off the coast for the present time, while they
decided how to resolve the impasse. Seeing no real commitments from
any countries, Malaysia increased security around the vessel and continued to threaten to tow the ship into open waters and abandon it.
Minister Cullen felt that "Malaysia was calling our bluff, and heaven
knows they had every right to, having accepted something in excess of
35,000 refugees."[61] Finally, under the condition that those on the *Hai
Hong* accepted by other countries be removed from Malaysian territory immediately, Malaysia agreed to delay towing the boat out to sea
while other countries made arrangements to resettle the refugees.

Controversy in Canada

As the Canadian media continued giving coverage to the *Hai Hong*,
the public began to respond. Newspapers pressed the government to
take action, and letters from the public "flowed into the [Employment
and Immigration] department."[62] But the consensus remained that,
while Canada should do something, it should not resettle the refugees.
There must be another solution.

Cullen worried that the UNHCR was delaying too long in deciding
what to do, and that Malaysia would get impatient and tow the boat
out of its territory, leading to greater loss of human lives. He decided
that Canada would spearhead the effort to resettle the refugees, despite the general lack of support and with a commitment "of such
magnitude that other countries would be encouraged to follow."[63]
There was further concern that if Canada took a strong leadership
role, it might well be saddled with the entire problem, but to his credit
Cullen decided to risk it. He also decided that the life or death predicament of those on the ship outweighed the perception of unfairness to
those waiting in the camps. Every day that passed, leaving the refugees
in limbo, increased the chances of illness, injury, or death. Cullen received some encouragement from Windsor's mayor Bert Weeks, who
wrote that "a special gesture of humanitarianism would appear to be
warranted" and suggested that Canada accept five hundred people
from the *Hai Hong*.[64]

Cullen described Couture's earlier announcement of Quebec's offer
to accept two hundred refugees from the *Hai Hong* as "the first real
break" for Canada. Three days after the Quebec National Assembly

announcement, the issue was discussed in the federal Cabinet. With the promise from Quebec to take two hundred or 30 per cent of the passengers as impetus, the decision was made to accept a firm six hundred refugees from the ship. During the Liberal convention, Cullen and External Affairs Minister Don Jamieson held a press conference to announce the commitment. Cullen and his colleagues were initially concerned that the announcement in this setting could be seen as a political move and that the overall reaction would be negative. To their relief, reporters treated it as a human interest issue and responded encouragingly. The following day newspapers were filled with positive stories lauding the government's move on the issue, such as "Canada First to Offer Haven" and "Selection of 'Lucky 600' Refugees to Begin Today."[65]

Alberta's minister of manpower, Bert Hohol, had told Cullen that Alberta would accept up to fifty refugees but only under strict conditions: the federal government must fully fund all health care expenses, language schooling, and job training.[66] In the public release of his statement, Hohol said that "it must be clearly understood that Alberta expects this support to be continued, if necessary, for up to three years, at which time these people can become Canadian citizens."[67] Viewed beside Quebec's generous readiness to take at least two hundred *Hai Hong* refugees, Alberta's stance outraged the Canadian public. Shocked by the reaction, Hohol found his efforts to revise his position fell on deaf ears. As the controversy raged, people began suggesting that Canada could, and should, accept far more Indochinese refugees than the current quotas allowed.[68] Ironically, Hohol's blunder enhanced public awareness of the plight of the Indochinese refugees and increased public support for a larger Canadian role.

The Operation

At this time, responsibility for immigration and refugee matters in Thailand, Malaysia, and Indonesia rested with the three visa officers stationed in Singapore: Ian Hamilton, Dick Martin, and Scott Mullin. Canada's high commissioner to Malaysia recognized that a decision was imminent and summoned the team to Kuala Lumpur. They were joined by Florent Fortin of the Quebec Immigration Service, who flew from Montreal for the operation. However, they were kept in the dark for the weekend as the High Commission inexplicably refused to open its communication centre to them. On learning of the Canadian government's decision and that charter flights were being organized immediately to comply with Malaysian demands, Hamilton and his officers proceeded to Port Klang.

Although Canada had publicly announced that it would take six hundred of the passengers and had the team on the ground, Malaysian authorities remained distrustful and greatly complicated the process for the Canadians. Malaysia would neither allow the boat to dock in its territory nor allow the Canadians to go aboard. When the team attempted to survey the boat from a mile away, their binoculars were confiscated by police. Hamilton's team did manage to send a large number of Canadian immigration applications out to the ship. After much prolonged negotiations, leavened with Hamilton's diplomatic skills and personal charm (and aided by handfuls of maple leaf pins), the Malaysians finally agreed to anchor a minesweeper between the shore and the *Hai Hong*, to which a police escort, armed with automatic weapons and cans of mace, would transport small numbers of refugees by boat to be interviewed and processed by the Canadian officials.

Starting before sunrise on 21 November, the team dealt with oppressive heat and torrential downpours as well as a six-hour unexplained delay but managed to process seventy-four people. On the second day, despite police interference and bureaucratic delays, in an era when twelve immigrant interviews a day per officer was the norm, Hamilton, Martin, Fortin, and Mullin interviewed and accepted 356 refugees. The team finished the third day, having accepted a total of 604 people including, at eighty-two years, the oldest passenger on board, as well as the two youngest, born on the *Hai Hong*.

On 23 November 3:00 a.m., Hamilton realized that, in their exhaustion, his team had mistakenly processed one family of fifteen twice, leaving them fifteen people short of their goal. Now on reasonable terms with the security police (all wearing Canadian maple leaf pins), he persuaded them to take him out to the *Hai Hong*, where he knelt in the dark and accepted fifteen more refugees to reach Canada's target and fill the four flights being dispatched from Canada. Distrustful to the end, the Malaysians refused to allow the refugees to bathe before boarding the planes, transported them from ship to plane under armed guard, and searched the Canadian airplanes for weapons before allowing the refugees to board.

The Longue-Point military base near Montreal, which in 1972 had welcomed 5,000 Ugandan Asians, was readied to receive this new wave of refugees. Upon arrival, they were welcomed by ministers Cullen and Couture and enabled at last to bathe, eat, and rest. Subsequently, they were given medical examinations and processed for permanent resident status. They were outfitted for winter before heading to their new homes across Canada, all within a few days of arrival. Despite the dramatic waiting, discussions, threats, fears, and delays, the entire process was in reality very quick; the first flight to Canada was on 25 November, just sixteen days after the *Hai Hong* first dropped anchor off of Malaysia. Three additional flights on 28 November and 1 and 5 December would carry the rest of the refugees to Canada.

Couture's gesture and Cullen's leadership gamble paid off. In short order, the Federal Republic of Germany accepted 657 *Hai Hong* refugees, France took 222, Switzerland accepted 52, New Zealand took nine, and Australia accepted eight. The United States took 897 people, including all of those left over after the other countries had completed their selection processes.

Impact

After the announcement that Canada would accept six hundred refugees from the *Hai Hong*, coupled with the media stories about the miserable conditions on the vessel, offers from the public poured in. Immigration service providers were overwhelmed with donations of clothing and furniture as well as offers of assistance with housing and childcare. Not wishing to turn down any offers of help, they announced that, although they had more than enough resources for the *Hai Hong* refugees, they would appreciate the public keeping in mind the steady flow of other Indochinese refugees arriving in Canada and needing such assistance.[69] The seventy families a month that Canada was already accepting had mainly arrived quietly, with little public awareness or support. But now, with an enhanced understanding of the problems facing refugees in Southeast Asia, many churches, organizations, and ordinary citizens began to discuss the growing crisis and the new private sponsorship program for refugees.[70]

Newspapers and other media more and more frequently published human-interest profiles of Vietnamese refugees already settled in Canada, highlighting upbeat stories of first Canadian meals and snowy winters, warming the Canadian public still further to accept and assist Indochinese refugees beyond those from the high-profile *Hai Hong* incident. The widespread discussion of the *Hai Hong* in Canada highlighted the need for continued assistance for the tens of thousands of people still waiting in refugee camps in Southeast Asia. In 1978 alone, 61,000 Vietnamese had landed in Malaysia, with another 49,000 arriving in Indonesia.[71] "The dramatic *Hai Hong* situation together with the increasing exodus from Viet Nam have heightened Canadian media and public interest in and sympathy for these people."[72] Concerned Canadians began to organize sponsorship groups.

The general perception that Vietnamese refugees could not possibly adapt to the Canadian life and climate now transitioned into a belief that as Canada "has been welcoming persecuted people for many years ... [we] should admit at least 10,000–20,000 of the refugees in a similar action as in 1956 from Hungary, in 1968 from Czechoslovakia, or refugees from Chile."[73] A *Globe and Mail* editorial argued that "the least we can do is commit ourselves to ... welcome 20,000 of the boat people to Canada as quickly as they can be brought here. Taking that number would be no reason for self-congratulation. But it would be a start."[74]

The *Hai Hong*, which had all the necessary elements for a gripping story (greed, corruption, human tragedy, happy ending), provided the catalyst for a dramatic shift in the Canadian media's coverage of the Indochinese refugee problem and humanized the refugees in the mind of the Canadian public. It demonstrated that Canada could, in fact, do something about their plight. Within the Immigration Department, Hamilton and his team established a "can do" model of compassion, creative adaptability, and steely determination that would become the hallmark of future resettlement operations in Southeast Asia. An iconic photograph of Hamilton descending the gangplank of the Hai Hong with a small refugee child captured Canadian imagination. At the political level, barely three weeks after he had welcomed the Hai Hong refugees, Immigration Minister Cullen would be in Cabinet with Canada's first annual refugee plan. The plan would put the Indochinese refugees at the centre of Canada's resettlement efforts and set a course for even greater involvement.

6

Canada Engages: Critical Decisions, 1978–1979

Deterioration of the Refugee Situation in Southeast Asia, 1978 and Early 1979

In the course of 1978–79, the political situation in Indochina worsened rapidly. In 1978 there were serious incidents along the Cambodian-Vietnamese border. Following a year of skirmishing, Vietnam decided to take definitive action, invaded Cambodia in December 1978, and in January 1979 replaced the Khmer Rouge regime by its own proxy, the "Kampuchean United Front for National Salvation." China had been a supporter of the Khmer Rouge and a traditional enemy of Vietnam,[1] while the USSR, attempting to contain China on its south flank, signed a twenty-five-year mutual defense treaty with Vietnam in November 1978.[2] In response, the Chinese invaded Vietnam's border regions in a destructive punitive expedition lasting from mid-February to early March 1979.

The main victims of these wars and inter-ethnic violence were the minority and "politically untrustworthy" populations of Vietnam and Cambodia, as well as those who simply stood in the way of invading armies. Among these, the most important were the ethnic Chinese minority population of Vietnam and any persons in Vietnam deemed suspect by the authorities, including Catholics, those associated with the former regime or the Americans, members of the urban commercial classes, professionals, and any so-called "bourgeois" elements. Starting in mid-1977, an outflow of small boats full of these people clandestinely left Vietnamese harbours and eventually washed up on beaches in Malaysia, Thailand, the Philippines, Indonesia, and Hong Kong. As long as the outflow of boat people was relatively small, these countries of first asylum (none of them signatories of the UN Refugee

Convention) temporarily accepted the Vietnamese refugees. However, numbers increased rapidly over the course of 1978. UNHCR's report on the Indochinese situation noted, "As the numbers grew, so did local hostility. Adding to the tension was the fact that several of the boats arriving ... were not small wooden fishing craft, but freighters ... chartered by regional smuggling syndicates and carrying over 2,000 people at a time."[3]

The flow of the Vietnamese refugee movement had two distinct aspects. In the North, many poor Chinese-Vietnamese went overland to China – by the end of 1978 their numbers were estimated to be 200,000. In the South, the Vietnamese Ministry of the Interior, through its Public Security Bureau, organized departures for payments of "3 to 5 taels of gold" (1 Canton tael = 37.5 grams) officially contributed to the national treasury but, according to reports by refugees, often pocketed by Vietnamese officials. The alternatives faced by the middle classes – including a majority of Chinese, but also many others – were leaving by boat or being deported to outlying "New Economic Zones" to perform punitive farm labour. More and more people chose to pay and leave on rusty, often semi-seaworthy freighters or small wooden fishing boats.[4]

Numbers tell the story. In August 1978, just under 3,000 boat people arrived from Vietnam in other Southeast Asian countries. In November 1978, over 21,000 arrived: a seven-fold increase of monthly arrivals. The majority sought asylum in Malaysia, but boat arrivals in Thailand also doubled during this period.[5] Loescher explains the attitude of local governments to these refugees: "Refugees in general were viewed as a domestic political liability throughout South-East Asia, and governments came under increasing pressure from local state, military and political leaders to take a firmer stance against them."[6] The countries of first asylum in Southeast Asia did not want to be burdened with large numbers of desperate, often penniless refugees belonging to ethnic groups, Chinese or Vietnamese, whose presence, because of long-standing historical animosities, could occasion serious social and political challenges to Malaysia, Thailand, Indonesia, and the Philippines.

As the boat-people crisis deepened, the human tragedies associated with it began to capture the world's attention. Newspaper and television journalists from many countries reported on people and corpses on beaches, piracy on the high seas, divided families, and lost children. The recollections of a Jesuit priest who had earlier served in

Indochina and had come back to help the boat people provide a graphic description of the situation at a refugee camp in Thailand close to the beach:

> Each morning we would go down to the beaches and there would be bodies – men, women and children – washed ashore during the night. Sometimes there were hundreds of them, like pieces of wood. Some of them were girls who had been raped and then thrown into the sea by pirates to drown. It was tragic beyond words ... Sometimes people would somehow still be alive. They would be on the beach exhausted or unconscious. They washed ashore at night, and we revived them and held them when we found them.
>
> Of course the weather took its toll on the boat people. The boats were terrible. Sometimes the refugees would be caught by Vietnamese authorities and towed back to Vietnam and put in jail. But the pirates were probably the biggest cause of the killing. The pirates stopped nearly every boat. They searched for gold first, even going so far as to take it out of the people's teeth. The next thing that attracted them was the young girls. The pirates were concerned about getting caught, and the best way of not getting caught was to destroy the boat and the people in it and maybe even throw the girls overboard when they were all through with them ... And then the bodies washed up on shore or just disappeared into the sea.[7]

The United States had a major political interest in attempting to find an international solution to the crisis: it wanted to continue to demonstrate the inhumanity of the regimes that emerged following the communist takeover. At the same time, however, the Americans were reluctant to engage alone in another major domestic refugee resettlement movement. During the initial outflow of 1975–76, they had shouldered the greatest part of the resettlement, and this time they wished to ensure that other developed countries would share the burden. On 28 November 1978, Malaysia, the country of first asylum and under the greatest pressure, urgently appealed to the US president. "Mr. Carter," urged the Malaysian home affairs minister, Ghazali Shafie, "please take the lead among nations of the free world ... Do something quickly!"[8]

The US response to the crisis and ASEAN (Association of Southeast Asian Nations) appeals was to pressure the UN High Commissioner for Refugees Poul Hartling to convene an international consultation meeting in Geneva in December 1978.[9] Before proceeding to Geneva for the UNHCR consultations, the Canadian delegation, led by Jacques Gignac, the assistant under secretary of state for external affairs, accompanied by Kirk Bell of the CEIC, travelled to Washington for exchanges with US officials.[10] The main elements of the US argument for the urgency of this meeting were communicated to Canada: "There exists a pool of 800,000 deeply discontented persons in Vietnam ... boat escapees from Vietnam [might] grow to 140,000 by the end of 1979 ... [with] similar flow levels for 1980 and perhaps even 1981. The consequent political, social and financial burden on countries of first asylum ... could well become unsupportable. There is a massive backlog of 130,000 overland refugees in Thailand and some 50,000 boat escapees throughout Southeast Asia, including 38,000 in Malaysia ... resettlement in Southeast Asia is improbable."[11]

The Geneva consultations of 12–13 December 1978 reached a general agreement on the need for "burden sharing" by developed countries and an expression by Southeast Asian countries to continue to provide first asylum to refugees as long as these would be resettled in third countries. Vietnam was present at the consultations and "expressed a willingness to cooperate in programs of family unification. Additional financial pledges of $13 million were made to the UNHCR ... and 80,000 new resettlement places were offered ... the US doubled its intake for 1979 to 50,000 and Australia said it would accept 11,000 [in 1979] ... in addition to the 12,000 already taken since 1975 ... Other countries offered more modest resettlement and financial pledges ... As a result, first steps were taken towards the UNHCR objective of a more broadly-based international response."[12]

The December consultations were modestly successful. As they came to a close, most participating countries did not yet fully admit – albeit all signs were pointing in this direction – that in 1979 they would witness a major growth of the Indochina refugee crisis. Within the next six months the international community, including Canada, would be called upon to undertake much greater efforts than agreed upon at the consultations to deal with this enormous international humanitarian emergency.

The Reaction of the Canadian Government, Private Sponsors,
and the Provinces

By the end of 1978, legal measures were in place to enable Canada to
react effectively to a growing refugee emergency in Southeast Asia.
The new 1976 Immigration Act was being fully implemented in the
course of 1978. The act incorporated the UN Convention Refugee
definition into Canadian law and gave the government the power to
designate classes of people for admission under the same terms as
refugees. On 7 December 1978, the Indochinese Designated Class
Regulations came into effect, providing the legal basis for accepting
Indochinese refugees without their having to satisfy the UN Convention Refugee definition.[13] Arrangements were finalized to establish a
visa office in Thailand with two Canada-based officers, Murray Oppertshauser and Robert Shalka, who arrived at the Canadian Embassy
in Bangkok on 11 November. Their principal responsibility was to
deal with Indochinese refugee cases.[14]

The rapid succession of events in November and December 1978
raised the profile of the Indochinese refugee problem within the
government and, in particular, within CEIC. Media across Canada
expressed satisfaction with the arrival of four flights of *Hai Hong*
refugees at CFB Longue-Pointe, and refugees on the first flight were
personally welcomed by Bud Cullen, the federal immigration minister, and Jacques Couture, the Quebec minister of immigration. The
UNHCR consultation on the growing crisis in Southeast Asia took place
a week or two later, and the high commissioner's assessment of the
problem formed part of the package of information presented a week
later to Cabinet.

For the first time, Canada was doing forward planning on refugee
issues rather than simply reacting to events. The first-ever Annual Plan
for Refugee Resettlement, including 5,000 places for Indochinese
refugees, was finalized in December 1978.[15] Based on the outcomes of
the Geneva consultations, the preparedness of CEIC both in terms of
legislative and on-the-ground implementation instruments, and the
annual refugee plan, Minister Cullen presented the main elements of
CEIC's Indochina plan to Cabinet on 21 December 1978. Cullen emphasized that with the extreme seriousness of the problem in Southeast Asia, the 5,000-place commitment in the refugee plan might not
be sufficient. Existing commitments by other resettlement countries

were proving inadequate, and effective action was needed. He advised that using the entire contingency reserve of 2,000 included in the refugee plan might also be required to increase Canada's Indochinese refugee intake above 5,000 places.[16] To reach this higher figure, private sponsorships and popular support for Indochinese refugee resettlement raised through the publicity of the *Hai Hong* incident might be important factors.[17]

On 21 December 1978, Cabinet approved the 1979 Indochinese Refugee Program, setting a target of 10,000 refugee admissions for 1979, of which 5,000 were to be from Indochina, and providing $4.5 million for supplementary funding for the Indochinese program. Accepting Cullen's warning about the seriousness of the situation, Cabinet instructed the minister to report back if higher numbers were needed and the contingency reserve needed to be used. In any event, whichever way the situation would evolve, Cabinet required Cullen to report again on Indochina in June 1979.[18] From December 1978, CEIC management, from the minister and the DM down to those directing operational and policy units, closely monitored unfolding events in Southeast Asia. As the number of arrivals in countries of first asylum mounted dramatically from month to month, the Government of Canada was fully informed of developments.[19] Thus, by the end of 1978, Canada was prepared to increase its commitment to Indochinese refugee resettlement by a magnitude that appeared at the time to be generous and significant. As well, Canada either already had in place or was prepared to rapidly apply resources and mechanisms that would enable the country to implement this commitment.

In a message of 19 December, Ernest Allen, director of CEIC's Asia and Pacific Bureau, advised that additional staff would be required in Southeast Asia.[20] Ian Hamilton, manager of the Singapore visa office, recommended the centralization of refugee operations covering Malaysia and Indonesia at the Canadian High Commission in Singapore. Hamilton reasoned that because of Singapore's geographic position and transport infrastructure, its visa office was the one best able to react to refugee-related exigencies in the enormous regions bordering the South China Sea, especially those in the Indonesian archipelago.[21] Canada's rapid response to the *Hai Hong* emergency had provided convincing proof of the country's ability to react quickly and effectively to unforeseen emergency situations that fell outside the planning process.

Responding to Cabinet's decision, visa officers, immigration doctors, and RCMP officers at Canada's diplomatic missions in Southeast Asia began to process large numbers of Indochinese refugees in early 1979, rapidly increasing refugee arrivals in the spring and early summer. In February 1979, Allen instructed the four Southeast Asian offices – Singapore, Bangkok, Hong Kong, and Manila – to select 420 unsponsored refugees (persons, not families) per month in order to meet the annual target of 5,000.[22] In large part, this was possible because the Indochina Designated Class regulation enabled Canadian officers working in distant refugee camps to process refugees under very difficult field conditions without a time-consuming examination of refugees' claims to well-founded fear of persecution. Indochinese refugees could become eligible for resettlement in Canada after a short interview.[23]

As of late 1978, the new refugee sponsorship provision of the Immigration Regulations remained virtually untested. In their 22 December 1978 press release on the Canadian response to the "Indochina refugee problem," Immigration Minister Cullen and External Affairs Minister Jamieson did not even mention the sponsorship program.[24] Within the next few months, however, the practical elements of implementing sponsorship arrangements were worked out and the Canadian public, exposed through graphic media reports to the suffering of the boat people, became committed to the program in a manner beyond any expectations of the politicians and civil servants. By June, sponsorships emerged as a critically important element of the Indochinese refugee movement.

The creation of the implementation mechanisms for the sponsorship of refugees started in February 1979, during negotiations with the Mennonite Central Committee of Canada (MCC). The first Canada Master Agreement between CEIC and MCC was signed on 5 March by Cullen and J.M. Klassen, MCC's executive director.[25] The MCC master agreement became the model for similar agreements concluded with other religious bodies.

Initially, there was a certain amount of resistance by some religious bodies to assuming responsibility for sponsored Indochinese refugees, fearing that the government was attempting to unload the costs of resettlement. However, the Mennonite agreement broke the ice, and a range of corporate religious bodies immediately opened negotiations with CEIC for their own master agreements. Within weeks, some thirteen Canadian churches signed master agreements based on the Men-

TABLE 6.1
Indochinese refugee arrivals January to July 1979

January	February	March	April	May	June	July
217	348	769	1,060	1,438	930	1,281

Source: Employment and Immigration Canada, *Indochinese Refugees: The Canadian Response, 1979 and 1980* (Ottawa: Department of Supply and Services 1982), 28.

nonite model.[26] An essential administrative fast track for rapidly processing applications to sponsor refugees was now in place. Nearly four decades after the signing of that initial agreement, the unique Canadian private sponsorship model remains a pillar of Canada's resettlement program.[27] A mechanism was required to assign destinations for refugees in Canada and to match them with sponsors, and the instrument established for this task in May 1979 was the central Refugee Matching Centre (RMC) located at CEIC headquarters in Ottawa. The matching system is also still in place to this day.[28]

An important issue to be addressed, given the absorption capacities of individual provinces, was the fair distribution of refugees across Canada. Initial refugee targets were arrived at in consultation with the provinces in line with the annual refugee plan, based first on each province's share of the immigration intake, and second, by estimating intakes above the annual refugee plan expected through sponsorships by the churches.[29] The initial provincial distribution plan for 1979–80 was Quebec, 33 per cent; Ontario, 30 per cent; British Columbia, 15 per cent; Alberta, 10 per cent; Saskatchewan, 5 per cent; Manitoba, 5 per cent; and the Maritimes, 2 per cent.[30]

In accordance with the Cullen-Couture Agreement of 1978, Quebec had separate, autonomous immigration selection and reception mechanisms, and the selection of Indochinese refugees destined to the province was reserved exclusively to Quebec officers. As of February 1979, Quebec agreed to accept fifty families of Vietnamese boat people and twenty families of overland refugees per month.[31] Over the next two years the provincial intakes were modified considerably, largely because non-church private sponsorships came to play an important role.

The International Community and Canada React as the
Refugee Crisis Explodes

At the end of December 1978, there were almost 200,000 refugees in
temporary camps throughout Southeast Asia.[32] The international undertaking to accept just over 80,000 of these for permanent resettlement in 1979 – including Canada's commitment of 5,000 – would
still leave the countries of first asylum with an enormous ongoing burden even if there were no more arrivals. But arrivals did not stop. The
greatest flows both overland and by sea, resulting from wars, regime
changes, and cruel policies toward national minorities, came during
the first half of 1979. Vietnam's expressed intention stated in Geneva
in December 1978, "to cooperate in programs of family unification,"
turned out to be an empty promise.[33] Canada received tangible proof
of Vietnamese obstructionism when in March 1979, after months of
correspondence with the Vietnamese government, a Canadian official
visited Ho Chi Minh City (Saigon) to arrange interviews for the family unification program. On a second visit later that spring, the visiting Canadians saw only minor signs of progress on the part of the
Vietnamese, who continued to place bureaucratic hurdles in the way
of the program.[34] Even as the Hanoi government was arguing that
they were open to the idea of "orderly departures," they closed their
eyes or colluded to ever larger numbers of boat people leaving Vietnam illegally during the first half of 1979.[35]

Media outlets worldwide reported on the Vietnamese actions and
attitudes toward the boat people. The *New York Times* described one
appalling example: "Official Filipino sources said today that Vietnamese troops killed 85 Vietnamese refugees, 45 of them children,
when their fishing boat ran aground ... on an island in the South
China Sea. ... only eight persons survived the June 22 massacre and
eventually found refuge in the Philippines ... The sources said Vietnamese troops opened fire on the refugees with mortars, machine guns
and automatic weapons."[36]

In January and February, around 20,000 Vietnamese refugees,
mostly of Chinese descent, arrived in Malaysia, Thailand, Indonesia,
and Hong Kong. By March the rate had increased to over 13,000 in
one month and escalated to over 26,000 in April, to 51,000 in May
and 57,000 in June.[37] The US estimate made in December 1978 for
total boat arrivals of 140,000 during 1979 was reached and exceeded
in the first six months of the year.[38]

As the numbers of Vietnamese boat people increased each month in late 1978 and early 1979, another refugee crisis was taking place in Thailand. In April–May 1979, large numbers of Cambodians – estimates vary between 50,000 and 80,000 – attempted to cross overland into Thailand, followed by tens of thousands of Cambodian-Chinese, all of them fleeing the new government installed in Cambodia by the Vietnamese. Many of the Cambodians suspected of being Khmer Rouge cadres or sympathizers were pushed back at the border, and large numbers perished. Thai refugee camps on the border were overwhelmed, and the new wave of refugees became a major political issue in Thailand.[39]

Given these rapidly growing numbers, the international resettlement response was inadequate. In May, as over 50,000 boat people arrived and tens of thousands of refugees streamed over the border to Thailand, the total number of refugees internationally resettled in all western countries was 8,500.[40] The apparent inability of western resettlement countries to react in a manner that corresponded to the magnitude of the humanitarian disaster in Southeast Asia elicited strong reactions from the countries of first asylum. Gil Loescher observes,

> By spring 1979, the number of new boat arrivals overwhelmed the South-East Asian asylum countries ... South-East Asian governments made it abundantly clear ... that their willingness to provide first asylum to the boat people depended entirely on firm commitments by Western countries to resettle Vietnamese outside the region. When no new significant pledges were made by the West, [member states of the Association of Southeast Asian Nations (ASEAN)] ... took dramatic actions to deter boat people. Malaysian officials termed the refugees "scum, garbage and residue" to be swept off the beaches and pushed back to sea and threatened to shoot boat people on sight. The Malaysian navy systematically towed heavily laden boats back to sea even though many were unseaworthy and would sink ... In the process, large numbers of Vietnamese died of starvation, thirst or exposure and many drowned ... [Others ended up stranded on distant, often uninhabited Indonesian islands, thereby increasing pressures on Indonesia] ... Others were murdered by Thai pirates.[41]

The media began to depict the boat people as victims of an "Asian Holocaust."[42] A typical newspaper report of March 1979 described an incident in Mersing on the east coast of Malaysia, confirming that Malaysian authorities were pushing Vietnamese refugee boats back to sea: "At 8:30 PM on a recent Friday, 219 Vietnamese pulled up to the dark dock in the river channel here in a 42 foot fishing craft. The refugees were confronted by Malaysian policemen armed with shotguns and pistols and told they could not land ... The refugees who had endured a 17-day voyage southwest across the South China Sea ... waited quietly. Two and a half hours later, the Vietnamese were told they could leave their boat and spend the night ashore. ... They had to wait two days ... On March 15, Malaysia's Prime Minister, Datuk Hussein Onn, announced that Malaysia would no longer allow Vietnamese 'boat people' to land."[43] The boat, with 219 refugees on board, was forced to leave Malaysia and sailed to the Indonesian Bintan Island. The Mersing incident was raised at diplomatic levels by the United States, and the Malaysians exercised their push-back practices selectively in April, May, and June 1979. As many boats were redirected to Indonesia and the Philippines, the situation progressively worsened: like Malaysia, neither Indonesia nor the Philippines wanted to be burdened with the boat people problem.[44]

Bintan Island, under Indonesian sovereignty, was one of the temporary camps for refugees; other Indonesian refugee islands were Galang – the principal refugee holding island in Indonesia – and Lombok; in the Philippines the main island of temporary refuge was Tara.[45] The United States had been urging the international community since January 1979 to adopt the concept of large temporary camps, or Refugee Accessing Centres, where refugees could wait until they were resettled in the West. Canada and other western resettlement countries supported this proposal.[46] But the temporary refuge concept could only work if Vietnam put a stop to boat departures – or at least slowed them down – and countries of resettlement guaranteed that refugees in temporary camps would be resettled in the West. As of June 1979, neither of these requirements was in place.

The attitude of the countries of first asylum continued to harden. The outflow of boat people had increased so quickly that for every refugee resettled during the first half of 1979, three more arrived in Southeast Asian camps.[47] An ASEAN foreign ministers' meeting in mid-May 1979 in Jakarta, with the UNHCR and a small Vietnamese delegation present, worked out the details for the establishment of the island transit camp in Galang. Importantly, the meeting attempted to get the Vietnamese to stop the refugee exodus; this effort met with very limited success, even though Vietnam had earlier intimated during several diplomatic meetings that it would put in place measures to mitigate the outflow.[48] Something needed to be done: the stability of the entire Southeast Asian region was being endangered by the exodus.

Since the *Hai Hong* incident and the media reports that followed it, the Canadian public had become progressively more aware of the crisis. In the press and on TV, Canada's significantly increased commitment to refugee resettlement, made in December 1978, was regularly publicized. Despite the unfolding tragedy, several opinion surveys through 1979 and 1980 indicated that the majority of Canadians were not in favour of increasing the number of Indochinese refugees being resettled in Canada. What the government policy did have, however, was the support of key influential groups: in July 1979, when the federal government opted to increase Canada's Indochinese refugee intake enormously – proportionately, more than any other western refugee-receiving country – it had the crucial support of Canadian churches, municipalities, some influential media outlets, and, despite what the opinion polls stated, many strongly committed groups of Canadians.[49]

As the situation deteriorated in the region, Canadian officials based in Southeast Asia witnessed, monitored, and reported the inhumanity and cruelty. Canada was fortunate in having an exceptional individual as the head of its Immigration Service. Deputy Minister Jack Manion watched as the crisis unfolded, named effective officials to administer and coordinate Canada's response, and fought battles within the public service to obtain the resources required at missions abroad. Of equal importance, Manion advised and counselled his political master, Bud Cullen, on every aspect of the evolving refugee emergency.[50]

The Progressive Conservatives took power after the federal election of 22 May 1979. The new PC government was headed by Joe Clark, at forty years of age Canada's youngest-ever prime minister. The new immigration minister, Ron Atkey, at thirty-eight, was even younger. Both Clark and Atkey had comparatively little political experience and both, along with Flora MacDonald, the new secretary of state for external affairs (SSEA), were "Red Tories" – conservatives with strong social consciences who believed in international humanitarian action. Outgoing Immigration Minister Cullen met privately with his successor and told him that the Indochinese refugee question was the most urgent and difficult file Atkey would be inheriting and that bold action was warranted.[51]

By late May, the Southeast Asia situation was reaching a breaking point. On 30 May, UN Secretary General Kurt Waldheim sent out a call to fifty-two nations, including Canada, to increase their financial contributions to the UN and make available increased numbers of resettlement places.[52] On 31 May, Prime Minister Thatcher of Great Britain, "concerned about the Southeast Asian situation, particularly its implications for Hong Kong, called for an international conference under the aegis of the UN secretary general."[53] Meanwhile, intelligence received from Canada's mission in Canberra on 18 May described a renewed expulsion campaign against Chinese-Vietnamese in both south and north Vietnam.[54]

The new Progressive Conservative Cabinet met on 18 June to consider an External Affairs/CEIC proposal to expand the Indochinese refugee program. Through close monitoring of the evolving situation during the first half of 1979 and of Canadian public opinion during the same period, Cabinet was aware that additional action and commitments were needed and accepted the proposal to raise Canada's Indochinese refugee target for 1979–80 to 12,000 for 1979, including 8,000 government sponsored refugees, 2,000 privately sponsored refugees, and 2,000 refugees accepted through family reunification.[55]

However, many Canadian media outlets still considered these latest government measures insufficient. Major newspapers urged Canada's government to do more to help the Indochinese refugees. On 22 June the *Montreal Gazette* called the Canadian effort to date a "drop in the bucket."[56] In a 28 June editorial, "It's Up to Us," the *Globe and Mail* stated, "The challenge to the Canadian conscience is clear and urgent … The challenge is to do all that we possibly, decently can … In preparing and leading the conference needed to get this program moving External Affairs Minister Flora MacDonald, Immigration Minister Ron Atkey and Finance Minister John Crosbie would have key roles to play … [In] dark times of trouble we are, most of us, refugees or the children of refugees. It's time to remember that."[57]

And indeed, Canada's political leaders, public service officials, churches, secular bodies, and NGOs as well as municipal and provincial authorities and a large part of the Canadian public did remember and were ready to respond to the plight of persecuted people on the other side of the globe. Even as the Southeast Asian countries of first asylum stated in tough language that they had reached the limit of their endurance and would not accept any new arrivals,[58] Canadian initiatives were being launched to rescue more Indochinese refugees and resettle them in Canada.

Late June and early July were extremely busy periods on the refugee front in Canada as private initiatives were launched across the country. Among these, Operation Lifeline was exemplary. It was initiated on 24 June in the living room of Howard Adelman, a young York University professor, where a number of Toronto residents representing a wide cross-section of the community came together to discuss drafting a letter to Minister Atkey demanding more action. Two CEIC settlement officers, André Pilon and Bob Parkes, sent by Atkey, arrived at Adelman's house and asked if they could attend the meeting. Once the concept of sponsorship was explained by the federal officials, those present at the meeting decided to organize a number of sponsorships. The following day a column on the meeting appeared in the *Globe and Mail*, describing Adelman's efforts as Operation Lifeline. News of the organization spread like wildfire. After eight days, fifty families were sponsored through the new organization. "Within two weeks, sixty chapters of Operation Lifeline were organized across the country, providing an information source and a structure for individuals who wished to sponsor refugees."[59]

A complementary initiative to Operation Lifeline was the establishment of municipal task forces that would organize groups to privately sponsor refugees in cities across the country.[60] One of the most important and successful of these efforts took place in Ottawa. Mayor Marion Dewar held a private meeting on 27 June with community, church, and business leaders and proposed the founding of Project 4000 to sponsor 4,000 Indochinese refugees.[61] On 4 July, Ottawa City Council unanimously supported the mayor's initiative. The organizers of a rally to launch the project at Lansdowne Park on 12 July set out six hundred chairs; between 2,300 and 3,000 people showed up.[62] Project 4000 was quickly established as a non-profit organization directed by a volunteer board of directors drawn from a cross-section of the community. In all, some 2,000 Indochinese refugees were resettled in Ottawa through this project. Also during this time, the Montreal Committee to Save the Boat People, a group of thirty-six prominent Montrealers including Charles Bronfman, Lionel Chevrier, and Maurice Sauvé placed an advertisement in the *Montreal Star* soliciting signatures for a petition urging Prime Minister Joe Clark "to increase significantly the quota on immigration of 'Boat People' to Canada."[63]

Thus, Canadian media reactions to the situation in Southeast Asia coincided with a sharp rise in civil society and municipal activism, while at the same time the new PC government was rapidly moving to a position based on humanitarian moral principles towards the Indochinese refugees – a rare occurrence in politics. By the time the international community reacted energetically to resolve the crisis in July 1979, Canada had the domestic elements in place to welcome a major increase in Indochinese refugee intake.

The fifth Group of 7 economic summit took place in Tokyo on 28–29 June 1979. At the summit, the G7 heads of government issued a special statement on Indochinese refugees, emphasizing that the crisis "constitutes a threat to the peace and stability of Southeast Asia. Given the tragedy and suffering which are taking place, the problem calls for an immediate and major response."[64] However, the only country to announce an increase in Indochinese refugee intake at the Tokyo summit was the United States. All the other countries represented – including Canada – agreed to the urgency of the issue and the need for greater resources if the refugee challenge were to be met, but none as yet ready to make statements of increased intakes. The summit provided Canada with the opportunity for consultations with other major industrialized countries. Flora MacDonald, Canada's secretary of state for external affairs, confirmed that Canada had increased its refugee resettlement commitment earlier that month (to 8,000 with a possible 4,000 sponsored). She encouraged other countries to increase their commitments and stated that Canada was actively considering further additional measures while watching developments.[65]

Following intensive consultations with governments and under the pressure of events in Southeast Asia, UN Secretary-General Waldheim convened a meeting on refugees and displaced persons in Geneva on 20–21 July.[66] During the three-week period between the Tokyo summit and the UN's Geneva meeting, intensive high-level consultations took place in Ottawa to define and further develop Canada's position on the Indochinese refugee crisis.

When MacDonald returned to Ottawa from the Tokyo summit, she already had a firm resolve, based on what she had learned in Tokyo, to substantially increase the number of Indochinese refugees Canada was accepting for resettlement. According to the recollection of David Elder, MacDonald's senior external affairs departmental assistant at the time, she was intent on using the summit discussions to show that dealing with the Indochinese refugee situation was an international issue of global importance in which Canada would do its share.[67] Her effort was reinforced by "messages of support – and even pressure – for Canada to do more along with offers of assistance and resettlement. She was receiving a very strong political message."[68] While conscious that not all in her party would support a significant increase in numbers, she also knew the non-government, community, and church sectors and understood that their members could effectively partner with the government to assist in refugee integration. As well, very importantly, both she and Atkey had tremendous support from Prime Minister Clark on this file.[69]

Atkey became convinced of the need for more radical action by Canada at about the same time as MacDonald. According to his recollection, prior to a Cabinet meeting in early July, DM Manion sent him a draft manuscript of the book *None Is Too Many* by Irving Abella. It described Canada's callous response to the persecution of Jews by the Nazis in the 1930s. Atkey went into the Cabinet meeting with Abella's manuscript and asked whether the ministers present wanted to be remembered in the same way as Canada's leaders during World War II who, by their inaction, consigned some of Europe's Jews to destruction.[70] The young minister's boldness paid off: Cabinet eventually accepted the proposal to raise Canada's Indochinese refugee target for 1979–80 to 50,000. In this action, historic memory played a real role.[71]

On 9 July CEIC sent a memorandum to the prime minister recommending a significantly increased Canadian Indochinese refugee resettlement program.[72] On the same day, Elder briefed André Préfontaine, the senior Canadian Press correspondent in Ottawa.[73] The next day, apparently based on the briefing, an article appeared in Montreal's *La Presse* stating, "Canada to welcome up to 55,000 refugees."[74] The possibility of resettling a high number of Indochinese refugees, beyond anything to which Canada had committed previously, was now in the public domain. At the 10 July External Affairs senior management meeting, Elder was "scolded" for allowing the press to publish a figure beyond what senior bureaucrats had then agreed to.

When he later reported to MacDonald what had happened, apologizing for placing her in a difficult position, "she laughed and said it was good to have press coverage allowing for the possibility of moving to 25,000 refugees; she would use that as a base because she wanted to move to 50,000."[75]

The final decision on the position that MacDonald took to Geneva was approved by Cabinet on 18 July, following the recommendations of a 16 July joint memorandum by the External Affairs and CEIC that included, for the first time, the one-for-one proviso: for each privately sponsored refugee, a government assisted refugee would be resettled.[76] The 50,000[77] would include the 8,000 approved in December and June, some of whom had arrived while others were in the pipeline, and 21,000 to be sponsored by private citizens, matched by 21,000 who would be settled by the government. In MacDonald's speech in Geneva to the sixty-five governments that met to try to heed the UN secretary-general's call to find an effective international response to the refugee crisis, she made the following dramatic statement:

> Mr. Chairman, my government recognizes that countries of first asylum must be encouraged to continue to accept refugees fleeing the brutality in their own lands. Asylum countries must be assured that resettlement places are available in other parts of the world. Recognizing that such assurance is necessary, two days ago my government announced that it will accept up to 50,000 Indochinese from this year to the end of 1980. This means, in effect, that the countries of first asylum can count on Canada to accept up to 3,000 refugees a month ... trebling the rate of acceptance of these unfortunate people. We challenge other countries to follow this lead ... The program we have introduced to fulfill this commitment is one of partnership between the Canadian Government and private citizens and organizations. The Government of Canada will sponsor one refugee for each refugee receiving private sponsorship.[78]

Minister MacDonald's speech shared with the world Canada's unique cooperative approach to Indochinese refugee selection, which included Canada's private sponsors in partnership with the government. This approach, the so-called matching formula, was described in a memorandum of 31 July to all CEIC staff.[79]

As one of the first nations to make a commitment in Geneva, Canada by its example of generosity played a substantive role in ensuring the meeting's success. "Worldwide resettlement pledges increased from 125,000 to 260,000. Vietnam agreed to try to halt illegal departures and, instead, to promote orderly and direct departures from Vietnam ... New pledges to UNHCR totaled about US$160 million in cash and in kind, more than doubling the total of the previous four years."[80]

The interaction between international, national, and local leaders in June and July 1979 was remarkable. On 18 June, two weeks after taking office, Atkey and MacDonald had announced that Canada would accept 8,000 refugees and called for private groups to sponsor an additional 4,000. In Toronto, Operation Lifeline was founded on 24 June, while in Ottawa, Mayor Dewar decided to launch Project 4000 on 27 June. On 28 June MacDonald was consulting with G7 leaders about the Indochinese refugee crisis at the Tokyo Summit. Over 2,000 people attended a rally to launch Project 4,000 on 12 July. Six days later, Atkey and MacDonald informed Canadians that Canada would accept 50,000 refugees, and MacDonald announced the commitment to the world in Geneva on 20 July. Seven days later, the government launched an airlift of over 2,000 refugees from Hong Kong.

At the end of months of intense efforts by political leaders, public servants, and civil society, with the continual urgings of Canada's media, the major commitment to resettle a very large number of Indochinese refugees in Canada in a short time had been made before the nations of the world. Faced with an unprecedented humanitarian emergency, Canada had increased its commitment sevenfold. This dwarfed the country's actions in the region to date.

But the really difficult work of implementing this commitment in course of the next one and a half years lay ahead.

7

Innovation on the Run

The government's decision of July 1979 to accept and resettle 50,000 Indochinese refugees by the end of the following year came as a shock to the staff of the Immigration Department. The last refugee movement of a similar magnitude that older employees could recall was the 37,000 Hungarians who arrived in 1956–57.[1] It was clear that normal ways of doing business would have to be quickly rethought.

The task was made easier by measures taken in the preceding twelve months. The implementation of the Indochinese Designated Class in December 1978 had already simplified the selection process in Southeast Asia. The master agreements for sponsoring refugees, beginning with the Mennonite Central Committee of Canada in April 1979 and quickly followed by agreements with other faith communities, eliminated a great deal of paperwork for thousands of sponsorships. The Refugee Matching Centre, established in Ottawa in May 1979 to bring refugees and sponsors together, had a great deal of promise, but the original system was cumbersome and needed to be recalibrated if eager sponsors were to be expeditiously linked with the tens of thousands of incoming refugees.

All these measures, however, were not enough to deal with the 3,000 refugees scheduled to arrive each month. A whole range of new ways of doing business had to be invented, implemented on the run, and constantly modified under the pressure of events. A series of innovations was put in place, most by late September, to meet the unprecedented refugee challenge. In 1979 and 1980 there were no cellphones, portable computers, or email. Communications were by time-consuming telexes and the occasional long-distance telephone call, if a connection were available. Yet the fact that procedures were not embedded in computer software meant that changes could be designed and employed very quickly. A high degree of individual responsibility was essential and encouraged; CEIC senior bureaucrats were receptive to innovations suggested by relatively junior civil servants.[2] The department as a whole always strove for consistency in applying the law but was highly receptive to operational flexibility in the delivery of the refugee operation.

Indochinese Refugee Task Force: Management and Coordination

CEIC deputy minister Jack Manion created a task force, which he initially chaired, that introduced an efficient organizational structure to deal with the unprecedented refugee challenge. Cal Best was named executive director, refugees, and reported to Manion. Kirk Bell, who had overseen the reforms to immigration legislation in 1976–78, was made deputy executive director, reporting to Cal Best. Five units came under Bell's authority:

1 Selection and Movement from Abroad, headed by Ernest Allen, an immigration foreign service officer with extensive experience in Asia. This division was officially known as the Asia and Pacific Division, Immigration Foreign Branch (IFAP), and was responsible for operations in the eastern Asia-Pacific area, including Hong Kong, Singapore, Bangkok, and Manila. IFAP provided operational directions to the visa offices and coordinated the negotiation and scheduling of the chartered airlift.
2 Reception and Settlement in Canada, initially headed by Bill Nauss, who was succeeded by Janet Zukowsky. This unit was responsible for the reception and settlement of the refugees after arrival in Canada and for managing the Matching Centre.
3 Public Relations – Information and Press Relations, managed by Rene Pappone, an experienced media relations officer of the Public Affairs Branch. Pappone oversaw media relations and the publication of the *Indochinese Refugee Newsletter* to keep sponsors and coordinating organizations informed of developments.
4 Refugee Policy, led by Doug Hill, an external affairs officer on secondment to CEIC. The division responded to policy challenges

and handled relations with the UNHCR and the Intergovern-mental Committee for European Migration (ICEM). Hill also handled policy coordination with other refugee resettlement countries.

5 Coordination, headed by Michael Molloy, designated as se-nior coordinator. Molloy managed a small secretariat that tracked and analyzed the enormous body of data generated by the program. The secretariat monitored press and public reac-tions and trends, responded to parliamentary queries, kept CEIC regional offices informed on broad policy matters, and issued statistical reports. The secretariat's real task, however, was to troubleshoot, to deal with everything that fell between the cracks, and to ensure that the different parts of the system in Canada and abroad actually worked harmoniously together.[3] Over time more officers were brought on board to handle special needs and operational challenges such as unaccompanied minors and refugees suffering from tuberculosis.[4]

Streamlining Documentation

By the summer of 1979, visa officers in Bangkok, Singapore, and Hong Kong were drowning in paper. Refugees were still being docu-mented like regular immigrants, and in a world without portable com-puters this meant a flood of multi-page carbon-paper forms. Key information about the assessment of the individual applicants was en-tered by hand on a multi-paged Immigrant Assessment Record. At the completion of each processing stage, a page was detached from the form, batched, and sent to Immigration Headquarters for entry into the departmental mainframe computer. Upon completion of all pro-cessing requirements, each family member in an application was is-sued an Immigrant Record of Landing and Visa, itself a multi-copied typed document. Resources were simply inadequate for the labour-intensive completion of the standard forms.

Gerry Campbell, who had served in Kampala during the Ugandan refugee movement a few years earlier, coordinating documentation and transportation, had spent two months in Singapore in the spring of 1979 on temporary duty. He was part of a small team that put into process several thousand refugees from camps in Malaysia to meet the initial 5,000 target. Upon his return to Ottawa, Campbell reported to the Refugee Task Force and described the massive paper burden that threatened to bog down the selection process in the camps throughout Southeast Asia. Interviewing officers had to travel to the camps, often on small fishing boats, with boxes of forms and files. If an officer had twelve minutes to interview a refugee family, Campbell said, fully ten minutes were devoted to filling in a myriad of standard immigration forms rather than in talking to the family. The problem continued when the officers returned to the visa offices in the region, since completing the complex immigrant landing records and other documents absorbed scarce resources and time. Campbell recommended that the task of completing the final documentation for refugees be shifted from the visa offices to the newly established staging areas in Edmonton and Montreal.[5]

Best grasped the seriousness of the issue and brought it to the attention of Deputy Minister Manion, who had coordinated the 1956–57 Hungarian refugee movement where formalities were cut to the bone. Manion immediately summoned a team to review the problem and propose a solution.[6] Within two days, a single new form had been devised that captured each refugee family's personal information, the visa officers' interview notes, and medical and security results. It then served as visa and travel document for the entire refugee family, who carried it with them to Canada. The Indochinese Designated Class Processing Record and Visa, assigned form number IMM1314, replaced four existing forms and could be completed by hand on the spot in the refugee camps. The IMM1314 reduced the paperwork of staff overseas by half, though it did require more work at the staging areas in Montreal and Edmonton. The new form was approved on 25 July and was in use in Southeast Asia by the end of August.[7]

The Airlift

Transporting to Canada the much higher numbers of refugees accepted in the course of 1978 became a major challenge. At first, block booking of seats on commercial airlines was used. Ian Hamilton, manager of the Singapore visa office, negotiated an agreement with ICEM to arrange refugee transports through Europe for refugees bound for Eastern Canada, and by way of the Pacific for those bound for Western Canada, thereby doubling the number of seats available. With the December 1978 cabinet decision to admit 5,000 refugees, a heavy schedule of charter flights to transport refugees from Singapore was put in place.

When, in July 1979, Indochinese refugee targets had increased to 3,000 arrivals per month, CEIC turned to the Department of National Defence (DND). DND responded with Operation Magnet II, providing eleven refugee flights, each carrying 201 passengers from Hong Kong.[8] Despite delays caused by Typhoon Hope, the Hong Kong visa office was able to meet the enormous challenge of filling the military planes, and over 2,000 refugees were transported to Canada in one month, between July 27 and August 26. A touching incident that brought back memories of the baby flights of April 1975 was the birth of a baby girl on the first DND flight on 27 July.[9] The DND flights from Hong Kong were a temporary expedient, buying time while the small visa offices in Singapore and Bangkok were reinforced and until arrangements could be made with commercial airlines for refugee transport.[10] The Department of Supply and Services issued contracts on behalf of CEIC with commercial carriers. Ernest Allen, assisted by Michael Francomb, played a key role in negotiating arrangements.[11] A tentative initial schedule, announced on 24 July, was for thirty-one Ontario World Air, seventeen Canadian Pacific, and eighteen Air Canada charters.

The airlines were highly cooperative. Wardair, which joined the operation a few months later, made its hangar in Edmonton available to other airlines at no cost so refugees could deplane in midwinter sheltered from the worst of the weather. Cabin staff of all the airlines went out of their way on behalf of the anxious passengers. Like most refugees coming to Canada before or since, they paid for their transportation through interest-free loans. Fares were set at $750 per adult, $375 per child, and $75 per infant. The loans were to be repaid over time once the refugees became self-sufficient.

The Refugee Matching Centre

Directing incoming refugees to sponsoring groups was a new activity for the Immigration Department, and it took several months to perfect the process. The initial plan to match sponsors and refugees at visa offices overseas quickly proved ineffective and interfered with the primary task of selecting and transporting the refugees. The Matching Centre was established and tasked with matching arriving refugees

TABLE 7.1
Number of charter flights, July 1979 to December 1980

Visa Office	1979	1980	Total
Bangkok	22	30	52
Hong Kong	23, incl. 11 DND flights	22	45
Kuala Lumpur (managed by Singapore)	31	25	56
Singapore	7	21	28
Total	83	98	181

Source: Employment and Immigration Canada, *Indochinese Refugees: The Canadian Response, 1979 and 1980* (Ottawa: Department of Supply and Services 1982), 11.

with sponsoring groups and assigning destinations to government assisted refugees. The centre began operations in May 1979 with a single officer, Don Milburn, as its head.[12] The system of recording of sponsorship applications in ledgers was subsequently replaced with index cards. With the increasing number of sponsorships and the soaring number of refugee arrivals, the cards too became difficult to manage. Analyzing trends and patterns on the basis of a stack of cards proved cumbersome, error prone, and time consuming.

Over the summer of 1979 the Matching Centre's staff rose to eight people, charged with receiving the information about refugees provided by the selection officers abroad and finding a workable match with a sponsoring group. Groups interested in sponsoring refugees completed applications at Canada Immigration Centres. A copy of the "Undertaking to Sponsor" was sent (initially by mail but later by telex) to the Matching Centre. There the details were recorded, and an eventual marriage of a sponsorship application was made with an incoming refugee family. Sponsors often defined the type and number of refugees they were willing and able to accept. Critical factors could include family configuration, school requirements, and employment skills when jobs had been identified. Efforts were made to send refugees to areas where their prospects for successful settlement were optimized.[13]

There were many initial problems. Forms were mailed, not telexed. Matches were made before refugees were medically cleared, causing

delays. Early in the movement, UNHCR did not coordinate refugee selection, which meant that often a refugee family applied simultaneously to the United States, Canada, France, and Australia. In hundreds
of cases, Canadian officers discovered that refugees promised to a
sponsor had left for another country, wasting precious resources and
causing disappointment at the Canadian end.[14] In addition, complex
procedures required several rounds of communication between the
sponsors, their local immigration office, the Matching Centre, and the
visa offices in Southeast Asia. With 3,000 refugees starting to arrive
each month, the situation was untenable. As one official said, "It became clear that we could move information or we could move people
but we couldn't do both."[15]

Recognizing that the matching system needed to be completely
redesigned, Molloy recruited Ian Thomson, an experienced visa officer with a flair for systems design, to overhaul it. After a week's
observations and analysis, Thomson presented a new twelve-page set
of instructions designed to create a more efficient system, inspired, as
it turned out, by the Berlin Airlift.[16] Thomson's revised procedures for
matching refugees with sponsoring groups were simple in concept and
complex in execution but worked. Henceforth, unless the sponsor
knew the name and location of a specific refugee, visa officers would
interview, select, and process refugee applicants without worrying
about whether they would be sponsored or where in Canada they
would be going. Refugees would not be referred to potential sponsors
until all selection criteria had been met and they were ready to travel
to Canada. The matching of refugees with sponsoring groups would
be completed exclusively by the Matching Centre, though the system
would "provide clear-cut and definitive information on refugees to
sponsor groups in Canada [to] hasten the acceptance of refugees on
their arrival."[17] The new operational procedures, which came into
effect on 10 September 1979, ensured that 80 per cent of the 13,820
refugees arriving on sixty flights between September and December
1979 were matched with private sponsoring groups.

The new matching system was at the heart of the success of the
1979–80 Indochinese refugee resettlement program. A minimum of
ten working days before a flight was ready to depart, the visa office
responsible sent by telex a Destination Matching Request (DMR) listing the details of every refugee who would be onboard the flight. The
DMR was sent to the Matching Centre, the Refugee Task Force, the

staging areas in Edmonton and Montreal, Health and Welfare Canada, the regional offices, and the responsible Canadian Immigration and Employment Centres. The DMR for each flight listed family clusters with file numbers, names, dates of birth, occupations, nationality, language, presence in Canada of family, sponsors (if known), and other relevant information. The format for the DMRs was precise and consistent, with codes and abbreviations following a standard format and order. Deviation was not permitted. While the management of local refugee operations in Southeast Asia and across Canada allowed local managers a great deal of latitude, the manner in which critical information about arriving refugees was communicated between the different parts of the system had to be absolutely consistent. A single DMR could carry information on anywhere from ninety to five hundred people.

On receipt of each DMR, the Matching Centre identified potential matches of refugees and sponsors and communicated these to the regional offices, which tasked the CIC in the appropriate community to contact the sponsors. The CIC asked the sponsors if they would accept the incoming refugees arriving a few days hence. Elaborate procedures guided the actions of the CICs in case the sponsors could not accept either the suggested individuals or the date of arrival. Refugees still unmatched by the time their flight arrived in Canada would be considered "government assisted" – seldom more than 20 per cent of cases.

The time lines were brutal and the logistics daunting:

- A DMR was sent ten days before a flight was due to depart.
- The Matching Centre had one working day to send proposed matches to the regional offices.
- The regional offices passed the proposed matches to the sponsors' local CIC, which immediately contacted the sponsor.
- The sponsors had forty-eight hours to decide.
- The regional offices had to respond to the Matching Centre with the results of the CIC-sponsor negotiations forty-eight hours before the flight arrived.
- The Matching Centre had to send details of the matches and destinations to the appropriate staging area twelve hours before the arrival of a flight.

In some cases the entire communications loop had to be completed in as little as forty-eight hours.

Meanwhile, as circumstances could and did change after the DMR had been sent by the visa office, a second definitive list of the refugees on a particular charter, called a Notification of Arrival Telex, or NAT, was sent forty-eight hours before the flight was due to take off. At any one time there could be DMRs and NATs in play for as many as eight charter flights, some involving Boeing 747s with up to five hundred refugee passengers.[18] Typically, each of the eight "matchers" at the Matching Centre in Ottawa dealt with a single DMR, but the matching units in the regional offices might have to deal with three or four Ottawa matchers (and three or four flights) at a time.[19]

The September transitional period was nerve-wracking, and the system itself placed intense pressure on the sponsoring groups and the Immigration Department, but it worked. Enormous pressure and excitement were injected into the matching process because it occurred when the refugees were ready to travel (if not already in the air) and would arrive within days. The Matching Centre attempted to match the preferences of sponsoring groups with the profiles of arriving refugees, but given the time pressures involved, flexibility was required by all.

Computerization

Although Thomson's new operational system made a huge difference, matching tens of thousands of refugees with thousands of sponsors on the basis of notes on index cards was highly problematic. Cards could easily be lost or misfiled, and transferring information from thousands of sponsorship forms to the cards took a great deal of time. As the number of refugees, flights, and sponsorships mounted, the system was again in danger of collapse. In 1979, commercially available computers were expensive and rare; there were long waiting lists and fierce competition within the bureaucracy for the few magical machines available. When Molloy put in an urgent requisition for a computer on behalf of the Matching Centre, a perception that the refugee task force was trying to jump the queue (which it was) led to a showdown over who would get priority. While some egos in CEIC were bruised, the support of Deputy Minister Manion ensured that a computer –

the size of a stove and accompanied by its very own nerd – arrived in September 1979.

The results were immediate and dramatic. Information arriving about new sponsorships or incoming flights could be transferred directly into the computer by feeding telex tickertape into the appropriate slot. Primitive by contemporary standards, the new technology was still a vast improvement over hand-transcribing the information. Moreover, from a situation of working virtually in the dark and having only a subjective, anecdotal understanding of the efficacy of the matching process, the Matching Centre suddenly found itself able to assess trends quickly, generate useful statistics, and work toward a more equitable distribution of incoming refugees. At the time it was nothing short of amazing.

In addition, as the visa offices in Southeast Asia were reinforced, and as they and their operating partners (UNHCR and ICEM) gained experience, they were gradually able to build up larger inventories of refugees ready to travel and able to provide more lead time to the Matching Centre and the sponsoring groups.

Initial Refugee Reception: The Staging Areas

As the likelihood of a major resettlement operation became apparent, CEIC management realized that one of the challenges was how to receive the arriving refugees in Canada, process their landed immigrant status, and attend to their needs before sending them to their final destinations. In the past, ad hoc reception procedures for dealing with large refugee movements and their special needs had been devised and then abandoned when the movement ended. Many of the people who had been involved in earlier movements and had developed procedures for handling large numbers of arriving refugees had retired or were on the cusp of departing. Over the winter of 1978–79, with commendable foresight, William Nauss, the acting director general of the CEIC Settlement Bureau, instructed Frank Wynen of his staff to interview knowledgeable people on the Immigration and the Employment sides of CEIC, including some retired officers, to tap their knowledge and experience in handling large influxes of refugees. By February 1979, "A Staging Operation Planning Guide" had been prepared.[20] Drawing on past experience, the guide outlined how to deal with a multitude of situations that might arise on the arrival of refugees in Canada. While the actual procedures employed in the reception and settlement of the arriving Indochinese refugees eventually deviated significantly from the guide, it formed a nucleus of knowledge around which preparations and planning could begin, and stimulated serious thinking about how to manage the arrival of large numbers of refugees.

From December 1978 on, refugees began arriving in larger groups – 217 in January 1979, 348 in February, 769 in March, 1,060 in April, 1,438 in May, 930 in June, and 1,281 in July. These numbers put serious stress on the limited capacity of CEIC's small reception facilities in Vancouver, Toronto, and Montreal. It became clear that one or more staging areas, as the large reception centres were called, were needed. With the decision in July to accept 50,000 refugees, the need for better reception facilities was immediate. The decision was taken to establish one staging area at Canadian Forces Base (CFB) Longue-Pointe in Montreal to serve Eastern Canada and a second at CFB Edmonton (Griesbach Barracks) to serve the West. (A detailed description of the establishment and operations of these two facilities is found in chapter 21.)

Refugee Liaison Officers

In the 1950s and early '60s, the Immigration Department had a group of settlement officers who worked out of local immigration offices with incoming immigrants and refugees in a hands-on manner. They picked new arrivals up at the airport or railway or bus station, found them accommodation, drove them to workplaces and factories, and personally introduced them to employers. It was labour intensive, possibly inefficient, but highly effective. With the creation of the Department of Manpower and Immigration (later Employment and Immigration), the settlement officers were absorbed into Canada Manpower Centres. There they were expected to work mainly from behind a desk in a corporate culture that tried, unsuccessfully, to minimize the distinction between Canadians looking for work and newly arrived immigrants and refugees.

After the July 1979 announcement of Canada's decision to accept 50,000 Indochinese refugees, there was an immediate recognition that success would depend in part on deploying employees capable of working with minimal supervision in the community rather than in the office. As a briefing note in late July pointed out, "the impact on communities of such substantial numbers of new people within such a short time frame requires a special resettlement effort at the local level to ensure successful adaptation." A corps of fifty-five refugee liaison officers (RLOS) was quickly recruited and deployed in refugee destination communities to liaise with sponsors and voluntary agencies and to facilitate the integration of the refugees at the community level. The RLOS were assigned to provinces in proportion to the number of refugees the federal government wished to settle there: British Columbia, 10 per cent; Alberta, 15 per cent; Saskatchewan, 5 per cent; Ontario, 30 per cent; Quebec, 33 per cent; and the Maritime provinces, 2 per cent.[21]

Most of the new RLOS were "community development workers" from CEIC Employment Development Branch (EDB). They were specialists in finding community-based employment opportunities for disadvantaged people. By the nature of their experience, they came with well-developed local networks that included government institutions, non-government agencies, and employers in their communities. The fit between community development workers and RLOS was all that could be desired. In addition to their networking skills, the RLOS were excellent coordinators, adept at winning the trust of both sponsors and refugees and helping them navigate issues that inevitably arose from cultural differences and conflicts rooted in differing expectations.

Naomi Alboim's description in chapter 23 of the role of the RLOS, as deployed by CEIC's Ontario Regional Office, provides a vivid account of the culture and accomplishments of this unique group of young people. Chapter 24 includes personal narratives of the challenges faced by two RLOS, Hulene Montgomery and Cheryl Munroe, in two widely different environments.

The Media Strategy

The government authorized a media campaign in support of the refugee operation on 17 July 1979, the day before it increased the Indochinese refugee target to 50,000. A memorandum to the minister outlining a strategy for keeping the public informed included plans for a weekly newsletter. The media strategy was to capitalize on the upswing of popular support for the "boat people" and sustain this interest, which the CEIC's public affairs team thought would be temporary. The strategy was also to reduce public reliance on the "unpredictable and uncontrollable press."[22]

The media spotlight was expected to remain focused during July before dimming in the face of other news. The expectation was that media attention would resurge and last until the end of August, to be followed by a slack period during September and October; then, from the end of October until Christmas, the pace would pick up again. It was believed that the support of the general public would decline with the rise of unemployment and the increasingly visible presence of refugees in Canadian communities. Some ethnic groups were also expected to be concerned that the Indochinese movement would jeopardize the flow of immigrants from their countries.

The Public Affairs team proposed an information plan to sustain a positive climate for the refugee movement, provide information to journalists through a news desk and answer inquiries. Announcements in the form of press releases or press conferences as well as the weekly *Indochinese Refugee Newsletter* would be used. The newsletters would provide an overview of CEIC's activities and statistics, including reports on the activities of private groups. Success stories were key to generating a receptive atmosphere for refugees. CEIC also wanted to show the contributions made to Canada by earlier groups such as the Hungarians and Czechoslovaks, as well as recent Vietnamese arrivals. Canada's ethnic population also had to be assured that the Indochinese movement would not interfere with the regular immigration program.

A range of communication tools was to be employed: material in thirteen foreign languages to all ethnic media in Canada; a speakers' bureau of MPs, the Public Affairs team chairman, the vice-chairman, commissioners and other skilled speakers to generate interest among associations, services clubs, and other groups. Audiovisual materials were prepared to animate presentations on how to sponsor refugees. Informational literature was prepared to provide guidance on the customs, culture, food, and philosophical outlook of Indochinese refugees.

The media was viewed as an uncertain reflection of public attitudes and sympathies, making it necessary for the government to establish strong liaison relations with community organizations to identify opportunities and counter obstacles. As it turned out, however, over the next two years the Canadian media provided informative and balanced coverage of developments in Southeast Asia and was unfailingly supportive of the sponsorship program.

The Indochinese Refugee Newsletter

The unprecedented involvement of thousands of Canadians as sponsors or volunteers in the dozens of coordinating organizations created by civil society presented the government with a unique challenge. For the overall national effort on behalf of the refugees to be effective, the government needed to keep Canadians, especially those directly involved in the sponsorship program, informed. In the pre-Internet world, the only effective option available was to create and distribute a newsletter by surface mail.

Minister Ron Atkey's conviction that information had to be made rapidly available to interested Canadians led him to issue "the first of a weekly series of reports on Canada's Indochinese refugee operations"[23] even before the decision to accept 50,000 Indochinese refugees. The first issue of *Newsletter: Indochinese Refugees*, released on 16 July 1979, reported that there were 350,000 Indochinese refugees in asylum countries in Southeast Asia. The newsletter gave statistics on Canada's refugee acceptances, listed the sixteen religious organizations that had signed sponsorship master agreements, provided phone numbers across Canada where information on sponsoring could be obtained, and described initiatives undertaken by various provincial governments, municipalities, and private groups. By the time the second newsletter was issued on 24 July 1979, it had a proper logo and banner. This issue reported on the UN Conference in Geneva and carried details of Canada's commitment to resettle 50,000 refugees over the next two years.

From the initial printing of a few hundred copies, the newsletter's circulation increased to 12,000. It became the centrepiece of the government's information strategy, although it was mentioned only in passing in the formal strategy document of 5 July. As problems arose, including a backlash against the numbers being admitted, health issues, and allegations of criminality in the refugee population, the newsletters provided a vehicle for the government to address the issues, often with the help of experts, such as tropical medicine specialist Dr Jay Keystone. The newsletter provided statistical and operational updates (including charter flight schedules), news about various initiatives, and helpful publications. In all, twenty-one newsletters appeared between July 1979 and May 1980, including special editions on health (March 1980) and language (May 1980). A minor disaster was narrowly averted when a sharp-eyed editor noticed that a list of useful phrases printed in Cambodian script had been glued upside down in the version sent to the printer.[24] Occasionally, a newsletter presented reports from the field that demonstrated with a great immediacy why Canada was accepting Indochinese refugees. An anecdote from the 22 August 1979 issue is one of these:

> Immigration Officer Colleen Cupples was supervising the embarkation of Indochinese refugees for their DND flight to Canada. She spotted a tiny Vietnamese girl in the lineup carrying a bucket almost as big as she was. One of Miss Cupples' tasks [was] ensuring that certain foodstuffs are not imported by the refugees contrary to Canadian regulations. She approached the child and gently asked what she was carrying. The child took the lid off the bucket. It contained water.
>
> "When we left Vietnam," she gravely explained to the interpreter, "we were all very thirsty. Now I am going to Canada. I don't know how far away it is but it is certainly a long journey and I am never going to be thirsty again."[25]

Policy and Implementation

The refugee provisions of the 1976 Immigration Act described in chapter 4 provided the legal underpinnings for the Canadian effort on behalf of the Indochinese refugees. The application of the Designated Class provisions to Indochinese refugees simplified the selection system. The newly created sponsorship program provided a practical way for Canadians to actually do something about the crisis unfolding every night on their TV sets. Absolutely indispensable was the political courage of the Clark government and the leadership of ministers Atkey and MacDonald for charting such a bold course for Canada.

The possibility that more would have to be done for the Indochinese refugees was something that immigration staffers had been quietly working towards well before the crucial decision of July 1979: witness Bill Nauss's handbook on reception arrangements and the design of the Indochinese Designated Class. But it was the magnitude of what the government proposed to do, and its insistence that large numbers of refugees must begin to arrive immediately, that surprised and then inspired the staff of the Immigration Department. The structure established by Jack Manion was designed to ensure that there was no division between CEIC's senior management and the Refugee Task Force; every senior manager essential to the enterprise was a member of both. Manion's decision, on the advice of a junior officer, to slash overseas paperwork allowed visa officers to focus on essentials and was a powerful signal to staff that innovation was the order of the day.

Most of the measures described in this chapter were designed and in place by late September. The staging areas, thanks to the competence of the Canadian military and CEIC's Alberta and Quebec staff, were up and running by mid-August. The airlift was delivering 5,000 refugees a month by October and November. Ian Thomson's redesign of the matching system, the core of the national endeavour, was primed to deliver 4,000 refugees to sponsors by October. With the help of a primitive computer and a herculean effort by the Ottawa and regional matchers, it delivered 3,578 refugees to waiting sponsors in October and 4,160 in November. It took time to recruit and extract the RLOs from the Employment Development Branch, but they were all working by early November.

Bold policy inspired bold implementation.

8

Mr Atkey's Fifty Thousand

This chapter reviews issues that arose under the leadership of Minister Ron Atkey between August and December 1979 and the evolving circumstances facing the CEIC teams operating out of visa offices in Singapore, Thailand, and Hong Kong. It also examines special groups within the refugee population that required special handling. The early months were chaotic: orderly ways of meeting an enormous refugee processing challenge needed to be established very rapidly. A media campaign by a right-wing organization against the refugee movement had lasting consequences.

The complexity of moving 50,000 refugees and matching at least half of them with sponsors by the end of 1980 was without precedent. In previous refugee movements, the refugees could typically be interviewed at a single Canadian visa office abroad, with the processing supported through the embassy's technical facilities. Without sponsorships, decisions on refugee destinations in Canada were made by working-level immigration officers implementing policies made by Cabinet and directions issued by the immigration minister. In contrast, the Indochinese refugees were scattered through seven countries around the South China Sea in over seventy distant camps, located on small islands or in jungle clearings far from Canadian missions. Those rescued by passing ships could be deposited as far afield as Japan and Turkey. Climatic extremes, including the seasonal monsoon rains and storms, added another level of difficulty to the challenges.

The Indochinese Designated Class Regulation and streamlined processing forms (the IMM1314) simplified selection and reduced paperwork. However, the public's concerns about possible health threats posed by the refugees and the legacy of the General Dang episode meant that normal medical and security screening requirements remained firmly in place. In some countries, local authorities and the international agencies were efficient and helpful, in others, less so. As well, this was the first operation where both federal and Quebec officers were involved in the selection process, adding another layer of complexity.

DM Jack Manion left CEIC on 1 September 1979 to become secretary of the Treasury Board. His experienced and steady leadership was sorely missed, but the innovations he had approved greatly facilitated refugee processing. While the policy decisions of July 1979 defined the course for the following eighteen months, Minister Atkey and the new DM, Doug Love, faced a number of subsidiary issues that needed attention.

The 50,000-Person Movement Gets Underway

The Canadian Forces airlift of more than 2,000 boat people from Hong Kong between 27 July and 26 August 1979 provided an immediate demonstration of the government's determination to make good on its resettlement commitment. Fortunately, the Hong Kong visa office had been instructed to pick up the pace of refugee selection in early June.[1] By late July, it was processing hundreds of refugees and was able to fill two hundred seats on the Canadian Forces planes every three days. The airlift allowed the Longue-Pointe and Griesbach Barracks staging areas (reception centres) to test and refine their systems and processes with manageably sized flights before the much larger commercial charters began. It also gave CEIC an interval during which reinforcements could be rushed to the small visa offices in Singapore and Bangkok. In addition to the arrival of extra visa officers, the hiring and training of more locally engaged support staff got underway.

Financial Strictures

By September 1979, the financial ramifications of accepting 50,000 refugees became apparent. CEIC had gone to Treasury Board on 28 August seeking funding.[2] The board approved CEIC's expenditure plan but declined to provide additional resources. The acting CEIC deputy minister, M.A.J. Lafontaine, informed the minister "that we may need to absorb most of the expenditures and staff requirements for this program from within the Commission's existing resources."[3] As it was, CEIC had originally underestimated costs for the staging areas, language training, and direct allowances to government assisted refugees, and the cost of the two-year Indochinese program had risen from $112,888,000 to $117,439,000.[4] The Treasury Board's unwillingness to provide supplementary funding for what was the Clark government's most visible initiative is surprising: that CEIC was able to find over $100 million from within its existing resources is even more so.[5] The lack of new funds for the resettlement operation meant that useful activities, such as occasional coordination and troubleshooting meetings between the managers in Hong Kong, Bangkok, and Singapore and their Ottawa counterparts, could not take place.

Conflicting Priorities: Private Sponsorships and Quebec's Commitment

By 24 August, CEIC had received 1,893 sponsorships for 10,600 refugees. Information available at the time suggested that there was sufficient momentum to reach the 21,000 sponsored refugees called for by the government, since family reunification cases were to be included in the overall sponsored target.

Within weeks of the 18 July decision, CEIC was faced with a number of conflicting logistical and political challenges. Transportation arrangements were in place to move 13,000 refugees by the end of 1979. By 7 September, the number of sponsored refugees had reached 14,044, but only 3,879 had been matched with sponsors. No one knew for certain whether the new matching system would be able to reach its design goal of matching 80 per cent of arriving refugees with sponsors. If it did, most of the sponsorships in the system would be filled by the end of the year. But giving priority to privately sponsored refugees meant that relatively few government assisted refugees would arrive before 1980, when CEIC would be facing an even tighter financial situation.

An early September memorandum to the minister from acting DM Lafontaine noted that officials now understood that the public's enthusiasm for the private sponsorship program was continuing and CEIC would soon be facing a large backlog of unmatched sponsorships.[6] At the same time, refugee arrivals would need to be speeded up: Lafontaine reminded the minister that Cabinet had set a target of 3,000 arrivals a month, but this number would have to be exceeded in October and November to compensate for lower arrival rates earlier in the year.[7]

There was, in addition, a special situation with regard to Quebec. Under the Cullen-Couture Agreement,[8] Quebec had the authority to select and integrate immigrants and refugees destined to that province. Quebec had committed to take 10,000 Indochinese refugees: 5,000 in 1979 and another 5,000 in 1980. While officers of the Quebec Immigration Service were working alongside CEIC visa officers in Southeast Asia selecting government assisted refugees for Quebec, comparatively few private sponsorships had been received from Quebec residents by September 1979. As a result, if the monthly cap of 3,000 arrivals was maintained and priority given to refugees destined to sponsors, the Quebec target for 1979 might not be reached, and most of the 10,000 would arrive in Quebec in late 1980, causing "major stresses in the province's ability to integrate the refugees rapidly."[9]

To attempt to resolve these issues, the Lafontaine memorandum recommended increasing the monthly rate of arrivals in 1979 and into the early part of 1980. Three limiting factors were identified: the capacity of the overseas selection system, the availability of flights, and the capacity of the staging areas. While Lafontaine had nothing to say about the latter two issues, his analysis with regard to the overseas system provides insights into what CEIC's senior executives understood about the challenges faced by the E&I teams in Thailand and Singapore: "It is extremely important that Canada not be seen to be accepting disproportionate numbers from the various Southeast Asian countries of first asylum. With the Singapore office already operating at maximum capacity, this leaves only the alternative of increasing selection to the extent possible from Bangkok, augmented as necessary from Hong Kong."[10]

Minister Atkey accepted Lafontaine's recommendation to increase the number of arrivals in December 1979 and January, February, and possibly March 1980, to accommodate both the privately sponsored and the Quebec-bound government sponsored targets.[11] The solution to meeting the competing demands of the Quebec commitment and the burgeoning number of sponsorships was to push visa offices in Southeast Asia to send ever-greater numbers of refugees to Canada. They responded to this challenge: 4,989 refugees arrived in October 1979, 5,385 in November, and 2,832 in December, followed by 4,006 in January 1980 and a record 6,133 in February.[12]

The Singapore visa office, covering Malaysia, Indonesia, and Brunei, was operating at maximum capacity. Al Lukie, E&I Singapore's new manager, was opening a second operational area in Indonesia while maintaining operations in Malaysia. Telex messages from Lukie reveal his frustration with the UNHCR's performance, especially its slowness in creating infrastructures to support resettlement operations in Indonesia.[13] The situation facing the E&I Singapore team was described in an undated ministerial briefing note of October 1979: "In Malaysia cooperation and active support of the government has been minimal and the United Nations in Malaysia has not been able to provide the support it has promised due to its inability to develop a local infrastructure. In Indonesia the large numbers of refugees did not build up until Malaysia had refused to accept any more Indochinese. However our officers have now started to select refugees from the camps controlled by Indonesia. Our officers have received excellent cooperation from the Indonesian government [which] is overcoming the problems posed in processing applicants from the remote locations."[14] Lukie's team of eight would shortly be managing two airlifts: one out of Kuala Lumpur for refugees from camps in Malaysia, and a second through Singapore for refugees from Indonesia.[15]

The perception in Ottawa that E&I Bangkok had additional processing capacity would create major problems for Bangkok's manager, Murray Oppertshauser, and his new team. By September 1979, the Bangkok operation, just ten months old and originally tasked with moving twenty refugee families a month, was now expected to select about one-third of the government's new commitment of 50,000 refugees. New officers and local staff were still arriving or being recruited and trained. In addition, while in Malaysia, Indonesia, and Hong Kong the UNHCR's "blue card" registration system reduced the problem of individual refugees being processed simultaneously, in Thailand the UNHCR used the blue card registration system only in Vietnamese boat-people camps. These people were but a fraction of

E&I Bangkok's mainly Laotian and Cambodian caseload. With no mechanism to signal whether Laotian or Cambodian refugees were being processed by other resettlement countries, the Bangkok visa office had to operate on the assumption that up to 30 per cent of the cases its officers put into process would go elsewhere.

An October 1979 briefing note outlined some of Bangkok's challenges: "Processing from Thailand has been the most difficult from the beginning. The government of Thailand has not allowed access to all Indochinese within its borders. UNHCR has not yet registered everyone in the camps to which it has access. The methods for transport and medical examination of the refugees devised by the Thai government and the United Nations together, have not been able to cope with the demands. While fighting along the Thai-Cambodian border has occasionally prevented our officers from conducting interviews it is mainly the logistical and geographical problems which have slowed processing."[16] Senior executives in Ottawa had the perception that the Bangkok visa office might have been mismanaged, as refugee selection in Thailand fell below expectations in the summer and early fall of 1979. This perception was corrected when Cal Best and Kirk Bell visited Hong Kong, Singapore, and Bangkok in October 1979 and saw for themselves the enormous challenges faced by the Bangkok team.

By the first week of October 1979, the Refugee Task Force secretariat reported that refugee arrivals in Canada since January 1979 numbered 12,845. Of those, 8,640 were government assisted, 487 were sponsored by relatives, and only 3,718 were destined to private sponsors.[17] This proportion was about to change as the new matching system took off. In October, November, and December, 9,958 of the 12,865 arriving refugees available for matching were matched with sponsors.[18]

As the number of refugees sponsored by Canadians approached the 21,000 target, the log kept by the Matching Centre for the week of 5 October provides a snapshot of the sources of sponsorships.[19] Collectively, churches that had signed master agreements had submitted 2,212 sponsorships asking for 12,204 refugees, with Catholics (764 sponsorships for 4,292 refugees), Mennonites (428 sponsorships for 2,356 refugees), and the United Church (230 for 1,282 refugees) leading the way. Quebec had created its own sponsorship program, which had generated 283 sponsorships for 1,415 refugees. Far and away the

TABLE 8.1
Sponsorships as of 5 October 1979

Sponsors	Sponsorships	Refugees sponsored
Total unaffiliated groups	967	5,324
Master agreement holders		
Mennonites	428	2,356
Presbyterians	127	717
Lutherans	149	790
Christian Reformed	231	1,296
Roman Catholic	764	4,292
Anglican	56	321
United Church	230	1,282
Baptist	110	554
Others	117	596
Total by master agreement holders	2,212	12,204
Total Quebec program	283	1,415
Grand total	3,462	18,943

Source: See note 19.

largest number of sponsorships up to 5 October came from organizations and groups of friends and neighbours not covered by master agreements: 967 sponsorships for 5,324 refugees.

Turning the Corner

By mid-October, despite the many challenges, both the newly reinforced Singapore and Bangkok visa offices and the long-established office in Hong Kong were in high gear. From Singapore, Al Lukie reported that there were 42,000 refugees on various Indonesian islands; only 6,000 of those people had been accepted for resettlement, 2,000 of them by Canada. In contrast to the situation in Malaysia, Indonesian authorities and the UNHCR were now providing excellent support. In the Bintan and Galang refugee camps, ICEM had established efficient medical examination facilities and was chartering ferries to transport refugees from the Indonesian camps directly to the airport in Singapore, eliminating the need to accommodate the refugees in Singapore overnight. Lukie and his team established good rapport with the Indonesian military and navy and insisted that UNHCR and ICEM ramp up their efforts in Indonesia. Their initiative paid off by giving Canada first access to the refugee population there.

In Malaysia, there were now 40,000 refugees, and all but 5,000 had been selected by a resettlement country. Malaysia continued to push refugee boats back out to sea; the survivors ended up in Indonesian camps. Lukie anticipated that the refugee population in Malaysia would be reduced to between 20,000 and 25,000 by December.[20]

Remarkably, at the same time, the Bangkok visa office was requesting *more* refugee flights. The Bangkok operation had hit its stride and located, selected, and put into process sufficient refugees to fill the six flights scheduled to the end of 1979 plus enough to fill another eight hundred seats.[21] In addition, E&I Bangkok asked to be informed about increased targets for January and February, as visits to refugee camps would have to be scheduled in November: "We hesitate to select refugees too far in advance of their anticipated departure as this tends to increase [the] loss rate to other countries."[22]

In late October 1979, a serious problem interfered with rapid refugee departures from Thailand. The lack of medical examination facilities in Thai camps meant that soon after being selected, refugees were moved to transit camps near Bangkok to be medically cleared. Thereafter, they would in theory be immediately ready to fly to North America. With Canada's high-speed refugee matching system, this was indeed the case. However, US-bound cases often remained in transit camps for weeks after being medically cleared until a US sponsor could be identified. The population of the transit camps became swollen as some refugees waited for US sponsors while others were delayed for medical reasons. An outbreak of diphtheria in Lumpini Transit Camp threatened to disrupt the flow of refugees to North America. A crisis was averted, thanks in part to the intervention of the Centers for Disease Control in Atlanta. This incident had the positive side effect of expediting a Thai government decision to create a separate transit facility for Canada-bound refugees, facilitating their rapid departure.[23]

Special Groups

The overriding preoccupation of the minister and the Refugee Task Force was the need to respond rapidly to the demand created by the thousands of sponsorships now pouring into Ottawa. The refugee processing system in Southeast Asia and the system for matching refugees and sponsors were designed to meet this objective. However, there were a variety of refugees with special needs. Selecting these refugees was more difficult, took greater resources, and more time.

Unaccompanied Minors

Starting in 1977, relatively early in the emergence of the boat people phenomenon, media reports and NGO observations had begun to surface about unaccompanied children under the age of eighteen, many of them orphans, among the refugees. Later, as the refugee crisis grew, rumours circulated in North America about large numbers of orphaned children. In fact, Canadian officers travelling in the region on refugee selection missions observed few unaccompanied orphaned children in the camps. Yet in 1979, UNHCR reported that there were 3,000 unaccompanied minor refugees – teenagers under the age of eighteen – in Malaysia. Of these, all but nine hundred had relatives in countries of resettlement other than Canada.[24]

Under pressure from NGOs, Quebec was the first province to be involved in the selection of unaccompanied minors. Since Quebec could select its own refugees, no special agreement was needed with the federal government, and in 1978, forty-four unaccompanied minors arrived in Quebec. Responsibility for their settlement was shared between the province's Centre de Services Sociaux and a group home under the auspices of the Order of Jeanne d'Arc.[25]

Later, the federal government and Ontario signed a formal agreement on unaccompanied minors (17 September 1979), and the Quebec government signed agreements with four NGOs outlining the conditions for the settlement of this group (22 October 1979).[26] To provide a legal basis for admission of individuals who met the broad designated class definition but were under the age of eighteen and were not accompanied by relatives, the Indochinese Designated Class Regulations were amended to include a provision requiring the sponsoring group or family to provide proof of approval by the provincial child welfare authorities and to extend the designated family sponsorship from one year to the age of majority of the child.[27] The amendment was rushed through the regulatory process and approved on 13 November 1979.[28]

Canadian officials in Southeast Asia were directed to concentrate their selection activities on the nine hundred unaccompanied minors without relatives in other countries of resettlement. A full-time officer, Warren Lloyd, was attached to the task force in Ottawa to coordinate the adolescent refugee program.[29] Selection and processing was complex and fraught with difficulties. Before the federal government could move unaccompanied minors to Canada, provincial concurrence was required. Questions of identity and the status of the minor's parents or guardians had to be resolved – difficult to do in the refugee camps where documentation was largely non-existent. As time passed, it became evident that desperate Vietnamese families were putting children, known as "anchor children," on departing boats in hopes that they would be accepted by a resettlement country and eventually facilitate the resettlement of the entire family. In a telephone conversation, Al Lukie spoke of the challenge of locating "genuine minors" for the unaccompanied minor program for Ontario: "The majority of those described by UNHCR as being seventeen years old are actually twenty-three and twenty-four years of age. On [the Malaysian island of] Bidong, only eighty bona fide minors for inclusion in the program have been located, and selection must therefore be made in Indonesian camps."[30] David Ritchie's account in chapter 13 documents the complications and reality of identifying young males suitable for placement in Canadian homes.

In October 1979, DM Doug Love suggested to the minister that Canada might be able to accommodate as many as five hundred unaccompanied minors.[31] By the end of 1980, 388 had arrived: 264 in Quebec, 108 in Ontario, fourteen in Newfoundland, and two in British Columbia.[32] In chapter 22, Naomi Alboim describes the measures that had to be put in place in Ontario to accommodate the arrival of unaccompanied minors and which served as a point of departure for negotiations with other provinces.

Single Refugees

A high proportion of the refugees arriving by boats were young un-accompanied males, and UNHCR put considerable pressure on reset-tlement countries to accept these young men. On 16 November 1979, Kirk Bell wrote to all refugee program managers in Canada and over-seas, pointing out that single refugees might encounter unique prob-lems of isolation and loneliness in Canada. The visa officers were to concentrate on selecting families with children, but Bell acknowledged that Canada must take some single young men. He noted, "Already some posts [visa offices] have begun to identify groups of friends on N.A.T. When these relationships are noted the Matching Centre has had good success in persuading sponsors to accept them despite a preference on the part of sponsors to accept mainly married couples with children."[33]

Bell instructed the visa offices to expand the practice of identifying groups of friends and sending them to Canada together. As well, he recommended bringing the problem of single refugees to the attention of new sponsoring groups; if they were willing to sponsor singles, this should be flagged for the attention of the Matching Centre.

"Named" Refugees

In November 1979, E&I Hong Kong drew National Headquarters' attention to the difficult issue of sponsorships for "named" refugees. It was not always possible for the visa officers to identify all members of a particular family before refugees departed for Canada. In other cases, once refugees informed their relatives that they had successfully arrived in a resettlement country, remaining family members might risk leaving Vietnam. Naturally enough, refugees in Canada asked their sponsors to sponsor their relatives, and naturally enough, spon-sors often did so, submitting a sponsorship application that "named" the desired refugees.

E&I Hong Kong identified two basic kinds of named sponsorships: "a) those arranged in Canada through groups with no obvious con-tacts in Hong Kong and b) those arranged by agencies/organizations through sister organizations or private individuals in Hong Kong."[34] Missionaries and aid workers throughout Southeast Asia had a ten-dency to send the names of refugees they had encountered to their coreligionists in Canada, often without providing the vital information that visa offices and the UN would need to track them down. Misspelled names and faulty information about where the refugees were caused many problems. In addition, some refugees travelled under false names. Even in Hong Kong, where the eighteen refugee camps were close at hand, it could take the UNHCR and the Red Cross up to three months to locate named refugees.

E&I Hong Kong requested that all CICs be advised that it was necessary for sponsors to provide both the specific locations of refugees they wanted to sponsor and the number of the boat on which the refugees had arrived. (All Vietnamese boats had registration numbers, and UNHCR registered refugees according to their boat number). Hong Kong also reported receiving sponsorships for people who were not in the camps and were, in fact, long-term legal residents of Hong Kong. E&I Bangkok reported similar issues in February 1980.[35]

The task force in Ottawa was besieged by sponsors demanding to know where "their" named refugee was. Efforts to track down an elusive group of alleged Cambodians in Thailand, sponsored by a group of Catholic parishes, went on for months. Little could be done. In the pre-computer age, there was no central registry of refugees in any of the asylum countries. Vietnamese boat people were registered on index cards, but only in the camps where they were residing and nowhere else. For much of 1979–80, refugees in Laotian and Cambodian camps in Thailand were often not registered at all. Over time, Canadian groups who had sponsored particular refugees grew increasing frustrated: how difficult could it be to find the Nguyen family in Malaysia? For CEIC managers in Southeast Asia (and their UNHCR colleagues) faced with the imperative of filling the seats on the charters, tracking down the named refugees who might or might not be interested in going to Canada consumed resources they could ill afford. There was no easy solution, but the steady stream of demands for information from frustrated sponsors in Canada had to be dealt with.

The Pagoda People

In 1975 and 1976 a group of Cambodians fled to Vietnam after the fall of Phnom Penh and took up residence in pagodas on the outskirts of Ho Chi Minh City. In the spring of 1980, following consultations with the UNHCR, Canada agreed to accept a number of these people. Extracting them from Vietnam and ensuring they were interviewed and screened before arriving in Canada was a complex but effective process. UNHCR provided files on one hundred "Pagoda families," 473 people, and arranged to fly them to Paris in June 1980, where their formalities were handled by the Canadian Embassy. Thanks to careful planning, the cooperation of UNHCR, the French government, the NGO Terre d'Asile, and the efforts of federal and Quebec immigration officers, the group was in Canada by September 1980.[36]

Opposition

Not everyone in Canada approved of the admission of so many Indochinese. In fact, public opinion polls revealed that for most of 1979 and '80 a slight majority of Canadians remained opposed. The government tracked the polls closely. For the most part, opposition was voiced in letters to the editor and on talk radio, but it became more public and vocal when the National Citizens' Coalition (NCC), "the most vocal and prominent of the groups calling for a tempering of Canada's humanitarianism took out a full page ad in the *Globe and Mail* and other Canadian newspapers stressing that Canada was simply unable to assimilate that many Indo-Chinese refugees and that there would be negative social and economic effects of such a large intake."[37] The NCC had little support among elites with influence on national policy or within the Canadian media. In this case, it used scaremongering tactics to attract public attention. The coalition claimed, for example, that each refugee received by Canada would sponsor fifteen additional family members within a short time. This was sheer nonsense, based on no evidence. Historical facts indicated that each new arrival in Canada generated an average of 0.8 additional persons over twenty years, a figure that would be lower for the Indochinese arrivals for such reasons as their difficulties in leaving Vietnam and CEIC's policy of accepting whole extended families whenever possible. Minister Atkey responded to the coalition with considerable vigour, stating that its allegations "smack[ed] of racial prejudice" and rejecting its claims as irresponsible.[38]

The end of the NCC's campaign came about as the result of "Operation Intellectual Kneecapping," an effort launched by Howard

Adelman and Joseph Wong of Operation Lifeline. Dr Wong knew one of NCC's financial backers. Wong and Adelman met with the financier, who agreed that the NCC campaign was racist and vowed to take care of the problem. He contacted a number of wealthy associates who also made contributions to the NCC. With their agreement, he phoned the NCC to advise that future funding would end if the coalition continued to stray from its focus on economic issues. The short-lived NCC campaign ended immediately.[39] Nevertheless, it would haunt the government, making it extremely wary of anything that would give those opposed to the refugees a reason to go public again.

Wrap-Up

Through the fall of 1979, under the direction of Minister Atkey, CEIC managed a complex set of variables including the government's direction to deliver 50,000 refugees and the need to match 21,000 refugees with private sponsors, to accommodate Quebec's target, and to respond to the resettlement needs of various special groups. Despite the challenges, by October it was clear that with the response of the Canadian public to the sponsorship challenge, the enthusiasm of CEIC's staff, and the robust design of the resettlement operation, Canada's objectives would be met.

By the end of December 1979, 24,828 refugees – half of the target – had arrived: 11,325 government assisted, 783 sponsored by relatives, and 12,720 sponsored by private groups. The arrival statistics through August to December demonstrate the impact of according priority to privately sponsored refugees and the effectiveness of the revamped refugee matching system.

There was, nevertheless, a growing chorus of complaints from sponsors who could not understand why it took so long for "their" refugees to arrive. In some ways the sponsorship movement was a victim of its own success. While over 12,000 refugees had arrived and been matched with sponsors by the end of December, there were unmet requests for over 17,000 refugees registered with the Matching Centre.[40] There were no new resources, human or financial, to devote to the operation, but CEIC staffers, including visa officers, Matching Centre employees, reception teams at the staging areas, Employment and Immigration counsellors, and refugee liaison officers in communities

TABLE 8.2
Refugee arrivals, August to December 1979

1979	Aug.	Sep.	Oct.	Nov.	Dec.	Total
Government assisted	1,889	1,087	1,266	1,139	512	5,893
Private sponsored	591	1,720	3,578	4,160	2,220	12,269
Relatives sponsored	110	182	145	86	100	623

Source: *Employment and Immigration Canada, Indochinese Refugees: The Canadian Response, 1979 and 1980* (Ottawa: Department of Supply and Services 1982), 28.

across Canada now had solid experience and were getting better at their jobs; the system was performing well. With the transportation that had been chartered for 1980, it seemed likely that most sponsors would have their refugees before June and the 50,000 target could be met by September. Until then, the complaints would simply have to be endured. However, two seemingly unrelated developments – the over-subscription of the sponsorship program and a vast humanitarian catastrophe in Cambodia – were about to collide.

9

To Match or Not to Match:
It's All about the Numbers

The response of Canadians to the plight of the refugees and the opportunity afforded by the new sponsorship system to do something concrete about it eventually created a conundrum for the Clark government, leading to a crisis in the relationship between the government and the sponsorship community. The issue from CEIC's perspective was first flagged in a memorandum of 22 October 1979 to Minister Atkey, alerting him that the number of private refugee sponsorships had reached 1,000 per week, and if this rate were to continue, by early November the total number would exceed the 21,000 figure set by Cabinet.[1]

The October memorandum presented three options to deal with this situation. The first was to advise potential sponsors that once the 21,000 target had been reached, the acceptance of additional sponsored refugees would have to wait until 1981. (This was not recommended, because it would disappoint the sponsoring groups concerned and stifle the public's good intentions.) The second was to admit the 29,000 government assisted refugees while still matching the 21,000 additional sponsored refugees. (This would exceed the 50,000 ceiling and was not recommended for fear of overloading provincial services and provoking a serious backlash). The third was to allow sponsored refugees to exceed 21,000 but reduce the government intake proportionally so that the 50,000 ceiling was not breeched. The remaining government cases would be admitted in 1981.[2] Atkey, in agreement with Secretary of State for External Affairs Flora MacDonald and Secretary of State David MacDonald, favoured the third option, thereby continuing the policy that would give precedence to privately sponsored refugees over government assisted refugees during 1979–80.[3]

Confronting New Demands

As the problem of what to do about the surprising number of private sponsorships occupied Canada's politicians, another major refugee crisis emerged in Southeast Asia. The Vietnamese defeat of the Khmer Rouge pushed large numbers of Cambodians to the Thai-Cambodian border. Some managed to make it into Thailand, but most remained pushed up against the border with the Thai military not allowing them to enter. These people were in a desperate situation, starving in extremely primitive camps. By December 1979, there were an estimated 600,000 to 800,000 refugees on the Cambodian side of the border and some 150,000 Cambodian refugees inside Thailand.[4] These refugees needed immediate assistance to survive but were not ready for third-country resettlement. As E&I Bangkok reported, "These people need medical personnel and food not immigration officers."[5]

The new Cambodian refugee situation would have major ramifications for the Canadian resettlement program. An emergency meeting on the humanitarian crisis on the Cambodian-Thai border was held in New York on 5 November. UN Secretary-General Kurt Waldheim chaired the meeting and Flora MacDonald led the Canadian delegation. MacDonald was originally authorized to pledge $5 million, but, recognizing the magnitude of the crisis and the urgent need for immediate help, without consulting her Cabinet colleagues, she raised Canada's pledge to $15 million.[6] By this time, she knew that, because of the higher than expected level of private refugee sponsorships, the federal government's financial commitment to the refugee resettlement program could possibly be reduced; therefore, part of the additional $10,000,000 to meet Canada's pledge might come from the resulting financial savings.

During the following week there were intense consultations between officials from CEIC, External Affairs, Finance, and Treasury Board. As the issue involved a fundamental change to the policy approved by the government in July 1979, it was necessary to return to Cabinet. Accordingly, Cabinet considered a new memorandum dated

13 November 1979.[7] Given the controversy it created, it is worth examining in detail the information and advice Cabinet received.

The memorandum reviewed the July decision to admit 50,000 Indochinese refugees to Canada, including 8,000 government assisted refugees who had already arrived or were being processed, plus an additional 21,000 government assisted refugees (for a total of 29,000) to match on a one-for-one basis 21,000 refugees to be sponsored by private groups. It noted that "both the volume and pace of sponsorship commitments exceeded the most optimistic expectations ... [By] November 9 the [sponsorship] figure was 23,510, more than enough to reach the 50,000 figure."[8] A total of 16,000 refugees had already arrived, and this number was expected to rise to 23,000 by the end of 1979.

The memorandum further noted that public opinion was sharply polarized. The unexpected level of sponsorship response indicated a strong base of support, but the size of the movement during a period of economic uncertainty had prompted a strong backlash. The fear of a backlash was in part the legacy of the National Citizens' Coalition ad campaign and in part what the public opinion polls were saying.

Opinion polls were regularly taken throughout the later stages of the Indochinese refugee movement. The opinions recorded contradict today's rosy public perception of all Canadians recognizing the plight of the refugees and everyone coming together to welcome and assist them. The reality was somewhat different. One of the earliest Gallup Polls was taken in late February 1979, following the government's announcement that 5,000 refugees would be accepted. The majority of those polled, 52 per cent, thought the number to be accepted was too high. Only 7 per cent thought the figure too low, while 37 per cent thought the number appropriate.[9] A Gallup Poll conducted in early July 1979, following the Clark government's announcement of a target figure of 50,000 Indochinese refugees to be accepted by the following year, showed a 49 per cent favourable response, while only 38 per cent were against the unprecedented intake. Interestingly, fully 57 per cent in Quebec indicated positive response.[10]

Further polls commissioned by CEIC followed in quick succession as the Indochinese refugee movement gained momentum. The 49 per cent favourable response of the July 1979 Gallup Poll would prove the most positive response to be received throughout the refugee movement. Polls taken in August, September, and October 1979 reversed the trend, resulting in a consistent average of 52 per cent of those polled being of the view that Canada was accepting too many Indochinese refugees, while only 36 to 37 per cent thought the target of 50,000 persons was appropriate.[11]

The government faced a dilemma. It would be difficult to justify discouraging sponsorships, but it seemed "equally inappropriate, on both domestic and international grounds, to expand the government's commitment at this time."[12] Public opinion was currently focused on Cambodia where "the main requirement is emergency food and relief supplies – not overseas resettlement."[13] Canada's resettlement program was considered "unexpectedly generous"[14] by the UNHCR and other countries: the number of refugees departing for Canada from Southeast Asia exceeded even those going to the United States. At the same time, new boat arrivals in Southeast Asia had fallen dramatically since July, down to 7,000 a month, while refugee departures for resettlement countries now exceeded 25,000 a month.[15]

With sponsorship pledges now beyond the 21,000 level and expected to rise significantly, Cabinet considered four options on how to deal with this situation:

a) Without extending the matching formula, the government could admit sufficient refugees to meet sponsorship requests above the 21,000 level while at the same time bringing to Canada before December, 1980 the 29,000 government supported refugees to which it was already committed. This would mean exceeding 50,000 admissions in 1979/80 by the number of sponsorships we receive beyond the 21,000 figure, a number impossible to predict, but potentially substantial. However there are obvious risks in exceeding the total intake of 50,000 in 1979/80 in the absence of a new and major crisis. With only 16,000 refugees now in Canada, the full impact of the July decision has yet to be felt. For this reason, the provinces would very likely object on the grounds that their social and educational services will be overtaxed by the time the 50,000 figure is reached. Moreover, an increased commitment is unlikely to broaden public support for the program, while those opposed would publicly become more strident and vociferous, making for a more difficult resettlement milieu.

b) The number of refugees sponsored privately could be allowed
to exceed the figure of 21,000 (without applying the matching
formula beyond this figure), while the number of government
supported refugees admitted in 1979/80 would be reduced
proportionately to keep the intake figure for 1979/80 at
50,000. This would be coupled with a firm pledge that the remainder of the 29,000 government assisted refugees would be
admitted after 1980 as part of the regular ongoing refugee
program.

c) The government could limit the total Indochinese refugee intake to 50,000, while allowing sponsorships to find their own
level within the present program, on the understanding that
each sponsored refugee above 21,000 would reduce the government's commitment by an equal number, and that the
funds thus saved would be diverted to provide food and medical aid for Indochinese refugees overseas, e.g. part of the $15
million commitment for Cambodian relief announced by the
SSEA [Secretary of State for External Affairs] on 5 November.

d) Since options (b) and (c) effectively appeal to two conflicting
constituencies, adoption of either as set out above could well
prove unacceptable to significant segments of the Canadian
public. Without fundamentally altering the thrust of option
(c), a variant is possible which might make it more generally
acceptable. This would be to convert the present program of
29,000 government and 21,000 sponsored to a matching formula on a 25,000/25,000 basis, thus leaving some scope for
sponsorship to rise from its current 23,500 level and commit-
ting the government to a firm 25,000 intake in 1979/80. Sponsors would be told that no further sponsorships would be
honoured above 25,000 until after 1980. Some financial savings, about $4.8 million, would still occur with the reduction
of the government's program from 29,000 to 25,000 and, in
a general way, the concept of the July challenge, one for one
matching, would be retained. The disadvantage of this option
which does not exist in (c) is that by announcing a ceiling on
sponsorship of Indochinese refugees at this time, those who
are now organizing to sponsor, of which there are still a significant number, will consider themselves to have been treated

unfairly. Further, it may be difficult to maintain this ceiling on sponsorships to the end of 1980 if subsequent events create in the public's mind a new and compelling need to respond.[16]

The final Cabinet decision took into account that many groups of Canadians were still getting organized to sponsor refugees. The first wave of sponsorships had been organized in the large urban areas and, if the submission of sponsorships were to be closed off, sponsoring groups now forming in smaller communities across the country, and particularly in Quebec, "would be caught in the close-off."[17] This would have an undesirable impact on the distribution of refugees across the country that could not be offset by sending government assisted refugees to smaller communities where it would be too expensive to establish support systems. Between 1 October and 9 November, an average of 61.9 per cent of new sponsorships came from non-urban areas.[18]

On 16 November 1979 the Cabinet Committee on Social and Native Affairs reported to the inner Cabinet its decision to agree to the following approach:

1 To limit total refugee intake to 50,000 while allowing sponsorships to find their own level within the present program, on the understanding that each sponsored refugee above 21,000 would reduce the government's commitment by an equal number.
2 That the funds thus saved would be diverted ... to provide food and medical aid for Indochinese refugees overseas [as] part of the $15 million commitment for Cambodian relief announced by the Secretary of State for External Affairs on November 5, subject to review by the President of the Treasury Board on the feasibility of other alternatives to provide a portion of the funding required as requested in 6036-79RD (NSD).[19]

Working-level members of the Refugee Task Force saw the decision as highly problematic and detrimental to relations with the sponsoring community. They saw the absence of any reference to the fulfilment of the original government commitment to resettle 29,000 refugees in subsequent years as damaging to the excellent relationship that had existed between the government and the public service on the one hand and the leaders of the sponsorship movement on the other. After the years of acrimony that had characterized government-refugee advocate relations over the Chilean movement, the prospect of losing the good will of a new generation of civil society leaders was disturbing. A conversation between Kirk Bell and Michael Molloy on how to limit the damage led to a recommendation that Minister Atkey and Minister Flora MacDonald brief a representative group of civil society leaders on the reasons for the decision at a breakfast meeting at the parliamentary restaurant on 5 December, 1979.

In the meantime, a meeting on 26 November 1979 of CIDA, External Affairs, CEIC, and Treasury Board officials evaluated the worsening situation on the Thai-Cambodian border. The $5 million the government hoped to recoup from savings at CEIC would not be realized until the 1980–81 fiscal year, but senior External Affairs and CIDA officials now believed "a further Canadian contribution in the range of $25 million may be needed for Cambodian relief in fiscal year 1980–81 on the basis of 'normal' burden sharing."[20] While most Cambodian refugees were expected to return home eventually, this could not be guaranteed because of the continuing instability of Southeast Asia. The bulk of any additional funding would likely come from CIDA, given Treasury Board's recognition that any reduction in CEIC spending for refugee resettlement would only occur in fiscal year 1980–81. Deputy Minister Doug Love counselled Atkey, "To minimize criticism it would be helpful if at the time of the announcement [of Cabinet's decision] you could indicate that the present $15 million [for Cambodian relief] will undoubtedly have to be augmented, and that the savings obtained from adjusting the matching formula will enable this augmentation to occur."[21]

The Breakfast Meeting

On 5 December, about forty individual leaders of the sponsorship movement from all parts of Canada assembled in the parliamentary restaurant for the meeting with Atkey and MacDonald. Speaking first, Atkey stated that the response of Canadians to the government's challenge for sponsorships had exceeded all expectations and the sponsorship program was permitting Canada to accept a larger number of refugees than would otherwise be possible.[22] As well, the sponsored refugees were benefiting from the personalized help they were receiving from sponsors and as a result were integrating more rapidly. Also, sponsorship meant a better distribution of refugees, particularly into rural areas. Atkey then announced that after extensive consultations it had been decided that the 50,000 target for 1979–80, "a very delicate symbol," should not be exceeded.[23] Despite the higher number of privately sponsored refugees, he said, the principle of matching would be maintained by transference of some money to voluntary agencies. "Moneys saved by the government through the extra efforts of sponsoring groups beyond 21,000 [will be used] for relief efforts overseas and particularly to relieve the terrible situation relating to the Cambodian refugees who are fleeing in large numbers into Thailand." Some 600,000 Cambodian refugees were in need of food, temporary shelter, and emergency medical treatment. Each additional Indochinese refugee sponsored by the voluntary sector would create a government saving of $1,300, and this money, "notionally saved," could be used to help the Cambodians. Atkey closed by noting that the talent that had been marshalled to support the program would "permit Canadians to continue to play an active role in helping refugees both directly by facilitating resettlement in Canada and indirectly by supporting Canada's relief efforts for food and medical aid overseas."[24]

Flora MacDonald then stressed the magnitude of the disaster unfolding in Cambodia in terms of its impact on children. Her example was that if a comparable disaster were to take place in Ontario, it would mean that "every child currently in grade 5 or below would be expected to die within the next few months."[25] She continued, "We are talking about the genocide of a race, we are talking about something that rivals the Holocaust, perhaps even surpasses it in the magnitude of what is going on there and so what we are trying to do is marshal both money and forces."[26]

The message that the two ministers delivered was not well received. On the one hand, participants were reassured that the government would continue to respect and act on current and future sponsorships, and that the 50,000 target would be met. No one disputed the gravity of the tragedy in Cambodia, but, on the other hand, the idea that the government would not meet its one-for-one matching commitment and would use the notional savings for humanitarian relief abroad was received with some scepticism and anger. A long and heated discussion continued after the ministers left the meeting, and the public servants who had accompanied them received the brunt of the participants' anger. Civil society leaders from all parts of Canada were deeply unhappy that the government appeared to be reneging on its matching commitment.

At the same time, there was a very useful discussion of the gaps in the settlement services network and the discrepancies between the situations facing government assisted and privately sponsored refugees. The discussion highlighted the need to get funding into the hands of the institutions that had emerged across the country to coordinate sponsorship and settlement activities for both streams of refugees at the community level. Kirk Bell, Doug Hill, and Michael Molloy also had an opportunity to brief participants on measures being designed or rolled out by the Refugee Task Force with regard to unaccompanied minors, single refugees, the handicapped, tuberculosis cases, and issues arising from refugees arriving with false identities.

Despite many critical comments, the meeting ended on a positive note, with several of the more seasoned leaders recognizing the remarkable achievement the government's program had made possible. Many civil society leaders accepted that the refugee situation in Southeast Asia demanded new responses from government and private sectors alike. Yet concern was strongly and frequently expressed that support for Cambodian refugees should not be at the expense of the refugee resettlement program in Canada. As well, there remained strong doubts whether the wider constituency would appreciate and accept the need for a shift away from the matching formula so soon after the program was launched. The civil society group was grateful for the opportunity to exchange views with ministers and officials about the future direction of the program and were strongly of the view that the process of consultation should be intensified in the future, particularly when new changes in direction deeply affecting the private sector were under consideration. A conclusion arising from the meeting was that, as a result of the government's decision, sponsoring groups might press private sponsorship to the limit in 1980, in hopes of persuading the government to raise the 50,000 ceiling.[27]

Neither the reaction of the participants at the breakfast meeting, nor a strongly worded letter of 11 December, signed by representatives of forty-eight organizations, diverted the government from its chosen course.[28] Still, the message about the need to get funding into the hands of settlement and sponsorship coordination agencies fell on fertile ground, both because the needs were obvious and because government wanted to make a conciliatory gesture. Almost everyone at the breakfast meeting spoke of the need for special or additional measures to ensure that the long-term integration of the refugees was as successful as possible. As well, they "expressed the view that there were notable gaps in our programs and services now available for refugees (which in most cases were not designed for the Indochinese emergency), and which in their view should have first claim on the funds saved by the changes in the sponsorship formula."[29]

Reaction and Damage Control

Actions in reply to the strongly expressed voluntary agency and civil society views were initiated immediately. Molloy and Hill were despatched to Montreal to attend the annual meeting of the Committee of Organizations Concerned for Refugees in Montreal on 10 December 1979, where they read a statement from Minister Atkey to the delegates. In the statement Atkey advised that he had ordered his officials to consult organizations involved with refugees to discuss "needs that are now not being met and the means by which this help could be best provided with a view to making an announcement regarding further help the government could provide early in the new year."[30] On their return from Montreal, Molloy and Hill reported on the damage done by the announcement at the 5 December breakfast meeting: "The (Montreal) meeting's tone was one of indignation at the recently announced alteration in the matching formula and the decision to divert settlement funds to the Cambodian relief efforts. Anger was focused on the perception that the government had struck a partnership with the voluntary sector and then unilaterally altered its terms and conditions. The idea of the one-to-one match and its underlying concept of working together with the federal government were extremely attractive to both the large sponsorship bodies and the individual local sponsors. These groups did not consider aid to the Cambodian refugees on the Thai border as an acceptable equivalent."[31] The atmosphere of trust and cooperation that had existed between the government and its voluntary sector partners had been shaken and was replaced by a tone of righteous moral indignation on the part of the voluntary sector. The following day, 11 December, Kirk Bell sent instructions to CEIC regional directors general requiring them to consult immediately with the major groups involved with the Indochinese refugees in each province "to provide us with detailed information ... on the needs of the refugees that are not being properly met and the means by which this assistance could be best provided."[32] Bell stressed that the information was urgently needed by the minister for a review of possible program changes; all regions were to report by close of business 19 December 1979.

The responses were remarkably consistent. There was a shortage of interpreters and translation services, especially after hours, on weekends, and in rural areas. Funds were needed to cover the expenses of those providing interpretation on a voluntary basis. There was a need for language training courses to be delivered on a more flexible basis – part time, after working hours – and for language training for stay-at-home spouses and the elderly. Both refugees and sponsors needed a handbook of useful words and phrases and a national translation hotline, like that established in British Columbia. Disparities in the availability of language training and supporting allowances for sponsored and government assisted refugees should be addressed. Sponsoring groups needed access to more orientation, cultural information, counselling, and reassurance, while the refugees required assistance in accessing health care and understanding the Canadian educational systems. There were concerns about medium-term settlement assistance because serious emotional and psychological problems tended to emerge long after the refugees arrived, when services supported by the federal government were no longer available. Funding available to immigrant serving agencies under the Immigrant Settlement and Adaptation Program (ISAP) was insufficient, inflexible, and difficult for smaller agencies to access. There were, in addition, countrywide concerns about the scarcity of services in small communities and rural areas and the need for more resources for follow-up sessions with government assisted refugees. Ontario Region's report also pointed to overworked volunteers dropping out and the need for more public education, including a special effort aimed at the medical community, as some doctors and dentists were reluctant to deal with refugees. British Columbia Region emphasized the needs of rural areas, home-school liaison, orientation to employment, orientation programs for mothers, and head start programs for preschool children, as well as recreational and cultural activities and library services.[33]

Bell and his staff analyzed and prioritized the issues and service gaps identified by the regional offices, and in the course of the coming months CEIC would respond to the concerns expressed.

Progressive Conservative Government Defeated

While this process was going on, the budget introduced in the House of Commons by Finance Minister John Crosbie on 11 December was defeated in a non-confidence motion on 13 December. The minority Progressive Conservative government had failed to notice that on the day of the budget vote, its MPs were outnumbered in the House of Commons. Prime Minister Joe Clark had no option but to dissolve Parliament. He called an election for 18 February 1980. The Conservatives were defeated, and Pierre Trudeau's Liberals returned to power with a comfortable majority.

Carrying On

In the month before the election, the business of government carried on, and CEIC made concerted efforts to strengthen refugee reception and settlement mechanisms. On 11 January 1980, a Treasury Board Submission was sent to Minister Atkey by Deputy Minister Love seeking authority to make an additional $600,000 available through purchase-of-service contracts under the Immigration Settlement and Adaptation Program (ISAP) for agencies providing direct services to Indochinese refugees. The submission also requested that provision be made to fund groups "which are primarily engaged in establishing links between the Indo-Chinese [sic] refugees and the voluntary sector in the community."[34] Because of the largely administrative nature of their costs and the indirect nature of their services (to sponsors rather than refugees), these groups could not be funded through ISAP, but "since the survival of these groups is essential to the identification of the full range of voluntary assistance in the community and the organization and coordination of this assistance, a new initiative is required to meet their needs."[35] The initial request to Treasury Board was for $900,000 from existing resources for the new program, dubbed the Indochinese Refugee Settlement Grants Program, but in the approval process this amount was whittled down.

On 8 February 1980, Minister Atkey announced the availability of $1,310,000 "to support and strengthen the work of voluntary, non-profit organizations involved in the adaptation and integration of Indochinese refugees resettling in Canada." Of this, $600,000 would be made available to coordinating groups in fiscal year 1979–80 and $710,000 in 1980–81. Treasury Board approved spending for the program for fiscal year 1979–80 (barely two months before the end of the fiscal year) on 14 February 1980, authorizing $300,000 for ISAP and $410,000 for support to coordinating organizations.

Looking Back

Forty years later, a question may legitimately be asked: was the PC government's decision to hold the line at 50,000 Indochinese refugees to be resettled in 1979–80 necessary, and could better choices have been made to accomplish this task? Because of the massive outpouring of help for the refugees by thousands of private groups participating in the sponsorship program, this was a question that would have faced the government regardless of the Cambodian crisis. But the need to find funds to meet the $15 million pledge to the Cambodian refugees made by Flora MacDonald complicated an already difficult issue.

The ministers of external affairs and immigration were well aware that half the Canadian population (including some of the Conservative Party's rank and file) opposed the admission of such a large number of refugees; the National Citizens' Coalition's anti-refugees campaign had stirred up and given voice to that opposition. They were anxious to ensure that this mainly passive opposition did not turn into something more active and potentially ugly and dangerous. The least damaging and most easily explained option was identified early in the review process: let sponsorships exceed 21,000, give sponsored refugees priority up to the 50,000 mark in 1979–1980, and meet the government's commitment in subsequent years. This sensible option was rejected partly because it would have required the government to admit publicly that eventually more than 50,000 refugees would be arriving in Canada and partly because a PC government, committed to reducing government costs, was unwilling to contemplate the future financial commitments that an increase in the number of refugees would imply.

The option chosen, to keep the 50,000 cap, to let sponsorships continue but to deduct one government assisted refugee for each privately sponsored refugee beyond 21,000 and apply the hypothetical savings to Cambodian relief, was complicated and convoluted. It was hard to explain and had something of a "now you see it, now you don't" air about it. The leadership of the sponsorship movement, the government's most valuable and creative allies, viewed it as a betrayal, and it played into the hands of those who opposed the whole notion of private refugee sponsorship and who had up to that time been sidelined.

The government (and the country) were fortunate that within the sponsorship movement there were responsible leaders who disliked the decision yet remained deeply committed to the program as a whole. In addition, Atkey and MacDonald showed political courage in conveying the decision to the sponsorship movement's leaders in person and hearing their reaction first hand. The exchange at the breakfast meeting, reinforced by the information gathered through the subsequent consultations across the country, provided both the evidence and the impetus to get desperately needed funding into the hands of service-providing and coordinating organizations across the country.

While the decision made in December 1979 to abandon the one-for-one matching deal left a bad taste that endured for a long time, it in no way diminishes the historic significance of the brave decisions of July 1979 to admit 50,000 Indochinese refugees and to intimately involve concerned Canadians in the process of resettling them in Canada. Looking back, it is the bold number and the mobilization of thousands behind the sponsorship program that constitute the enduring legacy.

10

Mr Axworthy Sees It Through

The election triggered by the defeat of the Progressive Conservative government over its budget took place on 18 February 1980, and the Liberals returned to power with a majority under Pierre Trudeau. The PC decision to abandon the one-for-one matching formula was only a minor election issue, but during the campaign the Liberal employment and immigration critic Robert Kaplan and senior Liberal politicians like Eugene Whalen promised to reinstate the formula.[1]

On 10 March 1980, the new minister of employment and immigration, Lloyd Axworthy, received a brief from several major sponsorship and refugee advocacy groups. They asked the new government to "redress the gross imbalance between the large private sector commitment and the current non-existent 1980 government sponsorship program." In addition, they asked for maximized positive support for the program. They requested that the minister maintain consistency with past practices to minimize disruptions, and that Axworthy lay the groundwork for deeper, meaningful, and sustained consultations with the voluntary sector in planning for refugee resettlement beyond 1980.[2] The brief demonstrated considerable sensitivity to the need to avoid provoking a vocal backlash, the very thing the PC government had worried about when it held the line at 50,000 admissions and scrapped the one-for-one formula.[3]

In the meantime, the sponsorship program peaked and began to taper off. A total of 3,891 refugees were sponsored in January 1980, declining to 1,759 in February and 1,095 in March. In April the total dropped below 1,000 and by July to less than 500, staying there until the end of the year.[4] Meanwhile refugee arrivals continued apace: 4,006 in January, a record 6,133 in February, 1,932 in March, 3,390 in April, and 4,520 in May.

Increasing Funding for Transportation Loans

Immediately on taking office, the Liberal government had to address the problem of financing refugee transport. The Transportation Loan Fund, which provided loans to refugees and certain types of immigrants, was capped at $20 million under Section 121(3) of the 1976 Immigration Act. As that ceiling had been reached in late January 1980, the previous government had introduced a bill to raise the ceiling to meet the demand for loans to cover the transportation of the remainder of the 50,000 refugees, but the bill died when Parliament was dissolved. In the interim, CEIC continued issuing transportation loans so as not to disrupt the flow of refugees, using funds obtained by the unusual expedient of a warrant issued by the governor general. To meet Canada's international commitment and avoid disappointing sponsors waiting for their refugees, a memorandum to Cabinet of 14 March 1980 recommended that the immigration act be amended "to increase the amount of funds that can be loaned to immigrants, including refugees, in the form of transportation loans from $20 million to $60 million."[5] The necessary legislation was quickly introduced and passed.

Increasing the Target

In a memorandum of 12 March 1980, Minister Axworthy asked Cabinet "to consider ways and means of restoring the principle of government leadership in the sponsorship of refugees."[6] He noted the following:

- As of 29 February 1980, the total 1979–80 refugee intake had reached 34,000 refugees: 12,400 government assisted and 21,600 privately sponsored.
- The remaining 16,000 of the 50,000 target would arrive by the end of September.
- Private groups had committed to sponsor 35,000 refugees, of whom 21,600 had arrived, with 13,400 still to come.
- The maximum number of sponsorships that could be accommodated was 36,000, of which the uncommitted portion, 2,600, could be reached by March.

Axworthy's memorandum also reported that Quebec had received only 3,200 refugees in 1979 and was insisting that its commitment to accept 10,000 be respected. Even if every government assisted refugee was directed to Quebec in 1980, that target could still not be met within the existing total target of 50,000. In this politically difficult situation, with the serious imbalance between privately sponsored and government assisted refugee arrivals and the shortfall of the Quebec target, cabinet was presented with three options:

The first: Stick firmly to the 50,000 level as already announced. This would entail a very early announcement that sponsorship applications beyond a given date or number could not be filled until 1981. The advantages: This decision would be supportive of a program commitment (50,000) that in itself had not produced widespread criticism. The disadvantages: Such a decision would be disappointing to the more committed sponsoring groups. It would fail to meet the expectations of the Quebec government. It would also make it virtually impossible for the new federal government to visibly express its concern about the need to restore the principle of government leadership in refugee sponsorship.

The second option: Maintain the 50,000 level for 1979–80 but permit additional sponsorships on the understanding that they would not begin to arrive until October 1980 and would be counted against the 1981 plan, which should be formulated in the summer in the light of refugee developments in Southeast Asia. The advantages: This option could be presented as one involving no change in the present 1979–80 ceiling. It would permit private sponsorship to proceed at its own pace. It would be unlikely to have any adverse effects in terms of international perceptions. It could help to meet the requirements of Quebec. The disadvantages: This option would not fully meet the Quebec requirement. It might well appear to be a half-hearted compromise among those committed to the sponsorship concept. It would do nothing to restore the balance between government and private sponsorship, and it would potentially create considerable confusion in the public mind about the effective ceiling, leading to criticism of a kind to which an effective response would be difficult.

The third option: Establish a revised program level for 1979 and 1980 of 60,000 on the understanding that the government was prepared to sponsor the additional 10,000 refugees. The advantages: This approach would be well received by sponsorship groups and would help to restore the role of government leadership in the program. It would provide some headroom for additional private sponsorships (about 2,600) in 1979–80. It would also make it possible to meet the Quebec commitment fully. The disadvantages: This option would represent a visible and clear-cut change of numbers and would therefore be the least satisfactory in terms of potentially adverse international reaction.[7]

As of 1 February, there were still almost 260,000 refugees in Southeast Asia, of whom over 100,000 were waiting for third-country resettlement. Therefore there were definitely 10,000 refugees available for resettlement in Canada. As well, it was expected that option 3 would create a more "congenial atmosphere" for consultations with private groups and the provincial governments regarding the 1981 refugee resettlement program. The risk of a possible adverse reaction on the part of Vietnam was acknowledged.[8] The "inevitability" of negative views from those opposed to more Indochinese refugees, a worrisome issue for the previous PC government, was mentioned only in passing. Taking all considerations into account, the government adopted the third option and raised the 1979–80 Indochinese refugee resettlement target to 60,000.[9] In retrospect, this was the most humane option, as well as the least dangerous and most expedient one, considered from the viewpoint of the delicate political situation inside Canada.

Prior to this decision, the Indochinese refugee resettlement program was on track to be completed by late September 1980. Now it would continue, albeit at a slower pace, until the end of the year. The initial estimate of the cost of the enlarged program was $26.2 million including an additional $200,000 for the Immigrant Settlement and Adaptation program. The final Cabinet decision approving the new 60,000 target was issued on 25 March 1980. The decision directed that the costs of the additional 10,000 government assisted refugees should come from the Social Development envelope, if necessary from funds earmarked in 1980–81 for employment programs of Employment and Immigration.[10]

Minister Axworthy announced the government's decision to accept 10,000 more Indochinese refugees in a news release of 2 April 1980: "My intention is to bring into better balance the partnership between the federal government and the private sector." While not placing a ceiling on private sponsorships, he noted that, within the 60,000 target, there was room for another 2,600 places for sponsored refugees, and any sponsorships beyond that would be "filled at the earliest opportunity at the beginning of 1981." Axworthy expressed the hope that private groups would be willing to assist the government's resettlement officers in helping the additional refugees to integrate. Looking ahead and beyond the 1979–80 Indochinese program, and responding to the demands of private groups and institutions for more consultations, the news release promised, "There will be extensive consultations with both provincial governments and private groups during the next few months, in developing the 1981 program to deal with refugee problems around the world."[11]

The Dynamics of Delivering the Increased Target

Immediately following Axworthy's decision, the department started to design the process of bringing 10,000 additional refugees for resettlement in Canada. On 24 March 1980, Axworthy was presented with the following four options for organizing the selection and transportation arrangements for the remainder of the year:[12]

Option 1: Backloading. Leave the existing transportation arrangements in place and bring in the 10,000 on new flights in October, November, and December. This option would provide longer lead times for the visa offices to gear up and would push more of the costs into the next year. On the other hand, the arrival of 10,000 refugees in three months would place considerable strain on federal, provincial (especially Quebec), and private settlement agencies.

Option 2: Frontloading. Organize additional flights to bring in all remaining privately sponsored refugees by the end of July and launch the movement of the 10,000 over the subsequent months through to December. This option would ensure that sponsors got their refugees more quickly during the summer, and some of the 10,000 would start arriving before winter. The impact on government settlement services would be spread over a longer time period and there would be a clean break between the private and government phases, making for better optics. Adding flights from April to July would put additional pressure on the visa offices, and keeping the two strands of the movement separate would increase the operational complexity. Having all the government refugees arrive at once would also put greater pressure on the government's refugee reception and settlement groups.

Option 3: Double Stream. Develop an orderly schedule of flights to ensure that all 60,000 refugees, including the additional 10,000 government assisted ones, arrive before the end of the year. Give priority to the privately sponsored but allow the government assisted to come on stream and gradually increase as the number of sponsored refugees declined. This option would mean a smooth flow that would be better for both the visa offices and the settlement agencies, especially those in Quebec. It could cause some frustration among the latest of the sponsors, who might have to wait a bit longer, and it could complicate the effort to rally support for the government assisted refugees at the community level.

Option 4: Deferral. Have some of the 10,000 arrive in 1981. This option would push some of the settlement costs into 1981 but would mean greater costs in maintaining the higher level of operational activities abroad, at the staging areas, and within Canada. It could mean that Quebec would have to wait until 1981 to get its full share of refugees, it would undercut the process of re-establishing government credibility, and it would undermine efforts to establish a global refugee plan in 1981 with the full involvement of the private groups and agencies.[13]

The deputy minister recommended option 2, frontloading, and the minister agreed. Because of operational exigencies, the final program actually consisted of a combination of the backloading and double-stream options, as demonstrated by table 10.1.[14] The concerted effort placed on matching incoming refugees with private sponsors from July 1979 to May 1980 had met its goal. By July 1980, a review conducted by the Refugee Task Force economist Tony Falsetto indicated that there were just 824 sponsors still waiting for 3,470 refugees.[15] By June, the number of arriving refugees classified as government assisted far exceeded those being directed to private sponsors.

TABLE 10.1
Indochinese refugee arrivals April to December 1980

	April	May	June	July	Aug.	Sep.	Oct.	Nov.	Dec.
Government assisted	663	1,710	2,130	1,563	1,609	2,005	2,028	881	389
Private sponsor	2,699	2,691	1,354	561	533	352	587	457	171
Relative sponsor	28	119	151	96	51	59	102	120	41
Total per month	3,390	4,520	3,635	2,220	2,193	2,416	2,717	1,458	601

Source: *Employment and Immigration Canada, Indochinese Refugees: The Canadian Response, 1979 and 1980* (Ottawa: Department of Supply and Services 1982), 28.

Adjusting to the Additional 10,000 Government
Assisted Refugees

The decision to add an additional 10,000 government assisted refugees before the end of 1980 was welcomed by the leaders of the refugee sponsorship movement. As well, it was a relief to the officials responsible for the program in Ottawa, as it eased strained relationships with sponsoring groups, whose efforts continued to be highly valued. Minister Axworthy stressed the need for a "congenial atmosphere" with both voluntary agencies and the provincial governments The decision did, however, require immediate operational changes.

The first set of instructions implementing the changes was directed at the CEIC's employment network in a message from Associate Deputy Minister M.A.J. Lafontaine on 14 April 1980.[16] Lafontaine stressed the importance of continuing cooperation with private groups in assisting with the settlement of the 10,000 government assisted refugees. The development of a more formal, structured approach to helping refugees develop personal links with individual Canadians would reduce the workload on the Canada Employment Centres and result in a higher quality of assistance to the newcomers. At the same time, it was important to maintain the two distinct resettlement programs for sponsored and unsponsored refugees and not to blur the distinction between the two by having private groups pay costs that were the responsibility of the government.

The biggest change initiated by Lafontaine's directive was the insistence that, since the 10,000 refugees would be resettled through the Canada Employment Centres, CEIC regional directors of employment services should become fully involved. They were instructed to work with their district and local employment service managers, refugee liaison officers (RLOS), and the regional directors of settlement in developing plans to engage the voluntary sector.

Kirk Bell sent a complementary set of instructions to the CEIC immigration network in Southeast Asia and across Canada on 29 April 29.[17] Visa offices in Southeast Asia were informed that while many of the new 10,000 refugees would go to communities where they had relatives, whenever possible government assisted refugees would be directed to reinforce refugee clusters established by sponsors in smaller towns. Decisions regarding destinations would be made at the staging areas, using guidelines and/or personnel provided by the regions. The instructions noted that retention of refugees in small towns improved in direct proportion to the ethnic and geographic homogeneity of the refugees, and the regions were asked to identify the ethnic mix in target communities. The visa offices were instructed to begin, both verbally and in writing, to inform the refugees now being selected that they were going to smaller communities and that their cooperation was required if Canada was to absorb such a large number of refugees.

To assist the destining process, a set of new codes was added to the Notification of Arrival Telexes (NATs) for heads of families regarding languages spoken by the refugees and their geographical origins. The visa offices were to do their utmost to include in the NATs accurate and detailed information on refugees' occupations. They were also to identify with the code "URB" those refugees who were long-term residents of large cities. This information was used not for selection purposes but to assign refugees to the most appropriate destination. It was suggested that employment counsellors in the western regions be seconded to the Griesbach staging area. From this point on, because of a lack of employment opportunities, government assisted refugees were not to be sent to the Atlantic provinces unless there was a specific reason to do so.

The same message instructed the directors of settlement across the country to identify the communities to which they wanted the government assisted refugees sent. The objective was to reinforce existing Indochinese communities and reduce drift to the major cities. Job opportunities, housing, existence of strong and successful sponsoring groups, and the potential for host programs or community based programs for the government assisted refugees were to be taken into account. It was important as well to identify communities where the refugees were beginning to organize or had exhibited good leadership potential. RLOs, CICs, and CECs in target communities were to compile quick reference guides on the ethnic mix of existing refugee communities for the use of the staging areas in making destination decisions.

The regional offices and the staging areas were encouraged to consult on how best to determine the destinations of refugees. In keeping with past practice, national headquarters did not wish to impose a single system, but simplicity and compatibility were essential. As this was a new and complex activity, a national coordinator with both overseas and domestic experience was required. Darrell Mesheau, New Brunswick Region's director of immigration, had the requisite experience and joined the Refugee Task Force.

As the program entered its second year, a series of new challenges arose. Both CICs and visa offices were indicating that an increasing proportion of refugees being sponsored by private groups had relatives previously admitted under the program. Visa offices were requesting that the names of the relatives already in Canada be noted on the sponsorship so the files could be cross-referenced.[18] The difficulties involved in tracking down refugees "named" by sponsors, in the absence of centralized refugee records in the asylum countries, continued.

During this period there was also a steady stream of communications between the regional settlement directors and CEIC headquarters about "misunderstandings" between refugees and sponsors and discussions of the possibility of creating mediation teams to assist the RLOs in resolving such problems.[19] At the same time, CEIC headquarters became aware that "some individuals misrepresenting themselves as Indochinese refugees have been successful in hiding their true nationality and gaining access to Canada illegally" and sought information from UNHCR and other resettlement countries regarding the extent of the situation.[20]

By early June 1980, the embassy in Bangkok was reporting a steady increase in small boat departures from Vietnam now surpassing 2,000 people per week, attributable in part to seasonal weather improvements.[21] The Vietnamese authorities were not thought to be complicit, but the official Vietnamese press attributed departures to an American decision to refuse to accept 32,000 Vietnamese granted exit permits by Vietnam under the Orderly Departure program. There were rumours that the Vietnamese government might be preparing to resume organized boat departures. E&I Singapore reported at about the same time that there was no hard evidence that the Vietnamese authorities were organizing departures, but that minor customs and police officials were turning a blind eye to boat departures for a price.[22]

Balancing Needs: Available Funds versus Useful Information for Refugees, Sponsors, and Officials

In the opinion of officials charged with coordinating the reception of refugees, the *Indochinese Refugee Newsletter* published by CEIC – now with a circulation of 12,000 – was providing useful and necessary information for refugees and sponsors, as well as officials most closely involved in refugee settlement work. The Refugee Task Force had already issued two special editions, one written mainly by medical experts on health issues, and the second a collection of useful words and phrases in Vietnamese, Laotian, and Cambodian and their equivalents in English and French. The list of problems and issues arising from the large refugee population that had arrived in Canada was growing. These included disagreements between sponsors and refugees, dissatisfaction about differences in the benefits received by government-sponsored and privately sponsored refugees, housing and job shortages, and a range of mental health issues. Many of the issues could only be addressed locally, but it was clear that Ottawa needed to provide more information and advice in the newsletter.

Against this background, with Minister Axworthy placing a high value on the cultivation of "congenial relations" with the voluntary sector and the deputy minister issuing instructions to engage civil society in the resettlement of the new wave of government assisted refugees, Executive Director Cal Best announced that he was shutting down the *Indochinese Newsletter* because it was costing too much. He disbanded the communications unit of the task force around the same time.[23] The loss of this simple but important communications tool at this critical juncture was deeply regretted by the staff of the Refugee Task Force, but Best would not be dissuaded. He had strong respect for the public purse, and the files indicate that he was deeply worried about having to manage the refugee program with resources scraped together from other parts of CEIC. It is not clear whether Axworthy even knew of the newsletter's existence.

Assessing the Impact and Looking Ahead

By June 1980, officials in Ottawa were beginning to think about what Canada would do within the context of the 1981 Annual Refugee Plan.[24] While the program in 1981 is beyond the scope of this book, planning for it took place in 1980. The process was influenced by the impact that the arrival of 60,000 refugees was having across the country. It brought to light a gap in perceptions between leaders and advocates of the sponsorship movement and the institutions and people delivering services on the ground. It also reflected CEIC's efforts to make good on Minister Axworthy's desire for comprehensive consultations and improved relations with the voluntary sector.

In June, Cal Best and Kirk Bell travelled to Geneva for consultations with the UNHCR to gather the information to develop a comprehensive set of recommendations for the 1981 Annual Refugee Plan. They reported that High Commissioner Hartling was "quite fulsome" in his praise of Canada's resettlement efforts in Southeast Asia.[25] They also reported that Hartling would probably ask Canada to maintain a refugee intake target of 30,000 Indochinese refugees per year in 1981 and 1982 to help in definitely solving the Indochinese refugee situation in Indochina. Hartling's assessment was that the Vietnamese boat people situation was under control and Vietnam was unlikely to "reopen the flood gate," as it did not wish to unduly upset Thailand, Malaysia, and Indonesia. The threat of resuming the boat people exodus was "perhaps a more effective weapon for the Vietnamese in political terms than actually allowing it to take place."[26] The number of boat people now arriving (5,000 to 6,000 a month) was considerably less than the outflow to resettlement countries (20,000 a month). If this situation continued, the Vietnamese refugee problem would be resolved within two years. On their return to Canada, Best and Bell launched a formal consultation process regarding the overall 1981 refugee levels and at the same time sought regional views about absorptive capacity for Indochinese refugees in 1981.

In July 1980, a paper titled "International Refugee Scene: The Resettlement Perspective" was sent to a wide range of religious institutions, refugee advocacy organizations, and ethnic associations, as well as the provincial governments.[27] Drawing on the consultations with UNHCR in Geneva, the paper provided a succinct review of refugee needs in Asia, Eastern Europe, Latin America, and Africa. With regard to the Indochinese refugees, the paper stated:

> The sustained international resettlement effort prompted by the 1979 Geneva Conference on Indochinese refugees has significantly reduced the heavy pressures on first asylum countries in Southeast Asia. Currently, some 25,000 Indochinese refugees are resettled overseas each month; the new inflow, while rising slightly in recent weeks, is about 6–7,000 monthly. However, leaving aside the large numbers of Kampuchean [Cambodian] refugees clustered on the Thai-Kampuchean border, whose future situation and needs are uncertain at present, there are still some 150,000–200,000 refugees seeking resettlement in camps from

Thailand to Hong Kong. For this reason, supported by the natural interest of the Indochinese refugees already in Canada (and their sponsors), a requirement for continuing Canadian involvement in this area obviously exists though probably not at the unprecedented level of the 1979–1980 program. Within the Indochina program, we envisage a greater emphasis in 1981 on the more difficult cases, through the Joint Assistance Program under the umbrella sponsorship agreements to ensure that we reach the broadest possible cross-section of refugees in the camps.[28]

The consultative process was designed to elicit the views of the senior institutions and leaders involved with refugee questions and sought in particular to obtain their views "on the relative weighting of refugee intake between different world areas."[29] Few of the responses survive, but those that do are an important mirror of the views of the Canadian refugee advocate community in 1980. Operation Lifeline's Howard Adelman, noting a rise in refugee arrivals in Southeast Asia, suggested that the "prime factor in determining the number of refugees arriving should be the need abroad."[30] Estimating that there were 100,000 refugees, he suggested that Canada's traditional 10 per cent share would indicate a minimum commitment in 1981 of 10,000, but since Canada had in fact taken 20 per cent of the Indochinese to date, it should be prepared to accept 20,000 going forward, divided evenly between the government and private sponsors. Canada's absorptive capacity should be "a very secondary but relevant consideration."[31] Adelman noted that "the increase in unemployment has an effect on the attitudes of Canadians and their willingness to remain passive and not oppose continued immigration and support for refugees."[32] Unemployment in Southwestern Ontario, where there were many Indochinese, was rising considerably due to problems in the auto industry, and there were employment problems in small towns. The memorandum suggested, wrongly, that the labour market out West "seems very favourable." There was "no problem" in the language training area, given increases in resources. Adelman's recommendations included that the government "sponsor" 10,000 refugees, while private sponsors would take 10,000 plus 4,000 that might be left over from 1980 and a 1,000-person contingency reserve. Further, the government's 10,000 should include an experimental program in which the government would cover expenses for the first three months, and then the private sponsors would take over for the next six months, with the government picking up the final three months if required. Adelman recommended that 5,000 to 6,000 refugees from other parts of the world be included in the government commitment; he closed by suggesting there was a need for a federally funded organization for fostering further private sponsorships to meet the suggested 15,000 target. While Operation Lifeline was planning to terminate its activities, the recommendations of its leader were upbeat, ambitious, and positive.

The Standing Conference of Canadian Organizations Concerned for Refugees sent a paper that began by suggesting the formation of a tripartite consultation committee. It would be made up of equal partners including NGO representatives appointed by itself, provincial representatives, and federal representatives to advise the government on refugee policy.[33] The presentation went on to critique the government's paper "as less specific than we had hoped and while we found ourselves often in agreement with the general statements we question the implementation and interpretation."[34] The organization asserted that many NGOs found Canada's response to the UNHCR inadequate. The Interchurch Refugee Concerns Committee called for the separation of refugee quotas and immigration levels and for a "modest increase over the 1980 program" of 50,000 refugees in 1981. In Southeast Asia it called for a rapid and effective family reunification program and mechanisms to guarantee refugees the support they need to sponsor their families.[35] The United Baptist Convention of the Atlantic Provinces found the approach taken by the government's paper "highly rational" and "acceptable" but stressed the need for "sufficient elasticity" to deal with sudden changes in "need and pressure."[36] The National Council of YMCAS[37] expressed its strong disagreement with the idea of a "paragovernmental body to be responsible for refugees to Canada and their integration" in light of the exceptional job the voluntary agencies had demonstrated and asked for clarification of the UNHCR's role in decision-making in the Immigration Department.

At the same time as the consultation paper was sent to provincial governments and NGOs, the regional directors of immigration were instructed on 11 July 1980 to take soundings within their regions. They were directed to consult with refugee liaison officers, key CIC and CEC people directly involved with refugee resettlement, a sampling of agencies receiving ISAP funding for direct services to Indochinese refugees, and a sampling of groups working with Indochinese refugees receiving resettlement service grants.[38]

Two memoranda from Deputy Minister Doug Love to Minister Axworthy, dated 4 September 1980, set the stage for the upcoming refugee plan. The first, "Indochinese Refugee Program, 1980–81," was based on the comprehensive summaries prepared by CEIC staff in each province in response to Bell's instructions of 11 July to consult those people in both the governmental and voluntary sectors most closely involved in providing direct services to the refugees.[39] The memorandum was accompanied by a chart summing up the results on the consultation regarding housing, labour market, language training, and potential assistance to non-sponsored refugees, common attitudes, and comment for each of the ten provinces. The memorandum noted that the movement of 1979–80 had awakened more public interest than any other refugee movement, and with 50,000 refugees now in Canada, public support remained high. Canadians recognized that the plight of the refugees was serious and they were "genuinely worthy of assistance"; the refugees had proven to be "industrious, law-abiding people who make tremendous efforts to become self-supporting family units."[40] It was apparent that many of the sponsor-refugee relations would endure beyond the one-year sponsorship agreements. Further, the systematic distribution of refugees throughout rural and urban areas meant that the burden of provision of services – federal, provincial, and local – had been shared more evenly than ever before.

While all of this was very positive, a number of factors would limit capacity in 1981. These included countrywide declining employment opportunities, especially for unskilled and entry-level workers. Moreover, a drought in Manitoba and Saskatchewan had resulted in a significant secondary migration of refugees to Alberta. Refugees emerging from language training were running into difficulty finding jobs. It was expected that many sponsors would remain engaged with their refugees for a second year, and there had been little response to the minister's appeal for sponsors to become involved with the additional 10,000 government sponsored refugees.

Beyond this, there was a widespread perception that Canada had already responded generously to the refugee crisis and had done its share for the time being. All of the summaries received from CEIC regional offices suggested that in the coming year the refugees who had already arrived, and their sponsors, would now be preoccupied with trying to facilitate the arrival of relatives who had reached refugee camps or others who would come directly from Vietnam.

The memorandum concluded that there were practical and perceptual barriers preventing an intake in 1980–81 on the same level as in the previous two years, and there seemed little prospect of securing "more than 5,000 sponsorships."[41] It seemed likely that, to handle even a smaller intake successfully, it might be necessary to institutionalize some services and programs that had been delivered on an ad hoc basis.

The second memorandum Axworthy received from his deputy, Doug Love, on 4 September, titled "Annual Refugee Intake 1981," noted that consultations with UNHCR, the provinces, and the principal private organizations were still in progress.[42] It was, however, desirable to anticipate the approximate scale of the 1981 government refugee plan to ensure that adequate funding was sought from Treasury Board before October when Cabinet would consider the total immigrant and refugee intake. The memorandum noted that Indochina would remain the principal focus for 1981 and that the UNHCR had indicated the hope that Canada would absorb another 30,000 refugees in each of 1981 and 1982 "even to the point of withdrawing from other programs, e.g. Eastern Europe."[43] This was not practical for reasons set out in the companion memorandum. While Operation Lifeline estimated that 10,000 refugees could be sponsored in 1981, CEIC's soundings suggested this was overly optimistic; 5,000 seemed a more realistic estimate. The memorandum suggested that an intake of 10,000 government assisted refugees represented the optimum commitment Canada could resettle without undue strain. Even so, to look after the refugees properly and to maintain the positive climate of acceptance that had characterized the Indochinese program to date would require an expanded program of settlement services. An intake of 10,000 government refugees combined with 5,000 privately sponsored ones would compare favourably with those projected by other resettlement countries. For refugees from the rest of the world, the memorandum suggested an intake of 6,000 to 7,000, with a contingency reserve of 1,000 to 2,000 for total government commitment in the range of 16,000 to 17,000. With 5,000 privately sponsored refugees, that would bring the total Canadian commitment to something like 22,000.

This robust commitment suggested by the department was not to be. In reviewing Canada's immigration levels plan for 1981, Cabinet decided that the overall government assisted refugee target would be set at 16,000, with 8,000 places allocated to Indochinese government assisted refugees.[44]

While the planning for the future was going on, the movement of Indochinese refugees to Canada continued over the summer and into the fall. June, July, and August saw the arrival of 3,635, 2,220, and 2,193 refugees, respectively. On 11 August 1980, the management of the Griesbach Staging Area began to wind down, and the interpreters and the last of the refugees vacated the barracks on 27 August.[45] In its year of operations, Griesbach had welcomed over 21,500 refugees. From that point on, the remaining refugees would arrive by charter at Longue-Pointe in Montreal, and that staging area in turn would close down at the end of the year.

1980 Year-End Situation

The vigorous resettlement activities of the international community brought about major changes in the refugee caseloads available for resettlement in Southeast Asia by the end of 1980. A briefing note drafted by Murray Oppertshauser, now stationed in Ottawa after two years of service in Bangkok, was forwarded to Minister Axworthy on 3 October 1980. It provided an assessment of the situation in Malaysia and Thailand as part of the planning process.[46]

Malaysia had 20,000 refugees remaining, including 6,000 in transit camps who had been selected for resettlement and would soon depart. Boat arrivals had dropped off, and Canadian officers were finding that most of the remaining refugees wished to go to the United States and were not interested in Canada or had already been refused for various reasons. Of the remaining refugee population of 7,850 in Indonesia, all but 1,350 had been selected for resettlement, and boat arrivals were down. In Singapore there were 2,000 refugees, and all had been approved for resettlement by one country or another. Hong Kong had 30,000 refugees, all but 12,000 in the process of resettlement to a third country. The American authorities were selecting 1,000–2,000 each month, so most of the 12,000 would be moved out quickly. Canadian officers working in Hong Kong (and Macau, with

3,000 available refugees) were now encountering refugees who were only interested in going to the United States.

In Thailand the picture was more complex, but the reality from a Canadian perspective was similar. There were 119,000 Laotian refugees in Thailand, of whom the majority (including 50,000 to 60,000 members of Hill Tribes) were not interested in resettlement and were hoping to stay in Thailand or go home when conditions improved. About 15,000 were interested in resettlement, but most of those appeared to be confident that they would be accepted by the United States. The Vietnamese population of Thailand numbered 7,000, but 2,700 were "overland Vietnamese" whose transport to Thailand, via Cambodia, had been facilitated by Vietnamese authorities. The Thai government was not allowing these groups access to resettlement countries in order to discourage others from using the overland route. Of the 5,000 remaining boat people, all were under consideration by resettlement countries, and boat arrivals were down. The Cambodian refugee population in Thailand included an "old" pre-October 1979 population of 6,300 (most of whom had ignored resettlement offers) and a "new" post-October 1979 population of 148,000. UNHCR's assessment was that most would go home when conditions improved. The Canadian resettlement program would focus on Sino-Cambodians who could not return, and on family reunification cases. Oppertshauser's briefing note concluded that while Canada would meet its 1979–80 target, by 1981 the E&I operations in Southeast Asia could be in the 5,000–8,000 range, focusing on Cambodians and boat people who would continue to arrive in smaller numbers.

The last element of the planning cycle involved consultations in late November 1980 with the managers of the resettlement operations: in Hong Kong/Macau, Gerry Campbell; in Thailand, Edward Woodford; and in Singapore/Malaysia/Indonesia, Al Lukie. Senior coordinator Michael Molloy travelled to Hong Kong to participate on 21 November 1980 in a workshop chaired by William Sinclair, the manager of immigration operations in Hong Kong.[47] The managers expected to concentrate their efforts in1981 on "those with the greatest claim to Canadian consideration," i.e., those with approved family class and assisted relative sponsorships, and named privately sponsored refugees, particularly those with relatives in Canada.[48] The managers were particularly concerned about the large number of cases on "medical hold" but hoped to move these to Canada in the first quarter of 1981, assuming that national headquarters could find a way to speed up the clearance of cases on hold for TB. It was evident that all three operations were moving to a program that involved more intensive work, clearing cases with complex medical problems, and time-consuming effort verifying family relationships. Some government assisted cases would be processed, with priority going to those without private or family sponsorships who nevertheless had close relatives in Canada. Staffing needed to reflect this new reality.

In November 1980, E&I Hong Kong had 1,400 persons in the resettlement process, including 900 on medical hold. It would move 1,000 refugees to Canada on four charters in early 1981 and an additional 1,500 on commercial flights during the balance of the year. E&I Singapore had 1,200 in process, including medical holds, and would move 1,000 on four charters by March and 2,500 on commercial flights in 1981. E&I Bangkok, with 700 refugees in process, would direct most of its efforts to meeting Quebec's monthly target of 215 arrivals. It would send 750 refugees to Canada on charters in the first quarter.

The report of the workshop included a blunt message: "It is apparent that high production in 79–80 was achieved at horrendous personal cost to officers, support staff and families. It will not be possible to expect staff to continue this pace or working long hours and weekends that have been the norm for past 18 months."[49] In late 1980, Molloy, wishing to coordinate decision-making between Ottawa and Canada's Southeast Asian embassies more closely, visited the refugee operations in Indonesia, Singapore, Malaysia, and Bangkok. He confirmed that the staff at Canada's visa offices there were indeed "running on empty."

Finale

The charters continued to carry refugees to the staging area at Longue-Pointe through the fall – 2,005 in September, 2,028 in October, 881 in November, and 601 in December. The majority were government assisted, but privately sponsored refugees also continued to arrive. The movement had included 32,281 refugees sponsored by private groups, 1,790 sponsored by relatives, and 25,978 resettled by the government. The estimated cost to the federal government was $137,140,000.

The sponsorship program had a strong impact on the provincial distribution of the refugees. In Ontario, non-church private sponsorships played an important role. In Quebec, private sponsorships had a relatively minor impact, while in Alberta, Manitoba, and Saskatchewan, church-based sponsorships played a major role. By the end of 1980, the three Prairie provinces received a higher percentage of the Indochinese refugee movement than their original allocation – 25 per cent instead of 20 per cent – while Quebec received a lower percentage – 21.8 per cent instead of 33 per cent. Ontario also received a higher percentage than its initial allocation – 37 per cent instead of 30 per cent.[50]

Like so many projects of this sort, it ended less with a bang than a whimper. Charter Flight 181 arrived at Longue-Pointe on 8 December 1980 carrying the last of 60,049 refugees admitted to Canada under the 1979–80 movement. Plans had been made to welcome the symbolic final refugees: two Cambodian brothers and their families – four adults and six children – destined to a Mennonite congregation in Goderich, Ontario. A day or two after arrival, the family was whisked off to Parliament Hill, where they were formally welcomed by Prime Minister Trudeau and Minister Axworthy.

Everyone smiled, the cameras clicked.

PART TWO

Resettlement Operations in Southeast Asia

Historic signing of the first master agreement for refugee sponsorship between the Mennonite Central Committee (MCC) and Employment and Immigration (E & I), 5 March 1979. *Standing*: Kirk Bell, E & I; *seated (left to right)*: Ken McMaster, Manitoba minister of labour and manpower; Bud Cullen, minister of E & I; J.M. Klassen, executive secretary, MCC; John Wieler, director, MCC; Art Driedger, associate director, MCC. Courtesy of Rudy Regehr, Mennonite Central Committee File: Refugees 1979–1990, Archived Photos MCC Canada 1960–2004.

Hai Hong refugees awaiting interview on Malaysian minesweeper *Brinchang*. When Minister Bud Cullen agreed to accept six hundred of the 2,500 refugees on a derelict freighter off Malaysia, it alerted the Canadian public to the plight of the boat people. Prevented from boarding the *Hai Hong*, Ian Hamilton and his team (Scott Mullin, Dick Martin, and Florent Fortin – Quebec) selected 603 refugees in three days. Courtesy of Ian Hamilton.

Pulau Tenga, Malaysia, spring 1979. Gerry Campell (*left*) and Dick Martin (*right*) with three Vietnamese interpreters. Campbell and Martin, along with Rod Fields, put over 4,000 refugees into process in the months before the big push began. Courtesy of Gerry Campbell.

Ka Ho Camp, Macau, 1979–80. Translator Edith Campbell (née Hung), unknown, Scott Mullin, and Raymond Hall (UNHCR Macau). The camp was run by the Catholic Relief Services, headed by the inimitable Father Lancelot Rodrigues. Courtesy of Gerry Campbell.

Kuala Lumpur Airport, Malaysia, spring 1979. Refugees waiting for the first Canadian charter of the year. Courtesy of Gerry Campbell.

Bill Lake (RCMP) and Florent Fortin (Quebec Immigration) boarding the boat to go to Pulau Bidong Camp. They bought bananas in Kuala Terengganu, where they stayed overnight, to bring for kids in the camp who had little fresh fruit. Courtesy of Margaret Tebbutt.

UNHCR acquired this fast boat, which reduced travel time to island refugee camps from three hours to one hour. The fast boat was safer and more comfortable than the fishing boats previously used. Courtesy of John McEachern.

Far afield: David Ritchie, John McEachern, and Ben Soave (RCMP),
photographed by Donald Cameron, prepare for a long helicopter flight to
the Anambas Islands. The team accepted over 10 per cent of the refugees
from Kuku and Air Araya camps and received a standing ovation from
the refugees. As the helicopter broke down, the Canadians and the more
than 1,000 refugees they had accepted were transported to Singapore
and Galang, respectively, on the rescue ship *Lysekil*.
Courtesy of Donald Cameron.

Arriving at the Pulau Tenganau dock, Malaysia, was relatively easy. In the early days Bidong lacked a dock, and officers waded through waist-high water, carrying files and briefcases above their heads.
Courtesy of Donald Cameron.

Opposite
Pulau Bidong, Malaysia. Young, single men like these typically had difficulty being accepted by resettlement countries, which preferred families with children. Courtesy of Margaret Tebbutt.

Laemsing Vietnamese Camp, Thailand. Malaysian officials damaged boats after they had arrived to prevent them from being used by Vietnamese to escape the island camps. Once beached, wooden boats were stripped of useable materials for shelters. The Malaysian Red Crescent Society took the larger refugee boats and painted them white for their own use. Courtesy of Robert J. Shalka.

Pulau Bidong, Malaysia. UNHCR Malaysian employees organizing refugee registration cards. The "blue cards" signalled whether a refugee was being interviewed by one or more countries and eliminated wasteful dual processing in the camps. In background, John McEachern and David Ritchie. Courtesy of Donald Cameron.

John McEachern interviewing at Pulau Galang, Malaysia. Officers often interviewed late by the light of an oil lamp and then, in the early days, slept on the work tables. Courtesy of John McEachern.

11

Singapore: The Early Years

Nearly forty years after the fall of South Vietnam, two of the veteran immigration foreign service officers who served as the E&I Singapore team from 1975 to 1977, in the relatively quiet period after the initial phase of the crisis, met to reminisce about their shared memories of dealing with Indochinese refugees during this time. The conversation, presided over by Stephen Fielding of the University of Victoria, and recorded over two afternoons in 2013, was extensive, broad, and compelling about how they coped with a small but widely dispersed refugee caseload at a time when almost no one in Canada was paying attention to Indochinese refugees.[1]

John Baker had opened the immigration office in Singapore in 1973, assisted by one locally engaged officer, a secretary, and two locally engaged clerks. The area of responsibility covered all of Southeast Asia except for Hong Kong and the Philippines. Until May 1975, when Bill Sheppit arrived as the second Canada-based officer, John had been dealing with the regular immigration program and was involved with the Indochinese refugees during the three months that followed the fall of Saigon.

Tove Bording, John Baker's successor, was the officer-in-charge, and Bill Sheppit was the junior officer, during that early phase of the Indochinese refugee movement. They became the pioneers in defining how Canada would respond to the crisis. Tove's informative reporting on what she and Bill were seeing and experiencing kept Ottawa closely informed of evolving events at a time when international news coverage of the refugee situation was sparse at best. In the course of her reporting, Tove seems to have coined the term "boat people." The two also developed the partnerships and operational procedures that carried the program at a time when the challenges of tracking down refugees with linkages to Canada were little understood at Immigration Headquarters in Ottawa. The conversation reveals the blend of toughness and compassion, willingness to take risks, and determination to do the right thing that would characterize the approach of the Canadian visa officers who delivered the Indochinese refugee program over the next fifteen years.

TOVE: I arrived in Singapore in July 1975 to replace John Baker, and we were permitted a two-week overlap to brief and prepare me for the regional operation. When I arrived, there was still no high commissioner, although Bob Thomson, a trade officer, arrived in late July and proved an excellent head of mission and was very supportive of the immigration program.

BILL: I was posted to E&I Singapore in 1975 as the second officer because the immigration program was expanding, but at that time it had very little to do with refugees. I had worked in immigration in the domestic service in Canada and had completed my overseas training during the spring of that year. E&I Singapore had a broad range of activities, but there was very little family sponsorship. I recall that the bulk of the immigration program consisted of what are now called skilled workers. There were also some students under the Colombo Plan.

When the Chilean crisis erupted in 1973, it was handled in much the same way. And we had the Canadian Council of Churches practically living in the minister's office on that one! And yet, when Cambodia and Vietnam fell, there was nary a peep from the Canadian churches. I was in Ottawa at the time; it was a quiet time. I had been told in January 1975 that I was being posted to Singapore, but there was no hint of a refugee program at that point.

In 1975 I was on my overseas training at E&I Tel Aviv. I had gone on a diving trip to the southern Sinai on Easter weekend. When we returned to Tel Aviv, there was a message waiting for me at the embassy, at my apartment, and at the bar where I drank, telling me to call Ottawa. I left Israel two weeks later in mid-May and arrived in Singapore in the middle of June. As the situation deteriorated in Vietnam, Vietnamese who wanted to leave Vietnam could not obtain exit permits. For one weekend in April 1975, all Canadian Immigration

Centres (CICS) across the country were open following a special advertising campaign aimed at the Vietnamese communities, urging them to sponsor any of their relatives back home. This occurred just before the fall of Saigon. The CICS were in touch with Saigon by telex and would send off a message saying "Nguyen Van So-and-So, head of family, male, eight kids." A number of Canadian immigration officers were on temporary duty in Saigon, and the embassy would write a letter to sponsored persons informing them of a sponsorship from a relative in Canada.

TOVE: Yes, and CEIC had two officers at the Pearson Building (External Affairs HQ) to process the flow of sponsorships, remaining there overnight and trying to catch a bit of sleep on bunks in the communications centre.

BILL: That was the start of what became the refugee program. John Baker picked me up at the airport when I arrived in June, driving an old clapped-out Ford Escort with a fuel gauge that didn't work. Ten minutes after my arrival, we ran out of gas. Wearing my jacket and tie, I found myself pushing this heap down the airport expressway in 40°C heat, wondering what I was doing there.

In Singapore, we shared an office floor with the Israeli Embassy. I remember coming to the office, getting off the elevator, to be met by people sitting in the lobby between the two embassies, waiting for the doors to open. You had to step over people who had wandered in to see what their chances were of going somewhere because they felt they could not return to Vietnam.

TOVE: Most of these people had little documentation beyond their identity cards, which showed their parents' names as well as their own birth dates. These were the only identification documents available to us. But they were better than most. As far as we could determine, those identity cards were quite reliable.

Communication at the time was considerably different than now. We had a communicator who worked office hours of nine to five, five days a week, and he was an External Affairs employee. The encrypted telexes would come from Ottawa, which he decoded, after which we received the messages. The communication limitation allowed us to have free weekends until the message traffic became very heavy, after which the communicator would have to work extra hours. Rarely, we received telephone calls from Ottawa – like messages from God. It just was not done. I think we received three or four telephone calls in the course of two years. The diplomatic bag with the classified material arrived every two weeks. Regular mail from Canada took about one month to arrive. Classified mail was brought and sent via diplomatic couriers who arrived at weekly or bi-weekly intervals. When we were in the camps, we had no means of communication at all. The Indochina operation was conducted in a technological era which seems primitive by today's standards of instant communications. The framework within which we worked and had to act required that officers abroad routinely made difficult decisions without consultation with headquarters.

BILL: I recently came across an old annual appraisal of mine where I was arguing that I deserved a better appraisal than I had received because I was on my own for seventy-eight weeks in two years. That reflects the extent to which we saw each other.

Going to the refugee camps was always a challenge. I was on one particular trip to Mersing, which was the nearest refugee camp to Singapore, about a four-hour drive away. I was in a rental car and was forced off the road by a timber truck, because the timber trucks in Malaysia rule the road. Fortunately they were widening the road at that point and had cut down trees on both sides. My car did a 360-degree turn and then rolled over. I was 50 feet off the road by the time the car stopped. I got out, a little shattered, nothing broken, but with glass in my hair, a little bit of blood, and covered in red mud with office files all over the inside of the car from my opened suitcase. I was picked up by an intercity taxi with a couple of German tourists in it and driven back to Singapore. When I walked into the office with the suitcase, covered in mud and blood, Tove, reflecting on my recent appraisal that year, suggested that I was obviously trying for an outstanding appraisal! [Immigration Headquarters had just ruled that an outstanding appraisal was the equivalent to a posthumous Victoria Cross. Bill came pretty close.]

TOVE: There were also occasions when the Malaysian navy were on the coast pushing the boats offshore. If some boats overturned and the people in them drowned, that was too bad.

BILL: E&I Singapore was responsible for the area from Burma through Thailand, Laos, Cambodia, Malaysia, Brunei, Singapore, and Indonesia. The refugee movement began by handling Vietnamese outside of their country at the time of the fall. This included students in Southeast Asia, as well as tourists and business people. They were primarily in the national capitals, staying with friends or relatives. As their local immigration status expired, they were held in immigration detention centres including the immigration holding centre at Lumpini in Bangkok, and the Hawkins Road immigration detention centre in Singapore, the town of Bogor in Indonesia, and the immigration detention centre in Kuala Lumpur.

Compared to Cambodia, there was relatively little exodus from Vietnam following the change of government. In Cambodia, there was an immediate forced mass evacuation of the cities and widespread slaughter, although not widely known at the time. Vietnam had experienced numerous regime changes in the previous five years of the South Vietnam regime, with little impact on daily life. As time went by, the new unified communist government in Vietnam began to sentence opponents to re-education camps. This lead to an increasing number of people leaving Vietnam in small boats.

Starting in early 1976, we saw the arrival of small boats up and down the Malay Peninsula (including Thailand) as well as along the southeastern Thai coast. Boat occupants who were not raped by pirates and reached the coast were detained at the local police stations of the towns. Some arrivals were detained on offshore islands in Malaysia and Indonesia. Some Vietnamese were also detained near Nongkhai on the Lao border, along with a few Lao escapees, as well as in another camp towards the eastern border. Most of these were ethnic Chinese.

This had us wandering all over our territory on lengthy, unproductive trips. Trips to Thailand involved a two-hour flight followed by a multi-hour drive to the camps. Trips to the east coast of Malaysia were a one-hour flight to Kuala Lumpur, followed by a one- to two-hour car trip to the east coast, or else a minimum four-hour drive from Singapore to the coast.

TOVE: There were a lot of Cambodians in Thailand in camps. Ottawa would inform us that a person had an uncle in a given location. We would set off into the wilds of the countryside to find the camp, and we might find the uncle, and we would then start processing.

BILL: And he might be a blood uncle, or he might be a friend of the family they called uncle!

TOVE: The first time when I went to Thailand, the Canadian Embassy gave me an embassy car, and away I went. I had letters in Thai for the governor of each province where there was a camp to visit. I had to go to the governor's office, and the governor had to write a letter to the manager of the camp telling them that I was admissible to the camp. Most governors were very cooperative. One governor kept me cooling my heels for half an hour, so I told my driver, "This is a waste of time, let's go on to the next camp." Amazingly, the governor found time to see me immediately! When I reached the camps, the managers said not to bother with the governors, just come directly to the camps! I think I visited four or five camps the first time.

The first two camps were in the Chantaburi area, because we stayed there one night. Then we drove to Khlong Yai on the Cambodian border at the bottom of the Gulf of Siam. The road was on a narrow strip of land with the mountains up one side and the gulf down on the other.

Khlong Yai was a tiny fishing village with no place for us to stay. It was monsoon season and the road was terrible. I thought it was under construction since we drove in and out of huge excavations. As we could not stay in Khlong Yai, we had to go back to Trat each night and then return to Khlong Yai the following morning, making four trips over that road. It was only after I returned to Singapore and spoke with a colleague at the Thai Embassy that I learned that the road wasn't under construction, but its rough condition was due to the fact that the road was mined and a minesweeper was sent over the road twice a day!

When we initially reached Khlong Yai, everybody had gone to the movies as they had not expected me in the current monsoon weather. Everyone immediately left the theatre to welcome me. A very nice lady acted as my interpreter – the Vietnamese were always very organized. There was a shed with two walls and a roof into which I backed my car out of the rain, and we worked out of the trunk of the car. We were sitting on orange crates or something similar.

The interpreter had a fan and she kept fanning me to keep the mosquitoes away. As the applicants crowded closer and closer, she periodically whacked them with her fan to make them back off.

The regional economy was poor with the Americans gone. The hotels and restaurants were appalling. You did not look too closely at the mattresses, but at least they had running water. Restaurants cut up the napkins into pieces and in one place I had a roll of toilet paper placed on the table. Food was consumed to survive but rarely enjoyed. The people in the camps were worse off. Food was poor and inadequate, and most had only the clothes they wore.

In another small town further up the coast, near the Cambodian border, we arrived in the early evening. There was only one hotel, and the owner said, "No, madame, you cannot stay there. It is not suitable for you." The hotel was a brothel. The owner also had some cottages, and he and my driver agreed that it would be a better place for me to stay. There were police barricades along the town perimeter to protect it from incursions from Cambodia. The cottages were outside the barricade. I got into the cottage and my driver left. There was one 15-watt light bulb hanging from the ceiling. One look at the sheet and mattress, and I wished I had left the light off. I remained there working on my files throughout the night.

The water in the room was in one of these dragon pots [almost indestructible glazed pots made in Thailand]. It smelled awful, and you used as little as possible. The morning after I had arrived, my driver picked me up and we went 50 kilometres north of Aranyaprathet where there was a family we had been directed to find in a temple. The only thing we saw on that road was an elephant. We saw no human beings, no buildings, no anything. This was because the Cambodians would raid anybody living there.

BILL: Putting this in context, Cambodia fell in mid-April 1975, Vietnam fell the 30th of April, and Laos sort of fell in December. Everybody was expecting that Thailand would be the next to fall, and the domino theory would have come true. The Americans had already pulled out. The Thai economy had tanked. Everyone was worried about the communists. The Pathet Lao, Khmer Rouge, and Viet Cong were thought to be poised to invade. The entire area was on a warlike footing. You encountered roadblocks everywhere, experienced coup d'états in Thailand, and lived under a state of emergency in Malaysia, which had been in force since the late 1950s.

TOVE: These areas were not the tourist destinations they have now become. Aranya had a very large refugee camp, but they were Cambodians. At that point, if you went into a Vietnamese camp, they would have a camp manager, you would give him a list of whom you needed to see, and in about five minutes he took control, and everybody was lined up in front of you. The Cambodians were mostly peasants exhibiting little social organization, although we did meet a number who were well educated.

But there were also a number of Cambodians who were upper middle class. One tragic case I encountered in Aranya was later written up in the *Readers' Digest*. This was a young girl whose parents had been slaughtered by the Khmer Rouge. She had two brothers and one sister. They had headed overland. The two boys became sick and ended up in hospital where one sister elected to remain with them. The other sister eventually continued with another group of refugees and she hit a landmine. The brothers died. The one sister managed to escape, the last member of the family. Her story was not unusual.

That first trip finally finished, and we headed back to Bangkok, a long drive. My driver was unwell, and I was just dreaming of the bathtub in the Sheraton Hotel where we stayed in Bangkok. We were in the midst of rice fields when the car died. It was a sunny day and my driver said we had to leave the car and walk back. I asked, "How far?" and he responded, "seventeen kilometres," and I said. "Oh, no, no ... we cannot do that because this is Canadian government property and my files are in this car ... we will have to stop somebody." "Nobody will stop," was the reply and I said, "Of course they will stop." So I tried to flag cars down and a truckload of police came by and they slowed down to look at us but didn't stop. Finally, I just got out in the middle of the road and stood with my arms stretched out. And somebody stopped but they couldn't help us, but behind them was a small truck with a motor in the back and a mechanic aboard who got us going.

With repairs concluded, we recommenced our journey. It was now raining hard, and the peasants were dressed in black and the wandering water buffalo were black. I remember thinking that if peasants or water buffalo are on the road, we're not going to see them and will end up in the rice paddies. We made it to the edge of a larger town when the car again died, but this time we were in front of a service station with a reasonable-looking hotel across the road, so we booked in. The next morning my driver knocked on my door at about 6 a.m. to say he had arranged for a mechanic, but repairs would require two days. The driver had also arranged with the mechanic to lend us his car and a driver to take me to Bangkok. I was loaded into an ancient but very clean Mercedes with a driver who didn't speak English and sent off down the road hoping to reach Bangkok. Later I found out that our car had earlier been in a bad accident and the embassy had just received it back and it hadn't been properly repaired before our trip.

BILL: The embassy in Bangkok provided assistance for us but did not have the resources to do anything substantial. We hired our own rental cars and drivers. Some camps were three to four hours from the nearest decent hotels, so days were long. On one trip I was trying to reach the airport to leave Thailand during the monsoon. The car was a nice Mercedes with absolutely no tread on the tires. It is well known that water buffalos are somehow drawn to the middle of the highway in monsoon season. I spent the entire trip in a panic as we regularly screeched to a halt to avoid a water buffalo.

I did two refugee postings in Southeast Asia: Singapore in 1975–78 and Bangkok in 1979–81. My last interview the first time was in Mairut on the Cambodian border. I spoke with a man who had walked from Phnom Penh starting with twelve in his family. As they walked out they were stopped by the Khmer Rouge and took some casualties. Two of the women were later murdered. Three of the family made it to the Thai border, only to encounter a minefield where two of them were blown up. The man I met was the only one in the group to survive.

At that point in the program, individuals had to demonstrate a well-founded fear of persecution based on religion, race, or national origin, or membership in a particular social group, to be considered a refugee. You cannot react to what you are being told, since the next applicant would provide an improved story. When I returned to my hotel at night and was sitting at dinner, I experienced a chill when thinking about what these people had gone through.

Life was difficult for everyone in the region. There was a big Lao camp in Nongkhai in northern Thailand, whose northern provinces were once part of Laos and remained ethnically Lao. Nongkhai eventually held 50,000 people, and the locals were trying to sneak into the camp because the refugees had a better life than those outside the camp. The camp had medical care, food, running water, and toilets. Canada did not have a program for Lao until 1978, apart from requests for specific individuals.

Operationally, we faced huge challenges dealing with other agencies throughout our time in Singapore. We had to secure permission from the local immigration offices to interview refugees who were in detention. If refugees were in camps, or police stations outside the capital, we had to deal with the UNHCR, the local governor's office, and/or camp commander, who might be police, military, or immigration.

In the early days, we had to determine if someone met the legal definition of "refugee." This involved detailed interviews to determine eligibility, as well as determining whether or not they were likely to "successfully establish in Canada." Once they were accepted for immigration, we had to arrange a medical examination for them. Apart from those in the capitals, where there were already local physicians authorized to perform medical examinations for us, we had to arrange for local physicians to conduct the examination. In most cases, we had to arrange for transport to the capital for medical examination. In some cases, when numbers warranted, we would visit local physicians and then seek authorization from the regional Canadian National Health and Welfare doctor based with E&I Hong Kong for approval of additional doctors.

There was a great reluctance to accept anybody who had exposure to TB until after we were sure that they were not infectious. People often remained an additional six months in refugee camps because they might have TB. If they didn't have TB when they were first tested, they probably would have six months later, even if they were being treated.

We also had to initiate the security clearance through the RCMP officer based with E&I Hong Kong. This started as a one-person operation in Hong Kong with responsibility for security clearances for all Vietnamese, wherever they were processed. Clearances took many months to complete. Sometimes by the time medical and security clearances were completed, the person had gone somewhere else. There was little coordination. More than one country might be processing an individual. Later, the UNHCR assumed a coordination role.

When somebody had cleared selection, medical, and security, we had to arrange transportation. This involved the International Red Cross in Malaysia, which issued travel documents; the Intergovernmental Committee for European Migration (ICEM), now the International Organization for Migration (IOM) in Bangkok, which arranged local transport; and the regional office of Canadian Pacific Airlines (CP Air) based in Hong Kong, which found places on the airplanes. We also required refugees to sign a travel manifest indicating that they promised to repay the cost of their transportation. This was quite a complex operation, with opportunity for delays and confusion.

TOVE: Critical in our deliberations was the humanitarian side. You made decisions which were "right" and didn't worry about it. I encountered four cousins who insisted that they would only go if all were accepted. Two of them had good employment prospects. They were going to Manitoba and I talked them into going ahead to get established before the next two cousins arrived. I had committed to taking the second two, one of whom I think was only seventeen. After a while, facing the grim realities in the camps, you didn't ask headquarters; you did the right things and sorted it out with headquarters later. When I was ready to visa the second two cousins, we received a message from headquarters saying they had changed their minds, not to take them because Winnipeg had said something. I sent them anyway because we had made a commitment to help.

You made these kinds of decisions. Shortly after arriving, I had a call from our embassy in Jakarta saying they had two excellent candidates. I think they were specialists in fisheries or something similar. Bill and I both had commitments and couldn't go to Jakarta to conduct an interview. Foolishly, I contacted headquarters to ask if it was acceptable to have an external affairs officer do the interview, if we provided the questions. I received a rocket from headquarters saying, "On no terms will you do that," so these skilled individuals went to another country. With some experience in the field, I would have just let the External Affairs officer do the interview. We had to make split-second decisions all the time, since there were no protocols in place. During those two years there were no guidelines.

BILL: And our selection quota would constantly go up as CEIC operations in Guam or Indiantown Gap in the United States concluded, with any unused quota transferred to us. We would sit one month unable to select anyone, and the next month we received more slots. It was a numbers game, with us constantly monitoring how many we could select.

It wasn't until bigger boats began arriving in 1977, I think. Up until then it was a small-scale operation. It was a tremendous amount of work with little to show for it.

TOVE: And then there was an epiphany. One weekend we received a telephone call from Ottawa (an unusual event), explaining there were four girls on a boat in Bangkok harbour and their brother in Canada was afraid they were going to be raped or sold into slavery. We were told to go and select them.

Logistics were always a stumbling block. Luckily we had a wonderful External Affairs officer in Bangkok who had learned a lot about immigration and did a lot for us because we had no presence there. He managed to receive authority from the Thais to remove the girls from the boat based on our commitment to take them, even though we hadn't examined them yet.

The boat was an old converted oil tanker and it started to sail and was off the coast of Singapore/Malaysia when it broke down. The Singapore authorities would not allow us to bring the girls ashore so we could have them x-rayed for TB. Finally, the doctor and I went out to the ship to interview them, and the doctor did his Mantoux tests and unofficially gave a bit of medical advice. Then he took a lot of photographs of the deplorable conditions on the boat. I received copies of them to send to headquarters where they went right to the minister's office. Those photographs became one of the contributing factors in Canada deciding to have a refugee program. That was the start of the "boat people," with the next big boat being the *Hai Hong*, which arrived in November 1978 on the west coast of Malaysia.

BILL: As time passed, our selection quota gradually increased, so that by early 1978 refugee arrivals were averaging approximately 3,000 per month within our territory. But the boats kept coming and became larger. The first large boat was a converted minesweeper which dropped some people on the Malay coast, with the Malays convincing them to get back on the minesweeper because it would be better if they went down to Singapore. The UNHCR knew the minute they left the shore of Malaysia that they would not be permitted to return, and would not be permitted to land in Singapore. And that's just what happened.

TOVE: The ship was moored by an island off the coast of Singapore and given supplies to look after themselves. If we needed to see someone from the ship, the authorities would bring them to our office. We weren't allowed to board the ship, and the refugees had to remain aboard until ready to depart Singapore.

I made one fascinating trip to an island off the coast of Malaysia. I was travelling with three men: one from the Malaysian Foreign Office, the last Malaysian military attaché from Saigon (with a gun down the back of his pants), and there was a third man. We started in Kota Bharu where the police had one woman and her four kids who had to be interviewed. I think the police were keeping her for their own purposes, but she wouldn't admit to it. From Kota Bharu we drove down the coast to opposite the island where there was an old British rest camp which was reasonably nice. We had lunch there and I was told to leave my luggage as we would sail out to Pulau Perhentian. When we had been sailing for about an hour I was informed that we were not returning to the rest house that night. I had only a little overnight case with me, but in it I kept a 40-ouncer of Scotch because I had learned that if I took a drink of Scotch first thing in the morning I didn't get Delhi Belly. I followed this habit throughout my visits to various hell-holes and never succumbed to intestinal troubles.

This was my first time in an Islamic country and I was cautious and asked, "You said there were no places to stay on the Island, so where are we going to stay tonight?" I was told, "Oh well, some of the refugees are gone, and there are some empty tents and the Australians stayed there," and I thought if the Australians did it, how bad could it be?

When we arrived on the island, there were three small tents on the bare sand. That's it. I said I'd take the middle tent, thinking they would take the ones on the ends. I began to conduct my interviews and looked forward to a grim night but assumed I could get through it. After sundown, the fellow from the Foreign Office told me that it was not safe for me to stay in the tents because some of the refugees were still armed.

There was a rest house on the island which the military had taken over. When I arrived there, I encountered female military, now wearing their sarong kebayas, cooking dinner for the men. I was allowed to sit with the male officers, but none of them spoke to me, except for the lieutenant in charge whose conversation focused on the inferiority of women.

The bathroom in the house was unreal. The bathtub had moss growing in it and comments on the sink or the toilet are best left unsaid. When the men left, one of the girls loaned me a sheet and a bed – she set up a cot for herself. At the crack of dawn, the girls were all in uniform, and I had to return the sheet.

I finished my interviews and the people I was travelling with were fiddling with a couple of refugee boats that they wanted to take to their summer cottages if they could get them going. Eventually we returned to the rest camp to get my luggage, where the managers of the camp wanted to charge me for the night. I was no longer worried about being diplomatic and said, "If you want the money, then you can collect it from those guys. I'm not paying." I hadn't slept there and I wasn't paying.

Back in Singapore, US Immigration had come to do a similar visit and asked for a briefing. Sure enough, the Malays tried the same thing on them. After sailing for an hour, the American was told they would not be going back to the rest house. The US immigration chap told them to turn around because unless he stayed at the rest house that night, the US would not take a single refugee out of Malaysia. Later, the guy from the Foreign Office phoned to ask when I would be making another visit and was told by our administration officer, "Well, after the way you treated her, I doubt that she is coming back, and I doubt that Canada is going to take any refugees out of Malaysia." Magically, our treatment suddenly improved!

BILL: We made comments or promises about our program that Ottawa was unaware of. We sometimes had to threaten to close down if assistance was not provided. As far as Malaysia and others were concerned, we spoke on behalf of Ottawa.

We tried not to become involved with the people we were interviewing. It was emotionally too straining, and we tried to look upon them not as people but cases. Our "cases" saw it differently. Some years after I had left Singapore, I encountered a Vietnamese in Banff who walked up to me and said, "Mr Sheppit, how are you? So good to see you!" I had no idea who he was ... not a clue – but he recalled our encounter.

TOVE: I had the same thing happen to me. On top of Sulphur Mountain in Banff, this young couple came up me and asked whether I was Miss Bording from Singapore. I had just left Singapore and I had interviewed them in Sabah. To them, we were a major turning point in their lives. They always remembered the interviewer.

BILL: And you're God. We were the start of a new life, while from our perspective they're one of thirty or forty or fifty or eighty people that we'd seen that day.

TOVE: I once went down to the Riau Islands where a refugee family had arrived. This was a restricted military area controlled by the Indonesian navy. The prospective interviewees were out in the country right where their little boat had landed, so the military loaded me in a Jeep with two guys and we drove to where this family was. The military wanted to listen to the interview, so I did it in French, and they became disgusted and left – my French was not very good. But the wife and daughter had also held up blankets so that the military couldn't see what we were writing, because they said if the military found out the refugees had anything of value, they would take it. There is no question that this was true.

BILL: Everything we did at the time was a precursor for what happened later.

I did one trip on the east coast with the UNHCR chap, and we were at the hotel having breakfast when he got a call that a boat had landed at such and such place. We were immediately on our way. We hadn't received specific instructions about this group; you just did what was right.

TOVE: Travelling with the UN provided some protection. If you found new arrivals and they wanted to go to Canada, you did the interview, and perhaps later a relative in Canada would emerge – at least a fictitious one. Operations were responsive to the needs – it was really by guess and by go, and you had to make snap decisions.

When I was in this area, it was possible for someone to fly to Thailand to select a child for adoption and complete legal requirements in two or three days. Many of these children were the offspring of US military personnel and local women from the years of the Vietnam War. These mixed-race children were unwanted by the Thais, and the US accepted no responsibility for them. Their futures were bleak at best.

Shortly before I left Singapore, I dealt with one such case that really touched me. Late one afternoon, I received a call from the Singaporean immigration authority informing me that they had detained a man and woman with two children they had just adopted in Thailand. They were all destined to Canada, but the children had no visas and could not be returned to Thailand, as that country would not readmit them. Thailand wouldn't give such children citizenship. I asked that they be allowed to come to our office, which at first was refused. I suggested that the Singapore authorities could hold the adults' passports if we could have forty-eight hours to process the children. On that basis they were allowed into the country, but only for twenty-four hours.

The next morning the two adults with two small children in tow appeared in my office. It turned out that the woman, although living in Canada, was in fact a US citizen, so I had no authority to allow retention of her passport but happily she made no objection. In addition, the adults were not a couple but two friends who had each adopted a child. The children, a little girl of about four and a boy of six or so, settled in a corner and played quietly with a few toys they had along. A call was made to one of our designated doctors, and immediate medicals were arranged for the children. As no x-rays were required, given their young age, this really just amounted to a physical examination, which the children passed. I had the required documents prepared to facilitate the travel – and then the problems began.

In order to arrange for travel, I asked the Singaporeans for a twenty-four-hour extension, which they refused, even though all relevant airlines out of Singapore appeared to be fully booked. A call to CP Air in Hong Kong produced space on their flight, although they too had been fully booked but would bump other passengers to help us out. However, to get to Hong Kong, the children required visas. I phoned my colleagues at the British Embassy, which was already closed for the day. They agreed to help initiate the visas, but then we found we couldn't get a flight to Hong Kong. Then suddenly we found we could get four seats on a Pan Am flight from Singapore to San Francisco, so now it was the US colleagues I called, and they too were prepared to do the necessary, so we were able to get all four on their way. Technically, as far as Canada was concerned, the legality of the adoptions was also questionable, but I sent them all off and advised headquarters to sort it out when they got there, which it eventually did.

Two sweet little children were saved after being rejected, through no fault of their own, not just by individuals but by entire countries.

But you also had to be on the watch for predators. There was one chap who was adopting young boys to start an orphanage in Canada, and he was in Thailand when I met him. He had two thirteen-year-olds in tow so I rejected them, because "orphans" had to be twelve or under. The next time he showed up, the identity cards had been altered so they now claimed to be twelve, but I maintained the refusal. He wrote headquarters a scathing criticism, but when the circumstances of the refusals were explained to Ottawa, it ended the story. Later, the embassy in Bangkok sent a blistering report saying that not only was he so aggressive to the local staff that he had been banned from the embassy but he was also a well-known pedophile. This was the kind of thing you had to watch out for.

BILL: The whole issue of unaccompanied minors became a challenge. Vietnamese families began to send out kids as anchors to allow the entire family to follow later. It was impossible to determine the truth with small children. They might be included in another family of a relative or claim to be an orphan.

Once they reached where they were going, they would turn around and claim to have found their parents, whom they wanted to sponsor. You can't turn them down, so you become harder with these cases initially. The international community ended up relying on the UNHCR to provide guidelines for the care, feeding, and resettlement of unaccompanied minors.

Throughout the time of our operation, we were relying on the goodwill of everybody: the host government, the local officials, the UN, and the Red Cross because they issued travel documents. Any one of them could make your life miserable.

TOVE: To succeed, we had to build good relationships. You had to develop trust with those with whom you interacted. Because of the logistical complexities, we had to rely on those with whom we worked.

When the Canadian sponsorship program was introduced, I found it amazing that the first churches to respond were the Mennonites and Lutherans and not the big church groups. At one point I asked headquarters what the Canadian Council of Churches was offering to do, and I received a reply that said they would offer moral support.

BILL: Yes, the Mennonite Central Committee did a wonderful job. Eventually they had staff working in our embassy in Bangkok, matching refugees with sponsoring groups in Canada.

Singapore was a wonderful place to be based, because everything functioned well and it was a transportation hub for the area. Everywhere else you went was a challenge. I found an old vaccination book of mine that had ten US $10 bills stapled in the back of it that I kept for when I was in Indonesia, just in case you needed to bribe somebody to get something done.

You could drink the water in Singapore. You'd go to Bangkok and I would find myself bargaining for a taxi or tuk-tuk and you're sitting there bargaining for five minutes over 25 cents. But you wouldn't want to lose face, so you bargained. When you returned to Singapore, you hopped into a cab and the driver flipped the meter. You paid the meter rate and tips were not expected. It was wonderful.

One of the nice things we didn't talk about was the joys of interviewing under a tin roof because Thailand in March-April gets to be about 40°C. Under a tin roof, you're just dripping sweat and you'd have your papers on the desk and they'd stick to your arms.

TOVE: During the monsoon season it was like a machine gun going off on the roof.

BILL: Unless of course it *was* a machine gun – that was not uncommon either.

Among the camps, Laem Sing stands out in my memory. It was in an arroyo near the beach, and we used to interview in what was normally the crematorium. The refugees had a sign made which had a fill-in-the-blank section reading, "A warm welcome to the _____ delegation." There were times we worked there when the furnace was still warm from the most recent cremation.

It is telling that in late 1975 the UN office in Bangkok consisted of three people. Within the year, it had grown to more than 150, plus a sub-office in Malaysia. Our growth was nowhere commensurate.

Finally, in early 1978, a new immigration act[2] came into force, along with new procedures for refugee processing. While we had been in discussions for quite some time with Ottawa, I first found out about the new program in a refugee camp. I was greeted with great excitement in Songkhla and was told that Canada had a new program for refugees. The refugees had heard it announced on Voice of America, and I had no idea that it was official.

TOVE: Our work in the early days of the refugee movement was challenging. The hours were incredibly long, the logistics were mind-numbing, the food and accommodations when on trips were barely tolerable. You faced threats to your health, and there was the ever-present danger of being caught in crossfire. But we knew we were making a difference.

I 2

The Canadian Refugee Program in Singapore, 1975–1980

Richard Martin

The best historical evidence is evidence recorded at the time.

Col. Charles P. Stacey, Canadian military historian.[1]

This chapter differs from others in the volume as it was written on the spot as events were unfolding. It was prepared by Richard Martin, a former journalist and visa officer who served at the visa office in Singapore from 1978 to 1980. He arrived just as the two-officer team at E&I Singapore was expected to produce a small number of refugees from an enormous territory including Thailand, Malaysia, Singapore, and Indonesia. He participated in the rapid transformation of E&I Singapore to the largest element of the 1979–80 resettlement operation.

Shortly before his assignment in Singapore ended, Martin took a few weeks in June 1980 to consult the office's policy and operational files and construct a history of refugee operations from the fall of Saigon to the summer of 1980. The report was never forwarded to headquarters, as the high commissioner directed that it be updated and submitted once the program ended in December 1980. However, that appears not to have happened, and Martin's report was quickly forgotten. Happily, David Ritchie, another visa officer serving in Singapore at the time, re- tained a copy and made it available to the authors.

Martin provides a fresh, frank, and unique description of the chal- lenges of working at the front end of Canada's refugee operations in Malaysia and Singapore. He is candid in describing misunderstand- ings between the staff in the field and headquarters, an occupational hazard in operations of this sort, and conveys how difficult it was for officers in the field to stay abreast of trends and public opinion in Canada. The report reveals the grit, initiative, and tough-minded determination required of Canadian officers and managers to meet the constantly rising targets imposed by the government and to complete the selection of 60,000 refugees, of which over 26,000 came through the Singapore operation. The footnotes in this chapter are substantially as recorded by Martin.

Martin's report provides examples of the analysis done by the staff as to where their base of operations should be located and the capacity of various locations to operate as jumping-off points for the refugee airlift. It offers an intimate glimpse into the issues that managers and staff confronted and reveals how and why decisions were made. While the size, scope, and shape of the Canadian commitment was determined in Ottawa, the decisions about how that commitment was delivered rested on the shoulders of the young field managers. The text almost inadvertently illustrates the burden of responsibility borne by two outstanding managers, Ian Hamilton and Al Lukie. It also provides the first and only account of Lukie's decision to shift resources and attention from Malaysia to the refugee camps of Indonesia and describes what it took to secure Indonesian, UNHCR, and ICEM support for the shift. One result of this decision was that Lukie and his staff had to simultaneously coordinate airlifts out of both Kuala Lumpur and Singapore.

This unique account,[2] drawing on many documents that never made it to the national archives, has been lightly edited to eliminate some bureaucratic terminology, but every effort has been made to preserve its original character.[3]

The Canadian Refugee Program in Singapore
1 July 1980

As I write this, E&I Singapore is wrapping up the biggest refugee movement ever undertaken by our government. In conjunction with posts in Bangkok, Hong Kong, and to a lesser degree, Manila and the United States, we will, by November, have delivered more than 70,000 Indochinese to the Canadian community since the fall of Saigon, in April 1975.

Curiously, this program, which at its peak airlifted approximately 4,500 people per month, to a large degree was not envisioned by either planners or politicians. As a matter of fact, this one began without reference to any specific quota or time frame objectives. In consequence of this staged development, completely unlike the department's traditional undertakings – for example, in Hungary and Uganda where the quota and deadlines were known – officers in place in Southeast Asia were obliged to develop a selection, processing, and movement package as events thrust the need to do so on them. This is quite unprecedented in Canadian immigration experience.

The development of this package was largely at the initiative of the Singapore office. Its execution here and at other posts is broadly based on patterns developed in Singapore. Given that instability and forced migration are likely to continue in several world areas in the foreseeable future, it is possible that the operational methods conceived, tested, and initiated here may have to come into usage with some frequency over the next several years.

The following is a record of refugee developments at this post for the most part for the period 1978 to 1980. Hopefully, this record of our experience will be of value to officers being briefed prior to departure on similar assignments to deal with refugee crises as they occur.

Beginnings, 1975–1977

The period from the fall of Saigon in April 1975 until mid-1977 was, in terms of refugee activity, tranquil in Singapore. In 1975, the post sent seventy-six persons displaced by the war in Indochina to Canada. The following year was even quieter, with only thirty-one Indochinese receiving visas. In 1977, the post returned to 1975 levels as seventy-one persons from the refugee camps throughout Southeast Asia began new lives in Canada.

The minimal level of activity outlined above is not surprising given Ottawa's reluctance to get more involved at the time. Immediately upon the conclusion of the war, Canada had deployed immigration officers to Guam and to various refugee processing military bases in the continental United States. Officers assigned to these locations had by mid-1976 selected close to 6,000 persons, almost all of them Vietnamese evacuated by air and sea from Vietnam during the collapse.

By October 1976, Employment and Immigration senior management had reached a consensus that "Canada had done its part in the Indochina problem except perhaps for help with the 'small boats' people if they had relatives in Canada."[4] The continuing problem of displaced Indochinese was regarded as one for the United States to resolve.

Given this perception of the plight of the displaced from Vietnam, Cambodia, and Laos, IDHQ [Immigration Department Headquarters], through to the close of 1976, encouraged a low profile by Singapore's two officers.[5] They were originally directed only to deal sympathetically with Vietnamese boat escapees who had been sponsored or nominated by relatives in Canada. This stance eased somewhat in late 1976 when 180 places which had not been used in the Guam quota were assigned to Singapore for unsponsored refugees.[6] The first priority was boat escapees having Canadian connections but lacking formal sponsorships.

While the department slowly and, it must be said, reluctantly began to accept that the Indochinese refugee problem was not going to go away, the UNHCR with large infusions of American money intensified activity in the area, particularly in Thailand. In November 1976, their Bangkok office, already the largest UNHCR field office in the world, noted that despite a heavy monsoon, more small boat escapees had landed around the South China Sea basin than during any previous month since the fall of Saigon. By mid-December, 4,659 Vietnamese had landed on the beaches of Southeast Asia.

With US and UN pressure for Canadian participation increasing, official reluctance to become involved in the Asian refugee plight eased markedly. While no new quota was proposed, on 12 January 1977, the Asia and Pacific Bureau (IFAP) advised that boat escapees no longer needed to have a connection with Canada in order to be selected.[7] In the same message, and in a much more positive manner than previous communications on the subject, posts were reminded that non-boat escapees, that is, predominantly Cambodians and Laotians, could be selected without quota under the ongoing refugee program.[8]

Unhappily, while this policy change (outlined in two brief paragraphs) marked a quickening of official interest in the region's displaced, Singapore for several more months, possibly through misunderstanding, did not aggressively pursue these new avenues to increase refugee intake, and as a result, the post's level of visa issuance did not respond to expectations in Ottawa. Increasing pressures from the Canadian public and international sources led to some irritation, again it seems not clearly expressed, concerning the lack of results here.[9]

Although selection levels remained low, the first half of 1977 saw the initiation here of operational measures which were to have important effects during the post's refugee build-up in 1978. In January, the OIC [officer-in-charge, i.e., manager] Singapore developed our first agreement to transport refugees from the region at inexpensive rates through facilities to be provided by the Intergovernmental Committee for European Migration (ICEM).

In a related effort one month later, Singapore obtained Ottawa's consent to use ICRC (International Committee of the Red Cross) documentation as travel documents for Canadian acceptances. This document remained key to our transportation system until the spring of 1979, when the sheer volume of airlift to Canada threatened to overwhelm ICRC staff, creating an unacceptable bottleneck that threatened to paralyze the system. To prevent this occurrence, we initiated the use of our visa as a travel document, gaining much greater flexibility and cutting a week off our processing time.[10]

Getting on Track

With the arrival of Ian Hamilton in Singapore in July 1977, a new sense of urgency dominated area refugee operations. Following a pattern that would intensify over the next two years, he and 21C [second-in-charge] Bill Sheppit increased the frequency of area trips, still concentrating heavily on Thailand. Their selection effort paid off very quickly, so that by mid-October "in process" totals threatened to exceed the Vietnamese/Cambodian (VNP/KRP) quotas, obliging IFAP to request that Asian posts less exposed to the refugee outflow release parts of their quota to Singapore.

Ironically, the two officers' success in selection immediately highlighted a remarkable weakness in the refugee processing system and again raised tension between the post and headquarters. The problem involved two factors. First, despite a long-term UNHCR presence in the area, particularly in Thailand, that organization had not yet evolved a system to record selection/processing status of refugees by receiving countries. Second, the Canadian selection system, particularly in relation to medical processing, was far too cumbersome for a refugee operation. The effect of the latter problem was that Canadian cases were in process an inordinately long time before visas could be issued. The effect of the former was that families, once visaed, were found to have departed to another country, which had not been aware that they had already been selected. Ottawa, on the other hand, for a long time not fully cognizant of these problems, and buoyed by ever higher levels of selections, could not understand why greater numbers of refugees were not landing at Canadian airports.

This was a most frustrating period for both officers, during which they repeatedly made exhausting trips to primitive camps; selected large numbers under appalling working conditions; returned to Singapore to complete paperwork and badger the UNHCR for medicals, the ICRC for travel documents; only to discover after months of effort that 90 per cent, and sometimes all, of their selection had left for other destinations.[11]

While Singapore strived to complete the VNP/KRP program, events of a much larger scale gradually overwhelmed the existing international relief effort, fundamentally changing the refugee problem in the South China Sea area. In a development that was not originally perceived as remarkable, Vietnamese boat escapees directly to Malaysia had steadily increased month over month throughout 1977. In all of 1976, only 1,028 small boat escapees had reached Malaysia. By mid-November 1977, however, figures had jumped to in excess of 5,000 arrivals. By September, Malaysian authorities had established major camps in Kota Bharu, Pulau Besar [*sic*] near Trengganu,[12] and in smaller locations within the city limits of Kuantan.

Although the refugee population in Malaysia was not in itself dramatic when compared to the numbers of displaced in Thai camps, the Vietnamese presence, as well as precursing the enormous influx later, had an immediate political impact upon the predominately Muslim and racially sensitive East Coast. Luckily, while selection levels by receiving countries were to this point very low in Malaysia, there was still sufficient international attention to Malaysia's plight to counterbalance calls to prohibit further landings. Throughout the year, the UNHCR steadily increased activity in Kuala Lumpur and, laterally, along the coast. In October, ICEM opened a Malaysian operation, extending their transportation service to European nations, the United States, and Canada.

Following the same pattern, the United States, Australia, and Canada shifted a much greater selection effort to Malaysia.[13]

It was fortuitous that our program build-up in Malaysia through the winter of 1977–78 coincided with the expanding international effort. As a result, our officers were able to influence the operational developments of related agencies and to integrate our own fledgling systems with theirs. In December 1977, we agreed with ICEM that Canada-bound refugees travel via the Pacific only to Western Canada and via Europe to Eastern Canada. This division of Canada at the Manitoba/Ontario border, which remained in effect until our scheduled charter flights began, effectively doubled our capacity to obtain aircraft seats even during peak (Pacific) tourist seasons.

At approximately the same time, medical processing was reorganized with the appointment of roster doctors in Mersing, Kuantan, and Kota Bharu. These appointments, together with the retention of an existing doctor in Trengganu, meant that we were no longer required to schedule refugee medicals with local doctors in Kuala Lumpur. This development alone cut a full month from our processing time in Malaysia.

Finally, in March 1978, the UNHCR implemented an indexing system allowing our and other delegations for the first time to be able to determine which refugees were free for selection and who were already in process by receiving countries. This in turn led to another decrease in our processing time when we agreed that Canadian decisions would not be deferred but finalized at interview and recorded on the blue cards.[14]

To summarize, Singapore's operation in Malaysia by mid-1978 had taken the form that would serve our needs adequately until the introduction of markedly heavier quotas in 1979 required a changeover to present operational methods.[15] In Thailand, however, our program remained minimal, as processing was still beyond our control. Given the distance involved from Singapore and the poor administrative assistance received from supporting agencies, there was little hope that we could improve our efficiency there. Happily, Ottawa in late spring 1978 came to the same conclusion and had initiated steps which by November saw the introduction of an independent E&I operation in Bangkok.

The implementation of the previously described processing methods in Malaysia through the first half of 1978 finally permitted our office to fulfill quota levels in the Small Boat Escapee (SBE) program in July 1978.[16] From this date onward, Singapore has never failed to reach any target or any new quota given by Ottawa.

Once our office reached quota level, the game completely changed. Temporarily freed of the problem of organizing related agencies' co-operation, both officers concentrated on selection activity, establishing a pace wherein each man was in the field for at least eight days per month.[17] Within two months we were, in Malaysia, routinely exhausting our quota and beginning a series of petitions to IFAP for ever-greater numbers. Ottawa reacted by raising our level to fifty families per month through to the end of January, but already this was not enough, and by October, we were routinely telexing Hong Kong and Manila for positions they were unable to fill each month. By late fall, as the availability of more quota positions dried up, our program was being overwhelmed by Canadian applicants among the now 10,000 SBES in Malaysia. To cope with this pressure and to assist the UNHCR, now being overwhelmed by the "Chinese Expulsion" which had quietly begun from Vietnam in October, we began selecting more Chinese ethnics who, with larger family configurations than Vietnamese ethnics, gave us more mileage on our family quota.[18]

None of these measures was successful for very long. Arrivals rapidly outpaced departures as escapees flooded Malaysia's shores. In an effort at least to rationalize the pressure on our "delegation" and to reserve the places we had for where we could do the most good, we introduced two new measures. First, only relatives of Canadian residents would be selected in Singapore.[19] Second, in Malaysia, we would deal on a priority basis with relatives of Canadian residents, interviewing other persons only if quota were available. The first ruling remains in effect, substantially unaltered, today. The second lasted about two weeks, by which time most Vietnamese had located or created relatives in Canada; again we tightened up, this time prioritizing according to closeness of relationship.[20]

Our level of selection activity, emphasizing relatives as it did, soon overwhelmed office staff in [E&I] Singapore. Telex traffic to confirm relationships and to report developments on the coast, together with flight reservations and visa processing, by mid-September routinely obliged twelve-hour days. Visa officers began to complete visa documentation by hand so that our three typists could cope with normal office activity.

Expansion of the Indochinese Program

Our team had barely returned to Singapore when the "back channel" from IFAP warned that bigger and better things were on the way. The office immediately initiated a series of plans to improve refugee selection and movement. Our first proposal, on 11 December, outlined the first phase of our current operating process. In this plan, we suggested, once security was passed (by now about two weeks), that the refugees be moved to Kuala Lumpur where a strengthened team of five local doctors would conduct medical examinations, forwarding the results to [E&I] Singapore. Simultaneously, our office would obtain travel documents, and through ICEM, book blocks of aircraft seats or charter aircraft at the rate of 160–170 seats per month. With this system, we were confident that time from selection to arrival in Canada would drop to seven weeks.

However, by this time, planning in Ottawa was far beyond ours. In a telephone exchange with Ottawa, while not provided with a target figure, we were queried concerning the possibility of increasing selection levels far beyond our planning. Our reply, quoted below [a long telex from Singapore to IFAP, 19 January 1979], broadly established the pattern of selection and movement which is used today:

Logistics (Ground-Air Movement)

Of the options discussed last night by you [Ernest Allen, IFAP] and Ian [Hamilton], i.e.,

(1) airlift from Kelantan, Kota Bharu or another East Coast Airport, or

(2) airlift from Kuala Lumpur;

Option two appears to us to be more advantageous.

Our reasoning is as follows re option (1);

1) Only Kota Bharu has jet capacity and that is limited to feeder planes, e.g., 737s. We doubt whether an international carrier (707, etc.) or even the air force in peace time would consider putting down here. Therefore, Kota Bharu could only stage at great expense to Kuala Lumpur.

2) In any event, Kota Bharu, on the Thai-Malaysia border, is strategically of benefit to movement only from the northern half of the country; i.e., camp Kota Bharu, Pulau Bidong, camp Besar [which is] (closing).

3) Trengganu airport in the centre of the East Coast is well placed to move people from all camps, both north and south. However, it has no radar and reputedly suffers from bad weather conditions (visibility).

4) Also Trengganu from our experience appears to be restricted to non-jets, i.e., a Fokker 747. Again, as in Kota Bharu, we would only have capacity to stage for Kuala Lumpur. Due to plane capacity, this would be more restrictive than Kota Bharu.

5) Other conveniently placed East Coast airports are defunct military strips built for the Second and Insurgency wars. Although we have not substantiated this information, we are told by Malaysian military sources that these fields cannot handle even a C-130.

6) Johore Bharu serves as the commercial strip for southern Malaysia. We believe that the reasoning used in points (1) and (2) stand for Johore Bharu with the further disadvantage that since it is located directly opposite Singapore, it is convenient only to Camp Mersing.

Re Option (2):

1) Kuala Lumpur is an international airport with full jet capacity, ground and maintenance crews, services, fuel, etc.

2) It is convenient to existing transit camps with the capacity to cope with the Canadian movement. Dr Holbrook has inspected these facilities.

3) It is convenient to five local doctors in Kuala Lumpur appointed by Dr Holbrook with a similar movement in mind. Telex 5656 Dec 11 refers.

4) A camp–Kuala Lumpur movement has been ongoing since the beginning of the SBE phenomena on behalf of Canada, the United States, Australia, France, and other countries. The UNHCR, ICEM, and the ICRC, agencies with whom we work and who are necessary to a commercial movement, are very experienced with this system. This experience includes that with large scale charters on behalf of the three major receivers [settlement countries] previously mentioned.

Logistics (Canadian Selection and Processing)

Not having an accurate picture as yet of the scope of the intended program, the following outline is based on the twice-monthly arrival of two hundred–plus capacity planes in Kuala Lumpur. For our purposes, we are predicating regular departures on the second and last Fridays of each month.

(1) Three interviewing officers, serving on a rotational basis, would interview twice monthly. They would be deployed either separately or in a two-man, one-man configuration, depending on camp populations and other factors.

(2) Trips would be for one week at the first of the month and for one week at mid-month, with the object of the first of month team filling the end-of-month plane (30th), and the mid-month team aiming for the following mid-month plane (15th).

(3) Immediately upon acceptance, the UNHCR and Red Crescent would be asked to move our PIS [prospective immigrants] to the Kuala Lumpur transit camp by bus.

(4) Upon their arrival, SBEs would be medically examined, utilizing the roster doctors, Kuala Lumpur labs, and the Canadian in camp x-ray facility.

(5) Either at the time of stage three or stage four, depending on the degree of medical refusal risk we may presume, we would simultaneously:

i. Advise ICEM to prepare AP [transportation loan] estimates, and passenger manifests for the appropriate flight; and

ii. Request travel documents from the ICRC.

(6) Medical reports would be sent by commercial courier once each week (e.g., on Mondays) to NH&W [National Health and Welfare immigration doctors] Singapore.

(7) [Stage] B documents would be sent as usual to the L.O. [RCMP liaison officer].

(8) Once medicals and [Stage] B [results] are received, visas would be issued and forwarded by commercial courier to ICEM. ICEM would, as now, oversee the transit of SBEs to the aircraft.

(9) Regular immigration, administration of the SBE program, advice re arrivals, etc., would be handled by the fourth rotational officer in Singapore.

Singapore – Kuala Lumpur Post

In terms of air, telephone, and telex connections, it is our view that Kuala Lumpur and Singapore are roughly equal.

However, we see genuine operational advantages in remaining in Singapore at least for the present. These advantages are:

(1) Singapore offers superior road communications to and from the East Coast than does Kuala Lumpur. This factor is very important and definitely not to be underestimated. Selection trips call for a north-to-south or reverse series of car trips from one camp to another, beginning or ending at Kota Bharu airport. The north-south roads in Malaysia are definitely superior to and less dangerous than the east-west roads, which must transit the spine of the peninsula.

(2) There already exists in Singapore a local staff of excellent calibre to serve as the nucleus of an increased paper operation. Just as there is internal advantage here, there is also an advantage in that our local staff has "long time established" understandings and cooperative agreements for efficient integration with outside agencies. The importance of this will be appreciated when one considers that the minimum damage (in the short term) which could come out of a transfer to Kuala Lumpur would be our appearance of incompetence to the Canadian public as we, while hiring and training, hiccupped rather than ran smoothly into the new pace.

(3) Given that the SBE phenomena of increased arrivals will continue, we should remain very sceptical that the increased Canadian and other third country efforts will persuade the Malaysians to be any more welcoming to the refugees than at present.

If this comes to pass, then the possibility of major arrivals in Indonesia remains very real. Should such a situation develop, then Singapore remains, as at present, the only post with the geographical position and communications to cope. A Jakarta post makes absolutely no sense in the context of selecting and processing SBE's.

In our view, this concern alone should preclude consideration of Kuala Lumpur as an E&I centre, at least until it is clearly established that Indonesia will not become an area of interest to our Commission.

(4) A final consideration in favour of Singapore over Kuala Lumpur, admittedly quasi-domestic, is that the "plant" of Kuala Lumpur City itself cannot assure its population, including us, of full and continuing phone service; access to the airport in convenient times; health services, etc., to the degree we require. Singapore provides, and probably always shall, these services in a superior manner, which enables our officers to react quickly to those emergencies which have in the past, as they will no doubt in the future, arisen.[21]

Immediately after this communication, the minister on 21 December announced a 1979 quota of 5,000 displaced persons from Indochina.[22] Assuming that Singapore would receive a substantial part of the quota, both officers flew to a monthly UNHCR organizational meeting on 18 January 1979. At this and at separate discussions held immediately afterward, we settled on the operations system, which with only a few subsequent changes, continues in effect in Malaysia. The results of these meetings were telexed to IFAP on 19 January:

Medical Examinations Facilities SBES

Have determined as a prelude to expanded refugee movement from Malaysia, ICEM Klmpr [Kuala Lumpur] has recently installed complete medical laboratory and x-ray facilities in Cheras, one of the current 2 transit centres in Klmpr (a 3rd transit centre is to be constructed and operational by 1 Mar). Total holding capacity of 3 camps approximately 7,000. An additional facility is under consideration for Pulau Tengah Camp in Southern Johore State.

ICEM has advised that their current facilities and staff of 2 doctors and 4 technicians would allow them to handle their present workload (American and small European programs) as well as the expanded Canadian quota of 320 per month. In addition, they feel they could handle double this number on behalf of the Canadian Government should this be required at a future date.

Cases furthered or rejected because of TB could be treated by the Tuberculosis Hospital in Klmpr with each case being transported daily from the transit or new holding centre to the TB centre by the Red Crescent Society until treatment complete. Treatment for positive serology could also be provided by ICEM at the transit camp site.

Our already instituted system of courier service transmission of medical forms, x-rays to Spore [Singapore] and visas to Klmpr can be readily expanded with no problems anticipated. We now completely by-pass Klmpr High Commission in transmission of documents to ICEM with considerable saving of time and man hours.

If we are to continue to use designated private physicians in Klmpr area, we feel volume of increased movement impossible to handle. Have spoken to several DMPs [designated medical practitioners] in Klmpr who feel maximum Canadian immigration workload they could handle per day would be 15 bodies. This would require vast increase of DMPs in area with the logistical problem of transporting small groups of people to various city locations for examination. Malaysian Red Crescent Society (MRCS) who supplies transport reluctant to undertake this cumbersome system with volume we have in mind.

Possibility of supplying Canadian examination facilities/doctors/technicians also impracticable for many reasons, not the least of which is cost. The possibility could exist at worst that the Malaysians would not allow Canadian lab and x-ray equipment to operate on Malaysian soil. At minimum feel this type of operation would be frowned upon by local authorities.

Considering all alternatives would recommend if acceptable to NH&W that the 2 ICEM doctors in the KLMPR transit centres be designated in the usual way as DMPs exclusively for refugee medical examinations. Non-refugee examinations would be handled in usual way by DMPs also appointed in area.[23]

Anticipated Movement – Expanded Program

For purposes of discussion with UNHCR/Red Crescent/Army/ICEM posited following Cdn schedule for expanded program.

(1) Charter planes of 160 capacity on 15th and 30th of each month.

(2) Six-week lead time for first flight.

(3) Upon announcement of operating details by Ottawa immediate selection of 360 people by E&I Spore [Singapore] to assure quote stockpile unquote in transit camps so as to preclude possibility of less than full plane leaving.

(4) Subsequent selection of approx 160 SBEs each two weeks by E&I Spore.

Given the above, the UNHCR/Red Crescent has undertaken to transport to K.L. [Kuala Lumpur] 160 SBEs each two weeks within two weeks of their selection. After "Task Force" discussion, we expect Army will move to assure that necessary buses are available.

ICEM has undertaken to complete and dispatch to Singapore medicals of each group of 160 within 60 hours of arrival in K.L. (See tel before this.) At the same time, ICEM will also arrange travel docs for each group so that upon completion, docs can be matched with visas.

We have undertaken to deliver completed visas to ICEM within one and half weeks of receipt of meds.

Objective is to have persons selected on first of month dispatched to Cda by 30th. All above-mentioned agencies have been advised and accept that Cdn medical furthered/rejected will not meet this schedule.[24]

Once the higher level of selection activity began in January 1979, the pressure to produce ever greater numbers did not ease until well into 1980. No sooner had we settled into a pace designed for 330 departures per month than on 30 January we received telexed instructions to have 1,300 SBEs ready to go by the end of March.[25] By mid-February, despite having lost Hamilton [to illness] at the first of the month, the post had, with the generous assistance of QIS [Quebec Immigration Service] Officer Florent Fortin, some 1,600 persons in process. At the beginning of March, the post confirmed to Ottawa our ability to fill all aircraft assigned here.

However, by this time, both officers and staff were having difficulty in keeping up despite remarkable stretches of overtime (unpaid) and bi-weekly trips to the coast. Needing greater efficiency, we asked repeatedly for improved communication facilities to Canada and for extra manpower. The former was provided immediately, the latter gradually over several months.[26] At our end, we eliminated the use of ICRC travel documents and again modified procedures to cut valuable days from processing times. Early in April, in a break with previous practice of flying medicals forms to ICEM after our selection trips, we began issuing medicals directly to refugee families at the time of their acceptance. This step allowed the Malaysian Red Crescent Society (MRCS) and the UNHCR to identify and prepare to move selectees prior to the receipt of official notice, cutting processing time by perhaps one day. Further, with these forms in hand, Canada-bound refugees were easily identifiable by ICEM doctors at Kuala Lumpur reception centres. This in turn meant that Vietnamese could be directed immediately to medical examination, saving another four to five hours, and a further day later when the completed medicals were flown to Singapore.[27]

Major Expansion of Singapore's Operations

In July 1979, several factors came together to significantly change both the scope and style of the Canadian operation in Singapore. Reacting to the enormity of the refugee problem in the South China Sea area and the strong sympathy within Canada, the Canadian government answered with a further intake of 50,000 Indochinese. Singapore was assigned 8,800 departures for the period 1 August to 31 December 1979, and a further 14,000 from January to 31 October 1980.

To facilitate this vastly increased program, the department negotiated the establishment of CFB Longue-Pointe, Montreal, and CFB Griesbach, Edmonton, as refugee processing centres to which all Canadian acceptances would be destined. Further, the officer staff and clerical support so long requested by this office began to come available.

While these things were developing, office organization and work roles underwent substantial changes which were generated by newly arrived OIC Al Lukie. Through Hamilton's tenure as OIC, Singapore's main preoccupations had been twofold. First, quotas had to be achieved and maintained; secondly, it had been necessary to establish a highly efficient system of selecting, processing, and moving refugees to aircraft. These goals had been met, but given our manpower, it was basically a seat-of-the-pants operation that probably could not maintain the pace for much longer.

Lukie's problem was to establish office systems, already informally in place, and field selection procedures, and develop a manpower utilization plan that would ensure our capability to exceed present processing volumes over a sustained period of time.

To accomplish these goals, office personnel were formally divided according to major functions so that individual officers and alternates were made responsible for selection activity, sponsorship, and other special case matching, and transportation. Further, reflecting a massive movement of refugees to Indonesia over recent months, selection and processing activity in that country and Malaysia were completely separated, each country being assigned to an operations officer. While these basic operational plans were being put into effect, OIC Lukie, hampered by the need to train large numbers of office staff, temporary duty officers, and, gradually, permanently assigned officers, initiated a field rotation system designed simultaneously to give all officers broad field experience yet allowing them to be in Singapore at least two weeks per month.

Despite these complexities, the post moved smoothly into the new selection pace, reaching record "in process" figures by late August, and maintaining month after month aircraft departure levels that would have been impossible as late as July. While we did accomplish our goals, the change of pace was not at all easy. Two factors now developed that forced our staff to a level of processing activity which had never before been required. Firstly, previous experience with monsoons in Malaysia had taught us that refugee transport from island camps was nearly impossible. Yet our aircraft schedule from Malaysia called for very substantial levels of departure at the height of the season in late October and November. To combat this, officers were obliged to select and move to Kuala Lumpur some 4,000 people by late September. The second development complicated this need immensely. Prior to late June 1979, tuberculosis had been only a minor problem among Canadian cases. Except in the most serious instances, our practice had been to render the ill non-contagious and use the Minister's Permit procedure to send them to Canada for follow-up. In June this procedure was rescinded, with the result that, by early fall, we had in the area of 350 TB cases tying up indefinitely some 1,500 in our transit camps.[28] The camp, designed for 1,800 persons, through the fall of 1979 held up to 4,000 Vietnamese destined for Canada.

Indonesia

Until April 1979, when Small Boat Escapee arrivals in Indonesia slipped over 5,000, E&I Singapore largely ignored developments there. Officers from Singapore had gone to refugee camps in Riau Province twice in the autumn of 1978 and once in the spring of 1979, each time selecting small numbers of Vietnamese. Aware that the United States and Australia were quietly selecting from the small community of perhaps 2,000 refugees, hardly any of whom had a connection with Canada, our office saw no practical reason to take any major initiative there.

However, once Malaysia in the spring of 1979 began pushing enormous numbers of Vietnamese back to sea, the situation in Indonesia changed dramatically. In May, 12,000 persons arrived on her shores. The influx did not slacken until late summer, by which time there were some 50,000 persons on the beaches of Riau Province. This change automatically meant that E&I Singapore had to develop a substantial presence in Indonesia to contend with the large numbers of people who wished to go to Canada or in whom Canada had an interest.

While we did draw upon our experience in expanding Malaysian operations in early 1979, the problems posed by Indonesia were unique. From our experience with small selections previously, we knew that an evacuation of large numbers through Jakarta was a most unlikely proposition; therefore Singapore had to be developed as our "air-base." This in turn meant that refugees, already spread over nine locations, separated in some cases by miles of sea, had to be transported to Singapore by boat. Finally, the infrastructure of Indonesia itself had to be quickly developed so that our officers could interview and process refugees in adequate numbers to maintain an airlift.

The first part of our problem was quickly solved on 28 May 1979, when Singapore, in a secret undertaking, agreed to allow Canada to transit up to 430 refugees, enough for a Boeing 747, for a maximum of two weeks. This understanding was conditional on our using Singapore facilities, other than for direct boat-aircraft transit, only when absolutely required.[29]

With this agreement in hand and with Malaysian operations running very well, we were free to organize in Indonesia. Throughout our transition period of July and early August, we waited, constantly barraging the UNHCR, ICEM, and Indonesian authorities, hoping for an indication that they would quickly establish the infrastructure on which a Malaysian-type operation could be based. By mid-August, it was apparent that without sufficient pressure from us, refugees in Indonesia were to remain out of reach for the indefinite future.

Realizing this, the office initiated an aggressive posture designed to impress Indonesia authorities with the seriousness of Canadian intent and to force related agencies through example into effective levels of activity. At the end of the month, the OIC dispatched a large selection team to the camps and initiated a series of Canada/agency meetings designed to immediately create adequate processing and transport facilities. By mid-September, we had established our operating plan:

> In past two weeks, E&I Officers have been in Tanjung Pinang. On first trip, approx 1,050 SBES were selected. On 2nd, efforts were made to assist UNHCR and ICEM in administering/expediting Canadian interest departures. Our intention is to effect departure of SBES at a rate of one plane/week; i.e., 190–300 persons per week via Spore. If experience with current selectees successful, will accelerate departure rate up to maximum of 3–400 persons per week using as many planes as necessary.
>
> Serious processing problems exist however:
>
> (A) ICEM, who handle both our transportation and medical examinations, can presently with a staff of two doctors examine only two hundred people per week. We are pushing for a third doctor and soonest deployment of two x-ray technicians.
>
> (B) ICEM does not yet have an x-ray facility. The machine is now in Spore and is scheduled to be sent to Tanjung Pinang within next few days. We anticipate that Indon[esian] customs may not be willing to extend duty free privileges, thereby delaying establishment this eqpt. US had made reps on this matter to MFA in Jkrta [Jakarta] and to Colonel Arifin, Defence Attache, Indon Emb, Spore. We have made similar approach.
>
> (C) UNHCR OIC Allan Simmance claims that UNHCR now has four x-ray machines in Tanjung Pinang. We have not been able to confirm this.
>
> (D) Of necessity, our selections on Bintan are spread through nine camps. Logistics to most camps are abysmal. We have therefore devised departure plan whereby SBES in Unggat, Air Raya,

Kilang (all in Tanjung Pinang area) will be medically examined
and evacuated first. We intend subsequently to use places vacated
in these camps to leapfrog SBEs from outlying camps into three
camps mentioned and to Cda. This is to expedite medical processing and assure availability of bodies for transport to Cdn
planes. This plan in line with Indon wish to depopulate and close
outlying camps but not in line with their wish that Viet population near Tanjung Pinang be reduced. Plan (1) removes Cdn interest from outlying camps, (2) due to leapfrog does not increase
Tanjung Pinang population, merely keeps it constant, (3) ultimately leads to reduction in Tanjung Pinang area in last stage of
our movement, (4) entire operation including anticipated future
selections in two more Bintan camps will be completed within
two months of the establishment of medical facilities. That is,
refugee population will be reduced by 1,300–1,400 persons on
Bintan if Indon co-operates on this matter. We believe it important for plan to succeed and to improve Indon morale generally
that small countries such as Cda and Australia be seen to effect
rapid departures. Australia has SBEs ready to go but sitting in
Unggat. We have asked them to move these people as soon as
possible. We are anxious, once next selections have exhausted
Cdn interest in Bintan (next two weeks), to divert heavy selection
interest to Galang. In this regard, doing all possible to encourage
deployment of UNHCR x-ray capability to Galang immediately.
As a poor second, we will settle for assured large volume access
to x-ray facilities in Tanjung Pinang. In this matter, we are alone
as the US does not anticipate they will require x-ray in Galang
until December. We need it now. We will undertake large scale selections in Galang (introductory paras refer) immediately medical facilities are in place. We are encouraging in every way
Indonesian transfer of Viets from Anambas to Galang.[30]

By mid-October, having applied tremendous pressure to supporting
agencies and to Indonesian authorities, the Canadian program was
off the ground. Our first two aircraft, cleared in the following telex,
left for Canada at the end of the month:

Wish to confirm that the completion of our last organization/
selection trip in Indonesia Oct 12, this post confident that full

scale selection/transportation should now be undertaken from Indonesia via Spore.

Team transport problems are solved with decision of Indon Navy to provide our del[egation] fast boats on request.

Refugee transport facilities are established by ICEM and have been tested in company with Cdn Officer.

Medical facilities are adequate, ICEM has the capability to undertake medicals at rate of up to 200 persons per day. System has been tested and proven. Indonesian Red Cross has guaranteed to provide 100 x-rays/day for Cda on demand. We already received up to 100/day from combination of general hospital and ICEM facilities. NH&W doctor happy with quality. Based on approx 1,000 meds received pass rate is approx 90 percent.

All agencies, including Indon civil and military, very co-operative at moment.

UNHCR/Indon Navy have reacted quickly to list submitted last week of Cdn "special cases." Navy dispatched ship Thursday to bring people to Galang/Bintan area from Anambas.[31]

In terms of selection, our rapid entry into Galang has put us in good position vis-a-vis the Australians and the US, making possible higher qualify selection than we have been accustomed to in recent past in Malaysia.

While we cannot guarantee that UNHCR will deliver Viets from Anambas to Galang rapidly enough to keep abreast of Cdn, US, Australian selections, present indications are that they will do so for foreseeable future. In any event, we have a back-up plan ready to present to UNHCR which will allow us to deploy officers to Anambas while ensuring rapid processing. Must emphasize that we see no need to deploy to Anambas at this time.

In summary, Indonesia, with 42,000 mostly unselected refugees and an in-place processing system, is a viable proposition for E&I Spore.

Malaysia, on the other hand, which has been the beneficiary of continuing endeavors by resettlement countries, now (according to most recent information from camp committees and other sources) has no more than 6,000 unselected SBEs, some of whom we expect we have already refused repeatedly as not likely to establish successfully in Cda. In our estimation, further concerted effort will be rather unproductive in the context of the rapid processing system which we have put into place.[32]

Our understanding has been that we were to make every effort to achieve an equitable distribution between Malaysia and Indonesia. Previous telexes such as yourtel log 2379 Sept 19 have supported this understanding by giving us the authority to divert aircraft to meet this objective (as long as you were given sufficient advance notice).

With the above in mind, in our negotiations with Indonesian officials in return for assurances of co-operation and support, we have assured them that we will make every effort to effect up to 1,000 departures per month through 1980. This, of course, pre-supposes that the situation does not change drastically and that Vietnam does not re-open the floodgates. It was considered that the Malaysian movement would be gradually scaled down as the Indonesian movement increased.[33]

Conclusion

With our Indonesian operation established by October 1979, E&I Singapore operations in both this country and Malaysia have settled into a regularly scheduled series of selection trips timed to move refugees not suffering health problems to Canada in about six weeks. While this average has not always held true, the lag has usually been due to periodic over-selections designed to guarantee the security of our movement through periods of rough sea conditions, etc., rather than to our inability to move quickly.

The system we have created has in any given months selected thousands of people in either country in a matter of weeks and loaded equally large numbers onto aircraft. Similarly, the flexibility of both operations has allowed us to shift at will from area to area in response to escapee or host government requirements without losing momentum.

The same flexibility will permit personnel here to expand or contract the movement of Indochinese to Canada on short notice as has been required of us in the past, and as will be required of us for the foreseeable future, at least until the termination of the IRP Program.

13

Singapore: Visas, Mounties, and Medicals

As the government increased the Canadian resettlement commitment from 5,000 to 8,000 to 50,000 between December 1978 and July 1979, CEIC, the RCMP, and Health and Welfare deployed additional officers to Singapore. Many were there on normal rotational assignments of two years, while others moved through the office on temporary duty for a few months. The accounts in this chapter record a remarkable effort to achieve Canada's commitment.

Several of the officers involved during this period have recorded their reminiscences of those hectic and rewarding days. E&I Singapore became the operational hub for the refugee operation in Malaysia and Indonesia and, until November 1978, Thailand. Tove Bording and Bill Sheppit were succeeded by Ian Hamilton and Richard Martin, whose assignments coincided with a gradual increase in Canadian refugee selection activity. The operation changed suddenly and dramatically following the media coverage of the *Hai Hong* affair, which acted as a catalyst to change Canadian public perceptions of the plight of Indochinese refugees.

Ian Hamilton was then succeeded by Al Lukie, a tough, no-nonsense, natural leader who proved to be an organizational genius as head of the operation from mid-1979 to 1981. While the success of the Singapore operation rests with the toil and achievements of the many officers who worked with little rest while confronting health risks and other threats to their lives, particular recognition must be given to Lukie. Richard Martin, who served with him, paints a brief but articulate portrait of Lukie's contribution to the success of the Singapore operation:

I have no idea of Al Lukie's skills as an immigration officer. Never once have I watched him work in that capacity. However, he was a splendid, natural manager. His ability rested on being able to recognize where he could contribute immediately, i.e., in exchanges with Ottawa, colleagues, foreign officials. Similarly, where he could not be at full speed – say, in the nuts and bolts of a seat-of-the-pants, evolving situation – he demanded thorough briefings, allowed others to speak for the Canadian side at meetings, and learned from what he heard. He was astute, assimilated information quickly, and always learned. By the time he had all the reins, I felt certain he knew the refugee operation in all respects. Also, he had the bonhomie to grease all this with lashings of booze and food at his house. He knew what his people were going through to ensure the success of the mission, and he was determined to ensure that they understood that they had his support and respect.[1]

What follows in this chapter records the experiences of some of those on the ground during those hectic days.

Singapore, Spring 1979

GERRY CAMPBELL

On a cold February day in Ottawa in 1979, I was sitting at my desk at CEIC Headquarters when I overheard the director general, Foreign Branch, Joe Bissett, and the director of personnel, Bill Sinclair, speaking about the need to find someone to go out to Singapore immediately on TD [Temporary Duty] to replace Ian Hamilton, who had been placed on sick leave.

I immediately volunteered (it only dawned on me as I began drafting this text many years after the event that I was probably set up by Joe and Bill, who were well aware of my aversion to spending time in Ottawa). I got my vaccinations updated at the Health and Welfare Overseas Medical Unit, and in a matter of a few days found myself on a flight to Hong Kong en route to Singapore, carrying with me in my bag a list of about eight charter flights scheduled to commence landing in KL [Kuala Lumpur] within two weeks or less of my arrival.[2] And so, for the second time in my career, I was sent out on short notice on a TD refugee program assignment halfway around the world to a place located almost on the equator.

I assumed responsibilities from Ian, who was more than hospitable despite the circumstances of his illness, and found a well-managed operation in place but with a limited number of Vietnamese refugee cases in process due to the relatively small selection quota previously assigned to missions in Hong Kong and Southeast Asia. Because of the small existing refugee quota, E&I Singapore was not prepared to deal with a substantial and immediate increase. The first challenge was resources; the decision to increase the Canadian target for Indochinese refugees to 5,000 places under Canada's first annual refugee plan occurred so quickly that authority had not been provided to missions to augment their staff. After briefing the head of mission, Robert Thomson, and despite the fact that visa operations abroad were at that time managed by CEIC rather than External Affairs, the high commissioner instructed his administrative officer to provide funds to hire temporary staff immediately. He deserved full credit for his decisive action in advance of formal authorization. That decision ultimately facilitated the speed with which E&I Singapore was later able to respond to the expanded refugee operations.

Along with Rod Fields and Dick Martin, who were already assigned to E&I Singapore, we headed off almost immediately after my arrival to Malaysia to select thousands of Vietnamese from the camps located along the east coast and on the offshore islands of Pulau Bidong and Pulau Tengah. On some of these trips we were accompanied by QIS [Quebec Immigration Service] officers Florent Fortin and Gerry Power, who were responsible for selecting refugees destined to the Province of Quebec. Cooperation was very close with our QIS colleagues, and we mutually selected refugees with connections or linguistic abilities for each other's programs.

These selection trips lasted up to a week at a time and started by flying through KL to Kota Bharu up in the northeast coast of peninsular Malaysia, and travelling down the east coast by car through Kuala Terengganu and Kuantan and back to Singapore through the land crossing at Johore Bharu. Kuala Terengganu provided the base for travel by local boats to the island refugee camps on Pulau Bidong, and Kuantan did the same for Pulau Tengah. At that time, the facilities along the east coast were underdeveloped, with the hotels very basic, or non-existent in the case of Bidong and Tengah. There were inland refugee camps at Kota Bharu and other locations on the mainland, but some were mainly transit camps for refugees already in process, pending medical and security screening. Boats were arriving constantly from Vietnam off the east coast and were either redirected or towed to two main islands offshore. The island of Bidong was overloaded with some tens of thousands of Vietnamese, their abandoned boats drawn up and beached on the sand. Aside from rudimentary shelters, there were no other facilities: no running water, toilets, or electricity.

We took local Malay boats to the island through rough seas and had to wade ashore on Bidong carrying our files and other documents above our heads. We worked as a team all day long and well into the night using kerosene lamps to select and process as many refugees as our limited time in a camp would permit. The heat and humidity were intense, amplified by the open working conditions and clamouring crowds of Vietnamese refugees, all hoping for a chance to get their families away from the terrible conditions in the camps as soon as possible. Pulau Tengah was slightly less intense, with a long open dock, and equally open latrines built of planks over the water. Our selection team was the first ever to stay overnight on Tengah, sleeping on tables under mosquito netting with rats running around below. It was a relief to return to the mainland and the one-star, Chinese-run hotels, the only places that were not "dry" in the staunchly conservative Muslim communities along the east coast. (The UNHCR representative, based in Terengganu, apparently ran afoul of strict religious observations and was forced to leave.) The trips were gruelling and exhausting. After long days in the camps, our return to Singapore was as welcome as arriving at an oasis in a desert.

Although during the early days of the Vietnamese exodus there were many refugees who were highly qualified with good linguistic skills in both English and French, we still had an unprecedented degree of flexibility in the selection of refugees. The sole criterion was their ability to establish successfully in Canada within a reasonable period of time – notionally within one year. The successful establishment criterion was applied with the utmost flexibility, taking into account the strengths of the entire family unit. In practice, it was applied more in reverse; only those cases that might have required long-term assistance were rejected, and many of these were subsequently sponsored by groups in Canada willing to take on cases that needed a longer-term commitment. At the same time, due to their close connections with the former South Vietnamese government or the Americans, many South Vietnamese had departed their homeland, often with impressive training and experience. I recall in particular helicopter mechanics trained in Texas who spoke English with a Texan drawl.

The challenges that E&I Singapore faced were significant for the staff and daunting logistically. From the moment that the Canadian government announced its decision to increase the Indochinese refugee quota from 5,000 to 8,000 in June 1979, we were under tremendous pressure to select a sufficient number of refugees to fill two dozen or so charter flights scheduled to begin arriving in Kuala Lumpur in short order.

Taking into account the primitive conditions in the camps, the large number of children, and the compelling humanitarian factors, our overriding objective was to approve as many refugee cases as possible. The selection acceptance rate probably approached 100 per cent at this time. From this historical distance, I cannot recall ever rejecting a single case on either Pulau Bidong or Pulau Tengah. The circumstances in which the refugees found themselves were truly appalling. The boat refugees had risked their very lives by embarking in leaky boats travelling on rough seas, evading pirate attacks, and then often being intercepted or towed back out to sea through the surf by Malaysian naval vessels. Some drowned in the process. The lucky ones made it to shore only to face the challenge of surviving on limited food and little water or medicine on the offshore islands where few amenities or shelters existed.

The selection of large numbers of cases had to be done rapidly over the first few weeks in order to feed the refugee movement pipeline and put enough cases in process to fill the looming flights. One lesson taken from my time in Kampala was that no matter what the circumstances, it was imperative to fill every seat on every charter flight: failure to fill flights, no matter what, triggered negative media coverage and political fallout. It was fortunate that ICEM [Intergovernmental Committee for European Migration, now the International Organization for Migration or IOM] was already on the ground in Malaysia, and arrangements were put in place for ICEM to manage the movement of selected refugees from the offshore islands and other refugee camps to transit centres set up in concert with (or by) the Malaysian government. ICEM, under the direction of Norwegian Hans Petter Boe, was a highly effective and reliable operational partner. With excellent planning and logistical preparations by all partners, despite the intensive schedule, the charter flights were filled to capacity.

Lessons Learned and Applied

After my two months of temporary duty in the Singapore region, Ian Hamilton was finally cleared to return to active duty, and I (reluctantly) returned to Ottawa, where I was immediately called upon to brief senior management on the situation. There was a great deal of interest in this high-profile operation and the challenges on the ground. It was clear that the operational circumstances obliging us to conduct selection interviews through interpreters under difficult conditions left little time for anything other than dealing with the multiple documents and other requisite bureaucratic formalities. This situation triggered a strong and supportive response from CEIC Deputy Minister Jack Manion and Assistant Deputy Minister Cal Best, who instructed headquarters staff to come up with a simplified process and single form that covered all requirements.[3] A new combined visa form that listed all family members was devised, designated, and deployed in a compressed time frame to all missions in the field dealing with Indochinese refugees. This form, the IMM1314, was a unique and remarkably non-bureaucratic initiative that saved immense time and effort in our field operations.

I returned to Ottawa around mid-April and subsequently was asked by Bill Sinclair, head of personnel, to return to Hong Kong to manage the Indochinese Refugee Program (IRP) out of E&I Hong Kong as deputy program manager under John MacLachlan. Somewhat ironically, given my subsequent career in the Foreign Service, I was a little reluctant to take this assignment after having spent time in Singapore, but Bill was always a highly persuasive personnel manager. I arrived in Hong Kong in July 1979 and ran the IRP in Hong Kong and Macau from then until November 1982, followed by two more postings there, the last as consul general, in what has long been acknowledged to be one of the most fascinating cities in the world.

Singapore and Region, 1979–81

DAVID RITCHIE

My introduction to Singapore in April 1979 was as the first of the many incremental resources sent to support the brave but exhausted two-man team of Ian Hamilton and Dick Martin. Within a week, Ian took me on my first refugee selection trip up the east coast of peninsular Malaysia. I reported the details (somewhat gloatingly) to my former officer-in-charge back in The Hague. As my letter to him reads, "I visited 5 camps in 4 days – 2 planes, 600 miles driving, 10 hours by boat on the South China Sea with 598 refugees selected for Canada."

In the next two years, I averaged a similar refugee interviewing trip every second week. How did we do it? It helped to be young and adventurous. However, I have never forgotten the advice given to me by Ian on that first trip. Selecting immigrants based on Designated Class Regulations was entirely new to me. Selecting individuals and families, largely via interpreters, from amongst thousands of boat people in an equatorial jungle island setting was mind-boggling. Mundane selection standards, such as family connections, language ability, and sponsorships of various sorts, were obviously necessary and important, but Ian's advice remained essential. He told me, "Choose them by the sparkle in their eyes."

Such a standard is at the core of a truly humanitarian program. The E&I Singapore program covered the far-flung archipelago of the island nations of Malaysia, Indonesia, and Brunei. As Ottawa gradually stepped up E&I Singapore's Indochinese Refugee Program team to as many as ten visa officers, three RCMP liaison officers, two National Health and Welfare doctors, and one Quebec immigration officer, it became a revolving door of comings and goings from Canada, and comings and goings from the camps. There was always someone new to introduce to the constantly changing field conditions. Over and over, we learned to trust our instincts when assessing the aptitude for Canada of the refugees before us.

I visited more camps than most. I saw the situation at its worst and witnessed the gradual improvements as selection countries, host countries, donor countries, and international agencies like the Red Crescent, the UNHCR, and the Intergovernmental Committee for Migration got organized.

In early 1979, there were dozens of refugee encampments in our region, many of them close to where the boat people made original landfall. Camps were in isolated backwater jungle areas, on previously uninhabited islands, and even in internationally disputed territory such as the Anambas Islands. Camps were in a flux of closure and relocation. Host countries marshalled their militaries to move refugees and consolidate them into larger and larger groups. On the sly, some militaries did what their foreign ministries hotly denied, and pushed off the boats, either to meet their fate at sea or wash up on someone else's beach.

When I made my initial selection trip along the eastern coast of peninsular Malaysia, there were an officially estimated 10,000 refugees. This number was not accurate. Of the two northernmost camps I visited, one would be closed within months. Penkalan Chapas (est. 3,000 refugees) remained a beachside encampment outside the Malaysian town of Kota Bharu, quite close to the Thai border. Cherating (est. 7,000 refugees) was an equally dirty, sand-flea hellhole behind barbed wire outside the Malaysian city of Kuantan. On a later trip to this camp, we heard of a young girl who had died overnight. Within an hour of our departure, the camp was medically quarantined, as the death was found to be a case of infectious meningitis. I have a handwritten list compiled by the Camp Committee's refugee volunteers. It lists the camp's inhabitants by their boats – all Vietnamese boats having a marine registration number prominently painted on their bows. At that point, Cherating's population consisted of 483 boats. Five of these boats had arrived during the past week. One boat, carrying seventy-nine people, arrived while we were interviewing refugees. Official numbers were consistently underestimating the reality we faced on the beaches.

The other two camps on that initial field trip included the famous island camp of Pulau Bidong. It was originally a two-and-a-half-hour one-way trip by leased Malaysian fishing boat from the city of Kuala Terengganu, and later, only an hour's travel by UNHCR motor launch. Bidong (est. 40,000 refugees) was much visited by Canadian VIPs and media. I escorted a CTV W5 crew and print reporters from the *Vancouver Sun* on such excursions. The island rose from shark-infested waters (yes – we saw the fins during transit) like a bald man's dome with the few remaining scraggly hairs represented by the few remaining palm trees. Blue plastic lean-tos followed meandering paths and tiny streams up the mountainside. I will not divert here into too many Bidong reminiscences; suffice it to say that we survived our long days with endless Chinese tea and instant noodles. At night, we sometimes slept on the same wooden tables at which we interviewed rather than face the rough sea journeys back to the mainland. On one such occasion, I lucked into the improved accommodation in the camp's wooden hospital. I was fortunate to get an upper bunk to avoid the rat traffic, which continued all night long. I do remember waking up to the camp's PA system wishing everyone a "good morning" in Vietnamese, Chinese, Malay, English, and French. Refugee volunteers brought us breakfasts of instant Nescafé and warm baguettes freshly baked over a wood fire in a metal cookie-tin oven.

The most southerly Malaysian camp (est. 10,000 refugees) was on the smaller island of Pulau Tengah, an hour off the coast from the Malaysian fishing port of Mersing. Tengah was a smaller, greener, quieter Bidong, which somehow kept just a touch of its original beauty. It had a fine, white-sand beach that might have suggested a tropical resort. Instead, the beach was littered with the rusting hulks of Vietnamese boats, many of them towed and dumped there by the Malaysian navy. At some risk, I surreptitiously photographed that navy towing a fully loaded Vietnamese boat *away* from the safety of the camp and escorting it southwards in the direction of Singaporean territorial waters. On another occasion, while over-nighting in Mersing and dining at the home of the UNHCR's local program officer, we were roused by one of his Malaysian employees to rush down to an isolated nearby beach. As we pulled up to the edge of the sand, our car headlights illumined a Vietnamese boat wallowing in the shallow surf. Dozens of young Vietnamese men began to shout their names, and the boat's registration number and home port. None of them dared venture out of the water. A lone Malaysian army private, gun in one hand and walkie-talkie in the other, stared at us in total shock and clearly took in the CD (Diplomatic Corps) on our licence plate. Whatever Malaysian authorities might have done under cover of darkness, that plan was now scotched. By dawn, a frigate was escorting the Vietnamese to Pulau Tengah. We Canadians were in the right place at the right time, and while we let the UN worker do most of the talking, I like to think that this was an unrecorded victory for Canada's "quiet diplomacy."

By late 1979 and early 1980, the E&I Singapore office was spearheading the establishment of a similar large-scale operation, selecting, processing, and transporting refugees out of Indonesia. Where once as many as nine camps had existed in that country, we were in the forefront of prodding and pulling Indonesia into centralizing a refugee population of 50,000 or more and building an infrastructure to permit our operation to work efficiently.

On the ground, I took part in two early aspects of this effort. One of these was to go to the neighbouring Indonesian province of Riau where the Indonesian government had been induced with international assistance funds to begin construction of a massive new camp and processing centre to be known as Galang. The Singapore government had quietly assented to the transit of selected refugees to board Canadian charters directly out of Singapore, and now we had to prime the pump and demonstrate to both governments our very serious intent. Galang was within a few hours' transport by boat to Singapore's bustling modern metropolis. By contrast, the nearest Indonesian town, both to Singapore and Galang, was the seedy old smugglers' port of Tanjung Pinang (TJP). Much of TJP was built on stilts out over the water. The coastal tidal flow was all that existed in terms of plumbing facilities. In this very rough-and-ready fish, lumber, and smuggling town, the refugee program was a whole new opportunity to turn a profit. TJP became our local base of operations, to the point that we jokingly established membership in the totally imaginary Royal Tanjung Pinang Yacht Club. The club did issue a very cool T-shirt with its membership fee.

On the first of my many trips to TJP and the growing plywood city of the huge, purpose-built camp of Galang, one of the UNHCR representatives convinced the RCMP liaison officer Dick Hawkshaw and me to interview a small number of refugees who had been left behind in a now-abandoned camp somewhere else in Riau province. We travelled by boat and then by a four-by-four vehicle deep into uncut tropical forest. At our destination, waist-high grass and creepers had reclaimed most of the old camp. The exception was the shelter, which was now home to the one hundred or so poor souls being nursed by the Indonesian Red Crescent for a variety of infectious diseases that prevented them from being moved to join Galang's growing population of 44,000. I remember that Dick and I, and the two refugee assistants (clerk and interpreter) who came with us, had to machete the entire open-air shelter that was to act as our interviewing area. Dust and flies and perspiration filled the equatorial air. None of us dared wipe the sweat from eyes, lips, or nose all day long, since most of our applicants were suffering from highly contagious conjunctivitis. Somehow we all escaped without succumbing to "pink eye." However, my medical luck ran out in TJP, when the wrong mosquito infected me with dengue fever. We normally took old-fashioned quinine tablets to ward off the more serious disease of malaria, but dengue fever put me on my back for a week.

In the waning months of my two-year posting, the E&I Singapore office turned more and more of its attention to Galang. This purpose-built camp was indeed a small city, with military-style wooden barracks row upon row on both sides of a shallow valley. On one hilltop, a Buddhist temple was built. On the other was a non-denominational Christian church. In between, actual kitchens and canteens were constructed for refugees and visitors. Refugees enjoyed running water, electricity, gyms, barbershops, libraries, and language labs. These were necessary because some of them would face many years of frustrating waiting before the United States permitted them entry. For those folks without close family in the United States or close affiliation with the former South Vietnamese regime, Canada and Australia beckoned with the opportunity to begin a new life.

Back in Malaysia, I made a one-man, one-time trip for the same reasons that we had visited Kuku (see below). I travelled to the East Malaysian city of Kota Kinabalu on the north coast of Borneo. When I arrived in Kota Kinabalu, I was directed to the chief of police. This tough Muslim insisted that I join him on a bar hop that ended late at night in an establishment where he seemed to receive all the free drinks he wanted. I remember him urging me to "visit" with the bar hostess behind a curtain in the back room, which I declined. Next morning I reported to a government pier at 8 a.m., somewhat hung over and in cut-off shorts and a T-shirt. My host, in full dress police uniform, with his uniformed crew lining the gunwale, ceremoniously welcomed me aboard what looked like a brand-new PT boat. A machine gun graced the launch's foredeck. The police boat quickly delivered me to the island and returned for me in late afternoon, leaving me with only the refugees, without guards or aid workers.[4]

The camp was a hot, rough, and miserable place, just off the sand. The island was still scrubby but lacking any fresh water. There was a small, temporary-looking dock. I was making the visit because several church sponsorships had resulted from an amazing refugee grapevine. On the island I found some delighted boat people sponsored by groups who were already assisting other family members who had recently arrived in Canada. Vietnamese boats had fanned out far and wide across the South China Sea, but the intrepid survivors always amazed me with their efforts to track each other down by boat number, the international grapevine, and old-fashioned mail.

Sponsorships from Canada, both family related and church promulgated, became a driving force as the government continued to match the number of private sponsorships. Because I had quickly become one of the old-timers in the E&I Singapore program, specialty or higher-profile subprograms were sometimes tasked to me. My colleagues kiddingly awarded me the titles of "Officer-in-Charge of Buddhist Monks and of Unaccompanied Minors." My search and selection of the former resulted from a one-off sponsorship from a monastery in Quebec, which had somehow heard that there were monks of their denomination on Pulau Bidong. They were correct, and I found them.

The subprogram for minors was a *cause célèbre*, because the Canadian media had reported that there might be "orphans" – children all alone in the camps. My search for minors became a top priority as sponsorships arrived from Canada from carefully screened Canadian families, who had met strict provincial tests to act as temporary foster families. We had the go-ahead to select as many as 150 of these young people.

In combing the camps for unaccompanied minors, I discovered that very few children were indeed alone. There were some who had been entrusted to the care of uncles or aunts during a risky night-time exodus from Vietnam, but they were best left in the care of their relatives in the hopes of eventual reunification with their parents. What I did find were several hundred unaccompanied young males, who might or might not have been under the age of sixteen. These teens reflected the efforts made by many Vietnamese families to avoid the forced military conscription of their sons. Many tactics were employed to confuse Vietnamese authorities in this regard. Identity documents were traded to exchange an earlier birth date for a later one. This tactic might delay the boy's draft call-up for a while, but in time the falsified birth date would bring up his name on the army's lists. At that point, out of desperation, many poor families were able to save just enough money to bribe the organizer of a clandestine boat departure to take along the one lad. In the camps, the UNHCR had trouble figuring out just who these kids really were and what their actual ages were. I encountered the same difficulties.

I hope that readers will be entertained and not shocked by the fact that I decided for this purpose to employ several former Saigon bar girls as my volunteer refugee clerks and interpreters. They were delightful women who had a shrewd eye and ear for anyone of the opposite gender. I was entertained by their easy way with GI English. Most importantly, I found these women's intuitive knowledge of young males invaluable in assessing the actual physical and psychological age of these young draft dodgers. Documents and IDs held by the young men were next to useless. However, some of these guys, coming from a war-torn country and the wrong side of the tracks, were simply too hardened to fit the expectations of a Canadian sponsor. The kids' reaction to the very attractive women sitting on either side of me told me a lot about their age of development, maturity, and worldliness. In the end, I managed to find several dozens of young guys who were indeed alone in the camps and truly in need of a foster family's love and protection.

I hold the Vietnamese that I encountered in these camps in high esteem. They were not only survivors but survivors with a smile and a positive attitude. They used the long indeterminate waiting period in the camps to their best advantage. They organized camp life to make the very best of a bleak situation. The refugees themselves organized forms of camp government. Elections were held. Committees were formed to ensure public safety, construction, health care, education, sanitation, entertainment, and assistance to the many international agency personnel and foreign delegations (like ourselves) who visited their temporary Vietnamese communities.

I grew fond of the Malaysian island camp of Pulau Tengah. Eventually, the Malaysians stopped bringing new arrivals to Tengah in favour of consolidating everyone in the larger Bidong camp. Near the end of my posting, I made a final area trip to Tengah to unofficially close our selection program there. I worked through the familiar UNHCR blue registration card files one last time, looking for anyone that we might have missed who had some kind of Canadian connection. Sometimes we deferred selection of part of an extended family group in the belief that the family might best be reunified in another resettlement country. Canada believed in family reunification, and, unlike some other countries, refused to knowingly split up families.

Tengah's population had fallen to 3,000 by this point, and, for most of those remaining, it was going to be a long wait for the United States. The refugees knew that this was their personal last chance for Canada. I remember the deep soul-searching by one of my interpreters. He was a bright young accountant who spoke excellent English and had worked with me on a previous camp visit. Based on my casual descriptions of life in Canada, he had studied up on Vancouver between my visits, and in the last hour of the day finally made the decision to present himself to me as an applicant. He put his trust in me and only asked that I please send him "somewhere warm." My photos record the poignancy and sadness as my boat left the camp's dock bound for the mainland. As always, there were brave smiles, but this time they were mixed with tears.

In Singapore itself, I was made responsible for the Hawkins Road camp, a British-built cantonment of two-storey wooden barracks, all neatly arranged, with World War II vintage cannons by the gates. The camp housed refugees rescued by commercial shipping and allowed landing in Singapore on condition that their stay be very brief. It was curious to me that both the UNHCR and the Singaporeans allowed some inmates to leave to shop, visit doctors, and even take on work. This camp was unimportant to our program, although we did take Canadian media and VIPs there because of its proximity, but it was not representative of the harsh conditions elsewhere.[5]

By the end of my two years in the Indochinese Refugee Program, the necessary ingenuity that was forced upon us in the beginning had gradually been transformed into established procedures. I said "no thanks" to extending my posting for another year. I was glad to leave at the peak of an exceptional, adrenalin-fuelled adventure.

The March 1980 Anambas Trip

DONALD CAMERON, DAVID RITCHIE,
AND JOHN MCEACHERN

A number of refugees had wound up on the uninhabited Anambas Islands, ownership of which was contested by several states. Their plight was unique, and Canada intervened to help as many there as possible.

We departed Singapore in a UNHCR chartered helicopter. The three of us boarded it, along with RCMP liaison officer (LO) Ben Soave and a UNHCR official. This was not a pleasure trip, since most of the spartan interior was filled by a very large gas tank for the long over-water flight. Our first stop was Tanjung Pinang, the Indonesian town about fifty miles from Singapore and closest to the largest Vietnamese refugee camp on Pulau Galang. There we cleared Indonesian customs and immigration and took off again for the Anambas Islands, 170 miles away to the north.

Two refugee camps created by the Indonesian authorities were on the previously uninhabited small islands. The Kuku camp had a rudimentary helipad, and we landed there, to be greeted by the Indonesian army officer in command of the camps, UNHCR officials, and the Vietnamese camp committee. We were the first foreign government officials to visit these camps to select refugees for resettlement, so our arrival caused much excitement. The camp population was about 7,000, and some of the people had been there for more than two years.

Interviewing facilities covered in palm-frond thatch had been built for us, and we set to work immediately seeing refugees who wanted to be resettled in Canada. As usual, we asked the UNHCR to refer applicants to us in the order in which they had arrived in the camp. After two days of interviewing applicants from dawn until late at night, we took a Zodiac boat to the much smaller Air Raya camp on a nearby island. There we saw in one day every Vietnamese who wanted to be resettled in Canada. Our principal recollections of that visit are the astonishing clarity of the water, enabling us to see the sea floor far below, and the incredible number of stars we saw in the night sky on the way back. The contrast between the outstanding natural beauty and the distress of the Vietnamese was stark.

After returning to Kuku, we continued interviewing applicants with the goal of seeing before we left every person who wanted to be considered for resettlement in Canada. We knew that it would be some time before another Canadian team would come. And we also learned within minutes of landing that the helicopter that had brought us had a history of mechanical problems and was now officially "broke down" and would be unable to take us back to Singapore.

While the UNHCR worked on an alternative exit strategy, we continued interviewing for as many hours each day as we had the strength to do so. The UNHCR then arranged for the Norwegian rescue ship *Lysekil* to transport the refugees we had selected to the refugee camp on Pulau Galang and to take us to Singapore. On our last day in the camp we still had a large number of Vietnamese to interview, and we set to work with a will. By the evening the number of Vietnamese gathered to watch us continued to grow. The list of those still waiting to be seen was long, and we continued to interview late into the night. At this point most of the camp population was pressed around us. When we finally finished the interview of the last refugee applicant at about 1:30 in the morning, the watching crowd erupted in cheers. We had selected over 1,000 people and were exhausted and stunned by the emotional response of the Vietnamese. It remains one of the highlight moments of each of our immigration careers.

Later that same day, we and those we had selected (over 10 per cent of the population of the two camps) were taken out to where the *Lysekil* was anchored and boarded the ship. Our collective recollections of the overnight voyage include air-conditioned accommodation, hot showers, cold beer, and steaks provided by our Norwegian hosts. We were taken directly to Singapore, and the refugees went on to Galang for medical examination and processing before they too would return to Singapore for their fights to Canada.

Malaysian Camp Rats

JOHN MCEACHERN

I didn't like Pulau Bidong and almost refused to stay there after my first visit. My problem was the accommodations and the rats. While camps in Indonesia were very structured and under government direction, those in Malaysia were a mess and largely reflected what the refugees had managed to create.

I first went there in late 1980 with Don Cameron and Dick Hawkshaw, our liaison officer from Singapore. By that time the accommodations had improved from the sleep-on-your-desk days to wooden houses for the foreign delegations – much better than what was available to the refugees. It was late when we went to bed, I in a top bunk and Dick in the lower. As we climbed into our bunks, we noticed at floor level what looked to be a rat hole in the wall. I had a full, heavy Samsonite briefcase with a double combination lock, and we shoved it against the hole. Dick and I got into bed but had trouble falling asleep. Don, an old hand, climbed into his bunk and was asleep in seconds.

Although I was in the top bunk, I could hear a rat walking within a foot of my head. Later there was hissing and shrieks as the rats fought each other. I could have coped with them near my feet but not by my head. The night passed slowly as I tossed and turned to the accompaniment of scratching and scrabbling, finally followed by the grating sound of sharp little teeth gnawing something. Dick (also awake) and I realized what it was – a rat attacking my briefcase. The noise suggested a lack of success against the hard plastic. Then – a sudden crack as my briefcase hit the ground. The rat had pushed it over! Recognizing that we were facing a rat strong enough to push over a large, heavy briefcase, Dick and I got up, in case of a more intimate attack. We didn't sleep the rest of the night but sat and talked until morning. Through it all, Don slept serenely.

The Boat People

DICK HAWKSHAW

There were three stages to the selection of refugees for resettlement in Canada. The "selection interview" was the cornerstone and could include elements of family sponsorship or provincial selection. The medical examination was also important and was directed at ensuring that risks to the health of Canadian society, or incurrence of undue health costs, were not introduced through arriving refugees. The final stage in the selection process was security, called Stage B in the parlance of the operational activities. Stage B was carried out at the time by members of the RCMP Security Service, the predecessor to the Canadian Security Intelligence Service (CSIS). Its role was to identify individuals who could pose a security or criminal threat to the nation. This could be a difficult task in the midst of a refugee movement where many of the individuals involved could produce few identification documents and where no reliable sources in the country of origin existed with which to verify information. The following recollection is by one of the security service officers who worked in Southeast Asia.

My first contact with refugees from Vietnam was as an assistant liaison officer while stationed in Hong Kong from August 1977 to April 1979. My involvement then was minimal, consisting of a couple of visa-vetting security interviews, or what is commonly referred to as Stage B processing. These interviews were my direct introduction to the refugee situation in Southeast Asia.

With the growing number of boat people arriving in Malaysia, Indonesia, and Singapore, there was an urgent need for an RCMP foreign service liaison office in the region. Canadian immigration authorities required, at that time, that a Stage B presence be accessible to assist with the refugee selection and resettlement process. Until the sudden escalation of arriving Indochinese refugees, security vetting was conducted by the liaison officers in Hong Kong. Being remote from the refugee selection process was a complicating factor for the time pressures under which the operation functioned. The processing urgencies resulted in my transfer to Singapore in April 1979 to open an RCMP liaison office. The operational territory included Malaysia, Indonesia, and Brunei. Concurrence for establishing a security service presence to cover the region was reached with each of the countries involved.

The decision to send me to Singapore was the result of my being in the right place at the right time – and my being single, which made much easier the haste with which the transfer had to occur. I was met in Singapore by four immigration officers stationed at our Canadian High Commission. Two were on regular assignment, while the other two were on temporary duty to assist with the escalating refugee situation. Additional immigration officers kept arriving throughout my assignment in Singapore. There was tremendous pressure to have a fully functioning operation in place to handle the heavy demands for processing Indochinese refugees, and within a very short time we had a permanent presence of myself as the liaison officer assisted by two assistant liaison officers, as well as support staff.

Our travel teams to the refugee camps varied but usually consisted of three or more immigration officers and a security service liaison officer. At times, a Canadian High Commission doctor also travelled with us. A visit to one or more refugee camps normally required a full week, with liaison reports and paperwork being completed afterwards. The pace was often hectic. Work in the camps was difficult, not only because of all that had to be accomplished but also because of the strains of working in the midst of so much human misery and so many harrowing tales of escape. After a full day in the camps conducting interviews in hot, humid, and at times rainy monsoon weather, all we wanted to do in the evening was to return to our base camp to have a shower and enjoy an ice-cold Tiger or Anchor "cleansing ale" and a meal.

Lunch at the camps often consisted of a quick bowl of noodles, rice, or soup – if anything. Sometimes we didn't stop to eat. Chinese green tea served us well during the day. Our initial tendency towards coffee or soft drinks we found only created discomfort with constant visits to the primitive facilities. Green tea seemed to have a cooling effect and was not disruptive.

Camaraderie was maintained with colleagues from other selection nations and UNHCR representatives. A couple of the UNHCR staff launched a virtual Royal Tanjung Pinang Yacht Club (RTPYC). Many of us joined and received an "official" membership card and could purchase an RTPYC T-shirt. The success of the RTPYC rested on the respite it provided from the stressful and highly demanding environment in which the Indochinese refugee movement occurred. It offered good-natured fun and camaraderie.

Life in the camps was otherworldly. There was a rudimentary structure to it, and politics were at play. The omnipresent vitality and enterprise were stunning. One local enterprise was the production of souvenirs, which were given or sold to those visiting the camps. Sadness mixed with hope was everywhere. Political leadership existed, as did a lucrative economy based on bartering and the black market – I heard of one refugee having a suitcase full of American dollars. The population of the camps included the "haves" and the "have-nots." Tranquility was maintained by an internal security and policing component. The refugees we encountered had overcome great adversity merely to have reached the camps. Their ambition and aspirations were amazing, and they were very adaptive people.

English language classes or tutoring were a part of camp life as individuals sought to enhance their chances of acceptance by speaking English during an interview. This sometimes resulted in humorous outcomes. In one of my interviews I began with "How are you?" which was met by the refugee responding by telling me how old he was. I laughed, the interpreter laughed, and once the question was translated, the refugee turned bright red. I couldn't fault him for trying.

My four years working out of Singapore on the Indochinese Refugee Program from April 1979 until June 1983 were fulfilling and rewarding and gave me deep respect for the refugees for all that they endured and experienced in seeking a better life.

Health Issues Related to the Early Indochinese Refugee Movements to Canada

BRIAN GUSHULAK AND EARL HERSHFIELD

The immigration medical program was administered and managed by the Immigration Medical Services Division of the Medical Services Branch of the Department of National Health and Welfare. The unit's headquarters was located in Ottawa, with the Asian regional managerial office, or zone office, in Hong Kong and regional operational offices in Manila, New Delhi, and Singapore. Much of the early health screening of Indochinese refugees was undertaken through the Singapore office, with management and supervision from Hong Kong and Ottawa. During the height of the movement, the Canadian medical officers in charge of the office in Singapore were Dr Farid Abdel-Sayed and Dr Mark Singer.

Managing the health issues of the camps, including basic medical screening for immigration clearance, was an effort cooperatively shared by local authorities, international agencies such as the UNHCR, and a variety of non-governmental and voluntary assistance organizations. As the programs developed, the Intergovernmental Committee for European Migration (ICEM) assumed a key role in delivering medical examination services in the camps and transit centres.

Medical Screening

The Indochinese refugee movement began while the Canadian immigration medical assessment and screening system was being revised. The promulgation of the 1976 Immigration Act necessitated an extensive review and modification of immigration medical screening and assessment. An organized and structured assessment process was implemented, including a numerical scoring of risks to public health and the potential demands on health and social services that might be "excessive." Application of this screening protocol included processes that deferred or denied access to Canada until potential risks or demands had been defined or managed. Depending on the outcome of the evaluations, admission could be permitted, denied temporarily, or permanently restricted.

In terms of public health, the arrivals of Indochinese refugees in Canada generated much discussion and concern regarding the potential impacts of pulmonary tuberculosis, tropical infections, and Hepatitis B infection. Rates of TB were decreasing in the Canadian-born population due to the success of national and provincial treatment programs, but tuberculosis was still common in Southeast Asia. Testing for Hepatitis B became available in the early 1970s; the prevalence of that disease was known to be higher in Indochina than in Canada.

Routine medical screening included age-specific chest x-rays to detect pulmonary tuberculosis, a test for syphilis for those over fifteen, and, for those coming from the tropics, stool screening for parasitic infections.[6] Additional screening was done for typhoid in certain situations.[7] If the initial x-ray screening for TB was determined to be suggestive or indicative of the disease, sputum samples were obtained and cultured to look for the presence of live tubercular bacilli in the sputum. Medical clearance to proceed to Canada required either a normal initial x-ray or a series of at least three negative sputum cultures for those with suspicious but unchanging (radiologically stable) chest x-rays. x-rays that changed during the evaluation period required another series of cultures. Access to laboratory TB services was location dependent, and in camp situations required forwarding the samples to larger centres. This process presented logistical and communication challenges among all of the involved locations.

While x-rays could be relatively easily obtained, the examination of the sputum and the culturing of the tuberculosis bacteria required skill and reliable laboratory services. The technology required long periods of culture incubation (a minimum of six weeks), making the screening process for those suspected of having pulmonary tuberculosis quite lengthy. Adequate treatment of active tuberculosis could be as long as six to twelve months, depending on the situation. During screening, culture determination, and treatment, the individual and his or her family were not allowed to proceed to Canada. The long processing delays were a challenge for the refugees and the processing teams trying to resettle them. Adding to the length of this complex process was the administrative validity of the information. Medical examination results were valid for one year, dated from the time of the initial examination. After that date, they were deemed expired, and a new medical screening evaluation was required. Cases where x-rays were suspected of indicating TB could involve repeated cultures.

In 1978, as the movement of refugees from Southeast Asia was developing, the Department of National Health and Welfare, through the director of the Immigration Medical Services, Dr Robertson, convened a committee to examine some of the issues of health and tuberculosis in refugees from Asia. This process drew on the experience of a medical task force established to assist with the development of the health aspects of the 1976 Immigration Act. The committee provided technical and public health advice on overseas screening as well as advice and recommendations for further medical management and follow-up after the refugees arrived in Canada.

Delays Resulting from Screening

In 1979, the exodus of refugees to countries in the region increased dramatically. Canada and other resettlement nations agreed to accept larger numbers of refugees. The expansion of the resettlement programs gave rise to two general areas of concern in terms of health. First, there were worries that there might be too much active TB arriving from the region, raising questions about the screening process. Second, the increased numbers of refugees being screened led to a larger and growing number of cases held back for TB review and cultures.

The long processing times, coupled with the one-year validity of the medical results, meant that some families could be held up in medical assessment and TB diagnosis and treatment for a period of several months to more than a year. Concerns about TB screening led to a temporary cessation of movements to Canada. The delays created a substantial accumulation of people (including family members) on "medical hold," which had programmatic implications for the camps and movement plans. Attention to these delays was heightened by the case of an individual involved in medical hold who took his own life to speed up the departure of his eight family members.

National Health and Welfare engaged Earl Hershfield, the director of the Manitoba TB program and one of the members of the medical advisory committee, to examine the process and issues. Dr Hershfield travelled to Asia, and in the Health and Welfare Singapore office he found large numbers of potentially abnormal x-rays under review and re-evaluation. Through his experience, assistance, and advice, those numbers were reduced to a more manageable volume, and case processing was speeded up. Dr Hershfield also visited processing camps and centres in Malaysia, Thailand, Indonesia, and Hong Kong. Diagnostic and treatment programs were established in the larger camps with the assistance of the medical services of ICEM and by non-governmental organizations such as the Mennonite Central Committee, who were in the camps providing cultural orientation. A single laboratory was selected to screen smears and cultures, and more streamlined screening protocols were developed, reducing variability and laboratory differences.

By the early 1980s Canadian medical screening in the camps and the region had become generally well organized. With the exception of some delays for complicated cases, usually due to active, infectious tuberculosis of the lungs, the movement of large numbers of people was accomplished with minimal impact on Canada or the refugees. Some cases of active tuberculosis were noted in resettled refugees, but these often resulted from the reactivation of old, non-infectious disease after arrival in Canada. Additionally, while the incidence of chronic Hepatitis B infection in some groups was noted to be higher than that of the domestic Canadian population, there was almost no measured transmission of these diseases beyond the refugee communities. The development and use of Hepatitis B vaccine in the 1980s also reduced much of the concern associated with the impact of any imported disease.

Many of the principles and practices developed and honed during the Indochinese refugee movements for Canada, the United States, and other nations have become basic standard operating practices for immigration medical screening associated with complex humanitarian events. They continue to be used in current refugee resettlement programs.[8]

14

Singapore: One Man's Refugee Movement

Donald Cameron

Donald Cameron was a seasoned foreign service officer, a superb observer of events, and an important member of a cadre of officers who served in Southeast Asia during this difficult period. His recollections of the Indochinese refugee crisis appear throughout this book. This chapter contains some of his critical observations of events in the region that have remained largely unknown to the public. He was in Hong Kong when South Vietnam was collapsing. He was in Immigration's Asia Pacific Bureau in 1976–77, which gave him a wealth of relevant experience and strong analytical skills. These skills were to stand him in good stead in coordinating selection activities in Malaysia when he was assigned to Singapore in August 1979.

Singapore Assignment

I arrived in Singapore as deputy immigration program manager in August 1979, shortly after Al Lukie, the new program manager, had arrived. Dick Martin, who had carried the refugee program in Southeast Asia until then with the former program manager, Ian Hamilton, remained for another year. The other newly posted officers included Rod Fields, David Ritchie, Rick Schramm, John McEachern, and Paul Trueman. Our Quebec immigration officer was Florent Fortin (later succeeded by Lucile Horner), and many temporary duty officers came and went. The RCMP officers were Dick Hawkshaw, Ben Soave, and Dave Francis.

By the time of my arrival in Singapore, all of the regulatory, policy, and administrative innovations that enabled us to meet our refugee delivery targets had been introduced. Some of these innovations were made in Ottawa and others at the post. There remained obstacles that were not within our power to influence but had to be addressed. These included the geography, the climate, and the infrastructure (or more correctly, the lack thereof). In both Malaysia and Indonesia almost all of the refugees were kept in camps on islands in areas of the country remote from the capital or other large cities. All the camps in Malaysia were off the east coast of peninsular Malaysia, although earlier there had been some refugees in the Malaysian states of Sabah and Sarawak on the north coast of Borneo. The distance from Singapore to Kota Bharu (the most northerly camp in Malaysia and close to the Thai border) was 350 miles, which took twelve hours to drive under the best conditions. A spine of mountains runs the length of the Malaysian peninsula separating the east coast from Kuala Lumpur; this meant long and painfully slow bus journeys for the refugees we had selected when they were moved to Kuala Lumpur (KL) for medical examination and their flights to Canada. In Indonesia the refugees were kept on islands remote from Jakarta but relatively close to Singapore.

The climate of both countries is tropical, with two monsoon seasons a year – the northeast monsoon between November and March, and the southwest monsoon between May and September. The resulting heat and humidity slowed down even the most energetic Canadians and seeped into our files so that the paper was too damp to write on. The monsoons also prevented us at times from reaching refugee camps to make selections because the sea was too rough for safe passage. On one occasion we waited in Kuala Terengganu, Malaysia, for several days hoping for better weather to make the trip by boat to Pulau Bidong. Eventually we, the UNHCR, and the Malaysian Red Crescent Society (MRCS) were so desperate to get to Bidong, each for our own purposes, that the UN ordered its boat captain to make an attempt, even though the local Malaysian fishermen were not venturing out. We strapped on life jackets and hung on tight as the UN boat headed for the mouth of the Terengganu River. When we reached it, a wall of water rolled toward us. Our boat went up the water wall and then crashed down on to the sand bar at the river mouth, breaking its windshield. The captain put the engines into reverse and opened the throttles wide – and that was the end of that. These sea conditions also prevented ICEM and the MRCS from removing from the island those refugees we had previously selected so that they could be medically examined and taken to our transit camp in Kuala Lumpur. Monsoon storms also prevented the MRCS from moving food and supplies to refugee camps. These interruptions in the flow of selected refugees to our transit camp in Kuala Lumpur caused us to come very close to not filling all of the seats on more than one charter aircraft.

In both Malaysia and Indonesia, the refugee camps were in less developed areas of the country. In Malaysia the east coast bordering the South China Sea was more thinly populated than the west coast bordering the Strait of Malacca, and the east coast roads were primitive compared to those in the west. These roads were prone to flooding and washouts, blocking us from reaching refugee camps. They were also heavily travelled by trucks overloaded (by Canadian standards) with very large logs. There were fewer towns on the east coast, which meant that we slept in refugee camps in the absence of nearby hotels. In Indonesia most of the refugees were on a small island off the coast of the province of Riau on Sumatra, southeast of Singapore. The nearest town, from which we went by boat to the Galang refugee camp, was so backward that staying in the refugee camp was preferable to the town hotels.

The Camps: Singapore

The Singapore government prohibited the landing of boat people from the commencement of the Indochinese exodus. Nevertheless, Singapore was singularly well equipped to house refugees because of the many military installations left vacant by the departure of the British earlier in the decade, which were easily converted to refugee transit camps.

As a result of Singapore's refusal to let refugees land, Singapore-destined freighters and tankers were reluctant to pick up refugees in danger at sea. Multilateral negotiations eventually created a program called DISERO,[1] under which Singapore agreed to land refugees picked up at sea by freighters on the undertaking that the refugees would be resettled elsewhere within ninety days.

I do not recall making a selection visit to the Singapore refugee camp, but I did once visit it to accompany a backbench Canadian member of Parliament who was on holiday in Singapore and wanted to see a refugee camp. He wasn't willing to undertake the uncomfortable trip to a Malaysian or Indonesian camp, so he was shown the one in Singapore. It was a former British army base with excellent housing, no overcrowding, and none of the usual odours to be found in a refugee camp. One can only hope that he took away with him a true understanding of the predicament faced by refugees, which was not fully evident in the well-maintained and well-organized Singaporean camp.

The Camps: Malaysia

By the time I arrived in August 1979, Vietnamese refugees were kept in several camps along the east coast of peninsular Malaysia. The camps, from north to south, were located at Kota Bharu, Pulau Bidong (Kuala Terengganu), Cherating (Kuantan), and Pulau Tengah (Mersing). The name in brackets is the closest town to the camp. "Pulau" means island. The Cherating camp, the only one not on an island, was inferior to the others and the most crowded. Although it was located on the sea, barbed wire prevented the refugees from reaching the beach.

The Camps: Indonesia

By August 1979 the main refugee camp in Indonesia was on Pulau Galang, near the town of Tanjung Pinang on Pulau Bintan in Riau Province. This location is closer to Singapore than to Jakarta. Indonesia consists of 17,000 islands, making boats the means of transportation to Tanjung Pinang and from there to the refugee camp on Galang. Two other refugee camps were located in the Anambas Islands, to the northeast of Singapore off the east coast of peninsular Malaysia. There were no boats or ferries travelling from Singapore to the Anambas, so UNHCR chartered a helicopter to take us there. This was my first time flying low over the water out of sight of land, and it was unnerving.

The refugee camps in Indonesia were managed by the navy or the army. Unlike some of my colleagues in E&I Singapore, I spent much more time in the Malaysian refugee camps than in those in Indonesia, so when I describe how we operated in refugee camps, my recollections come primarily from Malaysia. I should add by way of explanation that relatively few of the refugees we processed were selected in Singapore.

My strongest memory of the camps was their smell. It was unique and enduring, a blend of cooking odours, sweat, and raw sewage. A selection team returning from a camp brought to our Singaporean employees the unwelcome experience of the odours of a refugee camp. Although we could wash it off ourselves and our clothes, we could not eradicate it from immigration files that had spent several days in a humid, smelly camp. At the height of the monsoon seasons, the dampness made it difficult even to write without tearing the paper.

Living and Working Conditions in the Field

Shortly after my arrival in Singapore, I went with a refugee selection team to Pulau Bidong, the largest refugee camp in Malaysia or Indonesia with a peak population of about 40,000. Travel to Kuala Terengganu was either by air to Kuala Lumpur, with another flight from there to Kuala Terengganu, or by our van from Singapore up the east coast of peninsular Malaysia. Taking the mission van, teams could visit more than one camp on a single trip. Purchased for our use by the Department of External Affairs, the van was unsuited for our purposes in that it was seriously underpowered. It invariably made our road trips in Malaysia very exciting.

Arriving in Kuala Terengganu, we continued to Pulau Bidong by boat. UNHCR arranged for the boats and, not having yet obtained any of their own, they hired local fishing vessels to take us and our equipment to the island. Our equipment consisted of hundreds of files, hundreds of application forms, all of the office supplies we would require, right down to the paper clips, and our personal luggage for the overnight stays. The fishing boats were basic, slow, and uncomfortable. The trip took about four hours of noisy, unmuffled two-stroke engines, combined with the fumes from the exhaust, the heat, and the smell of fish. Anyone prone to seasickness quickly succumbed.

Later, UNHCR obtained its own boat, which reduced the discomfort and travel time, but it proved to be unsuitable in rough seas; however, even fishing boats could not safely exit the mouth of the Terengganu River during the worst of the monsoons. In the fall of 1979 I spent several days in Kuala Terengganu with a team capable of selecting several hundred refugees a day but unable to reach Pulau Bidong because of the weather. We and UNHCR searched unsuccessfully for any ports nearby from which we could safely depart for Pulau Bidong. Just as we were about to give up, the weather relented sufficiently for a fishing boat to take us on a corkscrew ride to Bidong. It was the only camp in Malaysia big enough for us to be able to select the numbers we required to fill chartered flights to Canada, and going to some or all of the other camps was not an option.

During my first two trips to Pulau Bidong, we used the same tables for working, eating, and sleeping on, and we interviewed applicants for as many hours as our strength permitted. On my first trip we were given thin mattresses on which to sleep, but on the second the Australians were in the camp when we arrived and they had taken all the mattresses. By my third trip, huts with bunk beds had been built to house visiting delegations. Similar huts were already available in other refugee camps where we stayed overnight – Pulau Galang and the Anambas Islands in Indonesia. In the case of Pulau Galang, the boat ride to Tanjung Pinang was short enough to allow us to return every night. However, after one night in the best hotel in Tanjung Pinang, I opted, as did many others, to stay in the refugee camp. We always worked in heat and humidity. Due to the crowded nature of the camps, we were usually located in rough shelters surrounded by people, so that not a hint of a breeze reached us.

Because of the number of bags we had to carry to bring our files and stationery, there was little room available to bring food. In some camps we ate what the refugees ate, while in some others (those which had a thriving private sector) we were able to purchase other food. On one occasion we arrived at the dock on Pulau Bidong to see a large barge already tied up. It contained hundreds of large plastic bags full of slaughtered chickens and, judging by the odour, it had been there in the hot sun for several hours already. Thereafter, I politely declined MRCS rations in that camp.

Returning from Pulau Bidong to Kuala Terengganu after one selection trip, our boat's engine cut out and could not be restarted. As the wind and waves pushed us closer and closer to the beach, we realized that we might ourselves experience a landing similar to that of the refugee boats. The waves at the beach were no more than a foot high, so I was not concerned for my safety, but I was very worried that the files of the hundreds of people we had just selected might be water damaged to the extent that we would have to go back and interview them all over again. We were about two hundred yards off the beach when we were spotted by a passing boat and towed to Kuala Terengganu. Ironically, the boat that rescued us was a refugee boat subsequently converted by the Malaysian Red Crescent Society to its own use.

Selection and Processing – Primarily Malaysia

At the time of my arrival in Singapore (August 1979), the innovations that enabled us to select and process large numbers of refugees were already in effect. These included:

- the creation of the Indochinese Designated Class, so that we did not have to devote time to making refugee eligibility determinations in each case;
- the help of ICEM (Intergovernmental Committee for European Migration) to perform the immigration medical examinations of selected refugees, to move visaed refugees from the camps to airports, and to ensure they boarded the aircrafts;
- the creation of the IMM1314 form to replace both our existing processing and data collection forms as well as the immigrant visa;
- the establishment of a system for tracking cases. Floor to ceiling white boards covered every wall of the office in E&I Singapore. As soon as the file of a selected applicant reached the office, the name and file number were recorded on the boards, and as the application progressed (such as passing the medical examination), each event was added to the boards. This system provided an instant snapshot of the status of every case, including the vital information of how many refugees were ready to receive their visas;.
- replacement of time-consuming and frustrating efforts by visa officers to find refugees who matched the group sponsorships received from Canada with the Matching Centre in Ottawa. Posts sent Destination Matching Requests (DMRs) to Ottawa with details of all cases ready for visa. The Matching Centre matched cases with sponsorships and informed posts of their destinations in Canada.

Refugees arriving in Malaysia and Indonesia were registered by UNHCR as soon as possible after arrival. Registration took the form of an index card containing the tombstone data for each family, along with the Vietnamese registration number of the boat on which they had arrived. The boat number became an important identifier. The card also contained notes made by the representatives of each country who interviewed the family. The US government contracted with a New York–based organization called the Joint Voluntary Agency (JVA) to provide staff to do the initial interviews, and they were usually the first to see arrivals. JVA employees were young, adventurous Americans, and their task was to classify each refugee in one of the many immigration categories that the United States had created. These categories ranged from 1(A) – such as President Nguyen Van Thieu – to 4(E), which was for people who had no claim at all on resettlement the United States. JVA teams often included a US government employee, many of whom had served in Vietnam before 1975 and spoke Vietnamese.

Until UNHCR had registered arriving refugees, they were not available to be interviewed by resettlement countries, so it became vital that registration occurred immediately after boat arrivals. At periods of peak arrivals, UNHCR could be as much as several weeks behind in registrations, making many recently arrived Vietnamese unavailable for resettlement. In order to interview applicants for resettlement, we (and all others) needed their UNHCR registration cards. Thus, if more than one resettlement country was present in a camp, both could not interview Vietnamese who arrived at the same time. When we informed UNHCR of our intention to visit a camp, they would inform us of the presence of other countries' resettlement officials so that we could alter our plans to avoid possibly not having access to the registration cards. However, on occasions our need to select very large numbers of refugees to fill charter aircraft seats overrode the inconvenience of having to share the registration cards with the officials of other countries (invariably Australia and the United States), and we went ahead with our proposed trip.

When a Canadian team (usually visa officers, an RCMP officer, and a Quebec immigration officer) arrived in a camp to select refugees for resettlement, UNHCR had already requested the camp committee to make arrangements for us. These included providing us with the rough furniture and shelters in which to do the interviews, providing interpreters and other clerical staff, and notifying the residents of the camp that the Canadian delegation would be interviewing those who had arrived aboard specified boats or between specified dates. Our objective was to interview applicants in the order in which they arrived, and during 1979 and early 1980 we were often several months behind arrivals. We also had lists of persons we wanted to see: those sponsored by relatives in Canada, those whose relatives had been selected in other camps, and those previously seen who required a follow-up interview.

The camp committees were created by the Vietnamese themselves to organize life in the camp and usually consisted of men of high status in Vietnam. I recall among them Roman Catholic priests, doctors, former armed forces officers, and professors. There were many subcommittees, including those to provide support to the visiting delegations of resettlement countries. Had they not existed, we could not have met our selection targets. In Pulau Bidong there was even a subcommittee devoted solely to supporting Canadian delegations. This system ensured that when visiting Bidong we frequently had the same interpreters and clerical staff as on previous visits, saving us precious time by obviating the need to train new staff.

We interviewed applicants using only the information on their UNHCR registration cards. The Application for Permanent Residence in Canada (form IMM8) was completed after the interview by those we had selected. Staff provided by the camp committee interviewed the selected refugees to obtain the required information for completing the form. Those selected were then interviewed by the RCMP officer. At the same time, the Quebec officer would be interviewing applicants sponsored by relatives or organizations in that province. The Quebec officers were very cooperative and when they had met their target for a visit, they volunteered to interview applicants on our behalf.

When interviewing an individual or family, the visa officer's first objective was to determine if they had any other relatives in the camp and to gather together all of the relatives to be interviewed. If applicants had relatives in other camps or countries, we gathered that information so that they could be given the opportunity to be resettled in Canada. The identity of each applicant was what had been declared to UNHCR when registered. In some cases, applicants still had Vietnamese identity documents to support what they had claimed upon registration, but many did not. Similarly, proof of claimed relationships was usually not available. From time to time, applicants produced a Promise of Visa Letter issued by the Canadian Embassy in Saigon (actually prepared at the Commission for Canada in Hong Kong) in late April 1975. I remember one of my colleagues showing me one with my signature on it. All such letters were honoured. Applicants were selected if the visa officer thought that they could successfully establish in Canada with government assistance during their first year. Our objective in 1979 and most of 1980 was for each visa officer to select one hundred persons per day. There were few refusals during this period.

US government policy had a negative impact on the number of our selections when the USINS (United States Immigration and Naturalization Service) decided that refugees in the lowest US immigration category 4E (into which fell the majority of Vietnamese refugees in Malaysia and Indonesia) would not be eligible for resettlement unless they had first been refused by Canada and Australia. To make matters worse, refugees who requested refusal by Canada or Australia would be banned from resettlement in the United States. The result was that visa officers would, after devoting valuable time to thoroughly assessing an application, inform the applicants of their acceptance, only to find them breaking down in tears because we had ruined their lives. Visa officers then faced the decision of whether to record on the UNHCR registration card that the applicants had requested refusal (which would prevent them from being accepted by the United States), accepting them despite their wish *not* to go to Canada, or recording that they were refused by Canada so that they could continue their dream of going to America. To record nothing on the registration card was not an option, since UNHCR staff, who controlled the cards, knew of the interviews and in the absence of a decision would schedule them to be interviewed by us again.

Following acceptance, refugees were given the standard Canadian immigration medical examination by ICEM doctors. To the chagrin of ICEM medical officers (who in Malaysia were from Norway and in Indonesia from Australia), the results of these examinations were sent to Canadian medical officers in Singapore for a final decision. In Malaysia, refugees accepted by Canada were moved from their camps to the transit camp at the Convent of the Holy Infant Jesus in Kuala Lumpur, while in Indonesia they were moved to or remained in Pulau Galang. While the medical officer-in-charge at E&I Singapore, Dr

David Holbrook, did his best to limit requests for additional tests after the initial examination, the frequent arrival of new or temporary medical officers at times resulted in such requests, which the ICEM physicians regarded as unrealistic in the conditions in which the refugees lived and medical examinations were conducted.

These problems paled, however, when compared to the Canadian approach to applicants whose chest x-rays revealed the possibility that they had or may have had pulmonary tuberculosis. Canadian visa officers learned early in their careers that even if an applicant's chest x-ray indicated the possibility that he or she might have had TB in the distant past, we would ask the applicant to have samples of his or her sputum cultured for several weeks and to have another chest x-ray three months after the first. Unless these tests showed no change in the applicant's condition over the three-month period, they were repeated until they showed that the applicant's condition was stable. In consequence, the applicant (and his or her accompanying family members) could wait at least three months and in some cases over a year before receiving the pass or fail decision on their Canadian visa application. In normal immigration cases, this is frustrating for the applicant, but the protection of the health of Canadians trumps the inconvenience caused to those seeking to live there. In the case of refugees in Malaysia and Indonesia, however, the request for further tests for TB meant that they and their families would be spending many more months in a crowded refugee camp. In Malaysia, that would be the Convent transit camp where, at its peak population, 4,000 people lived in small shelters on a soccer field. For any applicants who might have had TB, these were far from ideal conditions, both for their own health and for the health of their families and other refugees who were exposed to neighbours who might have or have had a contagious disease. From the point of view of selecting enough refugees to fill all of the seats on the charter flights, the delay caused by TB testing meant that not all of the people we selected would be ready after medical examination to be transported to Canada. After some selection trips to Pulau Bidong, half of the hundreds of refugees selected would not be available for movement to Canada for an unknown number of months because of this approach to TB. In late 1979 and into 1980, these delays caused us to come very close to not filling every seat on our flights. Thus for both health and operational reasons we needed to deal with the "TB problem."

The Australian government took a different approach to the problem, which we wished to emulate. Refugees whose Australian immigration medical examination revealed the possibility that they had or may have had TB were not sent for additional tests. Instead, they were treated with drugs for two weeks to render them non-infectious, and then they were transported to Australia for monitoring and treatment. Our Australian colleagues were present every day when the medication was administered in order to be certain that it was taken.

A solution briefly attempted was to inform applicants during selection interviews that, if further TB testing was required, they would be refused and be made available for resettlement in another country. Had they been placed on "TB hold" (as the refugees called it) and subjected to months of medical testing, they could not be selected by another country if their UNHCR registration cards did not list them as refused by Canada. Some refugees asked us to refuse them rather than subject them to the delays of TB testing. However, the first time I assembled a group of applicants we had recently selected and informed them that we were refusing them (rather than sending them for TB testing) so that they would be available to be selected by another country, I was shocked by their reaction. Some were devastated. We quickly abandoned that particular attempt to solve the "TB problem."

Having been involved in Saigon in April 1975 with the chain of events that led to the arrival in Canada of the notorious Vietnamese General Dang Van Quang,[2] I was particularly sensitive to the need to prevent the arrival of any other such persons. This situation was complicated by the absence of proof by many refugees of their identity. Apart from RCMP interviews, I relied on the index of Frank Snepp's *Decent Interval: An Insider's Account of Saigon's Indecent End Told by the CIA's Chief Strategy Analyst in Vietnam*, published in 1977[3] to identify potential high-profile applicants. While I did not find any bad guys, I did find the names of several of our US colleagues favourably mentioned for their heroic efforts in helping their Vietnamese associates to escape from Saigon in April 1975.

When refugees had completed all of our requirements and we had received a reply to the Destination Matching Requests (DMRs – described above), we scheduled their departure on a specific charter flight. At our peak we filled an average of three flights a week. The information about each refugee on a flight was sent to the two refugee reception centres (the Canadian Forces bases in Longue-Pointe, Quebec, and Griesbach

Barracks, Alberta), in what was called a Notification of Arrival Telex (NAT). I should add that the DMRs (and their replies) and NATs were several yards of telex paper long – which made the High Commission communicators the recipients of a lot of overtime.

The refugees' visas were given to ICEM, which arranged their movement from the camps to the relevant airport. Those in Malaysia went out through the Kuala Lumpur airport, while those in Indonesia were brought to the Singapore airport. Transporting refugees was a challenging task in Malaysia during the Muslim Haj when chartering buses was very difficult because they were being used to take pilgrims and their well-wishers to and from airports, but ICEM never let us down. Had we needed to move refugees in Indonesia to Jakarta to fly to Canada, however, I doubt if even ICEM could have overcome the lack of infrastructure in Indonesia to perform this task. The attitude of the government of Singapore toward Vietnamese refugees made obtaining its permission to transit refugees from Indonesia a challenge, and credit is due to those of my predecessors who secured it.

A hallmark of ICEM operations was the efficiency and speed with which they loaded refugees onto aircraft. Several Canadian cabin crews commented that they had never seen it done better. All of the charter flights were Canadian carriers, most with no previous experience flying to Singapore or Kuala Lumpur. Had we given ICEM the task of chartering aircraft, few if any Canadian carriers would have been utilized. Generally, the airlines performed well, although I was involved in one curious incident involving a Wardair flight at the Singapore airport. After ICEM had loaded the aircraft, the captain ordered the gangways removed and the doors closed. As he had not yet paid for the fuel that he had taken on board, this caused consternation, and a tractor was parked in front of the aircraft. The airport police were summoned, and the captain told them that the Canadian High Commission would take care of the bill. I went on board and told the captain that the bill was his responsibility. Reluctantly, he paid it in cash.

Intercepts, Push-Backs, and Tow-Offs

One of the deplorable chapters in the history of the Indochinese refugee movement was the hostility with which most of these unfortunate people were met by their neighbours in the region. The coun-

tries of Southeast Asia did not want to host the refugees. Malaysia and,
to a slightly lesser extent, Indonesia and Singapore physically forced
Indochinese refugees landing on their beaches in leaky boats to leave,
sometimes at gunpoint. While some of these boats successfully landed
elsewhere on the coasts of these countries under the watchful eyes of
foreigners, an unknown number of the unfortunates aboard the boats
drowned or were killed or raped by pirates.

By the time I arrived in Malaysia and Indonesia, there were fewer push-backs (refugee boats prevented from landing and pushed out to sea) and tow-offs (boats towed out to sea). This improved situation was a result of the efforts of Canada and like-minded countries to persuade the governments of Malaysia and Indonesia to permit refugees to land, on the undertaking that all would be resettled elsewhere.

However, I did become involved in a push-back from Thailand at a refugee camp in Kota Bharu, Malaysia, the northernmost city on the east coast of Malaysia and only a few kilometres south of the Thai border. I was approached in the camp by a Vietnamese man on crutches who asked if I knew Ron Button.[4] Ron and I had been friends since 1968 when we both arrived at the Canadian High Commission in London for postings there. I was taken aback by encountering half-way around the world a man asking me about my colleague. The Vietnamese man was a fighter pilot from the former Republic of Vietnam Air Force who had escaped with others on a boat that landed on the Thai coast just north of the border with Malaysia. They were detained on the beach by the Thai army. Ron, a former RCAF fighter pilot, had been informed of their presence there while he was working at the large refugee camp in Songkhla in southern Thailand, and he and a UNHCR official went south to find this group of refugees. Ron accepted them all for Canada so that Thai officials would permit them to remain in the country, and the UNHCR official promised to remove the refugees to a camp.

UNHCR returned only a week later, by which time the Thais had lost patience and pushed the boat off. The air force officer had broken his leg during this process. Fortunately the boat had landed again south of the Thai border. Hearing the officer's story, I recalled seeing a telex in Singapore from Ron in Bangkok asking us to be on the look-out for this group. Luckily, I had a copy of the telex with me and could reconfirm Ron's acceptance by Canada of all aboard the boat who wished to be resettled in Canada. On my return to Singapore, I informed a very relieved Ron in Bangkok.

My meeting the Vietnamese pilot had been pure chance. After completing a selection trip to Pulau Bidong, we had decided that I would go north to the Kota Bharu camp because no Canadian had been there in quite some time. The others went south to the Cherating refugee camp and would return to Kota Bharu the next day to pick me up. A last-minute spontaneous decision saved these boat people.

The navies and marine police of Malaysia and Singapore denied that they intercepted refugee boats at sea and redirected them to other countries. That was a lie. I interviewed a family in an Indonesian camp who showed me the Royal Malaysian Navy chart they were given by a Malaysian ship, which also provided them with fuel, food, and water and showed them how to reach a camp in Indonesia. It was widely reported in the Singapore media (usually reluctant to criticize the government) that a Singapore navy patrol boat had intercepted a sinking refugee boat but had left the refugees to drown. Some survivors were picked up by a passing freighter.

The international media joined the hunt for the story, with the Singapore government eventually acknowledging the incident while blaming the young conscript officer in command of the boat. Then, in order to prevent future public-relations disasters, the Singapore navy painted over the identifying numbers on their vessels.

The Boats

The "boat people" fleeing Vietnam by sea usually set off in wooden boats less than fifty feet (seventeen metres) long. These ranged from deep-sea fishing boats designed for rough weather to boats with very low freeboard and low bows designed only for use on rivers. Some were little more than sampans. Most carried far too many people and too little food, fuel, and water. They had no life preservers or navigation equipment, and the engines were often insufficient to steer the seriously overloaded boats against the wind and waves.

Vietnamese authorities actively attempted to prevent clandestine boat departures, and a number of refugees told me that they succeeded in escaping only on the second or third attempt. The closest destination for a boat leaving South Vietnam (apart from Cambodia) was Thailand, but the arrival destination often depended upon the weather or rumours about "Thai pirate" attacks or which country was least hostile to the arrival of Vietnamese refugees. The major weather factor was the two monsoon seasons, which not only affected where and when refugee boats arrived but also interfered with our ability to make selection trips to island refugee camps. If the sea was rough, refugee boats attempting landings often capsized in the surf, crushing or drowning people unfortunate enough to be underneath. There were also many incidents in which the local population actively opposed the landings of refugee boats.

I witnessed the arrival of a boat in a port on the east coast of Malaysia. The boat had been spotted at sea by the Malaysian police and escorted to the dock. It was a river boat about thirty-five feet (twelve metres) long with low freeboard and bow. Vastly overloaded, it provided standing room only. The boat had successfully crossed the Gulf of Thailand only because the weather was calm. The Malaysian police superintendent in charge informed me that the police had not boarded the boat because of the overcrowding but had been told there was an injured person aboard. As the boat was emptied, the police discovered a young woman who looked to me to be dead. Bloody rags were tied around the stump of one of her arms. She was alive but unconscious: a flywheel from the boat's engine had torn her arm off two days before. I told the UNHCR official at the scene that the young woman was accepted for resettlement in Canada. By chance I was at the Kuala Lumpur airport when she left for Canada and recognized her because of the missing limb; she had otherwise recovered.

Refugee Stories of Escape

The overarching condition of our refugee selection work was the unhappiness of the refugees. The extent of their sorrow varied depending upon their individual experience in Vietnam following the conquest of the South by the North in 1975, the difficulty of escape, the hazardousness of the voyage, and the nature of their lives in the camp. Because the Indochinese Designated Class relieved us of the necessity of determining whether applicants met the refugee definition, we did not ask questions about these matters, although some applicants wanted to tell us their stories. We also heard the experiences of refugees who worked with us.

One of our interpreters on Pulau Bidong introduced me to her father, who had been an officer in the South Vietnamese army. He had spent considerable time in "re-education." Although he survived where thousands of others did not, mentally and physically he was a broken man. Our interpreter and her father were the only members of the family in the camp. Because of his army service, he was in a higher US immigration category and could expect in due course to be resettled in America.

The journey from their homes resulted in many family separations among refugees as they tried to avoid detection by the Vietnamese authorities or simply got lost. Worry about missing relatives weighed heavily on many people. The passage over the South China Sea was always fraught with peril. An accurate figure of the number who left Vietnam but never arrived in a country of first asylum will never be known, but it is certainly many, many thousands. Apart from the weather, the principal threat was attack by pirates. At the very least, a pirate attack meant the theft of all of the refugees' gold and valuables. In many cases the pirates wounded, killed, and threw overboard refugees who attempted to resist, and they raped many of the girls and women. In some cases, rape victims were thrown overboard to drown, and in others they were taken by the pirates to brothels on shore.

On arrival in one camp, I was approached jointly by the camp leader, the UNHCR representative, and a Red Cross doctor, who asked me to waive the usual policy of selecting applicants in the order in which they arrived so that we would remove from the camp as soon as possible several recently arrived young women who had been repeatedly raped during a pirate attack. The doctor told me that the only reason they were alive was that their boat arrived directly at the camp where immediate medical attention was available. Otherwise they would have died from loss of blood. We did move the young women quickly to Canada, and they wrote to us after they arrived to inform us that they were doing well and were under the sponsorship of a supportive religious community.

Every adult resident of the refugee camps was marked by some or all of these harsh experiences in escaping from Vietnam. We were fortunate in being able to respond to the situation by selecting as many refugees as we could and moving them quickly out of the camps to Canada. Our camp visits brought relief not only to those we selected for resettlement but also to those who assisted us as interpreters and general helpers by providing them with useful work and an opportunity to converse with people from outside their enclosed existence. These conversations also gave us the opportunity to refute the countless negative rumours that circulated in all camps about the international effort to resettle the boat people.

The refugee camps in Malaysia or Indonesia were located in what might be described in travel brochures as tropical paradises, characterized by white sandy beaches, palm trees, warm and crystal-clear water, and (apart from monsoon storms) cloudless skies. But life in the camps was no picnic. Most of what trees had existed on Bidong were cut down by the refugees for firewood and to build shelter. There was no police force and there were no courts. There was also a criminal element at work in the camps. However, the governments of the countries of first asylum were not concerned with what happened inside the camp as long as it did not result in widespread disorder. Nevertheless, in all the camps there were children playing happily, oblivious to the tragedy that surrounded them.

The Royal Tanjung Pinang Yacht Club

Of all of the towns in Indonesia and Malaysia which we visited in the course of our work, Tanjung Pinang was the greatest contrast to our home base in Singapore. Where Singapore was modern, efficient, clean, affluent, and orderly, Tanjung Pinang was none of these. There were few diversions in Tanjung Pinang. To relieve the stress of working in a hot, humid refugee camp, a doctor with the Australian Intergovernmental Committee for European Migration created the Royal Tanjung Pinang Yacht Club. The RTPYC, what we today would term a "virtual" institution, existed only in the minds of its members. Club members devoted their spare time to obtaining for the club the patronage of the great and the good of the world and securing reciprocal privileges with other clubs around the globe. For example, the "Royal" in the club's name was due to the patronage of Prince Leonard of Hutt – an imaginary micro-nation in Western Australia. Although HM Queen Elizabeth and many presidents and prime ministers declined the honour of lending their names, one who did do so was the then US secretary of state, Alexander Haig. In consequence, the club created the Alexander Haig Billiard Room.[5]

Visitors

Many Canadian visitors came to observe the refugee selection process, particularly in the fall of 1979 and in early 1980. Most of the visits were of little consequence to us in terms of achieving our selection objectives; all of them, however, were significant in the visitors bringing back to their organizations the facts they had learned and the impressions they had gained of the situation on the ground and the roles and effectiveness of the many Canadian, foreign, and international governmental and non-governmental bodies involved.

Journalistic visitors fell into the two types I had previously encountered in my job in Hong Kong in 1974 when I inaugurated the Family Reunification Understanding with China. The first type was the "hit and run crowd." Usually inexperienced in the subject of the story or the part of the world in which it was set (or both), they were unwilling or unable to learn. I begrudged the time devoted to them because their stories would be inaccurate, misleading, and at times sensational. The second type was experienced and knowledgeable – or, if not, willing to learn and able to do so quickly. Journalists of this type were well worth the time spent with them.

The visit of greatest importance to us was that of Cal Best. Civil service titles can be obscure to the uninitiated, so he can best be described as the chief immigration officer of Canada. His boss was the deputy minister of employment and immigration, which meant that Cal was where the buck stopped with respect to developing immigration policy and the conduct of immigration operations at home and abroad. In other words, the responsibility for meeting the government's commitment to resettle 50,000 Indochinese refugees rested on his shoulders. The purpose of his visit was to see for himself what was happening and to determine if any changes needed to be made. He was accompanied by one of his directors general, Kirk Bell, who headed the policy-making shop.

I was with a selection team on Pulau Bidong when Cal and Kirk arrived in Singapore. When they reached Kuala Terengganu, Margaret Tebbutt and I returned from the camp to meet them and Al Lukie, the immigration program manager in Singapore. We went directly from the dock to their hotel without a much-needed shower, in order to bring them up to date on the current situation. The next morning the Malaysian government provided the biggest boat on which I ever travelled to Pulau Bidong to transport the VIPs in comfort to the island.

We were accompanied by the high commissioner, Ross Francis, and UNHCR officials from their local and regional offices. Cal was greeted on arrival by the camp committee and several hundred children waving Canadian flags. Al Lukie explained to our visitors how we operated and conducted them on a tour of the refugee camp, while the rest of us returned to selecting applicants for resettlement in Canada.

The final phase of the visit went better than we could have planned. After returning from Bidong, we took our two visitors to the Kuala Terengganu airport late in the afternoon for their flight to Kuala Lumpur. There they would overnight in a hotel and continue on to Bangkok the next morning. When we reached the airport, however, we found that their flight had been cancelled. (Of course, this happens in all countries, but in Malaysia the reason for the unavailability of the flight could be, as I once experienced, that the chief minister of the State of Terengganu wanted to fly to the capital, and so the rest of the passengers were prevented from boarding so that he could travel in solitude.) Consequently, Cal and Kirk, accompanied by Al, me, and much luggage, boarded our underpowered van for the trip to Kuala Lumpur across the mountain range that runs the length of the Malaysian peninsula. In view of his height and rank, Cal was given enough space to stretch out, while I recall sharing the back seat with the luggage. As we crawled up the hills in first gear, Cal made a pointed observation about how the Department of External Affairs had spent the money he provided to them for our use. Following an uncomfortable and endless night, we arrived in Kuala Lumpur just in time to have a quick breakfast before our visitors left for their flight to Bangkok.

One very human and humorous event is associated with the visit. In preparation for Cal Best's visit, the Pulau Bidong camp committee sought my advice on a painting they wished to present to him. It was almost complete in time for the visit and showed a roughed-in figure stepping onto the dock at the island, with children in the background waving the Canadian flag. The committee wanted to know what Mr Best looked like so they could complete the painting. I told them that he was a very tall man who towered over most other Canadian males and that he was black. They got the "tall," but the "black" did not register. I repeated the explanation in French but with the same result. To be fair to the Vietnamese, the only Canadians they had seen in the camp were Caucasian or Chinese. Visa officers are no strangers to problems of cross-cultural communication, and I attempted to solve this problem beginning with a history of black immigration to Nova Scotia during and after the American Revolution. Eyes glazing over, they either got it or pretended they did. When the visitors arrived, it became apparent to the artist that there was a problem with the painting. He rushed off and quickly completed a colour correction. To the surprise of all, the finished painting contained a reasonable likeness of Cal Best.

Local Heroes

Throughout Southeast Asia, the tremendous efforts of the visa officers, primarily from Canada, Australia, and the United States, were made much easier by the intervention of local individuals who recognized the humanitarian crisis and took steps to alleviate the hardship and suffering of the refugees. There were many such people in each of the Southeast Asian reception countries. A handful went beyond anything that could have been expected in their efforts to ease the burdens of the refugees. These persons earned a special admiration from all the Canadian officers serving in the area.

Sister Monica of the Order of the Holy Infant Jesus

Sister Monica was the mother superior of the Convent of the Holy Infant Jesus in Cheras, a suburb of Kuala Lumpur. When the Malaysian Red Crescent Society created a transit camp for Vietnamese refugees selected for resettlement in Canada on the convent's football field, Sister Monica had no official connection with the operation. However, without her involvement and commitment to helping the transitory population of the camp, the cost in unnecessary hardship and stress to these unfortunate people would have been much greater. She was a significant factor in the camp operating as successfully as it did.

By 1979 the convent had become a home for retired nuns, although Sister Monica had been a teacher for many years. She acted as the champion of the refugees in the camp, bringing to our attention cases that had gone off the rails. In particular, she brought to our attention the hardships visited upon the camp residents by the approach we took to those refugees whose initial chest X-rays showed that they may have had TB. She ensured that the best housing and more food was provided to those unfortunates who spent many months in the Convent camp. As well, she made known to every visiting official from Ottawa or a provincial government the human impact of our policy. She was also convinced that Canadian visa officers working in tropical settings performed best when served an ice-cold beer every hour on the hour. Sister Monica passed away in the 1980s.

Datin Paduka Ruby Lee, Secretary General of the Malaysian Red Crescent Society

Ruby Lee had been the head of the MRCS since 1965. (Datin Paduka is a title awarded by the government of Malaysia.) The response of the Malaysian government to the arrival of the boat people was initially highly unfavourable and prejudicial to their welfare. Eventually the Malaysians accepted that only by housing and feeding the refugees until their resettlement could be effected would there be a permanent solution to the problem.

The MRCS was chosen as the organization to create and run the refugee camps. The MRCS had never before been involved in such a large undertaking, which was complicated by the fact that most of the refugees in Malaysia were located on previously uninhabited islands off the east coast of the country. Nevertheless, Datin Ruby proved to be the right woman in the right place at the right time, and through her organization skills and force of personality, some 250,000 Vietnamese refugees were fed, housed, and cared for until the last camp closed in 1996. Datin Ruby passed away in 2009.

15

Bangkok, 1978–1979:
Operational Beginnings

The next two chapters describe the impact of the refugees from Cambodia, Laos, and Vietnam on Thailand and the experiences of Robert Shalka who, with Murray Oppertshauser, opened a visa office at the Canadian Embassy in Thailand in November 1978. For several months, along with two locally engaged employees, they were responsible for all immigration operations in Thailand and Burma. Initially staffed to process twenty refugee families each month, within ten months E&I Bangkok would be tasked with delivering over 18,000 refugees. Chapter 17 recounts the experiences of several officers who served in Thailand.

Thailand's geography – a shared border with Cambodia and Laos and proximity to Vietnam – precluded its isolation from events in Indochina. In addition, the diverse composition of the refugee populations making their way into Thailand by land and sea – Cambodians, Laotians, Hill Tribes, Vietnamese, and ethnic Chinese – produced unique political and operational complexities for the Thai government, international organizations, and resettlement countries. These factors in turn created an unusually difficult and little-understood environment for the resettlement operation that Canada eventually established in Thailand. The mass killings and displacement of Cambodians from 1975 onwards also had a profound impact on the Progressive Conservative government's management of its resettlement commitment and on relations between the government and the sponsoring community.

Throughout the Vietnam War, many feared that Thailand would become Southeast Asia's next tottering "domino" to succumb to communism. The country had experienced an active communist insurgency in the northeast and far south. Relations with Cambodia were tense, regardless of which regime held power in Phnom Penh, and large tracts of eastern Cambodia were seen as Thai by historical right.[1] Laos, because of its ethnic and linguistic ties to Thailand, was considered a natural sphere of influence. Vietnam presented a real military threat, one that became more serious once it invaded Cambodia in early 1979 and installed a client regime in Phnom Penh.[2] It was this conjunction of geography, history, and internal instability that made Thailand's situation unique compared to other countries of first asylum in the region.

The fall of the non-communist regimes in April 1975 produced the first wave of Indochinese refugees, of which significant numbers sought refuge in Thailand. Most were from Cambodia and Laos, but some Vietnamese also made their way to Thailand. Although their numbers were small compared to arrivals who reached Hong Kong and the US refugee reception centres in Guam, Wake Island, and the continental United States, they were sufficient to warrant the temporary dispatch of a Canadian visa officer, James Metcalfe, to Bangkok to process Indochinese refugees with connections to or sponsorships from Canada.

For a variety of reasons, refugee departures from Cambodia and Vietnam dropped off significantly after the initial wave following the fall of Phnom Penh and Saigon. The Khmer Rouge regime in Cambodia imposed extremely tight controls following the forced evacuation of the urban population to the countryside. Escape was almost impossible, limited to the luckiest and most daring. In Vietnam, those who had been hesitant or unable to escape adopted a position of wait-and-see with the new regime, although a trickle of people escaping by boat began arriving on the east coast of Malaysia and southern Thailand during the second half of 1975.

The situation in Laos was more complex. Irregular military forces recruited from the Hill Tribe minorities (Hmong, Yao, Khmu, and Thin) had been heavily involved in the American-funded "secret war" against the North Vietnamese-backed communist Pathet Lao. With the American withdrawal from Laos following the January 1973 Paris Peace Accords, the Pathet Lao made it clear that they considered the Hmong hostile and would take harsh measures to punish their "collaboration" with the Americans. As the Pathet Lao position grew stronger, the situation became increasingly precarious for the Hmong, leading to the air evacuation of their leadership in May 1975, first to

Thailand and eventually to the United States. Rather than remain in Laos and face severe repression, tens of thousands of Hmong and other Hill People followed their leaders and fled to Thailand, travelling on foot through the mountains and floating across the Mekong River. By the end of 1975, some 40,000 Hmong and other highland refugees had reached northern Thailand. How many died or were killed attempting to escape Laos is not known, but the flight of Hmong and other Hill Tribe refugees continued for many years and amounted to 400,000 persons by the 1980s. It is estimated that at least one-third of the Hmong population left Laos.[3]

The impact of the Pathet Lao takeover was less severe for the lowland Lao population, at least initially. Vientiane, the capital, was occupied only in August 1975, and the moderate stance of the Pathet Lao was viewed with considerable optimism. The shell of a coalition government was retained, there were no arrests or show trials, and private property was respected. Diplomatic relations with the United States continued, although aid stopped. Many members of the business class, military officers, officials, and others who had cooperated with the United States and had fled to Thailand between April and June 1975 returned in the hope that Pathet Lao promises of moderation and reconciliation would be honoured.

Although the flow of refugees – with the exception of the Hmong – into the countries of the region slowed considerably after the influx of April and May 1975, the movement never ceased completely. That said, the decline in refugee arrivals was such that by October 1976 senior managers in Ottawa responsible for the Canadian immigration program were able to pronounce that "Canada had done its part in the Indochina program except perhaps for help with the small boats' people if they had relatives in Canada."[4] With hindsight, this assessment would prove woefully premature, although it was arguably made with some justification based on the information then available.

The Second Indochinese Refugee Crisis

The lull in refugee arrivals following the rush of April 1975 was short lived. Small boats filled with refugees fleeing Vietnam began to arrive on the shores of neighbouring countries during the second half of 1975.[5] Numbers started as a trickle, 377 for the whole region in 1975, but increased steadily – 5,619 in 1976, 21,276 in 1977, 106,489 in 1978, and 292,315 by the end of July 1979. Southeast Asian governments at first tolerated the boat arrivals on their shores, especially as countries that had resettled Vietnamese in 1975 were prepared to accept these refugees in numbers that ensured that residual populations did not increase. This attitude changed to outright hostility as the trickle became a flood, raising fears that the mass influx of refugees, many of them ethnic Chinese, would upset the local racial balance or pose a security threat if they were not moved on quickly to third countries. While Thailand was the recipient of only a small number of boat refugees, the authorities adopted the approach of their neighbours to discourage boats from landing.[6]

The situation in Laos took a drastic turn in December 1975 when the Pathet Lao assumed complete control and proclaimed the Lao People's Democratic Republic. There was no more talk of elections. Non-communist newspapers were closed, and a massive purge of the civil service, military, and police followed. Thousands were sent to "seminar" – the Lao version of "re-education" – in remote parts of the country, where many died from harsh conditions, food shortages, and lack of medical care. These events prompted a renewed flight to Thailand as many of the urban professional, business, and intellectual classes who had initially been willing to work with or for the new regime decided to leave – something much easier to do from Laos than from either Cambodia or Vietnam. By 1977, some 10 per cent of the population had fled Laos for sprawling refugee camps just over the border in Thailand. In contrast to their stance on the Vietnamese, the Thai authorities were rather more relaxed toward Laotians. Nevertheless, the Thai government was adamant that, like the Vietnamese and Cambodians, the Laotians would not be allowed to stay permanently. Although arrivals from Cambodia came to a near halt by mid-1975, a sizeable population remained in camps along the Thai border. Resettlement, chiefly to the United States, continued, but some 14,000 Cambodians still remained in Thai camps in mid-1978.

After the forced evacuation of the urban population into the countryside, and the expulsion of the few remaining foreigners following the Khmer Rouge victory in April 1975, Cambodia became almost completely isolated from the outside world. Nevertheless, reports of Khmer Rouge brutality and appalling conditions in the countryside began to trickle out, chiefly through the accounts of the small numbers able to escape to Thailand. These accounts consistently described star-vation, brutality from Khmer Rouge cadres, a total lack of medical care, harsh conditions, and large-scale massacres of people deemed hostile to the new regime. Initially the accounts were greeted with some scepticism, being considered part of a campaign of atrocity propaganda concocted by the US Central Intelligence Agency (CIA) to discredit the new regime. In addition, a combination of fatigue over Indochina and the need to pay attention to other equally com-pelling crises, as well as the rapidly changing role of China, diverted US attention away from Cambodia. For its part, the Thai government refrained from negative comment as it sought to develop close rela-tions with the Khmer Rouge regime, if only to ensure that Cambodia remained a buffer between Thailand and Vietnam. As well, China, Vietnam, and the Soviet Union were not prepared to criticize the Khmer Rouge. In the first instance, China supported the Khmer Rouge as part of its broader anti-Soviet and anti-Vietnamese policies. In the sec-ond, although relations between the communist parties of Vietnam and Cambodia were never good, Hanoi had provided support during the war and, notwithstanding intractable differences over their coun-tries' border, refrained from anti-Khmer Rouge propaganda as long as there was a prospect of a peaceful resolution of differences.[7]

By late 1977, events forced more attention on Cambodia. Repeated Khmer Rouge military incursions across the Thai border accompa-nied by atrocities against Thai villagers made it unlikely that relations between the two countries would improve.[8] Similar attacks over the border with Vietnam escalated into open warfare. The formidable Vietnamese and Soviet propaganda machine, which for more than two years had been supportive of the Khmer Rouge regime and dis-missive of any mention of atrocities, was directed against Cambodia. Finally, the accounts of escapees became too numerous and credible to ignore.[9] Cambodia was evidently not the bucolic paradise where, as some of the regime's apologists claimed, any problems facing the new social model were entirely the result of "imperialist" disinfor-mation and the residual impact of the Indochina War.

By early 1978 it was obvious that the refugee situation in Southeast Asia was reaching crisis level. Malaysia, Indonesia, and Thailand – the principal countries of first asylum – were increasingly vocal in communicating to both UNHCR and principal countries of permanent resettlement their unwillingness to keep refugees on their territories in perpetuity. They also threatened that new arrivals would not be allowed first asylum unless departures matched or exceeded arrivals. Although most international attention focused on Malaysia and Indonesia, the government of Thailand was not shy in pointing out that it hosted the largest number of Indochinese refugees of all – some 100,000 by mid-1978 – and that all were expected to leave. Resettlement countries were lobbied to increase their efforts in Thailand.

A Refugee Program for Thailand

Meanwhile, interest and pressure within Canada to help and resettle Indochinese refugees gained momentum through media accounts about the experiences of refugees and their plight in crowded, often squalid camps.[10] Canadian missions in the region also reported the grim conditions within the three countries of Indochina.[11] The US government, representing the largest resettlement country, became increasingly active in urging other western countries to expand their resettlement efforts within the context of burden sharing. The American Embassy in Ottawa, headed by Thomas Enders, an "old Indochina hand," advocated strongly for a greater Canadian role.[12]

From the Canadian standpoint, the small, albeit increasing refugee program managed by two officers in Singapore was inadequate to meet Canada's growing commitment to Indochinese refugee resettlement, and more attention needed to be placed on Thailand.

In the light of changed circumstances, and a request by UN High Commissioner of Refugees Poul Hartling that Canada consider accepting Cambodian and Laotian refugees, discussions took place during the first half of 1978 among Ottawa-based officials from Employment and Immigration, External Affairs, and other departments about the desirability of establishing a special refugee program for Thailand.[13] Cabinet approved a modest program to resettle up to twenty families per month from Thai camps at a "metered rate" up to an unannounced total of 1,000 persons.[14] The numbers were considered sufficient to deal with a relatively small number of Vietnamese boat people, Cambodians, and Laotians of interest to Canadians. An important element in the program approved by Cabinet was that refugees selected for resettlement would need to be able to establish successfully in Canada with support available from the government and the Canadian public.

Bangkok: Setting up the Office and Early Operations, November 1978–July 1979

Planning for the new program began even before Cabinet gave its approval on 20 July 1978. An early decision was that two Canadian immigration officers would suffice to manage the Thai program. However, it was unclear whether the two officers would be based in Singapore or at a new office in Bangkok. Eventually, Bangkok was chosen, partly because the embassy there had space and accommodation available for two additional Canadian officers and support staff, but more significantly due to the urgings of Ambassador William Bauer, who had lobbied for a refugee program in Thailand. Two officers were assigned to the new office: Murray Oppertshauser, assistant officer-in-charge and consul at the Canadian consulate in Manchester, England, as officer-in-charge, and Robert Shalka, vice-consul at the Canadian consulate in Stuttgart, West Germany, as the second officer.[15] Neither had served in Asia, although Oppertshauser had interviewed Vietnamese in US refugee centres in 1975. Shalka's refugee experience was with Eastern Europeans in West Germany.

The new Immigration Section (visa office) in Bangkok was to be a small operation, in keeping with the limited scope of the Thai program. In addition to refugees, it would be responsible for all Canadian immigration operations in Thailand, Laos, and Burma.[16] The two visa officers would be assisted by only two local support staff. Unlike most other offices, Bangkok was to have no locally engaged immigration program officer (IPO).[17] The office's primary mission, apart from a small movement of immigrants, visitors, students, and temporary workers, was to select, process, and manage the monthly departure for Canada of Indochinese refugees at a metered rate of five Small Boat Escapee (SBE) families and fifteen Thailand Overland Refugee (TOR) families each month. This target was a refinement of Cabinet's approval of twenty families and generally reflected the distribution of the refugee population. A family was assumed to mean a "case" – which could be single persons travelling by themselves or heads of family accompanied by a spouse and/or dependent children. Refugees with a family sponsorship or nomination from Canada would be considered over and above the twenty families per month target. The same would apply to private sponsorships once this program was in place. Refugees were to be processed under the recently established

Indochinese Designated Class provisions, which would avoid the necessity of determining whether each applicant met the UN Refugee Convention definition.

Some months would pass before Oppertshauser and Shalka actually took up their new assignment in Bangkok.[18] Both arrived in Ottawa at the end of October 1978 for a week of briefings at Employment and Immigration and External Affairs. Throughout the briefings, the potential for successful establishment was emphasized as a primary consideration when selecting refugees in the camps for Canada. With respect to the TOR part of the program, no preference was given for Cambodians or Lao. That said, it was recommended that the first group of refugees with visas issued in Bangkok should include Cambodians destined to Ottawa. This recommendation was a reflection of the early interest in Cambodians among church groups in the national capital region, generated in part by US Ambassador Enders and his wife. It was also mentioned that Gaetana Enders had visited the Cambodian border camps, identifying refugees she considered suitable for resettlement in Canada. While well-meaning, her interventions were not considered necessarily helpful.[19] Generally speaking, Oppertshauser and Shalka were given wide discretion to manage and deliver their monthly target of twenty families and those with sponsors or contacts in Canada.

En route to Bangkok, Oppertshauser and Shalka spent several days in Singapore. Ian Hamilton, the officer-in-charge, greeted them at the airport with the words, "Am I glad to see you guys." Hamilton and his second officer, Richard Martin, had been managing a growing refugee program in addition to normal immigration activities and clearly welcomed the reduction of their staggering workload, allowing them to focus on Malaysia and Indonesia. Oppertshauser and Shalka spent three days reviewing files, being briefed on conditions in the Thai camps that Hamilton had visited a short time before and on the key personalities and organizations on the ground in Thailand, and becoming familiarized with operational logistics and procedures then in place. The time spent in Singapore was extremely helpful, allowing Oppertshauser and Shalka to avoid reinventing the wheel once the new office in Bangkok became operational.[20]

The two men finally arrived in Bangkok on 11 November 1978. At the airport, Ross Glasgow, a foreign service officer (FS) for External Affairs on his first posting, responsible for consular and administration matters, echoed Hamilton's greeting in Singapore: "Are we glad to see you guys!" The mission was being inundated with inquiries from refugees, the Thai government, other refugee receiving countries, and international organizations about Canada's new refugee program in Thailand.[21]

Canada's embassy in Bangkok in late 1978 was a mid-sized mission with seventeen Canadian officers and support staff along with about the same number of Thai employees. William Bauer, the ambassador, was an old Asia hand with no illusions about dealing with the Pathet Lao, Khmer Rouge, and Vietnamese communists, or, for that matter, with Thai politicians and officials. He had a well-deserved reputation for being plain-spoken and called matters as he saw them – very much out of step with the traditional External Affairs image of a diplomat. Bauer had pushed hard to establish a Canadian refugee processing capacity in Bangkok. His deputy, Sean Brady, had reported extensively on the refugee and human rights situation in Indochina based on interviews with recent arrivals in the camps on the Thai border. Along with the other Canadians in the mission, Brady was very helpful during the first months of the immigration program in Bangkok. The Thai administrative staff, long-serving local employees of the embassy, were less than enthused about the arrival of two additional Canadian officers and two new local staff, as this meant additional work for them without any extra resources. That said, they were professionals who rose to the challenge as required.

Oppertshauser and Shalka quickly set to work getting the new immigration section up and running. The first priority was to hire two Thai assistants. The embassy placed notices in Bangkok's English-language newspapers inviting applications to staff a new immigration and visa section dealing primarily with refugees; out of hundreds of applications, some fifty people were interviewed. The quality of applicants was impressive; most had studied abroad and spoke excellent English and, in some cases, French.[22] The first two assistants were hired and given rudimentary training in filing, form filling, and correspondence. After perhaps a month, Luan Tan, Singapore's experienced and capable Immigration Program Officer (IPO), came up for a week to assist in training.

Along with organizing a new office, the visa officers' early tasks included introductory calls on key players on the refugee scene to clarify the new Canadian program and mandate. First and foremost was the local office of the UNHCR, which was responsible for refugee protection and coordinating humanitarian aid to feed, clothe, and shelter the refugees. The International Committee for European Migration (ICEM) was responsible for conducting medical examinations and organizing transportation from the camps to the Bangkok transit centres, completing Thai exit formalities, and arranging transfers to the airport and flights to resettlement countries, including Canada.[23] The local office of the International Committee of the Red Cross (ICRC) was also important, as it provided the travel documents required by refugees leaving Thailand.[24] Working under the UNHCR umbrella or the aid programs of various western countries were a variety of international organizations conducting relief programs in the camps. These included World Vision, Caritas, Food for the Hungry, Médecins Sans Frontières, and others. Last but certainly not least was the Royal Thai Government Task Force for Displaced Persons in Thailand, responsible for all refugee matters related to security and camp locations. It was staffed by members of the Thai police and military; their cooperation was essential, as the task force controlled access to the camps.

Links were also established with representatives of other resettlement countries. The Americans had a large presence devoted to refugee screening and selection. The head of the US refugee program during this time was Lionel Rosenblatt, a foreign service officer who had spent part of his early career in South Vietnam. Although not posted to Vietnam at the time of the collapse in April 1975, he returned to Saigon at his own expense and was instrumental in organizing the evacuation of many of his old Vietnamese associates.[25] Much of the American program was devoted to determining whether refugees met the parameters of their program, a chief element of which was association with the US involvement in Indochina.[26] Australia operated the second-largest program. Their officers were from the Australian Immigration Department and operated in a manner similar to Canada's. Because of their colonial legacy, the French were also present and active. Their officers were French army colonels and followed an approach dependent on the varying whims of Paris. New Zealand, Sweden, and other countries also had small programs in Thailand.

The new office sparked considerable interest among the various players in the refugee relief and resettlement community. Explaining the Canadian refugee mandate was very much an exercise in managing expectations. Contacts often had an over-optimistic notion of the size and nature of the Canadian program, and it was necessary to establish a touch of reality. Once the initial scope of the program became known, the Thais in particular expressed disappointment with the small numbers that Canada was prepared to resettle. Another source of confusion stemmed from misunderstandings over the Canadian refugee and family reunification programs. Within a week of their arriving in Bangkok, Oppertshauser and Shalka received a visit from the head of the local office of the International Committee of the Red Cross. The purpose of the visit was to present a list of persons in Vietnam said to have close family in Canada and exit permission from the Vietnamese authorities. Oppertshauser had to explain that the Bangkok mission did not have responsibility for immigration from Vietnam, which came under the Hong Kong visa office, and that it was uncertain whether the persons on the list had valid sponsorships from Canada.[27] The best that could be done would be to forward the list to Immigration Headquarters in Canada.[28]

Relative to later events in the spring of 1979, the first months for the new Immigration Section in Bangkok were sufficiently calm to allow the new team to settle in and get operations underway. Ian Hamilton had conducted interviews in the Cambodian and Vietnamese camps in the autumn of 1978 and arranged for medical examinations for approved cases. Oppertshauser and Shalka arrived in Bangkok with two suitcases of these case files, which provided an inventory of near-visa-ready cases even before initial trips could be made to the camps. The first group of these refugees left for Canada with visas issued in Bangkok in mid-December and included Cambodians destined to Ottawa as suggested by headquarters. More would follow at something approaching the metered rate envisaged by the department.

Within a week of arriving in Bangkok, the new office also made its first foray into refugee selection, interviewing and accepting a small group of Vietnamese and ethnic Chinese detained on a Greek freighter in the Bangkok harbour. They had been rescued at sea, and Thai authorities refused to allow the ship to depart until all refugees on board had been accepted for resettlement. As a result of Canada accepting some of the group, UNHCR was able to persuade the Thai authorities to allow everyone to leave the ship and be placed in immigration detention.[29] The ship was then allowed to continue on its way. Beginning in December 1978, selection trips were made to several camps with the largest populations – Aranyaprathet and Surin for Cambodians, Songkhla and Laem Sing for Vietnamese, and Nongkhai and Ban Vinai for Lao and Hmong.[30] These trips put a sufficient number of refugees into process to meet the monthly target with a small reserve.

Another notable event during these early months was the arrival on the 1979 Easter weekend of a Thai merchant ship at the mouth of the Bangkok shipping channel with several hundred Vietnamese rescued at sea. Canada accepted well over one hundred of these people, either as SBES or persons with family or sponsorships in Canada. Also noteworthy was the week-long visit of Archbishop Plourde of Ottawa in early 1979. His objective was to witness conditions in the refugee camps first-hand and take charge of a young Cambodian refugee from the Aranyaprathet camp who had been sponsored by the Catholic Church in Ottawa – a precursor to what would become a major sponsorship effort by various Ottawa faith groups.

Although boat departures from Vietnam increased in late 1978 and into 1979, SBES did not land in Thailand in great numbers. As a consequence, Bangkok was somewhat insulated from the dramatic situation faced by the offices in Singapore and Hong Kong. Lao continued to arrive in Thailand, but in numbers considered manageable. At the beginning of 1979, the Vietnamese army invaded Cambodia, forced the Khmer Rouge from Phnom Penh and other cities, and set up a client regime of exiles and Khmer Rouge defectors. However, these incidents did not immediately result in significant numbers of new refugees crossing into Thailand. All in all, the situation appeared well in hand from the perspective of the two Canadian officers in Bangkok. Indeed, there was some concern that the number of refugees in process would mean that the small quota of twenty families per month would be filled some months ahead, especially as Immigration Headquarters was not prepared to increase Bangkok's target. This position would soon be overtaken by events.

Working in the Camps: The Refugee Selection Process

In the years following 1975 the visa office in Singapore had developed a practical approach to selection and processing of refugees in the scattered camps of the region. The fundamentals of the approach were adopted by the new office in Bangkok and remained in place throughout the life of the program, with modifications as necessary to meet changing circumstances. In its broad outline, before each camp trip, the visa office would inform UNHCR of the intended dates and duration to ensure the availability of the local UNHCR field officer to provide whatever assistance might be required. The Thai government task force was also advised, partly as a courtesy but also to ensure that there would be no difficulty in gaining entry to the camp. On occasion, Canadian teams might be informed that a visit was not advisable because of security concerns. This happened mainly in camps along the Cambodian border.

Like their colleagues in Singapore, Hong Kong, and Manila, Oppertshauser and Shalka found themselves trying to balance an overwhelming demand for resettlement with the limitations of the Canadian program. At this stage, a visa officer arriving at a camp of 40,000 refugees could accept only a small number for resettlement in Canada. It was thus critical that control over the interview and selection process be established at the start to avoid raising false hopes.[31] The best approach was to go in fast, work quickly from a list of people to be seen, and leave. It was also essential that Canadian officers acted, and were seen to act, in a fair manner. In keeping with these principles, a Canadian officer or a team of officers would arrive at a camp with a list of people to be interviewed. This document provided an essential element of order to the process and a rationale for who could be seen. Throughout the life of the program, the interview lists remained a basic mechanism for maintaining an orderly interviewing process. Refugees were placed on the list according to certain basic priorities: persons with Family Class sponsorships (form IMM1009) and Assisted Relative undertakings (IMM1010) or in private sponsorship from Canada; persons claiming close family members in Canada, including holders of Promise of Visa Letters; referrals from UNHCR or letters from refugees[32] sent directly to the embassy; persons claiming other connections with Canada such as study; persons with a knowledge of English and/or French and employable skills; and others, including unaccompanied minors.

In almost all cases, this approach generated more than sufficient numbers of people to interview and select. Others not on the list could be considered depending on the circumstances. For example, recent arrivals might come forward claiming a relative in Canada. In other instances, UNHCR or other agencies might refer people for urgent humanitarian consideration. Such cases usually occurred in the boat camps and involved women who had been victims of violence, including rape, at the hands of pirates.

In keeping with the Cabinet memorandum establishing the refugee program in Thailand, Canadian officers sought to follow the general guideline that any refugee selected should be capable of successful establishment in Canada with the settlement assistance available, including the existence of sponsors or because of their language and skill levels. (Anna N. Vu and Vic Satzewich in their article "The Indochinese Crisis of the 1970s and 1980s: A Retrospective View from NGO Resettlement Workers" explore some of the strategies employed by refugees to improve their prospects at the interview.[33]) During the first six to eight months, many refugees met this profile, at least in the Lao and Vietnamese camps, and selecting sufficient numbers with settlement potential to meet the target was not a major issue. For example, the lowland Lao camps (Nongkhai and Ubol) had a significant middle-class population of former civil servants, teachers, and small-business persons. Many had studied abroad, some in Canada. In addition, the Lao secondary education system prior to 1975 had retained a strong French influence, and anyone holding a high school diploma was expected to be fluent in French. The situation in the Vietnamese camps was similar. The long French and US presence meant that a significant number of refugees spoke French and/or English. Many were also from professional and middle-class backgrounds. As a result, it was relatively easy to find Vietnamese and Lao with good settlement prospects.[34] A steady influx of new arrivals continually replenished this pool. It was different in the Cambodian camps, where most of the population had arrived in 1975. New arrivals were few, at least until mid-1979. By early 1979, most English and French speakers had already been approved for resettlement by other countries, chiefly the United States. Most of the remaining Cambodian camp population had rural backgrounds with no English or French, primary education at best, and limited skills. In addition, the United States had made a commitment that it would resettle all "old" Cambodians – arrivals between 1975 and the end of 1978 – in Thai camps within a two-year period. For this reason, interest in Canada declined in favour of the US option.

In light of the above, E&I Bangkok decided to focus its efforts on the Lao and Vietnamese camps where pools of refugees meeting the program profile were readily available. The Cambodian camps were not ignored, but selection efforts were concentrated on refugees named by sponsors or with family identified in Canada.

The interview and selection process followed a set pattern that continued throughout the duration of the program. The arrival of a Canadian team (one officer in the beginning) was announced over the camp public address system, and the persons named on the list were called to come forward. Copies of the list were also posted around the camp. In the Vietnamese and Cambodian camps, persons whose names were on the list would present themselves quickly. The Lao camps were different; the first day of an interview mission was typically very slow, as it was not uncommon for Lao refugees to be outside the camp shopping, working, or tending crops. Once word got out that the Canadians were in the camp, the refugees would rush back and business would pick up.

Those whose names were on the list would appear, and the visa officer would verify identity and family composition. The refugees would be asked to present any documentation showing a connection to Canada, such as a relative or sponsor.[35] They would also be asked whether there were other close family members in the camp; the objective here was to avoid leaving family behind.[36] If everything appeared to be in order, the head of family would be given an application for permanent residence in Canada (IMM8) and supplementary family composition forms. They were asked to complete them and to return for another interview in a day or two with all family members. At this second interview, information would again be verified and any discrepancies or contradictions clarified. If all was in order, the refugee would be informed that his/her case was approved, subject to completion of medical and other requirements, and be asked to sign the application and transportation warrant.[37] As a final step, information was given about medical examinations, onward transportation to the Bangkok transit centre, and, finally, movement to Canada. Overall, this procedure worked quite well.

Processing after the Interviewing Trip

Every camp visit generated considerable paperwork upon return to Bangkok. Sponsored cases required telexes to the responsible CIC to inform sponsors or relatives of the results of the interview. In the case of new arrivals, claims about a relative or contact in Canada had to be verified. Telexes might also be sent to other Canadian missions in the area to confirm whether other family members had been accepted and their destination in Canada if they had already departed. Finally, a general report about the trip would be sent to Foreign Branch headquarters and External Affairs, providing information about the number of cases and persons selected, as well as any other matters of interest.

Refugees were required to undergo medical examinations and pass security and criminality screening. A major task for the Thai staff after each camp trip was the completion of medical examination forms to be sent to ICEM medical services in Bangkok. ICEM would arrange for the medical examinations and forward the results, including x-ray images, to the medical section at the Canadian High Commission in Singapore for review and decision. Initially, refugee medical examinations took place at local Thai hospitals near the camps, but once the refugee movement grew, applicants were brought to transit camps in Bangkok for completion of examinations.

Security screening in these early days was rudimentary. Because General Dang Van Quang was still a relatively recent memory, interviewing officers paid close attention to any applications from persons claiming to have been high-ranking military officers (lieutenant-colonel and above), as well as senior officials in the pre-1975 regimes. In point of fact, very few such cases came forward for Canada. Former military officers and officials were primarily interested in resettlement in the United States, which was prepared to accept them, and, to a lesser extent, France. Names of refugees provisionally selected were passed on to the RCMP liaison officer for vetting.

Moving Refugees to Canada

At the start of the Bangkok program, the logistics of moving refugees to Canada were quite basic and followed the system that had evolved in Singapore. Mass movements by charter aircraft were a later development. Deciding the Canadian destination of refugees was at first left to the discretion of the visa officer, although persons with a sponsorship, relatives, or a similar connection to a particular location would be sent there. French speakers were usually destined to Quebec (principally Montreal or Quebec City) and the national capital region. Officers from the Quebec Immigration Service (SIQ) were present only on an occasional basis, although this changed as the Cullen-Couture

Accord on Immigration came into effect.[38] Refugees without connections already in Canada were destined to centres chosen by the visa officer.[39] Once all requirements were completed for the refugees, visa and transportation warrants would be forwarded with a covering letter to the local office of ICEM. This agency was responsible for arranging transportation for refugees with visas from the Bangkok transit centre to the airport as well as travel on scheduled commercial flights via the Pacific or Europe to final destinations in Canada.

In the early days, ICEM was required to follow certain protocols. Refugees were not to arrive in Canada late at night or on weekends or holidays; transit time between arrival and departure to the final destination via domestic airline was supposed to be kept to a minimum. Once ICEM had made travel arrangements, the Bangkok visa office was informed of the details. It, in turn, would send a telex message listing the names and other relevant information about the refugees along with travel details to the port of entry (usually Vancouver, Toronto, or Montreal) and the Canada Immigration and Employment Centres at the final destination. Copies were also sent to Immigration Headquarters in Ottawa as well as overseas immigration offices en route (e.g., Hong Kong, Tokyo, London, or Paris), in the event of delays or if assistance was required. This rudimentary arrangement worked well enough for the small numbers involved.

The first six months of setting up operations and establishing the program in Bangkok were busy ones, but when compared to events from the summer of 1979, this early period was the calm before the storm. With the massive influxes of refugees that soon followed, it became clear that the staffing levels in Bangkok and elsewhere as well as the procedures in place were inadequate. Changes would be needed.

16

Bangkok, 1979–1980:
Crises and Growth

The modest resettlement program envisaged for Thailand by Cabinet in the summer of 1978 called for the arrival in Canada from Thailand, at a metered rate, of fifteen Thailand Overland Refugees (TOR) and five Small Boat Escapee (SBE) families per month, along with sponsored cases. Soon, however, the influx of refugees fleeing Vietnam, Laos and, eventually, Cambodia created a growing pressure from the countries of first asylum on resettlement countries to accept more refugees. As a first step, and in line with the Canadian government's decision to admit 5,000 Indochinese under the 1979 annual refugee plan, E&I Bangkok's monthly target was increased in February 1979 to sixty-five families: sixty TOR and five SBE. By the spring of 1979 the rising flood of new arrivals and pressure from Canada to process more and faster meant that even this increase would prove insufficient. It was also evident that a Bangkok operation of two Canada-based officers and two support staff simply could not meet the expectations.

In May, Immigration Headquarters decided that the Bangkok office would assume responsibility for immigration from Vietnam.[1] In practical terms this meant the assignment of René Bersma, an experienced and energetic visa officer who had been covering Vietnam from the Asia and Pacific desk at headquarters, to manage the nascent Family Reunification Program (FRP). He would be supported by one locally engaged employee. Although the Vietnam FRP would be Bersma's priority, it was also understood that he would assist with the refugee program. Accordingly, he was interviewing Lao refugees in the Ubol camp within a few days of his July arrival in Bangkok. Headquarters also advised that it proposed assigning two more officers and four support staff for a larger operation in Thailand. In the meantime, the office was swamped, especially as ever more refugee sponsorships, named and unnamed, were being received from Canada.[2]

While arrivals from Laos and refugee boats from Vietnam landing in Thailand continued at a high rate,[3] it was the Cambodian refugee dynamic that changed most drastically in the spring of 1979. Following the Vietnamese invasion of Cambodia in early 1979, the communist Khmer Rouge were pushed westward, accompanied by large numbers of hostage civilians. At first these population movements remained under the tight control of the Khmer Rouge, and there was no significant increase in the number of refugees crossing the Thai border. In April 1979, as Khmer Rouge control weakened, tens of thousands of Cambodian civilians as well as Khmer Rouge fighters began crossing into Thailand in consequence of being forced away from food-producing areas into the mountains and forests along the border. By September, when it became evident that insufficient rice had been planted earlier in the year, flight into Thailand became the only option to avoid starvation. This influx of people created a major refugee crisis and humanitarian disaster. Most new arrivals were in dire straits, having been on the move for months under short rations. The plight of these refugees, publicized worldwide by the media, made it clear that the first priority was to provide food, shelter, and medical care. From late May 1979, a major international effort through a joint mission, a consortium of international agencies (UNICEF, UNHCR, ICRC, and the World Food Program) along with non-governmental organizations (NGOS) was established to provide for these new arrivals. This effort, under various guises – the best-known being UNBRO (United Nations Border Relief Operation) – continued for many years and wound down only at the end of 2000.[4]

The new arrivals were housed in camps segregated from those holding the 1975 to 1978 refugee population. For some considerable time, access to these new arrivals for resettlement was problematic. Certain groups remained under Khmer Rouge control or were themselves Khmer Rouge. In addition, the Thai authorities maintained that the new arrivals would not be allowed resettlement. From the standpoint of the Thai military and security services, a significant population of Cambodian civilians and Khmer Rouge fighters along the border was a useful buffer and recruitment base for groups fighting against the

Vietnamese army. As a further complication, Thai authorities also engaged in periodic involuntary repatriations, forcing Cambodian
civilians back over the border, notwithstanding protests from the
United Nations and resettlement countries. Eventually international
pressure prevailed, and most Cambodian new arrivals were made
available for resettlement in third countries. From 1979 to the end of
1984, over 165,000 Cambodians departed Thailand for third countries (in 1979, 17,323; 1980, 27,200; 1981, 49,723; 1982, 20,411;
1983, 29,138; and 1984, 21,706). Of these, 62 per cent were resettled in the United States.

The Geneva Conference on Indochinese Refugees, 20–21 July
1979, resulted in an increase in global resettlement pledges from
125,000 to 260,000. The new Progressive Conservative government
of Joe Clark announced that Canada would resettle 50,000 Indochinese refugees by the end of 1980 as its contribution. E&I Bangkok's
share would move from sixty-five families a month set in February
to, by August, 4,000 persons for 1979 and then to 12,000 for 1980.
When the Trudeau government returned to power in April 1980, it increased the overall commitment by 10,000 to 60,000. E&I Bangkok
was assigned 4,000 of the increase, raising its total to 16,000.

The Bangkok operation would expand to eight Canadian visa officers and fourteen locally engaged staff. The Quebec Immigration
Service (SIQ) would also assign two officers to Bangkok with appropriate support staff in offices within the embassy. Since Quebec had
signalled a preference for Cambodians, E&I Bangkok was expected
to select and process large numbers of the Quebec target of 10,000.[5]

The newly assigned Canadian officers began to arrive only in mid-
September. In the interim, Bangkok received a stream of temporary
duty officers from both the domestic and foreign services in order to
meet assigned refugee targets. First to arrive were Brian Calvert from
Immigration Headquarters and Gilles Bibeau from CIC Winnipeg.
Their experience as new arrivals was repeated throughout the life of
the program. Both were met at the airport in mid-afternoon on a Friday, allowed a brief rest at their hotel, and then had dinner with the
Canadian immigration staff already in Bangkok. Saturday and Sunday
were spent at the office in briefings and orientation followed by an
early Sunday-evening departure on the night train to the Lao camp at
Nongkhai for four days of interviews.[6] Other trips to refugee camps
followed in short order.

Calvert and Bibeau were soon joined by Leo Verboven and Ron Button, foreign service officers from headquarters, Frank Seegers[7] from CIC Hamilton, and Jim Saunders from CIC Winnipeg. The last temporary duty officer to come to Bangkok was Gary MacDonald, an officer on posting in Belgrade who had been pulled from leave to go to Bangkok. They remained in Bangkok for varying times until well into the fall of 1979. Because their time there was expected to be temporary, they were worked hard and rose to the challenge in a strange and difficult environment.

Of the officers posted to Bangkok on a permanent basis, Bill Lundy from headquarters arrived to assume the role of deputy program manager of an expanded office. He was followed in short order by Ben Smith from Hong Kong, Bill Sheppit[8] from London, and Don Myatt from Athens. The last officer to arrive was Marius Grinius, a new immigration foreign service officer on his first posting. The RCMP also augmented its security screening capacity by sending additional resources on a temporary basis – Stu Sutherland, a Cantonese speaker from Hong Kong, and Doug Herda and Mike Oneschuk, both from Canada. One of them would accompany each interviewing team to the camps.

Faced with the need to deliver 4,000 Indochinese refugees for resettlement in Canada by the end of 1979, followed by another 12,000 in 1980 – later increased to 16,000 – and to fill a preordained schedule of charter aircraft, the Bangkok management team had to decide where to focus their efforts, based on the number and availability of the refugee population. In the late summer and early autumn of 1979, the largest available pool of refugees was in the Lowland Lao camps of Nongkhai and Ubon. For practical reasons, it was these camps that would receive major attention, even though the Lao did not spring immediately to mind as refugees among the Canadian population, the media or, for that matter, Immigration Headquarters. While the Cambodian and Vietnamese camps would not be forgotten, it was E&I Bangkok's decision that the principal focus would have to rest with the Lao in order to meet the numbers required. At this point, new Cambodian arrivals were by and large not available for resettlement, and their condition, especially in those camps controlled by Khmer Rouge cadres, was such that providing the basic necessities of life took priority over refugee selection interviews. This reality was not always appreciated in Canada, where knowledge was derived largely from media coverage. That said, selection trips would be made on a regular basis to the Cambodian camps at Aranyaprathet and Prasat, where the population was available for resettlement. The populations of the two Vietnamese boat camps – Laem Sing and Songkhla – were too small to meet the needs of the assigned target.

Although the refugee population in Thailand was the largest in any of the countries of first asylum, it was still often difficult to identify and process sufficient numbers to meet Canada's commitment. There were several reasons for this. Canada was not the only country actively resettling refugees from Thailand. In July 1979 other countries such as the United States, Australia, France, and even the United Kingdom had also greatly increased their resettlement commitments. Following the Geneva Conference of July 1979, a variety of countries not usually considered as major countries of refugee resettlement launched programs to accept thousands of refugees, albeit for a short time. As a result, significant numbers of refugees were resettled in West Germany, Italy, Spain, China, and Argentina.[9] Even Malaysia, whose government was adamant that no Vietnamese would remain in the country, accepted several thousand Cambodian Muslims from the Cham minority.

Refugee selection trips to the Lao camps became something of a race for numbers to meet the target assigned to the Canadian team in Bangkok. This happened in competition with other resettlement countries, all actively selecting from the same pool of candidates. As a consequence, it was not uncommon for refugees to be accepted by more than one country. Refugees themselves often had family members already resettled in several countries. Under the circumstances, as they wanted to maximize their resettlement options, they could not be blamed for failing to mention that they had already been accepted or were under consideration for another country. Also, it was not unexpected that refugees would opt for the country that would move them from the camp first. The result was that 25 to 30 per cent of the persons selected in the Lao camps were no-shows when called for movement to Bangkok for continued processing. Selections therefore had to be made on the premise that there would be considerable wastage before planes could be filled. A primary factor in this wastage was UNHCR's delay in establishing a registration system to monitor resettlement activity for individual refugees. UNHCR had never considered third-country resettlement as a viable option for the large Lao population. A comprehensive registration for resettlement purposes in the Lao and Cambodian camps was implemented only in the spring of 1980, by which time the major push for resettlement has passed.

The situation in the boat camps was very different; there was no question that the Vietnamese would be required to leave. Here UNHCR had developed an effective system at an early date – the so-called blue cards, which tracked the resettlement history of each refugee, including referrals to various resettlement countries, and the decision. As a general rule, a boat refugee selected by one country would not be poached by others.[10]

Logistics: The Camps

Thailand is a large country, and travel to the camps varied according to location and distance from Bangkok. The Songkhla camp for boat refugees in the extreme south required an hour and a half flight on Thai Airways to Had Yai, the regional centre, followed by a one-hour taxi ride to Songkhla itself. The Cambodian camps (Aranyaprathet, Prasat, Pong Nam Ron, and Trat), the Vietnamese boat camp at Laem Sing, and the "land" Vietnamese camp at Khorat could be reached only by embassy vehicle. Thailand had an excellent network of paved highways, thanks to American aid programs, which made road travel relatively simple, if lengthy. The camps in the far north were reached by a combination of air travel and a rendezvous with an embassy vehicle sent ahead with files, application forms, and supplies. The Lao camps at Nongkhai and Ubol could be reached by rail, embassy vehicle, or air. Each method of transport had its advantages and disadvantages. Embassy vehicle was the best choice if several camps were to be visited. Air had the shortest travel time, but it meant being at the Bangkok airport well before the usual departure time between 5:00 and 6:00 a.m. and not arriving at the camps until noon at the earliest. Trains, which were air-conditioned and had showers in the first-class carriages, left Bangkok in the early evening and arrived in Nongkhai and Ubol the next morning around 9:00 a.m., allowing almost a full day of work. As a matter of safety when travelling up-country, no driving took place after dark. Night-time road hazards included highway robbery and wandering villagers and animals. Even day-time travel was not without incident, as when an embassy vehicle almost collided with a group of working elephants coming around a blind corner.

Unlike in Malaysia and Indonesia, it was not necessary to stay overnight in the Thai camps. Hotels of varying quality ranging from primitive to excellent were to be found in nearby towns.[11] The food in small up-country Thai restaurants was uniformly excellent. A tasty meal with a cold beverage at the end of a long day of interviews was always more than welcome.

Trips to the most frequently visited refugee camps (e.g., Nongkhai, Prasat, Aranyaprathet, Songkhla, Laem Sing, and Ubol) became a matter of routine and differed from the system established at the opening of the Bangkok office only in scale. Upon arrival, meetings were held with the UNHCR field officer to confirm the availability of interpreters, assistants, and a place to work, followed by brief courtesy calls on the camp commander and the refugee camp committee. Lists of persons to be interviewed would be posted and an announcement made over the camp loudspeaker that the Canadian team had arrived. Interviewing facilities depended upon the camp. Basic requirements were limited access to avoid crowds of curious onlookers in close proximity to the interviews, a work table, and chairs or benches for officers, interpreters, and applicants. Ideally, there would be shade outside for those awaiting interview.[12] Interviewing conditions varied. For example, one trip to the Cambodian camp at Kamput took place during the rainy season, and the first priority was to find a place dry enough to work. A suitable hut was found with a thatched roof that did not leak. Unfortunately, the only table was already occupied by several chickens which had to be shooed away before interviews could start. At Laem Sing camp, located on the precincts of a Buddhist temple, interviews were held beside the crematorium or, if a funeral was taking place, on a boat grounded on the beach.[13]

Although the interviewing and selection of refugees for resettlement was a serious business, camp visits were not without lighter moments. On one trip to Nongkhai, it happened that three of the four-officer team were Dutch speakers (Bersma, Verboven, and Seegers). Shalka, the fourth officer, spoke German. In order to exchange information about cases free from eavesdropping, they decided to converse in Dutch and German. This caused considerable confusion among the refugees, who thought they were applying to go to Canada.

Those who assisted the selection teams as interpreters or helpers in the camps were themselves refugees and often quite remarkable people. They were young, well-educated, and enthusiastic. They were also prepared to work long hours in difficult conditions. Although there was no guarantee, many were accepted by Canada, or could have been, if not already selected by other countries.

Logistics: Transit Centres, Medical Holds, and Delivering the Target

Refugees selected by Canada and other resettlement countries were moved by bus from the camps to transit centres in Bangkok for medical examinations and preparation of onward travel arrangements. Refugees coming from camps in the far north or the south of Thailand could face a journey of twenty-four to thirty-six or more hours. Suan Plu, the Thai Immigration Detention Facility in Bangkok, was the initial transit facility and continued to be used for refugees destined to smaller countries (France, the United Kingdom, Norway, etc.). Although crowded, it offered basic facilities. With the massive expansion of resettlement programs following the Geneva Conference in July 1979, Suan Plu could no longer accommodate all the Indochinese transiting Bangkok, and UNHCR and ICEM established additional transit centres. The largest was a derelict Thai army barracks at Lumpini (quite close to the embassy), where refugees bound for Canada, the United States, and Australia were brought for medical examinations and to await final departure. The Lumpini transit centre too proved inadequate for the numbers involved and quickly became hopelessly overcrowded and unhealthy, including an outbreak of diphtheria.[14] By 1 November 1979, the Immigration Section of the embassy in Bangkok reported that the Canada-bound population in Lumpini had reached 2,400, largely to meet charter flight schedules for 1,680 seats in eight flights between October 17 and November 10.[15] The excess of some 800 refugees was due partly to meet the need for a reserve of applicants ready to move at short notice but also the result of medical furtherances[16] and a small number of security holds.

By 9 November, conditions had deteriorated to the point that Canadian Ambassador Bild signed a message (ZHGR2192) urging Ottawa to intervene with UNHCR to devise a solution that included increased transit capacity in Bangkok and medical examination and treatment facilities in the camps.[17] The result was the establishment of an exclusive temporary Canadian transit facility with space for 1,500 persons for the period 1 December 1979 to 31 March 1980 in a newly built but still unfurnished hotel, the Golden Dragon, on the outskirts of Bangkok.

For most refugees, the stay in the transit centres was mercifully brief, and those who passed medical requirements were soon headed for Canada. The overcrowded conditions in the centres were also mitigated by day passes granted by the Thais for shopping and other activities.[18] As a result, refugees with funds arrived in Canada with new clothes, electronics, and personal items, often to the dismay of the media, which expected them to appear destitute.

As discussed in the previous chapter, all refugees destined for Canada had to pass immigration medical requirements. Initially, medical examinations were arranged by ICEM at local Thai hospitals near the camps. In theory, ICEM would follow up for treatment and additional examinations as required.[19] With the expanded resettlement programs starting in the late summer of 1979, local hospitals near the camps could no longer cope. As a temporary measure, refugees were brought to Bangkok for completion of medical examinations prior to departure. Shortly after the Geneva Conference, UNHCR undertook to provide mobile units that would allow for medical examinations and treatment in the camps. Despite assurances from senior UNHCR officials that these mobile units were available at short notice, they did not arrive until well into 1980, when the bulk of the movement had already been selected and processed.

In the meantime, medical furtherances or holds for additional tests or treatment became a serious problem for the Bangkok transit centres, as one person with a medical issue could delay the departure of an entire family. Most issues involved possible tuberculosis, active or otherwise, and the testing and treatment process could be frustrating and time-consuming. In addition, the departure of some refugees could be held up for seemingly trivial reasons. For example, refugees might be furthered for corrective eyeglasses, as if these were readily available in a camp or transit environment. Many women were furthered for investigation of possible urinary tract infections. Given conditions in the camps, it was surprising not to have a urinary tract infection.

Although ICEM was efficient in completing initial examinations, it quickly became overwhelmed by work, and some time would pass before it could develop systems for follow-up and treatment. In the meantime, many refugees languished on medical holds in overcrowded transit centres. This situation not only contributed to serious overcrowding in Lumpini but also began to affect E&I Bangkok's ability to fill its scheduled charter flights. In October 1979, after consultation with Ottawa, a difficult decision was reached to split up families. The person on medical hold and one other family member would remain behind, while the rest of the family went forward to Canada. Immigration Headquarters in Canada was supposed to track the destination of the family to facilitate reunification once the person left behind was able to travel. Refugees facing longer medical holds, such as possible tuberculosis, were transferred to the Cambodian camp near Prasat, where care and treatment was supposed to take place. Unfortunately, this created additional problems. Most of the persons moved to Prasat were not Cambodian and found themselves in a strange environment surrounded by hostile and fearful refugees with whom they could not converse. Communication between ICEM and Médecins Sans Frontières (MSF), the organization providing medical care in Prasat, was poor. With considerable justification, MSF complained that large numbers of ill refugees had been dumped on them with little or no warning or information about what treatment was required. It took months to clear these Canada-approved refugees from Prasat. A new problem arose as persons on medical hold became ready to move to Canada and join their families. In some instances, it was found that the persons left behind had not really been part of the original family selected for Canada and had no interest in being reunited with people to whom they were not related.

For Bangkok, the early months of the expanded refugee program were a time of crisis that went beyond the issues discussed above. Selecting refugees in the camps was not in itself a major issue. Getting them ready to board the charter aircraft was, due to a combination of other factors. Unlike the well-established operations in Singapore and Hong Kong, Bangkok was a new office, and under-resourced from the start. The newly hired support staff, while eager and willing, were inexperienced and came on strength just as the office was expected to produce large numbers at short notice. As well, the infrastructure set in place by UNHCR, ICEM, other agencies, and the Thai government was not as efficient and effective as might have been desired. These factors were not fully appreciated by Immigration Headquarters, which led to an often less than favourable assessment of the performance of E&I Bangkok compared to that of Singapore and Hong Kong, both of which bore the heavy lifting during the early stages of the enlarged program.

As a consequence of Ottawa's concerns, Bangkok received the special scrutiny of two senior departmental officials during their tour of Indochinese refugee missions in November 1979 in the persons of Cal Best, executive director of immigration, and Kirk Bell, deputy executive director. Their visit proved opportune insofar as it sensitized Immigration Headquarters to the differences between operations in Thailand and the countries served by Singapore and Hong Kong. Murray Oppertshauser, the immigration officer-in-charge, arranged a full program for Best and Bell to give them firsthand exposure to the processing realities the Bangkok operation faced. Meetings were arranged with senior Thai officials, UNHCR, and ICEM. Best and Bell also accompanied Oppertshauser to the Bangkok transit centre and visited the refugee camps in Ban Vinai (Loei Province) and Nongkhai.[20] The visit made it evident that many of the difficulties faced by the Bangkok operation were beyond its control. The Thai government, for instance, had not devoted resources to support resettlement efforts in the same proportion that had been done in Malaysia, Indonesia, and Hong Kong. In addition, UNHCR and ICEM were still staffing up and readily admitted their shortcomings in providing support to the Canadian program, which was second only in size to that of the United States. One positive consequence of these meetings was commitment from the two key international agencies to increase effectiveness. Improvements were soon evident. ICEM, in particular, enhanced its medical examination and treatment programs, reducing the number of long-term medical holds. As well, Best acquired an understanding of the difficulties facing Oppertshauser and his team, and the messages from Ottawa became less strident.

Through the autumn of 1979 into the first quarter of 1980, the main focus of Canadian resettlement activity in Thailand was on the Lowland Lao and Vietnamese boat population. That did not mean that resettlement opportunities were denied to other groups, as periodic visits were made to the Highland Lao camps as well as to those holding Cambodians and to the land Vietnamese camp at Khorat. Nevertheless, meeting the targets set by headquarters and filling scheduled charter flights demanded a focus on those camps with large refugee pools available for resettlement. Accordingly, selection priority was given to Nongkhai, Ubon, Laem Sing, and Songkhla.[21]

Charters and Movement to Canada

Bangkok's first charter in late July 1979 was an Ontario World Airways operation that carried some 185 refugees to Toronto International Airport.[22] There would be no further charters from Bangkok until October. Although additional Canadian officers and local support resources were provided as part of Canada's increased resettlement program, it took time to build up inventories of refugees. Not until mid-October was there enough to fill regular charter flights. A charter-configured Boeing 707 could carry 185 passengers, a DC-10 could carry about 350, and a Boeing 747 Jumbo around 480. The number of passengers on any particular flight varied, depending on the number of children under age two and other factors.[23] By the beginning of 1980, Bangkok was able to accommodate up to six flights per month, for a total of 13,215 refugees destined to Canada by the end of the year.[24]

At first all refugee departures from Thailand took place from the main terminal of the Bangkok International Airport. As refugee charter flights became increasingly frequent, the Thai authorities changed arrangements, and departures were made from a semi-derelict building at a remote corner of the airport with only the most basic conveniences and no air-conditioning. Flight departures were also delayed until the small hours of the morning, around 2 a.m., when the air was cooler and flights were able to reach cruising altitude with less expenditure of fuel. Flights delayed until daylight had to refuel en route, adding thousands of dollars to the costs.[25]

The processing of each refugee from selection in the camps to movement to Bangkok and subsequent processing stages was a matter of some complexity. As the number of cases in process grew,

Bangkok developed a simple ledger or manifest book into which the particulars of each refugee selected for Canada were entered, with columns to record key processing information such as passing medical and all other steps leading up to flight departure. When all the blanks in the columns were filled, the case was ready for departure. The manifest book was a simple system that worked well in a pre-computer age where many hands touched each file between selection in the camps and final departure for Canada. With this system, few if any refugees fell between the cracks. Information in the manifest book also served as the basis for Destination Matching Request (DMR) telexes.

Cambodian Refugees: A Change in Focus

Although the Bangkok operation's resettlement focus from the last quarter of 1979 into the first quarter of 1980 was on the Lowland Lao and Vietnamese boat camps, events were unfolding that would ultimately result in a change in resettlement priority to Cambodians. As mentioned, by the autumn of 1979 the Khmer Rouge had lost control over ever-larger numbers of the Cambodian civilian population, resulting in a surge of arrivals along Thailand's eastern border. Cambodian civilians still under Khmer Rouge control were also moved closer to the border. Initially, the Thai authorities sought to keep these Cambodian new arrivals in makeshift camps in no man's land along the ill-defined border. As this population grew, so did the logistical difficulty of sustaining it. The United States, other western countries, and international agencies began exerting pressure on the Thai government to allow a significant number of Cambodians to take refuge within Thailand to relieve pressure on the border camps. In October 1979, Thai Prime Minister Kirangsak Chomanan announced an open-door policy to allow the Cambodians to enter Thailand and be accommodated in camps at specific locations.[26] The first of these camps, Sa Kheo, located in a large field on the road between Bangkok and Aranyaprathet, opened on 22 October 1979 with 8,000 refugees arriving at short notice. Thousands more arrived in the following days. Another camp, Khao I Dang, opened a month later on 21 November. The camp eventually was enlarged to accommodate 50,000 people but never housed more than 25,000.[27]

Initially, the Thai government was adamant that these refugees, or "illegal migrants," as the Thai authorities called them, were not eligible for third-country resettlement. However, it was not long before western governments began receiving representations on behalf of persons in the camps from relatives previously resettled. Notwithstanding pressure from western governments, the Thai authorities maintained their hard line. Then, suddenly, at the beginning of June 1980, the Canadian Embassy was informed that some refugees had been moved from Khao I Dang to a new camp at Trat, adjacent to an old camp that had existed since 1975. Canada was "invited to consider them for resettlement." A three-officer team – Bill Lundy, Don Myatt, and Florent Fortin (a Quebec immigration officer) – was promptly dispatched to Trat and selected some eight hundred persons over a three-day period.

By the late spring of 1980, US pressure to allow resettlement access to all Cambodians inside Thailand had begun to have an effect. The Thai government announced that a new resettlement camp would be established at Phanat Nikhom southeast of Bangkok. The camp opened in late July, and the first refugees, primarily from Khao I Dang, entered in August 1980. The first Canadian selection visit to Phanat Nikhom occurred in mid-August, and visits continued regularly until the camp closed.

Through the summer of 1980, the number of Vietnamese boat arrivals in Thailand declined to levels not seen since early 1979. Lao arrivals also decreased significantly. Camp visits continued to be made to the Vietnamese camps at Songkhla and Laem Sing. But while there had been no original intention to focus on Cambodians during 1980 and beyond, a visit to the Laotian refugee camp of Nongkai by Bill Sheppit and Marius Grinius in early September identified the need for a change in priorities. The pair returned to Bangkok after only three days, having selected fewer than three hundred refugees. According to Sheppit, the camp was empty, despite UNHCR data showing almost 20,000 refugees still resident. From that point on, Khao I Dang, with its largely Cambodian population, would become Bangkok's primary source for meeting its targets.

Staff Changes and Reorganization

Other changes were imminent, harbingers that the resettlement effort following the July 1979 Geneva Conference was about to run its course. Oppertshauser and Shalka both returned to Ottawa in the late summer of 1980, their two-year assignments at an end. Shalka was not replaced. Oppertshauser was succeeded as officer-in-charge by Ed Woodford, an immigration foreign service officer from headquarters. Woodford's low-key management style was in marked contrast to that of the more dynamic Oppertshauser. Woodford also appeared to have less enthusiasm for both Bangkok and the resettlement program. Within a month of arrival, he indicated that it was his preference, based on his understanding of views from headquarters, to scale back refugee selections, even if that meant not reaching the assigned refugee target.[28] This possibility met with objections from Ambassador Fred Bild, whose position was that Canada had made a commitment that he had conveyed personally to the Thai government in early 1980.

Faced with reduced targets for 1981, the number of officers devoted to the refugee program was already greater than needed. Bill Lundy, in his capacity as deputy officer-in-charge, proposed a reorganization of officer resources. René Bersma would be committed to the Vietnamese Family Reunion Program full-time, as this program was starting to show some movement. Ben Smith would be assigned responsibility for the Thai (largely visitor visas) and Burmese program, reporting through Lundy. The remaining officers, Lundy, Sheppit, Myatt, and Grinius, would continue to deliver the refugee resettlement program.

Summing Up

In the immediate years following the fall of Saigon, Phnom Penh, and Vientiane, Canadian refugee resettlement activity in Thailand was something of an afterthought, given the larger operations managed through Hong Kong and Singapore. Nevertheless, by mid-1978, circumstances had changed significantly. Pressures to respond to a growing refugee crisis and information about conditions in Cambodia prompted the Canadian government to establish a small program in Thailand delivered by two Canadian visa officers and two support staff. While adequate for the program originally envisaged, this establishment proved unable to cope with the realities of the crisis that unfolded in early 1979. As an integral part of Canada's response following the Geneva Conference of July 1979 and the remarkable upwelling of support from Canadians through the sponsorship program, the Bangkok operation grew rapidly and made a major contribution to meeting Canada's commitment at Geneva and beyond. This was achieved through a relatively small staff of Canadians and local Thai employees working long hours under often difficult conditions.

By the end of 1980, Canada's commitment to resettle 60,000 Indochinese had been met. By coincidence, the designated 60,000th refugee was a Cambodian selected by Bangkok and destined to a Mennonite sponsor. Of a total of 60,049 Indochinese refugees resettled in Canada between 1979 and 1980, Bangkok processed 18,379, or 30.6 per cent of the total.[29]

Bangkok's role as home of a major Canadian overseas immigration office did not end. A refugee program continued for many years, and responsibility for the Family Reunification Program (FRP) from Vietnam kept the office fully occupied as well. After a rough beginning, where official Vietnamese commitments did not always match delivery, the FRP served its goal of minimizing the need for persons with family in Canada to risk clandestine departure by small boat and face the hazards entailed. That, however, is another story.

17

Bangkok: Working in the Camps

The E&I Bangkok operation, like E&I Singapore, became a large enterprise involving a significant number of Canadian officers assigned for full postings or passing through on temporary duty for a couple of months. The lives of all who were involved in the operation were dramatically influenced by the experiences they encountered. The following recollections by five Bangkok officers reflect the broader experiences.

Into the Fray

DON MYATT

My first memory of Bangkok after I arrived in October 1979 was the heat. It was not the dry heat of Greece I had experienced during a four-year posting to Athens. This was really humid, making you always sweat and feel uncomfortable. It takes a lot to get used to a humid climate.

Settling in at a posting is a challenge, and Bangkok was no exception. I was lodged in the Montien Hotel with several other recently arrived colleagues. Accommodations were in short supply in Bangkok because of the heavy influx of expatriates and diplomats in response to the arrival of the boat people. The hotel was centrally located near Pat Pong and close to the office. I had never had a problem staying in a hotel for a few weeks, but this was different, as I remained at the Montien for almost half a year. It began to feel like my permanent residence.

Then a number of us moved into an apartment building at Soi 16 off Sukhamvit Road. The flats there were spacious, with large rooms and a long balcony off the living room overlooking the Thai Tobacco Monopoly pond. The balcony did not get much use due to the weather, although the sunsets and lightning storms made for spectacular views. Moving to an apartment meant finally receiving my shipment of personal effects, which had been sitting on the airport tarmac during monsoon season. Mildew had rendered a lot of things irreparable. Most of them could not be replaced easily, as buying local products was the norm in those days. Nonetheless, I was very glad to be in my own place at last. One vacant bedroom came to serve as a repository of unusable stuff that was slowly replaced, shipped home, or discarded.

No account of Bangkok is complete without mention of the traffic. In Bangkok you had to leave home at 6 a.m. to be at work before 7:30, or you could not make it on time. The office hours were 7:30 a.m. to 4 p.m. but we always worked much later. There was no end to the files. And weekends were not exempt, just to keep on top of the workload. The most striking memory of my arrival is of being met at the airport by my new boss, Murray Oppertshauser. Murray was an experienced, no-nonsense, professional foreign service officer of the old school. He believed that team-building required him to share the burdens of his staff. He met everyone on arrival. After a nice feeling of being made welcome by Murray, I was slapped on the back and handed an envelope containing a train ticket. I was to depart first thing in the morning for Nongkhai (up-country Thailand on the border with Laos) to select refugees. The train was leaving at 6 a.m., which was distressing since my plane had landed after midnight. By the time I reached the hotel, it was close to 2 a.m. Jetlag plus fear of oversleeping and missing the train made for little sleep that night. Soon I was on board a train travelling through the Thai countryside. My posting had begun.

Interviewing and processing the boat people meant working under arduous conditions. We worked from dawn to dusk, sitting on uncomfortable benches in open bunkers without air-conditioning in stifling, humid, 40-degree weather. Effective selection decisions demanded a detailed and comprehensive knowledge of program criteria and refugee resettlement objectives. The constant pressure of completing flight manifests and departure deadlines made one's caseload greater than normal.

We worked on weekends when the air-conditioning in the office was turned off. In an effort to cope, officers would show up in Bermuda shorts, and I recall Murray muttering that he was not paid enough to look at officers wearing shorts. To unwind, Murray held "Happy Hour" on Friday afternoons. He kept a bottle of scotch in his office bar, which he opened after 5 p.m. on Fridays. It was an appreciated effort to maintain morale by allowing officers to gather and share the week's stories. Such an approach to maintaining morale would not be permitted today.

Maintaining one's health could be difficult. I recall one trip up-country when I suffered serious food poisoning after eating ice cream from a vendor's wagon. Normally, the food in Thailand was safe, clean, and delicious, but not this time. I lay in the hot, dreary hotel room for three days with high fever and pain, alone in a remote area of the country. In retrospect, I consider myself lucky to have survived without medical attention or medicine. But to compensate for this experience after my recovery, I also recall eating an oyster omelette and stir-fried cashews with chillies at a restaurant on a beach in Songkhla while watching the fishing boats arrive with their fresh catches.

I was responsible for the movement of Khmer (Cambodian, also referred to as Kampuchean) refugees, which was expected to represent 50 per cent of the embassy's resettlement caseload, from camps to transit centres in Bangkok for departure. I first oversaw the movement of Khmer refugees from holding centres to the interview and processing centre in Phanat Nikhom. The Khmers were selected on the basis of close family connections, and therefore relationships had to be scrupulously verified before transfer to the processing centre. In the space of three months, I processed over 2,400 refugees. How I achieved this I cannot fathom, but there was very little down time during my posting. My memories are of work, work, and work with little play.

Our labour-intensive operation was exacerbated by constant status requests that required timely responses, forcing production of a considerable and endless volume of correspondence and telegrams. Countless inquiries were received from HQ, the public, other government departments, MPs, and ministers. We also had to maintain and service our useful contacts in the UNHCR, diplomatic community, local government, and NGOs as sources of information in order to stay current on program and political developments and be in a position to analyze and report on the refugee situation.

The plight of the boat people was an international humanitarian crisis, yet there is little public awareness about this operation nor understanding of the amount of work and effort that went into processing the Indochinese refugee movement. The demands we faced were unceasing. In addition to selecting the refugees, we monitored local policy for shifts affecting the refugees. As well, we sought ways to improve our operational efficiency, since staff resources were being reduced despite the growing workload. These achievements were due to the sacrifice of time and recreation by this group of foreign service officers. And it was not just us. All over Canada, church groups and organizations came together to sponsor refugee families, providing housing and jobs and resettling thousands, many of whom did not speak English or French and had no relatives in Canada. In many places in Canada where families settled, there were no Vietnamese communities.

We were all totally immersed in the work, and during my career I never again witnessed this kind of dedication.

Working in the Camps

LEOPOLD VERBOVEN

Letters were constantly received at the embassy from refugees in camps requesting resettlement in Canada. These letters played an important role in who would be invited to a selection interview and which camps would be visited. Some of the letters noted that the writers had relatives or friends in or on their way to Canada. Some letters were formally written and some arrived on scraps of paper.

Selection teams to refugee camps were comprised of a driver and two or three officers, depending on the assumed number of people to be seen. The locations of the camps were not always precisely known, but we were expected to find our way there and obtain accommodations if there were none readily available.

Once at the camp and having gained entry, we looked for persons who had sufficient command of English or French to act as interpreters. This was usually a simple matter, as word of our arrival and its purpose circulated quickly, and sufficient volunteers met us on arrival. After meeting with the camp authorities (Thai government personnel and the unofficial refugee camp authorities), we would be allocated space in which to conduct the interviews and given authority to enter and exit the camp.

We next met with the interpreters to discuss payment for their services and work procedures and whether they were interested in moving to Canada. We asked them first to find several of the largest, toughest young men in the camp and bring them to us. These were asked if they were interested in going to Canada, with the response invariably affirmative. We established their family makeup (not always obvious, as members became separated while fleeing Laos, were in other camps, or dead, or presumed so). When their current families had been ascertained and interviewed, we asked the large lads to act as security guards and gophers while we were in the camp – implying that if they worked well, they and their family would possibly be accepted to go to Canada. Their job would be to ensure that people who had written to us were available for interviews and that our "offices" remained intact overnight, and to carry out other administrative tasks, such as finding a tailor in the camp to mend torn pants.

Once the operational set-up tasks had been completed we began to interview families. Most of the refugees had fled Laos because of ongoing fighting. Some had supported the previous regime, while some had left because other members of their village had. Eligibility hinged on involvement with the previous regime, the nature of that involvement, and whether there was any chance of returning to Laos without problems. Determining successful establishment in Canada was influenced by the sufficient potential within the family unit for work and study. Family units, because of their potential for mutual support, were preferred.

Determining family configuration was complex. Our goal was to ensure that families were not separated, and we tried to find out who was where. This practice sometimes led to dealing with large units, as many distant members of split and broken families had become de facto dependants of surviving members. Extended families could include two brothers with wives and children as well as mothers and fathers on both sides and an assortment of never-married sisters and others attached to the family unit. The idea was to be able to identity young and able persons who could be the anchors for the family, with grandparents to look after the children who would be in school, leading to everyone successfully establishing in Canada.

One camp tour was particularly memorable. We were at Sob Tuang camp and on our way to Ban Nam Yao, both in Nan Province in the northeast of Thailand. Nan Province was one of the more isolated areas of Thailand, and stories tell of its conquest by the Thai authorities in the 1930s, one of the last campaigns conducted with the use of war elephants, taking place just before a French takeover of the area.

Poor and isolated, Nan was a stronghold of the Thai communist guerrillas until the 1980s, and many of them were still active when we visited. We encountered numerous roadblocks with Thai soldiers in full battle dress. Hill Tribes have traditionally inhabited this region, and it was natural for them to cross the border from Laos to seek sanctuary in Thailand. Among them were Hmong, Mien, Htin, and Khmu Hill Tribes, along with Yao and Lao. The refugee camps were constructed in the same fashion as each tribe would have built its villages in Laos, except that they were now all in the same location. However, each tribe stuck to its own community, and even among the Hmong there were divisions between White, Black, and Flower Hmong. Life was not easy, and having to live in close proximity to other tribes was a constant cause of friction. For the men, there were the additional factors of chronic boredom and loss of status. The daily routines for the women were likely more or less the same as they had always been.

On one trip to Nan Province, our team was staying in a hotel in the capital, Nan. A small nearby camp had some residents with family in Canada, and I was sent with a driver to complete any possible selections of refugees. The camp was small, its population mostly Flower Hmong, Yao, and a few Lowland Lao. After gaining access to the camp I located an interpreter and asked him to find the refugees with Canadian ties, which proved to be an extended family of brothers and sisters and offspring, totalling no more than ten.

The primitive infrastructure of the camp meant that no office, restaurant, or even shed was available in which to conduct interviews.

As there were so few interviews involved, I selected a handy log, which was also a bench (and in the shade), as my "office." While I was conducting an interview, there was a sudden commotion a few metres away as some young men beat the ground furiously. Not knowing what was happening, I stopped the interview to look. A cheer erupted, and one of the young men lifted up a large dead snake. The snake had also been escaping the heat (and avoiding camp residents) by sleeping beneath the log I was using as my "office." Perturbed by my intrusion, it had decided to move on and was immediately spotted by the locals – not me.

According to the young man who had killed the snake, it was going to go into the pot for dinner that evening, and I, seen as the person who had instigated this bounty, was invited to join the family for the meal. I would have liked to accept, but the danger of guerilla attacks after sunset did not allow me to stay. I regret missing this culinary delight.[1]

In these northern areas, the local Thai population was as poor as the people in the camps, and it was at the Ban Nam Yao camp that the Tom Dooley Foundation established one of its hospitals. It was Thai policy that no refugee camp should have a higher standard of living than the surrounding Thai population, so the hospital was shared by both the local and camp populations. As a result, it was one of the few opportunities for official egress from the camp. Other methods were common but required the active participation of the camp security.

Our office was in the Fertility Clinic of the camp – a somewhat misleading term, as it was meant to offer family planning services to the camp population. The large number of young children attested to the unintentional success of this program, and to its availability for our use as interviewing space. Our desks were sewing machine tables – without the sewing machines – and they and other benches were then transported to the "restaurant" for our lunch, invariably a variety of fruits, vegetables, and chicken. Each morning we were invited to choose a chicken from among those running around, and it would be prepared for our enjoyment.

As it was monsoon season, every day there was a tremendous downpour that would inundate our office. When necessary, we took a short break while the water was swept out and then continued our tasks.

Large families appeared before us, sometimes interrupted by one of the members screaming that they were not going to allow their child to be passed off as the son of another family unless they too were allowed to immigrate. If memory serves me correctly, I have a photograph of interviewing one extended family consisting of thirty-eight persons: two brothers, their spouses, children, parents, other siblings – the list went on.

At the end of one day, the guards asked if I could see a young couple who were not on our list but who would like some information. The guard mentioned that one of them spoke English. Intrigued, I agreed. The woman was a Thai citizen from a prosperous middle-class family, and he was a Lao refugee. She, an independent spirit, had rejected her family's proposed future of school, arranged marriage with a socially acceptable man, and future within the family business in Chang Mai. Instead she had taken a course in nursing at the Tom Dooley Institute, learned English, and after graduation became a nurse at the hospital in Ban Nam Yao. Her parents were horrified but felt that this was a passing phase and that she would return home. Instead she met the man who accompanied her to the interview.

He was a Lao who had become involved in the struggles in Laos while a teenager. His family and clan were nationalists and anti-communist. He had basic primary education and distant family members who had been involved with the American "Secret War." He managed to find employment, and avoid military conscription, by working in a hospital as a medical technician, specializing in minor wounds. When the Pathet Lao took power, he and his family fled. An uncle working with the Pathet Lao helped him reach Thailand, where he wound up at Ban Nam Yao. Single and active, he was soon hired by the hospital as an orderly.

There the young man and woman fell in love. The problem was that she was not allowed in the camp, while he was not allowed out of the camp. Their only means of contact was in the hospital where both worked. They went through a marriage ceremony performed by an NGO member, but it was not legal or possible for Thais to marry Lao refugees at that time. They had a room in the hospital which was their residence and future.

The challenge was how to help a young, intelligent couple in love. She spoke English and had a nursing diploma recognized in Canada, but as a Thai citizen, she was not a refugee. He was a Lao refugee and given his background, was admissible as such. In the end the young woman was processed as an immigrant and her "husband" as a refugee. The program manager managed to make travel arrangements for the young woman by having her work as a nurse on an American flight carrying refugees to the United States.

At that time refugees not directly sponsored by a group went to centres in Edmonton or Montreal and from there were assigned to resettlement areas. This applied to the young man. However, his eventual destination in Canada would be unknown. This was problematic as the woman was destined to Canada as an immigrant and required a specific destination. With a little creativity, an unnamed officer became a sponsoring group, with the woman destined to that location, while a notation was placed on the man's visa that he was destined to this same "group." Love conquers all when the selection team is sentimental.

Helping One Person at a Time

ROBERT SHALKA

I was alone in the Bangkok office in the early summer of 1979. Murray Oppertshauser was away on a selection trip to one of the refugee camps. It was a Friday afternoon when the embassy receptionist called to say that a young woman, who spoke no English, French, or Thai, was at reception holding a handwritten note from the United States Embassy explaining that she was Vietnamese and wanted to join her relative in Canada. I called Sean Brady, the chargé, to ask if he knew someone who spoke Vietnamese. Fortunately, the wife of one of his American journalist contacts was Vietnamese and available at short notice. She came in to interpret and the young woman's harrowing story unfolded. She had appeared at the main gate of the US Embassy earlier in the day, where a Marine sergeant, who had served in Vietnam and spoke some of the language, determined that she wanted to go to Canada where she had a sister. He gave her the explanatory note and put her in a taxi to the Canadian Embassy.

Her story was as follows. She was from Saigon, and her father, a former officer in the South Vietnamese Army, had been sent for "re-education." A sister had left Vietnam by boat some months earlier, had reached Malaysia, and was believed to be in Canada. The woman's mother made financial arrangements for her to leave by boat, which she did. After several days at sea, the boat was boarded by Thai pirates, who robbed the refugees of their belongings and took the younger women on board to their own boat to be raped, after which they were thrown overboard. The young woman decided that her best chance of survival was to become attached to one of the pirates, in the hope that he might protect her until they reached land. She picked the pirate she thought was the youngest and somehow made it clear to him that she would be his "wife" if he would protect her. This he did, and she stayed close to him for the rest of the time at sea. The fate of the other refugees was not known to her. The pirates eventually reached their home port somewhere in southern Thailand, and she managed to get her "protector" to understand that she wanted to go to Bangkok. He smuggled her ashore, and they reached Bangkok after a bus journey of several days, where he left her at the gate of the US Embassy.

After hearing this emotional story, I quickly prepared a message to our office in Singapore explaining the situation, with the names and ages of the sister and her husband who were supposed to have gone to Canada from Malaysia. I then decided that the best solution for the young woman was to remain somewhere safe in Bangkok pending confirmation of her story. I called Mario Howard, the UNHCR Protection Officer for Bangkok, to explain the situation and asked him to meet me at the Thai Immigration Detention and Transit Centre at Suan Plu. That seemed the best interim place for her to stay as it held other Vietnamese and provided protection by the UNHCR. Mario agreed this was the most sensible approach. We met at the detention centre with the young woman and arranged for Thai Immigration to arrest and detain her as an "illegal immigrant." It was explained to her that it would take some days to find out where her sister had gone and to make arrangements to be reunited.

Several days after the young woman was placed in the detention centre, I received a call from a colleague at the US Embassy to find out what had happened. It seemed that the wife of one of the senior officers at the embassy had heard about the incident and was upset that the young woman had been turned away. I assured my colleague that matters were under control and that the young woman was in the process of being reunited with her sister in Canada.

E&I Singapore soon confirmed that the sister and brother-in-law had been approved for Canada and had left only a month or two earlier. The responsible CIC at their destination was quickly contacted, to inform them that the younger sister was safe and to initiate unification. After rapid processing of her case, the young woman left for Canada on the first charter from Bangkok in late July. Being able to help people like this young woman placed our own hardships in perspective.

The "Newbie"

MARIUS GRINIUS

"You look lost. You must be Grinius." Thus Murray Oppertshauser, my new boss, greeted me upon my arrival at Bangkok's Don Muang International Airport on Saturday, 5 January 1980, at 10 o'clock at night. I was to be the last of the permanent staff to join Murray's team, which consisted of his Number 2, Bill Lundy, along with Bill Sheppit, Don Myatt, Bob Shalka, René Bersma, and Ben Smith. From a practical work approach, René was responsible for organizing the Orderly Departure Program for Vietnamese emigrants destined to leave Saigon, now Ho Chi Minh Ville, for Canada. Ben held the fort in Bangkok by focusing mostly on visa issuance for travellers out of Thailand or Burma. The rest of us were to spend much of our time up-country in the refugee camps throughout Thailand. At the height of the Indochinese refugee movement, there were sixteen camps, not counting those straddling the Thai-Cambodian border, which were off-limits for refugee selection. Separately, Thailand also hosted various camps along the Thai-Burmese border where the Shan and Karen minorities often sought shelter from the fighting inside Burma.

Instead of taking me directly to the hotel, Murray drove me to his house where those officers who were not up-country were enjoying a rare evening of good Thai food and relaxation along with spouses or significant others. As the new kid, I felt a certain standoffishness among the veteran officers gathered at Murray's, probably because not only did I not have any previous immigration experience but I was new to Asia and new to the Foreign Service. The learning curve began immediately with my introduction to Thai beer and to Mekong, the Thai whisky, which was considered aged vintage if it was more than two weeks old.

Murray dropped me off at the Montien Hotel at four in the morning. He advised me that, unlike himself and the rest of his team, I did not have to work that Sunday. I was to use the day to get over my jet-lag and report to the embassy the following morning. On Monday, Bob Shalka guided me to the embassy via a shortcut from the hotel down a back alleyway full of boisterous noodle stands and pungent smells of frying rice, fish sauce, and garlic. The odd mangy stray dog could be seen dodging cooks and tuk-tuks, the local three-wheeled taxi service.

"Here is your airline ticket," Murray greeted me at the embassy on the eleventh floor of the Thai Farmers Bank on Silom Road. "Your flight departs tomorrow at seven in the morning. You are going to Nongkhai refugee camp for the week. Bill Lundy, Sheppit, and Myatt are already there. Don't screw up like a previous TD [Temporary Duty] officer, who got off at the wrong airport. Do not get off at Ubol, which is pronounced "Ubon" and where there is also a refugee camp. Make sure that you get off at Udorn, which is pronounced Udon. Ubon–Udon. Got it? Here is your office, which you will share with Myatt. I will now introduce you to the locally engaged staff and in thirty minutes to Ambassador Fred Bild. Welcome to Bangkok and good luck."

I somehow managed to get off at the right airport up-country, where an embassy driver was waiting for me. We drove directly to Nongkhai refugee camp, situated near the Mekong River across from Vientiane, the capital of Laos. Nongkhai was host to the largest number of Lao refugees, about 30,000 at its peak. The driver took me directly to where Bill Lundy, Bill Sheppit, Don Myatt, and RCMP officers Doug Herda and Mike Oneschuk were interviewing Lao families. The Canadian officers welcomed me. Bill Lundy told me to sit in on an interview being done by Bill Sheppit and then another one by Don Myatt. "Okay, you have now seen how it is done," Bill said. "There is your interpreter. Now go select people for Canada."

In many respects, selecting refugees for Canada was relatively easy. The key was not to think too much about the yes/no life-changing decisions that you had to make thirty or forty times a day. Otherwise you risked being overwhelmed. The enormous press of numbers also ensured that one did not have the time to dwell on any philosophical or existential aspects. The criteria for acceptance were simple. By the end of the interview you had to decide whether the family, and it usually was a family sitting in front of you, could ultimately establish themselves in Canada. An ideal scenario was a family unit comprised of two able-bodied parents with at least grade-school education, a trade, and perhaps speaking French or English, one or two single siblings who could contribute to the family as wage-earners, and grandparents who could look after the children while parents were working. A tough, energetic grandmother and matriarch was always welcome. The family dynamics and the parents' willingness to work at no matter what job to start a new life in Canada invariably ended with a positive decision. Sometimes, however, as Bill Sheppit put it, "You made your decision based on the gleam in a child's eye."[2]

With my military background, I was rather partial to ex-military applicants. They and their spouses tended to have at least a high-school education. They had a trade and often spoke some English, often having been trained by American forces personnel. I was told a few years later that several helicopter pilots whom I had accepted eventually became successful bush pilots in Northern Canada.

All official refugee camps in Thailand were organized and administered by UNHCR representatives. They provided the basic documentation for all inhabitants of the camps. They also assisted in finding individuals or families who had sponsorships from Canada. Over the next two years, many of these UNHCR representatives became good friends and trusted colleagues.

While visa officers did the initial interviews, it was the job of the RCMP officers to vet those refugees who had been tentatively accepted for Canada to ensure that there were no security or criminal concerns. The final hurdle for any refugee tentatively accepted for Canada was the medical examination. Many families had to wait in situ or in holding camps in Bangkok if a family member was suffering from tuberculosis. Many had to wait and take the required TB medicine before they were cleared for Canada. Medicals were organized through the International Committee for European Migration (ICEM), founded at the end of World War II to facilitate the movement of European refugees and displaced persons – including my own Lithuanian family – to Canada and the United States. Subsequently, ICEM's mandate expanded to cover the rest of the globe. ICEM also was responsible for the actual travel of refugees from the camps to Bangkok and onward to their country of settlement.

Notwithstanding the best efforts of the UNHCR, the documentation process was a challenge, with some fraudulent family units being unrelated to each other, or so-called unaccompanied minors below the age of sixteen actually having families in the camp. While fraud was not rampant, one had to be alert and often question members of a family separately to confirm that they were indeed related. Occasionally their body language gave them away. One quickly noticed if a "sibling" was sitting well away from the rest of the family. Also, rumours within a camp could spread rapidly regarding how best to be accepted by Canada or any of the other countries taking refugees. On one sad occasion I interviewed several families in a row, all of whom were wearing bright yellow T-shirts with "Jesus Saves" written on them in large red letters. The rumour of the week had been that Canada and the United States were only accepting Christians. This rumour apparently had originated with a fervently religious NGO energetically proselytizing on behalf of their particular god.

Most NGOs, however, and there were many in Thailand, genuinely helped the Lao, Cambodian, Vietnamese, and Hill Tribe refugees in their time of need. In particular, I continue to have the highest respect and admiration for the Mennonite Central Committee of Canada. Jake Buhler, the MCC Bangkok representative with whom I had the privilege to work in Hanoi fourteen years later, basically told us that MCC would take those refugees that Canada would normally refuse. These would include such cases as a widow with, say, six young children, or a family with a child who was either physically or mentally incapacitated and would be normally refused by Canada. MCC did wondrous work. I so admire them.

For a year or more, we all worked seven days a week. At one point when I found myself flat on my back at the Bangkok Nursing Home, connected to an IV drip and suffering from an unknown fever, Murray came to visit and generously gave me the rest of the day off.

During my second year, things had slowed down to the point where we were all allowed every second Sunday off. The pattern of work was much the same. Sponsorships flowed in from Canada, either naming particular individuals or families (often with relatives already settled in Canada) or simply indicating family size or configuration that they could accept for resettlement. Private sponsorships were matched by government sponsorships. Once we had assembled enough case files for any particular camp, we would go there either singly or as a team, depending upon the workload. We fondly called the larger team visits "body grabs." Often one of the RCMP officers would accompany us. The routine was to alert the UNHCR to our visit so that they could prepare documentation for cases that we wanted to see and also to present cases they thought would be of interest to Canada. We would always need interpreters, who were organized by the local camp committee. We then simply got to work interviewing families and individuals. Initial interviews would spawn official applications, which would then be reviewed at a second interview, followed by an RCMP interview. The immigration forms would then become the key document for the file that eventually allowed the persons to settle in Canada. At the end of the day, and sometimes well into the night, it felt as if we had reached a limit to our quota of decision-making. Often exhausted, we would sit in the basic up-country hotel, cockroaches and all, not being able to decide where to go to eat (if there was a choice) or what to eat. Singha beer, however, seemed to be an always welcome nutrient.

Travel by road at night was discouraged, because of the very real danger of hitting a dark water buffalo along the road at high speed, as had happened to a crew from another embassy. It had the same effect as hitting a moose in Canada. Travel by car up-country in the daytime was also a challenge. Whenever my RCMP colleagues and I travelled by road between Bangkok and Nongkhai, a distance of some six hundred kilometres, we kept score of the number of accident scenes that we came upon. We awarded a half-point for any car-car or car-motorcycle collision and a full point for any truck-truck or bus-truck collision, as well as any single 10-wheeler rice truck or bus accident. Thai long-distance drivers had a habit of trying to keep awake by using amphetamines and then suddenly falling asleep at the wheel. And there was a reason why the Thai orange-coloured inter-city buses were nicknamed "Orange Crush." Our one-way scorecards averaged ten to twelve points.

Camp conditions varied but were never good. The "normal" camps consisted of rows of wooden barrack buildings, which always had far too many people living in them for their design. The latrines were invariably overflowing and revolting. There were usually common kitchens, with rice and a few vegetables as the daily fare. Some camps did have thriving local markets, run by local Thai or entrepreneurial refugees, where people could supplement their diets. Dog and fresh rat-on-a-stick were popular. The UNHCR brought in trucks with water tanks to distribute potable water, but there was never enough to bathe or shower in until monsoon season arrived. When the monsoon did arrive, the camp roads became rivers of mud, and latrine effluent was spread more widely. All of the usual diseases like malaria and dengue fever were ever present. Other, tougher camps consisted of tents or simply blue UNHCR tarpaulins thrown over bits of wood.

Perhaps because of their historic animosity, the Thai seemed to reserve the worst living conditions for the Vietnamese. Songkhla in the far south near the Malaysian border was a village of tents surrounded on three sides by barbed wire and guarded by local police with big side-arms. The camp faced the Gulf of Siam from whence those Vietnamese who survived the Thai pirates staggered ashore. Laem Sing, facing the northern part of the Gulf of Siam, was a rocky outcrop dotted with wretched little huts covered by the ubiquitous UN blue plastic. On one visit Bob Shalka and I were at least protected from the driving monsoon rain because we conducted our interviews in the crematorium. (On another occasion, I recall being in Laem Sing immediately after my "day off" at the Bangkok Nursing Home when, in the middle of an interview, I unexpectedly broke out in a sweat which totally soaked me and the documents before me. I stepped out of the interview, threw up, and then returned to continue the interview. I accepted the surprised family for Canada.) Despite difficult conditions, the Vietnamese camps were always the best organized. Upon our unannounced arrivals, the local camp committee would immediately ask how many interpreters we needed and in which language, English or French. We would then be given interview space to get on with it.

A third, special camp, located near Sikhiu, about 120 kilometres northeast of Bangkok, was reserved for Vietnamese ex-soldiers and their families. As a precaution, the Thai authorities wanted them separated from other refugees and interrogated, I would assume, about Vietnamese military dispositions in Cambodia after Vietnam's invasion of Cambodia in December 1978 when it routed the Khmer Rouge and pushed them back to the Thai border. As the Vietnamese tried to wipe out the last pockets of Khmer Rouge resistance along the Thai-Cambodian border in the area of Aranyaprethet, the fighting sometimes spilled over into Thailand. When Vietnamese artillery barrages occasionally strayed over the border, they were answered by Thai artillery barrages.

A fourth Vietnamese camp was located right on the Thai-Cambodian border. For a while, fleeing Vietnamese could bribe their way to Phnom Penh, and those who were not killed by the Khmer Rouge made it to the Thai border area near Aranyaprethet. The Thai authorities wanted to make living conditions in that particular camp as hard as possible so as to discourage any further arrivals via the Cambodian land route.

It was also off-limits to any refugee selection. Later the Thai authorities relented and moved sponsored Vietnamese families from that camp into normal processing centres further inside Thailand. My first visit to that camp, soon after it had been established, was almost my last. A black-clad militia guard, surprised to see a *farang* (foreigner) at the camp, immediately stopped me at gunpoint – an M-16 rifle, as I recall. With my hands up, I slowly, slowly pulled out the Thai Border Task Force 80 permit from my shirt pocket, only to find that the guard was illiterate. Thankfully, he had the wherewithal to call his commander who could read and confirm that I was allowed to visit the camp, and I was left intact.

If one was not up-country, the focus of our work tended to be the incoming 747s of Air Canada or Wardair, which we had to fill with those families ready to be sent to Canada. The logistics, through ICEM, flowed like magic from refugee camp to holding centre in Bangkok to 747 on the tarmac in Don Muang. The necessary paperwork always seemed to be complete, although a few no-shows occasionally caused unhappiness. One of us from the team was always present at each loading of the 747. This invariably took place in the middle of the night when Don Muang was quietest. ICEM representatives supervising the move of refugees onto the aircraft were accompanied by Thai immigration authorities. The Canadian representative checked off the names and ensured that all travel authorities and their obligations to repay had been signed. My lasting image has been that of a 747 fully loaded with refugees in their seats (no business class), yet seeing no one because they were so small. Both the Air Canada and Wardair aircrews seemed highly enthused and motivated by their special refugee flights. It was a special time for all of us. Both airlines also flew in Canadian beer, which was well used to host our various friends and contacts at Canada Day celebrations. Ambassador Bild, as official host, made sure that all embassy staff, including lowly third secretaries such as myself, were able to invite our counterparts to the Canada Day celebration.

While most of my responsibilities centred on Lao refugees, as well as keeping track of the large TB caseload, it was a singular privilege to visit the various Hill Tribe refugee camps. Ban Vinai, up-river from Nongkhai, was by far the largest and even boasted a separate leper colony. Ban Vinai was also the centre of the Hmong resistance movement in Laos, led by legendary Hmong leader Vang Pao, and later by his brother Vang Neng, long after the war in Laos had officially ended. While a number of Hmong did settle in Canada, trying to interview and then getting them to Canada proved to be particularly challenging. Most often an entire family, although they had a sponsorship from Canada, would not leave their camp if one family member, say, a grandmother, was still missing. One could only speculate about their fate in Laos. On various occasions I visited Hill Tribe camps located in Ban Vinai, Chiang Khong, Chiang Kham, Ban Nam Yao, and Sob Tuang, all in Northern Thailand.

No story of Indochinese refugees can be complete without mentioning the work of the embassy's locally engaged staff. Some were spouses of Canadian Embassy officers. Most, however, were local Thai staff. Theirs was the onerous responsibility of keeping thousands of files in order, up to date, and accessible without the benefit of computers. They too worked seven days a week, preparing files for camp visits, keeping track of incoming sponsorships, and liaising with the local Thai authorities in Bangkok, all with stoic patience, grace, and good humour.

Postscript: I mentioned earlier the Lao military pilots who became bush pilots in Northern Canada. Over the subsequent years of foreign service work, it has been my pleasure to meet the children of ex-refugees whose families settled in Canada. It is a familiar refugee success story, where the parents and older siblings work hard and sacrifice all to ensure a better future for their children. The children have not disappointed their parents. Many are graduates from higher education. They are doctors, engineers, nurses, civil servants, and even foreign service officers.

The Brotherhood of Fighter Pilots

RON BUTTON

On my first visit to Songkhla refugee camp, I was part of a three-man team with René Bersma and Don Myatt. While there, we received a message from Bangkok saying that south of Songkhla, on the Malay border, thirteen Vietnamese had come ashore. They were about to be "pushed off," and would we attempt a rescue action? As the senior officer present, I decided to go myself, accompanied by a UNHCR representative and an American religious NGO representative named Cy.

After a three-hour drive we reached the location, a small spit of land on which the Thais had built a beautiful open pagoda-like summer house. Sitting in the summer house were the thirteen Vietnamese who had come ashore, their boat on the beach in the background. Surrounding these thirteen unarmed and frightened people was an army of Thai soldiers with machine guns. We talked our way through the cordon and met the refugees.

The refugee interpreting for the group was a former F-86 pilot from the Vietnamese air force. I had flown F-86 in the RCAF, and there exists a strong fraternity among F-86 pilots.

We were with the refugees for almost four hours. Several of them had relations in Canada, so I decided that we would take them all. We informed the Thais of this decision to prevent the refugees being pushed out to sea. Their boat was in very poor shape – it looked like it was falling apart. We had them fill out applications forms, had them signed, and then, with Cy's assistance, prepared the Canadian immigration papers on the spot. Before leaving, we arranged with the Thais that the UNHCR representative would return within two days to move the refugees to a camp.

A week later, back in Bangkok, I received a telex informing me that things had gone terribly wrong. The UNHCR representative was new to his job, extremely bureaucratic in his ways, and did not arrange to pick up the refugees until seven days after our visit. By that time it was too late. The Thais had waited five days and then pushed the refugees and their boat back out to sea.

I cried that night. Full as my life had been of bureaucratic rules, I thought I had managed to save those lives, and now they were lost and probably dead. I was very depressed. But Bill Lundy was smart enough to say, "Hey, if they're lucky, they might just drift and hit the Malayan coast a few miles down, and the Malays won't push them off. Why don't you send Don Cameron (at E&I Singapore) a telex, tell him who they are, and maybe he'll run across them somewhere."

About six weeks later, Don picked them up in a Malay camp. He telexed us to say they sent their very best wishes, I was their friend for life, he'd taken on my commitment, and he was putting them through the system. Two of them went to the United States, but the rest of them came to Canada. In the midst of so much misery, we had a happy ending.

18

Hong Kong, Macau, Manila

The visa office of the Canadian Commission in Hong Kong, then a British Crown colony, was the third pillar of Canada's Indochinese refugee program. E&I Hong Kong was a long-established immigration office with staff of eight or nine immigration foreign service officers and a substantial complement of highly skilled and experienced locally engaged staff (LES) who provided the institutional memory and were largely responsible for the processing and documenting of immigrants selected by Canadian officers. They also knew the region, the local and regional bureaucracies, and the manner and style of conducting business, including government business, in Southeast Asia. The Hong Kong operation contributed a wealth of skills, knowledge, and experience to the entire regional operation throughout the duration of the Indochinese refugee movement.

Neither the Liberal nor the Conservative government wanted the special program for the Indochinese to impede the regular flow of immigrants and refugees from other parts of the world. As one of the offices processing all categories of Canada-bound immigrants, E&I Hong Kong had the unique challenge of maintaining both a large flow of immigrants and a substantial refugee program. It had the advantage of being able to shift staff back and forth between regular immigration activities and refugee selection as needed, and benefited from the support of competent Hong Kong authorities who attached a high value to Canada's resettlement efforts. The crowded refugee camps that E&I Hong Kong dealt with were close at hand, though moving around the small, crowded colony was never easy.

E&I Hong Kong played a pivotal role in the final days of South Vietnam, including the evacuation of the Canadian Embassy staff *from Saigon, the dramatic rescue of Vietnamese orphans, and the Guam operations. When Cabinet demanded a rapid response to its decision of 18 July 1979 to admit 50,000 refugees to Canada, it was E&I Hong Kong that, on a week's notice, was the source of the 2,000 refugees transported on the eleven-flight Department of National Defence airlift. Several of the persons who served in Hong Kong during the fall of Saigon in 1975 returned to Southeast Asia in 1979 and 1980, where their critical experience and knowledge added greatly to the success of the entire Indochinese refugee operation. E&I Hong Kong was also responsible for selecting immigrants, including refugees, from Macau, at that time still a Portuguese colony located about sixty-four kilometres from Hong Kong on the western side of the Pearl River Delta.*

The E&I Manila operation was smaller and geographically more remote from the Indochinese refugee storm unleashed with the collapse of Saigon. More than 1,000 kilometres across the South China Sea, far fewer Indochinese refugees survived a perilous journey of that distance in small, unfit, and overloaded boats. But some succeeded against all the odds.

This chapter recalls the stories of some of the Canadian visa officers stationed in Hong Kong and Manila, and their daily involvement in the unfolding Southeast refugee drama.

Hong Kong: The Early Days – 1975

ERNEST ALLEN

My posting at the Commission for Canada, Hong Kong, began in August 1974 as first secretary and deputy program manager of the immigration program.

In March 1975, Ottawa informed us that Hong Kong would be the intended destination for the Canadian evacuation flights from Saigon. Commissioner Bud Clark formed a working group to make the necessary arrangements for the flights and evacuees. The group consisted of Charles Rogers, counsellor (immigration), Pierre Ducharme, first secretary (political), Barbara Lonsdale, second secretary (consular and administration), RCMP Inspector Bruce James, and me. With so little time in which to prepare the many arrangements necessary to support the evacuation, other commission staff members were pressed into service. Because the commission's primary workforce were Immigration foreign service officers, these were the persons called upon to assist and included Donald Cameron, Scott Heatherington, Margaret Tebbutt, and Bill Bowden.

Prior to the imminent arrival of a Canadian Forces C-130 Hercules aircraft and crew diverted from a routine around-the-world training flight, it was necessary to secure over-flight clearances, ground servicing for the aircraft by Cathy Pacific Airlines, and the authorization of the Hong Kong government to allow the evacuation to be staged via the Crown colony. Hong Kong officials proved exceptionally cooperative.

Those of us who had volunteered to assist with the first evacuation flight to Saigon met early in the morning of 9 April at the Commission for Canada, then located at 1 Henessey Road on the edge of Wanchai's sleazy bar and nightclub district. My primary task in the operation was to ensure that persons being evacuated were admissible to Canada and thus eligible to board the aircraft. We were apprehensive about the task. Bud Clark came to the office to wish us well and, with sufficient time before departure from Hong Kong's Kai Tak Airport, invited the group for breakfast which, frugally, consisted of a bowl of congee at a nearby noodle shop.

John Baker, then stationed in Singapore with responsibility for Vietnam and neighbouring countries, had arrived in Hong Kong on the C-130 incoming flight from Saigon the previous day and joined us for the return flight. It had been necessary for him to come to Hong Kong to consult with us on the management of his suddenly expanding refugee caseload. Baker had attempted to assist the departure of many persons sponsored by Canadian relatives and friends, who had been named in a barrage of telex messages received in both Saigon and Hong Kong from immigration centres across Canada. Strict exit and passport controls that were maintained to the end of the South Vietnamese regime were a barrier to departure. The sponsorship messages eventually resulted in Hong Kong preparing some 15,000 Promise of Visa Letters printed on Canadian Embassy, Saigon, letterhead paper and hand-carried by Margaret Tebbutt, Don Cameron, and Bill Bowden for mailing in Saigon during mid-April. Many of these letters were produced in the months and years to come by Vietnamese boat people in camps throughout Asia as they approached our officers seeking refugee admission to Canada. The non-secure nature of these letters, however, rendered them open to abuse, making it difficult to ensure that the holder was the intended recipient.

The c-130 evacuation flight, piloted by Major Cliff Zacharias, crossed the South China Sea in bright, sunny weather. The low flight altitude provided an excellent view of numerous atolls en route. As we traversed Vietnam's coast approaching Saigon's Tan Son Nhut Airport, we reflected on the possibility of our aircraft, which had military markings, coming under attack from North Vietnamese surface-to-air missiles then positioned within some thirty miles of Saigon. We later learned that our travel to Vietnam coincided with the forces of North Vietnam reaching and shortly thereafter taking Xuan Loc, the ARVN's[1] final line of defence before Saigon. Our arrival at Tan Son Nhut was uneventful, and I recall being surprised at the relative calm of the airport despite South Vietnam's government being in absolute turmoil and its army in defeat. Adhering to Canada's unwritten policy regarding embassy closures and evacuations – never the first, never the last, and always in good company – our actions in Saigon that day were in step with those of Australia and the United States, which were also evacuating civilian nationals.

For reasons of security, Major Zacharias asked us to spend no more time than necessary on the ground, and immediately upon landing we commenced screening the intended evacuees. The small group of persons awaiting our arrival at Tan Son Nhut had been informed of the evacuation flight by the embassy through its consular warden network. Accompanied to the airport by Canada-based embassy staff, the evacuees included a number of Roman Catholic priests, a few CIDA officers and civilian aid workers, and a handful of Vietnamese-Canadians, all of whom held Canadian passports. In all, I believe the evacuees numbered no more than two dozen.

Our late-afternoon departure from Saigon took place without incident. Prior arrangements had been made with the Hong Kong authorities for the evacuees' entry to the colony. Consular staff members were on hand on arrival to provide assistance with temporary accommodation and onward flight arrangements to Canada.

Hong Kong, April–May 1975: "The First Person You Speak
to Is a Woman from Calgary"

MARGARET TEBBUTT

In 1975, I was a Canadian visa officer in Hong Kong and had flown
on a Canadian Forces Hercules to Saigon in April with Bill Bowden
to deliver Promise of Visa Letters and bring back a few Canadians
and their Vietnamese wives and children. [That same Hercules aircraft had transported Vietnamese and Cambodian orphan babies
bound for adoption in Canada]. A few days earlier, with others, I had
bathed the orphans flown in and then prepared Minister's Permits for
them overnight. [See chapter 2 for the stories of the Promise of Visa
Letters and the Canadian baby flights.]

On 4 May 1975, Hong Kong's British government established a
camp in Shek Kong, twenty kilometres from the colony's centre, in what
was called the New Territories, for 1,600 refugees who had come by
boat from Vietnam. The Commission for Canada in Hong Kong was
the first to set up in the camp to interview and select people amongst
the 800 families and 430 single men for refugee admission to Canada.

I was sent out to the new camp in the first week of May, and for
several days I conducted interviews, with the help of a volunteer Vietnamese interpreter, in our Canadian "office" – a tent with long tables
set up underneath. By coincidence, a reporter, Gunilla Mungan from
the *Calgary Herald*, visited the Shek Kong camp on 9 May. She interviewed me, the RCMP liaison officer, and a number of British officers
and soldiers from the Gurkha Brigade, famous for their organizational
skills, who ran the camp. As I was originally from Calgary, there was
a local interest angle for the Calgary paper, and as a result, an article
entitled "Canada Wins Friends at Hong Kong Refugee Camp" appeared in the *Calgary Herald* on 22 May 1975, with photos. This report may have been one of the earliest in the Canadian media on
Canada's actions to accept refugees.

To quote the *Calgary Herald*:

When you walk into the [Shek] Kong camp for Vietnamese
refugees, not far from Hong Kong, the first thing you see is a
Canadian flag and the first person you speak to is a woman from
Calgary [Margaret Tebbutt]. The Canadians are equally popular

among the refugees and among the British soldiers in charge of the camp.

About 80 per cent of the refugees in Hong Kong put down Canada as their preferred country to emigrate to.

Several British officers told me that they were impressed by the Canadian effort and surprised that the Canadians at the time were the only ones to expedite the re-establishment of the refugees. No other country, not even the US or Australia, has set up headquarters inside the camp.

One of the British soldiers speculated that this may be due to the red tape necessary to get the authorization from the Hong Kong authorities, who reportedly are not too happy with the way the Canadians simply cut through the red tape.

The Canadian attitude seems to be that people come first, for which they are honoured by all those actually in contact with the refugees.

Hong Kong: 1979 to 1982

GERRY CAMPBELL

After returning to Ottawa in mid-April following Temporary Duty in Singapore, I was asked by Bill Sinclair, head of personnel, to return to Hong Kong to manage the Hong Kong Indochinese Refugee Program as deputy program manager under John MacLachlan. I arrived in Hong Kong in July 1979 and remained until November 1982.

Hong Kong had one of the densest concentrations of Vietnamese refugees of any country of first asylum in Southeast Asia. Refugee boats, some the size of small freighters, had been landing in the colony since 1978. Some 50,000 Vietnamese were crammed into half a dozen or more very large refugee camps spread around Kowloon and the New Territories. Some of these camps, like Sham Shui Po, were former POW camps, and the refugees were housed in old Quonset huts left over from World War II.

Hong Kong had established a Refugee Coordinator's Office under the Security Bureau, led by Talbot Bashall. It was highly efficient and helpful, as were the UNHCR and ICEM representatives in Hong Kong. Unlike the Singapore and Bangkok operations, the commission managed both medical processing and transportation arrangements. Once cleared of medical and security requirements, refugees were moved to a transit camp run by the Prisons Department under Prisons' Superintendent Mak Pak Lam at Ma Tau Wai in Kowloon. Prisons and the Refugee Coordinator's offices managed the local transportation arrangements of Vietnamese booked on charter flights departing from Kai Tak Airport.

In response to the July 1979 Cabinet decision to increase Canada's acceptance of Indochinese refugees to 50,000, and since Hong Kong had a large concentration of refugees who could be quickly selected and processed in addition to its large immigration contingent, the commission was assigned an immediate and heavy frequency of charter flights, at one point peaking with two 747s on the ground at Kai Tak at the same time. Shortfalls in the pipeline in Bangkok and Singapore occasionally resulted in the diversion of some charter flights to Hong Kong, where there was a ready pool of processed refugees who could be transported on short notice. Virtually every departing flight was filled to capacity. The sole complicating factor in Hong Kong was the high number of cases furthered for lengthy and repeated medical tests for suspected TB. This was a blot on our record, as other major resettlement countries were less restrictive or more flexible in dealing with what were legitimate concerns about TB.

The Canadian refugee program operation in Hong Kong was in full swing before my arrival, having already completed a DND airlift of 2,000 refugees. The Hong Kong operation was a team effort and highly efficient, with the full support of the head of mission, Al Kilpatrick, E&I's John MacLachlan, and his deputy Del McKay. The RCMP based in Hong Kong handled security screening on the spot, and two of their officers, Don Kilpatrick and Dirk Doornbos, were key team players, as were members of the Quebec Immigration Service, including Gerry Power, who had been reassigned to Hong Kong, as had the IOM representative Hans Petter Boe. Hong Kong's locally engaged staff assigned to the refugee program were extraordinarily hard-working and efficient, and included Edith Hung, Rebecca Lam, Virginia Wong, and Ella Kwan. At its peak, the refugee camp selection teams included eight or nine commission staff plus a driver and camp interpreters, some of whom were commission locally engaged staff since many refugees were ethnically Chinese.[2]

UNHCR legal and resettlement officers, including Chooi Fong, Ulrich Freyschmidt, Terry Leckey, and Raymond Hall, were exceptional in their support. Perhaps the most outstanding help of all came from Macau, where the legendary Father Lancelot Rodrigues, in his capacity there as director of the Catholic Relief Services, was so hospitable, well organized, and supportive that it was hard to maintain a proportionate balance between the number of Vietnamese selected from the camps there and in Hong Kong.

The selection process in Hong Kong was simplified because the UNHCR conducted interviews of refugees and completed reports that we could review to preselect cases for interview. While the interviews were still not pro forma, the acceptance rate was high and, in cooperation with UNHCR resettlement officers, we sought a balance between better qualified Vietnamese and more difficult resettlement cases. The existing circumstances called for an unprecedented degree of flexibility in dealing with unique situations; family groupings often included members who were not part of the nuclear family, such as aunts, nephews, nieces, and other informally "adopted" children, even concubines. It would have been inhumane to leave these refugees alone in the camps, and ways were simply found to include them as part of the larger family group that had left Vietnam. Cases in obvious need of longer-term resettlement assistance were referred to the matching centre or at times directly to sponsoring groups in contact with our office. Many sponsoring groups were extremely helpful and willing to take on the most difficult settlement cases. Others had religious as well as humanitarian objectives, sponsoring refugees who had been converted in the camps and even assigning them numbers in their sponsorship queue. However, we had little flexibility in cases with a family member inadmissible on medical grounds.

A unique aspect of the Indochinese Refugee Program operation in Hong Kong was that most of the camps were "open." Refugees could come and go without restriction, while conversely only escorted visitors were allowed into the camps. This meant that we received many requests for assistance in arranging visits to the camps from Canadian-based groups, officials, and others with an interest in the refugee operation. I personally escorted between one hundred and two hundred persons through the camps, including CEIC Minister Lloyd Axworthy, a strong supporter of the program.

Conditions in the camps, where whole families were often housed in a single level of a bunk bed, along with all their possessions, were relatively good compared to other locations, but they were a shock to many visitors who had never been in a refugee camp. The visits were a burden but helped raise awareness and probably contributed to the number and nature of sponsorships. Many sponsoring groups responded with alacrity to difficult cases and deserved much credit for taking on long-term and challenging commitments.

Over time the nature of the refugee flow to Hong Kong changed. The proportion of northerners arriving grew higher. While still considered refugees by the UNHCR and under the Canadian Indochinese program, they were North Vietnamese fleeing the new Vietnam government. Many were ethnic Chinese feeling unwelcome after the China-Vietnam conflict along the northern border. Many had left rural areas in Quang Ninh Province in smaller vessels that followed the coast of China to Hong Kong. The northerners were unskilled, often farmers or coal miners from rural areas in Quang Ninh Province, or dock workers from the port of Haiphong. Many were functionally illiterate in their own language.

Some of those expelled from Vietnam stopped for periods of time in China, and Hong Kong immigration screened all arrivals to identify any mainland Chinese attempting to pass themselves off as Vietnamese boat refugees. Despite these efforts, some evidently slipped through the net and were referred for resettlement by the UNHCR. Some reached Canada and were only unmasked when it was discovered that they could not speak Vietnamese.

The Hong Kong authorities provided exceptional operational assistance, although sometimes things went awry. The Hong Kong Aviation Authority at one point decided to restrict landings of all charter flights to non-peak evening times and denied authorization for the landing of charter flights contracted out to Canadian carriers. This decision was quickly reversed after we informed the Hong Kong Security Bureau that the timing of these flights, already chartered, could not be changed, but their destination would instead be altered to Bangkok or Kuala Lumpur to pick up refugees there instead of from Hong Kong. We also received pleas to increase the Canadian refugee quota for Hong Kong, to which we could only respond that it was hard to make a case to increase our acceptance level when Britain had not managed to meet its own moderate quota of 11,000.

Overall, however, relations with the Hong Kong government were extremely good, and the Canadian contribution was acknowledged regularly and in generous terms at all levels. In 1993, when I was back

in Hong Kong as program manager, at the conclusion of a meeting between Commissioner John Higginbotham and Chris Patten, the last
British governor of Hong Kong, Governor Patten put his hand on my
shoulder and expressed his deep appreciation for all we had done.

The Hong Kong Camps

MARTHA NIXON

Although the camps in Hong Kong were better than in almost all
other places in Southeast Asia, it was not like staying at the Hilton.
In the part of the camps where people awaited decisions, they were
crammed into an area with layers of wooden bunks stacked high to
the ceiling – I don't recall how many layers, but it seemed to be around
three to four. Whole families lived on these beds; while they were free
to come and go, the overwhelming impression was one of warehous-
ing. How sad and tragic it must have been to live this way, in some
cases for years. Observing this reality was difficult, but it paled in
comparison to the horrors they had faced in the boats on an unfor-
giving sea. When I sat face to face with families, asking them questions
about their situation, I was reluctant to make a negative decision
about their entry to Canada.

Vietnamese Boat People in Macau

SUSAN LOPEZ

In April 1978, near the end of my three-year posting to Hong Kong,
I was sent on an area visit from Hong Kong to Macau to interview the
first boat people from Vietnam to land there. My duties in Hong Kong
had been directed at independent, nominated, and family class immigrants, as well as visitors and students; processing refugees was a new
experience for me.

The noisy hydrofoil from Hong Kong was an effective way to get
to Macau. I was met on arrival by the enigmatic Father Lancelot
Rodrigues, head of the Catholic Relief Services in Macau. He settled

me into one of the casino hotels, run by the Triads[3] but the only hotel that gave us a reduced rate. Macau casinos were the playground of the Hong Kong rich and famous, lots of dinner jackets, silks, and collars of diamonds flashing. They would gamble for hours in very large denominations. It was a noisy, cold, but convenient place to change money at any hour of the day or night.

The next morning Father Rodriguez drove me with my suitcase of files to the humid Quonset hut where the refugees were staying. These refugees all claimed relatives in Canada, which was why we were looking at their applications. I completed the interviews by about 1 p.m. with the help of Father Rodrigues's secretary, who served as translator. I think the applicants were all accepted, and the church would assist them through the medical examinations.

Then Father Rodrigues picked me up for a lengthy lunch with the Macau police chief at the church manse. Lots of Portuguese rosé, African chicken, and blackened shrimp were brought to the table and consumed until we could hardly get up. We then started to share our national songs with more wine. I remember singing "Un canadien errant," "I'se the B'y," "Red River Valley," and "Leaving on a Jet Plane." In his hearty fashion, Father Rodriguez drove me back to the hotel to check out and onward to the hydrofoil dock to catch my boat back to Hong Kong. The driver was wobbly, but he would not have been stopped anyway, as he was well known and a friend of the police chief. I did not see those cases through to completion, but they eventually made it to Canada.

Shortly before I left Hong Kong in September 1978, I interviewed an eighteen-year-old young woman sponsored as a fiancée by her Cambodian boyfriend, who had arrived in Canada as a refugee a few months earlier. They had been dating as teenagers before the fall of Phnom Penh. Their parents were small-business people who did what they could to get their children out of Cambodia before the worst happened. The young woman and her little brother were sent to Hong Kong, where they had an aunt. A mutual friend bumped into her in Hong Kong and knew how to contact the boyfriend, now fiancé, in Canada. We obtained the sponsorship and eventually sent the young lady and little brother to Canada. We all were a soft touch for love stories.

Macau, 1979

SCOTT MULLIN

On 16 February 1979, I made the first of what would be many refugee selection trips to Macau, the sleepy Portuguese colony one hour by jetfoil across the Pearl River delta from Hong Kong.

I was six months into my first posting at the Commission for Canada in Hong Kong and had two months earlier returned from Malaysia and Singapore where I had helped process boat people on the *Hai Hong*, after which Ian Hamilton and I did a tour of Malaysian refugee camps, including the infamous Pulau Bidong camp.

I was met at the Macau ferry pier that morning by a driver from the Catholic Relief Services, and we headed to their offices in "Centro." Doris Ho, assistant to the director, Father Lancelot Rodriques, ushered me into a small office. Father Lancelot rose from behind a desk stacked high with papers and, with a booming deep voice I can still hear, welcomed me to Macau. "Sit, you must sit down," he said, adding, "Do you take one or two lumps?" as Doris hovered by the door. I replied that I liked my coffee black. "Coffee?" he said with a wry grin. "We need a drink man, not a coffee. I guess you take yours neat," and out from under his desk came a large bottle of Johnny Walker Black Label. Doris came back with two glasses, and so began my first meeting with the director of Catholic Relief Services, the organization that administered the boat people camps in Macau.

Small groups of Vietnamese boat people began arriving in Macau in the spring of 1977. Macau had welcomed refugees for years, including waves of Chinese and some foreigners from Shanghai when the Communist Party took over China in 1949. The tiny Portuguese colony, only fifteen square kilometres at the time, was founded in 1537, three centuries before Britain planted the Union Jack in Hong Kong in 1842. It had a colourful history, including as a slave port for Chinese coolies shipped off to South America in the mid-1800s. There was a significant Eurasian community, the result of Portuguese intermarriage with local Chinese, then virtually unheard of in Hong Kong. In the late 1970s it was a sleepy place with only one casino, the Lisboa. Macau could have been the setting for a Graham Green novel: cafés along the waterfront of Praia, odd characters who rarely revealed their true provenance, and a hint of a sleazy underbelly lurking not far beneath.

The Macau government essentially outsourced the growing boat people refugee issue to the Catholic Relief Services (CRS), who managed the camps and, until the arrival of a UNHCR representative, dealt directly with consulates in Hong Kong. The outsourcing was total – over the course of some eight visits to Macau in 1979 and 1980, I never encountered, much less met with, a Macau government official. I selected a handful of refugees on my first couple of visits in the early part of 1979. Refugees were housed in various church properties including a CRS-built camp at Ka-Ho on Coloane Island, a short drive from the centre of Macau. Conditions were cramped, but basic needs were well taken care of by the CRS. Over time, a school, playground, and other amenities were built. The Ka-Ho camp would have been considered luxurious by refugees in Malaysia and Thailand.

In the summer of 1979, as both Hong Kong and Macau reeled from the huge influx of boat people, mostly ethnic Chinese "cleansed" from the north of Vietnam, we began a massive selection process to meet the government's boat people resettlement quota of 50,000 and decided to select some from Macau. The CRS did a reasonable job of pre-screening refugees for interviews, selecting the obvious candidates with relatives in Canada (although often "brothers and sisters" were in fact distant cousins), and those with some language skills. As we increased our interviews in response to the increased quota, we quickly found ourselves dealing mostly with very simple folk from northern Vietnam. A positive selection decision often hinged on a bright son or daughter who had learned a surprising amount of English in the CRS-run school.

In late 1979 the UNHCR established a one-man office in Macau, sending Michel Barton, a wonderful Swiss-American who tragically died of a heart attack in 2003 on a flight from Montreal to New York while working for UNESCO.

As in Hong Kong, we were often approached by CRS or the UNHCR to consider unusual cases. Our American colleagues operated under a rigid set of rules (and delighted in applying them strictly), and other countries took few refugees from Macau. In contrast, we were selecting people who, "in the opinion of the visa officer, will successfully establish in Canada." That flexibility allowed me to take cases such as an elderly man married to identical twin sisters. He had a son in the United

States, but the Americans would not take him, his wives, and his three other sons and their families, because of the second wife. Once I had established who was the elder of the two sisters, the younger wife became simply his wife's sister, and the family was accepted.

Father Lancelot Rodrigues appeared in late mornings during interview sessions in the camps, and if his staff told him the acceptance rate was low, he would announce – command, more accurately – that it was time for lunch, and off we would go to Fernando's restaurant on Coloane for amazing grilled prawns, sausage, and salad – and several bottles of vino verde.

In all, we took about nine hundred refugees from Macau between 1979 and 1981. Our "M4"[4] TB rate was lower in Macau than in Hong Kong, so there were fewer refugees backlogged waiting to pass our notoriously tough (and in my view unfair) medical examination. Refugees selected and approved for travel to Canada were taken to Hong Kong to meet our charter flights courtesy of STM, the jetfoil company owned by the Lisboa casino owner, Stanley Ho, who had deep connections to Canada. The logistics of the transfer from Macau to Hong Kong's Kai Tak Airport was one of those Macau "behind the scenes" events with which we had little to do.

Father Lancelot Rodrigues died in Macau on 17 June 2013. He was 89. He was honoured with an obituary in *The Economist* on 29 June. Describing his influence and outreach that had spanned some sixty years in Macau, it read in part, "Anyone was welcome who would help his cause. One young man from Montreal, sent to Macau to give Canadian visas to boat people, found himself plied with cognac at 11 in the morning to issue more visas faster." I wish I had known the obit's author as I would have corrected the story: it was Black Label, not cognac.

Manila: Vietnamese Refugees in the Philippines, 1975–1977

IAN RANKIN

The Vietnamese refugees who reached the Philippines between 1975 and 1977 were few and often had connections (business, government, military, and political) with the Americans. Refugees arriving in small boats, often in horrendous condition, increased after 1977.

Like most countries in Southeast Asia, the Philippines was not a signatory to the 1951 UN Convention related to the status of refugees. It did not have resources to settle large numbers of refugees, nor did it have a history of providing asylum. The Philippines wanted to co-ordinate its policies with ASEAN allies, none of whom were enthusiastic about providing asylum to large outflows of fleeing Vietnamese and others from Indochina. However, it was a Catholic country, and the church with its strong humanitarian traditions was an integral part of the fabric of the society.

E&I Manila's goal was to resettle Vietnamese refugees who might have connections to Canada, present a united international resettlement front, particularly with the Americans and Australians, and actively support the Philippine government's willingness to act as a country of first asylum. The Philippines is the United States' closest ally in Southeast Asia. Throughout the Vietnamese conflict, it was a major staging point for the American military. Angeles Airbase and Subic Bay Naval Base were major depots for the conflict in Vietnam. The government of Ferdinand Marcos, the president of the Philippines, had been closely allied with the Americans since World War II. Hence, as South Vietnam began to collapse, many Vietnamese who were aligned with the Americans sought safe haven in the Philippines. Many had funds and were not initially a settlement problem.

On 3 April, shortly before the fall of Saigon, President Gerald Ford ordered all US navy and air force resources to assist with the removal of 176,000 evacuees, mostly from South Vietnam. Initial staging was at US military bases throughout the region, including the Philippines, before transfer to the United States. The Philippines was willing to provide safe haven to fleeing Vietnamese, but their ability to provide settlement support was limited. In Manila, there was the Jose Fabella Centre Annex for refugees, run by Caritas and overseen by the Catholic bishop of Manila, Jaime Sin. Accommodations there were crowded and deplorable and could be compared to Manila's slums. However, the centre was in Manila, and, in the beginning, refugees residing there had access to the city and any work that was available. They were also close to refugee resettlement agencies and embassies of resettlement countries, including Canada. Other refugee camps were established in Lubang and Palawan, with the latter becoming the central refugee camp for the Philippines by 1980.

The Philippines saw a relative hiatus in the refugee movement following the initial surge after the fall of Saigon. Resettlement countries selected refugees at a relaxed pace; claimants were interviewed and counselled, and family connections were investigated. In the 1975 to 1977 period, Vietnamese refugees were selected on a case-by-case basis, with acceptance strongly dependent on family or resettlement abilities in Canada. Individuals were allowed forward only when a refugee allocation placement was received from headquarters or with the support from a non-governmental organization. Settlement support in Canada became quite important. No significant concerns about the Vietnamese were raised by Philippine government liaisons within the Ministry of Immigration. Western government resettlement efforts, including Canada's, kept decreasing the overall number of asylum seekers.

It is difficult to get an exact picture of how many refugees who fled Vietnam came to Canada from the Philippines in the initial years. A table in Manpower and Immigration's annual statistical reports indicates country of citizenship or last permanent residence and the country from whence immigrants came. In 1975, twenty-three South Vietnamese and three North Vietnamese arrived in Canada from the Philippines.[5] In 1976, seventeen South Vietnamese from the Philippines arrived.[6] In 1977, 110 South Vietnamese and 108 North Vietnamese came from the Philippines.[7] In 1978, fifty-six Vietnamese (no distinction whether from North or South) came from the Philippines.[8] In 1979 and 1980, E&I Manila selected and processed 1,428 Indochinese refugees.[9]

When I arrived in 1975 on my first major posting, among other duties, I assumed responsibility for the refugee movement. Roy McGrath was the program manager and was succeeded by Norm Derrick, with Kevin Burke and later Jim Hentschel as deputies. For most of my time in Manila, Gerry Maffre, Brian Beaupre, and Jim Norris were my colleagues. My UNHCR contact was Werner Blatter, who had arrived from Cambodia. He was a dedicated and hard-working man, mostly concerned with feeding and sheltering the Vietnamese refugees in the Philippines. He brought to our attention cases with Canadian connections but recognized that any push for Canada to accept greater numbers of refugees would come from Ottawa. My main interlocutor at the US Embassy was a deputy consul, Consular Affairs, and his assistant, a Canadian married to an American communications officer, who was indispensable and became a close friend.

As most refugees wanted to go to the United States, the Americans would contact me about refugees with Canadian connections. Several of these had family in Montreal or were guaranteed employment with former employers from Vietnam. The US Embassy also used the UNHCR representative to refer "difficult to place" cases to us, knowing that Canada had church or other non-governmental groups to provide support and assistance. Usually they would provide advance warning with a detailed backgrounder on the case.

What I remember most about our refugee work was the collegiality of our efforts. It was not a large movement at that time, but every effort was made to relieve pressure on the Marcos government to ensure that the Philippines remained a country of sanctuary. It was also important to maintain a multinational aspect to the movement so that the United States was not perceived as the only country to bear the burden. For the most part, this effort succeeded.

The initial evacuation of Vietnamese refugees in 1975 was massive and tremendously stressful. The exodus in small boats began in earnest at the end of 1977. The Philippines was largely spared the onslaught because of the dangerous passage across the South China Sea.

By the time that I left Manila in 1978, attitudes towards providing safe haven throughout Southeast Asia, including the Philippines, had hardened. Access into Manila for refugees was discontinued, and the Jose Fabella Centre was closed. Perhaps because of our cooperative resettlement efforts, the presence of the American government and, in particular, the strong advocacy for the right of asylum by Cardinal Jaime Sin and the Catholic Church, the Philippines continued to provide safe haven and allowed large holding camps to be created in Palawan and Morong Bataan for Vietnamese small-boat refugees.

Palawan Refugee Camp, Philippines

LINDA BUTLER

When I was posted as 2-I-C¹⁰ to E&I Manila in 1979, I knew little about the Philippines. I knew that the office had a heavy workload with temporary workers coming to Canada as nannies and nurses, family reunification cases, and independent immigrants. I did not realize that many Vietnamese boat people were in the Philippines with few rights. They could not hold normal jobs or buy homes or expect much in the way of education for their children.

In 1979, the Philippines opened a camp on the western Filipino island of Palawan near the city of Puerto Princesa, bordered by the ocean and an airport. This camp was to be a refugee processing centre, capable of holding up to 18,000 refugees while they were tested for tuberculosis and completed immigration requirements. Some English-as-second-language training was provided. During its ten years of operation, hundreds of thousands of boat people, including a high number of unaccompanied minors, had their applications processed for the United States, Australia, Canada, and elsewhere. In 1989, the camp was closed, and Vietnamese boat people refugees were no longer granted status, on the grounds that they were fleeing poverty, not persecution.

My involvement with Palawan began with the receipt of immigration applications from a number of Vietnamese boat people in the camp. A decision was made that my colleague Paul Anderson and I should go to Palawan to interview them. It was quite the adventure. A Philippines Air Force helicopter was to fly us to the island. Never fond of these noisy, shaky contraptions, my confidence was not boosted when the pilot asked whether I had ever been to Palawan, because he was not sure of the way! I thought he must be joking, but he did spend a great deal of time peering at a map and gazing down at the ground as if looking for some landmark. Eventually, he landed us on a navy ship, where we exchanged courtesies with the local commander before proceeding to the camp. I recall nothing of what was said, but the takeoff is vividly etched in my memory. The joystick came off in the pilot's hand, and we plunged towards the ship's rail, only to be lifted up at the last second by the actions of the co-pilot!

Our welcome at the camp was warm and enthusiastic. Residents were eager to end their time of waiting and make a start in a new land. Some were beginning to feel stranded in the Philippines, afraid to return to Vietnam and unable to find a new home. They thronged around us, hoping to persuade us to take them to Canada. Unfortunately, Paul and I could only interview the people whose applications we had already received. One of these families generously took the time and trouble to prepare and share their noon meal with us.

All too soon, we had to board the helicopter once more. This time I was confident that the pilot would be sure of his way. However, we soon ran into a thunderstorm, the helicopter tossing and turning and at times dropping like a stone. I was never happier to step out on solid ground than at the end of that trip – my first and last to Palawan.

A Manila Perspective

JAMES HENTSCHEL

I was in Manila from 1977 to 1979 when Asia experienced a dramatic outflow of Vietnamese. I recall the arrival in Manila Bay of a steamer with three hundred refugees on board. Norm Derrick, my supervisor, instructed several of us to identify as many potentially acceptable refugees as we could. Three of us boarded the ship one morning, and by day's end we had selected about sixty of those who had expressed an interest in Canada. We were proud of this achievement until learning three days later that the US Embassy had offered those same people a chance to settle in the United States. All but ten accepted! This placed the boat program in a more realistic light for me.

On a trip to the refugee camp on the island province of Palawan in the Philippines, my father-in-law, a doctor back in Canada, who was visiting us in Manila, asked to come along. At the camp we heard the tragic story of a Vietnamese boat that had been marooned in the South China Sea and arrived with only one female teenager alive. She stayed alive by eating the remains of her fellow passengers. I was asked to interview her to determine her prospects for resettlement. My father-in-law heard about the girl and asked if he could examine her to determine the impact of her experience on her physical and mental well-being, which the UNHCR granted. He was amazed by her excellent physical and mental condition after her traumatic experience.

19

Quebec Operations in Southeast Asia

The recollections in this chapter are those of Florent Fortin and Lucile Horner, officers of the Quebec Immigration Service, who worked in the refugee camps from the last month of 1978 into the 1980s.

From 1975 to 1980, relations between Canada's federal government and the government of the Province of Quebec were in a state of flux. In 1975, for the first time, the Parti Québécois (PQ), a sovereigntist party whose aim was to gain independence for Quebec, was elected. The first referendum on Quebec independence – a referendum on the concept of sovereignty-association – was held in May 1980. While the federalists won the referendum, during the five years preceding it the PQ government succeeded in increasing Quebec's autonomy within the Canadian federation. During this period, immigration was one of the important areas where Quebec successfully negotiated for autonomous authority.

Beginning in 1867, the British North America Act, today a part of Canada's constitution, recognized both federal and provincial legislative competence in the field of immigration. For the most part, provincial governments made no use of this common competence until 1971, when the Lang-Cloutier Agreement authorized a minor consultative role for Quebec immigration agents operating abroad. In 1975, the Andras-Bienvenue Agreement gave more power to Quebec by obliging the federal government to consult Quebec officers regarding the selection of immigrants destined to Quebec. In 1978, the PQ government negotiated the Cullen-Couture Agreement, which gave Quebec immigration officers the authority to select immigrants.

The Vietnamese boat people crisis was the first significant event in which Quebec could use its new powers of selection on the interna-

tional stage. As Florent Fortin points out, Quebec Immigration Minister Jacques Couture was the first political leader in Canada to offer resettlement to the desperate refugees on the Hai Hong freighter. Fortin's work with the refugees from that ship took place in close cooperation with his federal colleagues.

Federal immigration policy was different from the immigration policy of the Province of Quebec. As well, changing roles and personality differences occasionally gave rise to disagreements, and no one was immune to the tensions generated by the 1980 referendum. Faced with a humanitarian crisis, however, operational cooperation to rescue distressed human beings prevailed over political differences. Fortin's and Horner's recollections bear witness to that reality. With a few exceptions, Quebec and federal officials worked together in the camps in a spirit of goodwill and cooperation. The anecdotes of the two Quebec officers, like those of CEIC officers such as Campbell, Ritchie, Martin, and Cameron, demonstrate that in a challenging work environment, dealing with situations ranging from tragic to comic, relations between federal and Quebec officers were generally close and friendly.

The cornerstone of Quebec's immigration policy was the integration of new immigrants into Quebec's francophone society. According to Lucile Horner, the Quebec Ministry of Immigration had decided that refugees destined to Quebec should receive courses in the French language and an introduction to life in Quebec during the time between the acceptance of their applications and their departure. Horner describes the establishment and operation of the "Quebec School in Phanat Nikhom" in Thailand, designed to help prepare the refugees for the challenges they would face in their future lives in Quebec. That innovative school was among the first initiatives taken by the province to facilitate the reception and integration of refugees. As such, it played an important role in the history of Quebec immigration.

Indochinese Assignments

FLORENT FORTIN

In 1978, the maritime exodus of the Vietnamese people increased markedly, arousing the sympathy of the western world. This development occurred just after Quebec had signed an agreement with the

Government of Canada (February 1978), which finally provided Quebec with real selection powers for immigrants destined to the province. In this context, as a Quebec immigration officer, I was at the heart of the action. The network of Quebec offices abroad had not yet been set up; we were proceeding through itinerant missions.

Since the Cullen-Couture Agreement provided that Quebec give consent for refugees selected abroad to be resettled in the province, I was sent on a mission to refugee camps in Southeast Asia. I had already completed a one-year assignment in Argentina between April 1977 and April 1978, during which I had selected hundreds of Chilean refugees, and so I was perceived as an officer with experience in this area. Thus, I left Montreal on 7 September 1978, to return on 9 November. During those two months, I went to refugee camps in Thailand, Malaysia (three missions), Singapore, the Philippines, and even in Okinawa (Japan). Later on, after we opened an office in Singapore, I also went to Indonesian camps.

These initiatives would not have been possible without the extraordinary cooperation that I received from the federal officers of that time, who included me in their missions. In addition to Ian Hamilton, I am very grateful to Richard Martin, from the Singapore office, who helped me gain self-confidence and who acted as my friend in all circumstances. I did not have to deal with logistics, because the federal officers had organized transportation to the camps and coordination with the United Nations. As the agreement had just been signed, I wanted to ensure the federal officers did not perceive me as a troublemaker.

When we arrived at a camp, we first asked the local authorities to provide us with interpreters and interview rooms. Initially, I started the interview with the federal officer. If the applicants indicated that they wanted to settle in Quebec and met our requirements, I issued a Certificat de Sélection (CSQ) for the family and gave them some counselling about living in Quebec.[1] The only criteria that I used for my selection was the ability to adapt to Quebec.

In 1979, the federal officers from the Singapore office, who had limited staff and very high targets, realized that I had acquired sufficient experience to help them meet their goals, and so we modified our processes. I worked our mission independently; I hired an interpreter and two clerks, selected the successful applicants, and delivered all federal files to the Canadian officers at the end of the day. This meant additional work, but it provided me with great satisfaction. To refugees that I accepted, I gave a copy of the document "Vivre au Québec." This final step became well known, so that if I forgot to deliver the document, refugees asked me for it, because they believed that if they did not have it in their possession, they would not get a visa. These booklets made my luggage much heavier, which meant a considerable physical effort for a five-foot, nine-inch man weighing 115 pounds. I was thinner than some of the refugees! I stapled the applicant's copy of the CSQ to the federal file, so that it would be attached to the visa of the head of the family, and ensured that he or she had it for presentation on arrival in Quebec.

Working conditions in the camps were not easy. I remember my first series of interviews with Richard Martin in Pulau Bidong. We had a plain table set up outside in the sun, next to the garbage dump. The temperature was 35°C or higher. As refreshments, Cokes were brought to us. However, we couldn't really benefit from them, as the bottles quickly filled with flies. To reach the camps, we generally travelled on fishing boats. We did not know whether we would be able to return at night, and sometimes had to sleep on our tables, because the captain decided that the sea was too choppy for us to return to the mainland.

During our mission in fall of 1978, Richard Martin and I were the first foreigners to conduct interviews in some of the camps, such as Kuantan. We were sometimes able to go through the complete list of refugees who wanted to go to Canada because, initially, most refugees wanted to be selected for the United States. This attitude changed in 1979 when the camps became overpopulated. Pulau Bidong became so jam-packed that a "shack"-based real estate market developed. During that period, there were so many arrivals each day that there was a great accommodation shortage. Refugees who were going abroad would sell their spaces to the highest bidder among the new arrivals.

That mission ended in Japan. Some Vietnamese boats pushed by the currents and storms had ended up there, and the Japanese did not want to receive those unwanted guests. Thus, under the enthusiastic lead of Conrad Adams, the immigration officer based at the Canadian Embassy in Tokyo, I went to Okinawa on 6–9 November to select candidates for Quebec. (Thirty years later, I learned that I'd had the honour of having been accompanied by the father of someone who would become one of the world's most popular singers, Bryan

Adams, who had launched his first record two years earlier.) The Japanese Red Cross moved us zealously and followed us carefully during our entire mission.

Back in Montreal, newspaper headlines were focused on the arrival in Kuala Lumpur of the *Hai Hong*, carrying 3,000 refugees. Minister Jacques Couture announced in the Assemblée nationale (Provincial Parliament) that Quebec would accept two hundred refugees and would send an officer to Kuala Lumpur to carry out the selection. I was that officer, and I returned to Kuala Lumpur on 19 November to join the federal team, which had an objective of selecting six hundred refugees.

While we were waiting to start the first interviews, I was sitting next to the head of the Canadian delegation, Ian Hamilton, and we were hearing some unpleasant motor noises. A Malaysian sailor was trying to start the generator brought by the High Commission staff to provide electricity for the typewriter used during the mission. When I saw that the sailor was not being successful, I asked Ian Hamilton, "Should I get involved?" He answered, "You don't know anything about it." I responded, "Do you want to bet? Watch me!" I got up, went to the generator, turned the carburetor intake valve, and went back to my seat. From that moment, we heard a regular noise from the functioning generator. I did my best to hide a smile.

The Opening of Permanent Offices

The Indochinese refugee program was growing. To implement the new agreement, Quebec decided to set up offices in Southeast Asia. I was sent to open a permanent office in Hong Kong in January 1979. The mission head, François Dupré, would arrive three months later, followed by Lucien Beaumont and Louise Langlois. When time came for my departure from Montreal, I felt ill-equipped with few resources, vague terms of reference, and little or nothing in the way of directives. Paul Simard, deputy director of international services, who was very perceptive, saw some worry in my expression and encouraged me, saying, "Mr Fortin, don't worry, you know as much as we do!" Possibly this was not completely inaccurate.

In 1979, I went through all the refugee camps in Southeast Asia at a frantic pace. I wanted to ensure that we were selecting all the Quebec-destined refugees. Between January and December 1979, I crossed approximately forty borders. In August, I went to open an office in Singapore. In the following three months, I made sure that I was participating in all federal missions in Malaysia and Indonesia, cooperating with all the teams from mission to mission. I worked seven days per week. It didn't matter – I loved this exciting life. In November, when the office was well set up, I returned to Hong Kong and was replaced by Lucile Horner. During this time, Montreal sent Richard Dupont on a long-term mission to Bangkok, where a program for Cambodian and Laotian refugees had started and was now developing. Elsewhere, Hong Kong had been overwhelmed. During certain periods, up to 1,200 refugees were arriving in Hong Kong each day, and, the Hong Kong authorities allowed all those who were willing and able to find employment to work locally.

In August 1980, Quebec decided to make its office in Bangkok permanent, to deal with the Cambodian refugee movement that had followed the fall of Pol Pot and the Vietnamese invasion. I was named head of mission, and Gerry Power quickly joined me. The Quebec officer who had been on long-term mission before my arrival had difficult relations with his federal counterparts, which meant that I had to use all my diplomatic skills to recreate a good partnership. Fortunately, I was able to demonstrate our goodwill, and we cooperated very well. However, some federal officers in Bangkok always seemed to really dislike our presence. Some of them did not like our work style. I remember a comment on a minor child that we had selected, written by a federal officer: "Not too frisky but good enough for Quebec."

The Indochinese refugee movement led to a wave of generosity without precedent in our population. Sponsorship rules were fairly strict. However, group sponsorships were coming from all parts of Quebec. Sometimes, to our great surprise, the documents mentioned the names of villages that we had never heard of. We needed to do some research on maps to find their location. At first, the matching work for sponsorship groups and refugees required an exhausting exchange of communication with the central office. This is why, after a few months, I asked Jean-Pierre Tainturier, who was then our international services director, to proceed generically rather than through names. He accepted my suggestion, which made our work much easier. When the flight manifest arrived in Montreal, the Quebec civil servants on the ground contacted the sponsorship groups and invited them to come to Longue-Pointe to welcome the family that had been assigned to them.

This period of work with Indochinese refugees, which lasted from 1978 to 1982, was the most exciting and satisfying of my career.

The Wave

During my first mission in Southeast Asia, I went to a refugee camp in Malaysia with Richard Martin. To reach the place, we used a pleasure craft, starting on a river and sailing to the ocean. Richard and I were sitting in the back on the transom, talking, when suddenly we were submerged by a three-metre wave that went over the boat. Apparently this phenomenon is common in river estuaries where the rivers flow directly into the sea. However, no one had warned us of the possibility. Richard told me that he was certain that I was being swept overboard, and that he had desperately lashed out with his hands in the hope of catching me so that I would not drown. In fact I had managed to maintain a firm grip on the transom. In the following weeks we often looked back and laughed about this incident, which could have ended tragically.

The Coconut

During a mission on a Malaysian island, at the end of the work day, I was just getting seated in a skiff that would row us out to the fishing vessel taking us back to the mainland, when I was asked to make room for a comatose woman who needed to go to the hospital. She had been knocked unconscious by a coconut that had fallen on her head. There I was, sitting in the bottom of the boat, with this woman who had not regained consciousness in my arms, wondering how I would deal with this issue once we reached our destination. In the end, I never had to face that eventuality, because the captain decided not to leave the island in view of a bad weather advisory that had just been issued. Thus, I had to return to the island with the lady. The following morning I went to find out how she was and was informed that she had passed away during the night.

The Missing Woman

There was a period when boat arrivals in Malaysia became so numerous that Malay authorities were unable, or unwilling, to let all refugees enter the official camp. As a result, hundreds stayed on the beach for long periods of time. At the same time, I had been regularly receiving a request from my central office in Montreal to track down a certain refugee who never showed up for interviews, even though I had posted her name on my calling lists in all the Malaysian camps. One day, at the Kuantan camp, as I was waiting to begin my interviews, I spoke to the interpreter who had been assigned to me. Her French was excellent. She was confident and had a good sense of humour. At some point, I told her, "I forgot to ask your name." She responded with the name of the woman I had been looking for. I almost fell off my chair! She had been part of the group that had been waiting for months on the beach prior to being admitted to the Kuantan camp.

Child Interpreter

During a mission in Manila, I was assigned an adorable fifteen-year-old girl as an interpreter. She was surprisingly mature for her age. I asked her whether she had found a destination country, and she told me that her case was desperate, as nobody could do anything for her. I asked her why. She then told me that her mother was a prostitute. The girl had fled Vietnam with her younger brother and sister, but no country would take her because her father was in the United States. I asked her why she was not joining him. She explained that she had phoned him, and he had told her that he had started a new life and did not want her to contact him anymore. As we had a program for unaccompanied minors, I suggested that she make an application for Quebec. The following morning, she brought her twelve-year-old brother and her younger sister to see me. It was obvious that her story was true, as there was clear evidence of a specific genetic look in this little family. I asked the federal officer to build a file until we could confirm the identification of a sponsor. It did not take long to complete it. I never found out what happened to them after their move, but I would like to know that they went on to a happy life in Quebec.

The Ashes

I cannot remember precisely how it happened, but I was once asked to find a ninety-two-year-old refugee on Tanjung Pinang Island in Indonesia, who was sick and had been hospitalized. One day after my interviews, I went to the local hospital, and she was there! I was surprised to find her in reasonably good health and to be able to have a conversation with her as she was a fluent French speaker. A bit later, she passed away, and her grandson came from Canada to the Singapore High Commission to retrieve her ashes, which federal officers had brought back from one of their missions. Incredible!

Kilometre 21

Tanjung Pinang Island was a really boring place, at least at first glance. When we were travelling on the island, taxi drivers often offered to take us to Kilometre 21. We wondered what could be so attractive about that place. One night, the four of us decided to take a taxi to the famous Kilometre 21. In the middle of the jungle, out of nowhere, suddenly appeared a small village with two streets and fairly pretty houses. The taxi driver left us at the entrance of the village and stated firmly that he would await our return. As soon as we started to walk down the street, a bevy of pretty young girls came out of the houses, believing us to be unexpected clients. They even grabbed us in an effort to persuade us to venture inside. We quickly ended the excursion and went back to the hotel. We later learned that this village was used as a discreet sexual tourism site for many Singaporeans who did not have access to this type of service in their extra-pure city, controlled with an iron fist by Lee Kwan Yue. It still surprised us to see that such a village could exist in the heart of Muslim Indonesia.

Slaughter

One day when we arrived in Pulau Tengah, there was an old man on the pier who was gesticulating, obviously in a state of hysteria, and who seemed to want to tell us his drama. We learned that he had previously come ashore with his family in a small boat that held approximately 120 passengers. This old tub had been intercepted by the Malay navy, which took it in tow and made it capsize so that all the passengers were tipped into the ocean. According to credible sources, the Malay sailors enjoyed pushing back into the water all of those who were trying to scramble back on the boat. This ugly scene only ended when the sailors became bored with the show. They finally picked up approximately forty survivors and brought them to the camp. The old man was the only survivor of a family of twelve.

Richard Martin was very moved by this character and kept looking at him, repeatedly stating, "Poor bugger!" I was so shocked by this tragedy that after my return to Singapore I secretly phoned Pierre Nadeau from Radio-Canada, who connected me with Denise Bombardier. We did an interview on the radio to report this story. It was broadcast the following Sunday, but, of course, I was not identified.

Customs

The doctor responsible for the medical section of the Canadian High Commission, David Holbrook, ensured that all High Commission drugs that were close to expiry date were sent to refugee camps and not to garbage dumps. As there were always doctors among the refugees, this initiative contributed strongly to better health in the camps. During a mission in Malaysia, Richard Martin asked me to carry some drugs in my luggage because his suitcase was full. At the Kuala Terengganu airport, he told me, "I will go through Customs with the suitcase containing the drugs. Since I have a diplomatic passport, they will not search me." I only had a regular passport, and it was obviously better if the custom officers did not find a pharmacy in my luggage. However, after I had gone through customs with no search or difficulty, I suddenly noticed Richard, who was behind me in the queue, holding his luggage in his hands and having an intense discussion with the customs officer. Later, he told me that the officer had insisted that he open the suitcase. Richard had to argue at length to make the officer understand that he was a diplomatic passport holder, that he was accredited to Malaysia, and that as such he did not have to submit to an inspection of his luggage.

The Monk

When I was in Thailand, we received a sponsorship for a Cambodian Buddhist monk who was eagerly expected by the Cambodian diaspora in Montreal, which considered him a holy man. However, a zealous federal officer had verified the exact date when the applicant had reached Thailand, and had found out that he had crossed the border twenty-four hours before the date needed for inclusion in the Designated Class. As such, he was not eligible to be resettled in Canada in that class. Fortunately, the federal officers found that the monk was a member of the Lesser Vehicle sect of Buddhism, a persecuted minority. For that reason they decided to consider him a Convention refugee because he would face persecution in Cambodia because of his religion. Happy ending!

Learning

During a mission in Thailand, I met a Cambodian peasant in his fifties, semi-illiterate, who did not speak any French or English and who did not look too impressive. I asked him how he would be able to manage in our country with so few assets. He answered, "Sir, if I was able to survive for five years under the Pol Pot regime, you shouldn't worry about my ability to survive in Canada." How can you respond to that?

Indochinese Refugees and Quebec

LUCILE HORNER

In 1979, Quebec became concerned about the fate of the Vietnamese refugees who were fleeing their country on small boats, many arriving on the Malaysian and Indonesian coasts. The Canadian Immigration Office in Singapore was already organizing selection missions for the refugees scattered throughout the camps set up along the Malay coast. Quebec became involved in this operation and sent its officers to select a large number of refugees. In the context of this program, I was assigned to Singapore.

The Quebec Immigration Office in Singapore

The cooperation of the Canadian Immigration Office in Singapore facilitated our work. Al Lukie, the Singapore immigration program manager, was always making our task easier. There was a lot of work, and we had little time to organize travel for the refugees we selected. The arrival dates were determined by Immigration Headquarters in Ottawa. We were told of the dates when a plane would come to pick up our refugees. Medical examinations and security processes had to be completed by those dates, as Quebec departures were taking place at the same time as departures for other provinces. This coordination process required significant effort on our part.

In order to meet our objectives before the travel date, we simplified our process. The IMM1314 form simplified the paper portion of the selection process. That form was also used as a visa, so officers had only to complete one form. For Quebec cases, Florent Fortin, my predecessor, made special arrangements with our federal colleagues. He shared his interview list so that a single list could be used for all refugees, whatever their destination. Federal officers did the same but did not complete the additional forms required for Quebec cases. Florent completed the IMM1314 for each of his interviews, as well as the Quebec Evaluation Form (FEVAL). He also prepared a Quebec Selection Certificate (CSQ) for each case that he accepted, adding these daily tasks to the thirty interviews he had to complete each day.[2] In the refugee camps, it was difficult for CSQ holders to keep their precious documents clean and in a secure spot, so we decided that in all camps the original would be delivered to the federal officer, with a copy for the file. Upon arrival in Quebec, each applicant received a visa, and the CSQ was delivered to the principal applicant. This document was important as it gave to each applicant his or her right to be a Quebec resident.

When I succeeded Florent, I limited myself to my mandate and only did the interviews for refugees destined to Quebec. In 1979–80, as refugee arrivals were at their highest point, the Singapore immigration office was a real hive of activity. We had very long days, and one often saw officers still working at 11 p.m.

Rodney Fields was responsible for the departure list. I remember one night, as he completed his final list for the following day, he was advised that a family that had been in the camp for a very long time had now met all requirements and would finally be able to leave. One of the family members had required tuberculosis treatments, and this had delayed the departure of the entire family. Rod went back to the office to make the necessary changes, so they could leave the following day. It was a lengthy process: he had to remove all the names of a family of the same size that had already been registered for departure, and insert the names of this other family, without changing the global departure order. I also appreciated the humanitarian actions of Don Cameron. He made all necessary arrangements so that two young women, a sixteen-year-old and a twenty-two-year-old, who had been raped nine times by pirates, could leave for Quebec with the highest priority.

We usually took a plane to travel from Singapore to Kuala Terrenganu, but this mode of travel was dangerous in the rainy season. During the week preceding one of our trips, we learned that our plane had been struck by lightning during a violent storm. We thus decided to take one of the High Commission vehicles. I remember the pleasant atmosphere – we sang throughout the trip. We stopped at a Chinese restaurant to savour some fish and other wonderful dishes. Thanks to the size of our vehicle, we could, without any problem, use the roads that had been flooded by the torrential rains.

I also remember Christmas 1979 at the Lukies' home, where we consumed the traditional eggnog with some nice varied small dishes, all of which reminded us of home. The Lukies invited us regularly throughout the year.

Quebec Activities in Indochinese Refugee Camps on the Malay Coast

My first missions from Singapore were to the Kota Bahru Kelanten, Pulau Besar, and Pulau Tengah refugee camps, where we conducted interviews under very difficult conditions. In one of these camps, my work table was set up next to a crematorium. Sometimes a cremation was taking place during the interview. The odour of the smoke was troubling. I was particularly moved when the body of a child was brought to the crematorium. We were next to death on one side and to life on the other; our work had to continue.

I also remember a stressful exchange on the roadside between the UNHCR representative, a Canadian immigration officer, and a representative of the Malay government. The Malay wanted to turn back a refugee boat that had just arrived. To avoid this catastrophe, the UNHCR representative had to promise that these refugees would only stay temporarily on Malay territory and would be resettled in France, the United States, Australia, or Canada. The Canadian officer intervened and also promised that the great majority of these refugees would be considered for resettlement in Canada. The promises, made on the roadside, saved those refugees. This incident convinced me of the importance of our missions.

Later, agreements were concluded with the Malay authorities so that no boat could be turned back to sea. The camps were closed, and all boats were directed towards Bidong Island (Pulau Bidong).

Pulau Bidong Camp

Every two weeks, I joined the Canadian immigration team, managed by Don Cameron, on a five-day selection mission for Vietnamese refugees destined to Quebec. Initially we went to Kuala Terengganu on the Malay East Coast where we stayed in a small hotel with a pool. After a long day at work, the comfort of this simple haven was very pleasant.

Every morning, we used a leisure craft to reach Bidong Island, returning to our hotel at night. Each trip lasted thirty to sixty minutes. However, during the rainy season, we had to use a large fishing boat to deal with the restless sea, and the trip took two to three hours. In the rainy season, we had to stay in the camp for the entire five-day mission. My colleagues had told me that we would have to sleep outdoors on our work tables and that the rats would take advantage of this situation to have a party. As the only animals that I really fear are mice and rats, I was frightened of that happening. At the end of the day, however, the UNHCR representative was happy to announce the official opening of a house that would welcome all delegations. He showed us the site with pride. On each side there was a dormitory with bunk beds. One was assigned to Canadian immigration officers. As the only female, I was shown a small room with one bed and an adjoining bathroom. As there was no door, I was informed that there would be a sentry on guard all night. When I entered the room, I saw a big rat run from under the bed. Despite my fatigue, I hesitated to go to sleep. To calm myself, I put incense sticks all around my bed, hoping that the smoke would keep the rats away. I asked for a flashlight and eventually went to sleep. The following day, we were at our tables very early, ready to see applicants.

The refugees also had to sleep in small makeshift homes, often made of bamboo and covered with canvas, and generally had to share the space with strangers.

Vietnamese Refugees in Malaysia

I had limited knowledge of the lifestyle and mentality of these people for whom resettlement in a third country had become the last hope. I quickly learned of their courage, their tenacity, their faith in life, and their determination to access a better existence. Each of them had gone through very painful times: the difficult decision to leave their country, the fear of not surviving a risky sea voyage, the difficulties linked to a temporary stay in a foreign country, and finally, the feelings of anxiety and of hope linked to the permanent resettlement processes.

In one of those camps, I encountered evidence of human weaknesses. Federal officers had entrusted the distribution of Applications for Residence (IMM8) to refugees perceived as reliable. We were surprised to learn that some of those selected for this task had extracted monetary payments from other applicants. From that point on, only Canadian officers could distribute the forms.

I was able to select many refugees, thanks to the generosity of Quebecers who had committed to sponsor families or single applicants for a year following their arrival in Quebec. There were also foster families who had committed to temporarily welcome unaccompanied minors. We had been told to accept all refugees meeting our criteria until we had no more sponsors. However, we never ran out of sponsors. The main selection criterion was: Would they be able manage on their own, after a year in Quebec? Our selection was also influenced by additional family links in the province.

Indonesia: Pulau Galang Camp via Tanjung Pinang

Vietnamese refugees arriving in Indonesia were generally housed on Galang Island (Pulau Galang). The camp had a number of large cement buildings where each family was allocated a specific location. Dick Martin was the Canadian officer responsible for this sector. For each mission, he was accompanied by a team of two or three people. Every two weeks, I joined them. From Singapore we took a boat that carried us to Tanjung Pinang, a small village that became our base during our five-day mission.

As we disembarked on the pier, a group of young people ran towards our suitcases. At first I was alarmed, but I quickly understood that these young people only wanted us to show them which suitcases to put onto their luggage carts, which they then did for us. Once the immigration formalities were completed, we walked to the hotel together.

At the hotel, there were other surprises. Going to sleep, I did not have a sheet to cover me. Next day our boiled eggs arrived half raw. Early in the morning, we could hear the call to prayer at the neighbouring mosque. We had to get used to local conditions.

In the evenings the streets of Tanjung Pinang became outdoor restaurants. There were dozens of these establishments, each offering its own specialty. The dishes, especially the omelets, were delicious. Another feature of Tanjung Pinang was the many antique American cars on the island.

Every morning we took a fishing boat from Tanjung Pinang to Galang and used the same boat to return. Upon arrival at the camp, we were greeted by the refugee representatives, all elected by their peers. As in Pulau Bidong, our work tables were set up under a metal roof. The rain continuously drummed on it during the monsoon, obliging both interviewers and interviewees to speak much more loudly. Although it was exhausting, we joked a lot so as not to get discouraged. Rick Schramm was our comic expert.

Most of our interpreters, all well-educated, were also elected representatives with a great influence on the other refugees. In general they were cooperative and supportive and helped with classes, celebrations, and leisure activities. However, as with all populations, there were some of the best and some of the worst. One of the worst examples was the time we noted that a number of candidates had not shown up for their interview. We did not understand the reason for these absences, as the refugees had only one hope: to receive a notice for a selection interview. Then a Quebecer of Vietnamese background who was working for an NGO in the camp told us that some interpreters who had been receiving the interview lists prior to our arrival were extracting money from those on the lists. They were telling them that it was through their intervention that their names were on the list.

The following day, when my interpreter announced that a family was not responding to our call, I asked her to make an immediate announcement to be broadcast throughout the camp. She told me that this had already been done, but the family had not responded. I then told her that until the family showed up, I would not complete any other interviews, and that this would be the new process. Shortly thereafter, I had the family in front of me. The no-show problem was resolved when we decided to give our interview list only upon arrival.

I did not understand Vietnamese, but during some of my interviews I noticed a certain discomfort in my interpreter, who, instead of continuing to translate my questions and the applicant's responses, started another conversation with the applicant. The applicant then became more and more insistent. This was a difficult situation for the interpreter. Afraid of receiving a refusal, some applicants, instead of answering my questions, were asking the interpreter what they should say to be accepted.

Many Indonesians were working in the camp for international organizations such as the UNHCR, IOM, and the Red Cross, or for NGOs such as Save the Children and CARE. On many occasions, they organized events in the camp for the refugees. Snacks were served, and all were invited to dance to regional music. Contrary to those at other camps where we worked, the local workers from Galang not only tried to do a good job but also mixed with the refugees, for whom they had great affection. Their respect was reciprocated.

I spent Christmas 1980 in the Galang camp. The refugees had decorated with Christmas colours the large church that they had built. They had also decorated a Christmas tree with many lights and hung on it large lighted cardboard stars. Candles illuminated the road leading to the church where midnight mass was to be held. Although the many decorative lights caused an electrical breakdown during the ceremony, it did not diminish the humour and good cheer of our refugees.

That Christmas we prepared, with the help of the person in charge of the UNHCR Unaccompanied Minors (UM) group, a visit to children in each sector of the camp. The UM group manager had soap, a toothbrush, and some toothpaste for every child, and I had obtained some gingerbread men in a Santa Claus shape from the Goodwood Park Hotel where I was living in Singapore. What the children didn't know was that we were coming with Santa Claus. Our Vietnamese Santa Claus had a beard made of cotton wool and red pants and a shirt. He was small and slim and walked like an old man with a cane. He didn't look like the good fat Santa Claus that we know, but never was Santa happier to distribute small gifts to children whose eyes were shining with happiness. It was one of the best Christmases in my life.

It was also in Galang that I discovered the "Vietnamese telephone" that worked from camp to camp. One of the groups from the Montreal Archdiocese was offering sponsorships for seminary students. At Pulau Bidong, I had accepted a few seminarians. When one of the refugees I interviewed in Galang indicated that he was a seminarian and wanted to continue his studies, I thus accepted him. A few days later, however, we received a family sponsorship for this candidate.

We were asked to accelerate the process for the young man, as his fiancée was pregnant! I later learned that the candidate's sister, who was in Pulau Bidong, had written to tell him that seminarians were easily accepted. In the circumstances, we could understand, but we tried to make it clear to refugees that we expected the truth.

Cooperation with Canadian Immigration Officers in Singapore

We had good professional and social relations with our federal colleagues, discussing with them our files and our shared goal of helping the refugees.

During the year I was in Singapore, my superiors agreed that I could maintain my accommodation in a small apartment hotel, even when I was on missions to Malaysia and Indonesia. This arrangement gave me a fixed abode where I could leave personal effects and not have to live out of a suitcase all the time. However, my federal colleagues who were on temporary duty and also went regularly on missions in different locales did not have the same privilege. I gave them the opportunity to leave their suitcases at my place, which they greatly appreciated.

On 24 June 1980, Saint-Jean-Baptiste Day, I invited the federal immigration officers, members of the Canadian High Commission staff, international organizations and local NGOs, and other guests to celebrate Quebec's national day in the gardens of my hotel.

In May 1980, Quebec closed its Singapore office, which had opened in August 1979. All the files were transferred from Singapore to our Bangkok office in the Canadian Embassy, which already included three other Quebec immigration counsellors. We continued our missions in Malaysia and Indonesia, although there were now fewer refugee arrivals in those camps. From Bangkok, we also did some missions to the refugee camps housing Laotians and Cambodians.

Quebec Government Activities in Thai Refugee Camps

Vietnamese refugees arriving by boat in Thailand between 1976 and 1984 were admitted to the Songkhla or the Sikiew camp. My first mission was in Songkhla in 1979. The only equipment available to us for work consisted of picnic tables and benches. The refugee shelters were in poor shape. However, the camp was on a wonderful seaside beach.

The refugees took advantage of this location to go into the sea and play with balls, and the children built sandcastles.

Songkhla Camp

When interviewing, I sought to understand more about the refugees who had risked their lives in unsafe boats. Many families had been separated following their departure, which generally took place after nightfall to avoid detection by Vietnamese coastguards. Some had been robbed at sea by pirates, and girls and young women had been raped or kidnapped. On the boats they had to deal with promiscuity, lack of water and food, storms, and many other trials. I was troubled by these stories, but they made me realize how important and urgent our action was.

Cooperation with Canadian Immigration Officers in Songhkla

I completed my first mission in Thailand with Ian Hamilton, who had extensive experience working with refugees and gave me helpful advice when needed. In the evening after a very long day, we would have dinner in a small restaurant on the beach. The cook was happy to offer us freshly caught fish and seafood. Because of the linguistic barrier, he invited us into his kitchen so that we could choose our fish without words. Ian was very comfortable in this environment. He would set himself up in a beach chair in the sand and drink a cold Singha, the most popular beer in Thailand. For me it was a pleasant initiation, and I took advantage of the well-deserved break. Those evenings are part of my best memories from my years in Southeast Asia.

Khao I Dang Camp

This large camp was set up on the border not far from Cambodia. In 1980, it housed 160,000 refugees who had fled the Khmer Rouge atrocities. Responsibility for the camp rested with the Thai Ministry of the Interior and was managed by the Thai army. The UNHCR maintained close links with the Thai officials. The IOM, the Red Cross, and a number of NGOs were also in the camp to help the destitute refugees. They were responsible for schooling and training.

I conducted two or three missions to this camp. Suffering was evident in the emaciated faces of many of the refugees. Most had lost members of their family, killed by the Khmer Rouge or by injuries, hunger, or exhaustion. Many had changed their names to avoid arrest by the authorities. Often the youngest could not remember their real names or their date of birth, and it could be very difficult to complete the long interviews.

Ban Vinai and Ban Napho Camps

These camps were located close to the Mekong River, which constitutes the border between Laos and Thailand. Many of the refugees in the Ban Vinai camp were members of the Hmong Hill Tribe (mountain people), while those in the Ban Napho camp were Laotians from the plains. The living arrangements were quite comfortable; artisans sold items such as jewelry, embroidery, and quilts. Life had a normal rhythm, and conditions were reasonably pleasant.

Thai and Lao live on both sides of the Mekong and share a similar lifestyle; their cuisine and their habits are similar. Their languages belong to the same linguistic group and so they can easily communicate. We could see this in the camps, where the refugees were fairly free to move. Some would travel to Laos in the morning and then return to the camp at the end of the day. I was often unable to complete the scheduled interviews because the applicants were not showing up. One young man came to ask if I could postpone his interview to the following day so that he could bring all the members of his family.

During another mission, I was surprised to see a Lao government minister in the camp. She knew many people there and addressed them all informally. I found it strange that a country representative would visit people who had fled that country. Perhaps she was meeting with Thai representatives to discuss repatriation of the Lao who were in the refugee camp? I never found out what was really happening. However, despite the evident lack of separation of the Lao from their own country, a large number were recognized as refugees.

On one mission in the Ban Napho camp, Sunkran, the "Feast of Water," was being celebrated. This feast is a religious ritual that involves splashing oneself with water for purification purposes. As part of the ritual, a popular event took place in which everyone splashed their neighbours. Groups of young people in trucks filled with water buckets splashed others as they went through the streets. Refugees did not dare to splash me, but at the end of the day one of them finally did, and I celebrated with them by responding.

Phanat Nikhom Camp

This camp, only two hours from our base in Bangkok, housed Cambodian and Laotian refugees awaiting resettlement in countries such as France, the United States, Australia, and Canada. The refugee shelters were built to house only one family each. They were made of cement and appeared much more comfortable than most of those in camps where I had worked. On some days there was a market, and Thai businesses offered their products outside the gates around the grounds of the camp. Unlike other camps, Phanat Nikhom had three good restaurants that were operated by the Thai. In one of those restaurants, I ate the best Pad Thai I've ever had.

Cooperation with Canadian Immigration Officers

Generally, we had a very good relationship with our federal counterparts, but on one situation we were obliged to differ. Federal officers gave priority to Vietnamese refugees, as they had determined that Cambodians, in contrast to the Vietnamese, would eventually be able to return to their country of origin. On the Quebec side, however, Jacques Couture, then Quebec's immigration minister, had decided to give priority to the selection of Cambodian refugees.

Following an exchange between departments, the disagreement was resolved. Canada, as well as Quebec, finally accepted a large number of Cambodian refugees. Two years later, the Canadian immigration service received a plaque of acknowledgment from the Thai government, thanking it for having initiated the resettlement of Cambodian refugees in a third country.

The Quebec School in Phanat Nikhom

An international Quebec school was established in Phanat Nikhom through ICM in 1980. Our department had decided that during the period between selection and departure, refugees destined to Quebec needed to receive French language training and classes of initiation to life in Quebec. A large room was made available, and the refugees decorated it with Quebec symbols.

During the first two years, our department assigned two Quebec teachers to the school, each for a one-year period. After this time, we hired Quebecers travelling through Thailand with good pedagogical knowledge. Within a few years the school was well known. We even had two teachers from Quebec who offered their services after arriving in Bangkok. Our young educators did some marvellous work.

As a result, most refugees leaving the camp had a good grasp of French and were eager to reach Quebec to use their new knowledge. When Monique Gagnon-Tremblay, who was then Quebec's immigration minister, came to visit the school, she was very moved to hear the refugees welcome her by singing their adaptation of Gilles Vigneault's famous birthday song: "My dear minister, it's now your time to hear us speak of love to you."[3]

The school closed in 1993 after the Phanat Nikhom camp had been emptied. When I later met refugees in Quebec who had attended the school, they had fond memories and took great pride of their time there. Their stay at the school had made their adaptation to a new country much easier.

It was a great privilege for me to do selection work in the Indochinese refugee camps for a period of nine years. In my line of work, it is quite rare to deal directly with immigration applicants in such a difficult situation. A negative response to an application for permanent residence had an enormous impact on a refugee whose sole hope was to leave the camp to start a normal life. In those circumstances, it was sometimes difficult to give a refusal. The selection criteria that I had to apply were there to help me to keep the necessary balance.

20

Rescue at Sea[*]

Following the communist takeover of South Vietnam, escape by sea was the only available option for many Vietnamese desperate to leave. Those with financial resources could attempt to buy passage on a large freighter or substantial fishing vessel.[1] Many, however, were unable to pay for passage on a large boat; even after pooling their money, they could afford only small, poorly equipped vessels. These boats were filled to overflowing and often captained by individuals with little seafaring experience.

Those setting out in small boats, hoping to reach the shores of a noncommunist country, did so at the risk of their lives. They knew little of the route of their journey. Pirates boarded a considerable number of boats, looting, raping, and sometimes murdering. The international media carried accounts of Vietnamese refugee boats found sinking or near-to-sinking in the seas around Vietnam. In May 1980, UNHCR stated that in 1979 it had received reports of 8,627 refugees rescued at sea by 128 ships of 23 countries. Another 1,024 were rescued in the first three months of 1980.[2] While most refugees were disembarked by their rescuers in ports around the South China Sea, some ended up much further away. This chapter looks at refugees rescued on the high seas and disembarked in distant ports in Japan, Saudi Arabia, and Turkey.

Early in the Vietnamese exodus, officials of several departments met to determine how Canada could assist boat people rescued at sea. Initially, Transport Canada reminded Canadian ships' captains of

---

* CIHS is grateful to Laura May Roth for organizing and drafting this chapter.

their obligations to render assistance to those in need of aid as mandated by the Canada Shipping Act and various UN conventions that Canada had signed or was negotiating at the time.[3] In October 1978, officials at External Affairs, CEIC, and Transport Canada began joint discussions of the problem of boat refugees in distress.[4] A set of instructions, "Ship Safety Bulletin 2/79," was created and sent to ships' captains in 1979. The bulletin provided assurances that the Government of Canada would render assistance to masters of Canadian-registered vessels by obtaining permission for them to disembark rescued refugees at the first port of call. It also informed masters that Canada would accept and resettle Vietnamese rescued by Canadian owned and registered vessels.[5]

The immigration department's Refugee Policy Division issued complementary instructions to Canadian visa officers at the same time. Those rescued at sea would still be subject to the normal requirements of the Immigration Act regarding health and good character, but they would be interviewed as quickly as possible. Also, Canadian officials were instructed to assist masters of Canadian-owned ships under foreign registry to support the efforts of the country of registration to assist the refugees. Further instructions specifically dealing with refugees rescued at sea were issued to Canadian visa officers on 20 February 1979, soon after Canada's decision on 21 December 1978 to accept a further 5,000 Indochinese refugees: "As situations dictate, you are authorized to provide commitments to accept Vietnamese small boat escapees who may be picked up at sea by Canadian-owned or registered vessels. Canadian mariners have been informed of this policy which has been designed to encourage countries of first port of call to permit such refugees to disembark. A commitment to accept refugees in this situation may be made conditional upon the passengers being able to disembark and subject to them being of good health and character. No additional selection criteria need be applied in this circumstance, and refugees selected in this situation will be allocated quota positions from headquarters."[6] Significantly, this instruction exempted refugees rescued at sea from the normal statutory requirement that they be capable of successful establishment in Canada.

Canada took a further important step to aid refugees rescued at sea. In August 1979, under UNHCR auspices in Geneva, eight countries including Canada negotiated an arrangement establishing Disembarkation Resettlement Offers (DISERO). By signing DISERO, this group of countries agreed to guarantee the resettlement of refugees rescued at sea by merchant ships flying flags of countries that had not agreed to resettle refugees. According to the DISERO procedure, the eight signatory resettlement countries guaranteed to resettle these refugees within ninety days of disembarkation at the rescuing vessel's next port of call. By 1990, more than 68,000 people had been rescued and resettled using DISERO and its later companion program, Rescue at Sea Resettlement Offers (RASRO).[7]

Some people were not so fortunate. Many drowned at sea. The flight of others came to a tragic end after they arrived on a foreign shore only to be pushed off again by security officials.

The MV *W.A. Mather*, 1976

The case of the Canadian Pacific ship MV *W.A. Mather* and its rescue of a group of Vietnamese boat people sheds a rare light on the human dimensions of rescues at sea. The *Mather*'s captain, Bryan Oag Hunter Brown, a British citizen, made detailed notes of the rescue and subsequent efforts to aid the refugees, a task made more difficult by the early date of the event, before the attention of the world, and especially of resettlement countries in the West, was focused on the plight of the boat people. What is interesting in this case are the actions of a Canadian vessel, its captain, and its crew in rescuing a group of refugees from a small boat in distress on the high seas.[8]

On 2 September 1976, at 13h46, with the *W.A. Mather* positioned at 12 03N 113 6E, the watch officer noticed a small fishing boat drifting in the South China Sea with passengers signalling for help: "Mr. P. Griffiths, our Canadian Montrealer, on the bridge at the time spotted their distress signals and could hear their cries across the calm water. Captain B.O.H. Brown was summoned to the bridge and he quickly alerted the engine room and turned the ship round to stop and make a lee for the fishing boat ... Mr. P. Corney, Chief Officer inspected the boat to confirm that it was slowly sinking."[9]

On board the small boat was a large group of Vietnamese refugees. The group included the families of Mr T; Mr L, a storekeeper; Mr N, a male nurse; and Mr G, a chauffeur in the South Vietnamese Army. Although Captain Brown did not become aware of the fact until later in the voyage, all four men were originally from North Vietnam and had fled to South Vietnam to escape the communists. With the communist takeover of the South, they felt trapped. The four decided to buy a boat to flee Vietnam with their families and a few others. Mr T was already the owner and operator of a small fishing boat but was able to trade it for a larger one with a diesel engine in better condition. The men and their families boarded the vessel and fled via Nha Bay in South Vietnam, heading out to the South China Sea. The boat was 6.5 metres long and 1.5 metres wide and held more than thirty passengers. Two days into the journey, it ran out of fuel and was carried by the currents toward the Philippines. The group feared the worst. After a day of drifting aimlessly, they spotted a large ship with English writing on its side and signalled for help. The crew of the *Mather* came to their aid.

When Chief Officer Corney first saw the boat, it was leaking water and all the belongings stowed onboard were wet.[10] The group had clearly been at sea for several days. The effects of heat and exhaustion showed on the faces of the older women and younger children. Brown gave orders to the crew to take all distressed passengers on board. After bringing everyone onto the ship, the crew carefully checked the refugees' health. With rest, cooler conditions, and adequate food and water, the obvious signs of exhaustion began to disappear. The *Mather* sent a message to warn other ships that the hulk of the empty refugee vessel was still afloat and then continued to head southwest past Thailand and Malaysia toward Singapore.

After three days, the ship arrived at the tiny island of Pulau Bukum, five kilometres south of Singapore.[11] Captain Brown remembered the elation among the refugees. The crew members were also relieved, as they had been sharing their rations and had given up their cabins to the refugees. However, during docking at Singapore, local authorities informed the captain that the Vietnamese survivors would not be permitted to disembark unless they had unconditional acceptance for resettlement by another country. This was bad news.

Brown immediately reached out to the international community and local embassies, but in these early days of the boat people crisis, the responses were far from encouraging. From the British High Commission: *On the basis of the facts you have given us we regret there is nothing we can do to help.* The Canadian Embassy: *The survivors do not meet any of our requirements and cannot be considered for entry into Canada.* The American Embassy: *The families qualify for acceptance but it could take three weeks before they are processed. Meanwhile the families have to remain on board as this provisional acceptance is not sufficient for the Singapore government.* The French Embassy was the most positive: *We are most sympathetic and will do everything we can on humanitarian grounds to have them taken off the ship.*

Captain Brown was becoming increasingly frustrated with local authorities and the environment the refugees were forced to live under:

> The crowded conditions do not help good nursing and the survivors' harassment by the police and Immigration authorities do not help. These officials board every few hours day and night to check the party and have a variety of stupid questions which they ask them, only one has very limited English otherwise they speak no other language, and unless my officers head them off they call me too to ask either irrelevant questions or questions that have been answered previously to their superiors. One Immigration official asked to see all the party at about 3 a.m. [A six-year-old girl] had not slept for some considerable time [due to fever] but at last at this time was in a good sleep. I pointed out that if we entered the room she might be disturbed and since she was sick I wanted her to have her full sleep if possible. However, he insisted [and] opened the door which did awaken her and halfway through asked if I knew what her illness was. I replied I was not a doctor but thought it looked like leprosy. He nearly knocked me over in his rush to get back out of the doorway and kept wiping his hands on his trousers all the way to the gangway. I hope he had a very poor night's sleep.

While Brown appealed to the local embassies for resettlement help, and the crew prepared for the next leg of the journey to Japan, a doctor examined the survivors and pronounced them fit and well – a credit to the ship's crew after such an ordeal. The refugees were also vaccinated against smallpox. Within a few days, hopes were raised. Two families were told that an application had been made on their behalf and there was a possibility that they could go to the United States, but they would have to wait to hear more news.

In the meantime, the ship started to attract visitors. One of the first was an American man and his Vietnamese wife who came bearing gifts of fruit and sweets, which lit up the faces of the children. Other gifts followed from the Vietnamese community in Singapore, from the ship's chandler, and also from the ship's repair company. Still, none of the refugees was allowed to leave the ship. They had no choice but to wait.

Then Mme Fogarty from the French Embassy came to the *Mather* with new clothing for the children and some exciting news: the French Embassy was requesting permission for resettlement in France on humanitarian grounds for Mr G and Mr T and their families. However, Captain Brown noted, "Mr G is not too happy about this situation and through the interpreter from the French Embassy we now discover that he did undercover work for the c.i.a., posing as a Viet Cong and he is frightened that some free South Vietnamese may not be aware of this [the fact that he was only posing to be a member of the Viet Cong] and seek reprisals should he meet them in any other country but America." Good news also arrived from the American Embassy: the L and N families had met the resettlement requirements. But this news too had a downside, as security screening would take up to three weeks.

While dealing with these problems, Brown continued to treat the refugees with consideration. He also made detailed notes on them as individuals, pinpointing their skills. He assigned light duties to some of the men to keep them busy. They worked with the sailors washing paintwork, cleaning the forecastle store, and chipping rust. Mr T contributed by sewing canvas duffle bags for the group to store their new belongings.

Captain Brown provided an additional important service. The refugees had decided they could trust him and asked him to safeguard a bar of gold the size of a cigarette package. Brown put it in his safe, but knowing that his ship, including the safe, would be searched by the Singapore authorities, he worried that the gold might be confiscated. His solution, just before the customs officials came on board, was to place it in a lacquered cigarette box he kept in his cabin and cover it with cigarettes. When the officials came to search his cabin, he offered them a cigarette from the box. The gold bar went unnoticed and was subsequently taken ashore and converted to US dollars for the refugees, courtesy of the French Embassy.[12]

Unable to disembark in Singapore or follow up on their resettlement cases, the refugees were forced to remain on the *Mather* when it set out on the next leg of the journey to Japan on 14 September. Among the group was the six-year-old girl who had been ill and still had a fluctuating temperature. There were almost as many refugees on board as crew: thirty-three survivors and thirty-four crew. Captain Brown and his crew had made such accommodations as they could: "[The] ship [was] now fitted with extra life rafts, life jackets, extra provisions etc. in preparation for passage to Japan with all survivors onboard. Medical locker checked by Doctor and extra drugs (for use in minor children's complaints) being placed onboard. Bedding and four small tables ordered ... each person now has a thin mattress like a futong [sic] and a pillow."

On 13 September, Brown wrote: "Vessel is loading at Pulau Bukom. Police at foot of the gangway and a boat patrols offshore. However, I have heard unofficially that two of the Vietnamese borrowed passes from two of the crew and had a walk ashore and could have easily taken the ferry to Singapore. Since the passes are not handed in at the end of our stay, some of the crew had [extra] passes from the ship's previous visit."

On 14 September, the *Mather* left on the last leg of its journey to Japan with all the refugees on board. However, Singapore had one more problem in store for the ship. As Brown recorded in some anger, "'P 79' [a Singaporean warship] came close alongside our vessel about 400 meters off and asked by telephone if we had sighted or picked up a craft with Vietnamese refugees aboard which had been sighted this morning. After assuring them we had not, we were given permission to proceed with the thought 'Is P 79 under orders to sink the craft and drown the refugees or to pick them up?????' Who gives the orders in Singapore now? Hanoi???"

The next problem was not a human-made one but rather the weather: "Most of the party are seasick. Two of them ... have been given injections ... [and a] four year old ... has a nasty reaction to his [smallpox] vaccination and a temperature. His arm is swollen and red and has about a 3/8" hole of green matter. Poor wee fellow, normally cheerful, is very sad indeed. The good news is typhoon Iris is, as we had hoped, moving slowly NW'ly away from us and the rough weather we have been having should diminish." Avoiding the storm, the *Mather* passed north of the Philippines by Luzon and into the Pacific Ocean. During this final leg of the trip, Captain Brown was trusted sufficiently by the refugees to be able to collect their proper names to make a manifest for the Japanese authorities to pass along to interested embassies. (When fleeing Vietnam, the soon-to-be refugees had destroyed all personal papers and identification cards so that, if their attempt failed, the communist authorities would not be able to trace their relatives.)

As the *Mather* approached Japan, the Kobe agents of Canadian Pacific, the ship's owner, informed Captain Brown that they were making arrangements for the refugees to disembark in Kobe. Brown noted, "This has cheered the party up a lot." But soon came the disheartening news that, after all, Japan had refused them disembarkation. Instead, Brown was told that on arrival, an interpreter would board the vessel to assist in investigating the refugees and their applications to live in the United States and France. On 22 September, as the *Mather* anchored at Kobe at 13h33, the vessel was boarded by "fifteen Immigration Officers, four Japanese/Vietnamese interpreters, five police officers from special branch, five customs officers, agents from Dodwells and Cornes [sic], and photographers for Immigration requirements."

At this time, two teenage boys got into a fight and had to be separated by one of the crew, who was unable to find out what the fight had been about. Captain Brown wrote: "Have engaged the services of two students of Vietnamese to try to restrain the children who will all be locked up in hospital while we discharge [the cargo of oil] tomorrow. Problem is the Japanese Interpreters do not speak much English but we hope it is sufficient."

The next day, Brown learned from the Mizushima port authorities that they would not allow the ship to berth with the refugees on board. Brown then anchored in Kobe Bay to await further developments. While the government was not being cooperative, the eight men who connected the oil pipeline from the shore to the ship showed sympathy for the refugees, gathering money and buying candy for the children.

The refugees had now been living on the ship for three weeks, barely able to communicate with the crew and with no real knowledge of their ultimate fate. Brown grew increasingly frustrated with the many authorities he had dealt with in his attempts to help the refugees. Angrily he wrote, "The Americans are tardy and choosy. Is it because the Ford set up [President Gerald Ford's Administration] don't want adverse publicity about the touchy Vietnam Issue just before the election? The Japanese are hoping to do a lot of business with the Vietnamese in the near future. I wonder if they too are keeping their hands clean for the sake of the Yen … The Canadians are on[to] a good thing here too as if the Vietnamese do not qualify for entry to the U.S.A. then they do not qualify for Canada. That lets Trudeau off the hook nicely even if he does say Canada is independent of the U.S. How independent???"

Exploring one further avenue of assistance, Brown had earlier contacted Mr Dearlove of the British Embassy in Tokyo and Mr Rainbow at the British Consulate in Osaka. Both had promised assistance. On the evening of 23 September, the captain received a phone call from Dearlove, informing Brown that at last the British Foreign Office had granted permission to issue a *lettre verbal* to the Japanese government, by which the British government bound itself to pay for the cost of housing the refugees. However, there was one more delay: Brown was informed that the Japanese government required the justice minister to issue orders to the Immigration Department in Kobe. Brown delayed his ship's departure to wait for the Japanese government decision.

Finally (the date is not given in the manuscript), the refugees were allowed to disembark. Brown recorded the event:

> 1130 hours. Immigration boarded with Japanese Television company N.H.K. to film Vietnamese and record an interview with myself.
> 1300 hours. Amid some emotional scenes the party disembarked. The four heads of families through an interpreter thanked me for all that the company, ships staff etc. had done for them. They were taken onboard a special bus and driven about 350 miles to a refugee camp near Mount Fuji run by CARITAS the Catholic Mission in Japan, arriving there some eleven hours later.

The *Mather* then quietly proceeded on its voyage. The refugees were now the responsibility of the Japanese and, ultimately, western countries of resettlement. It is unclear from the memoir where all the refugees were resettled. However, at least two of the families made it to Canada, and two others were resettled in Britain (see below).

Captain Brown's memoir concludes, "The story for these Vietnamese is far from over but they were very lucky. They were originally from North Vietnam and flew south when the north turned communist. Now they have flown again this time, they hope and believe the American propaganda, to a land of freedom. They were taken from the sea with very little and left the ship loaded down with new clothes, new shoes etc. etc., some bought by the company, the remainder given by different sources in Singapore. They are alive, free and at least have some hope. How many have perished in their bid for freedom?"

A year later, Brown added this note to his memoir: "Jan 1977. Received a letter from Mr. N who with Mr. T have now both been granted permission to live with their families in Birmingham, England. Mr. L and Mr. G and their families are in Montreal, Canada." The document package that contains the memoir also contains a Hallmark thank you card. The printed inscription contains the words "How beautiful a day can be when kindness touches it." The handwritten message says:

Montreal, August 20th, 1977
Dear Captain, my savior. I never forget September 2nd 1976 you helped us. You worked hard for we have living good. I wish you and your family happy every time.
You saved we from death. I remember every day your kindness.
    L.T.V.

The Oil Tanker *Al-Nadji* in Saudi Arabia, September 1976

This account is the story of the odyssey across the Indian Ocean of Vietnamese boat people rescued in the South China Sea, the humanitarian actions of the captain and crew of an oil tanker, and the actions of Canadian officials – a visa officer and an RCMP officer – travelling long distances under challenging circumstances in order to resettle in Canada some of the Vietnamese refugees with family there. This narrative also shows how far-flung the involvement of Canadian embassies and especially Canadian visa officers became as the boat people crisis developed.[13]

In 1976, John M. Gibson was posted to the Canadian Embassy in Cairo. The summer before, on assignment in Los Angeles, he had been part of a small group of Canadian officials sent to the US Marine

Corps Camp Pendleton to select immigrants for Canada from a large group of Vietnamese refugees recently brought to the United States (see chapter 3). When Gibson left Los Angeles for Cairo, he did not expect to encounter another Vietnamese refugee. However, on 27 August 1976, he received word from the Canadian Embassy in Tehran, Iran, that an oil tanker had rescued a large group of Vietnamese refugees. Some of them said they had relatives or contacts in Canada. The last known whereabouts of the ship was somewhere in the Indian Ocean.

The Canadian Embassy in Jeddah, Saudi Arabia, did not have a visa officer. Gibson was thus the closest Canadian official responsible for interviewing refugees with a Canadian connection. As this was before the time of international computer communications or even fax machines, he had few resources at his disposal. Even the maps at the Cairo Embassy were outdated. Gibson felt that the oil tanker would most likely show up at Ras Tanura, Saudi Arabia's biggest oil port and the Saudi headquarters of Aramco, the world's biggest oil company. The closest airport to Ras Tanura was in the city of Dhahran. Gibson knew that both places were in northeastern Saudi Arabia, but had little information beyond this. Although it was the time of Ramadan, when all activities slow down in Muslim countries, Gibson's Cairo staff managed to get him a Saudi visa and a ticket to Dhahran quickly, and the Canadian Embassy in Jeddah, as well as American diplomatic officials in Dhahran, were informed of his travel plans.

With little knowledge about his destination, Gibson was on a plane on 2 September 1976. He arrived at a relatively modern air terminal with strict security regulations and was welcomed by a representative of the US Consulate in Dhahran, who helped him through customs and immigration formalities and took him to the American compound. There he met the American consul and was invited to stay at the compound while conducting his affairs. He was also informed that the *Al-Nadji* had left Ras Tanura for Iran to take on a partial load of crude oil but would return to the port.

It was now a week since Gibson had received the initial message from Tehran. In the next few days he spent fruitless hours trying to make contact with anyone who might know the tanker's whereabouts. His initial steps consisted of finding a translator – the Vietnamese wife of an American Aramco employee – and getting in touch with Aramco executives, who agreed to assist the refugees, including providing passes for them to leave the ship when the *Al-Nadji* did arrive in port. On his third day in Saudi Arabia, Gibson was joined by Laurie Cowan, an RCMP liaison officer from the Canadian High Commission in Kenya, who was responsible for the security and criminality clearing necessary for approving immigration to Canada, and – briefly – by an officer from the Canadian Embassy in Jeddah.

The following day, 3 September, the three Canadian officials made their way by car to the port of Ras Tanura, forty kilometres away. Gibson recalled the well-paved, straight highway, which he called "suicide alley" because their car passed eight relatively freshly wrecked automobiles on the side of the road. Happy to have arrived in one piece, the officials went to the Aramco harbour but could gain no further information on the *Al-Nadji*. They managed to track down the agent of the company (Kanoo) that owned the tanker and finally were able to obtain some specific information. The agent informed them that the tanker had left Iran, was somewhere in the Persian Gulf, and should arrive offshore at Ras Tanura sometime that evening.

Returning to Ras Tanura early the next day with the interpreter, Mrs Hoa Sims, they "first had to go through a long involved ceremony to obtain passes from ARAMCO and the local emir." Security clearance achieved, the party (Gibson, Cowan, Mrs Hoa Sims, M. de Caville, representing the ship's owner, and M. Engelken, a US consular official) boarded the *Confidence* 4, a powerful tug. Forty-five minutes later, they finally saw the *Al-Nadji*, a large oil tanker flying a Saudi Arabian flag, riding high in the water.

Gibson described the difficult process of boarding the vessel: "Balancing like ballet dancers we had to time [the ship's] rises and jump at the top of a rise to a rope ladder hanging down the tanker's rusty side, and from the ladder climb to a rather shaky metal gangway han[g]ing at a 45 degree angle from the ship's deck to the ladder. Slipping and sliding on my leather-soled shoes, and clutching my briefcase … in one hand, I made the jump successfully … followed by my companions." Once on board, they met Captain Mueller, who had himself once been a refugee, having fled communist East Germany for the Federal Republic of Germany. Mueller vented his frustration at the "Free World and its lack of sympathy and inefficiency in helping the downtrodden Vietnamese refugees," who had now been on board for twenty-five days. He calmed down as Gibson assured him that representatives of the "Free World" were now on board and ready to interview refugees with Canadian and American connections.

Captain Mueller described his encounter with the refugees. In rough seas six hundred miles off the coast of Vietnam, the *Al-Nadji* had encountered a small boat with an SOS sign painted on the roof of its little cabin. Mueller described how difficult it was to bring the refugees on board in typhoon-strength winds, putting his ship and crew in danger. When all forty refugees were safely on board, he used the *Al-Nadji*'s loading winch to lift the small boat from the heaving sea and deposit it on the tanker's deck. (Mueller was later able to sell the boat for $2,000 to a Saudi national and deposited the money in the ship's safe to be used by the refugees who most needed it.) For twenty-five days, the refugees were accommodated in the ship's cabins and Mueller's Philippine crew were on half rations; living conditions for them became difficult. Like Captain Brown of the *Mather*, Captain Mueller was angry that it had taken him so long to get help for the refugees from any government. His appeals had been ignored by officials in Singapore and Penang.

Gibson and Cowan began interviewing the thirteen refugees with links to Canada, while Engelken interviewed those with American links. One of the refugees, Mr L.D.H., fluent in Vietnamese, French, and English, proved to be a natural liaison person. Some of the group were concerned that the Canadians might be journalists – the refugees feared any publicity that might endanger friends and family left behind in Saigon. Mr L.D.H. helped by asking Gibson and Cowan to show their Canadian diplomatic passports to the group. He also explained why the interviews were necessary.

During the interviews, the story emerged of the refugees' difficult and dangerous escape. In Vietnam, they had carefully saved funds to purchase a small boat. One of the group, Mr N.V.C., played a crucial role in this. A law student before the communist takeover of Saigon, he had quickly switched to being a fisherman. Since only fishermen could buy boats, it was he who bought the fishing boat, complete with nets, on the group's behalf. The group then went to the countryside, ostensibly for a picnic, and slipped out to the South China Sea. They were able to evade patrol boats close to shore but then encountered the typhoon-strength winds that blew them an estimated six hundred miles out to sea. Their small boat would not have survived the storm much longer, they said; they owed their lives to Mueller and his crew.

In group sessions, the refugees were given counselling about Canada, including information about the Canadian economy and unemployment and the fact that refugees who had been teachers or had other skilled professions would not have their qualifications immediately recognized there. Also, because the refugees had very sketchy identity documents and the medical aspects of their immigration processing could not be finalized in the short time available, authorizations for the issuance of Affirmations for Visa[14] and Minister's Permits[15] had to be obtained from Immigration Headquarters in Ottawa.

The administrative needs were met and processing was done rapidly; Ottawa immediately approved the issuance of travel documents and permits, and airline tickets were bought. Finally, Saudi transit visas for the refugees were obtained and the group could go ashore. At a touching farewell ceremony, Mueller presented each family with a photo of the ship signed by all the crew members, and the refugees presented letters of thanks to the captain and crew. "Captain Mueller played his role of the gruff seadog to the letter," Gibson wrote, "all the Vietnamese bowed deeply, and there wasn't a dry eye in the house."

After a few days of hectic work by Canadian officials, the refugees were transported to Dhahran Airport and boarded a direct flight to Montreal. Given the conditions in Saudi Arabia during the Muslim month of Ramadan, the speed with which the operation took place may be considered a minor miracle.

A Turkish Cargo Ship, 1979[16]

The following short account of the aftermath of the rescue of some one hundred boat people from a Turkish ship in the South China Sea is another demonstration of how very far some of the rescued refugees had travelled and the crucial role played in assisting them by Canadian embassies in far-flung parts of the world. The narrative also highlights the extremely valuable assistance given to the refugees and Canadian officials by Caritas, an important international Catholic humanitarian organization.[17]

In 1979, Jean-Paul Delisle was posted as an immigration officer to the Canadian Embassy in Belgrade in the former Yugoslavia. The visa section at the embassy was responsible for visa and immigration affairs for a large region, including Turkey. One day (the exact date is unavailable) Delisle received a telex message from André and Viviane Dumezic[18] of the Caritas office in Istanbul, advising him that Caritas had just been informed "by the Turkish Ministry of the Interior that a Turkish-registered cargo ship sailing in the South China Sea, had, on its return voyage to Izmir [Turkey], rescued some 100 Vietnamese boat people whose ship was in the process of sinking."

The Turkish government had informed Caritas that when the ship reached Izmir in about one week's time, the refugees would be allowed to disembark with three-month temporary permits only if assurances as to their resettlement were received from refugee resettlement countries such as the United States and/or Canada. Apparently forty members of the group had relatives in Canada.

Delisle immediately contacted Immigration Headquarters in Ottawa, asking for instructions. His report states, "The immediate response was very clear – to do everything we can to support Caritas and process qualified applicants within the timeframe set by the Turkish authorities if this was possible." The shipping company's accounts of the refugees' rescue in the South China Sea left no doubt that they all qualified for Canada's Small Boat Escapee program.

Once the refugees arrived in Izmir, Caritas took over temporary responsibility for them. It bused them to Istanbul, where accommodations as well as facilities such as translators and medical staff were available. When Delisle arrived in Istanbul to interview the refugees, Caritas was able to provide an office and translators. It had also ensured that the refugees understood the process and helped them to complete application and other forms. Thus, Delisle was able to proceed quickly and efficiently with the actual interviews and the process of resettlement in Canada, even though, like most refugees, the families had little by way of documents related to their identities or work experiences. Information about relatives and contacts already settled in Canada was gathered during the interviews.

During the interviewing process, Delisle noticed that one of the women had a fresh bruise on her face. In reply to his probing questions, her husband admitted that a few days earlier the pressure of their long journey plus the uncertainty they faced had led to a dispute with his wife, during which he hit her. Both claimed that this had never happened before. The contrite husband said it would never happen again. Delisle explained that in Canada this kind of behaviour amounted to assault and that it was not only considered unacceptable but could lead to criminal charges against the husband. He counselled the wife that there were numerous organizations and shelters in Canada that offered protection and assistance to women and children in distress who felt threatened and, should it ever become necessary, she should not hesitate to seek protection. The couple reassured Delisle that this kind of behaviour would not be repeated.

Delisle's report narrates the final steps of the interview and application process:

> Following the completion of the interviews, I met with Caritas representatives and informed them that all was in order. We ... decided to convene the group in the inner courtyard of the facility in which they were being housed to inform them that they had all been accepted for resettlement in Canada. [The announcement was met with] ... an outburst of cheering, hugging, crying and celebration that would just not end ... During my wrap-up session with the Dumezics they informed me that the couple [questioned about the wife's bruise] wanted a few minutes of my time. After agreeing to this, I was approached by the husband and wife, along with a group of 4–5 adult persons from the group selected for Canada. The husband now had a fully shaved head, very much like a Buddhist monk. I was then informed by the interpreter that the husband was very contrite ... and had made a solemn vow to his wife, with other members of the community present as witnesses, that he would never hit her again. The shaving of the head was a symbol of the seriousness with which he had made his vow.

A Brief Analysis

The three reports above of rescues on the high seas, two from 1976 and one from 1979, clearly demonstrate the bravery of Vietnamese boat people. Even if they did not perish on the high seas, which many did, sea-going refugees experienced a great deal of suffering. After rescue, they still faced weeks, months, or even years of uncertainty about their future.

The ships' captains and crews who came to the assistance of small refugee boats on the point of being lost on the high seas acted with commendable resolution and courage and often went well beyond what was required of them by the Law of the Sea.

The accounts also illustrate that after the initial intense activity in 1975 – especially by the United States, and also by Canada – to resettle the refugees immediately after the fall of Saigon, interest in the fate of the boat people declined. Only in mid to late 1978, as the phenomenon reached catastrophic proportions and became a major international media event, did the international community react. In this context, the humanitarian actions of ships' masters like Captain Brown and Captain Mueller were highly commendable, as were the effective interventions by Canadian officials such as Gibson and Delisle.[19]

Laem Sing Boat Camp, Thailand. Boat people awaiting interview in the shade of a beached boat. Courtesy of Robert J. Shalka.

Nan Refugee Camp, Thailand. Hill Tribe people watching interviews. Courtesy of Robert J. Shalka.

Kuala Terengganu, Malaysia, October 1979. Headed to Pulau Bidong: *from left to right*: Director General Kirk Bell; Michael Phelps (UNHCR); David Hardinge; Philip Leung, Assistant Deputy Minister Cal Best (behind Leung); Bill Lake (RCMP); Al Lukie; driver; Margaret Tebbutt; and Ross Francis, high commissioner to Malaysia. The trip gave first-hand exposure to the challenges in Southeast Asia. Courtesy of Donald Cameron.

A Pulau Bidong souvenir. Enterprising refugees in the Malaysian camp created logos and other souvenirs to raise money. Courtesy of John McEachern.

Hmong refugee camp, Nan Province, Thailand. Visa officer Leo Verboven interviews an extended family with relatives in Canada. Courtesy of Leo Verboven.

Northern Thailand. With no camp office or communal area, Leo Verboven interviewed on a handy log in the shade. This snake crawled out from under the log and was promptly dispatched. Verboven declined an invitation to have it for dinner. Courtesy of Leo Verboven.

Pulau Bidong, Malaysia, 1979. Margaret Tebbutt was one of a handful of female Canadian visa officers. In Hong Kong in 1975 she assisted with attempts to rescue relatives of Canadian Vietnamese. In the fall of 1979, she interviewed refugees in camps in Malaysia and Indonesia. She then trained and managed refugee liaison officers in British Columbia (1979–80). Courtesy of Margaret Tebbutt.

David Ritchie with Vietnamese refugee children in Bidong. Of the 60,000 refugees in 1979–80, 32 per cent were children fourteen years old and under. Courtesy of David Ritchie.

Opposite
Pulau Bidong, Malaysia, October 1979. Family with children leaving Bidong camp on boat for Kuala Lumpur and a flight to Canada. Courtesy of Margaret Tebbutt.

Convent Transit Camp, Malaysia, November 1980. Preaching to the converted: Sister Monica describes the plight of refugees on TB hold to Senior Coordinator Mike Molloy and Singapore Manager Al Lukie. Courtesy of Donald Cameron.

Kuala Lumpur, Malaysia. An Air Canada DC-8 charter ready for takeoff. Airline companies had designated crews for the charter flights. Feedback from those crews indicated that the experience was a career highlight. Courtesy of Donald Cameron.

Arriving in customs hall at Mirabel Airport, Montreal, on the way to the staging area at CFB Longue-Pointe. Courtesy of Major (ret.) Jacques Coiteux.

Arrivals at Griesbach Barracks, Edmonton. Refugees typically arrived with just a small bag of belongings. Those from camps in Hong Kong arrived with more belongings as they had been allowed to work there.
Courtesy of Murray Mosher.

Refugees completing a medical questionnaire at Griesbach Barracks, Edmonton. Upon arrival, refugees had a medical examination and were tested for hepatitis. Courtesy of Murray Mosher.

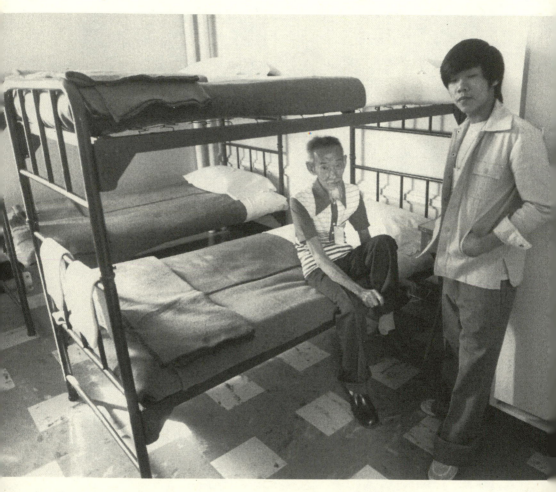

Accommodation at Griesbach Barracks, Edmonton. Refugees remained at the staging areas in Edmonton and Montreal for three to five days. Courtesy of Murray Mosher.

PART THREE

Welcoming the Refugees

Receiving the Refugees: The Staging Areas

When ministers Flora MacDonald and Ron Atkey announced the decision to admit 50,000 Indochinese refugees to Canada, they also informed the public that the government would establish two staging areas, or reception centres, one in the East, to open on 7 August 1979, and another in the West, to open on 14 August. These centres would receive and process the refugees on their arrival in Canada. Refugees would likely remain at the staging areas for two to seven days before continuing on to their final destinations in Canada.[1]

Preliminary work had been done in Ottawa over the winter of 1978–79 to review past experience with receiving large numbers of refugees, and a "Staging Area Planning Guide" was produced in February 1979.[2] Following the government's July 1979 decision, the Department of National Defence and the Canadian Employment and Immigration Commission were instructed on short notice to prepare the two staging areas, one at Griesbach Barracks in Edmonton and the other at Longue-Point Canadian Forces Base in Montreal. By the middle of August, following hurried preparations, both were operational and began to receive flights of Indochinese refugees. The cost of processing the arriving Indochinese refugees at the staging areas for roughly two to three days per person was estimated at $341 each.[3]

Longue-Pointe, one of four garrisons that make up Canadian Forces Base (CFB) Montreal, had in 1972 received and accommodated over 4,000 Ugandan Asian refugees and more recently had provided the initial reception and accommodation for the 604 refugees from the *Hai Hong*.[4] With that experience, the base was an obvious choice for the eastern staging area. Its central geographical location made it an ideal entry point for refugees destined to the Atlantic provinces, Quebec, and Ontario. Griesbach Barracks, part of the CFB Edmonton complex, was chosen as the point of entry for refugees destined for British Columbia and the Prairie provinces. In addition to its convenient location, its extensive facilities, including barracks with sixty rooms and a mess hall capable of feeding five hundred people at a time, made it the logical centre for processing refugees destined for Western Canada. All the early Department of National Defence (DND) flights carrying refugees from Hong Kong arriving from 7 August onwards and all subsequent charter flights would be destined to these two staging areas. DND provided ground transport, food, shelter, health services, clothing distribution, and general orientation. On-site CEIC staff included interpreters, reception and settlement officers, and employment counsellors.

Potential medical problems were always a worry. In response to concerns raised by elements of the medical profession and on the somewhat reluctant recommendations of a task force of federal, provincial, and independent health consultants meeting on 18 July, the government decided that incoming refugees would be screened for Hepatitis B at the staging areas.[5]

Preparations were in place for processing the refugees before the arrival of the first flights in early August. By the month's end, when the streamlining of overseas documentation processing took effect with the introduction of the IMM1314,[6] the two staging areas assumed responsibility for completing much of the paperwork traditionally done at the overseas visa offices, including completion of the landing records (Form IMM1000) and applications for social insurance numbers.

While it would have been possible to impose a standard approach to dealing with the incoming refugees at the two staging areas, the Refugee Task Force in Ottawa was content to define what activities needed to be completed and leave it to the local managers to organize the work flow as appropriate to local circumstances. The Longue-Pointe management team designed a Ford-style assembly line model, with refugee families moving from one work station to another to complete medical, documentation, orientation, customs inspection, and preparations for onward travel to their destinations across Canada. In contrast, the Griesbach team devised what manager Mike Fitzpatrick described as the dedicated team (Volvo-style) approach:

This ensured that there was always an individual interpreter available, along with a CEIC staff member. This greatly facilitated Customs clearance, and I think we were unique in that Customs came to our facility to do the clearances. The other important aspect to this was that we assigned refugees and their families to individual teams as soon as we received the flight manifests, which occurred before the plane left the refugee camp overseas. This allowed the CEIC staff members the maximum amount of time to notify the receiving sponsoring groups and the applicable CICs [Canada Immigration Centres]. If there was no known sponsor, we strategized as to where we should send the refugee and did the necessary notification to the Canada Employment Centre at the final destination, etc. As may be recalled, many sponsoring groups had been approved months in advance of receiving their refugees and we – CIC – had received criticism for not delivering refugees sooner and then only notifying sponsoring groups at the last moment. We now attempted to mitigate some of these difficulties. Our approach also provided a small measure of continuity to the refugees once they arrived as they dealt with the same interpreter/CEIC staff member while they were at Griesbach.[7]

The Longue-Pointe Staging Area

SERGE BERGEVIN

It was a great adventure: imagine receiving 60,000 refugees in the relatively short period of eighteen months. Such a large movement had never been experienced within our organization. It was almost too large to manage, but somehow we had to establish an organization capable of facing this challenge.

Some years previously, a centre for receiving Indochinese refugees had been established in the Queen's Hotel in Montreal. At that time a few hundred refugees were admitted. When the regional director general tasked me with the responsibility of coordinating the new Indochinese refugee reception activities, I immediately consulted my colleagues who had worked at the Queen's Hotel reception centre. Based on their experience, they made two important recommendations.

First, according to them, it would not be possible to manage the daily operation at the reception centre and at the same time assure the needed liaison with governmental and private organizations playing a role in this movement. Therefore, they suggested that a director should be appointed to be responsible for operations at the military base [Longue-Pointe] and that I should be personally responsible for relations with governmental and private organizations. Secondly, they recommended that the director of the reception centre should be present at the airport to greet the arrival of each refugee flight, identify himself as the person in authority at the reception centre, and be responsible for resolving any problems that might arise. I followed both recommendations.

Organizing the Work

At the outset we learned that two evening flights per week were expected to arrive, each with 150 to 200 refugees on board.[8] As one of two refugee reception centres in Canada, we would be responsible for at least 30,000 people. With the above information in hand, my director of local operations, Claude Bourget, and I met with Major Dussault, commander of the Longue-Pointe Military Base, to define the division of labour between our respective organizations. We decided that military personnel would be responsible for transporting the refugees from the airport to the military base and would also be responsible for later transporting them from the base to the airport, the bus terminus, or reception centres in Montreal. Accommodations, food, and sanitary and medical facilities would also be military responsibilities. Immigration Canada would administer and perform admission-to-Canada formalities, provide clothes, and organize onward transportation to the refugees' final destinations. As well, the Quebec Ministry of Immigration (MIQ) had established its own program of group sponsorship and wished to be present at the Longue-Pointe Staging Area (LPSA) to receive the refugees and direct them to MIQ group sponsors. Another organization wishing to have a permanent presence at the LPSA was the Department of Agriculture. When I told Major Dussault that these other organizations might wish to work at the base, he said he would be ready to accommodate them. Throughout the entire refugee reception project, Major Dussault was highly accommodating. At the end of our first meeting, he said, "I am going to buy five hundred beds." Without a doubt, he fully understood the scope of our task.

In addition to the work at the military base, we also had to organize reception at the refugees' final destination. We hired a dozen refugee liaison officers (RLOs). Before starting their work, they received a week-long training course that included dealing with sponsoring groups and establishing necessary contacts within CEIC as well as with the provincial government and with NGOs participating in our project. The course also dealt with the organization of reception arrangements at the refugees' final destination. RLOs who were dealing with refugees being settled in the province were posted to Quebec City, Trois-Rivières, Hull, and Montreal. The Central Operations Centre at Longue-Pointe dealt with refugees destined for the eastern half of Canada outside of Quebec. When we occasionally received refugee cases destined outside our zone of responsibility, we dealt with their reception as well.

I recognized that we would often have to step outside of established procedures to get the job done – to think "outside the box." All the organizations participating in our project knew this and acted accordingly.

Providing clothes to a large number of people every week was no small challenge. Buying them in a disorganized manner and assigning our personnel to oversee their distribution was not the most desirable approach. I decided instead that we needed to find a clothing supplier who could set up operations at the base. We met with several suppliers and proposed that we would supply the location at the base and they would supply the merchandise and the personnel. As well, we stipulated that their shop at the base must adapt its opening hours to our working hours. Miracle Mart accepted our conditions, and a few weeks after the start of our operations, we noted that the company was distributing toys free of charge to refugee children.

Our goal was to deal with most cases within three days. Of course, a small number of cases could not meet this target for a range of reasons, including problems with medical treatment, travel arrangements, and final destinations. However, in most cases we were able to meet our goal.

An Information Session at the Longue-Pointe Military Base

In order to ensure good collaboration for the efficient administration of the project, I considered it useful to hold an information session for all organizations involved in the reception of Indochinese refugees. At the outset, the base commander Major Dussault, Claude Bourget, and I were presented as the main administrators of the project, so that our collaborators could identify who we were. I explained each of our roles and how operations were to be organized at the base, including the number of refugees expected, when flights would be expected, and how changes in operations could happen at any moment. We replied to all questions. The session made it clear that not only was this project a matter of collaboration but we all had important roles to play.

The Inaugural Flight

We were ready. The first refugees were to arrive on a National Defence aircraft between 11 p.m. and midnight. Early that evening the regional director of immigration, the director of public affairs, and Claude Bourget and I all met at our office in Montreal. Media representatives had requested to be present at both the airport and the military base for the arrival. The deputy minister of Quebec Immigration had also asked to be at Longue-Pointe to welcome the first arrivals. This was to be an important event.

It was almost 6 p.m. when the telephone rang. The person on the other end of the line said he was calling from Trenton Air Force Base and informed me that the refugee flight had just passed over their control tower and should arrive in Montreal in an hour. We, of course, had planned for the arrival much later. Had there been a change without our being informed? I was told, "No, the flight is on time. You were given the arrival time in international Greenwich Mean Time, not local time. This is what we always use for our air operations."

We hadn't a minute to spare. In less than an hour, everybody was informed, we arrived at the airport, and those welcoming the refugees at the military base were waiting for us when we arrived with the refugees. The welcoming ceremony took place as planned. The next day I convened a meeting at the regional office to ensure that all future flight arrivals would be communicated using Montreal local time.

One may plan for everything, but a detail can derail all plans. I was very happy about how rapid the reaction time of our organization had been.

Adjusting Our Procedures

It was normal that with experience we would make some adjustments to operational practices. The first adjustment came about after the Transport Canada representative requested a change of airports for the arrival of refugee flights. We had initially chosen Dorval Airport because of its proximity to Longue-Pointe, but the representative stated that because of the refugee arrival project's high visibility, Transport Canada wanted to use the newly inaugurated Mirabel Airport, where it could provide us with all facilities that we would require. Although it was a greater distance, Mirabel was more modern and better adapted to the needs of our project. It operated around the clock, and the walking distance to the buses that would transport the refugees to Longue-Pointe was shorter. I accepted the change.

Making travel arrangements for refugees to their final destinations in many different Canadian cities was initially done by our staff on an individual basis and took a long time. I thought it would surely be more efficient to have a travel agent who could make these arrangements for us and contacted Air Canada to inquire whether it could provide us with this service. We agreed to a meeting date, and I asked a representative of the Department of Supply and Services as well as Claude Bourget to accompany me to the meeting. Air Canada proposed posting one of its agents to the Longue-Pointe Military Base to make travel arrangements and issue airline tickets. However, for this type of service, a guaranteed deposit of $100,000 would be required. I had no access to such funds. The representative of Supply and Services said, "I'll be responsible for this and provide the guaranteed deposit." Marvellous collaboration: the deal was quickly concluded. A few days later I received a call from the officer responsible for transportation loans at headquarters. I did not know that transportation costs inside Canada had to be registered separately. I apologized for my error; the officer needed to know the changes that we had instituted in our operations so that he could adapt his own procedures.

Finally, the Ontario Regional Office asked us to provide name tags for refugees destined for Toronto. Pearson Airport was a large, confusing place, and officials were having difficulty identifying arriving refugees. Of course we accommodated this request.

Some Anecdotes

As we were just starting to establish our organization, I was faced with two major problems: a freeze on public service hiring and a strike at Bell Canada.

We were authorized to hire only temporary employees, not permanent ones. However, for one of my positions, the clerk responsible for distributing money to the refugees, who handled large sums, I insisted on a permanent employee. The personnel department refused to make an exception, so with the support of the regional director of immigration, I presented my application directly to the executive director. He gave his approval, but I lost some friends in the personnel department.

And with Bell on strike, how could we operate a reception centre at Longue-Pointe without telephone connections and fax? This was well before the Internet age. Claude and I met with Major Dussault and explained our problem. "I'll get you your telephone system and your fax," he said. I don't know how he did it, but it was done.

The Department of Agriculture (DA) conducted checks on the refugees arriving at the military base. One morning, an urgent message was waiting for me on arrival at my office to call Claude Bourget in Longue-Pointe. Claude informed me that at five that morning, DA employees had seized all of the refugees' flip-flop sandals and burned them. There was confusion and panic at the base. What to do? I told Claude first to inform the refugees that we would get them new sandals and second to meet with DA officials to find a better solution. We had to find flip-flops, but it was almost winter and there were none in the stores. I gave a program specialist the responsibility to find a supplier willing to sell us about a hundred pairs. After searching all of Montreal, he reported that Zellers had agreed to open its warehouse and sell us the shoes.

We then met with DA officials. They told us that the soles of the beach shoes contained soil that could carry insects or other parasites that represented a danger. We replied by telling them of the panic the DA actions caused among the refugees. Was there some other way to proceed? After some discussion, somebody suggested fumigation. That became the new procedure applied to sandals.

This incident made us think. We had previously considered destroying the refugees' old clothes once new ones had been procured for them. But we now recognized that for these people their clothes were all they possessed. Consequently, the base commander provided them with laundry facilities.

Earlier I mentioned that the provincial government had its own program of group sponsorships. We received one family of refugees with documents indicating that they were destined to a group under the provincial program and at the same time to another group under the federal program – so where were they really supposed to go? We contacted our colleagues abroad to clarify the situation, but in the meantime the family could not leave the base and were waiting with some anxiety. As well, I was worried that our overseas officers had little time to spend on this type of problem. I asked a representative of Immigration Québec to meet to discuss this issue. What would happen as a result of our inquiry to our officers abroad? Our officers would meet with the Quebec officers, and one side or the other would cede the sponsorship. So why not do this ourselves in Canada? We agreed that in future whenever this type of situation occurred, we would alternate: one group would go to the provincial sponsor and the next to the federal sponsor. We would then inform our officers abroad of the decision taken. This solution satisfied everybody.

It will be recalled that the government had established a foundation to give the Indochinese project a high profile, with Cardinal Paul-Emile Léger and former Governor General Roland Michener at its head. A trip had been arranged for Cardinal Léger to visit the camps in Southeast Asia. Before his trip he asked to meet with us. I asked for the presence of a foreign service officer during the visit, and the executive director and the regional director of immigration also wanted to be present. Upon his arrival, Cardinal Léger held up a pair of pants and informed us that a manufacturer had offered to sell us at cost everything we needed to clothe the refugees. It took a considerable exercise in diplomacy to dissuade the cardinal from accepting the offer, given the situation abroad and at the military base. We told him to thank the manufacturer in our name. At the end of the discussion I took out a map of Southeast Asia and suggested that our foreign service officer should show the cardinal where the camps that he was going to visit were located. This allowed us to finish the meeting on a more positive note.

Somewhat later, I received a fax from an officer in Southeast Asia with a rather unusual request: "On the next flight to Canada, I am sending you Mr. So-and-So who is the overseer of a camp here. I promised him that he could visit Montreal; he will return here on the next returning flight." We agreed to the arrangement, and one of our security officers offered to take charge of the visitor. As he was departing, I was able to confirm that he was very satisfied with his visit to Montreal. Would there be others that we would have to organize, I wondered? I sent a fax to the officer who had requested the visit, telling him that I had been surprised by his request – was it really necessary? The reply I received was as follows: "How do you think I was able to arrange for Cardinal Léger to fly, in a helicopter, over the refugee camps?" I then understood, and no more questions were raised.

It was important for me to find rapid solutions to any crisis situation, having people talk and exchange their experiences. It is preferable that people talk about the solutions to their problems rather than the problems themselves. One day I received a phone call from our Quebec City refugee liaison officer, informing me that in Saint-Féréole-les-Neiges, a small town just outside Quebec City, a locally sponsored refugee family was in need of dental care. The only local dentist refused to treat them, claiming that he could catch a contagious disease through their blood. I contacted the director of national health, asking him to resolve this problem. The dentist was in due course assured regarding the state of health of the refugees. Sometime after this incident, I received a phone call from an Immigration Québec employee, stating that their reception centre in Montreal had received refugees suffering from leprosy. Again I got in touch with the director of national health. The refugees had scabies, not leprosy; the director contacted the reception centre and provided advice regarding the treatment of this disease.

It was winter and I was ready to go to sleep at 10:30 p.m. Suddenly Claude Bourget called from Mirabel Airport where he was waiting for a refugee flight to land. There was a problem: a snowstorm in our region meant insufficient visibility for the aircraft to land, and the pilot had refused the control tower's suggestion to do an instrument landing. What to do? The pilot had two options – to land in Toronto or in Boston. I advised Claude that if the plane could not land at Mirabel, the pilot should go to Toronto. I also told Claude to continue to attempt to persuade the pilot to land at Mirabel. For my part,

I contacted Ontario region to prepare them for the plane's possible arrival. My call created panic in Toronto, but there was no other choice. Fortunately, a half-hour later Claude called to let me know that they had succeeded in persuading the pilot to land at Mirabel, and I again called Toronto to call off their preparations. They told me that they had woken the regional director of immigration and begun to contact hotels in Toronto for accommodations. I apologized for disturbing them.

The next day I received a call from headquarters asking what had happened. We had no Plan B for these situations. On take-off, pilots received the names of two airports in case of landing problems. These were not always the same two airports. We met with the airline to ensure that pilots were well informed about the capacities of Mirabel Airport.

Our minister, accompanied by a press attaché, wished to visit the Operations Centre at Longue-Pointe, with the event being covered by the media. However, on the day chosen for the visit, only thirty refugees remained at the military base. I attempted to change the date of the visit, but this proved impossible. Commander Dussault, Claude Bourget, and I had another meeting. The commander suggested that we gather all the refugees in the same building. The minister, accompanied by the media, would shake their hands and exchange a few words with some of them. Then, as the ministerial party left, the refugees would leave by the back door and be ferried by bus to the next place the party would visit. Everybody including the refugees agreed with this approach. Nobody noticed that anything amiss, and the visit was a success.

During this entire project, only one person, a representative of the Montreal Roman Catholic Diocese, expressed disappointment. He told me that they had gathered $100,000 to help parishes that were sponsoring refugees and were expecting more difficult cases than they actually received. "So much the better," I told him. "This made the task of your parishioners easier." He agreed.

In closing, I must emphasize the constant availability and steady cooperation of Major Dussault, commander of the military base, throughout this project. His help in the organization of work and making physical arrangements at the base and his participation in resolving problems for the duration of the project were greatly appreciated. The devotion of all our employees should be highlighted, since it made our project a success. These were not nine-to-five jobs. I was happy and proud to be associated with the success of this project.

Griesbach Staging Area

GUY CUERRIER AND ELIZABETH MARSHALL

Guy Cuerrier and Elizabeth Marshall were both managers at the Griesbach Barracks Staging Area in Edmonton, Alberta. Because they described the same issues, their narratives have been blended into a single account.

In 1979, CFB Griesbach, located on the northern outskirts of Edmonton, was a vibrant military base often home to some of Canada's elite military units. Preparation for establishing the Griesbach Reception Centre began in 1978. Elizabeth Marshall, a foreign service officer, was posted to Edmonton as the foreign service liaison officer for the Alberta/NWT Region of CEIC. One of her duties was to participate in the establishment and management of the staging area.[9]

Shortly before the refugee reception centre opened, the Alberta/ NWT Region of CEIC was informed that small groups of Southeast Asian refugees would be arriving on regular flights for resettlement. One of the first groups involved forty refugees, a large number considering the near-absence of experience in settling refugees in the area. Vegreville, a small community about one hundred kilometres east of Edmonton, was selected as a suitable destination. The Vegreville CEC was asked to make local inquiries, and the results were overwhelmingly positive. A community meeting was quickly organized and exuberant planning began. The owner of a local farm machinery plant agreed to hire all the refugees. The Honourable Don Mazankowski, MP for the area, offered the use of a former convent that he had purchased. In countless ways the process of accepting the Southeast Asian refugees became a project involving the entire community. A CEC employee later informed Marshall that on his last check to see that all was ready, just before leaving for the airport to meet the refugees, he found Mrs Mazankowski on her hands and knees, giving the floor of the convent a last wipe so that it would sparkle for Vegreville's newest residents.

The mandate to establish the staging area was issued in July 1979 with two primary tasks: processing a large number of arriving refugees in a short time frame and monitoring the health of the refugees. Negotiations were commenced with CFB Edmonton's commander, Colonel Dan Munro, and the project was named Op Magnet II.[10] As a military base, the facility had its own rules and regulations. Nevertheless, the military continually impressed their civilian colleagues with their politeness, flexibility, and determination to make the operation a success.

The staging area operated from July 1979 (officially August) until August 1980, during which time 21,474 refugees were processed, the first arriving on 14 August. Some 310,884 meals were served at a cost of $400,085.72, or $1.28 per meal.[11] The facility took over the Spall Block, a two-storey barracks with an accommodation capacity for 550 people. The Kapyong Building, an indoor drill hall and shooting range with two offices, washroom and shower resources, and storage rooms, was identified for use as the main reception area. The dining facility (mess hall) for the use of DND personnel on the base was relocated to a different building, and major repairs and renovations were launched in the space to create a new dining service managed by the military food services personnel and dedicated for use by the refugees.

A large number of conversions and repairs were made to all the buildings to ensure the facilities would meet the refugees' needs. A chain-link fence was placed around the building used for Op Magnet II, not for security reasons but to ensure privacy for the refugees. The military went to great lengths to be helpful. At one point Marshall remarked quietly to a colleague that the Kapyong Building could use a fresh coat of paint. No request was made, but a military officer overheard the remark, and a day or two later a crew of soldiers was diligently painting the Kapyong Building and the Spall Block.[12]

Operation of the staging centre began in August with National Defence flights arriving at Namao Airfield, which was part of CFB Edmonton but located some distance to the north of the base and Edmonton itself. Commercial flights began operating in September, using the Edmonton International Airport, and involved Wardair, Air Canada, Canadian Pacific Airlines, and Pacific Western Airlines. Wardair disembarked their passengers inside a large maintenance hangar owned by the airline. Other planes stopped on the tarmac some distance from the terminal, and the refugees boarded buses to the staging area. CEIC staff, assisted by one or two interpreters as well as military police, always met the flights and accompanied the buses. As winter approached, Elizabeth Marshall and others overseeing the settlement process worried about the flimsy clothing and flip-flops that most refugees arrived in. The cost to rent the Wardair hangar for an hour or two for the other airlines' use was prohibitive. As the Canadian officials debated how to handle the problem of freezing refugees, they received a call from someone at Wardair. "It's getting pretty cold for those refugees to disembark on the tarmac," they were told, "I've told the other airlines to pull into our hangar to unload for the winter months. There won't be a charge."

Two flights of refugees arrived each week, normally on Sundays and Wednesdays. Each flight carried in excess of four hundred people. The arrivals all had to be processed at the staging area and sent on to their destinations prior to the landing of the next flight.

There was concern that the arriving refugees would realize that they were on a military base with all the negative implications that had in their backgrounds. In fact, the military aspect did not become an issue. Mainly young Canadian soldiers spontaneously showed up to help elderly and frail people disembark from the buses and to swing small children off. After helping to usher the arrivals into the arrival hall, the soldiers served soup, tea, and biscuits, along with soy milk and formula for infants and small children. Marshall remembered that some refugees had cached bits of airline meals, not sure where or when they would be fed again.

Play areas with donated toys were available for the children while their parents were directed to long tables, divided by languages, where they were assigned barracks rooms and the told about available facilities. Nurses circulated to perform triage as necessary.

Usually the refugees were allowed to rest before completing the documentation procedures. CEIC staff then conducted interviews with each family group in order to "land" them and prepare transportation arrangements to their final destinations. CEIC staff would process one family at a time, locating their luggage and directing them to the customs area. The immigration documents the refugees had in hand would be taken and placed on individual files (one file per family group). Rooms had been assigned to all refugees prior to their arrival, and the file would contain all pertinent documents, their name (head of household), their category, language, manifest number, room number, and final destination. After completing the processing and customs formalities, they went for their medical examinations and any necessary immediate treatment for parasites, infections, cuts, sores, and scabies. Children under ten years were administered polio vaccine. Health and Welfare staff insisted that the refugees shower in the Kapyong Building before their medical examination and going to the barracks building. The CEIC initially opposed this demand on exhausted people, until realizing that the refugees welcomed the showers as a luxury after their months in crowded camps.[13] Marshall recalls that they lingered in the showers and the hot water never lasted long enough for everyone to benefit.

Michael Molloy, the senior coordinator of the Refugee Task Force in Ottawa, tells a story about excessive health concerns during the arrival process and their consequences:

Guy Cuerrier handled public relations at Griesbach and was one of the most courteous and deferential officers I had encountered. I was shocked one February morning to arrive at my office to find a blunt telex from Guy which basically said, "Molloy, if you insist that we confiscate the refugees' underwear after their medicals, in future we are going to box it all up and ship it to you." It seems that zealous health officials had insisted that the underclothing worn on the incoming charters was to be taken away and destroyed. This had been going on for some time and there had been no complaints.

I immediately called Guy to see what had prompted his message. He told me that he had received an urgent call from Griesbach in the middle of the preceding night and had been informed there was a major disturbance in the barracks. Guy drove across Edmonton in the bitter cold to pick up an interpreter and proceeded to the base where a couple of worried military police rushed him and the interpreter to the barracks where they found all the refugees up and about and very agitated. Eventually they made their way to a room that seemed to be the centre of the disturbance to find a particular family, especially the mother, in great distress. It took time to calm the family down, but eventually the story emerged.

Before leaving Vietnam, they had sold all their possessions and used the proceeds to buy a large diamond. The diamond was sewn into the mother's bra, and it had remained hidden during the voyage to safety, months in a refugee camp, and the long flight to Canada. Unhappily, in the excitement of the arrival, she had forgotten the diamond and after her shower had dumped the bra in the collection bin, only to wake with a start hours later. Guy determined that a 747's worth of undies had been placed in a dumpster and moved to a hanger awaiting destruction. After a long and not very pleasant search, the missing bra with its hidden diamond was found and returned to the relieved family.

I related this story to my contact in Health and Welfare Canada in Ottawa and suggested that future underwear collections would be mailed to him. It was quickly agreed that if the refugees would agree to wash the clothes they wore on the flight in machines provided by the military, the offending instruction would be withdrawn.[14]

Solutions were always worked out to overcome anything that contributed to the unease of the tired, anxious arriving Indochinese refugees. With all the formalities completed, they went to a clothing depot to obtain one full set of clothing and a pair of shoes, a Red Cross personal needs kit, and a Bank of Nova Scotia passbook (a $10 account, donated by the bank, was provided to each head of household). An envelope with cash for the vending machines at the centre was also provided. Female soldiers were usually on hand to help dress the young children in the change booths along one wall.

Within days of the opening of the staging area, organizations had collected used clothing for the refugees. An Air Canada attendant who worked on the flights and was appalled at the clothing in which the refugees arrived had herself arranged for the collection of a number of large boxes of clothing. Air Canada flew the boxes to Edmonton and had them delivered to the centre free of charge. Space was found in the basement of the barracks where the clothing was sorted, cleaned, and repaired. During their stay, the refugees were encouraged to visit the used-clothing depot for wardrobe additions with which to start their new lives in Canada.

Elizabeth Marshall describes the next stage for the newcomers:

Decked out in their new clothes, the refugees were shuttled by van to the Spall Block and their appropriate rooms. Interpreters were available in the Spall Block to help and direct individuals to emergency dental care, prescription services, etc. The refugees were also informed that the rest of the day was left free to relax, to sleep or to watch TV. The children could play outside and people might go to eat in the dining hall.

On the first morning after their arrival, the refugees returned to the Kapyong Building in smaller groups to complete the processing of their immigration visas and to receive their landed immigrant status. Employment counsellors discussed their work history, the presence of family or friends in Canada, the proposed sponsorship that might be available, and settled on a final destination for family group. In January 1980, CP Air stationed a ticket agent on-site to do all reservations and ticketing at no cost and with equal usage of the various transportation firms. Some refugees who spoke English well might be offered employment as interpreters at the Centre or at CECs throughout the country. The novelty of being offered a government job, even if temporary, on their first day in Canada never ceased to amaze the refugees.[15]

The military prepared all meals in the mess hall. The cooks had experience in preparing Asian food but also decided to offer some western food. Surprisingly, many of the refugees wanted to try western "delicacies" such as hamburgers, fries, and pizza. Each newly arrived group had to be directed to pick up a tray and utensils to join a line to take food. Often nothing happened until it was explained that they could take as much as they wanted. The mess hall normally stayed open for snacks and tea outside the meal hours. Refugees were instructed that they could not take food back to their rooms for sanitary reasons but were free to help themselves to apples set out as snacks in enormous bowls by the door to the mess hall. The refugees were incredulous. Apples, not being Asian fruits, were rarely found in Asian markets and normally were very expensive. They could not believe that they were being offered such expensive food. The interpreters explained that these were Canadian-grown fruit, tasty and nutritious and free to be enjoyed. The apples disappeared in huge quantities.

Soldiers on the base took it upon themselves to entertain the refugees. In good weather, they were on the parade square in the afternoons and evenings to organize games such as soccer, baseball, dodge ball, and tag with the children and men. In winter, they showed the newcomers how to make snowmen and snowballs and organized many a hard-fought battle. The first winter the soldiers wanted to build little snow hills on the parade square to teach the children how to sled, but they had no sleds. CECs and CICs in the Alberta/Northwest Territories Region were canvassed for funds with promises that the names of contributing offices would be painted on the sleds. Soon the whoops of happy children rang as far as the Kapyong Building.

Once all the formalities of arrival had been completed, in most cases after two or three days, CEIC staff and interpreters put refugees on planes and buses to their final destinations. Airline staff and Greyhound bus drivers ensured safe connections and pickups at the other end. If lengthy travel was involved, box lunches were provided, as well as sufficient infant needs for mothers to last at least two days.

Most of the refugees successfully settled at their destinations and many remained there, although reunions with extended families occurred as they found each other in Canada. Settlement destinations covered all of Canada, including those for two couples who went to live on the edge of the Beaufort Sea where jobs and housing had been secured for them. One of the couples is thought to be still there.[16]

The story of one settlement experience bears repeating. Nanton, a town of 2,500 people, about eighty kilometres south of Calgary, decided to sponsor twelve refugees. They were offered employment at a mushroom farm, and accommodation and English language training were arranged. Upon their arrival, a large meal awaited the group in a local Chinese restaurant. Settlement in the community was a permanent success. Twenty years later, Marshall received a phone call from a man who asked if she was the one who had sent the Vietnamese refugees to Nanton: "He identified himself as the father in one of those Vietnamese families. He said that his eldest son was getting married in a few weeks and that it was their custom to invite to the wedding reception those who had helped them in their lives. He wondered if I would be available to attend as an honoured guest."[17]

22

Community Coordination

Federal, provincial, and municipal organizations across Canada were brought to bear to ensure the safe and successful settlement of the Indochinese refugees in their new surroundings. While immigration settlement services already existed to handle arriving immigrants from all points of the globe, the needs of the newcomers from Southeast Asia were unique because of the dramatic number of arrivals and the often traumatic history of their flights to safety. The success of the settlement undertaking owes much to independent officers doing what they thought was right, exercising flexibility in the face of unfamiliar challenges, and engaging the participation of others who were themselves often refugees or children of refugees and who could extend understanding and empathy. While broad operational guidelines were issued, their implementation often differed across the country.

This chapter begins with the experiences of Naomi Alboim, the officer responsible for organizing and coordinating settlement services across the Province of Ontario, and details the kind of work that was done by the settlement units at CEIC's regional offices across Canada. We were able to find former CEIC officials from British Columbia and Ontario, who worked at different levels and function, willing to write about their experiences after all these years.[1]

Coordination in Ontario

NAOMI ALBOIM

I was the acting director of the Employment Development Branch at Employment and Immigration Canada (CEIC) for Ontario in 1979 when David Conn, the director general of immigration for the region, called to ask whether I would coordinate the flow of Indochinese refugees to Ontario. I jumped at the opportunity. In those days CEIC was an organization with clear lines of authority and divisions of responsibility. The employment programs and labour market benefit programs of the department were implemented locally by Canada Employment Centres (CECs). All immigration programs pertaining to the selection of immigrants and refugees and the enforcement of the immigration act were implemented locally by Canada Immigration Centres (CICs). Each network of centres had its own reporting relationships, and they did not usually work closely together.

The Settlement Branch of CEIC in Ontario Region was a small unit headed by André Pilon with a few officers responsible for the delivery of the Immigrant Settlement and Adaptation Program (ISAP), liaison with CEC settlement workers who provided services to newly arrived immigrants and refugees under the Immigrant Adjustment Assistance Program (IAAP), and liaison with CIC officers on refugee issues. There was no direct reporting relationship between either the CECs or CICs with the Settlement Branch. However, the branch was the centre of expertise on all matters pertaining to the settlement and integration of immigrants and refugees, and it was unique in that it needed both networks to implement their programs to achieve its objectives. The responsibilities of CECs included reception, initial housing, and income support for government assisted refugees, as well as language and skills training, training allowances, settlement assistance, and help in finding jobs for newly arrived immigrants and refugees. CICs were responsible for reviewing, approving, and monitoring sponsorship agreements and for counselling sponsors.

The Settlement Branch was the poor cousin of the immigration operation. Its employees were seen as "softies" who had no real authority, except for ISAP, and only functional direction responsibilities. Bob Parkes and Pierre Gaulin were two program officers in the branch at the time who stayed on to play invaluable roles in the upcoming events. It was incumbent upon Settlement Branch to establish itself as the credible expert – accessible and friendly and understanding of the needs of both the CICs and CECs. They were under no obligation to do what we wanted them to do, but we needed the CECs and CICs to achieve our objectives. The cultures of the CECs and CICs were totally different, even though they were parts of the same department. We attended their meetings, provided training, and developed relationships to extend our advice. In most instances it worked.

The Indochinese movement would require a huge expansion of the resources, personnel, and mandate of the Settlement Branch, and I was to coordinate that exercise.

Our work for this new refugee endeavour required the ability not only to work with external stakeholders in a collaborative way but to work together with other branches across the federal government and with other orders of government. There were no manuals, rules, or precedents for how to bring in and settle 60,000 refugees in such a short period of time, with the largest numbers of them coming to Ontario, while ensuring welcoming and supportive receiving communities. We would have to make it up as we went along.

Building the team was an exciting opportunity. We recruited individuals from across the spectrum of the department, all of them young, eager, respected in their home branches, and willing to experiment and work very hard.

Recruiting, Training, and Supporting a Cadre of Refugee Liaison Officers

Early on in the process, it became clear that to successfully and rapidly integrate an unprecedented number of refugees in Canada would require the involvement of both the receiving communities and the refugees themselves. A decision was made at national headquarters to hire a cadre of refugee liaison officers (RLOs) to work in local communities with a broad mandate to bring together institutions, organizations, and community leaders to coordinate the successful integration of refugees in a geographic area.

In Ontario, we built upon the expertise of the Employment Development Branch (EDB) staff who were recruited to become the RLOs. The EDB was a discrete organization within CEIC, comprised of young people who had come of age in the 1960s with a commitment to social justice and experience working as community organizers, community developers, and bridge builders. Many of them had worked previously in the Company of Young Canadians (CYC) or in Canadian University Students Overseas (CUSO) or as program administrators for Opportunities for Youth (OFY) or the Local Initiatives Program (LIP) projects at the grassroots level. Staff of the branch worked independently in an environment that required innovation and creativity. The EDB was the least bureaucratic unit in the department.

Its employees had the inter- and intra-governmental connections, the networks across broad sectors, and the skills to be creative and innovative. They knew the communities in which they worked, and they were known and respected in those communities.

Settlement Branch trained the selected RLOs on the history, culture, politics, and sociology of Indochina and this refugee movement, and on immigration and refugee policies. Although each RLO worked in a different community and reported to the local CEC or CIC, they received functional direction from us, and we helped them to solve problems as issues arose. Some of these problems were a result of culture clashes within the department: between the local CIC, CEC, and RLO staff. The RLOs were seen as free spirits who identified more with the community groups and refugees than with the department. They were out in the community rather than desk- or office-bound. There were few precedents or rules to determine their role, and they were prepared to try new things without necessarily seeking permission in advance. Local CIC and CEC managers were not used to this kind of employee.

The cadre of trained RLOs would do the community development work necessary across the province to ensure welcoming and supportive communities. They would work with the Ontario provincial government and municipalities and with the settlement sector to recruit, approve, and support refugee sponsoring organizations. They would provide functional guidance to the network of CICs and CECs across the province, develop a program for unaccompanied minors, and implement a Joint Assistance Program for Hmong refugees.

The branch was in daily contact with the Refugee Task Force at national headquarters headed by Mike Molloy and assisted by Martha Nixon and Brian Bell. They understood our respective roles and provided the direction to do what was necessary to achieve the overall objectives.

The RLOs became their own community of interest, keeping in touch, sharing successes, and asking for help or support when necessary. They provided public education about the refugee movement; provided support to sponsors; convened local service providers to establish coordination mechanisms; worked with refugees to identify services gaps or helped determine ways to address such gaps; organized events that brought refugees and community members together; and worked with staff of other federal departments and provincial and municipal authorities. No operational standards existed for the RLOs. Each had a mandate only to facilitate the development of welcoming, supportive communities to enhance the settlement and integration of this group of refugees in their new home.

Provincial and Municipal Involvement

In Ontario we established a Settlement Planning Committee (SPC) made up of senior representatives at the regional level of the federal Department of Secretary of State, CEIC, the Province of Ontario, the Municipality of Toronto, the settlement sector, and the United Way, to work collaboratively in identifying the needs of the refugees and discovering how best to help them. Problems were brought to this table and resolved. We reviewed applications for funding from community groups collaboratively and determined who would fund what and how. Local coordinating groups were established in communities convened by RLOs, with settlement agencies, municipal, school board, health, and social service agency representatives.

The Ontario provincial government was actively engaged in the movement. CEIC's Settlement Branch worked closely with the Newcomer Settlement Branch of the Ontario Citizenship ministry and the Ontario Welcome House. The Newcomer Settlement Branch staff developed profiles on the Indochinese ethnic groups for public information and sponsor training purposes and prepared newcomer services booklets in Vietnamese, Laotian, and Cambodian as well as language training materials for the incoming refugees and teachers of English as a second language (ESL). Ontario Welcome House established ESL classes and nurseries for children, helped with Ontario Health Insurance Program (OHIP) registration, provided translation of documentation, and acted as liaison for all provincial ministries in contact with the refugees, such as Education, Health, Community and Social Services. A component existed for handicapped refugees, with provincial approval required for individual cases to be given the resources required to assist them effectively. The provincial government never refused to accept a handicapped refugee in need.

The municipal governments too had a role to play, particularly in the area of public health units' medical surveillance of refugees arriving with tuberculosis or other contagious diseases needing follow-up. Municipal libraries, community centres, and recreation facilities developed programs to respond to the influx of newcomers. The City of Toronto was particularly engaged, and mayors across the province actively championed the refugees and headed off any potential backlash. These activities were coordinated by the Settlement Planning Committee.

Work with the Settlement Sector

Bob Parkes and Pierre Gaulin were the initial program officers responsible for the implementation of the ISAP program. The Southeast Asian movement created an opportunity to reach out to the existing settlement sector and see how they could adapt to the needs of very different refugees from those they had previously dealt with, and to provide support to the very young, emerging refugee organizations which had little capacity but incredible commitment to provide services to their newly arriving community members. This led to the establishment, in collaboration with the Province of Ontario, of the first Vietnamese association, Lao association, and Cambodian association, with all the sensitive political negotiations necessary, given the lack of homogeneity of these communities. But immigrant settlement agencies and multicultural organizations across the province also hired, trained, and mentored emerging leaders in the Indochinese communities to better serve this clientele and created a cadre of confident, capable, culturally sensitive settlement workers who could in turn train their co-workers.

As part of the 1976 Immigration Act, local community organizations, groups of individuals, and affiliate groups of national organizations were for the first time given the authority to sponsor refugees from abroad to come to Canada. While in many cases the initiation of national sponsorship agreements was done at the national headquarters level, our branch conducted such negotiations with several organizations. We received calls from neighbourhood groups, groups of co-workers, and local faith communities who wanted information on how they could become involved. Members of the Settlement Branch attended community meetings or went wherever people congregated, to provide information and assistance. Operation Lifeline, founded by York University professor Howard Adelman, and Project 4000, founded by the mayor of Ottawa, Marion Dewar, played significant roles in the recruitment and support of sponsoring organizations.

Sponsoring groups had the energy and goodwill to find accommodation, furnish homes for the refugees, greet them at the airport, provide clothing, guide them on shopping for groceries, help register their children in school or register for health insurance, and help them find language training and employment. However, they occasionally encountered difficulties because of a lack of understanding of the culture, experiences, and expectations of the people they were sponsoring. Our team developed training sessions with provincial officials and organizations like Operation Lifeline to prepare sponsors for their roles and to troubleshoot.

Sponsorship applications were submitted to the CIC officers for approval, requiring us to train them to assess applications and counsel sponsors. In most cases, sponsoring groups indicated the size of family they could accommodate and support for a year. Once applications were approved, they were sent to national and regional headquarters to be matched with refugees from overseas.

Our matching team, ably led by Albert Lee, received Destination Matching Requests (DMRs) from the matching centre at national headquarters, identifying the names, ages, and gender of family units requiring resettlement, with perhaps a word or two identifying any special needs. Singles or families without special needs were referred to CEC officers as government assisted refugees to receive support from the settlement counsellors in those offices and from settlement agencies. Those with special needs were discussed with potential sponsoring organizations to ensure the additional support that could not be provided by civil servants. Sponsoring organizations were called, and, on the basis of limited information provided by visa officers abroad, were offered a family in need.

Some CEC settlement counsellors such as Ralph Talbot in Windsor and Deb Ashford in London went beyond what was required. They organized holiday parties for the refugees, ensuring that every refugee child received presents on Christmas (even if they weren't Christian). They arranged for each newborn child to receive a handmade baby blanket. They accompanied refugees on their first visit to a grocery store and provided transportation to workplaces even if it meant personally driving them. These people were public servants who did everything they could to create a welcoming environment for refugees coming to their communities.

Developing a Program for Unaccompanied Minors

I was contacted by Immigration Headquarters in Ottawa about the possibility of an Unaccompanied Minor Program to bring in child refugees who had become separated from the rest of their family members. Many of their parents had drowned or had sent the children ahead in order to save them or to establish a beachhead for the rest of the family to follow. In most cases, the parents' whereabouts were unknown. Because provinces have responsibility for the protection of minors, the federal government was unable to respond to the request of the UNHCR to accept these children for resettlement in Canada without the provinces' approval. I was asked to be part of the team that negotiated with the Province of Ontario for the development of such a program for that province. Victor Glickman from CEIC in the region and I met with the assistant deputy minister of the Children's Services Division of the Ontario Ministry of Community and Social Services, George Thomson, to negotiate an agreement for unaccompanied minors. Ontario was a willing partner, and many of the unaccompanied minors came to that province.

We had to create something that was neither an adoption program nor a traditional foster care program, since we did not know if the children's parents were deceased and because hosting families were doing this on a voluntary basis. The hope was that the children would ultimately be reunited with their parents. The families who would assume responsibility for the children had to understand the trauma that they had experienced and what some of them may have had to do to survive on the boats and in the refugee camps. Many were already teenagers going through life changes that are difficult to handle at the best of times, compounded by these particular circumstances. We also wanted to find families who would be interested in playing an active role in trying to reunite the children with their parents or other family members, and would allow the children to maintain contact with the Vietnamese, Laotian, or Cambodian communities in Ontario to retain their cultural identity.

Mary Jane Turner was hired by the province to coordinate this program, and she worked very closely with me. She had previously adopted a Vietnamese child and was familiar with many of the cultural issues involved. We collaborated closely with Sandra Simpson, the founder of Families for Children, who had enormous expertise and experience in that part of the world. She advised us every step of the way in the development of the program.

As there was no existing Vietnamese community on which to draw for the sponsoring families, Turner and Simpson and Simpson's counterpart in Quebec, Naomi Bronstein, set out to recruit Canadian families who might be willing to become involved. Interested families underwent intense home studies and training sessions before being approved. Once approved, they were then encouraged to put together scrapbooks with descriptions and pictures of their family, their home, their neighbourhoods, schools, and activities in which the children they were sponsoring would be involved. The scrapbooks would be given to the children on arrival at one of the staging areas and were used by the counsellors to familiarize the children with the Canadian families to whom they were assigned.

The selection of unaccompanied minors abroad was a complex procedure. As soon as it became known in refugee camps that countries were selecting unaccompanied minors for resettlement, young adults began presenting themselves as teenagers, and families intentionally put forward their children as if they were unaccompanied. Visa officers found it difficult to identify those who truly qualified. Many, often males, had survived on the basis of their wits alone, sometimes stealing or undertaking other illegal activities. Some of the female minors had experienced sexual trauma. These would be difficult young people to integrate into a typical Canadian middle-class family.

Some also had health issues, with a few being diagnosed with Hansen's disease (leprosy). Dr Jay Keystone, the director of the tropical disease unit at Toronto General Hospital, was enormously helpful in developing materials and speaking to families to reassure them about the minimal risk to their families and how to mitigate that risk if children suffering from that disease were brought into their homes.

The files of these children and their sponsoring families came to life for me, and I was thrilled when I was asked to go to Griesbach staging area in Edmonton to meet the first planeload of unaccompanied minors, all destined to Ontario. We had arranged all the protocols for how the children would be greeted and processed at the base, including the additional medical screening over and above the normal screening done for other refugees. We arranged for Vietnamese interpreters with the personal skills as well as linguistic skills to interact with the young people.

The children arrived on a blistering cold day in February 1980. They were wearing T-shirts and shorts, and many were barefoot or just wearing flip-flops. Big, burly soldiers from the base boarded the plane. When they emerged, they each tenderly carried a child wrapped in a blanket. The children were given hot drinks and met the interpreters who greeted them warmly with hugs. For the time in Edmonton, they were housed in barracks with bunk beds, the interpreters staying with them twenty-four hours a day. Some of the younger children slept nestled in the arms of the interpreters.

There were a few sibling units, and one in particular struck me: a young girl of fifteen and her seven-year-old brother. They were inseparable. They were going to the home of a former nun living in eastern Ontario, and I spent an afternoon with these two children and an interpreter, going through the scrapbook she had sent, explaining what all the pictures represented, and giving as much information as I could. The young girl impressed me as extremely intelligent, completely committed to her little brother and absolutely dedicated to doing whatever she had to do for his benefit and for the ultimate reunification of the family.

Years later, in 1998, I was called to jury duty, and as I sat waiting in the lounge in the Court House in Toronto, I heard a name being called. It was that young fifteen-year-old girl who had arrived with her younger brother at Griesbach. She was now in her thirties. I approached her and asked if she had come to Canada as part of the unaccompanied minor program with her brother, if she had initially lived with a former nun in Eastern Ontario. She was astonished by my questions, and answered in the affirmative. She asked how I knew and I told her that I had met her eighteen years previously. She looked at me, paused, and said, "You were the one that went through the scrapbook with me!" We both burst into tears.

She brought me up to date. She had gone to work as soon as she finished high school in order to help support her brother and to save money necessary to contribute to the sponsorship of her parents. They had come to Canada as a result of that sponsorship, and her brother had just graduated with a bachelor's degree in engineering. She was accepted for jury duty and I was not!

All the sponsoring families were monitored on a regular basis by a provincial home-study social worker and by someone from the local CIC, and all the reports were shared with our branch. I recall reading these reports as if they were detailing stories about my own children. Of course there were problems, and some children had to be reassigned to other homes, but most did enormously well. Many were ultimately reunited with their families in Canada through the efforts of the sponsoring families. Many went on to post-secondary education. I was invited to several weddings.

Implementing the Joint Assistance Program for the Hmong Community

The UNHCR and visa officers abroad began to identify groups of refugees whom they felt were in particular need of resettlement because of their vulnerability but were for the same reasons very difficult to settle. The Joint Assistance Program was established by national headquarters to assist groups like this, allowing for the federal government to provide financial support for one to two years while a sponsoring group provided all ancillary support for these individuals.

Among the vulnerable groups were the Hmong Hill Tribes from Laos. Their cultural practices were often at odds with North American ways; they were pre-literate, lived in polygamous units in large clans, and grew and smoked opium. They had acted as scouts for the American troops during the Vietnamese and Cambodian wars and were being massacred by the new Laotian regime. The United States, Australia, and Canada, the three major countries of resettlement, had agreed to resettle groups of Hmong, but each country had its own policy. The Americans were the first in the selection process, and they required the male head of family to choose one wife and that woman's children as the nuclear family to be selected for resettlement to the United States. The Australians took the remaining wives and their children for resettlement on the assumption that they would marry Australian men and integrate well. The

Canadians selected whole, intact polygamous family groupings but arbitrarily assigned fictitious roles to the women. There would be one "wife" plus "sisters-in-law," "sisters," "cousins," etc. This was not official policy, but it occurred. Motivated by compassion and the desire to keep family units together, the visa officers thought it best to select family units in this way. They believed that the situations could work themselves out after arrival in Canada.

Neither the Settlement Branch nor sponsoring organizations were advised of this selection practice. Many of the sponsoring groups assisting the Hmongs were churches affiliated with the Mennonite Central Committee and the Christian Reform Church. After arrival, many of the church sponsors were concerned to see "unusual" relationships between the various members of the family group. It became clear, particularly to the RLO in the Kitchener-Waterloo area, that something had to be done. The church groups were remarkably tolerant, given their own religious practices. The elders of the Hmong community understood that they could not live the way they had in Laos. The Hmong community itself, with the support of the RLO, Hulene Montgomery, and members of the sponsoring organizations, undertook a process to discuss which aspects of Hmong culture could not continue, which cultural practices were absolutely essential for them, and which were negotiable.

Over a period of months, this deliberative process resulted in decisions being made by the Hmong community: no polygamy in the next generation, no growing or use of opium, recognition of all wives in current polygamous relationships, and discouragement of underage sex play. We worked with the province and the federal government to ensure, to the extent legally possible, that the wives in the current polygamous relationships were not disadvantaged.

One of the most treasured pieces of art in my home is a handstitched and embroidered quilt commissioned by my staff and made for me by a group of Hmong women when I left the federal government. This traditional art form is practised as a storytelling device. The quilt I was given depicts the story of the Hmong starting with their pre-war agricultural life, the exploding bombs during the war, their escape across the river from Laos to Thailand, their life in refugee camps there, boarding airplanes to Canada, and their arrival here to the agricultural communities where they were sponsored. It is a stunning testament to their resilience. Seeing it in my home every day is a constant reminder of what a privilege it was to play a role in this historic refugee movement. It changed my life as it changed the lives of the refugees. It also affected the sponsors, community organizations, and ordinary Canadians who welcomed these people, and the thousands of public servants at all levels of government who worked behind the scenes in extraordinary ways to make this refugee movement the success that it was.

Settlement of Indochinese Refugees in London, Ontario

DEBORAH ASHFORD

Refugee settlement was a small part of my job in London until the Indochinese movement. However, by the summer of 1979, London was receiving between five and twenty-five Indochinese refugees two to three times per week. Additional positions were created, and by the end of the first year our settlement team of four had assisted over 1,000 boat people.

All in our twenties, we were young, energetic, and passionate. Most evenings found us on airport duty, moving a family into accommodation, dealing with a crisis, collecting donations, or doing community presentations. We thrived on the pressure and were supported by management, which gave guidance, encouragement, and the freedom to help our clients without bureaucratic barriers. Although our local settlement team reported through the Employment branch of Employment and Immigration Canada, our functional guidance came from the Settlement Branch of Immigration Regional HQ in Toronto. We developed strong and effective relationships with colleagues at the Settlement Branch and with immigration staff at various ports of entry and staging areas. Rules of hierarchy and protocol took second place to providing caring and responsive settlement assistance.

We developed a partnership with the London Cross Cultural Learner Centre (CCLC), which provided newly arriving refugees with a myriad of services including assistance with transportation, interpretation/translation, moving into permanent accommodation, registering children in school, finding doctors, and so on. CCLC provided hands-on assistance in helping newcomers to learn about shopping, buses, and social/recreational activities.

The overwhelming community response to the plight of the boat people generated many calls from the public wanting to help. We didn't have the capacity to respond, but we quickly arranged for women from one United Church to establish a volunteer action centre in the church basement with volunteers manning phones and handling offers of assistance.

Through our experience we grew to better realize the potential and risks associated with involving volunteers in settlement activities. Recognizing the importance of screening, matching, and training as key elements of successful volunteerism, we developed and implemented a model for volunteers to formally support government assisted refugees to become settled in our community. Similar initiatives were taking place in other communities, and the Host Family Program came into existence.

During our ongoing community outreach, we were easily able to promote "hosting" as a possible training ground for private sponsorship, and many sponsors became engaged in "hosting" a government assisted refugee while they awaited the arrival of a refugee family under the private sponsorship program.

It was amazing to work with colleagues dedicated to making a difference. It was a time of hard work but it was also a time of laughter, learning, and enormous satisfaction. The shared commitment made it a time of endless possibility, innovation, and hope.

My lasting memory is of that first Christmas, starting a tradition for the duration of the movement of reaching out to all our staff to provide toys for the refugee children. No child ever went without a new toy at Christmas.

Southeast Asian Refugee Settlement in Windsor, Ontario

RALPH H. TALBOT

In the fall of 1978 I was an employment counsellor in Windsor and volunteered for settlement responsibilities. Management, however, was reluctant to provide resources for a purpose that was not viewed as a priority in the delivery of "employment programs."

Windsor as a community did not initially welcome the idea of adding a large visible minority to the workforce, and some political and social encouragement was necessary. Shortly after the first arrivals (eighty individuals from September to December 1978), a meeting was arranged with the mayor and local church leaders from all denominations to discuss a strategy to assist the settlement of this group of newcomers. The Host Family Program later developed from this meeting's positive outcome.[2] Through a friend in the church community, I accessed congregations and groups and spoke at meetings to encourage assisting with refugee settlement efforts. The community responded quickly when I shed the "government bureaucrat" image by making myself available 24/7 to those in need of help. My duties were to attend at arrival point, arrange temporary housing, locate permanent housing, and arrange for ESL, then employment, while administering Adjustment Assistance Program funding.

There was initial tension and racial bias in the office directed at the refugees, as well as challenges in getting employers to accept the new workers. But word spread about the refugees' willingness to learn and work, and about their congeniality and desire to be accepted. The Southeast Asians became a desirable addition to a workplace. We maintained an 85 per cent employment rate within the first six to eight months of arrival for heads of households, the result of constant networking with employers and church groups.

We learned a great deal from the refugees. One of the great surprises for us was the realization that many of them were not poor peasants who had been living in grass huts but rather professionals or successful business people who had lived better than many of those helping them settle in Canada. It sometimes surprised sponsors that the newcomers didn't need instructions in flushing a toilet or using a light switch. We had to adapt our orientation sessions to the new reality.

Settlement in Kitchener, Ontario

JOHN WILKINS

I was an immigration counsellor at the Kitchener CIC and was invited with colleagues to a town hall meeting at a local church where Howard Adelman from York University spoke about group sponsorships for refugees. We hadn't been briefed or advised what our possible involvement might be. Mr Adelman spoke eloquently about the refugee situation and community involvement. This was a new age of sharing delivery of the settlement program with the public who could provide a more seamless contact with the arrivals. When we began, there was little direction or guidance, or even contact numbers within the broader bureaucracy.

Settlement in Cambridge, Ontario

DOUGLAS DUNNINGTON

My involvement with the boat people was as a settlement officer in Cambridge early in the movement of refugees to Canada. Lead time on arrivals could be as little as an hour or two, and there was always a paucity of information beyond ages, gender, and medical problems. Communication was difficult initially but we eventually recruited interpreters and settlement assistants.

There was only limited direction and help in the early days, and much of the settlement effort was through personal contacts and scrounging. The newcomers with solid skill sets were anxious to work, and we found employers willing to give them a chance.

Some cases I can still recall. A family of eleven was a last-minute arrival and included one very pregnant young woman. The baby was due within two weeks. The hotel where they were billeted was across the street from the Cambridge General Hospital. Having settled the family on their arrival, I said good night. I had barely arrived home when the hotel telephoned to say the baby's delivery appeared imminent and the young woman refused to go to the hospital. I somehow convinced her that the nurses across the street were my personal friends and she should go there immediately. Somehow it worked, and an hour later Cambridge had its first Vietnamese-Canadian baby girl.

Coordination in British Columbia

JAMES PASMAN

I was a regional manager of settlement in British Columbia, responsible for regional activities and coordination of immigration and employment services and liaison with federal departments, provincial counterparts, church and service organizations, and the media. The media took a great interest in the program, and I was invited to appear on many open-line radio shows to explain the government position and encourage people to become involved in the group sponsorship. The radio hosts, who were not always positive about federal programs, were very supportive of this one. The mayor of Vancouver got very interested, formed a task force to see how the city could help, and organized forums and gave positive support.

During the early stage (January–July 1979) we were responsible for the reception and processing of refugees destined to Western Canada, and we had to increase our capacity at the airport to document and care for arrivals until they could be placed on onward flights. This involved feeding them and providing them with clothing suitable for the new climate. We secured use of empty space in the airport and, with the assistance of Woodward's Department Store staff, stocked it with suitable clothing in a variety of sizes. Arrivals were processed and taken to the store to choose a wardrobe before proceeding on the final stage of their journeys. Later we leased space off-site and arranged transportation to the new "store."

At first we received refugees on commercial flights, and then the military flights were added, which provided us with lots of work and some days put a considerable strain on the space we had at the airport. It was on one of these military flights that we received our first Canadian citizen refugee, a child who had been born on the way to Canada on a Canadian plane. Fortunately, cabin staff on the military planes included a trained nurse, and mother and child were well cared for.

Although most refugees continued to their final destinations on the day of arrival, some were held over for various reasons, and we had to prepare for a large number of holdovers just in case. This meant arrangements with local hotels, and we even had a standby agreement (never used) with the University of British Columbia to have refugees housed in vacant dormitories. Eventually the reception facility at Griesbach in Alberta assumed our responsibility.

The Employment Centre in Vancouver was well organized to deal with new arrivals, as a centralized unit was already in place. But CEC and CIC field offices outside of Vancouver had to make new contacts quickly, provide information, and make arrangements with NGOs, churches, and merchants in their communities. This necessitated agreements with service providing organizations, under the Immigrant Settlement and Adaptation Program, to deliver settlement services to the newly arrived refugees. The Group Sponsorship Program for Indochinese Refugees was well received, and some officers began attending church to explain the program and then at the end of the service complete the necessary paperwork. The introduction of the master agreement feature was welcome, as it reduced the amount of paperwork and speeded up the approval of the applications.

Follow-ups to the sponsorships could be amusing. In one case the refugees told the immigration officer that things were fine but that they were cold while sleeping as there were no bed covers. The beds, it turned out, were well made with lots of covers tightly tucked in, and the refugees had been sleeping of top of them. Being very polite, they had been reluctant to raise their concerns directly with their sponsors.

The provincial authorities were kept informed of developments, and services were provided as needed. There was a time when the overseas offices raised the problem of delays in moving families because of one member having tuberculosis and asked if anything could be done to expedite the processing. When approached by us, the BC Ministry of Health quickly agreed to accept and treat where necessary the afflicted individual. They also arranged for a retired specialist to come back on contract to oversee the program and provide the necessary support. As I recall it, BC was the first province to respond positively to this request.

Vancouver Reception Centre

TOM STEELE

I worked as an employment counsellor at the Vancouver Immigrant Reception Centre (IRC) in late 1975, assisting indigent immigrants as well as government sponsored refugees. My task was to assist clients to find employment. Among our clients were early arrivals from Vietnam, Laos, and Cambodia. Their language skills made them difficult to place, but my respect for them grew after hearing what they had experienced in order to reach Canada. A lot of them had escaped leaving fathers or husbands who had been sentenced to re-education camps. Others had undergone elaborate and dangerous escapes leaving their whole families behind. Their main concern was to get their families out of danger. They willingly accepted whatever employment

I could arrange for them. I began to admire the strength and determination most of these people displayed.

When the Indochinese refugee movement accelerated a year later, we started recruiting as clerk/interpreters refugees who had come a year or two before. They had the required languages and understood the situation facing the clients. Other staff assisted the clients to register for assistance, locate accommodation, and register for English language training and employment assistance. Not all government employees were up to the task. Some were supernumerary from Employment Insurance; many did not want to be involved, and others were frustrated by the language difficulties or felt that the clients were not really refugees and were scamming the system.

Two things greatly influenced the success of our operation. The first was the contact made in early 1979 with Dr Libuse Tyhurst, a professor of psychiatry at the University of British Columbia and herself a Czech refugee from 1968. She had written extensively about the refugee experience in Canada, concluding that Canada was consistently ill-prepared for handling large influxes of refugees. After she shared her conclusions with me, I realized that we had to do the job differently. As a result of Dr Tyhurst's observations, we began to deliver services in a positive and more responsive manner.

Our services assumed a new format more suitable to dealing with a large volume of refugees. Our immigration colleagues provided functional guidance on Settlement Assistance funds and were supportive of our efforts to improve. Most facets of the settlement experience were restructured to enhance the independence of the refugees. Following English language training, for example, job search assistance and training in English interview skills and résumé writing were provided. Participants were encouraged to enter occupations related to experience in their country of origin, with volunteers helping them to develop English vocabularies for their intended occupation.

We also partnered with Health and Welfare Canada to receive flights of people we knew would have health issues. Public health nurses were sent to the IRC to receive refugees and to identify and assist the people who needed immediate medical attention. On first arrival at the IRC, the refugees and their families attended a welcome and orientation group session given in their own language. The types and order of assistance were laid out, and written information was handed out with illustrated flow charts about what services would be offered. Volunteers who spoke the various languages were recruited and coordinated through the Immigrant Services Society.

Private-sector providers were helpful as well. Motels and hotels covered taxi fares to the hotel, including them in the hotel room bills, which the government later paid. The hotels also advanced funds to purchase food until the government issued adjustment assistance cheques. This saved us labour and avoided delays. Arrangements were made with the Army and Navy Department Store to purchase essential clothing and household goods. To encourage decision-making and respect personal preferences, the clients were given a list of allowable household goods and clothing, with a maximum price for each item. They then selected their preferred colours and styles. Kitchen equipment lists were developed according to preferences expressed by the different ethnic groups.

23

The Refugee Liaison Officers

A fundamental key to the successful settlement of the Southeast Asian refugees in Canada was the dedication and commitment of thousands of Canadians: volunteers, members of sponsorship groups, local institutions, and government employees at all levels. It was the role of the Refugee Liaison Officers (RLOs) to ensure that the efforts of all these groups unfolded as harmoniously as possible.

The RLOs were the "ombudsmen" of the settlement process. No single job description can capture what these individuals accomplished. Each defined his or her own responsibilities under the supervision of a more senior officer in the local Canada Employment or Immigration Centre or regional office where they were stationed. Experienced community workers with deep knowledge of their communities and wide networks of contacts were recruited from CEIC's Employment Development Branch. Self-motivated and not easily confined within the normal, deskbound bureaucratic strictures of government, they were often something of a puzzle to conventional public service managers, but these very qualities contributed to their success. With broad authority for independent action, each of the RLOs identified problems and developed human solutions. They gathered a coterie of like-minded people from other levels of government and the voluntary sector who became their partners in achieving the best outcomes for thousands of people confronted by the daunting challenges of a new country, a new language, and a new culture. They were, in addition, a resource for Canadian sponsors involved in helping newly arrived refugees adapt to life in this country. When things went wrong, as the following accounts demonstrate, the RLOs were called upon to help find solutions.

This chapter records the experience of two of the RLOs *who had a positive impact on the newcomers, their sponsors, and the community-level institutions serving the refugees.*

Refugee Liaison Officer, Kitchener, Ontario

HULENE MONTGOMERY

When I first read the notice for a Refugee Liaison Officer position to work with the community to resettle Southeast Asian refugees, I was filled with enthusiasm. I was also awed by the sheer enormity of the challenges offered by the position, especially as it would take an entire community to make it work. Yet, with a group of people and agencies cooperating, we could create an environment where the refugees would be integrated. I began mentally listing the obstacles and opportunities, identifying champions and key figures and agencies I would need to get on board if I got the position.

I knew that an enormous amount of work was already being done by the local Canada Immigration Centre helping individual refugees and their sponsors find housing, doctors, language training, and so on and assisting with any and every need that arose. I also knew of "Friendship Families," the pairing of government-sponsored refugees with Canadians who provided friendship and lots of practical support. Others would have to be recruited as the circle of players grew. The Mennonite Central Committee (MCC), the only Canadian non-governmental organization present in Vietnam throughout the war and the first agency to sign an umbrella private sponsorship agreement with the federal government, would be among my first calls.

I thought back to my first exposure to refugees when I had been doing community work in Windsor. From time to time I had assisted American draft dodgers coming to Canada to evade involvement in the Vietnam War. In Kitchener-Waterloo (referred to by residents as K-W), I volunteered with a group to support Chilean and other Latin-American refugees, some of whom were now friends. I wondered how they would feel if I were working to welcome people who to them represented the opposite end of the political spectrum. I faced a moral dilemma: I had opposed the Vietnam War and I was now advocating for the government to open its doors to more Latin-American refugees. I was uncertain about my stance on this new refugee challenge. Eventually, however, I knew that my moral compass called on me to act compassionately with all refugees, to work with them to make a better world. My personal political views and assumptions about who the Southeast Asian refugees were would not stand in my way of helping them.

I began work as a Refugee Liaison Officer (RLO) in November 1979. Drawing on my past community involvement, I quickly identified a core group of advisors representing key organizations in the community: the Waterloo County Board of Education, the Department of the Secretary of State, the Kitchener-Waterloo Multicultural Centre, the Mennonite Central Committee, K-W Friendship Families, and Employment and Immigration staff. Following consultations, and reflecting past experience with short-term funding grants for projects, we opted for integrated and decentralized rather than segregated and specialized services. Our goal of having services in place for future refugees and immigrants would be best met if we worked with existing mainline services to expand their expertise and capacity.

My prior work experience had shown me the benefits of a community development approach. In an internal government report I wrote in 1981, I defined this as "a development or process approach that involves working with, not for, people to identify their needs and formulate solutions that enable them to take greater control over their lives and community, by mobilizing human and material resources, and facilitating the coordination and cooperative use of resources."[1] This model guided my work. I worked with refugees, service providers, and the community at large to identify needs and formulate solutions, helping them implement needed programs, and identifying ways to support the refugees' growth toward self-sufficiency.

Using a community development approach to support sponsors meant more initial work, since it meant contacting relevant employees in all community service agencies, introducing them to refugees and their circumstances, eliciting their sympathy and empathy, helping them see ways they needed to change, and keeping them informed. But the approach proved more effective in the long run; all the early work paid off, as there was less danger of refugee dependency on one person or agency.

Instead of one-on-one problem-solving sessions with individual sponsors, I organized workshops. In addition to the logistics of finding venues and organizing and running meetings, this meant locating and/or developing a lot of educational materials on refugees in general and Southeast Asian refugees in particular. It meant educating staff in the mainline organizations to the point where they could make meaningful, relevant presentations about the services being offered to the refugees and the citizens who wanted to support them.

The formation of a Kitchener-Waterloo Southeast Asian Refugee Coordinating Committee early in the resettlement process made a community development approach possible.[2] Formalizing the committee strengthened the informal links among an initial core group of consultants and advisors. While I officially reported to the Canada Employment Centre (CEC), the coordinating committee provided valuable direction and feedback both to me and to my immediate supervisor at CEC. Easy access to wise and knowledgeable advisors at the regional and national levels like Naomi Alboim and Martha Nixon also eased my burden. Their insight on policy issues and their willingness to listen, make connections, and suggest options were always beneficial.

The coordinating committee eased mobilizing and coordinating with community services and facilitated sharing of information and resources, identifying and planning long-term needs, and pinpointing and coordinating services and resources that were required. Our approach was to build a network of agencies and leaders that would spawn further connections and networks. Rather than focusing on the individual, we aspired to create a system or environment in which refugees could flourish and become active citizens. The coordinating committee also organized numerous necessary training sessions for agencies and individuals newly embarking on refugee resettlement. These factors contributed to Kitchener-Waterloo's response to refugee needs being "among the most ambitious and extensive" of any community in Canada.[3] By the time it was over, the Kitchener area had the highest per-capita intake of Southeast Asian refugees in the country.

Just two months after I started, I was plunged into what was one of the biggest challenges of my entire time as an RLO. In March 1979, the MCC had signed a master agreement with the Government of Canada for the private sponsorship of refugees.[4] MCC Ontario, located in Kitchener, received word that the first group of Hmong people to come to Canada would be arriving in December. The Hmong were regarded as very hard to settle. Many had acted as scouts for the American troops. They were being massacred by the new Laotian regime and could not be protected. MCC decided it would intervene to save their lives.

We were grateful for the background information about the Hmong provided by the CEIC regional office and by MCC, but it was limited. All we knew before the first six Hmong families arrived in December was that they had large, polygamous families and were subsistence farmers with little or no formal education. Theirs was an oral language that had not yet been transcribed. And they had no experience of an industrialized society.

My mind teemed with questions. How would this group adapt to an industrialized urban lifestyle? Would they be more comfortable if we could settle them with rural sponsors on farms? Were the people arriving from one or different clans? What was the relationship between different clans? How should we teach them English? Since they had not learned to read and write in any language, should we attempt to help them become literate in their mother tongue or Laotian before learning a second language? And, how would we work with the Hmong and their sponsors to discuss polygamy? My lack of knowledge of Hmong culture and language worried me and underscored how ill prepared I was to assist them. Several books and articles helped me understand the enormity of the change facing them in their integration to Canada.

We decided to resettle the six families as a group. A one-stop welcome centre at St Peter's Lutheran Church in downtown Kitchener was set up to welcome the families. MCC, sponsors, and the people from St Peter's as well as representatives from the CIC, CEC, Secretary of State, Waterloo Regional Health Unit, and Waterloo County Board of Education were all present. We had arranged to have tea and some food available. There was a room with warm clothing and boots from which the new arrivals could choose.

The families arrived wearing traditional colourful, hand-woven, and intricately embroidered clothing, their faces reflecting the long journey they had already made. I felt a sense of peace as the families and sponsors met, and I was grateful to the representatives of the various agencies for their flexibility and willingness to facilitate the paperwork and help set up future appointments at a time and in a way that worked for this group of people.

My anxiety continued about the challenges ahead and how well the older Hmong would settle. I worried how welcoming our community would be to a group who appeared so different; at that time, Kitchener had virtually no people of colour. The beautiful Hmong and Mien textiles we saw that first day made me realize how little we knew about these people in spite of our books and research.

"What Does It Mean to Be a Good Woman?"

Before the Hmong families arrived, workshops had been organized for the sponsoring families. These events later continued with both sponsors and Hmong together and contributed to Hmong adaptation and adjustment.

One workshop took place on a warm, early winter day. The newcomers' immediate needs had largely been met: housing had been found, some of the children had entered school, and some of the adults had begun language courses. Communication remained a challenge. This workshop had been organized to allow the Hmong families and their sponsors to problem-solve together and find mutual support.

Earlier in the day the Hmong families had met separately to share their experiences, ask questions, and identify concerns they wanted to discuss with sponsors. The sponsorship groups had done the same. Then the groups came together, and with the help of a Laotian translator, we sought understanding of the issues and ideas of what we could do.

The Hmong women had earlier asked for a session alone with the women from the sponsorship groups, and arrangements had been made. Slowly the women entered the room, the Hmong women's vibrantly coloured clothes contrasting sharply with the beige, browns, and blacks of their sponsors. The challenges these refugee women faced were staggering. To move from remote hill villages with an informal economy and no schools to an urban industrial region with two universities and one college was surely daunting. With the help of a translator, we went around the circle sharing our names and a bit about ourselves. The Hmong women had prepared a list of questions, which one of the older women posed. Some questions were practical, some intimate, some about immediate concerns, others about the future. After the list was shared, other Hmong women started asking questions. Most of the women from the sponsorship groups seemed comfortable answering as well as asking a few questions of their own.

One set of questions came from Hmong women understandably anxious about their children being hit by the cars and trucks that raced along the streets. We talked about finding routes to schools with less traffic, crossing at lights and with a crossing guard, looking both ways, and walking on the sidewalks. "How do you know the cars will not come on the sidewalks?" one young woman asked. To her, sidewalks seemed to be just smaller roads. These women had learned how to recognize and survive the risks of war and refugee camps, and I knew they would learn to identify and manage the risks of an urbanized environment – but it was a challenge.

As the end of the session approached, I recall feeling good about how successful it had been. Then a question was asked that brought silence to the room: "How do I know how to be a good woman?" The translator repeated the question.

The question reverberated around the room. Across the circle from me was an Old Order Mennonite woman wearing a long dark skirt, shawl, and bonnet. Next to her were several women in pant suits, and next to them was a woman in a miniskirt, tights, and a sweater. We were a diverse group with different educational, social, political, and economic backgrounds and perspectives, different faiths: Mennonite, Catholic, Buddhist, and secular. Some were feminist, some were not. I suspected different ideas abounded on what constituted appropriate behaviour for women.

The silence continued. The translator turned to me. I recall saying that in Canada there were many ways to be a good woman, just as many different forms of dress and behaviour were all acceptable and good. I spoke of how roles for women had changed and were continuing to change. The woman who had asked the original question explained how in Hmong culture there were defined roles and behaviours for women who were good. In Canada it was not clear what the norms were. It seemed confusing.

Other women shared their experiences, and we agreed that all in the circle were good women – even though that might not be apparent simply by looking at us. We needed to help these women learn about the various ways to be a good woman in Canada, wondering how we might provide further education and find ways to help them assume leadership roles here. I recall opening my local paper twenty years later and seeing a young Hmong girl being honoured as a student leader at her high school.

Forgiveness and Healing: A Response to Rape

My most painful RLO experience stemmed from the rape of a vulnerable Canadian woman by a group of Southeast Asian refugees, including three from Kitchener-Waterloo and others from Toronto.

The police called me late one night asking me to come to the station, along with another community member working with refugees. When we arrived, an officer informed us that the police had received a call that a woman had been raped by a group of Southeast Asian refugees. Two or three men were directly involved. Other men were sleeping in another part of the house where it had occurred when the police arrived. Alcohol and drugs were involved.

Our initial reaction was directed at helping the woman. A police officer assured us she was being cared for, and her family had been contacted. A social worker would see her in the morning. We asked if there was any help we could give her. The police officer gently and wisely pointed out that the woman might not want any help from people helping the very refugees who had harmed her.

Some of the refugees involved were terrified and weren't speaking. Some had refused to give their names, and the police sought our help in identifying them and contacting their sponsors. One of the young men recognized me, and his look of terror turned to relief. He was one of those who had refused to speak. On one hand I felt responsible and caring towards him, and on the other I was furious. So this is what happens when someone you care for commits a crime, I thought. My mind flashed back to the session with Hmong women in the fall: we should have had a session for the Southeast Asian male refugees and sponsors about "What does it mean to be a good man?"

The sponsors would need help in how to respond to the refugees in their care who had been charged with rape. And I recognized that I would have to help the refugees who had been accused. The emotions I experienced were traumatizing. I, too, needed help. But I never did seek help. That may be the reason I am crying as I write this memory thirty-plus years later.

After consulting colleagues on the Southeast Asian Refugee Coordinating Committee, and heeding the advice of Ray Schlegel, head of MCC Ontario, we asked the Victim-Offender Reconciliation Program, a recently formed restorative justice project, to help us.[5] Our first meeting with the sponsors of the accused K-W refugees was in a long rectangular room. The sponsors and a few of us from the coordinating committee sat quietly around the table. No one was chatting. Many of the sponsors had not met each other before. Dean Peachy, head of Community Mediation Services, was sitting at the head of the table to facilitate the meeting. There was a calmness about him. He looked slowly around the table at each person before speaking quietly. He gave a prayer asking for wisdom and compassion, then told us it was important we treat this room as a safe place where we could each share what we were feeling before we moved to discussing ideas about what we needed to do.

The first to speak was an Old Order Mennonite woman. Her church had sponsored one of the men involved in the rape, a married man with young children, now living in a small rural community. Their church group had met and prayed about what to do. They were very concerned for the woman who had been raped: how could they help her? They wanted her to know they were very sorry and that the man was extremely remorseful.

They had talked to the man about the harm he had done to the woman, how she had been vulnerable and how his actions had hurt her. They had talked to Legal Aid, who told them that the man might go to prison. If that happened, the church group told him, they would look after his wife and children. Then she talked about his wife, how she was almost hysterical, crying every night. The children were upset. The whole family thought they would be deported.

She talked about her faith and the belief that you had to accept that you had done something wrong, and you had to change. Their church had assured the man they would stand beside him and his family and help. He would not be alone. They believed he had done wrong but that he also had goodness in him. She spoke of her faith, her belief in forgiveness and the possibility of people to be restored.

The couple sitting beside this woman spoke next. Close to tears, they said that while they were horrified by the rape, they also loved the young man whom they had sponsored. Their clergyman had told them the incident was grounds to break the sponsorship agreement.

Under no circumstances was the church going to have anything to do with a man accused of rape. The couple was conflicted. They had been faithful members of the parish all their lives, but they loved the young man who had managed to survive on his own so many years without a family. They believed he was basically a good person who had done some bad things. To turn their backs on him would be like disowning their own son. They were grateful to be in the meeting, they said. Afterwards they told me their clergyman had advised them not to attend. "He doesn't know we're here," they said.

Dean told us how the restorative justice project worked. All parties to the incident would come together with a mediator, proposing a sentence that would restore relations in the community and help both victims and offenders. As part of any probation, the guilty would know how their actions had affected the victim, determine the terms of restitution, and ask for forgiveness. A recent case based on this approach had been the start of what is now known as Community Justice Initiatives. Dean asked if this was an approach we might want to consider.

Much of the rest of the meeting is a blur. Emotions overtook me. I remember my gratitude for Dean and being in awe of the Old Order Mennonite woman's calm conviction of what she felt called to do. To commit to help the man and his family while he was in prison was beyond the expectation the church had originally agreed to.

What Would You Do to Survive? The Refugee Experience Kit

Following a conversation with my nine-year-old daughter about refugees and good wars versus bad wars, and my difficulties in answering her questions, we launched a program to educate schoolchildren about these complex issues. My own thoughts were not clear about what constituted a "good" war, or what principles one would use to decide if war was justified.

An earlier conversation with Global Community Centre, a development education centre in K-W with programs in schools, churches, and the community at large, had focused on ways to help create a welcoming classroom environment for the refugee children. Hilary Lawson, Global's staff liaison with schools, helped identify persons with whom we wanted to explore this initiative further. She had experience working in the schools developing curriculum and knew which schools and teachers would be most supportive.

We organized a focus group of children to give us their questions about refugees and also tell us what kinds of activities they liked doing. From this information, we developed a kit with activities and games to help Canadian children understand what it was like to be a refugee, the many challenges Southeast Asians had overcome to get to Canada, and what it might be like to lose everything and have to start over in a new country. We also wanted to help children understand the global refugee situation and get a glimpse into its root causes. A curriculum was developed based on the book *The Refugee Child: UNHCR Projects for Refugee Children.*[6] The United Nations High Commissioner for Refugees in Geneva provided us with several thousand copies for our kits. The kits were used for a number of years. Word of them spread beyond the Waterloo Region, and they were distributed across Canada.

Children Grow Up Quickly

A much respected and valued member of the coordinating committee, Shirley Losee, a Waterloo County Board of Education ESL consultant, pointed out to us the impact of the refugee cycle on children. She explained that ten-year-old children were now de facto heads of households: because they were the only family members who spoke English, they were the ones negotiating car loans, discussing rents with the landlords, complaining about the cockroaches, explaining their mothers' gynecological problems to the doctor – subjects children would never have discussed in their own culture. This insight about needing to support refugee children not only academically but also socially was thoughtful and practical. One has to have enormous respect for these children who grew up too quickly and assumed so much responsibility so early.

There were other challenges for these young refugees. Our family knew a young Laotian man who had been very active in helping other refugee families and had a lot of responsibility for someone so young. He was a fine person. One evening, clearly distraught, he told my husband that in his culture boys are given knowledge about what it means to be man at different ages and stages of life. They received only the

knowledge needed for the age they were. He was just a teen when he
fled his country and had lost his parents as well as contact with the
elder men in his family. He was worried about how he would learn to be
a man and a father.

Negotiating Constant Crises: A Nine-Year-Old Finds Solutions

During the time that I was an RLO, all the boundaries between my
personal and professional lives were porous. Whether I was at home
or at work, my brain never stopping thinking about the refugees. I was
also totally stimulated and invigorated.

My family was very supportive and engaged with the refugee work
I did, but there was a negative side as well. Dinner was constantly interrupted by telephone calls, since this was when people knew where
they could find me. The calls disrupted the limited time I had with my
husband and nine-year-old daughter. One night there were no calls. It
was a relief. The calm continued for several nights. I was relaxing at
mealtime and expressed my surprise and pleasure at not being called
to the phone. Heather and Michael looked at each other and con-
fessed, "We unplugged the phone."

Our family shares many happy memories of this time. Our friendship with people from so many different backgrounds enriched our
lives. Several of our closest friends today date back to this period. We
were all influenced by the experience. Today our daughter is an active
community leader and social activist and sits on the board of a refugee
resettlement agency.

A community development approach was a key factor in the overwhelming success of the settlement effort in Kitchener-Waterloo. De-
centralization of the settlement process reduced the dependency on
any single support organization and stimulated existing agencies and
organizations to develop methods for positive interventions. One very
positive outcome was stimulation of volunteer involvement to aid in
successful settlement.

Conversely, the initial need for building strong networks and forming firm interpersonal dynamics meant that it took longer for positive
settlement results to make themselves apparent. And the entire process depended heavily on the availability of reliable volunteers whenever needed.

Refugee Liaison Officer, Charlottetown, PEI

CHERYL MUNROE

I was working in the Employment Development Branch as a project officer when I applied for the RLO position. I had a degree in Asian Studies and had taken some courses on government and politics in Southeast Asia, which spurred my interest. Consequently I thought I had some broader understanding to bring to the position. The position, a PM2 secondment, was initially located in the Canada Employment Centre (CEC), but to my everlasting joy it was relocated to the Canada Immigration Centre, where I had the pleasure of working with Janeth Crosby and Bill McPhail. I reported directly to Bill and was an RLO from October 1979 until September 1980. No training for the job was provided; I understood that I was to facilitate the integration of the refugees into the community by working with them, their sponsors, and affected communities and groups writ large. I was to be the link to the media and also the supervisor of a refugee liaison clerk who was, in reality, a translator. Over the course of the program, two individuals held this position – Maria Jones, a Shanghai-born, Chinese-Canadian woman, and David Kwan, a University of Prince Edward Island student from Hong Kong.

In general, I was responsible for the privately sponsored refugees, while the CEC handled those who were government sponsored; however, we did work with the government assisted refugees as well. I was the liaison for any group that acted as sponsors – St Pius X, the Sisters of St Martha, and at least one Protestant church, as well as various groups of five. Our sponsors were located all over the Island from Summerside to Souris, but most were in and around Charlottetown. The members of the sponsoring groups came from all walks of life, and one went on to become premier of the province.

My involvement generally started after the refugees arrived. There was no formal system in place for my position, so I adapted the existing Employment Development Branch site-visit system to record my visits to the sponsors and their refugee families. Perhaps in ignorance of liability and other legal concerns, I quite often took one refugee family to visit another living outside Charlottetown when the translators and I were undertaking our regular visits. We hoped to ease the feelings of isolation, and it seemed to work.

Inevitably there were clashes of culture; perceived differences in what was received from sponsors, either in material things or relative freedoms; actions taken by sponsors on behalf of the families which may or may not have been appropriate; and different ways in which the sponsors "guided" the families into Canadian life. However, all actions were done with the welfare of the families in mind. One of the most notable cultural clashes was a request from a family to have the wife undergo an abortion. For the sponsoring group, the Catholic Sisters of St Martha, the request was completely unacceptable. The reaction was predictable and explosive. Delicate intervention revealed that the couple believed the cost of having a child in Canada was very expensive, and they did not want to burden their sponsors further. The nuns pointed out that they would not be burdened and were able to cope with any expenses. All was forgiven, and the child was born.

The refugees quickly developed their own informal networks, which aided the settlement process but often centred in the early days on what was received in terms of shelter, finances, clothing, and on independence. Some sponsors were more paternalistic than others, while some gave the refugees almost complete freedom to run their affairs. It was not always easy to explain these differences to both sponsors and refugees, but no real anger ever erupted.

There was some reaction from the Department of Health, which was concerned about TB and other communicable diseases, and from dentists, who were concerned about hepatitis. The Department of Health revaccinated the refugees, although it was aware that they had already received the vaccinations. This the refugees did not understand. However, I believe that the health system and the dentists were genuinely concerned for the right reasons. Some dentists did indeed treat the families. Families expressed amazement that their children would get fillings in baby teeth – surely we knew that new teeth would replace them? Why bother?

I do not recall many negative responses from the community at large. People were curious but not especially nosy. Some community groups or individuals who were otherwise not involved put on large dinners as a way to welcome the refugees. All families and sponsors were invited to attend. One elderly refugee was moved to comment on how much Canadians loved sweet and sour sauce!

I truly believe that sponsors in PEI acted from a desire to do the right thing. They behaved in a manner that suggested a real concern for the welfare of the families at heart. I encountered no mean-spirit-edness in their actions and genuine sadness when some of the families chose to leave the Island. Sometimes that happened after a relatively short period of time. Some sponsors thought it was because the families thought that PEI was not good enough and their departure sig-nified a lack of gratitude. Considerable time was spent in discussion of why this happened as families chose to go to centres with larger Southeast Asian populations.

I was privileged to have had this opportunity. As government em-ployees, we engaged in an experience that was positive in intent and design. As Canadians, we worked together for something bigger than we were. Throughout, we did what worked, and we had the freedom to do so.

24

Adapting to Canada: The Long Struggle

An extensive account of the experience of the refugees themselves in remaking their lives in Canada is beyond the scope of this book, although in several places we have touched upon it. Nevertheless, this book would be incomplete without throwing some light on the subject by indicating how this experience has already been recorded and studied and suggesting directions for its further research

The first thing to note is that the "Indochinese" experience, as such, does not exist. "Indochina" is a geographic term that owes its existence to the colonial history of a region of Southeast Asia. The peoples of Indochina were thrown together by French colonial rule, but historically they lived in three separate, often warring states – Vietnam, Cambodia, and Laos. They spoke different languages and had distinct cultural traditions. In addition to Vietnamese, Cambodians (Khmer), and Laotians, the three states had large Chinese minority populations, as well as several smaller ethno-cultural minority groups, such as the Hmong Hill Tribe people in Laos. What brought these people together in resettlement countries such as Canada is, to some extent, their mutual struggles as Southeast Asian refugees[1] (the label the three communities prefer when referring to themselves collectively in Canada) in recreating their lives in the West.

Refugees from the three countries of Indochina suffered terrible experiences even before arriving in refugee camps. "Re-education" camps in Vietnam had high death rates; the mass murders by the Khmer Rouge in Cambodia and killings of Hmong people by the Pathet Lao in Laos were followed by dangerous escapes overland to Thailand and (and sometimes forced withdrawals back into Cambodian jungles) plus the exodus of the Hmong into Thailand along the

Mekong River. Unseaworthy refugee vessels often sank without a trace. There were pirate attacks accompanied by murder and rape and mass push-backs into the ocean. We have no exact records of mortality rates, but academic guesses suggest that between 20 and 40 per cent of those who tried to escape perished.[2] And then there were the long stays in camps with very difficult living conditions, waiting for acceptance by a distant country such as Canada for permanent resettlement. As Donald Cameron, a visa officer who worked in many camps, has stated, "Every adult resident of the refugee camps was marked by some or all of these harsh experiences."[3]

In a survey based on interviews with a large sample of Indochinese refugees in British Columbia over a ten-year period (1979–89), psychiatrist Dr Morton Beiser analyzed the resettlement and integration experience of the refugees in that province, with particular emphasis on their mental states.[4] While Beiser's study documented the difficulties faced by the refugees in adjusting to their new lives in a radically different cultural environment, it also demonstrated the great mental toughness of refugees – especially female refugees – in facing their difficulties.[5] Only a relatively small percentage of the refugees had become mental health casualties. Beiser demonstrated that the proposition – generally accepted before his study – that "immigration and resettlement are stressful enough to cause emotional disorder" was "too simplistic."[6] In fact, at the beginning of the study, rates of depression among the refugees (6.4 per cent) were only marginally higher than depression rates among the general Canadian population (5.2 per cent). By the end of the study, after a decade in Canada, depression rates among refugees (2 per cent) were actually much lower than the Canadian average.[7]

At the same time, the Beiser study did document a number of tragic cases: one case of murder, another of attempted suicide, and several cases of deep depression.[8] If we add to this the case of rape documented by RLO Hulene Montgomery (see chapter 23), we learn that not all Indochinese refugees integrated well. For some, the adjustment to new cultural patterns in Canada was too hard.

What were the main stresses that refugees faced during the first ten years after arriving in Canada? On leaving their homelands, most experienced an acute sense of loss.[9] Things may have been very bad at home and the journey may have been life threatening, but for some, the conditions in the camps made returning home seem preferable.

This option was quickly shown to be impossible when some who returned to Vietnam from Guam in 1975 were immediately thrown into "re-education" camps.[10] Refugees rapidly had to come to terms with the fact that, to continue their lives, their immediate choice was to stay in the camps or resettle in the West. For those destined to Canada, the only choice was to make a go of it or face personal failure.

Two obvious immediate challenges in Canada were climate and language. In the narratives from the Longue-Pointe and Griesbach reception centres, as well as the various reports from RLOs and sponsors, it is evident that the most important immediate task was to ensure that new arrivals had clothes appropriate to the harsh winter climate. This challenge was usually met relatively easily; the challenge of language acquisition was not. The refugees' mother languages were very distant from Indo-European languages like English and French. To learn English and/or French while mastering the tasks of daily life in a new country was very difficult. Most refugees did manage to learn basic English or French within a few years after arrival. However, learning the receiving country's language to a level of competency where it could be used to perform complex tasks required by sophisticated work environments proved to be much harder. Of the large Beiser interview sample (1,348 persons), only one-third could speak English fluently after ten years in Canada: "Among elderly refugees more than half spoke no English and a poorly-educated refugee was six times more likely to speak no English than a well-educated one."[11]

For most, not being fluent in the host country language meant problems in entering the labour market. To start with, many of their job skills were not easily transferable. But even when they were, without language skills they could not be used in the Canadian labour market. Frequent unemployment and a tendency to slide into lower-paying, lower-level jobs was part of the initial refugee experience. While statistics from Canada as a whole are difficult to obtain, detailed statistics from Quebec indicate that during their second year in Canada, 32 per cent of heads of refugee households were unemployed. Perhaps even more discouraging was the fact that after two years in Canada, most of them could only obtain low-paying service and factory jobs.[12] A 1984 study of 119 Indochinese refugees in Montreal found that after five years in Canada, 45 per cent had no knowledge of French and 66 per cent had no knowledge of English.[13] "More than two-thirds either worked in a factory as labourers (40%) or operated a machine (36%), while the rest flowed in and out of a variety of manual and unskilled jobs."[14] Many adult refugees remained in low-level jobs, relying on Canadian schooling for their children and the consequent full acculturation of the next generation for their resettlement experience to become entirely successful. Among the refugees who appear to have had the most successful resettlement experience were the abandoned orphans on the two baby flights of April 1975. As one of them, Thanh Campbell, has stated, in Vietnam, "with the inevitability of the Communist occupation of Saigon ... they would be killed or left to die."[15] Of course, their acculturation started immediately on arrival with their adoption by Canadian families. Yet as adults they have at times retained strong feelings of nostalgia for their roots in Southeast Asia.[16]

Although the refugees' individual earnings remained low, families succeeded by pooling their resources. Studies dealing with the ethnic groups of Indochina noted the importance of family belonging. Within refugee families there was a strong sense of personal responsibility for family success and for the welfare of family members. Earnings were often pooled, and individual self-interest was commonly subordinated to family interest.[17] Ethnic group cohesion was virtually as important as family cohesion. Ethnic associations – Vietnamese, Sino-Vietnamese, Cambodian, and Laotian – were rapidly established in refugee population centres across Canada, especially in the larger cities with core populations of Indochinese ethnic groups. These associations served not only as social centres – although having the opportunity to socialize with people who were culturally and linguistically similar to them was very important for the refugees – but provided information about and access to job opportunities. Refugees with limited language skills could often get information about available jobs through their better-educated and informed co-nationals.[18]

Although it is difficult to find studies fully documenting the movement of Indochinese refugees within all regions of Canada, indications are strong that during the first ten to fifteen years of the resettlement process there was a steady movement of refugees from rural areas and smaller towns toward larger population centres. The intention of the Canadian government was to balance resettlement across Canada evenly, in line with the populations and the relative reception capacities of Canada's regions. However, by the end of 1980, as a result of the major push by both church and secular private sponsors to receive refugees, this balance was being altered in favour of the Prairie provinces and Ontario. The next ten years saw steady movement of refugees to the larger urban centres and away from sparsely populated, rural Saskatchewan, the Atlantic provinces, and the Northern Territories. By 1991, according to a study by Louis-Jacques Dorais, "more than 90% of [Indochinese refugees were] living in an urban census metropolitan region (in contrast to 56% for all Canadian born). The three largest Canadian urban areas – Toronto, Montreal and Vancouver – alone had 57% of the Vietnamese, 56% of the Cambodians, 49% of the Laotians and nearly 60% of the Chinese from ex-Indochina."[19] Two local studies, in Victoria, BC, and New Brunswick, demonstrate this pattern at opposite ends of the country. Between 1980 and 1985, sixty-eight Indochinese arrived in Victoria from other parts of Canada, but 2.4 times as many (167) moved to other parts of Canada, 87 per cent of them to the large cities of Vancouver, Calgary, Edmonton, Toronto, and Montreal.[20] In New Brunswick, 1,400 Indochinese arrived between 1979 and 1986;[21] however, by 1991, only 370 Indochinese were living in the province.[22] In 1991, approximately 83 per cent of all Indochinese in Canada were living in Ontario, Quebec, and British Columbia; 12 per cent were in Alberta, 3.0 per cent in Manitoba, 1.4 per cent in Saskatchewan, and 0.6 per cent in the Atlantic provinces and the Northern Territories. The breakdown of settlement by ethnic group also demonstrates this pattern. By 1991 there were no Vietnamese living in Prince Edward Island, no Cambodians in Newfoundland, PEI, New Brunswick, or the Northern Territories, and no Laotians in Newfoundland, New Brunswick, or the Northern Territories.[23]

Despite the efforts of both the Canadian government and private sponsors to help with the acculturation and language acquisition of the refugees and the spread of refugee settlement across the country, the pattern described above was natural and largely inevitable. Most refugees, with strong ethnic group and extended family ties, made efforts to settle in places where their compatriots and extended families were already settled. As well, these were centres with economic opportunities and ethnic associations. Thus, by 1991, most Cambodians had resettled in Montreal, as had the greatest number of Laotians.[24] On the other hand, Toronto attracted most of the Indochinese of ethnic Chinese origin. Vietnamese settlement favoured all three of Canada's largest cities.[25]

The Hmong Hill Tribe community from Laos demonstrates how, once the core of a refugee ethnic group was well established in a specific locality in Canada, other members of that ethnic group would continue to gravitate to that locality and stay there. The original focus of settlement of the small (just over eight hundred) population of Hmong refugees was Kitchener-Waterloo, where the Hmong, with the help of private sponsors and CEIC officials, established family and ethnic networks. To this day, Kitchener-Waterloo remains the centre of Hmong settlement in Canada, with an active community life.[26]

Opinions differ on the efficacy of the two settlement schemes, private sponsorship and government assistance. Sponsor groups "typically provided a great deal of moral and material support to refugees";[27] the general view of "academics, government spokespersons and church leaders" is that "private sponsorship has been beneficial" for Indochinese refugees and should remain a part of Canada's refugee resettlement programs.[28] Yet "half of privately sponsored refugees and almost all of the government-sponsored refugees preferred to be government-sponsored, given the choice."[29] As Beiser observes, "Intrusiveness was one of the downsides of private sponsorships."[30] Some sponsors were insensitive to refugees' need for privacy. Often, they found housing for the refugees that proved unaffordable, "close to [the sponsors] rather than to the ethnic communities in which the refugees would have preferred to live."[31]

There are a number of individual stories of failed private sponsorships and just as many happier stories where the refugees and their sponsors remain close friends to this day three or four decades later. Overall, sponsorship was essential to the success of the 1979–80 resettlement program. Without it, Canada could not have resettled as many Indochinese refugees as it did. As well, private sponsorships were effective instruments that ensured that Canadians and Southeast Asian newcomers would get used to each others' cultural patterns on a person-to-person basis. Thus, despite some problems with individual sponsorships, they served as an important instrument for the long-term integration of Indochinese refugees into Canadian life.

From the arrival of the first Indochinese refugees in Canada in 1975 until the early 1990s, scores of researchers studied and conducted interviews with them and investigated their settlement and integration experience. Because of the enormously varied nature of the movement, both in terms of ethnic composition and settlement patterns across Canada, scholarly studies have tended to be limited to specific geographic areas, single ethnic groups, and limited time periods. Even Beiser's *Strangers at the Gate: The "Boat People's" First Ten Years in Canada*, probably the single most in-depth study of Indochinese refugee resettlement in this country, was limited to a single province and a single decade. As the Indochinese communities in Canada have matured, fewer scholarly studies have focused on them. Now, from a distance of several decades and with a new Canadianized generation, it would be valuable to examine how the various Indochinese ethnic communities have succeeded in becoming part of Canada's multicultural society. At the same time, preserving a record of the experience of the refugees, at a time when many of them are reaching advanced years, would be an important contribution to Canada's history.

Conclusion

In 1947, Prime Minister Mackenzie King could still insist on the unchanging, fixed nature of a Canada based on British values. Stating that "the people of Canada do not wish, as a result of mass immigration, to make a fundamental alteration in the character of our population," he specifically rejected the idea of immigration from Asia.[1] Yet, by the 1960s, the basic nature of Canada's social framework was undergoing fundamental change through the acceptance of a set of new political ideals, fuelled in part by recognition that Canada was already multicultural rather than bicultural and by a dawning familiarity with the concept of universal human rights. These evolving ideals had the effect of modifying Canada's largely British-based values by introducing an emphasis on pluralism and ethnic diversity (multiculturalism) while continuing to insist on the importance of good governance to hold together the disparate elements of Canada's body politic.

In response to these evolving values, Canada's immigration policies were gradually but steadily revamped. Regulation changes in 1962 removed most of the overt racial discrimination. The 1966 White Paper on Immigration recommended a universal, non-racially based immigration system and the ratification of the UN Refugee Convention. The point system introduced in 1967 facilitated the selection of immigrants from around the world using identical criteria. In 1969, Canada ratified the UN Refugee Convention and its new global Protocol and accepted the responsibility of applying a universal, non-discriminatory instrument for the protection of refugees. By 1970, Canada had adopted an immigration and refugee policy that reflected the policies of pluralism and ethnic diversity.

During the Vietnam War, Canada accepted as immigrants a large number of US war resisters (estimates vary between 30,000 and 40,000). Initially only "draft dodgers" were accepted, but later, under pressure from the domestic social justice constituency – in particular the NDP and the United Church of Canada – US army deserters were admitted as well. Many faith-based and grassroots refugee organizations in Canada actively helped US draft resisters come to Canada and aided them in settling successfully in this country. Large parts of Canada's political left, including some major press and electronic media outlets, saw the Vietnam War and the conflicts in Cambodia and Laos as the struggle of the small peoples of Indochina against US military might but failed to appreciate the totalitarian communist aspects of the Indochinese national liberation movements. Thus, during the decade of the 1960s and into the early 1970s, Canada's immigration program was already feeling the impact of the Indochinese wars.

When Vietnam, Cambodia, and Laos fell to communist forces in the spring of 1975, the immigration and refugee reforms of the 1960s and early '70s meant that critical elements of Canadian refugee policy were already in place to accommodate a refugee movement from Indochina. To summarize:

• By 1975, Canada's political leadership had succeeded, with the agreement of much of Canada's body politic, in significantly modifying Canadian values toward greater societal tolerance and the acceptance of pluralism and multiculturalism.
• The effect of this change was that Canadians, including many of the country's media outlets as well as faith-based institutions and communities, were now open to accepting non-European refugees with significantly different cultural backgrounds.
• Even though many Canadians were critical of US actions in Indochina, there was recognition that the United States remained Canada's most important ally and trading partner. As well, many prominent Canadians, especially in the foreign policy establishment, supported US actions against what they perceived as communist aggression. This meant that Canadian policy-makers were amenable to helping the United States cope with an Indochinese refugee outflow.

When Saigon, Phnom Penh, and Vientiane fell in 1975, the Canadian government responded to an American request to accept some refugees. Aware of conflicting sentiments within Canada vis-à-vis the Indochinese wars, the government handled the refugee issue very carefully, asserting the humanitarian, non-political nature of this decision and maintaining that admission of Indochinese refugees would not come at the expense of Canada's Chilean refugee program. In terms of numbers and duration, the only refugee movement undertaken by Canada comparable to that of the Indochinese refugees was the post–World War II resettlement of displaced persons from the camps of Europe. The 1979–80 phase of the movement was also unique because of the large numbers brought to Canada in such a short space of time, and the participation of civil society in taking responsibility for the initial resettlement of over half of the refugees through the new private refugee sponsorship program.

This book documents the complex challenges faced by Canada's government and public service during the Indochinese refugee movement and how these challenges were met. The six-year period under consideration saw two closely related yet distinct movements. The first began immediately before the fall of Saigon in April 1975, peaking and diminishing rapidly to a low point in 1977. The second phase began in 1978, as arrivals in neighbouring countries increased from month to month. The 1975–78 movement to Canada was much smaller than the later 1979–80 movement (9,000 in 1975–78, compared to 60,000 in 1979–80) and differed in some important ways. The first movement was characterized by reliance on the US government and its facilities and a strong family reunification component. Both movements benefited from hands-on political leadership and enthusiastic implementation by officials (and in some cases, their family members). The second, much larger movement was shaped by a high degree of legislative and operational innovation, an exceptionally difficult operating environment, close cooperation with international organizations, and unprecedented civil society participation.

During the first phase, many of those who escaped as Saigon fell were former South Vietnamese officials, military personnel, and their families, or others with close connections to the US military. The second phase included a much broader spectrum of Vietnamese society including Sino-Vietnamese and refugees from the north along with Laotians, Cambodians, and Hill Tribes.

In April 1975, following the lead and urging of Immigration Minister Robert Andras, Cabinet rapidly adopted a program to resettle Vietnamese and Cambodian family members of Canadian residents. Andras later expanded the program to include 3,000 government assisted refugees, insisting that Canada's motivation was "to alleviate human distress, without regard to political or any other considerations."[2] In April 1975, immigration officers and support staff across Canada worked around the clock, and as mountains of requests for help flowed into Immigration Headquarters in Ottawa, immigration employees, with the lead of Minister Andras and Deputy Minister Gotlieb, worked long hours to ensure that the requests to rescue family members were sent to Saigon as rapidly as possible. From a Canadian standpoint, the most dramatic event accompanying the collapse of the Cambodian and Vietnamese was the "baby lift" that brought some 120 orphans from Phnom Penn and Saigon through Hong Kong to waiting families in Canada.

A Canadian team from Hong Kong selected and transported 1,400 refugees from Guam to Canada in May 1975, and Canadian officers accepted several thousand from reception camps in the continental United States. Then the arrival in Canada in May 1975 of the notorious South Vietnamese lieutenant general Dang Van Quang soured Canada's attitude to the Indochinese refugee movement for several years. Canada fulfilled its initial commitment of 1975, but by 1977 the flow of refugees, confined mainly to those with relatives in Canada, had significantly dwindled. By the end of 1977, officials concluded that this refugee problem would soon be over. However, conditions in Indochina were deteriorating. The war may have ended in 1975, but with the Vietnamese-Chinese standoff growing sharper and with the bloody reign of terror by the Khmer Rouge in Cambodia, the region was on the verge of new military conflicts. The Vietnamese communist government exerted intense pressures on "class enemies," meaning middle-class people and especially members of the Chinese minority. Starting in mid-1977, boat departures were being actively encouraged by Vietnam, and by late 1978, marginally seaworthy large vessels organized by smuggling syndicates and full of refugees were arriving in ports around the South China Sea.

Canada was the first country to react to the UNHCR request to accept some of the 2,500 mainly Vietnamese-Chinese refugees from the semi-derelict freighter *Hai Hong*. Encouraged by an offer from Quebec (under its new powers in the Cullen-Couture Agreement), Minister Bud Cullen instructed Canadian officials in Singapore to accept six hundred of the refugees, and the United States, Germany, and France rapidly accepted the rest. The *Hai Hong* incident can be considered the first step in the process of large-scale Canadian engagement with the second wave of Indochinese refugees. In December 1978, a UNHCR consultation on the crisis added impetus to Canada's commitment to accept 5,000 overland and boat refugees in 1979.

By late 1978, a new set of selection and resettlement tools rooted in the refugee provisions of the 1976 Immigration Act were in place, including the Indochinese Designated Class Regulation and guidelines for the sponsorship of refugees by citizens and civil society organizations. In April 1979, the Mennonite Central Committee signed the first master agreement for refugee sponsorship, and dozens of churches rapidly followed.

At the beginning of 1979, the number of boat people arriving in Southeast Asian countries escalated. Many thousands perished at sea, and a new refugee outflow emerged on the Cambodian-Thai border following the defeat of the Khmer Rouge by Vietnamese forces in January 1979. Malaysia, Thailand, and Indonesia began pushing off arriving refugee boats, causing many deaths and demonstrating that they would no longer bear the burden alone.

In June 1979, under the newly elected government of Joe Clark, Canada increased its resettlement commitment to 12,000 Indochinese refugees. A month later, as the situation continued to deteriorate, the UN secretary-general convened an international emergency conference in Geneva. Intensive media coverage inspired initiatives within Canada to promote the sponsorship of refugees by faith communities, civil society organizations, and citizens' groups, notably Operation Lifeline in Toronto and Project 4000 in Ottawa. In a deliberate effort to exercise international leadership, Flora MacDonald, secretary of state for external affairs, announced at the UN conference Canada's commitment to resettle 50,000 refugees. This total would consist of the 8,000 government assisted refugees announced in December and June and 21,000 privately sponsored refugees, to be matched on a one-for-one basis by 21,000 government assisted refugees.

The main factors impelling Canada to take this unprecedented step were threefold. First, the international community recognized that dramatic action was needed to ease the refugee crisis. The new PC government saw an opportunity to play a prominent role on the international stage. Second, media focus on the crisis was intense. Canadians were regularly exposed to pictures of suffering and death on their TV screens, while newspaper editorial pages urged the government to take bold measures. And third, during the first six months of 1979, Canada's faith-based institutions had begun to make firm commitments to relieve the refugees' suffering through the new private refugee sponsorship program. The potential for great citizen support and participation was evident.

Once the announcement was made, the Immigration Department faced the daunting and complex task of delivering on the government's policy. The size of the commitment came as a surprise to public servants, but it was enormously helpful that immigration officials had been quietly planning for a bigger role in Southeast Asia for at least a year. It was evident from the outset that selecting refugees to meet both government and private targets would require a complex balancing act. The operational problems were many. The large number of refugees to be processed in extremely primitive conditions of the refugee camps in the depth of jungles or on distant islands, under severe time pressures, made it imperative to streamline operational processes and simplify formalities. Once refugees had been selected, adequate transportation arrangements and efficient reception facilities had to be put in place. Matching incoming refugees with eager sponsors was a new and unfamiliar challenge, as was the need to ensure that support services for refugees and sponsors alike were effectively coordinated at the community level. Finally, deploying and training personnel for rapidly expanding visa offices like those in Singapore and Bangkok required deep professionalism on the part of visa office managers and their assistants.

The central management challenges fell to the Immigration Department's Indochinese Refugee Task Force. The task force provided operational directions to the field abroad and inside Canada, planned and contracted for the transportation and reception of the refugees, and coordinated with domestic and international partners, along with handling communications and media relations.

The introduction of the Indochinese Designated Class Processing Record and Visa (IMM1314) dramatically reduced the paper burden and streamlined refugee processing in Southeast Asia. The redesign of the matching system so that only travel-ready refugees were referred to sponsors simplified and accelerated the process. With the cooperation of the Department of National Defence, staging areas were established at military bases in Montreal and Edmonton, where the refugees were welcomed, granted permanent residence status, and outfitted for the Canadian climate. An effective network of Refugee Liaison Officers (RLOS) was rapidly deployed to coordinate local settlement services and assist refugees and sponsors in the difficult task of initial settlement. Designed and rolled out in the space of one month, the system worked amazingly well. Empowered managers sorted out problems that arose abroad, CEIC's regional offices coordinated responses at the provincial and metropolitan levels, and the RLOS dealt with problems at the local level. The Refugee Task Force ensured that the widely dispersed elements of the resettlement operation worked effectively together.

The Canadian program was operating at full speed by October 1979. As the personal accounts in this book demonstrate, officers working in Southeast Asia faced enormous challenges with good humour and determination. The visa office managers in Singapore, Bangkok, and Hong Kong Asia deserve credit for providing training and leadership to their teams, planning and overseeing complex work schedules and processes, coping with operational partners that were not always up to the task, and getting 60,000 refugees onto 181 charter flights with never a seat left empty.

Success created its own problems. By November 1979, the target of 21,000 private sponsorships needed to reach the government's goal of 50,000 had been exceeded. At the same time, the rhetoric of the National Citizens Coalition ads had, in the government's view, done considerable damage, and polling indicated worrisome anti-refugee sentiments. After considering various options, the government decided it would not turn away the sponsorship groups still forming in the smaller towns and rural areas; however, it could not afford to go beyond the 50,000 target without the risk of turning the mainly silent opposition into something more vocal and dangerous. A complex challenge became more difficult when Flora MacDonald exceeded her authority by pledging $15 million instead of $5 million for Cambodian emergency relief. The solution arrived at – to let the sponsorships continue but to deduct one government refugee for each sponsored refugee over 21,000, and to use the savings for Cambodian relief – was viewed as a betrayal by leaders of the sponsorship movement.

While socially progressive refugee advocates could not in good conscience object to famine relief for Cambodians, they did object to the government reneging on its commitment to the one-for-one matching formula only a few months after its introduction.

How the relationship between the government and its civil society partners would have evolved from this point will never be known, because the minority PC government was defeated on a budget vote on 13 December 1979. Following an election on 19 February 1980, the Trudeau Liberals were returned to power, with Lloyd Axworthy as the new immigration minister. The new Liberal government rapidly solved the problems of the matching formula, refugee numbers, and Quebec-destined refugees in the simplest way possible: on 25 March 1980, Minister Axworthy raised the Indochinese refugee figure by 10,000.

On 8 December 1980, the last of the 60,000-plus refugees had arrived in Canada. The UNHCR was hoping the country would commit to accepting another 30,000 in 1981, but Canada politely declined. The people who sent the refugees to Canada, and those who welcomed them and helped them to settle, were exhausted. They were running on empty.

This book has examined the movement of Indochinese refugees to Canada between 1975 and 1980 in the context of wars, changes of governments, and other cataclysmic historical events in Southeast Asia. It has concentrated on Canadian government policies and the actions of politicians, officials, and the Canadian people in accepting refugees and managing their movement to and reception in Canada. It has focused in particular on the immediate, hands-on experiences of those Canadians who worked, often under circumstances requiring considerable personal humanitarian commitment, to select the refugees, arrange their transportation, and receive them in Canada. Overall, this is a "feel-good" story, a story of considerable efforts by groups of Canadians successfully reacting to a major international humanitarian challenge. Especially – and this needs to be emphasized – it is a story told for the first time of how bold policy initiatives and their innovative and energetic implementation could successfully accomplish a range of complex operational tasks, rescuing people of different cultures and languages in dreadful situations and moving them to new lives in Canada. However, the experience of the refugees themselves, the full story of their reception in Canada and integration into Canadian society, remains to be told. In the 1980s and '90s, when refugees from the former Indochina were still in the initial stage of finding their places in Canadian society, a number of researchers analyzed and documented their resettlement experience. The mental and physical stresses faced by different refugee communities in various Canadian locations during their first decade in Canada have been well documented in a range of scholarly articles and at least one major book-length study. Yet all these studies have focused either on individual locations within Canada or single ethnic groups, or both. The one exception that has dealt with all Indochinese ethnic groups was again limited to a single region of the country, British Columbia. This regional approach was probably inevitable, given the size of Canada and the complex ethnic composition of the Indochinese refugee movement, containing four major and at least one minor cultural and linguistic groups.

After the 1990s, as the Indochinese communities in Canada matured and a new, Canadianized generation of Vietnamese, Sino-Vietnamese, Cambodians, and Laotians, including the Hmong, were becoming part of Canadian society, scholarly interest in these refugee communities waned. Now, four decades after the arrival of the first Indochinese refugees in this country, the process of acculturation of a major element of Canada's population remains unexamined. It is a task that it deserves to be undertaken, and we hope that scholars and the communities themselves will make efforts to research and record the experience.

Most Canadians today, including most Indochinese refugees and their children, remember the story of Indochinese resettlement in Canada in a positive manner. This view, however, does not reflect the attitudes of a narrow majority of Canadians at the time.[3] By 1979, however, it was the response of Canadians motivated by the plight of faraway people in terrible circumstances, and their enthusiastic engagement though the private sponsorship program, that set the tone for a memorable moment in Canadian history. Canada had progressively become a more open, multicultural, diverse society that did not accept open racism but could and did accept a major influx of non-European refugees whose cultural patterns and languages were very different from what was at the time the Canadian norm.

Lessons

What are the lessons of the Indochinese resettlement movements of 1975–78 and 1979–80?

Leadership

The role of Prime Minister Joe Clark in backing his ministers, Flora MacDonald and Ron Atkey, in the face of sceptical Cabinet colleagues has received less attention than it deserves. The courage and leadership of MacDonald and Atkey in fighting for an unprecedented commitment, and in inspiring officials and ordinary Canadians to deliver on it, cannot be overstated. Equally impressive was the way that leaders emerged at other levels of government, in the civil service, and throughout Canadian society to take up the challenge.

The Media

Once the *Hai Hong* episode caught the attention of the media, it stayed focused on the suffering and danger faced by the refugees. In addition, the media took a strong, supportive approach to the sponsorship program and the experiences of arriving refugees. The impact of the media in informing the public about the crisis and championing the efforts of private groups was a positive factor in setting the stage for the Clark government's bold program and in sustaining the public's interest over the next two years.

Communications

Minister Ron Atkey was the first to recognize the critical importance of getting information rapidly into the hands of those organizing and coordinating the sponsorship movement and the settlement of government assisted refugees. In the pre-Internet era, the weekly *Indochinese Refugee Newsletters* kept stakeholders informed of the latest developments, schedules, and statistics and ensured that promising ideas and initiatives that were developed in one part of the country were recognized and publicized across the country.

Private Sponsorship

The unique Canadian private refugee sponsorship program was rolled out just in time and, despite some initial hesitation, was rapidly and enthusiastically adopted by faith communities and private citizens alike. It became the defining feature of the movement despite the fact that over 40 per cent of the refugees were resettled by the government. Over the years, private sponsorship has become an important component of Canada's humanitarian response to refugees and today has global significance, given how few countries actively resettle refugees. Interestingly, while there is nothing magic about the design of the sponsorship program, it has proven difficult if not impossible to transfer to other countries. Apparently the magic is in the Canadian people.

The Public Service

Bureaucracies everywhere are often vilified for rigidity, adherence to routines, and slow, hierarchical decision-making processes. However, over the summer of 1979, Deputy Minister Jack Manion threw away the book, and innovation, empowerment of local managers, and speed of implementation became the order of the day. Time-honoured systems and processes were set aside, and new ideas from relatively junior staff members were adopted and implemented with alacrity. Managers in the far-flung visa offices, the staging areas, and regional and local offices were given their objectives and left to decide how best to achieve them in their local environments.

Professionalism

Finally, this account demonstrates the importance of a motivated, well-trained public service staffed by intelligent, professional, and innovative people. The dedication, skill, compassion, good judgment, and determination of the immigration professionals in Southeast Asia and the hardships they endured, sometimes just to reach the jungle or island refugee camps, stand out. So do the rules they devised to guide their work: keep families together, do the right thing, leave no seats empty on the charters heading for Canada. But much the same can be said for those who staffed the national and regional coordination units, the staging areas, and the matching centres, and for those special community workers, the Refugee Liaison Officers.

Despite the many Canadians who were opposed or indifferent to the decision to settle 60,000 refugees in Canada in 1979–80, those who rose to the challenge, whether as private citizens, elected officials, or civil servants, set the tone for a special moment in Canadian history. It is probably fair to say that before 1979 multiculturalism was a rather vague concept to most Canadians. However, for the tens of thousands of Canadians deciding to welcome these rather exotic strangers into their communities, their churches and synagogues, and ultimately their homes, multiculturalism ceased to be an idea and became a living reality. The Indochinese refugee movement was the first very large non-European refugee movement to Canada and contributed significantly to transforming Canada into a well-functioning, open multicultural society.[4] It is not surprising that today most Canadians are proud of this movement and regard their fellow Canadians of Vietnamese, Cambodian, and Laotian backgrounds as members of the larger Canadian family.

The Nansen Medal of 1986 was awarded in recognition of decades of Canadian efforts on behalf of refugees since the end of World War II. That the award was to the "People of Canada" rather than a single individual or institution was a recognition of the initiative of thousands of Canadians in responding to the bold challenge issued by Ministers Atkey and MacDonald. The refugees did their part by adapting to this cold but welcoming country and by raising children who are today found in every walk of Canadian life as productive citizens, proud of being Canadians. For the civil servants who planned, managed, and delivered the Indochinese refugee movement between 1975 and 1980, that is enough.

Our book has ended but the story has not. The Canadian Immigration Historical Society collects and preserves stories and memoirs about the Canadian immigration and refugee experience. Readers with a memory or anecdote about the Indochinese refugee movement are encouraged to contact the society.[5]

The Indochinese Refugee Movement to Canada
Chronology, 1954–1980

This chronology covers the period from 1954 to 1980, ending with the completion of the program to resettle 60,000 Indochinese refugees in Canada.*

1954–1974

1954
Capitulation of French garrison at Dien Bien Phu (May), followed by Geneva Conference Accords (July), ends French military involvement in Indochina. Poland (communist), India (neutral), and Canada (western) become members of the International Control Commission (ICC), mandated to report on the progress of the ceasefire and on violations. Canada remains a member of the ICC until March 1973, just after the 1973 Paris Accords, when the ICC collapses.

November 1955
Beginning of US involvement in South Vietnam with deployment of military trainers under the Military Advisory Assistance Group (MAAG). Mission is training only.

1961–64
Steady increase of US military presence in South Vietnam, primarily as trainers/advisers. By July 1964, numbers reach 21,000.

---

* Sources of statistics: Employment and Immigration Canada, *The Indochinese Refugees: The Canadian Response, 1979 and 1980* (Ottawa: Department of Supply and Services 1981); *Indochinese Refugee Newsletter*, vols. 1 and 2 (16 July 1979–14 February 1980), CIHC Collection.

August 1964
Gulf of Tonkin incident, an alleged North Vietnamese attack on US
warships, provides rationale to increase US military involvement.

March 1965
US Marines land at Danang as first combat units to deploy to
South Vietnam.

1967
400,000 US troops in Vietnam.

January 1968
Tet Offensive is a tactical victory but strategic defeat for United
States and South Vietnam. United States begins gradual "de-escala-
tion" and "Vietnamization" with the intention of transferring the
main responsibility for the military aspects to the South Vietnamese
Armed Forces.

March 1970
Prince Sihanouk of Cambodia is deposed in US-backed military
coup. US and South Vietnamese "incursion" into Cambodia follows
to disrupt North Vietnamese supply lines into South Vietnam.
Ongoing massive bombing campaign begins in eastern Cambodia.
Beginning of Cambodian civil war, which culminates with Khmer
Rouge victory in 1975.

January 1973
Paris Peace Accords end overt US military involvement in Vietnam.
US forces leave Vietnam in following months. The functions of the
ICC are replaced by an International Commission of Control and
Supervision (ICCS) staffed by military officers from Canada, Hungary, Poland, and Indonesia. Canada withdraws in July 1973 and is
replaced by Iran. Over the next two years, the positions of the
regimes in South Vietnam, Cambodia, and Laos deteriorate in the
face of declining US aid and mounting communist strength.

1975

April
Communist forces in Indochina initiate a final offensive. Pro-western regimes in Cambodia and Laos collapse. On 30 April, Saigon falls to North Vietnamese forces. Approximately 140, 000 people flee South Vietnam to US evacuation fleet and neighbouring countries.

In Cambodia, the Khmer Rouge occupy the capital, Phnom Penh, on 17 April and immediately initiate a forced evacuation of the urban population into the countryside, ostensibly to create a new communal agrarian society. Phnom Penh and other cities are largely empty. In Laos, impact of the Pathet Lao victory is slower, except on the Hill Tribes (chiefly Hmong), accused of collaboration with the United States.

Desperate Vietnamese students from Montreal go to Ottawa to lobby the government to rescue their relatives in Vietnam. The government sends visa officers to Saigon to assist, but few relatives are able to leave Vietnam because of strict government exit controls. Over a two-week period in April before the fall of Saigon, immigration officials send Promise of Visa Letters to 3,500 heads of family in Vietnam encompassing approximately 15,000 family members.

6 April
First group of Indochinese orphans arrive in Canada.

12 April
Second group of Indochinese orphans arrive in Canada.

24 April
Canadian staff at Saigon Embassy is evacuated.

May
United States moves some refugees to Guam and others to the continental United States. Canadian officials from Ottawa and the Canadian consulates in Los Angeles and New Orleans accept several thousand from Camp Pendleton, Indiantown Gap, Fort Chafee, and Ellis Air Force Base and arrange transport to Canada. The notorious Vietnamese general Dang Van Quang arrives in Canada from the United States to join family members in

Montreal. The resulting controversy dampens public and political support for Vietnamese refugees.

In Laos, US military evacuates Hmong leadership to Thailand and later to the United States. Hmong and other Hill Tribe members begin fleeing to Thailand.

Freighter *Troung Xuan* escapes Vietnam crammed with 3,700 refuges and begins to sink some days later. Passengers and crew rescued by Danish freighter *Clara Maersk* and taken to Hong Kong, where those with Canadian relatives (number unknown) are immediately accepted by Canadian visa officers.

1 May
Robert Andras, minister of manpower and immigration, announces that, in addition to those Indochinese nationals already sponsored by relatives, Canada will accept 3,000 Vietnamese and Kampuchean refugees without relatives in Canada. Two thousand will be selected from refugees evacuated to US refugee centres and 1,000 from other countries.

2 May
Team from the Canadian Commission in Hong Kong arrives in Guam to deal with Vietnamese refugees evacuated by the US military. Between 7 and 23 May, they document and arrange transport of 1,401 persons to Canada on nine charter flights.

May–June
Beginning of "re-education" of members of former South Vietnam's military and officials. New Economic Zones in countryside are announced, along with a partial ban on private trade. People start fleeing Vietnam in small boats in the beginning of the "boat people" phenomenon.

May–December
Thai authorities make repeated efforts to normalize relations with Khmer Rouge regime in Cambodia in order to maintain a buffer with Vietnam. These efforts meet with only limited success.

December
Extreme cold followed by drought causes rice shortage, resulting in hunger and economic disruption in Vietnam.

Pathet Lao proclaim the Lao Popular Democratic Republic. End of moderate regime, with arrests, repression, and establishment of "seminars," a Lao version of "re-education." Many urban middle-class members flee to Thailand. By 1977, some 10 per cent of the Lao population have fled to Thailand.

1976

October
Minister Andras announces in May 1975 that 180 residual places in the Indochinese target of 3,000 are applied to boat people arriving in increasing numbers in neighbouring countries.

November
A group of Cambodian refugees, turned back by Thai authorities at the border and handed over to the Khmer Rouge, is reported to have been killed.

Thai military begins providing help to anti-communist Khmer (Free Khmer) guerillas along the border.

December
Between May 1975 and December 1976, a total of 6,353 Indochinese refugees have arrived in Canada: 3,601 in 1976 and 2,752 in 1977; 4,200 are accepted under family reunification and 2,300 as Convention refugees. Of these, some 4,500 arrived in the immediate two-month period following the fall of Saigon. Senior immigration officials conclude that Canada has done its part but will continue to accept "boat people" with relatives in Canada.

By end of 1976, 5,619 boat people have arrived in neighbouring Southeast Asian countries.

1977

For Vietnam, the year is marked by poor weather and related natural disasters, bad food harvests, and economic collapse. Numbers of people fleeing in small boats increase sharply.

July
Border disputes break out between Vietnam and the Khmer Rouge–
ruled Cambodia, with similar incursions along the border with
Thailand.

August
Government authorizes resettlement in Canada of 450 additional
boat people.

October
Intergovernmental Committee for European Migration (ICEM;
later the ICM and today the IOM) opens an operation in Malaysia
to support resettlement activities of United States, Canada, France,
and Australia.

December
The expulsion from Cambodia of large numbers of ethnic Vietnamese leads to heavy fighting between Vietnam and Cambodia;
Vietnamese troops advance on Phnom Penh but eventually
withdraw.
    More than 21,000 boat people arrive in neighbouring Southeast
Asian countries.
    The mayor of Windsor, Ontario, establishes a thirteen-person
committee to help resettle Indochinese refugees in that city.
    Agreements are made between ICEM Singapore and Canada to
book seats on commercial flights. Refugees for Western Canada will
fly via the Pacific and those for Eastern Canada across the Atlantic,
doubling the number of seats available to the Canadian program.
    Total number of Indochinese refugees arriving in Canada in 1977
is 854.

1978

January
Rising tensions between China and Vietnam. The Khmer Rouge is a
client of China, while Vietnam is aligned with the Soviet Union.

13 January
Under its "metered approach," Canada will accept fifty "Small Boat Escapees" families (program identifier: SBE), per month. Processing is initially slow, and lack of UN coordination results in several countries processing the same refugees.

25 January
Employment and Immigration Minister Cullen approves plan to establish a Private Refugee Sponsorship Program and authorizes CEIC to consult potential sponsoring organizations.

February
UNHCR implements "blue card" registration system in Malaysia to reduce processing of the same cases by multiple resettlement countries. A similar system is introduced in Thailand during the summer of 1978 for boat people only.

10 February
US official reports that Canadian SBE program has had a "multiplier effect" on US decision-making.

March
Hanoi nationalizes remaining – mainly ethnic Chinese – private businesses, placing increased pressure on this community.

14 March
CEIC initiates design of a Small Boat Escapee Designated Class Regulation under Section 6(2) of the 1976 Immigration Act to simplify procedures. This classification evolves into the Indochinese Designated Class.

April
Ethnic Chinese in northern Vietnam begin "returning" to China. The government claims the returns are voluntary, but most returnees say they were expelled from Vietnam. China accuses Vietnam of persecuting ethnic Chinese.

July
China cancels all aid to Vietnam, withdraws its remaining techni-
cians, seals its border, and claims it has accepted 160,000 ethnic
Chinese refugees.

Canada's refugee sponsorship program is initiated with release
of pamphlet "Sponsoring Refugees: Facts for Canadian Groups
and Organizations."

Cabinet instructs CEIC to promote involvement of Canadians in
assisting Indochinese refugees. Officials hold briefings across
Canada, and approaches are made to faith communities, voluntary
agencies, and parliamentarians to promote awareness of refugee
problem and new sponsorship program.

20 July
Responding to requests from the US government, UNHCR, the
Thai government, and interested groups in Canada, Cabinet approves proposal to initiate a refugee program in Thailand for Lao
and Cambodian refugees in addition to that already in place for
Vietnamese. Processing of refugees in Thailand is to commence
when a visa office is opened at the Canadian Embassy in Bangkok
in November 1978. The Bangkok operation envisages that under a
monthly "metered rate," twenty families of Thailand Overland
Refugees (program identifier TOR) and five Small Boat Escapee
(program identifier SBE) families will be settled in Canada. The
unannounced ceiling is 1,000 persons.

September
Freighter *Southern Cross*, chartered by a Hong Kong smuggling
syndicate, leaves southern Vietnam with 1,200 refugees on board
and eventually beaches on an Indonesian island. Immigration officers from the Canadian High Commission in Singapore accept
eighty-one refugees with links to Canada.

14 September
Paper prepared by CEIC, "Towards an Integrated Canadian Refugee
Policy," recommends an "Annual Refugee Plan" as part of the
Annual Immigration Levels Plan required by the 1976 Immigration
Act, and argues for closer coordination between External Affairs,
CIDA, and CEIC.

October
Worst flooding in recent Vietnamese history; 1978 rice crop is short by 7.5 million tonnes; further economic hardship.

Detailed instructions outlining selection criteria for SBES and TORS under the forthcoming Indochinese Designated Class Regulations stress need to keep extended families together.

November
Freighter *Pacific Conveyor* rescues 156 boat people at sea. A second freighter, the *Hai Hong*, organized by a Hong Kong syndicate, leaves southern Vietnam with 2,500 refugees (mostly ethnic Chinese) on board and arrives off Port Klang, Malaysia. After urgent debate within government, E&I Minister Bud Cullen announces Canada will accept six hundred refugees from the *Hai Hong*. Operating in adverse conditions, four federal and Quebec officials accept 603 refugees in three days. Media attention makes this a pivotal event, raising awareness in government, media, and the public of the growing Indochinese refugee problem.

Mennonite Central Committee in Canada meets to discuss the new private refugee sponsorship program.

11 November
Two Canadian visa officers arrive in Bangkok to establish a CEIC operation at the Canadian Embassy. Their mandate is to process SBE and TOR refugees from camps in Thailand, along with carrying out other immigration programs in Thailand, Burma, and Laos.

23 November
Edmonton Interfaith Immigration Committee holds workshop on sponsorship of Vietnamese refugees.

December
After months of escalating border skirmishes, Vietnam launches a full-scale invasion of Cambodia. Khmer Rouge resistance proves ineffective.

A third freighter, the *Huey Fong*, arrives off Hong Kong with 3,318 refugees on board. Again, most are ethnic Chinese.

December 7
Indochinese Designated Class Regulations approved by Governor-in-Council establish a simplified basis for selecting and processing Indochinese refugees.

11–12 December
UNHCR consultation meeting in Geneva draws attention to growing number of Indochinese refugee arrivals in first asylum countries in the region and the need for more resettlement opportunities.

20 December
Cabinet decides that 5,000 Indochinese will be admitted under Canada's first Annual Refugee Plan. Charter flights will transport the increased numbers to Canada. This commitment is announced on 22 December.

By the end of 1978, the number of boat people arriving in Southeast Asia totals 106,489.

Refugee arrivals in Canada in 1978 total 1,944 including 604 from the *Hai Hong*.

Total number of Indochinese refugees resettled in Canada, 1975–1978: 9,151.

1979

January
In the course of a short military campaign, Vietnamese forces occupy Phnom Penh. The Khmer Rouge flee to the western part of Cambodia. The Vietnamese military installs a pro-Vietnamese client regime headed by Heng Samrin.

February
Sino-Vietnamese War. China describes fighting as "punishment" imposed on an erring "younger brother" for invading Cambodia. "Punishment" fails to result in Vietnam withdrawing from Cambodia.

17 February
A fourth seagoing freighter, the *Skyluck*, arrives off Hong Kong
with 2,630 refugees on board.

March
Mennonite Central Committee (MCC) signs sponsorship master
agreement with Employment and Immigration Canada, simplifying
sponsorship procedures for its congregations. Other churches
follow quickly. Meanwhile Canadian visa officers in Hong Kong,
Bangkok, and Malaysia put thousands of refugees in process to
meet the target established under the Annual Refugee Plan.
    China announces phased withdrawal of forces from northern
Vietnam.

April–May
The flood of Cambodian refugees into Thailand begins as Khmer
Rouge are forced out of food-producing areas within Cambodia.
Numbers increase with realization that insufficient rice has been
planted to sustain the population.

April–June
Dramatic increase in boat arrivals in countries surrounding the
South China Sea: from 26,602 in April, to 51,139 in May, to
56,941 in June. The number of ethnic Chinese arriving in China
reaches 250,000. Evidence grows that the Vietnamese authorities
are actively facilitating the departure of boats, large and small, filled
with "class enemies" and ethnic minorities, especially Chinese.
Many boats are lost at sea; many refugees perish.

May
In response to growing Canadian refugee resettlement program, especially in the number of private sponsorships, a Matching Centre
is established at Immigration HQ to pair refugees with sponsors
and destine unsponsored refugees to communities across in Canada.

22 May
Canadian federal election. No political party wins a majority in the
House of Commons, but the Progressive Conservatives, led by Joe
Clark, have the largest number of seats and form a minority govern-
ment. The Liberals become the official opposition.

26 May
A fifth seagoing freighter, the *Sen On*, runs ashore on Hong Kong's Lantau Island with 1,400 refugees on board.

4 June
Clark government sworn in. Ron Atkey is appointed minister of employment and immigration, and Flora MacDonald becomes secretary of state for external affairs. Both become very active on the Indochina file.

8–12 June
Thai military forcibly repatriates 42,000 Cambodian refugees across the border. Canada enters discussions with international agencies about food aid to Cambodians along the border and within Cambodia. Action is complicated by political factors.

18 June
The new government announces an increase in its annual target for Indochinese refugees from 5,000 to 8,000 and asks the voluntary sector to sponsor an additional 4,000 refugees under the new Private Refugee Sponsorship Program.

24 June
Howard Adelman of York University hosts founding meeting of Operation Lifeline. CEIC Ontario region officials attend and inform meeting about new refugee sponsorship program.

27 June
Ottawa mayor Marion Dewar meets community leaders and commits to take half of the 18 June target of 8,000: hence, Project 4000.

28 June
Mennonite, Christian Reformed, Lutheran, and Presbyterian Churches submit 388 sponsorships for 1,604 Indochinese refugees.

Late June
In response to ever-increasing arrivals, ASEAN member countries (Thailand, Malaysia, Indonesia, Philippines, and Singapore) an-

nounce they have "reached the limit of their endurance and decided that they would not accept any new arrivals."

1 January–10 June
Total Indochinese refugee arrivals in Canada over this period: 4,319.

July
Canadian government charters seventy-six flights to transport 15,800 refugees by the end of 1979. The monthly rate of arrival increases from 1,000 to 3,000 and then to 5,000.

National Defence and Employment and Immigration establish staging areas (reception centres) at Canadian Forces bases at Longue-Pointe (Montreal) and Greisbach Barracks (Edmonton) to receive refugees arriving on charter flights.

12 July
City of Ottawa's Project 4000 launched with thousands attending Lansdowne Park rally.

16 July
Cabinet decides to accept 60,000 refugees over three years. Before the announcement, number is reduced to 50,000. Immigration Minister Atkey launches regular newsletter on Indochinese refugee program.

18 July
Ministers Flora MacDonald and Ron Atkey announce that Canada will resettle 50,000 Indochinese by the end of 1980. The program will be based on a "matching formula" in which the government will accept one refugee for each refugee brought in under private sponsorship. The 50,000 will include the 8,000 announced in June and 21,000 sponsored by private groups matched by 21,000 to be resettled by the government.

20–21 July
With the principle of "first asylum" under threat, the United Nations hosts a conference in Geneva to consider the problem of Indochinese refugees. The Geneva Conference averts the immediate

crisis and concludes with a three-way international understanding between countries of origin, countries of first asylum, and countries of resettlement: 1) ASEAN countries will continue to provide temporary asylum; 2) Vietnam will try to prevent illegal departures and promote orderly departures; 3) Developed countries will accelerate rate of third-country resettlement. This regional and international consensus lasts into the late 1980s.

At Geneva, Minister Flora MacDonald announces that Canada will accept 50,000 refugees.

25 July
The Refugee Task Force is established at Employment and Immigration Headquarters and charged with coordination of all Indochinese refugee activities.

31 July
3,800 refugees are sponsored by 747 sponsorship groups in Canada.

27 July–26 August
Hong Kong airlift. In response to pressing demands for immediate action and because of a lack of immediately available commercial aircraft, CEIC arranges for eleven charter flights with National Defence aircraft to transport refugees from Hong Kong. This allows time to reinforce the visa offices in Singapore and Bangkok and to build inventories of travel-ready refugees to fill commercial charters in the fall of 1979 into 1980.

August
The Canadian team in Singapore shifts its focus to the growing refugee population in Indonesia. By the fall, the Singapore visa office is coordinating airlifts out of Kuala Lumpur and Singapore. In Geneva, Canada participates in negotiating and joining the Disembarkation Resettlement Offers (DISERO) scheme to facilitate rapid resettlement of refugees rescued by ships of countries that do not resettle refugees.

8 August
First charter flight arrives at Longue-Pointe, Montreal.

14 August
First charter flight arrives at Griesbach Barracks, Edmonton.

30 August
Matching system is redesigned to allow the Matching Centre to handle 5,000 arriving refugees a month and match 80 per cent with sponsors.

By the end of August, 10,643 refugees have been sponsored by 1,893 sponsorship groups in Canada.

21 September
17,147 refugees sponsored by 3,122 sponsorship groups in Canada.

October–November
Between 600,000 and 800,000 starving Cambodian refugees arrive on the Thai border, setting off a new humanitarian crisis.

13 November
Cabinet considers the implications of sponsorships exceeding the 21,000 target. Because of fears of backlash, it decides government will no longer match each privately sponsored refugee with a government assisted refugee and will subtract one government refugee for each sponsored refugee over 21,000 to hold the 50,000 ceiling. The savings will be applied to Cambodian relief.

29 November
In Canada, 4,622 sponsorship groups sponsor 25,059 refugees, surpassing the 21,000 target for private sponsorship.

5 December
Ministers Atkey and MacDonald announce the Cabinet decision of 13 November at a breakfast meeting of sponsorship movement leaders. The reaction is negative.

13 December
Minority Progressive Conservative government loses confidence
vote in the House of Commons. General election is called for
February 1980.

End of 1979
Indochinese refugee arrivals in Canada by year end: privately spon-
sored, 8,211; relative sponsored, 615; government assisted, 10,043.
Total: 23,583.

1980

4 January
In Canada, 33,114 refugees (most of whom have not yet arrived)
have been sponsored by 6,003 private sponsors.

8 February
$1.3 million is allocated to cover administrative costs of organiza-
tions coordinating sponsorship activities under a new Indochinese
Refugee Settlement Grants Program and to top up the Immigrant
Settlement Assistance Program.

16 February
Joe Clark's Progressive Conservatives lose the election to Pierre
Trudeau's Liberals.

3 March
Liberal government takes office. Lloyd Axworthy becomes minister
of employment and immigration.

2 April
Minister Axworthy announces that 10,000 additional government-
assisted refugees will be accepted by the end of 1980, bringing the
total 1979–80 target for Indochinese refugees to 60,000.

July
Thai authorities open Phanat Nikhom camp as a central processing centre for Cambodians under consideration for third-country resettlement.

August
Greisbach Barracks staging area phased out. Remaining flights arrive at Longue-Pointe.

8 December
Flight 181 from Bangkok, the final charter of the program, arrives at Longue-Pointe carrying the last of 60,049 refugees. The symbolic 60,000th refugee is a Cambodian who, with his brother and their families, is destined to a sponsoring church in Goderich, Ontario.

Sponsorships: By the end of 1980, 7,675 sponsorships have been filed by private sponsors for 39,904 refugees, some of whom will arrive in 1981.

CHARTER FLIGHTS

	1979	1980	Total
Bangkok	22	30	52
Hong Kong	23	22	45
Kuala Lumpur	31	25	56
Singapore	7	21	28
Total flights			181

International Effort

Between July 1979 and July 1982, more than twenty countries, led by the United States, Canada, France, and Australia, have resettled 623,800 Indochinese refugees.

In 1986, the UN High Commission for Refugees awards the Nansen Medal to the people of Canada "in recognition of their essential and constant contribution to the cause of refugees within their country and around the world."

Notes

INTRODUCTION

1 Molloy was at the first discussion of this issue in Geneva in
1983, representing the Immigration Department, when a
UNHCR funding official asked whether Canada would fund the
following year's Nansen award. Molloy rejected the request,
pointing out that despite all that Canada and Canadians had
done for refugees since 1947 in terms of funding, resettlement,
and policy development, UNHCR had never seen fit to award it
to a Canadian. His statement led to a discussion in which the
contribution of Canadian civil society in sponsoring more than
half of the 60,000 Indochinese in 1979–80 was front and centre. Ultimately, this is why the award was given to the "people
of Canada" rather than to a prominent politician or humanitarian. Few Canadians had heard of the Nansen Medal until then.

2 Some of the most interesting and influential of these publica-
tions include Morton Beiser, *Strangers at the Gate: The Boat
People's First Ten Years in Canada* (Toronto: University of
Toronto Press 1999); Louis-Jacques Dorais, *The Cambodians,
Laotians and Vietnamese in Canada* (Ottawa: The Canadian
Historical Association 2000); Louis-Jacques Dorais, Kwok B.
Chan, Doreen M. Indra, eds., *Ten Years Later: Indochinese
Communities in Canada* (Canadian Asian Studies Association
1998); and Kwok B. Chan and Doreen Marie Indra, eds., *Up-
rooting, Loss and Adaptation: The Resettlement of Indochinese
Refugees in Canada* (Ottawa: Canadian Public Health Associa-
tion 1987).

3 *Indochinese Refugees: The Canadian Response, 1979 and 1980*
   (Ministry of Supply and Services Canada 1982).
4 The federal government's immigration program has had many
   homes and names during its long history, all reflecting its purpose at the time: Agriculture, Interior, Colonization, Mines and
   Resources, Employment, External Affairs, Public Security,
   Citizenship and Immigration, and, most recently, Immigration,
   Refugees and Citizenship. From 1975 to 1977, the immigration
   program was part of the Department of Manpower and Immigration (M&I). To make things more complicated, the department became the Canadian Employment and Immigration
   Commission (CEIC) in 1977. As a commission, CEIC had a
   chairman rather than a deputy minister and an executive director rather than an assistant deputy minister. For purposes of
   clarity, standard departmental public service titles have been
   used throughout the book. The organization within CEIC
   responsible for immigration and refugees in 1979–80 was
   formally known as the Immigration and Demographic
   Policy Group.
       M&I and CEIC had comprehensive service networks in
   Canada and abroad. Within Canada, regional offices in each
   province managed a network of Canada Manpower Centres
   (CMCs), later called Canada Employment Centres (CECs), as
   well as Canada Immigration Centres (CICs). Among other
   things, CECs provided settlement services to immigrants and
   government assisted refugees, including language and skills
   training. CICs performed an array of immigration functions
   from facilitation to enforcement including assessing and processing sponsorship applications and following up once the
   refugees had arrived. (Their officials are referred to as immigration officers.) Abroad, the department operated a network of
   visa offices located in Canadian embassies, high commissions
   (as embassies to Commonwealth countries are called), and consulates on six continents. These were managed and staffed by
   Immigration Foreign Service officers (visa officers) assisted by
   locally hired staff. For the purposes of this book, the visa
   offices are referred to as, for example, E&I Bangkok or E&I
   Hong Kong. Overall operational and program coordination for
   immigration and refugee affairs as well as policy formulation

and development were the responsibility of National Headquarters (NHQ) in Ottawa. Officials working in far-flung locations had to coordinate their efforts to facilitate the rapid
resettlement in Canada of the Indochinese refugees.

CHAPTER ONE

1 Among a number of books on the topic of Canadian refugee
policy, we'd like to highlight in particular Ninette Kelly and
Michael Trebilcock, *The Making of the Mosaic* (Toronto: University of Toronto Press 2010); Valerie Knowles, *Strangers at
Our Gates* (Toronto: Dundurn Press 2016); Freda Hawkins,
Canada and Immigration, Public Policy and Public Concern
(Montreal and Kingston: McGill-Queen's University Press
1988); and Gerald E. Dirks, *Canada's Refugee Policy: Indiffer-
ence or Opportunism* (Montreal and Kingston: McGill-Queen's
University Press 1977). Articles are available in a number of
journals. We would also like to highlight the Canadian Immigration History Society's website at http://cihs-shic.ca, in particular the CIHS-SHIC *Bulletin* and the collection of Indochinese
refugee documents found on the website.

2 Freda Hawkins, *Canada and Immigration*, 93.

3 Citizenship and Immigration, *Annual Report 1959*.

4 Between 1951 and 1970 the Canadian refugee definition was a
person who "(a) as a result of events arising out of World War
II, was displaced from one European country to another and
has not been permanently resettled; or (b) because of fear of
persecution on religious, racial or political grounds, left the
Soviet Bloc countries since the International Refugee Organization terminated its activities on December 31, 1951, and has
not been permanently resettled" (Memorandum to Cabinet,
"Selection of Refugees for Resettlement in Canada," 27 July
1970, LAC RG2, vol. 6373, file 1023-70).

5 "Ellen Louks Fairclough: Canada's First Female Federal Cabinet Minister," *Electoral Insight*, March 2003, http://www.
elections.ca/res/eim.

6 The Hon. Jean Marchand, "White Paper on Immigration"
(Ottawa: Queen's Printer 1966).

7 Under the point system, numerical values were assigned for
age, education, occupation, skill level, intended destination,

ability to function in French and/or English, presence of relatives in Canada, and arranged employment. The applicant
had to achieve fifty points overall to be accepted. The system
included discretionary authority for instances where the
interviewing officer believed the points did not reflect the
applicant's true prospects for successful establishment; the interviewing officer could award additional points for personal
qualities like adaptability and motivation. This provision
was particularly important in the case of refugees.

8 Memorandum to Cabinet, "Selection of Refugees for Resettlement in Canada," 27 July 1970, LAC RG76, vol. 6373, file
1032-70.

9 The 1967 regulations recognized that there would be circumstances when the points total did not reflect an applicant's
prospects for successful establishment. Officers could override
the system by explaining their assessment in the box provided
on the case processing sheet (Imm.1067) and having it en-
dorsed by their supervisor.

10 Operations Memorandum 17, "Refugees," 2 January 1971.

11 Prime Minister's Statement, quoted in External Affairs Cable
EXTOTT 35924, August 1972, CIHS Collection.

12 Roger St Vincent, "Seven Crested Cranes," CIHS 2012,
https://arc.library.carleton.ca/sites/default/files/exhibits/Seven
CrestedCranes-RogerStVincent.pdf.

13 Bill C-24, an Act Respecting Immigration to Canada, 2nd
Session, 30th Parliament, 25–26 Elizabeth II 1976–77.

CHAPTER TWO

1 The "domino theory" was a popular Cold War theory that
held that if one country in a region fell to a communist
takeover, the neighbouring countries would "fall like domi-
nos." President Eisenhower referred to the "falling domino"
principle in a speech in 1954. The first Asian domino to fall
was China. During the Vietnamese War, it was believed that if
communist forces prevailed in one country, all of the countries
in Southeast Asia, including Thailand, Malaysia, Burma, and
Indonesia, would fall as well.

2 US foreign policy during the post–World War II era was defined by Cold War ideology that required fighting the spread of

communism everywhere in the world, including Indochina. This policy, formulated in the "containment thesis" by US diplomat George F. Kennan in the famous "long telegram" of 1946 from the US Embassy in Moscow, is restated by Kennan in "The Sources of Soviet Conduct," *Foreign Affairs* 25 (4): 566–82. Kennan argued that "Soviet pressure against the free institutions of the Western world is something that can be contained by the adroit and vigilant application of counterforce at a series of constantly shifting geographical and political points." The Eisenhower doctrine, http://www.presidency.ucsb.edu/ws/index.php?pid=11007&st=&st1, elaborated by President Eisenhower on 5 January 1957, reiterated the practical implementation of the containment thesis ideals, singling out the communist threat and insisting that "a country could request American economic assistance or aid from U.S. military forces if it was being threatened by armed aggression from another state."

3 One of the most complete bibliographies of the Indochina War is Richard Jensen's "Vietnam War Bibliography," July 2008, http://tigger.uic.edu/~rjensen/vietnam.html.

4 See ibid.

5 Peter H. Koehn, *Refugees from Revolution: U.S. Policy and Third-World Migration* (Boulder, CO: Westview Press 1991).

6 Ronald Frankum, *Operation Passage to Freedom: The US Navy in Vietnam, 1954–55* (Lubbock, TX: Texas Tech University Press 2007).

7 Gil Loescher, *The UNHCR and World Politics: A Perilous Path* (Oxford: Oxford University Press 2001), 188–9.

8 W. Courtland Robinson, *Terms of Refuge: The Indochinese Exodus & International Response* (London and New York: Zed Books 1998), 7.

9 Ibid., 8–10.

10 Ibid., 7–20.

11 Guy S. Goodwin-Gill, *The Refugee in International Law* (Oxford: Oxford University Press 1983), 7–10.

12 Loescher, *The UNHCR*, 188–9.

13 Goodwin-Gill, *The Refugee*, 9.

14 Loescher, *The UNHCR*, 191–3.

15 Robinson, *The Refugee*, 8.

16 Memorandum to Minister, 9 April 1975, "Report from Cana-
    dian Embassy Wash DC," LAC RG 76, vol. 991, file 5850 3-5-
    641, part 1.
17 Ibid. Re UNHCR attitudes, see Loescher and Goodwyn-Gill.
18 Privy Council Office, Record of Cabinet Decision, 1 May
    1975, "Refugees from Cambodia and South Vietnam," PCO
    267-75RD, CIHS Indochinese Document Collection (hereafter,
    CIHS Collection).
19 Privy Council Office, Memorandum to Cabinet, 29 April 1975,
    "Refugees from Cambodia and South Vietnam," PCO 267-
    75MC, CIHS Collection.
20 Ibid.
21 Privy Council Office Situation Report, 16 June 1975, "Refugee
    Movement from Chile, Cambodia and South Vietnam," PCO
    381-75RD, CIHS Collection.
22 Ibid., Annex "A."
23 John Baker, "Description of Events in Saigon," unpublished
    narrative, 2014, CIHS Collection.
24 Vietnamese students who were in Canada in 1973 obtained
    permanent residence status through a status adjustment pro-
    gram initiated by Minister Andras that year (interview with
    Tho Cuc and Mai Nguyen, 9 September 2016).
25 Ibid.
26 Tove Bording, "Description of Events at Immigration HQ,
    Ottawa," unpublished narrative, 2014, CIHS Collection.
27 Baker, "Description of Events in Saigon."
28 Ernest Hébert, "Events Leading Up to the Evacuation of the
    Canadian Embassy in Saigon," unpublished narrative, 2015,
    CIHS Collection.
29 According to former CIA agent Frank Snepp, "The under-the-
    table payments required to gain a passport and exit visa
    jumped six-fold, and the price of seagoing vessels tripled."
    Snepp, An Insider's Account of Saigon's Indecent End (New
    York: Random House 1977).
30 Hébert, "Events Leading Up."
31 Ibid.
32 Baker, "Description of Events in Saigon."
33 Hébert in his unpublished narrative notes that there were six
    flights by CAF 130 cargo planes during the month of April

from Hong Kong to Saigon and back to Hong Kong. Two of these flights were "baby flights" (see later in this chapter), and the last was the final evacuation flight on 24 April.

34　Ernest Allen, "Description of Events in Saigon and Hong Kong," unpublished narrative, 2014, CIHS Collection.

35　Charles Rogers, "Events in Saigon and Hong Kong," interview, 2014, CIHS Collection. See cihs-shic.ca for an example of the Promise of Visa letter.

36　Allen, "Description of Events."

37　Murray Oppertshauser, "Situation at Canadian Diplomatic Missions in South-East Asia," interview, 2014, CIHS Collection.

38　Truong Nhu Trang, *A Viet Cong Memoir* (San Diego: Harcourt Brace Jovanovich 1985), 153–4; Stephen T. Hosmer, *Viet Cong Repression and Its Implications for the Future* (Santa Monica, CA: Rand Corporation 1970), 72–8.

39　Larry Engelman, *Tears before the Rain: An Oral History of the Fall of South Vietnam* (Oxford: Oxford University Press 1990), x–xi.

40　Ibid., xii.

41　Snepp, *Insider's Account.*

42　Fox Butterfield, "Reporter's Notebook: Six Days in the Evacuation from Saigon," *New York Times*, 5 May 1975.

43　Donald Cameron, "Description of Events in Saigon and Hong Kong," unpublished narrative, 2014, CIHS Collection.

44　Ibid.

45　"Interview of 24 April, 2000 with Ernest Hébert," CBC Archives, http://www.cbc.ca/player/play/1631531066.

46　Peter Kent, CBC *News Report*, http://www.cbc.ca/archives/entry/canadians-pull-out-of-saigon-vietnam.

47　Hébert, "Events Leading Up." All aspects of the Saigon embassy's evacuation are convincingly covered in Hébert's narrative.

48　Allen, "Description of Events."

49　Hébert, "Events Leading Up."

50　Engelman, *Tears before the Rain*, x–xi, 19–25; see especially Susan McDonald's gripping firsthand testimony of the American babylift.

51　Hébert, "Events Leading Up."

52　Engelman, *Tears before the Rain*, x–xi, 19–25.

53 According to Hébert's narrative, the main child help organiza-
    tions and individuals with Canadian connections operating in
    Saigon in 1975 were "Rosemary Taylor, 'Friends For Children'
    of Naomi Bronstein, Phumy, ISS, World Vision, Holt. Victoria
    Leach and Helen Allen of the Department of Community and
    Social Services of Ontario were also very much involved." For
    Hébert's role in arranging the first baby flight, see Tarah
    Brookfield, "Maverick Mothers and Mercy Flights: Canada's
    Controversial Introduction to International Adoption," *Journal
    of the Canadian Historical Association* 19, no 1 (2008): 324–5.

54 Gerry Bellett, "We Just Weren't Going to Leave without
    Them," *Vancouver Sun*, 18 April 2015. "Canada House" and
    the Charet sisters are discussed in a CBS Walter Cronkite video
    from 1975, available on YouTube at https://www.youtube.com/
    watch?v=xbxcNofeyLE. The Charet sisters' role (see CBS re-
    port, *Vancouver Sun* article) has not yet been mentioned in the
    scholarly literature. Brookfield in "Maverick Mothers and
    Mercy Flights" discusses the role of Families for Children
    (FCC) and Naomi Bronstein as well as the Kuan Yin Founda-
    tion (KYF), mentions Canada House in Phnom Penh in passing
    but omits the role of the Charet sisters.

55 Judy Jackson, *A Moment in Time: The United Colours of Bron-
    stein*, documentary film, Telefilm Canada, 2001.

56 Ibid.

57 Anonymous (at interviewee's request) interview with a witness
    to the baby flight, 2013.

58 Katie Daubs, "From Saigon to Toronto – Revisiting Vietnam
    War's 'Orphan Flights' 40 Years Later," *Toronto Star*, 3 April
    2015.

59 Elizabeth Heatherington, unpublished narrative on the Cana-
    dian Baby Flight, 2014, CIHS Collection.

60 Ibid.

61 Brookfield, "Maverick Mothers and Mercy Flights." According
    to Brookfield, Victoria Leach spent the early 1970s investigat-
    ing international adoption practices in Vietnam, concentrating
    her investigations on KYF, the main Ontario private agency for
    adoptions from South Vietnam. However, Brookfield does not
    mention the important role of Leach and her staff in arranging
    adoptions from South Vietnam as Saigon was falling to North

Vietnamese forces. Brookfield does not mention the second Canadian baby flight, arranged by Leach; it is, however, documented in Thanh Campbell, *Orphan 32* (Hamilton, ON: Hope for the World Productions 2013) and through the recollections of Hébert.

62 Victoria Leach to Joan Campbell, letter reproduced in Thanh Campbell, *Orphan 32*, 41–3. Unless footnoted otherwise, all information and quotes in this section are taken from Leach's letter.

63 Scott Heatherington, "Persons Evacuated from S. Vietnam/ Cambodia to Canada via Hong Kong," flight manifest, Commission for Canada Hong Kong, 13 April 1975, CIHS Collection.

64 Hébert, SAIGON to EXTOTT SAG0411 of APRI 1/75, private collection of Ernest Hébert.

65 Judy Jackson, *A Moment in Time*.

CHAPTER THREE

1 Privy Council Office, Record of Cabinet Decision, "Refugees from Cambodia and South Vietnam," 1 May 1975, PCO 267- 75RD, CIHS Collection. The decision authorized – in addition to the admission of relatives of Vietnamese (and Cambodians) in Canada – the admission of 3,000 Convention refugees without relatives, including 2,000 from camps in the United States and 1,000 from Asia.

2 Department of Manpower and Immigration, *Immigration Annual Report 1975/76*.

3 W. Courtland Robinson, *Terms of Refuge: The Indochinese Exodus and the International Response* (London and New York: Zed Books 1998), 18–19.

4 Richard Martin, "The Canadian Refugee Program in Singapore," *E&I Report*, 1 July 1980, CIHS Collection. Reprinted here as chapter 11.

5 The American military sustained the refugee population in Guam by flying in 2,000 tons of supplies a day. Accommodation for the refugees included 3,968 tents, two hospitals, five cinemas, eight dining facilities, and a bank to purchase the refugees' gold. *Viet-Bao, Revue Mensuel du Project I.A.R.V.*, Montreal, May 1976, CIHS Collection.

6 Charles Rogers, article in *M&I News*, August 1975.

7 Charles Rogers, interview on Guam, 2013. A SEA hut is a 16 foot by 32 foot wood-frame tent modified with a metal roof and extended rafters, developed by the US Army during South Asian (SEA) military operations.

8 Scott Heatherington, unpublished memoir on the Guam operation, 2013, CIHS Collection.

9 Ibid.

10 Joyce Cavanagh-Wood, unpublished narrative report on Guam, 2013, CIHS Collection.

11 Scott Heatherington, memoir.

12 Cavanagh-Wood, narrative report.

13 Charles Rogers, article in *M&I News*, August 1975, CIHS Collection

14 Pham Ngoc Luy, *Truong Xuan's Last Voyage*, published in 2009 at http://www.baixan.com/chuyenhomqua/Truong-Xuan.pdf; Donald Cameron, unpublished narrative report on the *Clara Maersk*, 2013, CIHS Collection.

15 Pham Ngoc Luy, 53–4.

16 Ibid., 66–7.

17 Cameron, *Clara Maersk*.

18 Marlene Massey, unpublished narrative report on Camp Pendleton, 2013, CIHS Collection.

19 The late John Sheardown, an air force veteran and career immigration foreign service officer, would subsequently be awarded the Order of Canada for his role in sheltering American officials in Tehran during the American hostage crisis after the Iranian revolution.

20 Massey, narrative report.

21 Ibid.

22 Ibid.

23 Joyce Cavanagh-Wood, unpublished narrative report on Camp Pendleton, 2013, CIHS Collection.

24 Ibid.

25 Murray Oppertshauser, extended interview on his activities in Southeast Asia and the United States, 2013, CIHS Collection.

26 Daniel Marvin, "General Quang Van Dang – Victim of Subterfuge," *The Unconventional Warrior*, part 18, 6 January 2003, http://expendableelite.com/UW_archives/UW_archive.0018.html.

27 John Pilger, *Heroes* (New York: Random House 2010), 223. Pilger's picture of General Dang as a corrupt drug dealer is contradicted by the views of Green Beret captain Daniel Marvin and CIA operative Merle L. Pribbenow. See note 25 above and Merle L. Pribbinow, "Drugs, Corruption and Justice in Vietnam and Afghanistan: A Cautionary Tale," 11 November 2009, http://www.washingtondecoded.com/site/2009/11/drugs-corruption-and-justice-in-vietnam-and-afghanistan-a-caution ary-tale.html.

28 Donald Cameron, unpublished narrative report on the fall of Saigon, 2013, CIHS Collection; John Baker, unpublished narrative report on the fall of Saigon, 2013, CIHS Collection.

29 Robert Trumbull, "Canada Studying a Saigon General," *New York Times*, 31 May 1975.

30 "Canada to Oust Ex-Saigon Aide," *New York Times*, 8 July 1975.

31 Pribbenow, "Drugs, Corruption and Justice."

32 Tove Bording and Bill Sheppit, recorded conversation on early days in Singapore, 2013, CIHS Collection. See chapter 11 for an extended interview with Bording and Sheppit.

33 Ibid.

34 WCRP Report, 22 April 1977, LAC RG 76, vol. 1838, file 8700-15.

35 UNHCR note 77/KL/261, LAC RG76, vol. 1835, file 8700-1.

36 Memorandum, W.K. Bell, Director-General, Recruitment and Selection Branch, to J.B. Bissett, Director-General, Foreign Branch, 19 October 1976, CIHS Collection, as quoted in Richard Martin, "The Canadian Refugee Program in Singapore," 1.

37 Memorandum to the Minister, "Request for Authority to Apply the Vietnamese/Cambodian Refugee Quota to Persons Escaping Indo-China in Small Boats," 5 October 1976, LAC RG76, vol. 1835, file 8700-1.

38 The 76,000 in Thailand included 3,000 Vietnamese, 10,000 Cambodians, 19,000 Laotians, and 44,000 Laotian Hill Tribes people. Memorandum to the Minister, "Refugees in Indo-China," 6 May 1977, LAC RG76, vol. 1835, file 8700-1.

39 Ibid.

40 Ibid.

41 In 1977, Manpower and Immigration Canada (M&I) became the Canada Employment and Immigration Commission (CEIC).

42 Letter from UNHCR representative J. Terllin, 15 July 1977, LAC RG76, vol. 1838, file 8700-15.

43 Press release 77-24, 2 August 1977, LAC RG76, vol. 1835, file 8700-1.

44 Richard M. Tait to J.B. Bissett and W.K. Bell, "Vietnamese Refugees," 18 August 1977, LAC RG76, vol. 1835, file 8700-1.

CHAPTER FOUR

1 Robert Andras, "An Historical Sketch of Canadian Immigration and Refugee Policy," in *The Indochinese Refugee Movement: The Canadian Experience*, edited by Howard Adelman (Toronto: Operation Lifeline 1980), 4, 7.

2 For a concise description of the process leading up to the 1976 act, see Kelly and Trebilcock, *The Making of the Mosaic*, 2nd ed. (Toronto: University of Toronto Press 2000), 352–79.

3 Ibid., 7.

4 Robert Andras, "Canadian Immigration and Population Study" (Ottawa: Manpower and Immigration/Information Canada 1974).

5 As mentioned in the introduction, the challenge facing Canadian authorities as officers began to select refugees from around the world to meet Canada's labour market needs was how to improve consistency in decision-making. The solution was the point system, under which numerical points were given to applicants based on their age, education, occupation, skill level, intended destination, ability to function in French and/or English, presence of relatives in Canada, and whether the applicant had arranged employment. Out of 100 available points, applicants had to achieve a certain total, usually between 39 and 41, to qualify for an interview. The interviewing officer could award additional points for personal qualities such as adaptability and motivation, and the applicant had to achieve 50 points overall to be accepted. The same criteria were applied to people all around the world, and potential immigrants from traditional sources like the United Kingdom or Europe were now assessed on the same basis as applicants from other regions. The system included a discretionary authority provision for instances where the interviewing officer believed the points did not reflect the applicant's true prospects for success-

ful establishment. This provision was particularly important in the case of refugees.

6   Unlike ordinary immigrants, refugees were provided with a living allowance until they found employment, along with assistance in finding employment, counselling, English or French language training, and, in some cases, skills upgrading.

7   Memorandum to Cabinet, "Selection of Refugees for Resettlement in Canada," 16 September 1970, LAC RG2, vol. 6374, file 116–70.

8   Canada, Immigration Act, 1976, Section 2(1).

9   Ibid., Section 3(g).

10 The processes and procedures to be followed when someone applied to be recognized as a Convention refugee at the border or within Canada were elaborated in detail in sections 45 to 48 of the Immigration Act, 1976.

11 Immigration Act, 1976, Section 6(2).

12 The UNHCR recognizes three durable solutions: *voluntary repatriation* to the country of origin under conditions of safety and dignity; *local integration* in the country of first asylum; and *resettlement* in a third country.

13 Canada, Immigration Regulations, 1978, 2(1).

14 See Raphael Girard, "Designated Classes: A Regulatory Device to Target Humanitarian Resettlement Program," CIHS *Bulletin* 47 (November 2005): 4, http//cihs-shic.ca.

15 Ibid.

16 For an interesting study on how Canada's use of alternative definitions has evolved to the present day and has impacted on international resettlement practice, see Robert C. Batarseh, "Inside/Outside the Circle: From the Indochinese Designated Class to Contemporary Group Processing," *Refuge: Canada's Journal on Refugees* 32, no. 2 (2016), http://refuge.journals. yorku.ca/index.php/refuge/issue/view/2311.

17 Bud Cullen, Minister, Annual Report of the Department of Manpower and Immigration, for Fiscal Year 1975–1976, Ministry of Supply and Services Canada, 1977, MPI - 1976, 21, CIHS Collection. The initial refugee movement to Canada during 1975–76 consisted overwhelmingly of Vietnamese nationals.

18 Memorandum, Acting Director, Refugee Policy, to W. Black, Director Legal Services, "Regulations under 6(2) and 115 1(d)

and (e) of the *Act* – Small Boat Escapees," 14 March 1978, LAC RG76, vol. 1838, file 8700-15.

19 Memorandum to the Minister, "Indochinese Refugee Program," 26 April 1978, LAC RG76, vol. 1835, file 8700-1.

20 Indochinese Designated Class Regulations, established by PC 1978–3661. For the text of the regulation, see http//cihs-shic. ca/indochina.

21 For a description of these later developments in the late 1980s (beyond the scope of this book), see W. Courtland Robinson, *Terms of Refuge: The Indochinese Exodus and the International Response* (London and New York: Zed Books 1998).

22 Interview with Michael Molloy, 20 February 2014; Roger St Vincent, "Seven Crested Cranes," *CIHS Bulletin* 65 (August 2012): 1.

23 Section 115(1)(k.1).

24 Ibid.

25 Interview with Michael Molloy, 20 February 2014.

26 Interview with Raphael Girard, 15 February 2014.

27 W.K. Bell, Director General, Recruitment and Selection Branch to Director Generals and Senior Directors of the Immigration and Demographic Policy Group, "The Sponsorship of Refugees and Humanitarian Cases," 19 August 1977, LAC RG76, vol. 1831, file 8630-1, part 1.

28 Memorandum to the Minister, "Soviet Jews in Italy," 22 August 1977, LAC RG76, vol. 1831, file 8630-1, part 1.

29 Shauna Labman, "Private Sponsorship: Complementary Protection or Conflicting Interest," *Refuge: Canada's Journal on Refugees* 32, no.2 (2016): 68, http://refuge.journals.yorku.ca/ index.php/refuge/issue/view/2311; *Refuge – Special Issue on the Indochinese Refugee Program*, 2016, 3.

30 Memorandum to the Minister, "Soviet Jews in Italy," 22 August 1977, LAC RG76, vol. 1831, file 8630-1, part 1.

31 Ibid.

32 A prophetic observation. The original process, based on characteristics of the Ongoing Refugee Program where most of the Eastern Europeans refugees were safe and well cared for in camps in Austria and Italy, envisioned a complex and leisurely exchange of communications between sponsors, their local

Canada Immigration Centre, and the visa office abroad, with a half dozen exchanges in the course of the process. As predicted, the system had to be ruthlessly streamlined to deliver the Indochinese special movement in 1979–80.

33 Memorandum to the Minister, "Soviet Jews in Italy" (see also note 29).

34 Memorandum to the Minister, "The Sponsorship of Refugees and Humanitarian Cases," 25 January 1978, FS5200-5R, LAC RG76, vol. 1831, file 8630-1, part 1. In fact B'nai Brith was unable to deliver, but JIAS stepped in and fulfilled the agreement.

35 Ibid. and attached undated paper, "The Sponsorship Provision for Refugee and Humanitarian Cases."

36 Memorandum, R.M. Tait to Deputy Minister J.L. Manion, "The Refugee Sponsorship System – Reaction of Potential Sponsors," 28 April 1978, LAC RG76, vol. 1831, file 8630-1, part 1.

37 Ibid.

38 Memorandum, J.C. Best, Executive Director, Immigration and Demographic Policy, to Regional Directors of Immigration, "Refugee Sponsorship System," 22 August 1978, LAC RG76, vol. 1831, file 8630-1, part 1.

39 Memorandum to the Minister, "Refugee Sponsorship," 17 November 1978, FS5200-11, LAC RG76, vol. 1831, file 8630-1, part 1.

40 See http//cihs-shic.ca/indochina for text of paper.

41 Circular letter to Edmonton pastors from Alice Colak, Edmonton Interfaith Immigration Committee, 26 October 1978, CIHS Collection.

42 Ibid.

43 Interview with Michael Molloy, 20 February 2014: "The meeting began with a lay member of the bishops' organization setting out arguments as to why it was the responsibility of the government to pay for refugee resettlement. As he listened, Mr. Best became more and more agitated. He suddenly slammed the table and announced to his startled guests, 'I'm paying for lunch, I'll speak first.' His passionate presentation on the merits of the sponsorship program and its humanitarian potential won the bishops over. About six weeks later the Catholic

Church's endorsement of the refugee sponsorship program was communicated to every parish in Canada in the form of an editorial in the monthly missalette."

44 Memorandum to the Minister, "Refugee Sponsorship Program," 17 November 1978, LAC RG76, vol. 1831, file 8630-1, part 1.

45 For text of the sponsorship brochure, see http//cihs-shic.ca/indochina.

46 Some early documents show the abbreviation as MCCC. Consultations with Mennonite officials confirm that MCC is the correct abbreviation.

47 Undated note from Gordon Barnett to Michael Molloy, CIHS Collection.

48 William Janzen, "The 1979 MCC Canada Master Agreement for the Sponsorship of Refugees in Historical Perspective," *Journal of Mennonite Studies* 24 (2006): 211–22.

49 Ibid.

50 Memorandum, Kirk Bell, Director General, Recruitment and Selection Branch to J.C. Best, Executive Director, "Refugee Sponsorship," 15 February 1979, file 5780-9; and attached six-page instruction, "Refugee Sponsorship Program," 15 February 1979, LAC RG76, vol. 1831, file 8630-1, part 2.

51 An "organigram" mapping the original sponsorship process can be found at http//cihs-shic.ca/indochina.

52 Refugee Sponsorship Agreements, 5 March 1970 to 3 March 1980. Other early signers of master agreements included Canadian Lutheran World Relief, the Catholic Archdiocese of Ottawa, the Anglican Diocese of Ottawa, World Vision Canada, the Catholic Diocese of Pembroke and of Montreal, the United Church of Canada, the Baptist Convention of Ontario, the Ukrainian Canadian Committee, and the Catholic Archdiocese of Toronto, Hamilton, and London, and the Catholic Bishop of Saskatchewan. CIHS Collection, Briefing Book, Indochinese Refugee Task Force, July 1979.

53 E-mail, Zal Kakaria to Michael Molloy, "Re: Chapter 4," 10 August 2015.

54 It is worrisome that changes to the sponsorship system imposed by the Harper government may have eroded some of the value-related underpinnings of the sponsorship program, in-

cluding keeping the government and private streams distinct, counting them separately, and reducing the ability of sponsors to reach out to the refugees of their choice.

55 Barbara Treviranus and Michael Casasola, "Canada's Private Sponsorship of Refugees Program: A Practitioner's Perspective of Its Past and Future," *Journal of International Migration and Integration* 4 (2003).

CHAPTER FIVE

1 Memorandum to the Minister, "Vietnamese Small Boat Escapees," 10 November 1977, LAC RG76, vol. 1838, file 8700-15, Refugees and Displaced Persons, Special Movements, Indochinese. Well into 1977, refugees without family sponsors were admitted under spaces left over from the 1975 Cabinet decision to admit three thousand unsponsored refugees. The term "metered approach" was coined in an effort to define a new commitment whereby the refugees would arrive in a predictable, steady monthly steam. It was hoped this would be more manageable for both the visa officers in Southeast Asia and those providing settlement services in Canada. In practice, the metered approach did not work particularly well for a variety of reasons, including initial instructions that were apparently unclear, and, frankly, it was too small to be efficiently delivered by the visa offices. It was superseded in 1979 by the first annual refugee plan.

2 Memorandum to the Minister, "Indochinese Refugees," 13 January 1978, ibid.

3 The city of Windsor, under the leadership of Mayor Bert Weeks, established a committee to resettle boat people in the summer of 1977, two years before Project 4000 or Operation Lifeline. See Giovanna Roma, "The Indochinese Refugee Movement: An Exploratory Case Study of the Windsor Experience in Refuge," *Canada's Journal on Refugees* 32, no. 2 (2016), http://refuge.journals.yorku.ca/index.php/refuge/issue/view/2311.

4 Memorandum to the Minister, "Vietnamese Small Boat Escapees," 10 November 1977, LAC RG76, vol. 1838, file 8700-15, Refugees and Displaced Persons, Special Movements, Indochinese.

5 R.M. Tait, memorandum to Regional Directors General, "The Resettlement of Refugees and Displaced Persons," 17 January 1978, LAC RG76, vol. 1838, file 8700-15, part 1, Refugees and Displaced Persons.

6 Ibid.

7 Ibid.

8 Ibid.

9 Minister of Employment and Immigration, Press Release 78-7, 26 January 1978, LAC RG76, vol. 1838, file 8700-15, Refugees and Displaced Persons, Special Movements.

10 Letter, W.K. Bell to Geoffrey Pearson, "Indochinese Refugees," 2 February 1978, LAC RG76, vol. 1838, file 8700-15, Refugees and Displaced Persons, Special Movements.

11 This involved some looking ahead, as consultations with Canadian churches and others on the sponsorship program had not yet begun, and instructions to the regions on evaluating sponsoring groups were only dispatched a week later. Telex, W.K. Bell to Regional Directors General, "Refugee/Humanitarian Class Sponsorship System," 9 February 1978, LAC RG76, vol. 1839, file 8703-1, part 1

12 Ibid.

13 Letter, Lionel Rosenblatt, US Department of State, to Richard M. Tait, 10 February 1978, LAC RG76, vol. 1835, 8700-1.

14 Memorandum, W.K. Bell to J.B. Bissett, "Small Boat Escape Program," 3 April 1978, LAC RG76, vol. 1838, file 8700-15, Refugees and Displaced Persons, Special Movements.

15 Memorandum to the Minister, "Small Boat Escapee (SBE) Program," 7 June 1978, LAC RG76, vol. 1838, file 8700-15, Refugees and Displaced Persons, Special Movements.

16 Memorandum to the Minister, "Press Release – Boat Refugees," 2 June 1978, LAC RG76, vol. 1838, file 8700-15, Refugees and Displaced Persons, Special Movements.

17 Memorandum to the Minister, "Indochinese Refugee Program," 26 April 1978, LAC RG76, vol. 1838, file 8700-15, part 1, Refugees and Displaced Persons, Special Movements.

18 Ibid.

19 Ibid.

20 Privy Council Office, Memorandum to Cabinet, "Democratic Kampuchea (Cambodia) Human Rights and Refugees," 8 June 1978, PCO 305-78MC, CIHS Collection.

21 Ibid.

22 Interestingly, the memorandum focused on Cambodians as a priority but couched the new program in terms of all Indochinese refugees in Thailand, including Lao and Vietnamese, though in practice the Vietnamese came under the SBE program for fifty families a month divided among E&I Hong Kong, Singapore, Manila and, eventually, Bangkok.

23 "Successful establishment" would become a key factor in refugee selection from Thailand during the early months of the program.

24 The memorandum did not mention that a significant number of Vietnamese were in fact ethnic Chinese.

25 Privy Council Office, Memorandum to Cabinet, "Democratic Kampuchea (Cambodia) Human Rights and Refugees," 8 June 1978, PCO 305-78MC, CIHS Collection.

26 Ibid.

27 Ibid.

28 Privy Council Office, Report to Cabinet, 15 June 1978, "Democratic Kampuchea (Cambodia): Human Rights and Refugees," PCO 305-78CR (R), CIHS Collection.

29 Privy Council Office, Report to Cabinet, "Democratic Kampuchea (Cambodia) Human Rights and Refugees," 10 July 1978, PCO 305-78CR (TB), CIHS Collection.

30 Privy Council Office, Record of Cabinet Decision, 13 July 1978, "Democratic Privy Council Office, Kampuchea (Cambodia) Human Rights and Refugees," PCO 305-78RD, CIHS Collection.

31 Treasury Board, Record of Committee Decision, 19 July 1978, confirmed by Cabinet 20 July 1978. "Democratic Kampuchea (Cambodia) Human Rights and Refugees," PCO 305-78RD (C), CIHS Collection.

32 Letter, Cullen to Hartling, 26 July 1978, LAC RG76, file 8700-1.

33 Memorandum to the Minister, "Establishment of CEIC Facilities in Bangkok, Thailand, and the Thailand Overland Refugee Program," 10 November 1978, FS5780-1-2/629, LAC RG76, vol. 1838, file 8700-15, part 2.

34 Telex, W.K. Bell to Regional Directors General, "Indochinese Refugee Movement," August 1978, LAC RG76, file 8700-1.

35 Telex, "Small Boat Escapee – Procedures," EANDI OTT.IFAP. IFAP, FS5850-3-5-641, LAC RG76, vol. 1838, file 8700-15,

Refugees and Displaced Persons, Special Movements, Small
Boat Escapees.

36 The text of "The Small Boat Escapee Program" can be found
at http://cihs-shic.ca/Indochinese.

37 Memorandum and attached paper, Ivan Timonin, Acting Director, Recruitment and Selection to J.C. Best, Executive Director,
"Small Boat Escapee Program," 21 August 1978, LAC RG76,
vol. 1838, file 8700-15, Refugees and Displaced Persons, Special Movements, Small Boat Escapees.

38 Memorandum and attached paper, W.K. Bell to Regional Directors General, "Small-Boat Escapee Program," 13 September
1978, ibid.

39 Memorandum, J.B. Bissett to J.S. Cross, 28 August 1978,
"Small Boat Escapee Program (SBE)," FS5850-3-5-641, LAC
RG76, vol. 1838, file 8700-15, Refugees and Displaced Per-
sons, Special Movements, Small Boat Escapees.

40 Memorandum, J.S. Cross to J.B. Bissett, "Small Boat Escapees
(SBE)," 6 September 1978, FS5850-3-641, LAC RG76, vol.
1838, file 8700-15, Refugees and Displaced Persons, Special
Movements, Small Boat Escapees.

41 Letter, Allan Gottlieb to J.L. Manion, 19 July 1978, LAC RG76,
vol. 1815, file 8620-8, Refugees and Displaced Persons, General, Annual Refugee Plan.

42 Memorandum and attached paper, "Towards an Integrated
Canadian Refugee Policy," 14 September 1978, FS5780-1,
LAC RG76, file 8620, Annual Refugee Plan.

43 Memorandum, J.C. Best to J.L. Manion, 30 October 1978,
LAC RG76, vol. 1815, file 8620-8, Refugees and Displaced
Persons, Annual Refugee Plan.

44 A fascinating account of the suffering of the refugees on the
Southern Cross may be found in Carina Hoang, *Boat People:
Personal Stories from the Vietnamese Exodus, 1975–1996*
(New York: Beaufort Books 2013).

45 Singapore telex, "*Southern Cross*," UCIM 5082, 27 September
1978, SPORE to HKONG, MANIL, and EANDI OTT/ IFAP, LAC
RG76, vol. 1838, file 8700-15, Refugees and Displaced Persons, Special Movements, Small Boat Escapees.

46 Telex, "*Southern Cross* SBES," UCIM 191, 13 October 1978,
SPORE to EANDIOTT IFAP, LAC RG76, vol. 1838, file 8700-15,

Refugees and Displaced Persons, Special Movements, Small Boat Escapees.

47 Circular Memorandum, "Small Boat Escapees – Procedures" 25 October 1978, FS 5850-3-5-641, LAC RG76, vol. 1838, file 8700-15, Refugees and Displaced Persons, Special Movements, Small Boat Escapees.

48 Memorandum, "Circular Memorandum on Designated Classes," 19 December 1978 (and attached draft CM dated 19/12/78), C.A. Thorlakson, LAC RG76, vol. 1839, file 8005-2-1, Act and Legislation Designated Class Regulations, Indochinese.

49 The account has been lightly edited, and some material not available to Marcus has been added.

50 Sara E. Davies, *Legitimising Rejection: International Refugee Law in Southeast Asia* (Leiden: Martinus Nijhoff 2008).

51 Roland-Pierre Paringaux, "Entassés dans un petit cargo, 2,500 fugitifs vietnamiens dans une situation dramatique," *Le Devoir*, 16 November 1978. Original reads: "on marche littéralement sur les gens, hommes, femmes, enfants et vieillards, étendus ou accroupis, visiblement épuisés et angoissés, mais demeurant, sans exception, d'une grande dignité."

52 Letters to the Editor, "Welcome More Viet Refugees, Reader Urges," *Toronto Star*, 11 December 1978.

53 Editorial, "Asian Refugees Must Be Helped," *Toronto Star*, 15 November 1978.

54 "Refugee Freighter Ordered to Leave," *Montreal Gazette*, 15 November 1978.

55 "Ottawa May Allow Some in Canada," ibid.

56 "Malaysia Ignores Appeals for Refugee Ship," *Montreal Gazette*, 16 November 1978.

57 Valerie Knowles, *Strangers at Our Gates: Canadian Immigration and Immigration Policy, 1540–2006* (Toronto: Dundurn Press 2007).

58 Teletype, Canadian Press, "Vietnamese with Vars [*sic*] Refugees," 16 November 1978.

59 Rene Pappone, "The *Hai Hong*: Profit, Tears and Joy" (Ottawa: Employment and Immigration Canada 1982).

60 Ibid.

61 Ibid.

62 Ibid.

63 Ibid.

64 Letter from Mayor Weeks to Bud Cullen, 14 November 1978, CIHS Collection. The *Windsor Star* reported on 10 January 1979 that a family from the *Hai Hong* had arrived in Windsor ("Vietnamese Get a Neighborly Welcome").

65 "Canada First to Offer Haven," *Toronto Sun*, 11 November 1978; "Selection of 'Lucky 600' Refugees to Begin Today," *Ottawa Journal*, 20 November 1978.

66 "Alberta's Refugee Policy Called Racist," *Ottawa Journal*, 4 December 1978.

67 Gordon Jaremko, "Hospitality Took Back Seat to Cash," *Charlottetown Guardian*, 5 December 1978.

68 "Welcome More Viet Refugees, Reader Urges," *Toronto Star*, 11 December 1978.

69 Pappone, "The *Hai Hong*."

70 Nicole Chénier-Cullen, *I Found My Thrill on Parliament Hill* (Bloomington, IL: Universe Inc. 2009).

71 W. Courtland Robinson, *Terms of Refuge: The Indochinese Exodus and the International Response* (London and New York: Zed Books 1998).

72 Privy Council Office, PCO 630-78RD, CIHS Collection; T.R.J. Moulton, "Indochinese Refugee Program 1979," 21 December 1978, CIHS Collection.

73 Ibid.

74 Editorial, "At Our Own Door," *Toronto Globe and Mail*, 6 December 1978.

CHAPTER SIX

1 Stephen J. Morris, *Why Vietnam Invaded Cambodia: Political Culture and Causes of War* (Chicago: Stanford University Press 1999), 110–11.

2 Robert Scalapino, "The Political Influence of the Soviet Union in Asia," in *Soviet Policy in East Asia* (New Haven: Yale University Press 1984), 71.

3 UN High Commissioner for Refugees, *Fifty Years of Humanitarian Action* (Oxford: Oxford University Press 2000), 82–3.

4 Robinson. *Terms of Refuge*, 41; Theresa C. Carino, "Vietnam's Chinese Minority and the Politics of Sino-Soviet Relations,"

Praxis 5, no. 1 (1980); Gil Loescher, *The* UNHCR *and World Politics: A Perilous Path* (Oxford: Oxford University Press 2001), 205.

5   Loescher, UNHCR, 204.

6   Ibid.

7   http://www.historynet.com/joe-devlin-the-boat-peoples-priest.htm, 12 June 2006. Originally published by *Vietnam Magazine*, April 1999.

8   Henry Kamm, "Malaysia Appeals to Carter on Asylum for Vietnam Boat Refugees," *New York Times*, 28 November 1978.

9   Loescher, UNHCR, 206.

10 Ibid., 3.

11 Jack Manion, Memorandum to the Minister, "UNHCR Consultations on Indochina Refugees," 13 December 1978, LAC RG76, vol. 1836, file 8700-12-1.

12 Privy Council Office, Memorandum to Cabinet, "Indochinese Refugee Program 1979," 18 December 1978, PCO 630-78MC(R3), CIHS Collection.

13 "Indochinese Designated Class Regulations," LAC RG76, vol. 1836, file 8005-2-1.

14 Jack Manion, Memorandum to the Minister, "Establishment of CEIC Facilities in Bangkok, Thailand and the 'Thailand Overland Refugee Program,'" 10 November 1978, LAC RG76, vol. 1839, file 8700-15, part 2.

15 Privy Council Office, Memorandum to Cabinet, "Annual Plan for Refugee Resettlement," 15 December 1978, PCO 613-78 (MC), CIHS Collection.

16 Jack Manion, Memorandum to the Minister, "Refugee Submissions to Cabinet: Indochina Plan," 20 December 1978, LAC RG76, vol. 1830, file 8700-1, part 1.

17 Ibid.

18 Privy Council Office, Revised Record of Cabinet Decision, "Annual Plan for Refugee Resettlement," 15 December 1978, serial no. 613-78RD (R), CIHS Collection.

19 Michael Molloy, personal recollections of developments in 1978–79, April 2015.

20 Ernest Allen to Director, Refugee Policy, 19 December 1978, LAC RG76, vol. 1839, file 8700-1, part 1. Allen's message was

sent after the opening of the Bangkok visa office with two officers, demonstrating that Immigration Headquarters did not consider the increased staff in Bangkok sufficient.

21 Hamilton provided a detailed analysis of all possible contingencies as seen from the viewpoint of a Southeast Asian field office; 19 December 1978, LAC RG76, vol. 1839, file 8700-1, part 1.

22 Telex from director, Asia Pacific Bureau to EANDI SINGAPORE, HONG KONG, MANILA, BANGKOK, 20 February 1979, CIC File 5850-3-7/641. Note that the processing focus was on Singapore, with a target of 320 persons per month. Bangkok received a monthly target of eighty persons, and Manila and Hong Kong received monthly targets of only ten persons each.

23 Indochinese Designated Class Regulations, LAC RG76, vol. 1836, file 8005-2-1.

24 Minister of Employment and Immigration, press release, 22 December 1978, LAC RG76, vol. 1839, file 8700-1, part 1.

25 William Janzen, "The 1979 Canada Master Agreement for the Sponsorship of Refugees in Historical Perspective," *Journal of Mennonite Studies* 24 (2006): 211.

26 Ibid. Eventually, over thirty master agreements were signed.

27 C&I brochure, "Citizenship and Immigration Canada Private Sponsorship of Refugees Program," C&I 2025-11/14 Ci4-70/2014E-PDF ISBN 978-1-100-23429-8 2.5, 7.

28 Employment and Immigration Canada, *The Indochinese Refugees: The Canadian Response, 1979 and 1980* (Ottawa: Department of Supply and Services 1982).

29 Memorandum from J.C. Best to J.L. Manion, "Refugee Program: Ministerial Initiatives," 1 February 1979, LAC RG76, vol. 1811, file 8620-1.

31 Telex from Director Asia and Pacific Bureau to EANDI SINGAPORE, HONG KONG, MANILA, BANGKOK, "Indochinese Refugee Program 1979," 20 February 1979, LAC RG76, vol. 1835, file 8700-0.

31 Ibid.

32 Jack Manion, Memorandum to the Minister, "Indochina Refugee Situation," 21 December 1978, LAC RG76, vol. 1836, file 8700-12-1.

33 Privy Council Office, Memorandum to Cabinet, "Indochinese Refugee Program – 1979," 18 December 1978, PCO 630-78MC (R) 3.

34 Jack Manion, Memorandum to the Minister, "Immigration from the Socialist Republic of Vietnam (SRVN)," 17 January 1979, LAC RG76, vol. 1836, file 8700-12-1; Minister's Speeches, Briefing Notes, "Family Reunification Program – Vietnam," n.d. (probably June 1979), LAC RG76, vol. 1837, file 8700-12-2.

35 James P. Sterba, "Refugees Face Guns at Pier in Malaysia," *New York Times*, 25 March 1979.

36 Henry Kamm, "Vietnamese Reported to Kill 85 Grounded Boat People," *New York Times*, 23 July 1979.

37 Loescher, *UNHCR*, 206.

38 Jack Manion, Memorandum to the Minister, "UNHCR Consultations on Indochina Refugees, 13 December 1978, LAC RG76, vol. 1836, file 8700-12-1; Loescher, *UNHCR*, 206.

39 Robinson, *Terms of Refuge*, 44–50.

40 Loescher, *UNHCR*, 206.

41 Ibid., 207.

42 Ibid.

43 Sterba, "Refugees Face Guns."

44 KLMPR XJGR0264 TO EXTOTT GPL, "Mersing Incident," 16 April 1979, LAC RG76, vol. 1839, file 8700-15, part 2.

45 A. Missbach, "Waiting on the Islands of 'Stuckedness': Managing Asylum Seekers in Island Detention Camps in Indonesia from the Late 1970s to the Early 2000s," *Austrian Journal of South-East Asian Studies* 6, no. 2 (2013): 281–306.

46 EXTOTT UNS0156 TO GENEVA, "Indochina Refugees: USA Demarche: UNHCR Role," 11 January 1979, LAC RG76, vol. 1839, file 8700-15, part 2; HKONG XBIM2620 TO EXTOTT UNS, "Viet Refugee Sitrep," 17 April 1979, LAC RG76, vol. 1839, file 8700-15, part 2.

47 UN High Commissioner for Refugees, *Fifty Years*, 84.

48 V.A. Sims to Charles Rogers, "Report – Southeast Asia Refugee Movement. Indochinese Refugee Situation," 16 May 1979, LAC RG76, vol. 1836, file 8700-12-1. The idea of "orderly departures" from Vietnam had been discussed with the Vietnamese since at least December 1978. Canada had been seeking a family

reunification program with Vietnam, modelled on a similar arrangement with China. There were UNHCR visits to Hanoi,
with attempts to arrange family unification by
several countries, including the United States, Canada, and
France. But progress was very slow, as the Vietnamese appeared to be dragging their feet. See Missbach, "Waiting," 288.

49 For the purposes of this book, the increase of refugee intake
by Canada is stated in per capita terms, taking into account
Canada's population. In absolute terms, the increase of US
refugee intake in 1979–80 was considerably higher.

50 Documentation for this book from LAC provided a large number of memoranda from Manion to the minister, of which only
a small number have been cited.

51 Ron Atkey, paper presented at the Conference on the Indochinese Refugee Movement and the Private Sponsorship Program,
1975–80, York University, Toronto, Ontario, 21–23 November
2013.

52 A.E Gotlieb, Memorandum to the Minister (SSEA), "The Indochinese Refugee Situation," 6 June 1979, LAC RG76, vol.
1836, file 8700-12-1.

53 "Indochinese Refugee Situation," CONFIDENTIAL, Report of
Indochina Developments in First Half of 1979 (undated but
from context of report, between 1 July and 10 July 1979), LAC
RG76, vol. 1836, file 8700-12-1.

54 CANBRA YAGR1422 to EXTOTT PS, "Viet[nam]: Refugees," 9
May 1979, LAC RG76, vol. 1835, file 8700-1, part 1.

55 Privy Council Office, Cabinet Document, Record of Committee
Decision, Meeting of 18 June 1979, "Indochinese Refugees,"
PCO 336-79RD (C), CIHS Collection.

56 *Montreal Gazette*, 22 June 1979.

57 "It's Up to Us," *Toronto Globe and Mail*, 28 June 1979.

58 Joint communiqué issued at the Twelfth ASEAN Ministerial
Meeting in Bali, Indonesia, 29–30 June 1979, as quoted in UN
High Commissioner for Refugees, *Fifty Years*, 83; see also
http://asean.org/?static_post=joint-communique-of-the-twelfth-
asean-ministerial-meeting-bali-28-30-june-1979.

59 Howard Adelman, *Canada and the Indochinese Refugees*
(Regina: L.A. Weigl Educational Associates 1982), 86.

60 Ibid.

61 This was three weeks before the government announced the target of 50,000. An immigration official had told Dewar that Canada was accepting 8,000 refugees and that 4,000 had arrived. The mayor decided to commit Ottawa to accepting the remaining 4,000; hence, Project 4,000.

62 Brian Buckley, *How Ottawa Welcomed the Vietnamese, Cambodian and Laotian Refugees* (Renfrew, ON: General Store Publishing 2008), 37.

63 James Powell, "Project 4000, 27 June 1979," https://todayinot tawashistory.wordpress.com/?s=Project+4000, 3 October 2014; "No Man Is an Island," *Montreal Star*, undated, CIHS Collection.

64 G7 Summit, Tokyo, "Special Statement of the Summit on Indochinese Refugees," 28–29 June 1979, LAC RG76, vol. 1836, file 8700-12-1.

65 G7 Summit, Tokyo, EXTAFF Report, 28 June 28 1979, LAC RG76, vol. 1836, file 8700-12-1.

66 UN High Commissioner for Refugees, *Fifty Years*, 84.

67 David Elder, "Narrative Summary of Flora MacDonald's Decision to Accept 50,000 Indochinese Refugees in Canada," 2015, CIHS Collection.

68 Ibid. The Mennonite Central Committee, among others, had contacted MacDonald, arguing for a large increase in Canada's commitment.

69 Ibid.

70 Atkey, paper presented at the Conference on the Indochinese Refugee Movement and the Private Sponsorship Program, 1975–80, York University, 21–23 November 2013.

71 It should be noted that developments in June and July took place extremely rapidly. In early July, briefing notes to civil servants talked of a commitment of 20,000 Indochinese refugees, equally divided between government sponsored and privately sponsored refugees in accordance with a one-to-one matching formula. Within a few days of the mention of the 20,000 number, the number was increased to a commitment of 50,000 (see notes 74 and 76). See "Briefing Book," Indochinese Refugee Task Force, July 1979, CIHS Collection.

72 Memorandum to Prime Minister, "Indochina Refugees," 9 July 1979, LAC RG76, vol. 1836, file 8700-1, part 1.

73 Elder, "Narrative Summary."

74 "Le Canada pourrait accueillir jusqu'à 55,000 réfugiés," *La Presse*, 10 July 1979. Original reads: "Le Canada pourrait accueillir jusqu'à 55,000 réfugiés."

75 Elder, "Narrative Summary."

76 Privy Council Office. Memorandum to Cabinet, "Indochina Refugees," 16 July 1979, PCO 380-79MC (E), CIHS Collection.

77 Cabinet first agreed to 60,000 but lowered the target to 50,000 when it was pointed out that the Clark government's election platform called for a reduction of the civil service by 60,000. It was felt by some that the opposition would have a field day conflating the two 60,000s (Atkey-Molloy conversation, June 2016).

78 Secretary of State for External Affairs, "Notes for a Speech by the Secretary of State for External Affairs," Flora MacDonald, the United Nations Conference on Refugees, Geneva, July 20, 1979." http://dfait-aeci.canadiana.ca/view/ooe.sas_1979 0720ESt/1?r=0&s=1.The formal objectives of the Canadian delegation to Geneva were "to encourage larger contributions to meet the immediate crisis ... to ensure the maintenance of an open-door policy in the first asylum countries ... to persuade the Vietnamese ... to cooperate more fully in arranging orderly departures [from Vietnam]." Briefing Book, Indochinese Refugee Task Force, July 1979, CIHS Collection.

79 Briefing Book, "Memorandum to All Staff, Indochinese Refugee Task Force," 30 July 1979, CIHS Collection.

80 UN High Commissioner for Refugees, *Fifty Years*, 84.

CHAPTER SEVEN

 1 Other significant movements included Czechoslovakian refugees (11,943), Ugandan Asians (7,069), and the South American/Chilean movement (7,016).

 2 The senior refugee coordinator Michael Molloy recalled in an interview on 20 February 2014, "It did not take us long to recognize that we could not micromanage the selection and processing operations in Southeast Asia – conditions from country to country were just too different and were subject to continuous change. We had to trust the managers and their teams to understand the objectives and figure out how to achieve them."

3 *Panorama* 2, no. 6 (August 1979).

4 An organizational chart of the Refugee Task Force can be found at http://cihs-shic.ca/indochina.

5 Molloy, "Emergency Innovations and Lasting Lessons: The *1976 Immigration Act* and the Launching of the Indochinese Refugee Movement of 1979–80," prepared for but not presented to the Metropolis Conference 2012, CIHS Collection; and "Processing Streamlined," *Panorama* 2, no. 6 (August 1979).

6 The team was headed by Herb Uren, a senior project officer from CEIC's Management Consultant Services Directorate and included Campbell. Much of the technical design fell to Elizabeth (Liz) Boyce, a former immigration foreign service officer in charge of form design, among many other things, at headquarters. The 1314 form was designed over a weekend and printed on a rush basis. Boyce herself delivered the first forms to the visa offices in Southeast Asia.

7 A sample of the IMM1314 can be found at http://cihs-shic.ca/Indochinese.

8 CEIC needed to make transportation arrangements at extremely short notice in summer 1979 for enormously increased refugee numbers. A shortage of available aircraft was aggravated by the grounding of all DC-10s for safety inspections during this period. Nevertheless, the government demanded a rapid demonstration from the public service of the seriousness of Canada's commitment.

9 *Newsletter: Indochinese Refugees*, 31 July 1979, 8. The baby girl was born to a nineteen-year-old widowed refugee, Nguyen Kiet Anh.

10 The decision to accept 50,000 refugees pushed the transportation requirement to a whole new level. Early talk of chartering a large passenger ship came to nothing (happily).

11 Ernest Allen, "Description of Headquarters Operations in 1979–80," unpublished narrative, 2014, CIHS Collection.

12 *Panorama* (October 1979).

13 Susan McKale, "The Refugee Matching Centre: Deciding Who Goes Where," *Panorama* (undated); Sponsorship Matching Centre," narrative contribution to the CIHS Indochina Project, CIHS Collection.

14 See Richard Martin's description of this problem in chapter 12. Martin asserts that at times 90 per cent of the cases interviewed by the Singapore team were lost before UNHCR established the "blue card" control system in February 1978.

15 Molloy, "The Indochinese Refugee Program – Introducing a New Act and Computers to Refugee Processing," undated, CIHS Collection.

16 See http://cihs-shic.ca/Indochinese for Thomson's explanation of how he found inspiration in the Berlin Airlift.

17 Ibid.

18 May 1980 seems to have been the most demanding period, with fourteen flights – two from Kuala Lumpur, two from Singapore, two from Hong Kong, and a whopping eight from Bangkok.

19 An example of the first page of a NAT can be found on the CIHS website at http//cihs-shic.ca/indochina. Names and file numbers have been altered for privacy reasons.

20 "A Staging Operation Planning Guide," 20 February 1979, LAC RG76, vol. 1811, file 8620-1.

21 Actual percentages by province: BC, 12.3; AB, 12.9; SK, 5.5; MB, 6.7; ON, 37.1; QC, 21.8; NB, 1.3; NS, 1.7; PE, .2; NL, .5.

22 J.L. Manion, memorandum to the Minister, "Information Strategy – Indochinese Refugees," 25 July 1979, LAC RG76, vol. 1836, file 5780-1-726.

23 Ibid., plus an attached paper entitled, "Information Strategy Indochinese Refugee Movement," 2; *Newsletter: Indochinese Refugees*, 16 July 1979, 7–1.

24 Designed as an ephemeral information source, the newsletters are a rich source of historical information. Thanks to the diligence of Rene Pappone, the Canadian Immigration Historical Society has an almost complete set. A comprehensive summary, prepared by Martha Nixon, of the contents of the twenty-one newsletters can be found at http://cihs-shic.ca/Indochinese.

25 *Newsletter: Indochinese Refugees* 1, no. 6 (22 August 1979).

CHAPTER EIGHT

1 Telex instruction from IFAP to E&I Hong Kong, "Indochinese Refugee Program 1979," 7 June 1979, LAC RG76, vol. 1835, file 8700-0, Refugees and Displaced Persons, Special Movements, Indochinese, Policy and Procedures.

2 M.A.F. Lafontaine, memorandum to the Minister, "Indochinese Refugee Program Financial Implications," 5 September 1979, LAC RG76, vol. 1836, file 8700-12-1.

3 Ibid.

4 Ibid., attachment.

5 Where exactly the money was found is unclear from the files examined, but the Employment side of the commission often had large sums allocated for manpower training programs that lapsed for various reasons.

6 M.A.J. Lafontaine, memorandum to the Minister, "Indochinese Refugee Program," 13 September 1979, LAC RG76, vol. 1836, file 8700-12-1.

7 In fact, 4,989 would arrive in October and 5,385 in November.

8 Agreement between the federal government and Quebec under which Quebec became responsible for selection and integration of economic migrants destined to Quebec and, by extension, for refugees. See Ninette Kelly and Michael Trebilcock, *The Making of the Mosaic*, 2nd ed. (Toronto: University of Toronto Press 2010), 387. This agreement was replaced in 1991 by the Canada-Quebec Accord.

9 Ibid.

10 Ibid.

11 Actual arrivals flowing from this decision: December 1979, 2,832 (the system stood down for two weeks over Christmas); early 1980, January, 4,006; February, 6,133; March, 1,932; April, 3,390; May, 4,520.

12 Employment and Immigration Canada, *The Indochinese Refugees: The Canadian Response, 1979 and 1980* (Ottawa: Department of Supply and Services 1982), 28.

13 Singapore telex 1871, "UNHCR Delays," 7 September 1979, LAC RG76, vol. 1839, file 8700-1, part 1.

14 Briefing note, "Indochinese Refugees – Sources of Intake," LAC RG76, vol. 1837, file 8700-12-7, part 1, Refugees and Displaced Persons – Special Movements, Indochinese Reports and Statistics, Ministerial Speeches.

15 E&I Singapore oversaw thirty-one flights from KL in 1979 and twenty-five in 1980. Through Singapore it launched seven flights in 1979 and twenty-one in 1980 (EIC *Indochinese Refugees*).

16 Ibid.
17 "Indochinese Refugee Statistics, 1 January – October 7, 1979," LAC RG76, vol. 1837, file 8620-1, part 2, Refugees and Displaced Persons, General.
18 EIC, *Indochinese Refugees*, 27.
19 "Indochinese Statistics, Sponsorship Program," 5 October 1979, LAC RG76, vol. 1837, file 8700-12-7, part 1, Refugees and Displaced Persons – Special Movements, Indochinese Reports and Statistics, Ministers Speeches, Indochinese Refugees – Sources of Intake.
20 Ernest Allen, memo to file, "Record of Telephone Conversation with Al Lukie/Singapore – Re. Operations in Indonesia and Malaysia," 12 October 1979, LAC RG76, vol. 1835, file 8700-1, part 1, Refugee and Displaced Persons, Special Movement, Indochinese, General.
21 Newsletter, *Indochinese Refugees*, 7–2, 24 July 1979, appendix A, 2, CIHS Collection.
22 Telex BNGKK ZHIM4604 to IFAP, File 47-1 "Transportation of Refugees," 15 October 1979, CIHS Collection.
23 Bangkok telex, "Lumpini Transit Camp – Diphtheria," 20 October 1979, CIHS Collection.
24 Memorandum to the Minister, "Meeting with Robert L. Wennman, MP, Regarding a Temporary Wardship Program in BC," 5 October 1979, LAC RG76, vol. 1836, file 8700-12-1.
25 Howard Adelman, "Issue of 'Refuge' on Unaccompanied Minors," *Refuge: Canada's Journal on Refugees* 4, no.1 (1984).
26 Ibid.
27 W.K. Bell, memorandum, "Amendment to Designated Class Regulations," 17 September 1979; G. Van Kessel, memorandum, "Amendments to Indochinese Designated Class Regulations," 25 September 1979, LAC RG76, vol. 1837, file 8005-2-1, Act and Regulations, Designated Class Regulations, Indochinese.
28 File no. 1979-2996, LAC RG76, vol. 1837, file 8005-2-1, Act and Regulations, Designated Class Regulations, Indochinese.
29 Ibid.
30 Ernest Allen, memo to file, "Record of Telephone Conversation with Al Lukie ...," 12 October 1979, LAC RG76, vol. 1835, file 8700-1, part 2, Refugee and Displaced Persons, Special Movement, Indochinese, General.

31 Memorandum to the Minister, "Meeting with Robert L. Wenn-
    man, MP …; "Temporary Wardship," Proposal for a Canada –
    United Nations Demonstration Project Regarding "Unattached
    Refugee Children," LAC RG76, vol. 1836, file 8700-12-1.

32 EIC, *Indochinese Refugees*, 30.

33 W.K. Bell, telex message, "Single Refugees," 16 November
    1979, LAC RG76, vol. 1839, file 8703-1, part 1.

34 Hong Kong telex XBIM4855, "Named Refugee Sponsorships,"
    21 November 1979, LAC RG76, vol. 1838, file 8705-1, part 1.

35 Bangkok telex ZHIM7431, "Named Sponsorship Program," 22
    February 1980, LAC RG76, vol. 1838, file 8700-0, Indochinese
    Policy.

36 EIC, *Indochinese Refugees*, 10. The meticulous planning that
    went into this little sideshow puzzled UNHCR officials, but it
    worked.

37 http://citation.allacademic.com/meta/p_mla_apa_research_
    citation/0/9/8/2/5/pages98250/p98250-22.php.

38 "STATEMENT: In Response to the News Release and Advertise-
    ments the National Citizens' Coalition," undated but likely late
    August 1979, LAC RG76, vol. 1836, file 8700-12-1.

39 Howard Adelman, presentation to the Indochinese Refugee
    Movement and the Private Sponsorship Programme 1975–80
    Conference, York University, 21 November 2013, jointly spon-
    sored by the Canadian Immigration Historical Society and the
    York University Centre for Refugee Studies.

40 Requests for an additional 10,000 would be received in 1980.
    See EIC, *Indochinese Refugees*, 28, 29.

CHAPTER NINE

1 Number of refugees sponsored in this period: October 1979,
   4,968; November, 4,040; December, 2,443; January 1980,
   3,891.

2 Doug Love, Deputy Minister, memorandum to the Minister,
   "Indochinese Refugee Program," 22 October 1979, LAC RG76,
   vol. 1839, file 8703, part 1.

3 Ibid. A handwritten note by Atkey in the margins of the October memorandum reads: "I favour this option [3]. So does
   David & Flora MacDonald with whom I have consulted. To
   counter criticism we can emphasise our new initiatives – provide food aid to Cambodians through UNICEF or Red Cross.

Also we can emphasise task ahead in resettlement of remaining 35,000 not yet here. [Initialled] R A. 24/10/79."

4 W. Courtland Robinson, *Terms of Refuge, The Indochinese Exodus and International Response* (London and New York: Zed Books 1998), 45-50, 68-74.

5 Bangkok telex, 22 October 1979, "Telecom Molloy-Shalka," 19 October 1979, CIHS Collection.

6 Howard Adelman, *Canada and the Indochinese Refugees* (Regina: L.A. Weigl Associates 1982), 41-4.

7 Privy Council Office. Minister of Employment and Immigration, Memorandum to Cabinet, PCO 693-79MC, "Indochinese Refugees," 13 November 1979, CIHS Collection.

8 Ibid.

9 Message EXTOTT UNS 0445, 3 March 1979, LAC RG76, vol. 1835 file 8700-1, part 1, Indochina General, Public Opinion Survey.

10 CIHS, *Summary of Employment and Immigration Indochinese Refugee Newsletters – July 16, 1979–February 14, 1980 – Public Affairs Division*, vol. 1, no. 5 (15 August 1979); Adelman, *Canada*, 1.

11 CIHS, *Summary of Employment and Immigration Indochinese Refugee Newsletters – July 16, 1979–February 14, 1980 – Public Affairs Division*, vol. 1, no. 5 (15 August 1979).

12 See note 7.

13 Ibid.

14 Ibid.

15 Ibid.

16 Ibid.

17 Memorandum to the Minister, "Cabinet Submission on Sponsored Refugees – Speaking Notes," 15 November 1979, LAC RG76, vol. 1827, file 8700-12, part 2, Refugees and Displaced Persons, Special Movements, Ministerial Statements and Statistics.

18 Ibid., attached paper, "Distribution of Indochinese Sponsorship Applications."

19 Privy Council Office, Report to Inner Cabinet, "Indochinese Refugees," 16 November, 1979, CIHS Collection (badly damaged PCO document, serial number illegible).

20 Memorandum to the Minister, "Indochinese Refugee Program

and Aid to Cambodia," 26 November 1979, LAC RG76, vol. 1827, file 8700-12-1, part 2, Refugees and Displaced Persons, Special Movements, Departmental Statistics.

21 "Cabinet Submission on Sponsored Refugees – Speaking Notes," 16 November 1979, LAC RG76, vol. 1837, file 8700-12-1, part 2, Refugees and Displaced Persons, Special Movements, Indochina, Departmental Statistics.

22 Transcript of breakfast meeting with representatives of various groups across Canada, Wednesday, 5 December 1979, 77 pp., LAC RG76, vol. 1839, file 8703-1, part 1.

23 Ibid., 3.

24 Ibid., 5, 6.

25 Ibid., 7.

26 Ibid., 8.

27 Memorandum to the Minister, "Indochinese Refugees – Consultation with Voluntary Agencies," 10 December 1979, LAC RG76, vol. 1838, file 8700-14-4, part 1.

28 Letter to the Prime Minister, Hon. Flora MacDonald, Hon. David MacDonald, and Hon. Ron Atkey. Montreal, 11 December 1979, LAC RG10, vol. 1832, file 8630-6, part 2.

29 Ibid.

30 "Statement to be made by Mr. Molloy on behalf of the Minister at meeting of voluntary agencies concerned with refugees, Montreal, 10 December 1979," LAC RG 76, vol. 1838, file 8700-14-4, part 1.

31 Memorandum to the Minister, "Committee of Organizations Concerned for Refugees – Annual Meeting December 9, 1979," 12 December 1979, LAC RG76, vol. 1837, file 8700-12-1, part 2, Refugees and Displaced Persons, Special Movements, Indochinese.

32 Telex, W.K. Bell to all Regional Directors General, no subject line, 11 December 1979, LAC RG76, vol. 1838, file 8700-14-4, part 1.

33 Executive Director, Ontario Region, Memorandum, "Voluntary Groups Involved in the Provision of Assistance to Indochinese Refugees – Comments on Settlement Needs," 18 December 1979, LAC RG76, vol. 1838, file 8700-14-4, part 1. For example, Ontario Region reported, "Without exception groups contacted expressed a need for financial assistance in

defraying administrative expenses – administrative staff, program supervisors, interpreters, transportation, rent, materials and supplies. Funds to cover these expenses are considered to be basic and in addition to programs and services that are deficient due to lack of funds." Also British Columbia Region, "Settlement Input from Agencies and Sponsors on Indochinese Refugee Needs," 19 December 1979, LAC RG76, vol. 1838, file 8700-14-4, part 1.

34 Memorandum to the Minister, no subject line, 11 January 1980, LAC RG76, vol. 1838, file 8700-14-4, part 1.

35 Ibid.

36 Press release, 8 February 1980, LAC RG76, file 8710-1-4, part 2, Refugee and Displaced Persons.

37 Denise Moncion, Assistant Secretary, Treasury Board, letter to J.D. Love, Deputy Minister/Chairman, CEIC, 14 February 1980, LAC RG76, vol. 1838, file 8710-14-4, part 2, Refugees and Displaced Persons.

CHAPTER TEN

1 Some refugee advocates argued for making the PC decision an election issue, but they were dissuaded by Howard Adelman who argued that making the number of refugees an election issue could easily backfire by giving those opposed to the refugees opportunities to speak out against them (Adelman to Molloy, email, 7 June 2015).

2 "Proposal for a March 10, 1980 Government Refugee Policy for Southeast Asia in 1980." Signing/endorsing institutions included representatives of the Vietnamese Association, Operation Lifeline, the United Church, the Anglican Church, the Canadian Council of Churches, the Standing Conference on Refugees, World Vision, the Christian Reformed Church, the Canadian Jewish Congress, and others. LAC RG76, vol. 1836, file 8700-1, part 3.

3 Gallop Report, 21 May 1980, LAC RG76, vol. 1836, file 8700-1, part 3. The voluntary agencies' concern was not without cause: a Gallop Poll of 21 May would report that 63 per cent of Canadians opposed the admission of more Indochinese refugees, even if private sponsors could be found.

4 Employment and Immigration Canada, *The Indochinese Refugees: The Canadian Response, 1979 and 1980* (Ottawa: Department of Supply and Services 1982).

5 Privy Council Office, Memorandum to Cabinet, "Transportation Loans to Refugees," PCO 208-80MC, 12 March 1980; Report of Committee Decision (Cabinet Committee on Social Development); "Transportation Loans to Refugees," PCO 208-80CR, 14 March 1980, CIHS Collection.

6 Privy Council Office, Memorandum to Cabinet, "Indochinese Refugee Program 1979–1980," PCO 207-80MC, 12 March 1980, CIHS Collection.

7 Ibid.

8 An issue that was taken into account in considering option 3 was the fact that the Vietnamese government was pressuring resettlement countries like Canada to accept greater numbers of non-family reunification refugees while placing difficulties in the way of family reunification from Vietnam. The fear was expressed by the Department of External Affairs that if Canada were to raise its refugee resettlement target, Vietnam might again allow a greater outflow of refugees as a pressure tactic against western countries.

9 Privy Council Office, Memorandum to Cabinet, "Indochinese Refugee Program 1979–1980," PCO 207-80MC, 12 March 1980, CIHS Collection.

10 Privy Council Office, Record of Cabinet Decision, "Indochinese Refugee Program 1979–80," PCO 207-80RD, 25 March 1980, CIHS Collection.

11 Minister of Employment and Immigration, news release, 2 April 1980, LAC RG76, vol. 1836, file 8700-1, part 3.

12 Memorandum to Mr. Axworthy, 24 March 1980 with attached discussion paper, "Indochinese Refugees – Selection and Processing Options," 18 March 1980, and a draft press release, LAC RG76, vol. 1836, file 8700-1, part 3. (On his arrival in office, Axworthy directed that the standard "Memorandum to the Minister" format be replaced by "Memorandum to Mr. Axworthy.")

13 Ibid.

14 Adapted from chart in EIC, *Indochinese Refugees*, 28

15 Tony Falsetto to W.K. Bell, memorandum, "Unfilled Sponsor-
    ship Requests," 14 July 1980, LAC RG76, vol. 1839, file 8703-
    1, part 1.

16 Memorandum to Regional Directors General, "Indochinese
    Refugees," 14 April 1979, LAC RG76, vol. 1836, file 8700-1,
    part 3.

17 W.K. Bell, telex, "Indochinese Refugees: Destining of Unspon-
    sored Refugees," 29 April 1980, LAC RG76, vol. 1836, file
    8700, part 3.

18 Bangkok telex ZHIM7431, "Named Sponsorship Program," 22
    February 1980, LAC RG76, vol. 1836, file 8700-0, Indochinese
    Policy.

19 W.K. Bell, memorandum, "Mediation of Misunderstandings
    between Refugees and Their Sponsors," 12 March 1980, LAC
    RG76, vol. 1839, file 8705-1, part 1. See also memorandum
    of 28 April 1980 from Chief, Settlement, Alberta Region, and
    memorandum of 27 March 1980 from Chief, Settlement,
    Manitoba Region, LAC RG76, vol. 1839, file 8705-1, part 1.

20 Task Force telex, "Non bona fide [sic] Indochinese refugees,"
    29 April 1980, LAC RG76, box 1837, file 8700-13, Refugees
    and Displaced Persons, Special Movements, Indochinese
    Refugees.

21 Bangkok telex ZHGR 1637, "Indochinese Boat People, In-
    creased Small Boat People Departures from Vietnam," 2 June
    1980, LAC RG76, vol. 1839, file 8700-15, part 3, Refugees and
    Displaced Persons, Special Movements.

22 Singapore telex UCIM2500, "Increased Small Boat Departures
    from Vietnam," 13 June 1980, LAC RG76, vol. 1839, file 8700-
    15, part 3.

23 Rene Pappone, former head of the Refugee Task Force Commu-
    nications Unit, wrote in an email to Michael Molloy on 9
    February 2015, "The decision to shut down the newsletter mid-
    way through a major refugee movement may seem perplexing,
    but it is not surprising. If money was an issue, what happened
    was consistent with common practice in which communications
    activities were often the first items on the chopping block when
    government departments wanted to cut costs."

24 While all attention in 1979 was fixed on the Indochinese
    refugees, 2,225 Eastern Europeans, 432 Latin Americans, and

264 refugees from elsewhere were admitted under the 1979 Annual Refugee Plan. The 1980 Plan called for 3,000 Eastern Europeans, 500 Latin Americans, and 500 from other sources. The 1980 contingency reserve (1,000) had by July been allocated to Eastern Europe (400) and Cuba (300). Briefing note, Resettlement Activities 1980, LAC RG76, file 8620, part 2, Refugees and Displaced Persons, General.

25 Memorandum to Mr. Axworthy, "World Refugee Situation," 11 July 1980, LAC RG76, file 8620-1, part 2, Refugees and Displaced Persons, General.

26 Ibid.

27 Refugee Policy Division, "International Refugee Scene: The Resettlement Perspective, July 1980," LAC RG76, vol. 1815, file 8620-9 (1981), Refugees and Displaced Persons, General Annual Refugee Plan.

28 Ibid.

29 Ibid.

30 Memorandum from Operation Lifeline's Howard Adelman to Andre Pilon, 7 August 1980, LAC RG76, vol. 1815, file 8620-8 (1981), Refugees and Displaced Persons, General, Annual Refugee Plan.

31 Ibid.

32 Ibid.

33 Standing Conference of Canadian Organizations Concerned for Refugees, 27 August 1980, LAC RG76, vol. 1815, file 8620-8 (1981), Refugees and Displaced Persons, General Annual Refugee Plan.

34 Ibid.

35 Inter-Church Refugee Concerns Project, "Presentation to the Refugee Policy Group, Employment and Immigration," 28 August 1980, and Inter-Church Refugee Concerns Committee, "Presentation to the Refugee Policy Group, Employment and Immigration Canada," 28 August 1980, LAC RG76, vol. 1815, file 8620-8 (1981), Refugees and Displaced Persons, General Annual Refugee Plan.

36 Keith R. Hobson, United Baptist Convention of the Atlantic Provinces, letter to W.K. Bell, 24 July 1980, LAC RG76, vol. 1815, file 8620-8 (1981).

37 Rick Patten, National Council of YMCAs of Canada, letter to

W.K. Bell, 18 August 1980, LAC RG76, vol. 1815, file 8620-8 (1980).

28 W.K. Bell, telex to Regional Executive Directors, "Absorptive Capacity – Indochinese Refugees," 11 July 1980, LAC RG76, vol. 1836, file 8700-1, part 3.

39 Memorandum to the Minister, "Indochinese Refugee Program – 1980–81," 4 September 1980, LAC RG76, vol. 1836, file 8700-1, part 3.

40 Ibid.

41 It is not clear whether this number refers to the number of sponsorship applications or actual refugees, but the companion memorandum presents this as the number of refugees who would be sponsored.

42 Memorandum to Mr. Axworthy, "Annual Refugee Plan 1981," 4 September 1981, LAC RG76, vol. 1815, file 8620-8, Refugees and Displaced Persons, General, Annual Refugee Plan, 1981.

43 Ibid.

44 Employment and Immigration Canada, Annual Report, 1981–82. As a matter of interest, 1981 saw the arrival of 6,400 Indochinese refugees of all categories, supplemented by 591 relatives who arrived directly from Vietnam. While the program continued into the 1990s, the glory days were over.

45 Memorandum, Guy Currier to Reg Gates, Director General, Alberta Region, 11 August 1980, CIHS Collection.

46 Memorandum to the Minister, "Refugees Southeast Asia – Briefing," 3 October 1980, LAC RG76, vol. 1836, file 8700-1, part 3.

47 Sadly, both Woodford and Sinclair passed away while this book was in preparation.

48 Hong Kong telex XBIM6539, "Refugee Workshop HKONG, 20–21 Nov," 24 November 1980, CIHS Collection.

49 Ibid.

50 EIC, *Indochinese Refugees*, 27.

CHAPTER ELEVEN

1 The editors of this book are grateful to Stephen Fielding, the first CIHS Gunn Essay prizewinner, for conducting the interview.

2 The 1976 Immigration Act took two years to implement.

CHAPTER TWELVE

1   Stacey, quoted in Col. Strome Galloway, *With the Irish against Rommel* (Langley, BC: Battleline Books 1984).

2   In the literature of Canadian refugee operations, the only comparable account is Roger St Vincent's *Seven Crested Cranes: Asian Exodus from Uganda*, https://arc.library.carleton.ca/exhibits/uganda-collection/seven-crested-cranes-roger-st-vincent; also CIHS *Bulletin 65*, August 2012.

3   With the exception of references to documents, all notes are as they appear in the original report.

4   Memorandum from W.K. Bell, Director-General, Recruitment & Selection Branch, to J.B. Bissett, Director-General, Foreign Service Region, 19 October 1976.

5   O-I-C Tove Bording and Bill Sheppit.

6   Through the years 1976–77, headquarters gradually came to appreciate that a unique E&I program based in Southeast Asia would be necessary. However, the commitment was twice postponed by this and a later transfer of 359 unused quota places from continental US camps in March 1977.

7   IFAP Log 1939, 12 January 1977.

8   Selection of Indochinese under the ongoing refugee program was at best an uncertain undertaking, as Ottawa several times seemed to reverse itself concerning the appropriateness of this program to Southeast Asians. With the implementation of the Small Boat Escapee (SBE) program in December 1977, all efforts to locate Convention refugees were stopped.

9   The greatest change really occurred in July 1977 with the arrival of the new OIC, Ian Hamilton, armed with clear verbal instructions. This change, however, did not fully resolve the problem of unclear communications. Differences in understanding continued to occur, such as with the definition of "quota." Hamilton believed he was to select thirty-five SBE families per month, while Ottawa wanted the delivery to Canada of thirty-five families per month. It was only with the advent of the *Hai Hong* incident, when a pattern of frequent phone consultation was put in place, that continuing clear understanding was established.

10 This was one of several initiatives taken by Gerry Campbell (temporarily assigned to Singapore during the OIC's illness in

February 1979). Campbell, who had been responsible for transportation arrangements during Canada's Ugandan airlift, used his experience in setting up the system for airlifting the Indochinese refugees.

11 Similarly, so as to ensure that selected persons would not be unduly delayed in processing, we obtained on 1 June 1978 Ottawa's agreement that persons selected for the newly begun Sponsorship Program would go to Canada immediately their visas were ready, regardless of whether sponsors had agreed to accept our choices.

12 Now Terengganu.

13 The futility of their effort was graphically demonstrated to me during a file purge immediately upon my arrival in July 1978. Entire shelves of visaed files were scheduled for destruction marked, "cancel, gone to ..." A "blue card" control system was inaugurated by UNHCR in Malaysia only in February 1978. In Thailand, the system was implemented that summer, but only for Vietnamese boat people, perhaps 6,000 of the 100,000 refugees in Thailand at that time.

14 To emphasize their concern and to ensure an orderly departure from Malaysia, the Australians, by mid-January 1978, had quietly selected all boat pilots and navigators in camps (Singapore Area Visit Report, 2 February 1978).

15 The SBE program was introduced on 21 December 1979. Under this program, Singapore was to deliver to Canada thirty-five families per month beginning in January.

16 Since 9 July 1978, Hamilton and myself. Until December, Hamilton worked almost exclusively in Thailand, I only in Malaysia.

17 Vietnamese ethnic acceptances average two people per case, Chinese between three and four.

18 The SBE Program was introduced on 21 December 1979. See note 15.

19 [The Government of] Singapore has consistently maintained a hard stand vis-à-vis Vietnamese arriving in this country. An escapee is either guaranteed departure to a third country, usually the nation whose flag carrier rescues him, or he is driven back to sea, often brutally. In reaction, we took the position that Vietnamese in Singapore were guaranteed resettlement and

therefore were ineligible for Canadian acceptance barring a bona fide Canadian connection.

20 The period from October to December 1978 was particularly disheartening for selection officers on the coast of Malaysia. To ensure equal opportunity for all camp populations, we decided to use our files on a per capita basis – one file (family) for each 1,000 persons. With this ratio, we would quietly enter, for example, camp Kota Bharu with two files, or Bidong with twenty, rapidly select the fortunate few, and then escape to our boat or car, leaving behind angry mobs of relatives for another thirty days.

21 Memorandum, Singapore to IFAP/Allen, 19 December 1978.

22 The Canadian government's timing in this instance was right on the nose. For the first time, the volume of the influx from Vietnam, together with 50,000 SBES already on Malaysian beaches, threatened the international relief effort with massive failure; the Malaysian government was becoming very jittery.

23 Telex from Singapore to IFAP, log 5114, 19 January 1979.

24 Ibid.

25 These jumps in demand became routine due to (1) the tremendous (and unexpected) effort of refugee sponsoring groups in Canada; and (2) the irregular schedule of aircraft departures. While these changes regularly caused us to scramble, they were never totally impossible to meet due to our continuing effort to try to maintain an extra aircraft load in transit camp.

26 Due to HQ response time and the difficulty of finding staff, program staffing supply simply never caught up to workload demand. To by-pass interdepartmental difficulties, i.e., in getting permanent positions into place, TD officers were rotated in and out by Foreign Branch HQ (E&I) on a two-month basis until December 1979. In January 1980, the full complement of permanent staff was finally in place. This included the External [Affairs] Administrative Officer, who was provided well after his talents were urgently needed to locate housing, furniture, and provide administrative services to the rapidly expanded program. Existing staff had to cope themselves with the additional burden of administration.

27 By March, the planned schedule of moving medicals by air from ICEM, Kuala Lumpur, to us in weekly bundles had been

522 NOTES TO PAGES 223–32

overtaken by events. They now came irregularly as required. In at least one instance, we flew a man to K.L. on the 0630 shuttle, where he met a courier with medicals and caught a plane back fifteen minutes later.

28 This problem remains unresolved. In Indonesia and Malaysia, we now have 983 persons tied up with tuberculosis. The provinces reluctantly permit the entry of perhaps a score per month. To prevent further people languishing in our camps, the department, effective 1 February 1980, has ordered that all acceptances after that date having TB are to be refused.

29 In fact, we have exercised this agreement only rarely – in those instances when aircraft mechanical failures obliged delays after refugees were already in transit from Indonesia [to Singapore].

30 Telex from Singapore to IFAP, log 6923, 13 September 1979.

31 From the moment of our arrival in Indonesia, the UNHCR has argued strongly that we put teams into the Anambas [Islands]. As this isolated archipelago had no medical facilities and no possibility of guaranteed swift transportation to our aircraft, we declined, preferring to focus on the Bintan/Galang area. However, to relieve UNHCR pressure on us to go, we initiated a program of moving down all Anambas refugees in whom Canada had expressed an interest via Indonesian troop transport. This scheme alone accounted for close to 2,000 Canadian selections in the fall of 1979. Finally, once the UNHCR had guaranteed immediate departures of our selections to Galang, in early 1980 a team helicoptered to Galang and selected 1,200 persons in one week.

32 A miscalculation. While the figure of 6,000 was accurate, we did not anticipate the possibility of a continuing major exodus from Vietnam to Malaysia. This movement over the last few months has been reaching 2,000 persons per month.

33 Telex from Singapore to IFAP, log 7378, 16 October 1979.

CHAPTER THIRTEEN

1 Dick Martin to Michael Molloy, email, 22 September 2014. Sadly, Al Lukie passed away in September 2016.

2 Memorandum to the Minister, "Indochinese Refugee Program – Transportation Arrangements," 19 March 1979, with attached undated (probably January 1979) copy of an earlier

memo of the same title, LAC RG76, vol. 1863, file 8700-12-1. E&I Singapore was responsible for eight flights and Manila for one. The Immigration Department anticipated the arrival of 5,000 refugees under the Annual Refugee Plan and another 2,000 sponsored by relatives or private groups. Campbell and two Singapore-based officers were tasked with selecting and sending to Canada 80 per cent, or 6,500 refugees. Five of the KL flights were to arrive between 27 March and 18 April 1979.

3 Gerry Campbell modestly omits to mention that it was his recommendation and design ideas that led to the IMM1314, the Indochinese Designated Class Processing Record and Visa. In addition, his suggestion that completion of the final immigration landing records be shifted from the visa offices to the staging areas in Edmonton and Montreal was accepted by senior management and had an enormous impact, freeing up the visa offices in Hong Kong, Singapore, Thailand, and Manila to concentrate on their core responsibilities – finding, selecting, and moving the refugees to Canada.

4 David Ritchie to Michael Molloy, email, 13 January 2015.

5 David Ritchie to Michael Molloy, email, 12 January 2015.

6 National Health and Welfare Canada, "Guidelines for the Control of Intestinal and Other Parasitic Infections in Immigrants," *Canada Diseases Weekly Report* 3 (1977).

7 J.S. Keystone, "Imported Disease in Vietnam Refugees," *Ontario Medical Review* 46 (1979): 369–70.

8 The kind editorial assistance of Dr Vincent Keane, an ICM/IOM medical officer who worked with the programs and in the area at the time, is gratefully acknowledged.

CHAPTER FOURTEEN

1 Under the Disembarkation Resettlement Offers (DISERO) agreement negotiated in Geneva in August 1979, "a number of countries (Canada included) jointly agreed to guarantee resettlement for any Vietnamese refugee rescued at sea by merchant ships flying flags of states that did not resettle refugees." See W. Courtland Robinson, *Terms of Refuge: The Indochinese Refugees and the International Response* (London & New York: Zed Books 1998), 59.

2 See chapter 3.

3 Published in Toronto by Random House Canada.

4 Ron Button was a foreign service officer. For his account of this story, see chapter 17.

5 I'm not making this up. See http://www.democraticunder ground.com/discuss/duboard.php?az=view_all&address=389 x7758242.

CHAPTER FIFTEEN

1 The Thai and Cambodian kingdoms had fought a series of wars in the pre-colonial period and with France at the end of the nineteenth century. More recently, a short war between Thailand and Vichy France (December 1940 to January 1941) had resulted in the annexation of much of eastern Cambodia. With the defeat of Japan in 1945, the border was restored to its pre-1941 status. The border itself was poorly demarcated, and each side tended to adopt an interpretation of the boundary favouring its position.

2 For years after the Vietnamese invasion, a Thai priority was to maintain a continued viable Khmer Rouge presence along the common border to act as a buffer against the Vietnamese and their Cambodian clients. The many displaced Cambodians along the border were pawns in this larger game.

3 The United States resettled the largest number of Hmong, chiefly in Montana, Minnesota, and California. By the 2010 US Census, some 260,000 Hmong were resident in the United States (see http://www.hndinc.org/cmsAdmin/uploads/ dlc/HND-Census-Report-2013.pdf). Smaller numbers were taken by other countries. By 2005, there were estimated populations of 15,000 in France, 2,000 in Australia, 1,500 in French Guiana, 835 in Canada, and 600 in Argentina. See Jacques Lemoine, "What Is the Number of Hmong in the World?" *Hmong Studies Journal* 6 (2005).

4 Memorandum, W.K. Bell, Director General, Recruitment and Selection Branch, to J.B. Bissett, Director General, Foreign Service Branch, 19 October 1976, as quoted in Richard Martin, "The Canadian Refugee Program in Singapore," *E&I Report*, 1 July 1980, CIHS Collection; reprinted here as chapter 11.

5 See Bruce Grant, *The Boat People: An "Age" Investigation* (London: Penguin Books 1979).

6   The Royal Thai Navy actively intervened to divert boats south toward Malaysia and Indonesia. The crews of Thai fishing boats also engaged in piracy. This threat diverted many refugee boats away from the Thai coast.

7   Much of southern Vietnam, including the Mekong Delta, had been under Khmer rule until the eighteenth century; hence Cambodia's claim over much of southern Vietnam.

8   The Khmer Rouge regime's response to official Thai protests about the incursions and atrocities was that these never happened, and in any event the alleged incidents took place inside Cambodia and were of no concern to the Thai authorities.

9   See William Shawcross, *The Quality of Mercy: Cambodia, Holocaust and Modern Conscience* (London: Fontana/Collins 1984), for a detailed account. Reaction to events in Cambodia is covered in Shawcross's chapter 3, "Views from Outside." Of particular interest is his discussion of the persistent reluctance of many on the "progressive Left" to accept any accounts of atrocities as credible. Once the horrors inflicted by the Khmer Rouge could not be denied or minimized, leftist analysts were forced to resort to convoluted mental gymnastics in explaining their position. Shawcross gives one notable example of this sophistry (p. 56) from the Australian academic Gavin McCormick writing in 1980 in the *Journal of Contemporary Asia*: "The Western media and press worked hard on Kampuchea. But, and here is a tragic irony, it becomes increasingly likely that some of the most malicious fantasies of propagandists, conceived with little or no regard for truth, may actually be close to the truth. This is a difficult and unpalatable conclusion."

10 Accounts about the Southeast Asian refugee camps often noted that there was a risk of the creation of a long-term, Palestinian-type refugee situation.

11 Canadian diplomatic missions reported extensively on refugee arrivals as part of their ongoing reporting responsibilities. Bangkok, in particular, produced a series of reports on conditions in Laos and Cambodia based on interviews with residents in the camps.

12 Thomas Enders, the US ambassador to Canada from 1976 to 1979, and his spouse, Gaetana, were very active on behalf of

Indochinese refugees, especially Cambodians. Both had a special connection to Cambodia, where Enders had served as deputy chief of mission at the US Embassy from 1971 to 1973. Gaetana Enders had been very involved in aid and relief work among those displaced by the fighting. On returning to Washington, she was appointed by President Ford to the Committee for Refugees, overseeing resettlement of Indochinese refugees in the United States. The Enders continued in their efforts while in Canada, bringing the plight of Indochinese refugees to the attention of Canadian politicians, senior government officials, and church and community leaders. Their efforts were instrumental in the Catholic Archdiocese of Ottawa sponsoring many Cambodians. See http://www.tinyrevolution.com/mt/archives/000478.html; http://en.wikipedia.org/wiki/Thomas_O._Enders; http://gaetanaenders.com/.

13 Memorandum to Cabinet, "Democratic Kampuchea (Cambodia): Human Rights and Refugees," 8 June 1978, serial no. 305-78MC, CIHS Collection.

14 Modest indeed, considering that background information provided to Cabinet indicated that there were some 100,000 Indochinese refugees in Thailand. Of these, 14,000 were Cambodians (mostly arrivals from 1975). The remaining 80,000 were largely Lao, including Hill Tribes, and Vietnamese. The Hill Tribes, who were described as primarily subsistence farmers, were not at that point considered suitable for resettlement in industrialized third countries.

15 Although no announcement had yet been made, both Manchester and Stuttgart immigration offices would close as part of government-wide austerity in the second half of 1978.

16 The existing immigration program in Thailand has been discussed above. There was no immigrant or visitor activity direct from Laos beyond the occasional official visitor. Visitor and student visas from Burma were issued at the British Embassy in Rangoon. Yearly area trips dealt with a small immigrant movement.

17 IPOs at the time performed most functions of Canadian visa officers except for issuing visas. The presence of a highly capable and experienced IPO in Singapore (Mrs Luan Tan) relieved the

two Canadian officers of much of the routine immigrant and visitor work and allowed them to concentrate on refugees.

18 An apparent lack of urgency to get both officers to Bangkok was seen in instructions that they take up to four weeks home leave before reporting to Ottawa.

19 Gaetana Enders made two trips to the Cambodian camps in February and October 1978. During her first trip, she identified a group of fifty Cambodians in the Aranyaprathet camp whom she felt had linguistic and occupational skills to resettle easily in Canada. Interviews by a Canadian immigration officer found the group were part of a paramilitary force trained by the Thai army for the purpose of cross-border forays into Cambodia. None spoke English or French or possessed any skills. Mrs Enders had also distributed mimeographed letters on US Embassy letterhead promoting the Canadian program and implying favourable treatment by Canada. None of the refugees identified by her were found acceptable for Canada. Her second trip was lower key, chiefly directed toward identifying a Cambodian orphan for adoption by the archbishop of Ottawa. These activities provoked a minor bilateral irritant, which resulted in the US authorities curtailing her activities. In any event, the Enders' assignment in Ottawa came to an end during the summer of 1979. See Memorandum to Minister, CEIC, "Programs in the U.S.A. and Southeast Asia," 14 June 1979, LAC RG76, vol. 1836, file 8700-12-1.

20 Although the refugee situation was relatively quiet at the time, there were definite inklings that this was about to change, as Hamilton was frequently called away from briefings to take calls from UNHCR about the progress of a large ship filled with refugees approaching the Malaysian coast. This ship was the *Hai Hong*.

21 At some point in July 1978, a public announcement of Canada's new program for Thailand was picked up by the media, including the BBC and Radio Free Asia. The announcement prompted a flurry of letters from refugees to the embassy in Bangkok pleading for consideration.

22 One French-speaking applicant was a graduate of l'Université Sainte-Anne in Nova Scotia. She was eventually hired. Although

only two assistants could be hired in the beginning, those interviewed formed a pool of candidates who were readily available
when the office expanded in the late summer of 1979.

23 ICEM eventually changed its name to IOM (International Or-
ganisation for Migration) to better reflect its global rather than
European mandate.

24 ICRC travel documents could be prepared for each refugee as
long as the numbers remained at a relatively low level. As
refugee departures expanded, the ICRC was hard pressed to
cope. Eventually, arrangements were made that eliminated the
need for individual ICRC travel documents.

25 See David Butler, *The Fall of Saigon: Scenes from the Sudden
End of a Long War* (New York: Dell 1986), 270–5.

26 Because of this requirement, most Hmong and officers from the
former military of South Vietnam, Laos, and Cambodia qualified for settlement in the United States. This diverted many potential security cases away from Canada.

27 From the outset, Canadian policy toward family reunification
from within Vietnam was to consider only persons named in a
Family Class Sponsorship or an Assisted Relative Undertaking.

28 A Canadian visa officer, René Bersma, was to be assigned to
the region with special responsibility for the nascent Vietnamese Family Reunification Program. At this point, however,
the plan was that he would take up his duties in Hong Kong. It
was only some months later that it was decided to move responsibility for relations with Vietnam to the embassy in
Bangkok. The ICRC list was an early indicator of how lists
would become the bane of the Vietnamese Family Reunification Program. The oldest list comprised persons issued Promise
of Visa Letters by the Canadian Embassy in Saigon in April
1975. Another list, compiled in Ottawa, consisted of urgent
priority cases holding valid Family Class or Assisted Relative
undertakings. The Vietnamese authorities also presented their
own lists of persons whose departure they were prepared to
allow. Not surprisingly, there were numerous inconsistencies
between the lists.

29 For the officer interviewing this group on board the ship, it was
evident that the guidelines provided by headquarters about establishment potential did not always fit the reality in the field.

None of the group appeared to possess any skills to suggest rapid establishment in Canada. In the end, the interviewing officer selected two family groups of siblings who had been active in doing odd jobs on the ship such as cleaning. Their initiative was a positive element.

30 One large Lao camp, Ubol, was not visited until July 1979 by agreement among resettlement countries due to concerns about the safety of interviewing teams. Australian interviewing officers had been forced to terminate operations after being physically attacked by frustrated refugees. Without security guarantees, resettlement countries decided it was best to place a moratorium on visits to Ubol.

31 Oppertshauser was particularly insistent that Canadian interviewing officers maintain tight control over the process in the camps. He believed that a loss of such control had allowed the notorious General Dang Van Quang to slip through and arrive in Canada in 1975, an incident that caused the government of the day considerable embarrassment.

32 Every camp developed a cottage industry operated by English or French speakers who, for a small consideration, would prepare letters including bio-data and other information making a case for resettlement.

33 In *Refuge: Canada's Journal on Refugees* 32, no. 2 (2016), http://refuge.journals.yorku.ca/index.php/refuge/issue/view/2311.

34 Once the refugee sponsorship system took off, many of the refugees selected on the basis of their language, educational, and skill levels were matched to sponsors who, quite frankly, had expected refugees in much greater need of assistance. Some expressed disappointment that the refugees coming were not sufficiently needy.

35 Typically, these were letters, but during an early visit to Nongkhai Camp, one refugee, a former college professor from Vientiane, presented his old Laotian passport with a Canadian Non-Immigrant Visa issued at the British Embassy in Vientiane. He had been a delegate to the Super Françofête held in Quebec City in the summer of 1974.

36 It was not uncommon for a refugee arriving in a camp to be joined later by other family members.

37	When it was explained that the transportation to Canada was in the form of a loan, many refugees would ask the rate of interest. They were always relieved to know that it was interest free.

38	Regional SIQ representation consisted of two officers posted in Hong Kong, who were expected to cover all of East Asia. The first Quebec visit after the opening of the Bangkok operation took place in the spring of 1979.

39	An effort was made to distribute refugees evenly across the country. In addition, the office tried to ensure that several refugees travelled to their final destination together.

CHAPTER SIXTEEN

1	The Immigration Section at the Canadian Commission in Hong Kong had been responsible for immigration matters from Vietnam. At the same time, responsibility for general relations was also transferred from the Canadian Embassy in Beijing to Bangkok. These changes were in response to the practical difficulties of dealing with Vietnam through China, as they had just concluded a war on their border.

2	Unnamed or open sponsorships generated considerable work at this stage, as a refugee family had to be matched to the sponsor, followed by correspondence with the sponsor through the CIC to verify that the sponsor would agree to the refugees proposed. It would also happen that a family matched to a sponsor would not proceed to Canada, opting for another destination, requiring additional correspondence.

3	This period saw some of the most dramatic small boat arrivals in Malaysia, including the "Mersing Incident," in which many refugees drowned after Malaysian authorities refused their boat permission to land.

4	For a good overview of the situation along the Thai/Cambodian border as well as links to other sources, see *Thai/Cambodia Border Refugee Camps 1975–1999: Information and Documentation Website*, http://www.websitesrcg.com/border/border-history-1.html. See also William Shawcross, *The Quality of Mercy: Cambodia, Holocaust and Modern Conscience* (London: Fontana 1985).

5	Prior to these changes, the Quebec refugee program was served on an itinerant basis by officers from Hong Kong. SIQ officers assigned to Bangkok for varying periods included Florent Fortin, Richard Dupont, Michel de Montigny, Jerry Power, Lise Langlois, and Lucile Horner.

6   On this first trip, Calvert and Bibeau, accompanied by one of the officers based in Bangkok, selected some five hundred refugees in Nongkhai camp.

7   Seegers had immigrated to Canada from the Netherlands in the 1950s. As a conscript in the Dutch Army after 1945, he had served in the Dutch East Indies and had picked up some Malay. This might have been helpful in Malaysia and Indonesia but was not in Thailand.

8   Sheppit had been on posting in Singapore from 1975 to 1977 and was already experienced with Indochinese refugees.

9   The experience of the Lao refugees selected from the Thai camps by Argentina was problematic. Probably under the impression that their Lao were villagers from the countryside, the Argentine authorities placed the refugees in remote rural areas near the border with Paraguay. In fact, most were ethnic Chinese from Vientiane and other towns, with a background as shopkeepers and traders. Not surprisingly, they quickly gravitated to Buenos Aires and sought to move on to the United States and other countries.

10 As an aside, it should be noted that at various times the United States would not consider boat refugees unless they had exhausted all other resettlement options. Since the United States was the preferred destination for most, refugees would often ask that their blue card be noted as "rejected by Canada."

11 A note on Thai hotels: During the Second Indochina War, large US air bases had been located near Nongkhai and Ubol in the northeast. Modern hotels in the style of a Holiday Inn had been built to cater to an American clientele and were still in operation, although beginning to show a certain seediness. Hotels near the Cambodian camps were more rugged and followed up-country standards – no air-conditioning, although a ceiling fan provided some comfort, with the draft keeping the mosquitoes away – and bathroom facilities best described as rustic. For example, the bathroom at the so-called Prasat Hilton consisted of a shower head on the ceiling, a Turkish

toilet in the floor, and a mirror on the wall. This configuration made shaving an interesting experience. The Chai Suk Bungalows at Aranyaprathet were located between the town and the Cambodian border, allowing a close-hand view of periodic tracer shells being fired across the frontier. Most pleasant of all was the Samila Beach Hotel in Songkla, with comfortable rooms and excellent seafood restaurants nearby.

12 In the Lao camps at least, the entrepreneurial spirit was alive and well as vendors quickly set up operations selling snacks, ice cream, and cold drinks to applicants awaiting interview.

13 A feature of life in the Lao and Vietnamese camps was the emergence of a real-estate market. Families with a hut in a desirable camp location would often find willing buyers prepared to pay a premium for right of occupation upon the departure of the occupants for resettlement. The market fluctuated with the rate of resettlement. High departure rates in the latter part of 1979 saw the major collapse of the property market in the Lao camps.

14 Telex (draft number not assigned), W.R. Lundy, "Lumpini Transit Centre – Diphtheria," 20 October 1979, CIHS Collection. The outbreak coincided with a visit by US First Lady Rosalyn Carter, who had been sent to Southeast Asia by President Carter to investigate and report on the refugee situation.

15 Telex, Lundy to IFAP, ZHIM487, 1 November 1979, CIHS Collection. A major interview effort had been made in the camps to ensure enough refugees would be selected to fill charter aircraft scheduled to depart Bangkok to Canada in the final months of 1979.

16 Immigration medical examinations could have three outcomes: passed, failed or, "furthered." When the examination revealed that a refugee or immigrant had a condition requiring further investigation or treatment before a final decision could be made by the Health and Welfare doctor, the case was said to be "furthered."

17 UNHCR had promised to provide mobile medical units that could be used to conduct medical examinations in the camps. The arrival of these units was seriously delayed for reasons that remain unclear.

18 Because of its proximity to the Lumpini Transit Centre, the

Canadian Embassy's air-conditioned waiting room was often occupied by a number of Canada-bound refugees, usually former interpreters or helpers in the camps.

19 Unfortunately, a significant number of refugees fell through the cracks as the ongoing treatment and examinations did not always take place in the camps.

20 Best and Bell were shocked by the situation at the Hmong Camp in Ban Vinai. The camp was in a state of chaos, as much of the leadership had recently left for resettlement in the United States. A new leadership was yet to emerge. In marked contrast, Nongkhai was a well-run operation. Two officers from Bangkok (Shalka and Verboven) had been sent ahead to conduct what might best be called model interviews. The workload for the two officers was remarkably light, as a five-officer Canadian team had been in the camp the week before and had selected over 1,000 persons. That said, a sufficient number of refugees presented themselves for interview to give the two Ottawa visitors a picture of how selection interviews were conducted.

21 In an interview with journalist Max Brem in Ottawa in late 1980, Oppertshauser explained the imperatives behind deciding on processing priorities as follows: it made little sense to send an officer to a camp for days and select only sixty persons when the same officer could travel to another camp (e.g., Nongkhai) and select two hundred in the same number of days.

22 This flight was not without comic relief. Ontario World Airways' single aircraft typically flew between Toronto and the Caribbean. In this, its first foray into Asia, the carrier had neglected to secure flight clearance over Indian and Burmese airspace. The pilot managed to bluff his way over India. Rangoon Air Traffic Control was adamant in refusing permission to over-fly Burma, necessitating a long detour.

23 The largest load carried by a Boeing 747 was 512 persons, twenty-seven of them children under two.

24 As an aside, it can be mentioned that for 1980 Wardair received a contract to provide transportation services after a competitive bidding process. For its refugee flights, the company used the same porcelain and cutlery provided on its regular charters. According to Max Ward, the company's CEO, this

was a deliberate decision, as the refugees would eventually become successful in Canada with money to spend on holidays and should have a good memory of the airline that brought them to Canada.

25 Flights to the West Coast crossed Vietnamese air space via the so-called Amber One route, which required over-flight permission from the civil aviation authorities in Hanoi. As Canadian carriers were not familiar with the region, the Bangkok Embassy was asked by the airlines for assistance in securing over-flight permission. Typically, this simply meant forwarding a request to Hanoi along with payment arrangements for the use of Vietnamese air traffic control. That said, it was sometimes necessary to sensitize Canadian carriers to the region's political realities. For example, Canadian Pacific asked for embassy help for clearance to transport "Vietnamese refugees" over Vietnamese air space. The embassy had to suggest changing the wording to "passengers."

26 See Shawcross, *The Quality of Mercy*, 169-90. Sa Kheo's population was in a particularly desperate condition and was under the control of Khmer Rouge cadres. Their plight justifiably raised demands from the media and the broader public for effective and immediate action. When conditions in Sa Kheo were first reported in the Canadian media, Robert Shalka was the senior Canadian officer at the Immigration Section in Bangkok, as both Murray Oppertshauser and William Lundy were away in refugee camps. Shalka received an urgent telephone call from Mike Molloy of the Refugee Task Force in Ottawa – this was an era when international phone calls were very much a rarity – asking for an update and whether it would be possible to select some of these refugees for Canada. Humanitarian organizations in Canada were urging the government to charter aircraft to rescue these refugees on an urgent basis. Shalka sought to calm the situation, stressing that the physical condition of the Sa Kheo refugees was so dire that they needed food, shelter, and medical help as a first priority before immigration could be considered. Oppertshauser and Lundy reiterated the same message on their return a few days later. In any event, the Sa Kheo population would not be made available for resettlement for some time.

27 The rapid construction of both Sa Kheo and Khao I Dang was
   due to the efforts of Mark Malloch Brown, a British citizen
   serving as the UNHCR field officer in the area. He would rise to
   the position of deputy secretary general of the United Nations
   under Kofi Annan (another UNHCR veteran) and was appointed to the British Cabinet and House of Lords by Prime
   Minister Gordon Brown in 2007.

28 Whomever the source of the advice given to Woodford at headquarters, it was singularly ill-advised, given the furor that arose
   when government reneged on the one-for-one matching formula. Had E&I Bangkok failed to meet its target, the consequences for the manager would have been severe.

29 See Employment and Immigration Canada, *The Indochinese
   Refugees: The Canadian Response, 1979 and 1980* (Ottawa:
   Department of Supply and Services 1982).

CHAPTER SEVENTEEN

1 Leopold Verboven to Michael Molloy, email, 8 April 2015.

2 This was a refrain often repeated by selection officers seeking
   to impart operational wisdom to new selection officers. Essentially the same sentiment is repeated by another officer (chapter
   18) at a different E&I mission.

CHAPTER EIGHTEEN

1 Army of the Republic of (South) Vietnam.

2 Staffing details are contained in an email from Gerry Campbell
   to Michael Molloy dated 14 December 2013.

3 In the sense used here, "Triads" refers to transnational organized crime organizations based in areas inside and outside
   Asia where large Chinese ethnic communities exist.

4 The medical screening results were divided in seven categories:
   M1, unconditional acceptance; M2, minor risk regarding
   public health but generally acceptable; M3, some risk regarding
   demand on services but generally acceptable; the dreaded M4,
   inadmissible because of risk to public health but with treatment could be reviewed after X months; M5, inadmissible because of high demand on public services but with treatment
   could be reviewed after X months; M6, inadmissible because
   of danger to public health which is not likely to change with

treatment; and M7, inadmissible because of demand on public services which is not likely to change with treatment. Source: National Health and Welfare Medical Officer's Handbook, CIHS Collection.

5 Manpower and Immigration, *Immigration Statistics 1975*, table 10, 24–5, http://epe.lac-bac.gc.ca/100/202/301/immigration_statistics-ef/mp22-1_1975.pdf.

6 Ibid., table 8, 20–1, http://epe.lac-bac.gc.ca/100/202/301/immigration_statistics-ef/mp22-1_1976.pdf.

7 Ibid., table 9, 20–1, http://epe.lac-bac.gc.ca/100/202/301/immigration_statistics-ef/mp22-1_1977.pdf.

8 Ibid., table 10, 20–1, http://epe.lac-bac.gc.ca/100/202/301/immigration_statistics-ef/mp22-1_1978.pdf.

9 Employment and Immigration Indochinese, *Refugees: The Canadian Response, 1979 and 1980* (Ottawa: Ministry of Supply and Services 1982), 20.

10 2-I-C: second-in-charge, or deputy program manager, in contemporary parlance.

CHAPTER NINETEEN

1 Once the Cullen-Couture Agreement came into force, selection of candidates for immigration to Quebec became the responsibility of Quebec, which led to the creation of the CSQ document. On arrival in Canada, the original was delivered to the principal applicant, and the number of accompanying dependents was recorded. One copy went to the federal authorities and another copy was kept in the Quebec file. On receiving the copy, the federal officer opened a file and initiated the process for the medical and security examinations (these latter were federal domains). Depending on the results of these examinations, the federal authority could decide whether to issue the visa.

2 The FEVAL document was equivalent to the federal form IMM1067. In this document, following the category to which the applicant belonged, the Quebec immigration counsellor wrote down the points attributed to each applicant for the seven or eight criteria on the selection grid. The work was simplified for refugees, as only one criterion was considered: the adaptability of the applicant.

3 Vigneault's lines, beginning, "Ma chère [nom], c'est à ton tour / de te laisser parler d'amour," have become an informal Quebec anthem.

CHAPTER TWENTY

1 Chapters 3 and 18 include accounts of the rescue, soon after the fall of Saigon, of 3,700 refugees from the *Clara Maersk*, a large Danish freighter in the South China Sea. While the *Clara Maersk* operation was the first major Vietnamese refugee rescue operation on the high seas after the fall of Saigon, it belongs more properly to the chaotic refugee flow immediately after the fall, rather than the small boat people phenomenon that started in 1976, gathered steam in 1977, and became a major humanitarian catastrophe in 1978.

2 UNHCR memorandum, "Indochinese Refugees Rescued at Sea by Merchant Shipping in 1979," 12 May 1980, LAC RG76, vol. 1839, file 8700-15, part 3. According to the UNHCR record, seven German ships rescued 763 persons; six Greek ships, thirteen; fourteen Dutch ships, 756; twenty-six Norwegian ships, 1,472; nine Panamanian ships, 440; eight US ships, 650; and sixteen UK ships, 2,036.

3 The present Canada Shipping Act (CSA), based on principles contained in a previous CSA in force in 1978, states: "Every qualified person who is the master of a vessel in any waters, on receiving a signal from any source that a person, a vessel or an aircraft is in distress, shall proceed with all speed to render assistance and shall, if possible, inform the persons in distress or the sender of the signal." Canada was a signatory to the 1958 UN Convention of the High Seas and in 1978 was negotiating the 1982 UN Convention on the Law of the Sea. The latter contains Article 98 on Duty to Render Assistance on the High Seas.

4 David Wilson, External Affairs Consular Operations, to Doug Hill, "CEIC Refugee Policy," 19 October 1978, LAC RG76, vol. 1838, file 8700-15. The negotiator for Transport Canada was Captain T.H. Brooks.

5 "Ship Safety Bulletin," Ship Safety Branch, Nautical Division Number 2/79, LAC RG76, vol. 1835, file 8700-15, part 2.

6 Instructions from IFAP to Singapore, Hong Kong, Manila, and Bangkok, Indochinese Refugee Program, 1979 (IRP/79), 20 February 1979, LAC RG76, vol. 1835, file 8700-0, Refugee and Displaced Persons, Special Movements, Indochinese, Policies and Procedures, para. 5.

7 W. Courtland Robinson, *Terms of Refuge: The Indochinese Exodus and the International Response* (London & New York: Zed Books 1998), 59, 192. Countries participating in DISERO included the United States, Canada, Australia, New Zealand, Germany, France, Switzerland, and Sweden. DISERO provided assurances to authorities at the first port of call; RASRO provided parallel assurances to ships' captains.

8 All information and quotations in this section, with a few exceptions referred to in notes 10 and 12, are from the late Captain B.O.H. Brown's memoir, "Rescue," given to the CIHS by his family in 2014.

9 Captain Brown's son, Ken Brown, informed CIHS that in ordering Chief Officer Corney to "confirm" (not investigate) whether the fishing boat was seaworthy, the captain handed him an axe from the fire rack. Corney returned on board without the axe.

10 On the vessel were "four families, Mr. and Mrs. L and their five sons of 20, 14, 7, 4 & 2 years and daughters of 20, 17, 11 & 6 years; Mr. L's sisters: Mr. and Mrs. T and their four sons of 22, 16, 10 & 8 and daughters of 18 & 12; Mr. and Mrs. N and their four sons of 8, 6, 4 & 2 and one girl of 10; Mr. and Mrs. G and their two sons 16 & 4 and two daughters of 14 & 6 years" (Brown, "Rescue," p. 1).

11 Captain Brown noted the date as 13 September. Since the refugees were picked up on 2 September, he probably meant to write 5 September, not 13 September. The confusion is easily explained by noting that the *Mather* was in fact ready to depart from Pulau Bukum on 13 September.

12 Email, Ken Brown to Mike Molloy, 26 July 2014.

13 All the information in this section is reproduced, in a somewhat edited form, from a report by John M. Gibson, immigration counsellor at the Canadian Embassy in Cairo, written in September 1976, now in the CIHS Collection.

14 An Affirmation for Visa was a device used by Canadian Immigration to facilitate travel to Canada for people without passports.

15 Minister's Permits were used to authorize the admission to Canada of, for example, people who had not completed all required immigration formalities. In this case the refugees had not passed an immigration medical examination.

16 Jean-Paul Delisle confirmed in an email to Michael Molloy, 9 May 2015, that he is unable to recall the name of the Turkish ship.

17 All the information and quotations in this section are reproduced from Jean-Paul Delisle's report, "Vietnamese 'Boat People' refugees in Turkey," now in the CIHC Collection.

18 The late André and Viviane Dumezic of Caritas in Istanbul were in the forefront of assisting refugees in Turkey for many decades.

19 By late 1978, the distinction had largely disappeared between the large numbers of very small, often unseaworthy boats carrying small groups of refugees, and the much smaller number of large boats carrying thousands of refugees. Boat people were boat people whether they escaped on tiny boats or big freighters. The phenomenon that started with the *Clara Maersk* and its 3,700 thousand refugees assumed a highly publicized profile for the people of Canada with the *Hai Hong* and its thousands of refugees.

CHAPTER TWENTY-ONE

1 *Newsletter: Indochinese Refugees*, 24 July 1978, 4, 5.

2 See chapter 7, section "Initial Refugee Reception – The Staging Areas."

3 Memorandum to the Minister, 18 December 1978, LAC RG 76, vol. 1837, file 8700-12-1, part 2.

4 See chapter 7.

5 *Newsletter: Indochinese Refugees*, 31 July 1979, 3, 4; 29 August 1979, 4.

6 See chapter 7, section "Streamlining Documentation."

7 Michael Fitzpatrick to Mike Molloy, email, 3 October 2014.

8 Once Boeing 747s began to arrive, the passenger load could exceed five hundred.

9 Elizabeth Marshall, narrative contribution to the CIHS Indochina Project, CIHS Collection.
10 Guy Cuerrier, narrative contribution to the CIHS Indochina
   Project, CIHS Collection.
11 Ibid.
12 Marshall, narrative contribution.
13 Ibid.; Cuerier, narrative contribution.
14 Michael Molloy, interview, 20 February 2014.
15 Marshall, narrative contribution.
16 Ibid.
17 Ibid.

CHAPTER TWENTY-TWO

1 The Canadian Immigration Historical Society would be pleased
   to receive accounts from people who performed similar work
   in other parts of Canada with the federal, provincial, or municipal governments.
2 The need for a program to link newly arrived government assisted refugees with Canadians was recognized first at the local
   level across the country by people like Ralph Talbot and Deborah Ashford, who simply made it happen, sometimes under the
   rubric of "friendship families." The merit of these initiatives
   was quickly recognized at national headquarters, which
   brought them under the Host Family Program.

CHAPTER TWENTY-THREE

1 Hulene Montgomery, memo, "Report of the Refugee Liaison
   Programme in Kitchener-Waterloo, 1981."
2 Some of the founding members were Ari Ariariatnam, Multi-
   cultural Centre; Ray Schlegel and Ruby Weber, Mennonite
   Central Committee Ontario; Theron Kramer, Secretary of
   State; Shirley Losee, Waterloo County Board of Education;
   Lorna van Mossel, Friendship Families; Sue Coulter and Tim
   Little, Citizenship Participation; and Gary Green, CEC. Tuan
   La and Lao Vang, community workers hired by MCC to sup-
   port the Vietnamese and Laotian communities, later played
   key roles.
3 Brian Bell, chief of policy, Settlement Branch, Canada Employ-
   ment and Immigration Commission, interview with Kae Elgie,
   October 1982.

4 William Janzen, "The 1979 Canada Master Agreement for the Sponsorship of Refugees in Historical Perspective," *Journal of Mennonite Studies* 24 (2006): 211–22.

5 Now known as Community Justice Initiatives, VORP was the first restorative justice program in North America. It formed in 1974, and in 1982 it "expanded to provide mediation and conflict resolution services for individuals, neighbours, families, and groups in the community." See Community Justice Initiatives, https://cjiwr.com. See also the Centre for Restorative Justice, Simon Fraser University, "Russ Kelly's Story," http://www.sfu.ca/crj/news/stories/russ-kelly.html.

6 Poul Hartling, *The Refugee Child: UNHCR Projects for Refugee Children* (Geneva: United Nations High Commissioner for Refugees 1979).

CHAPTER TWENTY-FOUR

1 As we note in the introduction, this book refers to "Indochinese refugees," since this was the generally acceptable term used by the media, academia, and governments at the time the refugee movement was taking place. In a book that describes the history of this refugee movement, replacing "Indochinese refugees" with "Southeast Asian refugees" would be unhistorical. However, people who have settled in Canada as "Indochinese refugees" now prefer to be known as Southeast Asians, since today "Indochinese" has unpleasant colonialist connotations for many of them. Therefore, in this one place, when talking about their long-term settlement in Canada, "Southeast Asian" is used as the preferred term.

2 The UNHCR in *The State of the World's Refugees 2000: Fifty Years of Humanitarian Action*, 1 January 2000, chapter 4, 98, http://www.unhcr.org/4a4c754a9.html, provides accurate figures of the number of refugee arrivals in first countries of asylum. However, neither the UNHCR nor any other scholarly work specializing in the Indochinese refugee movement provides reliable estimates of how many refugees perished along the way: most estimates are anecdotal. The 20–40 per cent figure comes from table 6.1A in R.J. Rummel, *Statistics of Democide: Genocide and Mass Murder since 1900* (Charlottesville, VA: Center for National Security Law, University of Virginia), https://www.hawaii.edu/powerkills/NOTE5.HTM#FIG. While

Rummell is highly respected by some academics, others are critical of his methods. All the same, before his death in 2014 he was the major analyst of all forms of war and civilian deaths in conflicts of the twentieth century. In order to be as careful as possible, we have taken low (20 per cent) and intermediate (40 per cent) estimates of the numbers of Indochinese refugee deaths he provides, omitting his high estimate.

3 See Donald Cameron, chapter 14, section "Refugee Stories of Escape."

4 Beiser, Morton, *Strangers at the Gate: The "Boat People's" First Ten Years in Canada* (Toronto: University of Toronto Press 1999).

5 Ibid., 82.

6 Ibid.

7 Ibid., 81–2.

8 Ibid., 3–5, 54, 84–92, 113–21.

9 Kwok B. Chan and Lawrence Lam, "Psychological Problems of Chinese Vietnamese Refugees Resettling in Quebec," in *Uprooting, Loss and Adaptation: The Resettlement of Indochinese Refugees in Canada*, ed. Kwok B. Chan and Doreen Marie Indra (Ottawa: Canadian Public Health Association 1987), 31.

10 See chapter 3, first section, "The Beginnings of the Post-1975 Refugee Movement to Canada."

11 Beiser, *Strangers at the Gate*, 151.

12 Gilles Deschamps, "Economic Adaptation of Indochinese Refugees in Quebec," in *Uprooting, Loss and Adaptation*, ed. Chan and Indra, 105–6.

13 Kwok B. Chan, "Unemployment, Social Support and Coping: The Psychological Response of Indochinese Refugees to Economic Marginality," in *Uprooting, Loss and Adaptation*, ed. Chan and Indra, 118.

14 Ibid., 119.

15 Thanh Campbell, *Orphan 32* (Hamilton, ON: Hope for the World Productions 2013).

16 Ibid., 137–8.

17 Norman Buchignani, "Towards a Sociology of Indochinese Canadian Social Organization: A Preliminary Statement," in *Ten Years Later: Indochinese Communities in Canada*, ed. Louis-Jacques Dorais and Doreen M. Indra (Canadian Asian Studies Association 1988), 16–17.

18 Ibid., 22–8. As well, see several studies in *Ten Years Later* and in *Uprooting, Loss, and Adaptation*. Articles in both books deal with Indochinese ethnic associations.

19 Louis-Jacques Dorais, *The Cambodians, Laotians and Vietnamese in Canada* (Ottawa: Canadian Historical Association 2000), 11.

20 Yuen-fong Woon, Helen Wong, and Donna Woo, "Loose Sand: The Ethnic Vietnamese and Sino-Vietnamese Community in Greater Victoria (1980–85)," in *Ten Years Later*, ed. Dorais and Indra, 41.

21 Tran Quang Ba, "The Indochinese of Southeast New Brunswick," in *Ten Years Later*, ed. Dorais and Indra, 190.

22 Dorais, *The Cambodians*, 11.

23 Ibid.

24 Ibid.

25 Ibid.

26 Melanie Heu, "Challenges of Volunteerism within a Cultural Community: Case Study of Young Hmong Adults in Kitchener-Waterloo," thesis paper 891, Wilfrid Laurier University, 2008.

27 T.J. Samuel, "Economic Adaptation of Indochinese Refugees in Canada," in *Uprooting, Loss and Adaptation*, ed. Chan and Indra, 71.

28 Yuen-fong Woon, "The Mode of Refugee Sponsorship and the Socio-Economic Adaptation of Vietnamese in Victoria: A Three Year Perspective," in *Uprooting, Loss and Adaptation*, ed. Chan and Indra, 141.

29 Ibid.

30 Beiser, *Strangers at the Gate*, 121.

31 Ibid.

CONCLUSION

1 Freda Hawkins, *Canada and Immigration: Public Policy and Public Concern* (Montreal and London: McGill-Queen's University Press 1972), 93.

2 Privy Council Office, situation report, "Refugee Movement from Chile, Cambodia and South Vietnam," 16 June 1975, PCO 381-75-RD, CIHS Collection.

3 Martha Nixon, "Summary of Employment and Immigration Indochinese Refugee Newsletters – July 16, 1979–February 14, 1980" (CEIC Public Affairs Division, vol. 1, no. 5, 15 August

1979), http://cihs-shic.ca/indochina/; Howard Adelman, *Canada and the Indochinese Refugees* (Regina: L.A. Weigl Educational Associates 1982), 1.

4 Canada accepted 6,000 refugees from Uganda in 1972, and 7,000 refugees from Chile and other Latin America countries in the 1970s. The Indochinese movement was larger than either of these movements by a factor of ten.

5 By email, info@cihs-shic.ca.

Contributors

Writing Team

MICHAEL J. MOLLOY, president of the CIHS, is an adjunct professor at the University of Ottawa. His Canadian Foreign Service career included assignments in Japan, Lebanon, Uganda, Minneapolis, Geneva, Jordan, Syria, and Kenya. He led design work on the refugee provisions of the 1976 Immigration Act, including the private sponsorship program. During the 1979–80 Indochinese refugee movement, he was senior coordinator of the Immigration Department's Refugee Task Force. He established the Canadian Embassy in Syria and directed immigration operations in Ontario. He was ambassador to Jordan and Canada's Middle East Peace Process coordinator. In retirement he co-directed the Jerusalem Old City Initiative, teaches a course on refugee resettlement, and researches immigration history and Palestinian refugees.

PETER DUSCHINSKY is a retired visa officer. As a graduate student of history, before joining the Immigration Foreign Service, he was the principal researcher, along with his wife, Christiana Epp Duschinsky, of John Norris's *Strangers Entertained: A History of the Ethnic Groups of British Columbia* (Vancouver: Evergreen Press 1971), published by the BC Centennial Commission. Between 1975 and 1996 he had overseas postings in Paris, Chicago, Cairo, and Budapest. Between 1998 and 2001 he served in Ottawa as director, International Liaison, responsible for the international multilateral relations of the Department of Citizenship and Immigration. He is a board member of CIHS.

KURT F. JENSEN spent his career in the Canadian diplomatic service, initially as an Immigration Foreign Service officer. After several years he transferred to the political stream at Foreign Affairs, where he was primarily involved in foreign intelligence matters, initially as an intelligence analyst, while later serving as head of Current Intelligence and ending his career as deputy director for Intelligence Coordination, a collection section. Dr Jensen's foreign assignments included Stockholm, Bonn, Port of Spain, and Boston, and various other locations for briefer durations. He holds graduate degrees from the University of Alberta, Boston University, and Carleton University. Following his diplomatic career, he became an adjunct professor at Carleton University in Ottawa. He is a board member of CIHS.

ROBERT J. SHALKA received bachelor's (honours) and master's degrees in history from the University of Alberta and a PhD in modern European history at the University of Wisconsin (Madison). Returning to Alberta, he worked as senior historical researcher for the Fort Edmonton Outdoor Museum Project from 1972 to 1974. He joined the Immigration Foreign Service in 1974 and was posted to Stuttgart, West Germany. Along with another Canadian officer, Dr Shalka was transferred to Bangkok in late 1978 to open a new program for Indochinese refugees in Thailand and remained until September 1980. His posting covered the most critical period of the Indochinese refugee crisis. He completed other overseas immigration management assignments in Moscow, Singapore, Kyiv, Riyadh, Bonn, and Berlin, as well as at Immigration Headquarters in Ottawa. He retired after thirty-six years of service in July 2010.

GAIL KIRKPATRICK DEVLIN has an MA in Canadian Studies from Carleton University. She spent over twenty years as a Foreign Service spouse on postings in Malaysia, Bonn, Berlin, Moscow, Barbados, and Prague. From 2003 until her retirement in 2012, she was the policy analyst on federal skilled workers with responsibility for the language testing file. For more than twenty years she was also the technical editor, proofreader, and researcher for *Documents on Canadian External Relations,* published by DFAIT. She is a board member of CIHS.

Contributors

NAOMI ALBOIM is an adjunct professor and chair of the Policy Forum at Queen's University's School of Policy Studies. During the Indochinese refugee movement, she was the director of settlement for CEIC Ontario Region. Naomi worked for twenty-five years at senior levels of the federal and Ontario governments and was deputy minister of three portfolios with the latter. A senior fellow of the Maytree Foundation, she leads policy work on immigration issues and is vice chair of the Toronto Immigrant Employment Council.

ERNEST ALLEN joined the Department of Citizenship and Immigration in 1957 and served in London, Cologne, Bonn, and Hong Kong. In 1977 he was director of the Asia and Pacific Bureau, providing operational direction regarding the selection, processing, and transport of Indochinese refugees to Canada. Subsequently, he managed immigration operations in New Delhi (1980–83) and Singapore (1983–86) returning to direct the Asia Pacific Division in External Affairs (1986–89). He later managed immigration operations in Nairobi, the Africa Middle East Division at Immigration HQ, and the immigration program in Islamabad. He retired in 1996.

DEBORAH ASHFORD spent most of her career involved in refugee resettlement matters with CEIC. She assisted thousands of government assisted Indochinese refugees to settle in and around London, Ontario, while providing support to privately sponsored refugees. In 1999, Deborah spent three months at Camp Borden assisting with the reception and initial settlement of the Kosovar refugees.

JOHN BAKER joined the Immigration Foreign Service in 1967. A visa officer in London, Belfast, and Hong Kong, he served as immigration program manager in Singapore, where he participated in efforts to extract relatives of Vietnamese in Canada as Saigon was falling. After assignments in Barbados and Nairobi, he managed the Bangkok operation, processing Indochinese refugees and family immigrants from Vietnam under the Family Reunification Program. Later, he managed the visa operations in New York. During three Ottawa assignments, he helped to draft the 1976 Immigration Act and trained the Foreign Service in its application. He also served as director, Immigration and

Refugee Affairs, at Foreign Affairs, and director-general, Case Management, at Citizenship and Immigration.

GORDON BARNETT joined the federal public service in 1968, the manpower side of the Department of Manpower and Immigration as a CR4. In 1975 he transferred to the immigration foreign program where he was responsible for federal-provincial relations. He negotiated the first private refugee sponsorship master agreements. In 1980, he worked at the Privy Council Office, with the team responsible for the Charter of Rights and Freedoms. He was with the Department of Indian and Northern Affairs from 1982 until 1984, then returned to Citizenship and Immigration Canada as director general (Settlement, and later Enforcement), and retired in 1996.

TOVE BORDING joined the Immigration Foreign Service in 1965 and was posted to Copenhagen and to Port of Spain. She was executive assistant to the director general of the Immigration Foreign Service before being assigned to the Asia and Pacific Bureau (1973–74) during the lead-up to the fall of Saigon. She managed the small visa office at the High Commission in Singapore (July 1975 to November 1977) where she was responsible for tracking down relatives of Indochinese residents of Canada in Indonesia, Malaysia, and Thailand. The graphic reports and photographs she sent to NHQ had a profound impact on policy. Subsequently she served in Bonn, the department's Inspection Service, and Seattle. She spent several years as litigation adviser before a final posting to Los Angeles (1992–95). Sadly, Tove passed away while this book was being written.

LINDA BUTLER joined the Foreign Service in 1972. After doing her training in Stuttgart, she was posted to Buenos Aires, the regional immigration office for Chile, Peru, Bolivia, Paraguay, Uruguay, and Brazil. She served as Latin America desk officer and as chief of refugee policy in Ottawa before being posted to Tel Aviv and Manila. In 1981 she returned to Canada to attend Emmanuel College. She is currently a minister at Richmond Hill United Church.

RON BUTTON began his career as a fighter jet pilot with the Royal Canadian Air Force, serving in France from 1954 to 1960. After earning a BA (hons.), he joined the Immigration Foreign Service and served in Hong Kong, London, Beirut, Ottawa, Santiago, and Hong Kong.

DONALD CAMERON joined the Immigration Foreign Service in 1967 and served in Glasgow, London, and New Delhi where he worked on the Tibetan refugee movement followed by a tour in Ottawa. In Hong Kong from 1974 to 1977, he helped establish the family reunification program in China and was sent to Saigon as that city was falling to communist forces. Back in Ottawa, he was deputy director of the Asia Pacific Bureau and worked in the personnel division. In 1979 he was assigned to Singapore, where he oversaw operations in Malaysia at the height of the refugee movement. He later served in Tel Aviv, Nairobi, Mexico City, and Seattle.

GERRY CAMPBELL joined the Manpower and Immigration Foreign Service in 1971. Posted to London in 1972, he was almost immediately deployed with the Canadian team in Kampala for the Ugandan Asian refugee movement. He was posted to Port of Spain from 1974 to 1977. He served in Ottawa during 1977–79, spending two months helping gear up the Singapore refugee operation in the spring of 1979 before being assigned to Hong Kong to manage the Indochinese refugee movement there. Assigned to Jamaica from 1982 to 1985, he returned to Ottawa as deputy director of Refugee Affairs at External Affairs, followed by a posting to Geneva from 1988 to 1992, where he handled Refugee and Humanitarian Affairs (UNHCR, IOM, UNBRO, and ICRC). He managed immigration in Hong Kong from 1992 to 1994. Gerry was also ADM, Immigration Operations (1994–98), and high commissioner to Kenya (1998–2000), then high commissioner to Bangladesh (2002–04), and consul general in Hong Kong/Macau (2004–08).

JOYCE CAVANAGH-WOOD joined the Immigration Foreign Service in 1967, was posted to Paris, but spent several months in Vienna in 1969 working on the Czech refugee movement, followed by a posting to The Hague. In 1975, while in Ottawa, she was ordered to Hong Kong and, after a few days working in a refugee camp, went to Guam (and Wake) and finally to Camp Pendleton, California, processing Indochinese refugees. After a hiatus from 1978 to 1982, she returned to Immigration Headquarters in Ottawa and later had senior assignments in Bridgetown, Mexico City, Guatemala City, Bangkok, London, Port of Spain, Buffalo, and again at Ottawa NHQ.

GUY CUERRIER was born in Montreal, raised in Alberta, and graduated from Concordia University with a BComm. He completed the management assignment program (1977) under Manpower and Immigration and was assigned the task of coordinating the Indochinese movement of 1979–80 to Western Canada at the Griesbach Staging Area in Edmonton. Later in his career (1999), while working in the Refugee Branch at Ottawa NHQ, he coordinated the seven sites used for housing the Kosovar refugees.

COLLEEN CUPPLES joined Manpower and Immigration in 1967 and the Immigration Foreign Service in 1971. She served in Paris (1971), London (1972), and Nairobi (1975–78). While posted to Manpower Services Branch in Ottawa in 1978–80, she was temporarily assigned to Hong Kong to assist with Indochinese refugees from July to October 1979. She was consul in Los Angeles (1980–81). In Buenos Aires (1981–84) she was involved in gaining the release and resettlement of political prisoners. She later managed immigration operations in Colombo (1984), Damascus (1984–86), and Rome and served as ambassador to the Congo (1987–89), followed by senior assignments in Ottawa and Rome. Colleen died in September 1997.

JEAN-PAUL DELISLE joined the Immigration Foreign Service in July 1973, and during a twenty-five-year career served in Jamaica, former Yugoslavia, Nigeria, France, Egypt, and Hong Kong. He resigned in July 1997 after completing his posting in Hong Kong where he started his own security consulting company. He joined Microsoft in the summer of 2001 and remained with them until his return to Canada in 2009. Jean-Paul still runs a security consultancy business dealing with the prevention of counterfeiting and brand protection.

DOUGLAS DUNNINGTON joined the Immigration Foreign Service in 1968. He served in Manila and London before returning to Canada. He eventually joined the domestic side of the department, spending much of his service at the CIC in Kitchener. After retirement, he established an immigration consulting firm.

DAVID C. ELDER joined the Department of External Affairs 1973 and was a member of the Foreign Service until 1998, when he was appointed assistant secretary to the Cabinet (Machinery of Government)

in the Privy Council Office. His assignments with the department included postings to Canadian missions in Dakar, Sénégal, and Harare,
Zimbabwe, and as deputy permanent representative of Canada to the
Organization for Economic Cooperation and Development. At headquarters, he served mainly in the Economic Policy Bureau and in Personnel. He was also the department's senior assistant to the minister,
including when the Hon. Flora MacDonald was secretary of state for
external affairs. He retired from the public service in 2004 and is now
an adjunct professor and fellow in the School of Policy Studies at
Queen's University.

FLORENT FORTIN worked for the federal government between 1971
and 1976 as a manpower counsellor in the Department of Manpower
and Immigration and Economic Development Counsellor in the Department of Indian Affairs. From 1976 to 2010 he was an immigration counsellor in the Quebec Immigration Ministry. Following a year
of training, he was posted for one year to the Quebec Immigration
Office in Buenos Aires. In 1978, he had a mission to Southeast Asia,
and in January 1979 he was posted to the Quebec Immigration Office
in Hong Kong. He opened Quebec's Singapore office in August 1979,
returned to Hong Kong in October 1979, and was transferred to
Bangkok in August 1980. He returned to Montreal in 1982. He later
had postings to Mexico, Rome, and Hong Kong. From 1992 until his
retirement in 2010, Fortin had various responsibilities at Quebec Immigration's Montreal headquarters.

JOHN M. GIBSON, the late "Gibby" Gibson, was a fighter pilot with
the RCAF from 1941 to 1946 and an air force flight instructor from
1951 to 1966. He joined the Immigration Department in 1966 and
served in Munich, Rome, Budapest, Islamabad, Los Angeles, Cairo,
and Mexico.

MARIUS GRINIUS joined the Foreign Service in mid-1979 following
twelve years in the Canadian army. Six months later he found himself
in Thailand, "up-country" in his first refugee camp. Subsequent postings included Brussels (NATO), Bangkok again, and Hanoi. He later
was ambassador to Vietnam, to South Korea and concurrently to
North Korea, and to the United Nations in Geneva. After many ad-
ventures, he retired in 2012 and is now a gentleman of leisure.

BRIAN GUSHULAK completed his service with the Immigration Medical Services in the early 1980s. From 1996 to 2001 he worked in the international sector as the director of Migration Health Services of the International Organization for Migration in Geneva. Dr Gushulak was involved in refugee and complex humanitarian emergencies in Eastern Europe, the Balkans, Asia, and Africa. From 2001 until 2004 he was the director general of the newly created Medical Services Branch in the Canadian Department of Citizenship and Immigration.

DICK HAWKSHAW joined the RCMP in 1959. In 1965, he transferred to the "K" Division – Security & Intelligence Branch – spending time in both Edmonton and Lethbridge. From 1974 to 1976 he attended the University of Alberta to complete a bachelor of arts degree. He was transferred into the RCMP Foreign Services in 1977, leading to postings in Hong Kong (1977–79) and Singapore (1979–83). He joined the Canadian Security Intelligence Service (CSIS) in July 1984 and was posted to New Delhi. Dick retired in 1993.

ELIZABETH HEATHERINGTON attended Queen's University (BA, art history). She worked at the Agnes Etherington Art Centre in Kingston and for Parks Canada in Ottawa. She accompanied her husband, Scott, a Foreign Service officer, on many postings, including an assignment as ambassador to Latvia. During her husband's postings, she worked at the University of Hong Kong, the US Embassy in Moscow, Catholic Relief Services in Thailand, the US Embassy in Bonn, the Centre for International Briefing at Farnham Castle, and the British Nutrition Foundation (London). She currently works as an official events officer in the Bureau of Protocol, Global Affairs Canada.

SCOTT HEATHERINGTON joined the Immigration Foreign Service in 1972 and was serving in Hong Kong when Saigon fell. He was involved in refugee selection there and was a member of the team sent to Guam in May 1975 to select refugees. He concluded his varied overseas assignments and responsibilities in Ottawa as Canadian ambassador to the Republic of Latvia, with accreditation to Lithuania and Estonia, from 2008 to 2012.

ERNEST HÉBERT joined the Canadian Foreign Service in 1965 after obtaining a bachelor's degree in political science at the Université de

Montréal. He served in various positions in Ottawa and abroad in Canadian diplomatic missions, including in the Congo (1966–68); in Ottawa as special assistant to the minister of justice, the Right Honourable John N. Turner (1969–71); in New York at the Permanent Mission to the United Nations (1971–73); in Vietnam in 1973 as head of the Canadian Delegation in Danang and in 1974–75 as charge d'affaires, a.i.; and in Belgium as minister-counsellor (1978–80). He was appointed ambassador of Canada to Cote D'Ivoire, Mali, Niger, and Burkina Faso (1980–84). In 1984 he was elected director general of La Francophonie in Paris after which he served in Ottawa (1986) as Canada's coordinator for the first francophone summit in Versailles and then deputy chairman of the Organizing Committee of the 1987 Québec Francophone Summit. He was appointed assistant secretary to Cabinet for Foreign Policy and Defense in the Privy Council of Canada (1987–89) and ambassador of Canada to the Hellenic Republic (1989–93) and to the Kingdom of Denmark (1993–96).

JIM HENTSCHEL entered the Immigration Foreign Service in 1967. He served as visa officer in Beirut, Lebanon (1968–70), with the Department of External Affairs in Lagos, Nigeria (1970–72), in Ottawa (1972–74), in Islamabad Pakistan, as O-1-C (1974–77), and in Manila as 2-1-C (1977–79). After an assignment in Ottawa, he returned abroad to New Delhi as 2-1-C (1984–85); subsequently as O-1-C in Bonn, Germany (1985–90); and then as O-1-C in Bangkok (1990–93). He returned to Ottawa from 1993 to 1995 and served out his career as O-1-C from 1995 to 1999 in Damascus, Syria.

EARL HERSHFIELD was professor of medicine in the Department of Medicine, University of Manitoba. From 1967 to 2004 he was the director of tuberculosis control for the Province of Manitoba and from 1976 to 1983 he was executive director of the Canadian Lung Association (formerly the Canadian Tuberculosis Association).

LUCILE HORNER was a director-announcer at the French-language International Service of Radio Canada between 1963 and 1976, directing and hosting Canadian news programs to Europe and Africa. From 1976 to 2009, she was an immigration counsellor for the Quebec Immigration Ministry. From April 1977 to June 1979, she was posted to the Montréal-Étranger section at Quebec Immigration Headquarters, undertaking missions to Boston and New York every two weeks. Following a mission to Milan (June–October 1979), she was posted to Singapore (October 1979–January 1981). Back in Montreal until April 1981, she reported on the needs of Indochinese refugees, based on her experience in Singapore. Following this, she was posted as immigration counsellor, later manager, to Quebec's Bangkok office (April 1981–August 1982). From 1983 to 1989 in Montreal, she was responsible for special cases. From 1989 to 1993, she was again director of the Bangkok office. Back in Montreal in 1993, she worked at the Ministry's General Secretariat. She was director of the Brussels office (July 1995–December 1997). Finally, from 1997 to 2009, she undertook missions in Europe and North Africa from the ministry's Montreal headquarters.

SUE LOPEZ joined the Immigration Foreign Service in 1975 and served in Hong Kong, Port of Spain, London, Kingston (Jamaica), and Detroit. She was later part of the team that trained staff in the first computer processing system at missions abroad. She retired in 2007. A talented singer, she has performed at Carnegie Hall.

DARA MARCUS has a BA in Spanish from Bard College and an MA in Public and International Affairs from the University of Ottawa, where she specialized in urban agriculture policy. In 2013, her term paper on the *Hai Hong*, written for a class on refugee policy, won the CIHS–Wilfrid Laurier University Gunn Prize. Following this, her article "Saving Lives: Canada and the *Hai Hong*" appeared in *bout de papier* (vol. 28, no. 1). She is presently project manager of the Canada-Europe Transatlantic Dialogue, a research project housed at the Centre for European Studies (EU Centre of Excellence) at Carleton University.

ELIZABETH MARSHALL, a native Southern Albertan, earned a BEd (University of Calgary) and an MA (Université Laval) before serving as an Immigration Foreign Service officer in Belgium, France, Tunisia, Chile, Haiti, and at the Edmonton Refugee Reception Centre. She then became manager of the Edmonton Canada Immigration Centre and then manager of the Community Futures Program in Alberta/Northwest Territories before working as a regional officer for the Commissioner of Official Languages.

RICHARD MARTIN joined the Immigration Foreign Service in 1971. After service in Lisbon and headquarters assignments, he was posted to Singapore during 1978 until 1980, at the height of the Indochinese refugee crisis. He left the Foreign Service after the Singapore assignment to pursue interests in media, writing, teaching, and the corporate world. Now retired, he maintains his interest in international affairs and the effects of human foibles.

MARLENE MASSEY joined the Immigration Foreign Service in 1974 and was sent to Los Angeles, where she had her first of many encounters with refugee movements. She served in Glasgow and then in Milan and Athens, both of which had active refugee programs. Following a stint in Ottawa, she served in Budapest and then in South Africa as program manager, processing refugees in the frontline states. A second assignment in Ottawa was followed by postings as deputy program manager in New Delhi and then consecutive assignments as program manager in Islamabad, Kyiv, and Rome. Refugee processing was a major activity in Pakistan and Rome. Her final assignment was in Canberra. She retired in 2006 and settled in Australia with her Australian husband.

JOHN MCEACHERN joined the domestic immigration service in 1976 and switched to the Foreign Service in 1978. His first posting was to Singapore in 1980, immediately followed by the selection and processing of Indochinese refugees in Malaysia and Indonesia. Later assignments were to Hong Kong, Manila, Detroit, Georgetown, New Delhi, Taipei, Moscow, Tokyo, and again to Singapore before retirement in 2005.

HULENE MONTGOMERY was the refugee liaison officer (RLO) in the Kitchener-Waterloo area between 1979 and 1982. She has also held leadership positions in the voluntary, government and university sectors working at the grassroots, national, and international levels. Hulene has lived and worked in southern Africa (Botswana), France (Strasbourg), and West Africa (Ouagadougou, Burkina Faso). She lives in Waterloo, Ontario.

SCOTT MULLIN spent nineteen years in the Foreign Service and was involved with the Indochinese refugee movement while serving in Singapore and Hong Kong. In Hong Kong from 1979 to 1980, he conducted the majority of refugee interviews. He returned to Hong Kong in 1993 as senior trade commissioner after having acted as spokesperson for the Minister of Foreign Affairs. Later, he was Canada's senior diplomatic representative in Tehran. He also served in Nairobi and Beirut. After leaving the Foreign Service, he served as vice president, Public Affairs, with the Canadian Bankers Association before becoming vice president, Government Relations, with the TD Bank Group.

CHERYL MUNROE spent her career in several departments with assignments in Prince Edward Island, Nova Scotia, and Ontario, where she ended her service in C&I Ontario Region as regional director of programs. In PEI she was the RLO during the critical 1979–80 period of the Indochinese refugee movement.

DON MYATT joined the Immigration Foreign Service in 1973 and served in Bangkok (1979–81) during the boat people movement, immediately following his posting to Athens. After a full career of seven overseas postings and thirty-five years, he is retired and pursuing his dreams of travel.

MARTHA NIXON spent many years in a variety of social programs and policy areas, including a challenging assignment with the Indochinese Task Force, which included a temporary duty tour interviewing refugees in Hong Kong. She went on to work with the Refugee Policy Division and capped her career with four years as assistant deputy minister, Operations, for Immigration and Citizenship Canada.

MURRAY OPPERTSHAUSER joined the Manpower and Immigration Foreign Service in 1969 and was posted in 1970 to Vienna, working with refugees from Eastern Europe. From April to October 1975 he was assigned to the first Vietnamese Task Force and processed applications from refugees relocated to military bases in the eastern United States, including Eglin Air Force Base, Florida; Fort Chafee, Arkansas; and Indian Town Gap, Pennsylvania. Following an assignment in Manchester, he established the visa office in Bangkok in November

1978, managing the processing of over 12,000 Indochinese over the next eighteen months. Subsequent assignments included a year as chief, Refugee Operations. He later managed immigration operations in Belgrade, Warsaw, Port of Spain, Georgetown, Manila (where he dealt with boat people rescued by HMCS *Provider*), Rome, New Delhi, Buffalo, Hong Kong, and again Manila. He retired in 2001.

JAMES PASMAN began his immigration career in London, Ontario, in 1957 when he accepted a temporary (three-to-six-months) job in a Hungarian refugee relief position. His immigration career ended in 1987 when he took early retirement from the Metro Vancouver manager position to become involved in health care administration. In the interim he worked on some interesting and rewarding assignments such as serving as an examination officer at Niagara Falls, visa officer in London, England, O-I-C in Grande Prairie, Alberta, appeals officer and enforcement policy manager at NHQ, member of the External Affairs audit team, and various responsibilities in the British Columbia and Yukon Territories regions. His main involvement with the Indochinese refugee program was as manager of settlement for British Columbia.

IAN RANKIN served for thirty-six years in Europe, Asia, and North America as a Foreign Service officer. In Manila in 1974 he was responsible for the Indochina refugee movement. Among his later assignments were special representative to the Immigration Appeal Board and working on intelligence-related issues in the Privy Council Office. While posted to Washington, he worked with the Congressional Judiciary and Labor Committees on the labour mobility chapters of the Free Trade Agreement and the future North American Trade Agreement.

DAVID RITCHIE joined the Immigration Foreign Service in 1974 and served in New Delhi and The Hague before being assigned to Singapore in 1979.

CHARLES ROGERS joined the Immigration Department in 1958, among the first university-educated Immigration Foreign Service officers. He served in Cologne (1959–62), Hamburg (1962–64), and Cologne again (1966–67). After a short assignment in Ottawa

(1966–67), he was immigration attaché, Port of Spain (1967–69), followed by another Ottawa assignment (1969–71). He managed immigration operations in Vienna (1971–73), Brussels (1973–74), and Hong Kong (1973–75). In 1975, as South Vietnam fell, he flew to Saigon to oversee efforts to evacuate people with relatives in Canada, and then led the Canadian Immigration team to Guam to process 1,400 refugees for Canada. This was followed by a series of director-level assignments in Ottawa (1975–79). From 1979 to 1984 he was minister counsellor (Immigration) in London and consul general in Buffalo until his retirement in 1989.

LAURA MAY ROTH is a writer and graduate of the University of Ottawa's School of Public and International Affairs. In 2013, she made a substantial contribution to this book by cataloguing thousands of memoranda to Cabinet, official documents and press releases collected by the research team, organizing them into a highly usable format. In addition she prepared the initial drafts of chapter 20, "Rescue at Sea." She worked as part of the CIHS team preparing the 2012 Indochinese Refugee Conference at York Centre for Refugee Studies in Toronto. She has since worked at Citizenship and Immigration Canada and the Department of Foreign Affairs on Southeast Asia and African issues.

BILL SHEPPIT joined the Immigration Foreign Service in 1974. He was posted to the Canadian High Commission in Singapore at the end of the Vietnam War in May 1975, at the start of the Small Boat Escapee program, and remained there until 1978. After a one-year assignment to London, he returned to Southeast Asia and a posting at the Canadian Embassy in Bangkok from 1979 to 1981. He later served in New York and Jamaica, followed by an Ottawa assignment from 1987 to 1991. He subsequently served in Hong Kong from 1991 to 1996 and later in Ottawa handling complex cases and security issues. From 2000 to 2004 he was responsible for immigration liaison in Washington, including border and perimeter security issues.

TOM STEELE began his varied career as a manpower counsellor in New Westminster (1974–75). From 1975 to 1982, at the height of the Indochinese refugee movement, he was an immigration settlement officer at the Immigrant Reception Centre in Vancouver, where he administered the intake of government sponsored refugees, found accommodation, registered refugees for language training, and provided Adjustment Assistance payment. He served as a visa officer in Birmingham (1982–84) and Hong Kong (1984–85). Returning to Vancouver, he was a foreign worker program officer (1986–90) and worked as a consultant from 1990 to 2006.

RALPH TALBOT was a counsellor at the Canada Employment Centre in Windsor, Ontario, and between 1978 and 1994 was involved in re-settling more than 5,000 government-assisted refugees from fifteen different countries. After retirement in 1994, he managed the Windsor Reception House Services until 2003.

MARGARET TEBBUTT joined the Foreign Service in 1972 and served in Hong Kong, Haiti, Ottawa, Singapore, and Vancouver. From 1983 to 1988 she worked as a commercial officer at the Canadian Embassy in Washington and then returned to Canada to work at Western Economic Diversification, retiring as director of Client Service. In the past decade she has led workplace mental health initiatives for the Canadian Mental Health Association.

LEO VERBOVEN was educated at Université de Montréal (Loyola College) and at Oxford University (Hertford College). He served as an officer or program manager in Bonn, Birmingham, Belgrade, Ankara, Prague, and Beirut, with a tour on secondment to the UNHCR in Geneva. He remains the departmental expert on Dinka Cow Songs (true but strange).

JOHN WILKINS began service with CEIC in 1972 as a border examination officer in Fort Erie. He received increasingly senior assignments, including as CIC manager in London. His service included an assignment as a migration integrity officer in Pretoria, RSA. He retired in 2007.

Index

acculturation, 445–6, 457

Adams, Conrad, 350

adaptation, 165, 368, 443–5, 460.
See also Immigrant Settlement and
Adaptation Program (ISAP); refugee
challenges

Adelman, Howard, 421, 514n2;
*Canada and the Indochinese
Refugees*, 4; Operation Lifeline,
117, 150–1, 179–80, 413, 472

Adjustment Assistance, 73–4, 87,
408, 421, 426

adoption, 414–15; organizations, 36,
486n53, 486n61; in Thailand, 203–
5; of war orphans, 35, 40–2, 445

Agriculture, Department of, 392, 396

aircraft: Boeing 747, 130, 225, 304,
533n23; C-130 Hercules 48–9; CF-
130, 37, 42; charter planes, 48,
126, 130, 186, 221, 266, 304–5,
464, 474, 477; military planes, 28,
36, 37, 42, 48–9, 423; Philippines
Air Force helicopter, 345–6; safety
inspections, 507n8; USAF C-5A
Galaxy, 28, 36. *See also* airlines;
baby flights

airlines: Air Canada, 48, 325, 395,
404; CAF (Canadian Air Force), 34,
48, 484n33; Canadian Pacific Airlines (CPA), 48, 198, 204, 405,

534n25; Nordair, 48; Ontario
World Airways, 533n2; Pan Am,
48; Transair, 48; Wardair, 325, 402,
533n24. *See also* aircraft; baby
flights

Air Raya camp, 226, 244

air transport: from Guam, 47–9, 464;
to/from Hong Kong, 37–8, 41–2,
121, 126, 139, 204, 334, 474;
Saigon evacuation flights, 33–4,
328, 329–31; schedules, 171–2,
521n25; from Singapore, 125–6,
266, 474, 509n15; to staging areas,
101–2, 108, 183, 185–6, 392, 394–
5, 475, 477; from Thailand, 304–5,
325–6; across Vietnamese air space,
534n25

Alberta: refugee intake, 100, 111,
181; refugee liaison officers (RLOS),
133

Alboim, Naomi, 133, 147, 407, 430;
coordinator of CEIC Ontario Region, 408–9, 430; creation of Settlement Planning Committee (SPC),
411–12; Hmong community and,
417–19; outreach to settlement sector, 412–13; training refugee liaison
officers, 409–11; unaccompanied
minors program, 414–17

Allen, Ernest, 34, 110, 123, 126, 216;